# Guide to English Language Teaching

# 2008

# Guide to English Language Teaching

# 2008

KEYWAYS
PUBLISHING

**Guide to English Language Teaching 2008**

**This Fourth Edition**
**Published 2007 by:**      Keyways Publishing Ltd
                           PO Box 100, Chichester, West Sussex, PO18 8HD, UK
**Tel:**                   +44 (0)1243 576444
**Fax:**                   +44 (0)1243 576456
**Web**:                   www.CareersInELT.com
**Email:**                 info@KeywaysPublishing.com

Fifth edition 2008

© Keyways Publishing, 2008

Editor                     Simon Collin
Editorial Director         Peter Collin

Design                     Keyways Publishing

**Section Acknowledgments:**
Training:                  Mary Ellen Butler-Pascoe, Susan Matson.
Working Overseas:          The British Council, James Beetham, Roger Chrisman, Guillaume Gazembetti,
                           Chung Han, Michael Howard, Alistair Kennedy, Dianne James, Ian McNamara,
                           Martha Oral, Edward Prados, Mark Sigrist, Yuri Tambovtsev, Celia Thompson,
                           Mark Warschauer,  Colin Underwood, Paul Vreeland, Joe Ziegler,
                           Brian Garity, Tony Donovan.
Career Development:        Tina Carver, Lin Lougheed, Andy Martin, Mark Peterson, Mona Scheraga,
                           Barbara Stipek.

**British Library Cataloguing-in-Publication Data**

A catalogue record for this book is available from the British Library

ISBN 1-898789-21-5

Printed by Nuffield Press, UK

NOTE: Every effort has been made to ensure that the information contained in this book is accurate and up-to-date at the time of going to press. However, details are bound to change, especially with regard to information that refers to visa requirements, state certification, exchange rates and working conditions. The publisher is not responsible for any problems or disappointments encountered during your training, qualifications or travels.

If your school is mentioned in this guide and you would like to update your information for the next edition of the guide, please visit our website **www.CareersInELT.com** where you can update your information using the forms online.

# Contents

*continued*: WORKING AROUND THE WORLD

# Foreword

B eing an English language teacher can be whatever you want it to be: a passport to world travel; a stable and fulfilling career; a way of helping others or the first step to owning your own business. This guide will help you choose how best to get qualified, find a job, develop professionally and travel the world. World demographics will result in sustained demand for teachers of English for at least the next twenty years – that's about as secure a job market as you will find these days.

Like it or not, English has become the world's language and it is growing in importance every day. Globalization and developments in communications are fuelling demand for the language around the world. About 85% of the Internet's web-pages are in English and everyone has acknowledged that English is essential for efficient use of the web – recently the governments of Japan and Korea announced policies to encourage all of their working populations to acquire a basic level of English.

If you are looking for a way to travel and work overseas, then teaching English is an obvious path. There are teachers from the UK, USA, Canada, Australia and New Zealand working as English teachers in almost every country in the world. Hundreds of thousands of young people have used teaching English as a means to see the world and understand other cultures.

By the year 2050 it is estimated that half the world's population will be competent users of English. This learning frenzy will not take place because of some love for the language, but due to the realization that people will be left behind in work and social situations unless they can communicate with the rest of the world.

And even in native-English-speaking countries, the demand for learning English is high: for example, in the UK, there are hundreds of ELT schools that gain most of their student intake from overseas visitors combining lessons with travel – from young learners visiting with a school for a week to professionals learning business English for their job development. And in the USA, teaching people to speak English accounts for almost half of all adult education!

This book will show you how you can work in English language teaching: if you are looking for a stable, long term career; to give something back to your community or to the rest of the world through voluntary work; or a good way to pay for your round-the-world adventure, this guide will explain how to do it through teaching English.

# Using This Guide

This *Guide* is designed for use by people thinking of becoming teachers as well as those who have started training and experienced teachers. Although you can read the *Guide* from cover to cover, you may find it easier to start with the section that is most suited to your own particular needs.

**One: Training to Teach (p.12)** – is aimed at readers who are thinking of becoming teachers of English as a second or foreign language and who are interested in getting qualified to teach. We provide an overview of the different training courses on offer including short term introductory and certificate courses.

**Two: Finding a job (p.24)** – explains how best to find a job as a newly qualified teacher. This covers job agencies, applying directly to schools and using the Internet. Country-specific information and a directory of schools to approach for a job are listed in section 4.

**Three: Preparation – before you go (p.34)** – covers the topics that you need to address before you set off and travel the world! This includes insurance, tax issues and how to handle problems when you reach your school.

**Four: Working Around the World (p.42)** – is written for readers who want to explore the exciting prospects of combining teaching with travel. The section provides detailed profiles of over 100 countries, together with their work prospects, regulations (including tax and visas), contact details of the local embassy and British Council office and, most importantly, a directory of the main job prospects: the schools in the country together with their contact details.

**Five: Career Development (p.176)** – is the section intended for language teachers with experience who want to develop their skills and professional lives. We include directories of Diploma/Certificate courses, universities that provide Master's courses and doctorates. We also cover specialist English subjects, including young learners and business English. Lastly, we cover school management and how to get published.

**Appendix (p.230)** contains a list of useful websites, addresses for teacher-associations, schools, publishers, suppliers, travel-related sites, British Council offices, Canadian embassies and US embassies around the world.

# Acronyms

For many new teachers, the first lesson is to learn the acronyms that are used in the profession. Here are some of the more common acronyms.

## Basic

**CALL:** Computer Assisted Language Learning.

**DOS**: Director of Studies

**EAP:** English for Academic Purposes–The study or teaching of English with specific reference to an academic (usually a university- or college-based) course.

**ECIS**: European Council of International Schools

**EFL:** English as a Foreign Language–English language programmes in countries where English is not the common or official language. It is used in American university programmes where international students study English although the use of the word "foreign" is now avoided in some schools because of its xenophobic connotations.

**ELICOS**: English Language Intensive Courses for Overseas Students. Acronym used in Australia to refer to EFL.

**ELL:** English Language Learner–a term that has become popular in California designed to replace the acronym "LEP" (see below) which many teachers felt to be pejorative.

**ELT:** English Language Teaching or Training– a term coined in the UK and designed to replace EFL. It is in use around the world but has yet to catch on in the USA.

**EOP**: English for Occupational Purposes

**ESL:** English as a Second Language–English language programmes in countries where English is the dominant or official language. In the U.S. programmes designed for non-English-speaking students in the U.S. are ESL programmes; in the UK, this term is not used - ESOL is used instead.

**ESOL:** English to Speakers of Other Languages – in the U.S. this acronym is often used to describe elementary and secondary English language programmes; in the UK it refers to a specific type of English language teaching for newcomers to the country who might have complex requirements (perhaps asylum seekers or refugees) and learn English to integrate and take further education. It is sometimes used to distinguish ESL classes within adult basic education programmes.

**ESP:** English for Specific Purposes–a term that refers to teaching or studying English for a particular career (like law or medicine) or for business in general.

**IEP:** Intensive English Program–refers to an intensive course designed to help non-English-speaking students prepare for academic study at a university or college.

**L1**: First language (**L2**: Second language)

**LEP:** Limited English Proficient–a term used for many years to designate children in the school systems for whom English was not their first language. Now replaced by terms like ELL.

## Teacher Training

**ACE**: Access Certificate in Education. An entry-level training certificate being piloted by Pitmans/City and Guilds in the UK.

**CELTA:** Certificate in English Language Teaching to Adults. Widely-recognised certificate course developed in the UK by University of Cambridge ESOL (UCLES) and RSA. DELTA is the advanced Diploma course.

**CELTYL:** Certificate in English Language Teaching to Young Learners. A certificate course developed in the UK by University of Cambridge ESOL (UCLES); normally taken as an add-on option with CELTA.

**Cert.TEB:** Certificate in Teaching English for Business. A certificate course developed by LCCI for teachers specialising in business English (see LCCIEB, below)

**Cert.TESOL:** Certificate in TESOL. Widely-recognised certificate course developed in the UK by Trinity College London. The advanced version for experienced teachers is the Lic.Dip.TESOL.

**Cert.TEYL:** Certificate in Teaching English to Young Learners. A certificate course extension developed by Trinity College London; normally taken as an add-on option with Cert.TESOL.

**COTE:** Certificate for Overseas Teachers of English. A certificate-level course developed by University of Cambridge ESOL (UCLES) - now replaced by ICELT

**DELTA:** Diploma in English Language Teaching to Adults. The advanced (post-experience) qualification from University of Cambridge ESOL (UCLES)

**FTBE:** (Further Certificate for Teachers of Business English) - awarded by LCCIEB

**ICELT**: In-Service Certificate in English Language Teaching - certificate for teachers awarded by CambridgeESOL, designed to replace COTE, and used to help improve a working teacher's skills

**LTCL.Dip.TESOL:** Licentiate Diploma in TESOL. The advanced (post-experience) qualification from Trinity College London

**TEFL:** Teaching English as a Foreign Language – a term that refers to teacher training programmes in EFL.

**TESL:** Teaching English as a Second Language–a term that refers to teacher training programmes in ESL.

**TESOL:** Teaching English to Speakers of Other Languages–a term that is used to distinguish English language teaching as a professional activity that requires specialized training. Also refers to the teacher examinations developed by Trinity College London (Cert.TESOL and LTCL.Dip.TESOL)

**TKT**: Teaching Knowledge Test - flexible award developed by Cambridge ESOL to provide and test the basic teaching requirements of any teacher.

## Associations

**AAIEP:** American Association of Intensive English Programmes is a group of university and college-based intensive English programmes

**ACELS:** Advisory Council for English Language Schools in Ireland

**ARELS:** Association of Recognised English Language Schools in the UK

**BASELT**: British Association of State English Language Teaching schools in the UK

**CRELS**: Combined Registered English Language Schools of New Zealand

**ELTAs**: English Language Teacher Associations groups for teachers in Germany and Austria

**IATEFL:** International Association of Teachers of English as a Foreign Language is based in the UK with members around the world.

**JALT**: Japanese Association for Language Teaching

**JET**: Japanese Exchange and Teaching Programme

**NABE:** National Association for Bilingual Education is an association that represents the interests of bilingual teachers in the USA.

**NEAS**: National ELT Accreditation Scheme, for course providers in Australia

**RELSA**: Recognised English Language Schools Association. The organisation of independent language schools in Ireland

**TESL**: Teaching English as a Second Language, Canada – national federation of teachers and providers in Canada

**TESOL**: US-based international association of teachers of English as a second or foreign language. There are regional affiliates and many countries have their own affiliated associations.

## Exams/Exam Boards

**Assessment and Qualifications Alliance (AQA) (formerly AEB & NEAB)** Certificate in English Language Skills (ESOL), JET SET, range of graded exams for ESOL. www.aqa.org.uk

**Cambridge** *see* University of Cambridge

**Chauncey Group** (part of ETS, below) US-based group that administers the TOEIC student examination. www.toeic.com

**ESB (English-Speaking Board International)** Oral assessments in (spoken) English www.esbuk.demon.co.uk

**ETS (Educational Testing Service)** Based in Princeton, NJ, the world's biggest examination board, administrators of the TOEFL student examination. www.ets.com

**City & Guilds** Based in the UK, offers a wide range of student exams and the ACE certificate for teachers.

**Institute of Linguists** Diploma in English for International Communication. www.iol.org.uk

**International English Language Testing System (IELTS)** Managed by UCLES, the British Council and IDP Australia for academic and vocational English. www.ielts.org

**London Chamber of Commerce and Industry Exam Board (LCCIEB)** Range of business and specialist English examinations. www.lccieb.com

**London Examinations – Edexcel International** London Tests of English range of exams graded from basic to proficient. www.edexcel.org.uk

**Pitman Qualifications** Range of general ESOL exams, including spoken English and business English. www.pitmanqualifications.com

**RSA** Royal Society of Arts is a body that works with UCLES (*see below*).

**Trinity College London** Responsible for the Certificate in TESOL and the Licentiate Diploma in TESOL examinations. www.trinitycollege.co.uk

**UCLES** (University of Cambridge Local Examinations Syndicate) Syndicate of local examination centres around the world that administer the University of Cambridge ESOL examinations. www.ucles.org.uk

**University of Cambridge ESOL** (administered locally by UCLES) is a British-based organization responsible for developing a number of important English language exams (including PET, FCE, CAE) and teacher training programmes including TKT, CELTA, CELTYL, and DELTA examinations. www.cambridgeESOL.org

# Training To Teach

This chapter offers a comprehensive guide to achieving one of the teaching credentials that will be essential for your working career. Although the profession is not governed by a single body or a single qualifying entrance exam, there are many ways to become a qualified teacher – the following sections explain how.

Whether you plan to teach in your own country or travel overseas, you will need to consider the type of training you will require in order to be employed; opinions within the teaching field are varied on this question.

Some teachers argue that you don't need a TEFL Certificate to teach English around the world. Others argue that a Master's degree is an unnecessary waste of time and money and that it is easy to get a job at a school or college without one. Teachers of this mindset are convinced that the teacher training industry is some sort of vast conspiracy set up in order to fleece unsuspecting students of their money by conning them into taking courses for qualifications which are almost useless. The reality is that you can get a job teaching English without a formal qualification, though it is increasingly difficult.

And another consideration: Do you really want to start teaching with no idea of what you are doing? Is this fair on you? Is it fair on your students? There are gifted teachers born with a natural ability, but even these teachers need guidance and feedback from peers and mentors.

This section of the *Guide* is designed to give you an idea of the courses and programmes on offer and which qualification suits your needs best when training to be a teacher. For post-experience courses (i.e. once you have taught for several years and want to develop your career), see page 176.

The English language teaching profession is not governed by a single body. Instead of a single qualifying entrance exam, there are multiple routes to qualification as an English language teacher. You can start with a simple introductory course – often designed to help you decide if this is the career for you – then move on to a basic certificate course. You can then teach around the world, before perhaps working on a diploma, Master's degree or postgraduate qualification.

# Training and Qualifications

There are several ways to become a qualified English language teacher and your choice of qualification route mainly depends on where and who you want to teach. The time you have to train and the cost of training are also important considerations.

### Can anyone be an English language teacher?

It is still possible to get a job teaching EFL/ESL without any formal qualification, but this is becoming increasingly rare. There is a global shortage of teachers, but unqualified teachers are only recruited locally and the pay is usually poor. In major cities and tourist centres only qualified teachers will be taken on.

### Is there a standard TEFL qualification?

No. There are many routes to qualification as a TEFL teacher ranging from intensive 3-weekend Certificate courses to two-year Master's Degrees. In the USA and some of the Far East, a good first degree is adequate; whereas in Europe, the Commonwealth and South America teachers are preferred to have taken a TEFL course. Of these TEFL courses, the two best-known practical teaching certificates are CELTA and Certificate in TESOL, validated by University of Cambridge ESOL (administered around the world by UCLES) and Trinity College London respectively. Once you have experience as a teacher, you can move on to a post-experience course such as the Diploma in ELT (from Cambridge) or the Licentiate Diploma in TESOL (from Trinity College London) – see page 176 for details of these courses, MAs and doctorates in ELT.

### Am I too old to teach ?

Many middle-aged people faced with redundancy or early retirement decide to embark on a career in English language teaching. Although age can be a barrier in some parts of the world, most schools welcome the added depth of life experience that a more mature teacher can bring to the classroom.

### I'm not sure if I want to commit to long course.  What should I do?

There are a number of introductory courses in teaching EFL/ESL offered by various institutions including Oxford Seminars (www.oxfordseminars.com), if you think that you might not want to commit yourself to a career in teaching, but many employers may not consider you qualified unless you have at least a Certificate  (see below).

# Choosing a Course

How do you choose a Certificate course? There are hundreds of schools, several accredited courses and various levels and ways to study.  However, they will all cost you money and take a couple of months (or longer) of study to complete.

Those teachers who want to grow, personally and professionally, are turning to TEFL Certificate courses. But not every course will be right for you – and you can only find a suitable course by asking the right questions. Here are some essential questions to ensure you choose the best school for you:

### What are the qualifications of your trainers?

A Diploma or Master's degree (MATESOL) for all or most trainers is a good sign. If those who will be your role models only have a TEFL Cert. themselves, look deeper into the curriculum offered and ask about their years of experience.

While a Master's is not a guarantee of good training, it does suggest deeper understanding about the theory behind the methods and a clear commitment to the field.

### Have any complaints ever been filed against your school?

If you are studying in the USA, any complaints must, by State licensing agencies, be reported – justified or not. The nature of the complaint will tell you what the programme may not publicly advertise.

### What about the duration of your programme and practicum?

Ask about both classroom time and practicum hours. Intensive programmes can run 120 to 150 hours. The more practicum hours, closely supervised, the better. It is very difficult for a teacher to learn from his or her mistakes if given only three or four opportunities to teach. The ideal programme will allow you chances to work with beginning, intermediate, and advanced speakers of English. Note: part-time programmes lack the immediacy of feedback seen in intensive, full-time programmes.

### What is your hire/placement track record?

Proprietary programmes are required to keep close records on how many graduates get jobs. The vast majority, over 80%, should be getting jobs within two months of hire, given the intense market for EFL/ESL teachers.

### Tell me about your job network

At minimum, a school should have an extensive list of employers throughout the world and access to Internet postings. Some programmes also offer job counselling, CV advice, and a means of providing feedback from graduates who are now teaching overseas.

### In the USA, are you licensed by any state agency?

If you are studying in the USA, this is an important point: licensure for proprietary schools does not mean that you will qualify for a public school job, but rather that the school meets stringent state standards. For example, in California, these include standards for qualifications of trainers and administrators, strict record keeping, and a refund procedure.

### How are trainees tested?

If you do poorly at written tests, you won't perform well in a TEFL programme that requires passing a test for graduation. All programmes should have highly specific criteria for evaluating you, particularly in the area of practicum teaching. These should be in written form, to help prevent any bias on the part of an observer. And if you do find there is a chance of failing, you'll want to know it early on, while there is still a chance to get a refund or improve your performance.

## What kind of coursework and topics do you have?

A comprehensive programme will at least introduce you to the basics of classroom management, lesson planning, student evaluation, and techniques for teaching grammar, reading, writing, listening, speaking, and pronunciation.

## What is your trainee/trainer ratio?

The programme should allow for easy exchanges in class work and for closer counselling as needed. Classes of more than 15 trainees may make it more difficult to get the best from your teacher. Your practical classes should be observed by more than one trainer, as opinions on your strengths and weaknesses will vary.

## How do you get your students for the practicals?

The ideal is students who really do not know the material you will be teaching, so that their responses will be genuine. Make sure you will have a guaranteed number of students for your practical sessions in order to do pair and group work.

## How are refunds handled?

Many unanticipated events may force a drop-out – family crisis, illness, or a mismatch of trainee and programme goals. The best programmes allow you to leave within the first few days with few, if any, financial penalty. Others will pro-rata the amount coming back to you depending on the time spent in the programme.

## What will I receive on completion?

Trainee teachers disperse quickly after a course ends. An efficient programme will make sure that on graduation day, they receive a certificate, a letter of recommendation, and, perhaps, a transcript of courses taken and the results.

## How much will it all cost?

Of course you will want to know about course tuition, but don't forget to add in extras such as books and day trips, and accommodation.

# Training: Types of Course

Before you start to teach, you should take an initial teacher training course; when applying for a job, some school do not require any qualifications of their teachers, but with a qualification you will find it easier to get a job, easier to manage classes and organise lessons and essential if you want to offer good training for you and your prospective students.

## Introductory Courses

Introductory courses are designed for prospective teachers who want to experience teaching before making the decision to train formally and obtain qualifications. The courses usually last from a week up to four weeks. These are not certificate courses and you will not be regarded as a qualified teacher after completion of your Introductory course. You will, however, be able to say that you have had some experience of English language teaching. Some schools require trainee teachers to take an introductory course before starting a Certificate course.

## Certificate courses

The majority of trainee teachers who would like to teach take a certificate course in teaching EFL/ESL. A certificate course provides basic grounding in teaching, lesson development, managing students and, in particular, the different stages of teaching English. Certificate courses are great for trainee teachers who have no experience of teaching – perhaps have a degree or experience in a totally different field – and want to ensure that they are well prepared for their first 'real' class (as a trainee teacher, part of your certificate course will be to experience practical teaching in a classroom). Most certificate courses are intensive and run over a four or six week period. You can take distance-study courses or take a certificate course on a part-time basis over several months.

Once you have a certificate in teaching English, you can start to apply for jobs at schools around the world. Although there is no single qualification, there are two main certificate courses: University of Cambridge CELTA and Trinity College London Cert.TESOL. Either one is well recognised around the world.

Aside from these two main certificate qualifications, many school, colleges and universities have their own certificate course developed in-house. Make sure that you ask the course provider about their qualification and if they will provide assistance finding a job once you have completed your course.

As well as the basic certificate course, you can also study for additional modules that will gain you experience and qualifications in specialist subjects (see also the section on ESP); for example, teaching young learners or teaching business English.

# Certificate Qualification Providers

When you look at the different courses on offer you will find they provide a range of different certificate courses. There are a number of certificates awarded by different organisations - they have different names, provide emphasis on different types of teaching but all have the same goal to ensure that you are able to manage your first class teaching English. The main organisations offering certificate awards are:

## University of Cambridge ESOL

### TKT
The TKT (Teaching Knowledge Test) is a new award from Cambridge. Its focus is on the core teaching skills and requirements needed by teachers of English and provides a foundation for new or prospective teachers who could then progress on to CELTA or ICELT awards.

### CELTA
The Cambridge CELTA (Certificate in English Language Teaching to Adults) is the longest established qualification for English language teachers and has over 8,000 student-teacher enrolments per year. It was developed by the University of Cambridge ESOL and managed around the world by the University of Cambridge Local Examination Syndicate (UCLES).

The CELTA is a pre-experience course, usually run on a four-week intensive basis, though some schools do run part-time courses. CELTA is run in over 40 countries around the world and is externally validated by University of Cambridge ESOL; a course normally costs between £700-1000 ($1300-1900).

A CELTA course is normally a 4-week intensive programme, with an examination at the end (the fee for the examination is normally included as part of the course fee). There are a few part-time CELTA courses, but these are very much the exception.

CELTA courses are, like the Trinity College London Certificate course (see next page), based on practical teaching – with observed teaching practice integral to any course. Pass rates are generally high, since applicants are carefully selected: when applying, you will be interviewed and might have to take a language awareness test. Candidates are assessed over the duration of the course (with moderation by external examiners), and there is no final examination. Successful candidates are awarded a Pass, a Pass B or a Pass A.

Many candidates are recent university graduates, but the course attracts a wide range of applicants, including mature professionals looking for a change of career or even an alternative to retirement. Although certain levels of previous academic achievement are recommended by the administrators, there are no specific entry requirements, and admission is at the discretion of the course provider. Most centres will accept non-native speakers who can demonstrate an acceptable level of written and spoken English.

The course is available throughout the year in more than 50 countries, and is taken by more than 10,000 candidates annually. It consists of a minimum of 114 hours, and includes an element of teaching practice to genuine ESOL students.

## CELTYL

Cambridge CELTYL (Certificate in English Language Teaching to Young Learners) is administered by the University of Cambridge Local Examination Syndicate (UCLES). This course provides a course in teaching age groups of 5–10, 8–13 or 11–16. Some candidates are new to TESOL, others are practising teachers who wish to develop their skills. Most of the details given above about the CELTA also apply to CELTYL. As an alternative to the full CELTYL course, successful CELTA candidates can take a Young Learners extension course (CELTYL Ext).

## COTE

Cambridge COTE (Certificate for Overseas Teachers of English) is a pre-experience course that is taken as an alternative to CELTA by non-native-speakers who already have teaching experience in their own language. You will probably still see this in brochures and advertisments, but it has now been replaced by the similar ICELT examination (below).

### ICELT (In-service Certificate in English Language Teaching)

An in-service award for practising teachers who want to improve their skills in the context in which they are currently working. Candidates taking ICELT courses are normally assessed teaching their own classes. A modular option enables courses to focus on language for teaching purposes only or for the full award to be gained in two phases. ICELT replaced the broadly similar COTE (Certificate for Overseas Teachers of English) from the start of 2004.

**University of Cambridge**
ESOL Examinations
1 Hills Road
Cambridge, CB1 2EU, UK
**Tel:** + 44 (0)1223 553355
**Fax:** +44 (0)1223 460278
**Email:** esolhelpdesk@ucles.org.uk
**Website:** www.cambridgeESOL.org

# Trinity College London

## Certificate in TESOL

The Certificate in TESOL (Teaching English to Speakers of Other Languages) – often referred to as *certTESOL* is administered by Trinity College London. It has over 4,000 student-teachers enrolments per year and is, like the CELTA (above) a well-recognised Certificate in practical ELT teaching. Trainees are expected to take courses in a foreign language, to understand the difficulties in teaching a foreign language. No two courses are the same, as course designers can introduce their own ideas and elements, so you will need to verify the details of the specific course. Cert.TESOL courses are usually full-time intensive and last between four to six weeks, although part-time courses are available at a few centres. The costs are very similar to a CELTA, £700-1000 ($1300-1900).

## Certificate in TEYL

The Certificate in Teaching English to Young Learners is administered by Trinity College London. This is a pre-experience course that is normally taken as an add-on module to a Cert.TESOL course and is designed for teachers who would like to specialise in teaching to young learners of English (which is a strong market that is growing rapidly, especially in Italy, Korea, Japan, and Greece).

## Trinity-ARELS One-to-One Certificate

A one-week/25-hour course for teachers of individual students on a one-to-one basis. Most candidates have an initial certificate (for example CertTESOL), but relevant experience is in some cases acceptable as an alternative. Availability is limited at present, but may increase.

**Trinity College London**
89 Albert Embankment
London , SE1 7TP, UK
**Tel:** +44 (0)20 7820 6100
**Fax:** +44 (0)20 7820 6161
**Email:** info@trinitycollege.co.uk
**Website:** www.trinitycollege.co.uk

# Pitman / City & Guilds

## ACE

The Access Certificate in English language teaching (ACE) is a Pitman/City & Guilds qualification developed with Manchester University in the UK. It offers a initial-level certificate for people who have never taught before or for teachers with some experience who want a formal qualification or for teachers experienced in teaching another subject who want to switch to teaching English. The training is in two parts covering theory and practical teaching activities.

**City & Guilds**
1 Giltspur StreetLondon, EC1A 9DD, UK
**Tel**: 020 7294 2800
**Fax**: 020 7294 2400
**Email:** enquiry@city-and-guilds.co.uk
**Website:** www.city-and-guilds.co.uk

# School for International Training (SIT)

### SIT TESOL Certificate

SIT is a US-based international organisation offering two qualifications for teachers of English (TESOL). The SIT Certificate in Teaching English to Speakers of Other Languages is available from a few dozen test centres around the world; the course of study is normally offered as an intensive four-week course. SIT also offer an advanced diploma (the IDLTM - International Diploma in Language Teaching Management) as a graduate-level diploma.

**SIT**
Kipling Road, P.O. Box 676,
Brattleboro, Vermont  05302-0676, USA
**Tel**: (802) 257-7751
**Fax**: (802) 258-3248
**Website:** www.sit.edu

# Private Language School Certificates

Some chains of private language schools offer their own 'in-house' training courses and certificates. As a general rule, if these are free and likely to lead to employment or promotion within the organisation, they may be well worth considering. If, however, fees are payable, it is not really advisable to accept any, often vague, assurances that the certificate is internationally-known or respected or that it is equivalent to a CELTA or Cert.TESOL.

Ask to see a list of employers who accept the qualification and contact them to ask if they really do consider this to be a full equivalent of an independent, mainstream certificate.

The best private language school TESOL courses leading to in-house certificates tend to be offered as a supplement to mainstream qualifications (for example, a refresher course) rather than as an alternative.

# University Certificate Courses

University Certificate courses are usually short courses running from one to six months and are an alternative to the Cambridge or Trinity certificates (above). These are the most common pre-experience courses available, with almost every university and college in the UK offering some form of English language teaching course. There are also 'in-service' certificate courses available for those teachers who have classroom experience but no formal qualifications.

## Distance Learning Courses

Some training courses in English language teaching are offered on a distance basis, though these are not generally popular with employers unless they include an observed period of teaching practice and are externally validated. But if you are already teaching English abroad, they can be a viable option.

## Certificates for Teaching English for Business

There are a number of different examinations for teachers who would like to train to teach English for business: Chauncey group, LCCIEB, Pitman and University of Cambridge ESOL all offer specialist qualifications. These are covered in detail on page 176 in the section on Professional Development.

## Do I need a degree?

In some countries such as Japan and Korea a university degree is a legal requirement (the requirement is for a degree in any subject rather than in TESOL/TEFL). In Spain some schools look for teachers to have a degree because government contracts demand it. We cover degrees, diplomas and post-graduate qualifications in chapter 5.

# University Degree Courses

Although qualifications in TEFL/TESL and TESOL are usually offered at the postgraduate level, there are a few programmes which enable undergraduate students to study for a Bachelor's degree in this area. Contact individual universities for information regarding admission requirements. For Diploma and post-experience university courses, see the chapter on Career Development.

## NEW ZEALAND (+64)

**Victoria University, Wellington**
PO Box 600, Wellington 6001, New Zealand
**Tel:** 4 472 1000
**Website:** www.vuw.ac.nz
**Courses Offered:** B.A. Linguistics.

## UK (+44)

**Coventry University**
Priory Street, Coventry CV1 5FB
**Tel**: 024 7688 7688
**Website:** www.coventry.ac.uk
**Courses Offered:** English and TEFL BA (Hons)

**De Montfort University**
**The Gateway, Leicester, LE1 9BH**
**Tel:** (0116) 255 1551
**Website:** www.dmu.ac.uk
**Courses Offered**: Education Studies and TEFL

**Northumbria University**
Ellison Place, Newcastle upon Tyne, NE1 8ST
**Tel**: 0191 238 6002
**Website:** www.northumbria.ac.uk
**Courses Offered:** TESOL BA

**Nottingham Trent University**
Burton Street, Nottingham NG1 4BU
**Tel:** 0115 941 8418
**Website:** www.ntu.ac.uk
**Courses offered**: English and TESOL BA (Hons)

**University of Wales Swansea**
Singleton Park, Swansea, SA2 8PP
**Tel:** 01792 205678
**Website:** www.swan.ac.uk
**Courses Offered**: English and TEFL BA

**University of Sunderland**
Edinburgh Building, City Campus, Chester Road, Sunderland SR1 3SD.
**Tel**: 0191 515 3154
**Website:** www.sunderland.ac.uk
**Courses Offered**: English and TESOL BA

**University of Middlesex**
North London Business Park, Oakleigh Road South, London N11 1QS
**Tel:** 0208 411 5000
**Website:** www.mdx.ac.uk
**Courses Offered**: English and TEFL BA

**University of Manchester**
Department of Linguistics, Oxford Road, Manchester M13 9PL, UK

**Tel:** 0161 275 3187
**Website:** www.manchester.ac.uk
**Courses Offered:** B.A. Linguistics; B.A. English Language.

## University of Sterling
centre for English Language Teaching, Stirling FK9 4LA, Scotland UK
**Website:** www.stir.ac.uk
**Courses Offered:** B.A. ELT; B.A. EFL

## University of Sussex
Falmer, Brighton BN1 9QH, UK
**Tel:** 01273 678195
**Fax:** 01273 671320
**Website:** www.sussex.ac.uk
**Courses Offered:** B.A. Linguistics.

## Wolverhampton University
Wulfruna St., Wolverhampton WV1 1SB, UK
**Tel:** 01902 322222
**Website:** www.wlv.ac.uk
**Course Length:** 3 years.
**Courses Offered:** B.A. TESOL.

## USA & CANADA (+1)

## Brigham Young University, UT
Dept. of Linguistics, 2129 JKHB, Provo, UT 84602-6278
**Tel:** (801) 378-4789
**Website:** www.byu.edu
**Courses Offered:** B.A. Linguistics.

## Brigham Young University, HI
Hawaii Campus, P.O. Box 1940, Laie, HI 96762.
**Tel:** (808) 293 3614
**Website:** www.byuh.edu
**Courses Offered:** B.A. TESOL.

## Cal. State, Northridge
Linguistics Program, 18111 Nordhoff St., Northridge, CA 91330-8306
**Website:** www.csun.edu
**Start Dates:** Any semester.
**Courses Offered:** B.A. Linguistics.

## Caroll College
161 N. Benton Ave., Helena, MT 59625
**Website:** www.caroll.edu
**Courses Offered:** BA TESOL.
**Start Dates:** Any semester.

## Central Washington University
400 E. 8th Ave., Ellensburg, WA 98926-7562.
**Website:** www.cwu.edu
**Start Dates:** Any quarter.
**Courses Offered:** B.Ed. TESOL.

## Eastern Kentucky University
Case Annex 270-1340, Richmond, KY 40475
**Website:** www.eku.edu
**Start Dates:** Any semester.
**Course Offered:** B.A. English with TESL.

## Eastern Mennonite University
1200 Park Road, Harrisonburg, VA 22802–2462
**Tel:** (540) 432 4000
**Website:** www.emu.edu
**Start Dates:** Any semester.
**Courses Offered:** Minor in TESL.

## Iowa State University
300 Pearson Hall, Ames, IA 50011.
**Tel:** (515) 294 4555
**Website:** www.iastate.edu
**Courses Offered:** Linguistics; K-12 ESL Teaching

## US International University
10455 Pomerado Road, San Diego, CA 92131
**Tel:** (858) 635 4772
**Courses Offered:** B.A. TESOL.

## University of Florida
Gainesville, FL 32611
**Tel:** (352) 392 3261
**Website:** www.ufl.edu
**Courses Offered:** B.A in Linguistics/Minor in TESOL

## University of Rochester
Dept. of Linguistics, 503 Lattimore Hall, P.O. Box 270096, Rochester, NY 14627-0096.
**Tel:** (716) 275 8053
**Website:** www.rochester.edu
**Courses Offered:** B.A. Linguistics.

## University of Texas, Austin
Dept. of Linguistics, Austin TX 78712-1196.
**Tel:** (512) 471 1701
**Courses Offered:** B.A. Linguistics.

## University of Calgary
2500 University Drive NW, Calgary, Alberta, T2N 1N4, Canada.
**Tel:** (403) 220 5110
**Website:** www.ucalgary.edu
**Courses Offered:** B.A. Linguistics

# Finding a Job

This chapter gives you leads and ideas on how best to find a job as an English language teacher. The main employers are ELT/ESL schools around the world, but there are also jobs in large international companies, and other specialist organisations. You can find jobs on our website, apply directly to a school or through a recruitment agency, use one of the hundreds of websites, or look for adverts in the trade newspapers and journals.

One of the great advantages of being an English language teacher is that you can travel the world and still get a job; almost every country has a requirement for English language teachers – some need teachers specialising in a particular accent (British or American), others have a focus on a particular age-range. However, once you have either a recognised qualification (see previous chapter) or basic experience, you can travel and find work around the world. This means that any ELT job section must cover travel and working practice around the world (see the next chapter) as well as covering agencies that can get you a job in a particular country. Over the next few pages, you will see how to find a job, how to get through an interview, how to get a job in a different country and how to prepare for the culture shock of travelling and teaching in a new environment.

## How Do I Find A Job?

Probably the easiest way to find a job is to use the resources we provide! Either contact the schools and teacher recruitment agencies listed in this book or visit the Oxford Seminars teacher placement service (www.oxfordseminars.com) or visit our sister magazine websites (www.eslmag.com for American English teachers and www.etprofessional.com for international English language teachers) and view 100s of job vacancies online.

To apply directly to a school, use the information listed in the country sections of this guide – you'll find this starting on page 42. If you want to teach English abroad as a volunteer, turn to page 31 for more information. When it comes to preparing your CV, be sure to stress any practical teaching you may have as well as any qualifications you have earned.

## What Should I Do When I Receive A Job Offer?

Ask your prospective employer if you can contact teachers who are working at the school for references. If the school is reputable, the owner or principal should have no problems with this request. If no other native-speaking teachers are currently employed at the school ask to speak to former employees. If this request does cause a problem, then you should be wary about accepting a job offer from this school. Another point to remember is that some teachers do criticize schools they have worked for even if the problems were mostly of their own making. Lazy and bad teachers do exist – even if they speak the same language as you do! Use common sense in a situation where you are confronted with conflicting stories from schools and teachers. After all, you're going to have to rely on your own judgement when you are living and working in a new environment.

## What If A Dispute Arises?

No single aspect of teaching EFL overseas causes more heartache, grief, and anguish than disputes between teachers and employers arising from contractual problems. Historically, certain countries, such as South Korea, were notorious for such disputes although there have been moves to stop these unpleasant episodes from arising. A few words of advice: don't be surprised if you find yourself caught in a dispute over a matter like wages, hours or accommodation. It has happened to thousands of EFL teachers before you and you won't be the last. Try to make sure you have a written contract and insist that it is translated into English. In many countries, the English language contract will not be valid so try to find a third party who knows both the language of your employer and English who can check that both contracts say the same thing.

If a dispute arises, try to be civil and courteous with your employer. Again, if you can find a third party to mediate the dispute this may help diffuse the situation. Some experienced teachers have reported that yelling at an employer has brought about the desired results but this is not advisable unless you are confident you can find a job if you get fired! If you find that your employer is consistently underpaying you or is increasing your hours without giving you money then start looking for another job. Unless you are in a remote region, there will probably be other language schools that will welcome your experience.

# Recruitment Agencies and International School Groups

There are plenty of commercial recruitment agencies specialising in the English language market – working for a school to help find teachers or helping a teacher find a job. The agencies are normally paid by the employer (the school), though make sure that you check before you sign up! Agencies normally cover a particular area or country – and will help you put together a good CV, send you new job opportunities and even advice on relocating, accommodation and visas.

Almost all the jobs for ELT or ESL teachers are with English language schools. The majority of all schools are run on an individual basis, with the director of studies also the person who interviews and appoints new teachers. But there are some major chains of schools who have their own internal recruitment agencies who can help you find a job within the schools in their group. Once you have a job in the group, the internal job-agency often works to help find a job in another school within the group or in a different country.

The biggest ELT employer in the world is the British Council, which has its own recruitment service – see page 27 for more details on the British Council.

As a good starting point, try these commercial agencies and major international school groups:

## Anglo Pacific
Suite 32, Nevilles Court, Dollis Hill Lane, London NW2 6HG
**Tel**: +44 (0)20 8452 7836
Agency that specializes in recruitment in SE Asia

## Avalon House
8 Denmark Street, London WC2H 8LS
**Tel**: +44 (0)20 7279 1998
**Email:** info@avalonschool.co.uk
**Web**: www.avalonschool.co.uk
Recruitment for its schools in China, France, Spain, Poland, UK

## Bell Educational Trust
Overseas Department, Hillscross, Red Cross Lane, Cambridge, CB2 2QX
**Tel**: +44 (0)1223 246644
**Fax**: +44 (0)1223 414080
**Email:** info.overseas@bell-schools.ac.uk
**Web**: www.bell-schools.ac.uk
Major group that has schools around the world; most schools recruit locally, but this office can provide contact information

## Benedict Schools
3 Place Chauderon, PO Box 270, 1000 Lausanne 9, Switzerland
**Tel**: +21 323 6655
**Fax**: +21 323 6777
**Email:** info@benedict-schools.com
**Web**: www.benedict-schools.com
Major group with over 80 schools (in Europe, Africa and America); most schools recruit locally, but this office can provide contact information

## Berlitz
Lincoln House, 296-302 High Holborn, London WC1V 7JH
**Tel**: +44 (0)20 7915 0909
**Fax**: +44 (0)20 7915 0222
**Web**: www.berlitz.com
Major group that has over 400 centres around the world; teachers are trained in the Berlitz way of teaching

## Billington Recruitment
1 Mariners Close, St James Court, Victoria Dock, Kingston upon Hull, HU9 1QE

**Email:** bill1312@hotmail.com
Agency that covers Europe

## British Council
Education and Training Group, 10 Spring Gardens, London SW1A 2BN
**Tel**: +44 (0)20 7389 4596
**Fax**: +44 (0)20 7389 4594
**Email:** assistants@britishcouncil.org
**Web**: www.languageassistant.co.uk
Provides language assistants to schools around the world. (See section on British Council on next page)

## CG Associates
83 Clarence Mews, London
**Tel**: +44 (0)7802 211542
**Email:** info@christopherg.co.uk
Agency offering worldwide coverage.

## CIEE
52 Poland Street, London W1F 7AB
**Tel**: +44 (0)20 7478 2020
**Fax**: +44 (0)20 7734 7322
**Web**: www.councilexchanges.org.uk
Looks after the JET (Japan Exchange Teaching) programme as well as Teach in China and Teach in Thailand programmes

## EF - English First
Teacher Recruitment, 36-38 St Aubyns, Hove, East Sussex, BN3 2TD
**Tel**: +44 (0)1273 201431
**Fax**: +44 (0)1273 746742
**Email:** recruitment.uk@englishfirst.com
**Web**: www.englishfirst.com
Major group that has schools around the world

## ELS Language Centers
400 Alexander Park, Princeton, NJ 08540
**Tel**: +1 609 750 3512
**Fax**: +1 609 750 3596
**Email:** info@els.com
**Web**: www.els.com
Major group that works with Berlitz for its language centers – however its 40-plus schools still recruit through this central address

## ERC Recruitment
New Tyning, Stone Allerton, Axbridge, BS26 2NJ

**Tel**: +44 (0)1934 713892
**Email**: info@erc-recruitment.co.uk
**Web**: www.erc-recruitment.co.uk
Agency offering worldwide coverage

### GEOS English Academy
Compton Park, Compton Park Road, Eastbourne,
BN21 1EH
**Email**: info@geos.com
**Web**: www.geos.com
Major group that has over 500 schools around the
world

### GTCE
52 Loampit Hill, Lewisham, London SE13 7SW
**Tel**: +44 (0)20 8691 6569
**Email**: info@gtce.co.uk
**Web**: www.gtce.co.uk
Agency that concentrates on China

### International House
106 Piccadilly, London W1V 7NL
**Tel**: +44 (0)20 7518 6970
**Fax**: +44 (0)20 7518 6971
**Email**: hr@ihlondon.co.uk
**Web**: www.ihworld.com
Major group that has over 120 schools around the
world

### Linguarama
Personnel Department, 89 High Street, Alton,
Hampshire, GU34, 1LG
**Tel**: +44 (0)1420 80899
**Fax**: +44 (0)1420 80856
**Email**: personnel@linguarama.com

**Web**: www.linguarama.com
Major group that has schools around the world

### Protocol Professional
**Tel**: +44 (0)115 911 1177
**Email**: recruitment@protocol-professional.co.uk
**Web**: www.protocol-professional.co.uk
Agency that specializes on the UK

### Saxoncourt
124 New Bond Street, London W1S 1DX
**Tel**: +44 (0)20 7491 1911
**Fax**: +44 (0)20 7493 3657
**Email**: recruit@saxoncourt.com
**Web**: www.saxoncourt.com
Major group of schools and recruitment centre that
places over 500 teachers per year around the world

### Sterling Recruitment
49 Sudbury Ave, Wembley, Middx, HA0 3AN
**Tel**: +44 (0)20 8903 4424
**Fax**: +44 (0)20 8903 3566
Recruitment Agency for jobs in London

### Wall Street Institute
Paca de Catalunya 9, 4th Floor, 08002 Barcelona,
Spain
**Tel**: +93 306 33 00
**Fax**: +93 302 08 29
**Web**: www.wallstreetinstitute.com
Major chain of over 400 schools around the world.

# The British Council

The British Council has over 60 language teaching centres, offices in over 100 countries and is
the by far the biggest ELT employer in the world, with over 7500 staff (most of whom are
involved in teaching). The Council is funded by the British Government, but works in a
non-political way promoting British English and culture around the world.

For job-hunters, the British Council can help in two ways:
**1.** Each local office is a mine of information about local schools, job opportunities and
conditions of work. Many offices have pre-printed information for prospective job-hunters and
sometimes provide contacts to known schools in the country. For a list of local offices, see our

directory on page 302 or visit www.britishcouncil.org

**2.** The British Council has over 60 teaching centres and it recruits around 300 teachers per year. For more information, contact Educational Enterprises, British Council, 10 Spring Gardens, London SW1A 2BN, Tel: +44 (0)20 7389 4931, Fax: +44 (0)20 7389 4140, Email: teacher.vacancies@britishcouncil.org

The British Council also publishes a wide range of leaflets and information packs about training to be an English language teacher and opportunities within the organisation. Either visit the information-packed website (www.britishcouncil.org) or contact its information centre: Bridgewater House, 58 Whitworth Street, Manchester M1 6BB, Tel: +44 (0)161 957 7755, Fax: +44 (0)161 957 7762

# UK Summer Schools

The UK has a very strong summer-school industry (with several hundred schools working the season) that always has a need for qualified teachers. The summer schools cater for students who want to learn English over a summer holiday; these students can be either young learners or young adults – but, even with the current downturn in international travel, the summer schools are still very busy – as is their requirement for teachers.

The rates of pay for work in summer schools is often higher than usual. In the past, some summer schools have not offered very good quality teaching, but with the work of industry associations, particularly English UK (www.EnglishUK.com) - the newly-merged organisation previously known as ARELS (Association of Recognised English Language Schools) and BASELT (British Association of State English Language Teaching) - and the British Council (www.britishcouncil.org), the schools are being accredited and standards are now high.

With so many schools on their lists, it's impossible to fit all these into this book: the best way to search for a suitable school to approach for a job is to use a site such as English in Britain (www.EnglishInBritain.com) or the English UK (www.EnglishUK.com) websites – both have search features.

# Jobs in Canada

To teach in most private language schools in Canada you will need a TESOL or TESL certificate. To find a list of schools, the simplest route is to use the Internet. The next few pages include ESL job sites in Canada. Alternatively, use the website directory for the individual states to search for schools in the state.

# Jobs in the USA

In the USA, each state has its own requirements for teacher qualifications (read the requirements later in this *Guide*). The schools within a state must also be registered with their state education body – and each state, again, has its own requirements for schools operating in their area.

# Jobs on the Internet

There are hundreds of websites specialising in the ELT/ESL job sector. Some simply provide advice, others offer help with interviews, others provide lists of jobs available in a particular region or country.

## Starting Points

Try these sites for a varied flavour of what the Internet offers job-hunters – these are some of the main sites from each of the following sections.

**British Council Vacancies**
www.britishcouncil.org/teacherrecruitment.htm

**English Teaching Professional**
www.etprofessional.com

**ESL Magazine**
www.eslmag.com

**International House Recruitment Services**
www.ihworld.com/recruitment/

**Oxford Seminars**
www.oxfordseminars.com

**Peace Corps**
www.peacecorps.gov

**Saxoncourt**
www.saxoncourt.com

**The Times Educational Supplement**
www.tesjobs.co.uk/homepage.asp

**VSO (Voluntary Service Overseas)**
www.vso.org.uk/volunteering/education_tefl.htm

## Career Advice

**Starting a Career in TESOL (tesol.org)**
www.tesol.org/careers/counsel/

**Teaching English Abroad**
www.cal.org/ericcll/digest/snow0001.html

**Best Bets for Teaching Abroad**
www.uci.edu/~cie/iop/teaching.html

**Creating a CV**
www.onestopenglish.com/Jobs/

**200 FREE Cover Letters For Job Hunters**
www.careerlab.com/letters/

## Finding a Job – all-in-one sites

**BestPeople**
www.bestpeople.co.uk

**CareerCentral**
www.careercentral.com

**CareerMosaic UK**
www.careermosaic-uk.co.uk

**Gradunet-Virtual Careers Office**
www.gradunet.co.uk

**JobHunter**
www.jobhunter.co.uk

**Jobs Unlimited**
www.jobsunlimited.co.uk

**JobSearch**
www.jobsearch.co.uk

**JobSite UK**
www.jobsite.co.uk

**Monster**
www.monster.co.uk

**Reed Online**
www.reed.co.uk

## ELT-specific Jobs

**All English Job**
www.allenglishjob.com

**Canadian Institute for Teaching Overseas (CITO)**
www.nsis.com/~cito/CITO.html

**Dave's ESL Café: Job centre**
www.eslcafe.com/jobs/

**Easter School Agency**
www.easterschool.com

**Edufind ELT Job Centre**
www.jobs.edufind.com

**EFLTeachingJobs.com**
www.eflteachingjobs.com

**English Club ESL Jobs Centre**
http://jobs.englishclub.com

**English Job Maze**
www.englishjobmaze.com

**English Teacher Recruitment: Greece**
www.teach.english.freeservers.com

**English Worldwide – Recruitment & Training**
www.englishworldwide.com

**English-International.com**
www.english-international.com

**Erudite Café Job centre**
www.eruditecafe.net/job_centre1.php

**ESL Career.com**
www.eslcareer.com

**ESLclassifieds.com**
www.eslclassifieds.com/esljobsoffered.html

**ESL Employment**
www.eslemployment.com

**ESL Job Search**
www.esljobsearch.com

**ESL Magazine**
www.eslmag.com

**ESL Resume Database**
my.globalesl.net/

**ESL Teachers Club**
www.eslteachersclub.com

**ESL WideWord Teach English**
www.eslwideworld.com

**ESLworldwide.com**
www.ESLworldwide.com

**ETNI – Advertising Teaching Positions in Israel**
www.etni.org.il/anntchadver.htm

**Foreignteacher.com**
www.foreignteacher.com/currentjobs.htm

**Global ESL Network**
www.globalesl.net

**Jobs Offered**
www.englishclub.net/cgi-bin/jobs/jobs_o.pl

**Russian School Placement**
www.sv-agency.udm.ru/svfiles/school.htm

**Saxoncourt & English Worldwide**
www.saxoncourt.com

**TeachAbroad.com**
www.teachabroad.com

**Teaching Abroad**
www.teaching-abroad.co.uk

**Teaching Abroad .net**
www.teachingabroad.net

**Teaching ESL at Kuwait University**
www.iteslj.org/Articles/Martin-Kuwait

**TEFL Job Placement**
www.tefljobplacement.com

**TEFL Jobs**
www.tefljobs.net

**TEFLnet**
www.tefl.net/jobs/

**TEFL Professional Network**
www.tefl.com

**University EFL/ESL Positions**
www.ultimateenglish.com

**Work Abroad ESL.com**
www.workabroadesl.com

## ELT Jobs in Asia

**Collection of Teaching Positions in Taiwan**
http://esltaiwan.20M.com

**Ding Ding Dang Recruiting**
www.dingdingdang.com

**EFL in Asia**
www.geocities.com/Tokyo/Flats/7947/eflasia.htm

**English Teaching programme in Thailand**
www.taiteach.com

**EnglishWork.com**
www.englishwork.com

**ESL City**
www.eslcityjobs.com

**ESL House: China**
www.eslhouseonline.com

**HBS Consulting: Korea**
www.hbscompany.com

**International Avenue Consulting**
www.iacc.com.tw

**Japanese Jobs**
www.japanesejobs.com/textonly/index.html

**Jobs in Japan**
www.eltnews.com/jobsinjapan.shtml

**KOAM Academy: Korea**
www.koam.org

**O-Hayo Sensei: Japan**
www.ohayosensei.com

**Reena Recruiting Co. Ltd.**
www.reena-recruit.com

**Russell Recruiting**
www.asiangateway.net

**Taiwan Teacher**
www.geocities.com/Athens/Delphi/1979/

**Teach English in South Korea**
www.teachenglish.co.uk/jobs.htm

**teacheslabroad.com: Korea**
www.teacheslabroad.com

**Teaching English and Educating in Korea**
www.keepro.com

**Teaching English in China**
www.EnglishTeachersExpress.com

**teach-in-thailand.com**
www.teach-in-thailand.com

**TeachinginJapan**
www.teachinginjapan.com

**teachkorea.com**
www.teachkorea.com/mb.htm

# Volunteer Programmes

In some countries the demand for adult English language teachers outstrips the supply; as state-funded programmes struggle to provide needed services with shrinking funds, the role of volunteers in teaching English becomes crucial. And this happens in developing countries as well as western countries such as the USA and Canada.

The following organisations arrange for volunteer teachers to travel and teach in volunteer programmes around the world, particularly into China and Africa. There are also volunteer groups providing support and teachers into local communities, for example, into regions of the USA where there is a great need for volunteer teachers. The volunteer groups should help arrange your travel, training, accommodation and any visas.

## AmeriCorps

www.americorps.org

AmeriCorps is a United States-based organization. The domestic Peace Corps has more than 40,000 Americans in intensive, results-driven service each year. AmeriCorps has built its foundation on teaching children to read, attempting to make neighborhoods safer, building affordable homes, and responding to natural disasters. AmeriCorps serves with projects such as Habitat for Humanity, the American Red Cross, and Boys and Girls Clubs. After a term of service, AmeriCorps members receive education awards to help finance college tuition or pay back student loans.

## AmeriSpan Unlimited

www.amerispan.com

AmeriSpan has become a major force for anyone wanting to study language abroad in Latin America. AmeriSpan's network offers language programmes in nearly every Spanish-speaking country in the Americas.

## Amity Institute

www.amity.org

Amity Institute was founded in 1962. It is a non-profit educational exchange programme that gives young people around the world the opportunity to represent their countries, by sharing their languages and cultures in language classrooms of all levels. Amity tries to encourage and enhance international understanding and friendship through the study of world languages and cultures.

## Christians Abroad

www.cabroad.org.uk

Provides advice and information for volunteers of any faith who are considering working abroad as a volunteer. It provides job vacancies through a monthly listing newsletter – the majority of its postings are to Asia and Africa. Also visit www.wse.org.uk for online information packs.

## Colorado China Council

www.asiacouncil.org

The primary focus of CCC is to send people to teach English in China, as well as other academic subjects, at universities and secondary schools throughout the country. The Council has placed over 200 teachers, making it one of the U.S.'s largest non-religious providers of teachers to China.

## Cross-Cultural Solutions

www.crossculturalsolutions.org

Cross-Cultural Solutions offers short-term and long-term programmes that give volunteers from all over the world the opportunity to come face to face with global issues and become part of productive solutions. CCS has close partnerships with social service pioneers in our host countries. The focus of CCS's work is health care, education and social development

## Friends of World Teaching

www.fowt.com

Friends of World Teaching helps teachers find jobs around the world. Friends of World Teaching works with English-speaking schools and colleges throughout the world that offer employment opportunities to American and Canadian teachers. There are some student teaching programmes as well.

## Global Routes

www.globalroutes.org

Global Routes is a tax-exempt non-profit, is a non-governmental, non-sectarian organization whose aim is to strengthen the global community. It has designed community-service/cross-cultural-exchange programmes that bring people with different world-views together.

## India Literacy Project

www.ilpnet.org

India Literacy Project is a US-based non-profit, volunteer organization that focuses on literacy in India. Its aim is to empower every individual we serve with functional literacy and an understanding of their basic rights and responsibilities. India Literacy Project's goal is 100% literacy in India.

## Intl. Foundation for Ed. & Self-help

www.ifesh.org

The International Foundation for Education and Self-Help (IFESH) was established as a non-governmental, nonprofit, charitable organization. IFESH aims to reduce hunger and poverty, empower people through literacy, train and place the unskilled and unemployed in jobs, provide preventive and basic health care to individuals in need, deal with population and environment problems, develop employment through economic development activities, foster cultural, social, and economic relations between Africans and Americans, particularly African Americans, and others.

## International Rescue Committee

www.intrescom.org

International Rescue Committee was founded in 1933. The IRC is a nonsectarian, voluntary organization that provides relief, protection and resettlement services for refugees and victims of oppression or violent conflict throughout the world.

## Intl. Schools Internship programme

www.tieonline.com

A TIE subscription gives you immediate access to the most prominent schools looking for staff: from 90 to 150 schools are always on the Job Ads web page. And the TIE Resume Bank means over 200 headmasters of International schools can access your file; and from there they can contact you through email, phone, your website, etc. Schools can, and often do, change their vacancies weekly at so you can be the first to know when a vacancy in the country you want opens up!

## Laubach Literacy

www.laubach.org/home.html

Laubach Literacy Action (LLA), the U.S. programme Division of Laubach Literacy, is the largest volunteer-based literacy organization in the United States. We provide a full range of literacy services to more than 175,000 students annually through more than 1,000 local member programmes, 45 state organizations. Instruction is provided by a national network of more than 80,000 volunteer trainers and tutors .

## Literacy Volunteers

www.literacyvolunteers.org

Literacy Volunteers of America, Inc. has served adults at the lowest levels of literacy and their families since 1962, and has assisted more than half a million people to acquire literacy skills. LVA offers a professionally designed and field-tested workshop that enables volunteers to tutor adults in English for speakers of other languages. After being matched with an adult learner or a small group of learners, tutors receive regular support and opportunities for additional training through the local LVA affiliate.

## National Adult Literacy Database

www.nald.ca

The National Adult Literacy Database Inc. (NALD) is a federally incorporated, non-profit service organization which fills the crucial need for a single-source, comprehensive, up-to-date and easily accessible database of adult literacy programmes, resources, services and activities across Canada. It also links with other services and databases in North America and overseas.

## PeaceCorps

www.peacecorps.org

As an English teaching volunteer, you will help expand the horizons and opportunities of students and teachers alike in Peace Corps' largest programme. There is no other experience like helping a middle school, secondary school, or university. More than 7,000 Peace Corps volunteers are serving in 76 countries. They are working to bring clean water to communities, teach children, help start new small businesses, and stop the spread of AIDS. Since 1961, more than 161,000 Americans have joined the Peace Corps, serving in 134 nations.

## Volunteer Adventures
www.volunteeradventures.com
VolunteerAdventures provides a range of projects across Africa, Asia, Central and South America, and Oceania. There are projects focussing on community development, conservation and TEFL. The TEFL-based projects include options to gain teacher qualifications and certification.

## VolunteerMatch
www.volunteermatch.org
VolunteerMatch, ImpactOnline's main service, uses the power of the Internet to help individuals find volunteer opportunities posted by local non-profit and public sector organizations.

## Volunteers in Asia
www.volasia.org
VIA is a private, non-profit, non-sectarian organization whose aim it is to increase understanding between the United States and Asia. Its Volunteer Programs in Asia have provided young Americans with an opportunity to work and live within an Asian culture while meeting the needs of Asian host institutions, since 1962.

## VSO (Voluntary Service Overseas)
www.vso.org.uk
The VSO is one of the biggest and best-known of the volunteer agencies. It works in over 70 countries around the world, with a current majority of postings to China and Africa. The VSO offers volunteers a complete package, including basic training (volunteers are expected to have a degree or be experienced TEFL teachers), airfares and, importantly, in-country support centres.

## VSO Canada
www.vsocan.com
People are what VSO Canada is all about– and you just might be one of them. VSO's people share their skills in developing countries.

## WorldTeach
www.worldteach.org
WorldTeach is a non-profit, non-governmental organization based at the centre for International Development at Harvard University which provides opportunities for individuals to make a meaningful contribution to international education by living and working as volunteer teachers in developing countries.

Gap year travel (huge in the UK, still relatively unknown in Canada and the USA) is a way for students to take a year out and travel before settling down to their studies at university, often working as a volunteer (and teaching English is a popular option). The needs and expectations of both sides (agency and volunteer) are very different for gap year compared to a qualified teacher taking a career break or travelling, so there are agencies that specialise in this work. For information about working in your gap year, visit these websites:

The gap year company    www.gapyear.com
GAP Activity projects    www.gap.org.uk
Gap Challenge    www. world-challenge.co.uk

# Preparation: Before you go

This section covers the preparation you need to consider before you head off on your travels around the world: in particular, income tax on earnings and insurance.

## Before you go

If you are thinking of teaching English in another country, you should have a lot of questions on your mind. Here are some of the most frequent questions asked by prospective teachers and the answers.

### When Should I Plan To Go?

This depends on where you want to teach. In many countries, everything shuts down during certain months of the year, usually in the summer. Our country profiles, later in this book, provide general information about the best time to apply for jobs. You can apply for jobs from home or you can turn up on spec. Both approaches have their own merits and drawbacks depending on the country you want to teach in. The country guides offer more detailed answers to this question.

### What Should I Take With Me?

Essentials – like obtaining health insurance valid for your stay overseas – are dealt with later in this chapter. Do remember to check if your passport will be valid for the period of time you plan to be away – it's amazing the number of teachers who forget to do this!

Make sure you take clothes appropriate for the climate you will be living in. Remember that a country that is hot and sunny in the summer can be freezing cold in the winter. Clothing may be expensive in your new country so take a good supply of things you like to wear. Check with the school to see if you will be required to dress formally when you teach. If you will be going out to look for a teaching job on spec it would not hurt to take clothes that you would wear to an interview. Appearance really does count when you are job hunting, almost as much your CV in some cases! You might want to invest in some ESL/ EFL teaching books as these may be hard to obtain in your destination country – they may be in short supply. A good dictionary and a grammar guidebook will always come in handy when you are faced with any awkward questions about word definitions or the nature of past participles. Also, make sure you have a few good novels for your leisure time. If you are learning the language of your destination country (it's a good idea), then take along some tapes, books and a Walkman.

### Will I Need A Teaching Qualification?

It's a good idea to get some training before you go or why not take a teaching course while you are on your travels? Whether you train in your home country or while you are away is your decision, but if you plan to train in another country make sure that there are appropriate courses on offer.

# Insurance

When planning to travel abroad you should you have adequate health insurance. With so many different types of coverage available it can be very confusing deciding which plan is right for you. Here's what to look for.

### Don't leave home without it

All European Union citizens are entitled to the same level of medical care in any other country of the EU as they would receive at home. To secure this coverage as a UK citizen, you must obtain form E111 from the Department of Health and Social Security before you leave the UK.

If you plan to stay for more than a few months, you should check what your local social security contributions entitle you to and decide whether you need to take out a private health care scheme. A private scheme gives you more flexibility about where you are treated, but you should check carefully exactly what your coverage is. It is also possible to obtain coverage for repatriation in a real emergency.

### Home Country Coverage: your existing health plan cover

This section will be of particular importance to citizens of the US (and other countries that do not have a good, free, state-funded health service) who typically have their own private health and medical insurance polices.

For US citizens, if you already have strong benefits at home, it is wise to double-check what exactly is covered while you are out of the country. Most health plans limit coverage to a maximum of 30 or 60 days outside the States, and HMOs and PPOs will likely impose severe – out of network – penalties for all but the most basic emergency care. More importantly, you will want to insure you have 24 hour access to emergency evacuation if you are sick or hurt in an area where quality care is not available. For those over 65, Medicare will not cover treatment outside the U.S. If you do not have any domestic coverage, travel insurance is a must. Once you have answered these questions, you will need to know what benefits and policy provisions to look for in a travel medical plan.

### Short Trips (two weeks or less)

Assuming you have solid coverage at home you may only need a small supplemental plan, with features like emergency evacuation and 24 hour worldwide assistance, along with a limited benefit for medical expenses (£10,000 to £50,000 is typical). These plans are readily available through your travel agent and may include lost luggage and trip cancellation protection too. Be wary of plans that require you settle all bills yourself and then seek reimbursement when you return home.

### Intermediate Trips (two weeks to six months)

The longer you are away the less likely it is your own plan will cover you and therefore the more importance you should place on the medical benefits of the plan. In addition to a higher emergency evacuation benefit, your plan should cover between £100,000 to £1 million in medical expenses. Other features to look for include coverage for a family member to come to your assistance if you are taken to hospital in a foreign country and an option to include "hazardous activities" such as scuba diving, skiing and bungee jumping.

### Longer Trips (six months+)

The travel insurance you purchase will most likely be your primary or only health insurance. Be sure that your plan includes all of the above, with higher maximum benefits (£1 million or more) as well as some provision for coverage when you return home. If you spend a year abroad but return home for a vacation, make sure you are still covered.

### Multiyear or Open Ended Trips

Standard medical plans are usually limited to one year, with the option to renew for another. If you anticipate being abroad for a longer period of time, look into a permanent international major medical plan. This type of coverage contains all the benefits of a travel medical plan, but once you are accepted you can maintain coverage year after year simply by paying the premium. Most importantly, you are covered for medical treatment anywhere in the world, including back at home. Note that these plans are medically underwritten, and people with prior health problems may have trouble obtaining coverage.

All of the plan types discussed share some common features; you will normally have a deductible and co-insurance payment or premium to meet, and pre-existing conditions are usually excluded. Worldwide assistance is sometimes done by the plan administrator, or through an independent assistance company. The market for these plans is growing rapidly and new companies enter the market all the time. Be sure the company you are dealing with has at least five to ten years' experience in the international market. Doing a little research before you go can mean security and peace of mind while you are away, and allows you to concentrate on the exciting and fulfilling adventure that international travel and work can be!

*Brian Garity, founder of International Health Insurance.com, has specialized in international health insurance for over ten years.*

# Tax

If you are planning to work abroad, it is important that you know your financial position, especially what your liability for tax will be. In the directory of countries, page 87, we note any special requirements of local tax authorities – often, you will have to register with the local tax office before starting work. However, there are plenty of potential problems when declaring your earned income in your home country. Regulations differ for citizens of different countries. Here are some guidelines for teachers from some Commonwealth countries and from the USA.

## Australian nationals

If you are an Australian national, you have to fill in your own tax return. If you work abroad for less than a full tax year, when you return you will need to declare your earnings and tax, and will either receive a tax credit for the excess tax you have paid or be taxed for the shortfall. If you are abroad for longer periods, there will be a break in your tax requirements in Australia for the period you are away. But check your social security arrangement as payments made overseas will not be credited.

## Canadian nationals

If you are a Canadian national, you will need to consider what your residency status is while you are working abroad. If you work abroad for a short term but keep your ties with Canada, you are considered a factual resident and will be liable to pay federal taxes, etc. If you work abroad for a longer period, you can be considered a non-resident. In this case your tax position in Canada will change. You will need to check with the authorities or consult a financial advisor to confirm your position, however the following general advice applies to anyone who works abroad.

If you move abroad (therefore live abroad for a significant period), taxation is complex - especially if you retain assets in Canada. Double taxation is one major concern - however, most countries have taxation treaties with Canada so this is relatively straightforward to explain to the tax department.

If you plan to move abroad, you might consider the radical step of establishing non-resident status with Canada to be able to take advantage of the (often lower) tax rates in other countries. However, this has serious implications on your return to Canada, so you should talk through the implications with the tax office or a tax advisor. For the latest regulations, visit: www.cra-arc.gc.ca/tax/nonresidents

Lastly, if you work abroad for a period of time then move back to Canada, you could still reclaim some taxes (for up to six years' absence) - again, visit the www.cra-arc.gc.ca for more details and forms.

# UK nationals

It is most important to check whether or not the country you are going to has a reciprocal tax agreement with your home country.

If you are a UK national, you will get tax relief (even up to 100%) if you are out of the country for at least 365 days and do not stay in the UK for more than 62 consecutive days in the tax period. There is a difference between non-resident status and exemption from tax in the UK. If you are classed as a non-resident, you are not liable for tax on unearned income from abroad but you are still considered to be domiciled in the UK. To qualify as a non-resident you must work overseas for more than a full tax year without being in the UK for more than six months in that tax year or three months in each year if your stay abroad spans the tax year.

Many countries have agreements with the UK to prevent the double payment of tax. Credit against UK tax for payment already made abroad will be given if there is no such agreement. (See Inland Revenue form IR6 – Double Taxation Relief).

When you are teaching abroad, it is important that you think about maintaining your UK social security payments so that you qualify for the state pension. You should get form N139 from the Department of Social Security (form SA29 if you are working in the EU).

# US Nationals

The U.S. income tax system (and forms) are well-known to be complex area – and for U.S. citizens working and travelling the world as teachers, this can be particularly difficult. As a U.S. citizen or resident alien, your worldwide income generally is subject to U.S. income tax regardless of where you are living. Also, you are subject to the same income tax filing requirements that apply to U.S. citizens or residents living in the United States. However, several income tax benefits might apply if you meet certain requirements while living abroad. You may be able to exclude from your income a limited amount of your foreign earned income. You also may be able either to exclude or to deduct from gross income your housing amount (more later). To claim these benefits, you must file a tax return and attach Form 2555, Foreign Earned Income. If you are claiming the foreign earned income exclusion only, you may be able to use the shorter Form 2555-EZ, Foreign Earned Income Exclusion, rather than Form 2555.

You may be able to claim a tax credit or an itemized deduction for foreign income taxes that you pay. Also, under tax treaties or conventions that the United States has with many foreign countries, you may be able to reduce your foreign tax liability.

### Income Earned Abroad

You may qualify for an exclusion from tax of up to $70,000 in income earned while working abroad. However, you must file a tax return to claim the exclusion. In general, foreign earned income is income received from services you perform outside of the United States. When we use the term United States, that includes Puerto Rico, Northern Marina Islands, Republic of the Marshall Islands, Federated States of Micronesia, Guam and American Soma. While not all of these countries are part of the United States, they have special tax status. Excluded from gross earned income is your housing costs allowance which are over a certain base amount. Generally, you will qualify for these benefits if your tax home (defined below) is in a foreign country, or countries, throughout your period of bona-fide foreign residence or physical presence and you are one of the following:

1) A U.S. citizen who is a bona-fide resident of a foreign country or countries for an uninterrupted period that includes a complete tax year, or

2) A U.S. resident alien who is a citizen or national of a country with which the United States has an income tax treaty in effect and who is a bona-fide resident of a foreign country or countries for an uninterrupted period that includes an entire tax year, or

3) A U.S. citizen or a U.S. resident alien who is physically present in a foreign country or countries for at least 330 full days during any period of 12 consecutive months.

## Tax Home

Generally, your tax home is the area of your main place of business, employment, or post of duty where you are permanently or indefinitely engaged to work. You are not considered to have a tax home in a foreign country for any period during which your abode (the place where you regularly live) is in the United States. However, being temporarily present in the United States or maintaining a dwelling there does not necessarily mean that your abode is in the United States. For details, see Publication 54.

A foreign country, for this purpose, means any territory under the sovereignty of a government other than that of the United States, including territorial waters (determined under U.S. laws) and air space.

Waiver of time requirements: You may not have to meet the minimum time requirements for bona-fide residence or physical presence if you have to leave the foreign country because war, civil unrest, or similar adverse conditions in the country prevented you from conducting normal business. You must, however, be able to show that you reasonably could have expected to meet the minimum time requirements if the adverse conditions had not occurred. See Publication 54 for a list of foreign countries that individuals have had to leave due to these conditions.

## Travel Restrictions

If you violate U.S. travel restrictions, you will not be treated as being a bona-fide resident of, or physically present in, a foreign country for any day during which you are present in a country in violation of the restrictions. (These restrictions generally prohibit U.S. citizens and residents from engaging in transactions related to travel to, from, or within certain countries.) Also, income that you earn from sources within such a country for services performed during a period of travel restrictions does not qualify as foreign earned income, and housing expenses that you incur within that country (or outside that country for housing your spouse or dependents) while you are present in that country in violation of travel restrictions cannot be included in figuring your foreign housing amount.

Currently, these travel restrictions apply to: Cuba, Libya, and Iraq.

## Exclusion Of Foreign Earned Income

If your tax home is in a foreign country and you meet either the bona fide residence test or the physical presence test, you can choose to exclude from gross income a limited amount of your foreign earned income. Your income must be for services performed in a foreign country during your period of foreign residence or presence, whichever applies. You cannot, however, exclude the pay you receive as an employee of the U.S. Government or its agencies. You cannot exclude pay you receive for services abroad for Armed Forces exchanges, officers' mess, exchange services, etc., operated by the U.S. Army, Navy, or Air Force.

## Foreign Credits And Deductions

If you claim the exclusion, you cannot claim any credits or deductions that are related to the excluded income. You cannot claim a foreign tax credit or deduction for any foreign income tax paid on the excluded income. Nor can you claim the earned income credit if you claim the exclusion. Also, for IRA purposes, the excluded income is not considered compensation and, for figuring deductible contributions when you are covered by an employer retirement plan, is included in your modified adjusted gross income.

## Foreign Amount Excludable

If your tax home is in a foreign country and you qualify under either the bona fide residence test or physical presence test for a tax year, you can exclude your foreign income earned during the year up to $70,000. However, if you qualify under either test for only part of the year, you must reduce ratably the $70,000 maximum based on the number of days within the tax year you qualified under one of the two tests.

## Foreign Income Taxes

A limited amount of the foreign income tax you pay can be credited against your U.S. tax liability or deducted in figuring taxable income on your U.S. income tax return. It is usually to your advantage to claim a credit for foreign taxes rather than to deduct them. A credit reduces your U.S. tax liability, and any excess may be carried back and carried forward to other years. A deduction only reduces your taxable income and may be taken only in the current year. You must treat all foreign income taxes in the same way. You generally cannot deduct some foreign income taxes and take a credit for others.

## Foreign Tax Credit

If you choose to credit foreign taxes against your tax liability, complete Form 1116, Foreign Tax Credit, (Individual, Estate, Trust, or Nonresident Alien Individual), and attach it to your U.S. income tax return.

Do not include the foreign taxes paid or accrued as withheld income taxes on line 55 of Form 1040.

## Foreign Tax Limit

Your credit cannot be more than the part of your U.S. income tax liability allocable to your taxable income from sources outside the United States. So, if you have no U.S. income tax liability, or if all your foreign income is exempt from U.S. tax, you will not be able to claim a foreign tax credit.

If the foreign taxes you paid or incurred during the year exceed the limit on your credit for the current year, you can carry back the unused foreign taxes as credits to 2 prior tax years and then carry forward any remaining unused foreign taxes to 5 later tax years.

Foreign taxes paid on excluded income. You cannot claim a credit for foreign taxes paid on amounts excluded from gross income under the foreign earned income exclusion or the housing amount exclusion, discussed earlier.

## Foreign Tax Deduction

If you choose to deduct all foreign income taxes on your U.S. income tax return, itemize the deduction on Schedule A (Form 1040). You cannot deduct foreign taxes paid on income you exclude from your U.S. income tax return.

More information. The foreign tax credit and deduction, their limits, and the carryback and carryover provisions are discussed in detail in Publication 514, Foreign Tax Credit for Individuals. For more information and to download publications and forms mentioned, visit www.irs.ustreas.gov/forms_pubs/index.html

# Country Profiles

*To find a particular country, see the index on the next page*

# Country Profiles

| | | | |
|---|---|---|---|
| Argentina | 153 | Honduras | 166 |
| Australia | 122 | Hong Kong | 128 |
| Austria | 49 | Hungary | 81 |
| Azerbaijan | 74 | Indonesia | 129 |
| Bahrain | 97 | Ireland | 58 |
| Bangladesh | 126 | Israel | 99 |
| Belarus | 74 | Italy | 58 |
| Belgium | 50 | Jamaica | 166 |
| Benin | 115 | Japan | 131 |
| Bolivia | 154 | Jordan | 99 |
| Brazil | 155 | Kenya | 118 |
| Bulgaria | 75 | Korea (South) | 135 |
| Burkina Faso | 115 | Kuwait | 100 |
| Cameroon | 115 | Laos | 138 |
| Central African Republic | 116 | Latvia | 82 |
| Chile | 158 | Lebanon | 101 |
| China | 126 | Lithuania | 82 |
| Colombia | 161 | Madagascar | 118 |
| Congo | 116 | Malaysia | 139 |
| Costa Rica | 163 | Mali | 118 |
| Croatia | 76 | Malta | 102 |
| Cyprus | 77 | Mexico | 167 |
| Czech Republic | 77 | Moldova | 83 |
| Denmark | 51 | Mongolia | 139 |
| Ecuador | 164 | Morocco | 103 |
| Egypt | 97 | Mozambique | 118 |
| El Salvador | 165 | Nepal | 140 |
| Eritrea | 116 | Netherlands | 61 |
| Estonia | 79 | New Zealand | 123 |
| Ethiopia | 117 | Norway | 63 |
| Finland | 52 | Oman | 104 |
| France | 53 | Pakistan | 141 |
| Georgia | 80 | Palestinian Authority | 99 |
| Germany | 54 | Peru | 73 |
| Ghana | 117 | Poland | 84 |
| Greece | 56 | Portugal | 64 |
| Guatemala | 165 | Qatar | 105 |

# Country Profiles

| | | | |
|---|---|---|---|
| Romania | 88 | Tanzania | 120 |
| Russia | 89 | Thailand | 144 |
| Saudi Arabia | 106 | Togo | 120 |
| Senegal | 119 | Tunisia | 108 |
| Singapore | 142 | Turkey | 108 |
| Slovakia | 92 | Ukraine | 95 |
| Slovenia | 93 | United Arab Emirates | 111 |
| South Africa | 119 | United Kingdom | 71 |
| Spain | 66 | Uruguay | 173 |
| Sweden | 70 | Venezuela | 174 |
| Switzerland | 70 | Vietnam | 151 |
| Syria | 107 | Yemen | 112 |
| Taiwan | 142 | | |

# Work the World

The following section of this guide will show you all you need to know to get a teaching job in almost any country in the world.

A s a qualified English language teacher you can travel the world and find work in almost any country you choose to visit. English learners gain a valuable opportunity to interact with a native speaker and pick up all the little nuances that they would otherwise miss. This section of the Guide will prepare you for travel around the world as an EFL/ESL teacher.

Teaching English as a Foreign Language has developed into a vast global business. In many countries around the world, the development of English language skills throughout society is considered crucial to economic success. People want to learn English because they see it as a key, opening doors to new opportunities that they would not otherwise enjoy. Governments around the world are insisting that their children learn English from a very early age: Korea, Japan and Italy are just three countries that have recently announced initiatives designed to get people to learn English.

Teaching English has always had one great advantage over any other form of teaching: the travel element. The requirement for teachers in just about every country around the world leads to great opportunities for well-qualified teachers who can travel and, often, a very enjoyable lifestyle exploring countries and new cultures.

This section of the book provides thorough, in-depth profiles of all the main markets for teachers of English. We include a short description of the country and its prospects for teachers, together with details of the visa requirements, salary expectations, medical conditions, cost of accommodation and local English-language newspapers. We also include details of the main schools in the country that could offer you a job. Use this information to contact the schools with your curriculum vitae and a covering letter to find a job as a teacher.

Once you have selected the country or region where you would like to work, flip back to the 'Finding a Job' chapter earlier in this book for more details on how best to apply, how to search for jobs online and even how to travel!

# Country Profiles

The countries over the following pages are organized geographically. If you already have your heart set on going to a particular country, look it up in the index at the end of this book and go straight to that section. If you have an idea of where you would like to go, but need more information before you decide, read about all of the countries in that area, because you may well find that another country is more suited to you. If you are unsure about where you would like to go, browse through all of the sections and you should get a good idea of countries that you would like to teach in.

## Country-specific information

In these country sections we have tried to give you the information that you need, rather than personal opinions, so there will usually be a brief summary of the country's economic position and how that relates to the demand for English language teachers.

Next, there is information on visas and work permits, which reflects the position in the country at the time of writing. Please note that we do not recommend working illegally in any country, even though it is mentioned where teachers do tend to work without the correct paperwork. Not all countries have such a clear policy on the working rights of foreign nationals, so consult the relevant embassy for full details.

The cost of living information is intended as a guideline to enable you to establish if your local salary will be just enough to support you or will boost your savings account. Costs are described in comparison to western European and North American norms, so this information must be read in conjunction with salary information. And some teachers manage to live on tight budgets in poorer countries by adapting quickly to the local way of life.

Salaries vary enormously, even within the same town, so figures given here are averages. Where figures are quoted in UK pounds, remember that exchange rates can change very quickly, so the Sterling equivalent will also change, but the salary should still remain the same in relation to local costs.

Some employers pay teachers in US-dollars, but the vast majority of employers pay in local currency. Taxation is not set at a standard rate in some countries, so it too will vary depending on the type of institution you are working for and your contract terms.

Accommodation causes as many problems overseas as it does at home. Prices given in this section are what teachers typically pay for standard accommodation in safe areas. Obviously, luxury penthouses in chic, central areas will cost you a lot more. If you do have problems finding somewhere to live, think of alternative options, such as living with a family, which can save you money and enable you to integrate with the local community very quickly. Ask around at universities and schools – something will soon come up.

Health insurance is advisable whenever you are travelling. Travel agents, embassies and airlines should be able to provide you with up to date details of any particular health issues in the countries you are visiting.

English language newspapers are good places to look for teaching jobs and accommodation. They are also a great way to keep up to date with the local (and international) news if your grasp of the local language is not good enough to read the local papers.

At the end of each country sections, there is a list of schools to contact for jobs. The national telephone dialing code appears in brackets at the top of the list. You should also look in the 'Finding a Job' chapter earlier in this book for more details on how to apply for a job and websites listing job vacancies.

# Western Europe

Demand for English as a second or foreign language is strong among the member states of the European Union. English is the working language of the EU despite efforts to promote other languages such as French, Spanish and German.

It has become more difficult for non-EU citizens to work in Western Europe. Work-related laws that are designed to make it easier for Europeans to work in member states have tightened up with regard to Americans, Canadians, and to a lesser extent, Australians.

Job prospects for native speakers from the UK are particularly good in Western Europe, but rather more difficult for Americans and Canadians with American-English qualifications (although many countries, Spain for example, have 'international' schools teaching American English). However, there are jobs available for any teacher – although schools much prefer someone with qualifications (i.e. someone who has passed at least a certificate-level course) – especially if you are flexible and don't expect to land a high-paying permanent teaching position right away. If a school wants to keep you on as a full-time and legal employee, there is usually a way to cut through the bureaucracy, even if it is time-consuming.

The traditional strong areas of the countries around the Mediterranean still attract a lot of prospective teachers, but some countries have had some economic problems recently, particularly Spain which has seen a number of its major schools shut down in the past year.

Any EU citizen can travel freely within western Europe and work in any other country – enjoying its local health system and social security benefits. However, your school will be able to advise of the local tax laws which normally require any visitor planning to work to register with the local tax authority (and often with the police, too). Non-EU citizens looking for work should contact the country's embassy and ask for current visa information. Your prospective employer is often in the best position to request (and push through) a visa application on your behalf.

## AUSTRIA

It is nearly impossible for non-EU citizens to live and work in Austria on a part time, freelance basis unless married to an EU citizen or in possession of a special visa (e.g., for the arts) and nearly all teaching positions are freelance. If you have a student visa for a university in Austria, this might give you eligibility to work. There is stiff competition for teaching jobs from the expatriate community. The most commonly available work is part-time and company-based.

### Embassy in UK:
18 Belgrave Mews West, London SW1X 8HU,
**tel**: +44 (0)20 7235 3731
www.austria.org.uk

### Embassy in USA:
3524 International Court NW, Washington DC 20008
**tel**: +1 202 895 6700
www.austria.org

### British Council office:
Schenkenstrabe 4, A -1010 Vienna
tel  +43 (1) 533 2616
Www.britishcouncil.at

⮑  **Visa/Work Permits:** For non-EU nationals intending to work or study in Austria, a residency permit is required. Contact the Embassy or Austrian Consulate General. US citizens may enter Austria as tourists and apply for a residency permit with the relevant authorities in Austria.

⮑  **Requirements:** College Degree, experience and a TESOL/TESL Certificate

⮑  **Currency:** £1 = € 1.49,  $1 = € 0.76

⮑  **Cost of Living:** Austria is a relatively cheap European country.

⮑  **Salaries/Taxes:** Expect to earn around £10 per hour but this depends on your qualifications. If you are contracted expect to earn £600 a month. Income tax and social security deductions are around 40%.

⮑  **Accommodation:** A one-bedroom apartment in Vienna or Salzburg will cost around £250 per month.

⮑  **Health advice:** Insurance coverage is advisable.

⮑  **English Language Media:** The Vienna Reporter

### Schools in Austria (+43)

#### Alpha Sprachinstitut Austria
Schwarzenbergplatz 16/ Canovagasse 5, A-1010 Vienna. **Tel:** 1 503 69 69, **Fax:** 1 503 69 69-14.

#### American International School
Salmannsdorferstrasse 47, A-1190 Vienna. **Tel:** 1 603 02 46.

#### Amerika-Institut
Operngrasse 4, 1010 Vienna. **Tel:** 1 512 77 20

#### Austro-British Society
Wickenburgasse 19, 1080 Vienna. **Tel:** 1 431 141.

#### Berlitz Sprachschule
Rotenturmstrasse 1-38, 1060 Vienna.

#### Berufsforderungsinstitut
Kinderspitalgasse 5, 1090 Vienna.

#### Business Language Centre
Trattnerhof 2, 1010 Vienna.

#### Danube International
Guderunstrasse 184, A-1100 Vienna.

#### Didactica Akademie Fur Wirtschaft Und Sprachen
Schottenfledgasse 13-15, 1070 Vienna. **Tel:** 1 526 2287.

#### English Courses And Seminars
Salzachstr. 16, Salzburg, 5020.
**Tel:** 66 2629995.

#### English For Kids
23 Anton-Baumgartner-Str. 44, Vienna, 1230.
**Tel:** 1 222 66 74579.

#### English Institute Linzerg 27
Salzburg, 5020. **Tel:** 66 2872195.

#### English Institute Sprachreisen Schoenberg
31 Michaelbeuern, 5152. **Tel:** 6 274 8236.

#### English Language Centre
In der Hagenau 7, 1130 Vienna. **Tel/Fax:** 1 804 1869.

#### Graz International Bilingual School
Klusemannstrasse 25, A-8053, Graz. **Tel:** 316 1050.

#### inlingua School of Languages
Neuer Markt 1, A-1010 Vienna, **Tel:** 1 512 22 25 / 1 512 94 99, **Fax:** 1 513 94 56.

#### Innsbruck International Highschool
Schonbeg 26, A-6141, Innsbruck. **Tel:** 05225 42013992.

#### Institut CEF
Garnisongasse 10, 1090 Vienna. **Tel:** 1 42 04 03

#### International Language Services
Getreidemarkt 17, A-1060 Vienna. **Tel:** 1 585 53 47, **Fax:** 1 585 53 47.

#### International Montessori Preschool Vienna
Mahlerstrasse 9/13, A-1010 Vienna. **Tel:** 1 512 8733.

**International Summer School Gmunden**
Postfach 182, A-4810 Gmunden, **Tel:** 1 494 9994

**Jelinek & Jelinek**
Privatlehrinstitut, Rudolfsplatz 3, 1010 Vienna.

**Kindergarten Alt Wien**
Am Heumarkt 23, A-1030, Vienna.

**Lizner International School**
Aubrunnerweg 4, A-4040 Linz. **Tel:** 732 245 8670.

**Mini Schools & English Language Day Camp**
Postfach 160, 1220 Vienna. **Tel:** 227717.

**Multi Lingua Language School and Translation Bureau**
Hardtgasse 5/2, A-1190 Vienna. **Tel:** 1 369 15 41, **Fax:** 1 369 15 42.

**Privat Institut Venetia Erwachsenenbildung**
Große Neugasse 8/19, A-1040 Vienna. **Tel:** 1 586 82 57, **Fax:** 1 586 82 579

**Salzburg International Preparatory School**
Moosstrasse 106, A-5020, Salzburg. **Tel:** 662 844 485.

**Sight & Sound Studio**
Schubertring 12, 1031 Vienna. **Tel:** 1 512 67520.

**SLL Institut Super Language Learning**
Florianigasse 55, A-1080 Vienna. **Tel:** 1 408 41 84

**Spidi (Spracheninstitut Der Industrie)**
Lotringer Strasse 12, 1031 Vienna. **Tel:** 1 715 2506-0, **Fax:** 1 89 17431.

**Sprachstudio J-J Rousseau**
Untere Viaduktgasse 43, 1030 Vienna. **Tel:** 1 712 2443

**Sprachinstitut Vienna**
Universitatstr. 6, 1090, Vienna. **Tel:** 1422227

**Sprachschule BriBou**
Barichgasse 26/3, A-1030 Vienna. **Tel:** 1 710 8829.

**Super Language Learning Sprachinstitut**
Florianigasse 55, 1080 Vienna. **Tel:** 1 408 4184

**Wiener Volkshochschulen Verband Wiener Volksbildung**
Hollergasse 22, A-1150 Vienna. **Tel:** 1 891 740.

**Young Austria**
Alpenstrasse 108a, A-5020 Salzburg. **Tel:** 662 625 7580

## BELGIUM

Currently there is little demand for teachers in Belgium. English is taught at secondary school level and school leavers usually have enough English to get by with the demands that will be made on them later in life. Some of the private language schools are struggling to survive and are often a one or two-person business. Often it is only freelance work, which is available at private language schools. This is for a number of reasons. The first is that English is an asset but not essential to work in Belgium. Also, the UK is very close for those who want to travel to the UK to learn the language and newsagents are well supplied in English magazines and the British press. Last but not least, the country has cable television and this includes a wide choice of programmes in English (British and American). Many teenagers therefore learn the language by watching British and American soaps and viewing films in the original version with subtitles in their own language.

**Embassy in UK:**
103 Eaton Square, London SW1W 9AW
**Tel:** +44 (0)20 7470 3700
www.diplobel.org/uk

**Embassy in USA:**
3330 Garfield Street NW, Washington DC 20008
**Tel:** +1 202 333 6900
www.diplobel.org/usa

**British Council office:**
Leopold Plaza, Rue du Trône 108 / Troonstraat 108
1050 Brussels
**Tel:** +32 (2) 227 08 41
www.britishcouncil.org/belgium

➲ **Visa/Work Permits:** If you're a non-EU citizen you'll need to apply for a work permit. This means you'll have to prove no EU citizen is able to do your job–it is best to leave this paperwork to your prospective employer. There are two main types of work permit (permis de travail/werkvergunning), normally you will get a B permit which is valid for only one employer and must be renewed each year. After several years you should be able to transfer this to an A permit which is valid indefinitely and allows you to work for any employer you like. Contact the Ministère de l'Emploi et du Travail for information and application forms for work permits.

➲ **Requirements:** College Degree and a TESOL/TESL Certificate

➲ **Currency:** £1 = € 1.49  $1 = € 0.76

➲ **Cost of Living:** Expect to pay a third more than in the U.S. for basic living costs. Belgium is not as cheap as it used to be.

➲ **Salaries/Taxes:** Salaries are negotiable according to experience, but on contract expect to earn around £600 a month. Employers will pay your tax and health insurance only if you are on a contract.

⮁ **Accommodation:** Schools rarely assist in finding accommodation. Outside Brussels rents are quite reasonable from a minimum of £150 per month for an apartment to £400 for a small house. An apartment in Brussels costs around £200.

⮁ **English Language Media:** The Bulletin (weekly)

## Schools in Belgium (+32)

**Access Bvba Taalbureau**
Atealaan 5, 2200 Herentals. **Tel:** 14 22 61 92

**Applied Language Centre**
21 rue du Trone 238, 1050 Brussels.

**Belgo-British Courses**
Rue d'Ecosse 21, 1060 Brussels. **Tel:** 2 537 8775.

**Berlitz Language Centre**
Avenue Louise 306, 1050 Brussels.

**Berlitz Language Centre**
Place Stéphanie 10, 1050 Brussels. **Tel:** 2 512 44 04.

**Berlitz Language Centre**
Britselei 15, 2018 Antwerpen.

**Berlitz Language Centre**
Leuvenselaan 17, 3300 Tienen.

**Bilingua**
6 rue Renier Chalon, 1060 Brussels. **Tel:** 2 347 4534.

**British Council**
rue de la Charité 15, 1210 Brussels. **Tel:** 2 227 0840.

**British School of Brussels**
Leuvensesteenweg 19, 3080 Tervuren. **Tel:** 2 767 4700.

**Brussels Language Centre**
55 Rue Des Drapiers, 1050 Brussels.

**Crown Language Centre**
9 Rue Du Béguinage, 1000 Brussels.

**The English Institute**
77 Rue Lesbroussart, 1050 Brussels.

**inlingua School of Languages**
62 Limburgstraat, 9000 Gent.

**Institute of Modern Languages and Communications**
20 Av. de la Toison D'or, Bte. 21, 1060 Brussels.**Tel:** 2 512 6607.

**Institut Pro Linguis SC**
Place De L'eglise, 6717 Thiamont.

**Linguarama**
Avenue des Arts, Kunstlaan 19, 1040 Brussels. **Tel:** 2 17 9055, **Fax:** 2 17 9523.

**May International**
40 rue Lesbroussart, 1050 Brussels. **Tel:** 2 640 8703.

**Mitchell School of English**
rue Louis Hap 156, 1040 Brussels. **Tel:** 2 734 8073.

**Peters School**
87 rue des Deux Eglises, 1040 Brussels. **Tel:** 2 280 0021.

**Phone Languages**
65 rue des Echevins, 1050 Brussels. **Tel:** 2 647 4020.

**Practicum**
Reep 24, 9000 Gent. **Tel:** 9 223 5442.

**Pro Linguis**
6717 Thiaumont. **Tel:** 63 22 0462, **Fax:** 63 22 0688.

**School Voor Europese Talen**
28 Charlottalei, 2018 Antwerpen. **Tel:** 3 218 7370.

## DENMARK

A recent study found that Denmark ranked as the number one place in the world to live in terms of its ability to provide basic social and material needs for its citizens. However, there are few jobs and prospects for non-EU teachers are particularly poor. Children of school age are decreasing in numbers and schools and universities are cutting back on staff. You may be successful if you look for work in institutes running part-time courses and evening classes, particularly in business English.

**Embassy in UK:**
55 Sloane Street, London SW1X 9SR
**Tel:** +44 (0)20 7333 0200
www.demarkemb.org

**Embassy in USA:**
3200 Whitehaven Street NW, Washington DC 20008
**Tel:** +1 202 234 4300
www.demarkemb.org

**British Council office:**
Gammel Mønt 12.3, 1117 Copenhagen K
**Tel:** +45 (33) 369 400
www.britishcouncil.dk

⮁ **Visa/Work Permits:** The same criteria apply as in other EU member states.

⮁ **Requirements:** College Degree and a TESOL/TESL Certificate

⮁ **Currency:** £1 = 11.13 / $1 = 5.69 Danish Krone

⮁ **Cost of Living:** The cost of living in Denmark is very high with a beer costing around £4 in major cities and towns and a cheap meal costing about £4-5.

⮑ **Salaries/Taxes:** Salaries vary according to the institution you are working for. Taxation rates run about 55%.

⮑ **Accommodation:** A room in the capital city of Copenhagen can cost around £600 per month.

⮑ **Health advice:** Excellent medical facilities are widely available in Denmark. You should have medical insurance to cover any expenses you may incur.

⮑ **English Language Media:** Copenhagen Post.

## Schools in Denmark (+45)

### Access
Hamerensgade 8, 1267 Copenhagen K. **Tel:** 14 22 6192.

### Activsprog
Rosenvægets Alle 32, 2100 Copenhagen - also Odense, Ärhus & Aalborg.

### Babel Sprogtræning
Vordingborggrade 18, 2100 Copenhagen.

### Berlitz International
Vimmelskaftet 42a, 1161 Copenhagen.

### Bis Sprogskole
Rolfsvej 14-16, 2000 Frederiksberg.

### Cambridge Institute Foundation
Vimmelskaftet 48, 1161 Copenhagen.
**Tel:** 33 13 33 02

### Centre for Undervisning
Ärhus amt, Ulla Sørensen, Vesterskovvej 4, 8660, Skanderborg. **Tel:** 86 511511, **Fax:** 86 511047

### Elite Sprogcentret
Hoffmeyersvej 19, 2000 Frederiksberg.

### Erhvervs Orienterede Sprogkurser
Betulavej 25, 3200 Helsinge.

### European Education Centre Aps (Inlingua)
Lyngbyvej 72, 2100, Copenhagen.

### FOF
Sønder Allé 9, 8000 Ärhus C. **Tel:** 88 86 12 29 55.

### Frit Oplysningsforbund
Vestergrade, 5000 Odense C. **Tel:** 66 13 9813.

### Linguarama
Hvilevej 7, 2900 Hellerup.

### Master-Ling
Sortedam Dossering 83, 2100 Copenhagen.

# FINLAND

The Finns are eager to speak English well and many spend their spare time brushing up on the language. There are plenty of opportunities to teach here as long as you are prepared to be flexible.

Finding a teaching job in Finland without qualifications will be very difficult but if you look in the bigger cities like Helsinki and Turku you may be able to get hired by a company to teach their employees. The best time to look for work is in the spring, when schools start recruiting for the following September. Before setting off and looking for work, it is advisable to contact language schools in advance as you may find it hard once you're in the country. Be prepared for taking on a lot of freelance work and the comparative instability associated with this.

**Embassy in UK:**
38 Chesham Place, London SW1X 8HW
**Tel:** +44 (0)20 7838 6200
www.finemb.org.uk

**Embassy in USA:**
3301 Massachusetts Ave NW, Washington DC 20008
**Tel:** +1 202 298 5800
www.finland.org

**British Council office:**
Hakaniemenkatu 2, 00530 Helsinki
**Tel** +358 (9) 774 3330
www.britishcouncil.fi

⮑ **Visas/Work Permits:** A visa is not required for tourist or business stays up to 90 days. Any non-Scandinavian wishing to work in Finland must apply for a residence permit and a work permit before entering the country. The process usually takes 6 to 8 weeks and costs around £100.

⮑ **Requirements:** College Degree, experience and a TESOL/TESL Certificate

⮑ **Cost of Living:** Go to Finland with plenty of cash reserves. The cost of living is not cheap (as with all Scandinavian countries) and going out, eating and drinking will seriously dent your wallet.

⮑ **Currency:** £1 = € 1.49  $1 = € 0.76

⮑ **Salaries/Taxes:** Teaching rates moderate ranging from £8 - £12 per teaching hour. If you are planning to spend less than 6 months in Finland you must pay income tax at 25%.

⮑ **Accommodation:** Ask if your employer will provide you with a place to live as accommodation is very expensive throughout the country.

� ✆ **Health advice:** There is a standard fee (relatively low) for medical services. Your insurance policy will cover it.

✆ **Tip:** As a rule, Finns are quite shy and you may find it takes some time before you start to make friends.

## Schools in Finland (+358)

### AAC-Opisto
Kauppaneuvoksentie 8, 00200 Helsinki. **Tel/Fax:** 9 4766 7801.

### The Federation of Finnish-British Societies
Puistokatu 1bA, 00140 Helsinki, **Tel:** 639625.

### IWG Kieli-Instituutti
Hämeenkatu 25 B, 33200 Tampere. **Tel:** 31 214 7573, **Fax:** 31 212 3519.

### Kielipiste Oy
Kaisaniemenkatu 4A, 00100 Helsinki. **Tel:** 90 177266, **Fax:** 90 174885.

### Linguarama Suomi
David Eade, Annankatu 26, 00100 Helsinki. **Tel:** 9/6803230, **Fax:** 9/603118.

### Lingua-Forum Ky
Fredrikinkatu 61 A 36, 00100 Helsinki. **Tel:** 694 8426, **Fax:** 694 8417.

### Lansi-Suomen opisto
Loimijoentie 280, 32700 Huittinen. **Tel:** 2 567866, **Fax:** 2 566409.

### Richard Lewis Communications
Itätuulenkuja 10 B, 02100 Espo, Helsinki. **Tel:** 455 4811, **Fax:** 466592.

## FRANCE

The French have become more demanding of their teachers and expect them to be experienced and professional. "Student centred" teaching methods are not in vogue and you really need to be au fait with the rules of English grammar before you take on an English language teaching job in France.

Many Americans and other non-EU nationals despair of finding a teaching job in France. But if you are determined and are not above a bit of minor rule-bending, you can work as an English language teacher in France. Reports suggest that one route for job finders is to contact all the language schools they can find in the Yellow Pages and arrange to send a CV, photo and hand-written cover letter to the relevant person. Some schools are prepared to pay foreign teachers in cash and if you can find part-time jobs at three or more schools you may find yourself rolling in Euros.

**Consulate in UK:**
21 Cromwell Road, London SW7 2EN
**Tel:** +44 (0)20 7073 1200
www.ambafrance.org.uk

**Embassy in USA:**
4101 Reservoir Road NW, Washington DC 20007
**Tel:** +1 202 944 6000
www.info-france-usa.org

**British Council office:**
9 rue de Constantine, 75340 Paris cedex 07
**Tel** +33 (1) 4955 7300
www.britishcouncil.fr

✆ **Visas/Work Permits:** A visa is not required for a tourist/business stay up to 90 days in France, Andorra, Monaco, and Corsica. Non-EU citizens must find an institute that is willing to put them on a contract before they can obtain working papers.

✆ **Requirements:** College Degree and a TESOL/TESL Certificate

✆ **Cost of Living:** Living costs in the major cities are often surprisingly high, but rent and food (particularly wine!) are cheaper than in the UK and USA.

✆ **Currency:** £1 = € 1.49  $1 = € 0.76

✆ **Salaries/Taxes:** Salaries for teachers vary immensely in France and will usually be considerably lower in the provinces than in Paris, due to the lower cost of living. Contracted teachers can expect between £500 and £750 per month, while freelancers can expect £12 per hour.

✆ **Accommodation:** Expect to pay from around £350 per month for a one-bedroom apartment in Paris.

✆ **Health advice:** You will need insurance to avoid big bills if you fall sick or have an accident.

✆ **English Language Media:** International Herald Tribune, Paris Passion, The News (monthly)

## Schools in France (+33)

### AABC
20 rue Gonot de Mauroy, 75009 Paris. **Tel:** 1 42 66 13 11.

### Academie des Langues Appliquées
60 rue de Laxou, BP 373 65- 40 98, Nancy.

**Alexandra School**
32 rue Amiral de Grasse, 66130 Grasse. **Tel:** 93 36 88 01.

**Alpha Formation**
51 rue Saint-Ferreol, 130001 Marseille. **Tel:** 91 33 00 72.

**American Centre**
Belomeau, Avenue Jean-Paul Coste, Paris. **Tel:** 1 42 38 42 38.

**Anglesey Language Services (ALS)**
1 bis Avenue Foch, 78400 Chatou. **Tel:** 1 34 80 65 15, **Fax:** 34 80 69 91.

**Arc Langue**
Chemin de la Haie, 64100 Bayonne. **Tel:** 59 55 05 66.

**Audio-English**
44 allée de Tourny, 33000 Bordeaux **Tel:** 56 44 54 05

**BEST**
24 Bd Béranger, 37000 Tours. **Tel:** 47 05 55 33, **Fax:** 47 64 40 27.

**British Connection International**
279 rue Crequi, 69007 Lyon. **Tel:** 72 73 02 55.

**British Council**
9/11 rue De Constantine, 75007 Paris. **Tel:** 49 55 73 00.

**British Institute (University of London)**
11 rue de Constantine, 74340 Paris, Cedex 07.

**Business English Service & Translation**
24 Bd Béranger, 37000 Tours. **Tel:** 47 05 55 33.

**BTS Language Centre**
226 Route de Philippeville, 6001 Marcinelle. **Tel:** 71313076.

**Centre D'Etudes Des Langues**
ISF Montfoulon, 61250 Damigny. **Tel:** 33 80 84 00.

**Cybée Langues**
7 rue d'Artois, 75008, Paris. **Tel:** 89 18 26

**Collegium Palatinium**
Dept EFL/CP, Chateau de Pourtales, 61 rue Mélanie, 67000. Strasbourg. **Tel:** 88 31 01 07.

**EF Corporate**
3 rue de Bassano, 75016 Paris. **Tel:** 47 20 18 01, **Fax:** 1 47 20 18 80.

**Executive Language Services**
20 rue Sainte Croix de la Bretonnerie, 75004 Paris. **Fax:** 1 48 044 55 53.

**Fontainbleau Langues et Communication**
15 rue Saint-Honoré, BP 27, 77300. Fontainbleau. **Tel:** 64 22 48 96.

**Formalangues**
106 Blvd Haussmann, 75008 Paris. **Tel:** 45229912.

**Forum**
66 Rue De La Bretonnerie, 45000 Orleans. **Tel:** 38625245.

**International House Nice**
62 rue Geoffredo, Nice, 6000

**Linguarama**
6 rue Roland Garros, 38320 Eybens. **Tel:** 76 62 00 18, **Fax:** 76 25 89 60.

**Metropolitan Languages**
151 rue de Billancourt, 92100 Boulogne. **Tel:** 46 04 57 32. **Fax:** 46 04 57 12.

**Rapid English**
2 rue du Maréchal Gallieni, 76600 Le Havre.

**Regency Langues**
1 rue Ferdinand Duval, 75004 Paris. **Tel:** 48 04 99 97, **Fax:** 48 04 34 96.

**Rothman Institute**
21 Avenue du Major Général Vanier, 1000 Troyes. **Tel:** 258 03041.

**Sarl Executive Language Services**
25 Blvd Sébastapol, 75001 Paris.

**Unilangues**
1 le Parvis-Paroi Nord, 92044 Paris la Défense Cedex 41. **Tel:** 47 78 45 80, **Fax:** 49 00 03 16.

## GERMANY

Many institutions in Germany are looking for qualified and experienced teachers with a specialization in an area such as business English. But even newly qualified English language teachers with Master's degrees, certificates and diplomas are being hired. Many teachers are employed on a freelance basis, often teaching in-company outside office hours. There are lots of private language schools looking for teachers.

Recent reports suggest that it is relatively easy (when compared to other EU countries) for non-EU teachers to find teaching jobs and work legally in Germany. For Americans, USIA Fulbright programme organizes for US graduates to work as teaching assistants in high schools

**Embassy in UK:**
23 Belgrave Square, London SW1X 8PZ
**Tel**: 020 7824 1300
www.german-embassy.org.uk

**Embassy in USA:**
4645 Reservoir Road NW, Washington DC 20007
**Tel**: 202 298 4000
www.germany-info.org

**British Council office**
Hackescher Markt 1, 10178 Berlin
**Tel** +49 (30) 311 0990
www.britishcouncil.de

⮕ **Tip:** Materials in American English are often hard to find. Bring some books and tapes over with you from the States. Your students, who may be used to British English, will appreciate working with different materials and they may even like your accent!

⮕ **Visa/Work Permits:** U.S. citizens must arrange employment and apply for a work permit before they leave. This may take a couple of months.

⮕ **Requirements:** College Degree, experience and a TESOL/TESL Certificate

⮕ **Cost of Living:** Contrary to popular belief, living costs in Germany are lower than you might expect, and lower than in the UK or USA.

⮕ **Currency:** £1 = € 1.49  $1 = € 0.76

⮕ **Salaries/Taxes:** All employees with their residence in Germany have to pay tax on their income in accordance with the German tax laws. The rates of wage or income tax are graduated progressively according to the particular wages or salary. Expect to earn £6-15 per teaching hour at a private language school and £15-20 as a freelancer. Freelancers often tend to work outside the social security and tax structures. This tends to imply high earnings but not much in the way of statutory health cover and benefits. The situation has become more complicated since 1999 when a law dating back to 1913 was resurrected by the German Social Security Administration, which requires that freelance teachers pay nearly 20% of their income into the state social security system. This law is being applied retroactively—some teachers report they have been hit with high tax bills. Many freelancers have left Germany claiming it is no longer worth their time to teach there. The situation remains uncertain at the time of writing so consult a lawyer if you have any specific questions or problems.

⮕ **Accommodation:** In any of the big cities a one-bedroom apartment will cost around £500. You will usually have to pay three months rent as a deposit

⮕ **Health advice:** Foreigners in Germany are placed on an equal footing with German employees when it comes to social protection. They generally have to be insured against sickness and unemployment and included in the statutory pension scheme by their employer on taking up the employment. The contributions to the social insurance scheme are borne half by the employer and half by the employee. The employee share is deducted from the gross wage and paid to the social insurance provider together with the employer's share. The employer also has to insure you against accident with his trade association: premiums for accident insurance are paid by the employer alone. In practice, many private language schools do not comply with the law and do not make contributions on your behalf. Of course, freelancers are afforded no protection and should carry their own medical insurance.

⮕ **English Language Media:** Handelsblatt (English edition), Munich Found (monthly), Spotlight, World Press

## Schools in Germany (+49)

**American Language Academy**
Charlottenstr. 65, 10117 Berlin. **Tel:** 30 20 39 78 10, **Fax:** 30 20 39 78 13.

**Anglo-German Institute**
Christopherstr 4, 70178 Stuttgart. **Tel:** 711 603 858 **Fax:** 711 640 9941.

**ASK Sprachenschule**
1 Kortumstr 71, 44787 Bochum. **Tel:** 234-12910.

**Bansley College**
Str Des Friedens 35, 03222 Lubbenau, Brandenburg. **Tel:** 354-244 407, **Fax:** 354 244 408.

**Benedict School**
Gurzenichstr 17, 50667 Koln. **Tel:** 221-212 203.

**Berlitz**
Friedrich-Willhelm-Strasse 30, 47051 Duisburg.

**British Council**
Hardenbergstr 20, 10623 Berlin. **Tel:** 3110990.

**Christopher Hills School of English**
Sandeldamm 12, 63450 Hanau. **Tel:** 49-6181 15015, **Fax:** 49-6181 12121.

**Collegium Palatinum**
Adenauerplatz 8, 69115 Heidelburg. **Tel:** 62 2146 289, **Fax:** 62-2118 2023.

**Didacta**
Hohenzollernring 27, 95440 Bayreuth. **Tel:** 921-27 555.

**English Language Centre**
Bieberer Strasse 205, 63071 Offenbach am Main. **Tel:** 69 85 87 87, **Fax:** 69 85 72 02.

**English Language Institute**
Sprachenschule 4, Ubersetzer Am Zwinger 14, 33602 Bielefeld. **Tel:** 521-69353.

**Europa-Universitat Viadrina**
Sprachenzentrum, Grosse Scharrnstr 59, 15230
Frankfurt (Oder).

**FBD Schulen**
Katharinenstr 18, 70182 Stuttgart. **Tel:** 711-21580.

**GLS Sprachenzentrum**
B Jaeshke, Pestalozzistr 886, 10625 Berlin. **Tel:**
30-313 5025.

**Hallworth English Centre**
Frauenstrasse 118, 89703 Ulmponau. **Tel:** 731-22668.

**inlingua Spachschule**
Konigstrasse 61, 47051 Duisburg. **Tel:** 203 30 53 40.

**Intercom Lang Services**
Muggenkampstr 38, 20257 Hamburg.

**International House**
Prolog Sprachenschule, Hauptstrasse 23/24, Berlin,
D-10827.

**International House**
LGS Sprachkurse, Werderring 18, Freiburg 79098

**International House**
Poststrasse 51, 20354 Hamburg. **Tel:** 352041.

**Knowledge Point**
Hohenzollernstrasse 26, 80801 Munchen **Tel:** 89 33
3405.

**Linguarama Sprachinstitut**
Kant Strasse 150, 10623 Berlin. **Tel:** 30 621 81 48,
**Fax:** 30 312 94 91.

**Lingotek Institut**
Schlueterstrasse 18, 20146 Hamburg. **Tel:** 40 459 520.

**Neue Sprachschule**
Rosastrass 1, 79098 Freiburg. **Tel:** 761-24810.

**NSK Language and Training Services**
Comeniusstr 2, 90459 Nurnburg. **Tel:** 911-441552.

**Sprachstudio Lingua Nova**
Thierschstrasse 36, 80538 Munich. **Tel:** 89-221 171.

**Stevens English Training**
Ruttenscheider strasse 68, 45130 Essen.

**Vorbeck-Schule**
77723 Gengenback. **Tel:** 7803 3361.

**Wirtschaftwissen-schaftliche Fakultat
Ingolstadt**
Auf der Schanz 49, 85049 Ingolstadt.

**Yes Your English Services**
Altonaer Chaussee 87, 22559 Schenefeld, Hamburg.
**Tel:** 408 393 2116, **Fax:** 408 393 2117

## GREECE

For many years, Greece has been one of the most
popular destinations for English language teachers. Of
all the candidates for the Cambridge First Certificate
and Cambridge Proficiency exams worldwide, one
quarter are in Greece. In most parts of the country,
English language teaching in state schools is
inadequate for these exams and children often attend
private language schools (frontisteria) as a supplement.

There are estimated to be more than 5,000 of these
schools in the country. You must be a graduate to teach
and a certificate, diploma or MA in TESL is desirable
although not absolutely necessary. Recruitment is
normally done locally in May/June or September.
Those less qualified may well have more success
finding work in January, as many native speakers do
not return to their jobs after the holiday break.

**Embassy in UK:**
1a Holland Park, London W11 3TP
**Tel:** 020 7221 6467
www.greekembassy.org.uk

**Embassy in USA:**
2221 Massachusetts Avenue NW, Washington DC
20008
**Tel:** 202 939 5800
www.greekembassy.org

**British Council office:**
17 Plateia Philikis Etairias, PO BOX 3488, 10673
Athens
**Tel** +30 (21) 0 369 2333
Www.britishcouncil.gr

➲  **Visa/Permits:** Non-EU citizens are supposed to
apply for a work permit before they come to the
country, for which they will need to present an
employment offer from a Greek school, at their local
Greek consulate. In practice, many teachers work
while they are waiting for their permits to be
processed. Americans of Greek descent can obtain
residency permits but should check to make sure they
won't have to serve in the army.

➲  **Requirements:** College Degree and a
TESOL/TESL Certificate

➲  **Cost of Living:** Greece is no longer a cheap place
to live in although it is less expensive than other parts
of Europe. The cost of living in Athens depends to a
large extent on the price of the accommodation. You'll
need around £400 per month to cover your living
expenses and rent.

➲  **Currency:** £1 = € 1.49  $1 = € 0.76

⊃ **Salaries/Taxes:** Expect to earn approximately £400-500 a month at a language school. You can augment your income with private lessons.

⊃ **Accommodation:** Apartments in Athens can be relatively expensive starting at around £200 per month. In smaller towns, some schools offer free accommodation but check to make sure the building has a roof and is adequately heated in winter.

⊃ **Health advice:** Greek hospitals are notoriously overcrowded. Make sure you have a good medical insurance plan because if you fall sick or are injured, you will want to get back home as soon as you can.

⊃ **English Language Media:** Athens News, Kathimerini (English edition).

## Schools in Greece (+30)

**A Trechas Language Centre**
20 Koundouriotou St., Keratsini. **Tel:** 1 432 0546.

**Alpha Abatzolglou Economou**
10 Kosma Etolou St, 54643 Thessaloniki. **Tel:** 31 830535.

**A Andriopoulou**
3, 28 Octobrio, Tripolis.

**Anglo-Hellenic Teacher Recruitment**
PO Box 263, 201 00 Corinth **Tel:** 741 53511, **Fax:** 741 86989. **Email:** info@anglo-hellenic.com

**Athens College**
PO Box 65005, 15410 Psychico, Athens.**Tel:** 1 6714621, **Fax:** 647 8156.

**British Council**
Ethnikis Amynis 9, PO Box 50007, 54013 Thessalonika. **Tel:** 31 235 236.

**English Tuition Centre**
3 Pythias St., Kypseli, 1136 Athens.

**Enossi Foreign Languages (The Language Centre)**
Stadiou 7, Syntagma, 10562 Athens. **Tel:** 3230 356.

**Eurocentre**
7 Solomou Street, 41222 Larissa.

**Featham School of English**
PO Box 12, 50 Ep. Marouli St., Rethymnon, Crete. 74100. **Tel:** 831 23428, **Fax:** 831 23922.

**Hambakis Schools of English**
1 Filellinon Street, Athens. **Tel:** 1 3017531/5.

**Hellenic American Union**
22 Massalias St., GR-106 80 Athens.

**International Language Centre**
35 Votsi St., 26221 Patras.

**Institute of English, French, German and Greek for Foreigners**
Zavitsanou Sophia, 13 Joannou Gazi St, 31100 Lefkada.

**Institute of Foreign Languages**
41 Epidavrou St., 10441 Athens.

**Kakkos School of English**
Papastratou 5, Arginio 30100. **Tel/Fax:** 641 23449.

**Makris School of English**
2 Pardos G Olympion St., 60100 Katerini. **Tel:** 35122859.

**G. Michalopolous School of English**
24E Antistasis, Alexandria, 59300 Imathias, Thessaloniki. **Tel:** 33 3 322890.

**New Centre**
Arkarnanias 16, 11526 Athens

**Omiros Association**
52 Academias St., 10677 Athens. **Tel:** 362 2887, **Fax:** 362 1833.

**Peter Sfyrakis School of Foreign Languages**
21 Nikiforou Foka St, 72200 Ierapetra, Crete. **Tel:** 842 28700.

**Polyglosso Language School**
73 Agylis St., Neos Kosmos, Athens. **Tel/Fax:** 1 9214982.

**Polyglosso Language School**
96 Ag.Varvaras St., Dafne, Athens. **Tel/Fax:** 1 9766542.

**Protypo English Language School**
22 Deliyioryi Street, Volos 38221.

**School of English**
8 Kosti Palama, Kavala 65302.

**School of Foreign Languages**
12 P Isaldari St, Xylokastro, 20400 Corinth. **Tel:** 743 24678.

**SILITZIS School of Languages**
42 Koumoundourou, 412 22 Larissa.

**Skouras Language School**
7 G. Miltiadi St., 67100 Xanthi. **Tel:** 541 26112, **Fax:** 541 23721.

**Strategakis Schools**
24 Proxenou Koromila St, 54622 Thessaloniki. **Tel:** 31 264276, **Fax:** 228848.

**Universal School of Language**
66 M. Alexandrou St, Panorama, Thessalonika 55200. **Tel:** 31 341 014

**Zoula Language Schools**
Sanroco Square, 49100 Corfu. **Tel:** 661 39330

## IRELAND

Many language students study English in Ireland in the summer months and the country is experiencing a boom. It is difficult for non-EU citizens to find jobs in Ireland unless they are in the I.T. industry, construction or nursing.

**Embassy in UK:**
17 Grosvenor Place, London SW1X 7HR
**Tel:** 020 7235 2171

**Embassy in USA:**
2234 Massachusetts Ave NW, Washington DC 20008
**Tel:** 202 462 3939
www.irelandemb.org

⮕ **Visas/Work Permits:** Ireland is a member state of the EU so you will need an EU passport to work here. Americans and Canadians of Irish descent can qualify for an Irish passport if they were born in Ireland or have parents or grandparents who were. If you do not qualify for an Irish passport your employer will have to prove that you are doing a job that another EU citizen could not do.

⮕ **Requirements:** College Degree and a TESOL/TESL Certificate

⮕ **Cost of Living:** Ireland can be an expensive country to live in.

⮕ **Currency:** £1 = € 1.49  $1 = € 0.76

⮕ **Salaries/Taxes:** Low wages for teachers and high taxation rates make it difficult for teachers to survive here.

⮕ **Accommodation:** It can be very difficult to find an apartment or room in Dublin over the summer months. Rents run around £50-100 per week per person in a shared house.

⮕ **Health advice:** Good medical facilities are available.

### Schools in Ireland (+353)

**American College Dublin**
2 Merrion Square, Dublin 2. **Tel:** 1 6768939, **Fax:** 1 6768941 **Email:** pmullins@amcd.ie

**Centre Of English Studies**
31 Dame Street, Dublin 2. **Tel:** 353 1 6714233, **Fax:** 1 6714425 www.cesireland.ie

**Cork Language Centre International**
Wellington House, Wellington Road, Cork **Tel:** 21 4551661, **Fax:** 21 4551662
www.corklanguagecentre.ie

**Dublin School Of English**
10-12 Westmoreland Street, Dublin 2. **Tel:** 1 6773322 **Fax:** 1 6795454 www.dse.ie/dse/

**English Language Institute**
99, St. Stephen's Green, Dublin 2. **Tel:** 1 4752965, **Fax:** 1 4752967  www.englishlanguage.com

**Galway Language Centre**
The Bridge Mills, Galway. **Tel:** 91 566468, **Fax:** 91 564122.

**International House Dublin**
Griffith College Campus, South Circular Road, Dublin 8. **Tel:** 1 454 9260 / 454 9261, **Fax:** 1 454 9262 www.ihdublin.com

**The Language Centre Of Ireland**
45 Kildare Street, Dublin 2. **Tel:** 1 6716266. **Fax:** 1 6716430 www.lci.ie

**Waterford English Language Centres**
31 John's Hill, Waterford. **Tel:** 51 877288, **Fax:** 51 854603  www.waterfortd-net.ie

## ITALY

There is a great demand for English language teachers in Italy but it can be hard to find work, especially in the major cities. Generally, teachers need to be native speakers with at least a TESL certificate. Schools are trying to save money so recruitment from overseas is much less common than it was in the past, as schools tend to recruit locally. September is the best time to arrive in Italy to start your job search. Italian schools and companies prefer to recruit locally and there is a strong demand for English teachers in the corporate sector.

**Embassy in UK:**
14 Three Kings' Yard, Davies Street, London W1K 2EH
**Tel:** 020 7312 2200
www.embitaly.org.uk

**Embassy in USA:**
3000 Whitehaven Street NW, Washington DC 20008
**Tel:** 202 612 4400
www.italyemb.org

**British Council office:**
Via Quattro Fontane 20, 00184 Rome
**Tel** +39 (06) 478 141
www.britishcouncil.it

⮕ **Visas/Work Permits:** It is now easier for Americans to arrive in Italy, find a teaching job, and then apply for a work permit without having to return to the States as was once the case.

➲ **Requirements:** College Degree and a TESOL/TESL Certificate

➲ **Cost of Living:** Italian cities are generally more expensive than their American counterparts but life in rural Italy is quite cheap.

➲ **Currency:** £1 = € 1.49  $1 = € 0.76

➲ **Salaries/Taxes:** Schools usually provide 25 contact hours a week at £10-15 per hour. A typical monthly salary is around £6-800 (with overtime paid extra). Schools often provide accommodation for the first month and some even give a ticket home at the end of the contract. Tax is payable at 20% with a 10% additional social security deduction.

➲ **Accommodation:** Accommodation is easy to find but tends to be expensive. Milan is the most expensive city and a one-bedroom apartment can cost about £700 a month but accommodation can be found for £300-400. Elsewhere, rents are cheaper.

➲ **Health advice:** Insurance is advisable.

## Schools in Italy (+39)

**Academia Britannica**
Via Bruxelles 61, 04100 Latina. **Tel:** 773 491917.

**Anglo American School**
Piazza S. Giovanni in Monte 9, 40124 Bologna.

**Anglocentre**
Via A de Gasperi 23, 70052 Bisceglie.

**Arlington Language Services**
cp99, 29100 Piacenza.

**Bari Poggiofranco English Centre**
Viale Pio XII 18, 70124 Bari.

**Benedict School**
Via Sauro 36, 48100 Ravenna. **Tel:** 544 38199, **Fax:** 544 38399.

**The British Council**
Via Manzoni 38, 20121 Milan. **Tel:** 39 2 772221.

**The British Council**
Palazzo del Drago, Via Quattro Fontane 20, 00184, Rome. **Tel:** 6 478141.

**British Institute**
Fontane 109, Rome. **Tel:** 6491979. **Fax:** 64815549.

**British Institute of Milan**
Via Marghera 45, 20149 Milan. **Tel:** 2 48011149.

**British Institute of Florence**
Palazzo Feroni, Via Tornalbuoni 2, Florence. **Tel:** 55 298866.

**British Institute of Rome**
Via 4 Fontane 109, 00184 Rome.

**The British Language Centre**
Via Piazzi Angolo Largo Pedrini, 23100 Sondrio. **Tel:** 342 216130.

**The British Language Centre**
Via Piazza Roma 3, 20038 Serengo.

**The British School of Bari**
Via Celentano 27, 70121 Bari. **Tel:** 080 5247335, **Fax:** 080 5247396.

**Cambridge Centre of English**
Via Campanella 16, 41100 Modena. **Tel:** 59 24 1004

**The Cambridge School**
Via S Rochetto 3, Verona. **Tel:** 458003154

**The Cambridge School**
Via Mercanti 36, 84100 Salerno. **Tel:** 89 228942, **Fax:** 89 252523.

**Canning School**
Via San Remo 9, 20133 Milan.

**Centro di Lingue**
Via Pozzo 30, Trento. **Tel:** 461981733. **Fax:** 461981687.

**Centro Internazionale di Linguistica Streamline**
Via Piave 34/b, 71100 Foggia. **Tel:** 88124204.

**Cento Lingue di Vinci Antonella**
Via San Martino 77, Pisa.

**Centro Lingue Tradint**
Via Jannozzi 8, S Donato Milanese Chandler, Viale Aventino 102, 00153 Rome.

**CLM-Bell**
Eugen Joa, Via Pozzo 30, 38100 Trento. **Tel:** 461 981733, **Fax:** 461 981687.

**English Centre**
Via Promis 8, 11100 Aosta. **Tel:** 165 235416.

**The English Centre**
Via P Paoli 34, 07100 Sassari, Sardinia. **Tel:** 79 238154, **Fax:** 79 238180.

**The English Connection**
Via Ferro 1, 30027 San Dona di Piave.

**English For Business Snc**
Via Magnani Ricotti, n.2, 28100 Novara. **Tel:** 321 627186 **Fax:** 321 398061.

**The English Institute**
Corso Gelone 82, 96100 Siracusa. **Tel:** 961 6085.

**English House**
Via Roma 177, 85028 Rionero, Potenza.

**English Language Centre**
Viale Milano 20, 21100 Varese. **Tel:** 332 282732, **Fax:** 332 236385.

**The English Language Studio**
Via Antonio Bondi 27, 40138 Bologna. **Tel:** 51347394, **Fax:** 51505952.

**English School**
Via dei Correttori 6, 89127 Reggio Calabria. **Tel/Fax:** 965 899535.

**Eurolingue**
Via Chiana 116, 00198 Roma.

**European Language Institute**
Via IV Novembre 65, 55049 Viareggio (LU).

**Filadelfia School**
Via L. Colla 22, 10098 Rivoli.

**Home School**
Via F. Malvotti 8, Conegliano (TV).

**Inlingua**
Piazza XX Settembre 36, Civitanova Marche (MC).

**Inlingua**
Corso Vittorio Emanuel II 68, Torino.

**Inlingua**
Via Leoncino 35, 37121 Verona.

**Inlingua**
Via Monte Piana 42, Venezia.

**International British School**
Via Santacaterina 146, 89100 Regio Calabria.

**International House Livorno**
Piazza Folgore 1, 57128 Livorno. **Tel:** 336 709682, **Fax:** 586 508060.

**International House Pisa**
Via Risorgimento 9, 56126 Pisa. **Tel:** 50440 40.

**International House Rome**
Via San Godenzo 100, 00189 Rome.

**International House Turin**
Via Saluzzi 60, 10125 Turin. **Tel:** 39 11 669 95.

**International Language School**
Via Tibullo 10, 00193 Rome. **Tel:** 687 6801, **Fax:** 683 07796.

**Language Centre**
Via Milano 20, 21100 Varese. **Tel:** 332 282732.

**Language Centre**
Via G Daita 29, 90139 Palermo.

**Lb Linguistico**
Centro Insegnamento, Lingue Staniere, Via Caserta 16, 95128 Catania, Sicily.

**Lingua Due Villa**
Pendola 15, 57100 Livorno.

**Living Languages School**
Via Magna Grecia, 89100 Regio Calabria. **Tel/Fax:** 39 965 330926.

**London School**
Fabiola Cordaro, International House, Viale Emilia 34, 90144 Palermo. **Tel:** 39 91 52 524

**Lord Byron College**
Via Sparano 102, 70121 Bari. **Tel:** 80 238696.

**Managerial English Consultants**
Via Sforza Pallavicini 11, 009193 Rome.**Tel:** 6 654 2391, **Fax:** 6 6871159.

**Modern English School**
Via Borgonuovo 14, 40125 Bologna. **Tel:** 51 227523, **Fax:** 51225314.

**Multimethod**
I Go Richini 8, 20122 Milan. **Tel:** 2583042.

**Oxford School**
San Marco 1513, Venice. Fax: 41 5210785.

**Oxford School of English**
Via S. Pertini 14, Mirano, 30035 Venice. **Tel:** 41 570 2355, **Fax:** 41 570 2390.

**The Professionals**
Via F Carcona 4, 20149 Milan. **Tel:** 2 48000035, **Fax:** 2 4814001.

**Regency School**
Via dell' Arcivescovado 7, 16121 Turin. **Tel:** 11 562 7456, **Fax:** 11 541845.

**Regent International**
V.U. Da Pisa 6, Milan.

**Regent International**
Corsa Italia 54, 21047 Saronno.

**RTS Language Training**
Via Tuscolana 4, 00182 Rome. **Tel:** 6 702 2730, **Fax:** 6 702 1740.

**Scuola The Westminster**
Via Tevere 84, Sesto Fiorentino.

**Spep School**
Via della Secca 1, 40121 Bologna.

**Studio Linguistico Fonema**
via Marconi 19, 50053 Sovigliana-Vinci. **Tel:** 571 500551.

**Studio professionale Apprendimento Linguistico Programmato**
Via Ferrarese 3, Bologna. **Tel:** 051 360617, **Fax:** 513 68413.

**Summer Camps**
Via Roma 54, 18038 San Remo. **Tel/Fax:** 184 506070.

**Unimoney**
Corso Sempione 72, 20154 Milan.

**Victoria Language Centre**
Viale Fassi 28, 41012 Capri.

**Wall Street Institute**
Piazza Combattento 6, 4100 Ferrara. **Tel:** 532 200231.

## THE NETHERLANDS

The current employment situation for English language teachers is good. There is quite a demand for teachers of English who are native speakers and there may also be possible opportunities for qualified teachers in a new type of school. There are forty of these at present and they teach children in English and Dutch. The Dutch term for the schools is "Twee Talig Scholen." Most work opportunities available to foreign teachers tends to be teaching Business English as the levels of English in the school system are very high. Schools depending mainly on long-term freelance teachers. Self-employed teachers typically work for a number of schools or agencies and their incomes can fluctuate considerably. To find work, go through the list of language schools below as well as those in the Dutch Yellow Pages. It is likely you will have to give an observed lesson before you are given the job.

**Embassy in UK:**
38 Hyde Park Gate, London SW7 5DP
**Tel:** 020 7590 3200
www.netherlands-embassy.org.uk

**Embassy in USA:**
4200 Linnean Ave NW, Washington DC 20008
**Tel:** 202 244 5300
www.netherlands-embassy.org

**British Council office:**
Weteringschans 85A, 1017 RZ Amsterdam
**Tel** +31 (20) 550 6060
www.britishcouncil.org/netherlands

◗ **Visa/Work Permits:** The Employment of Foreign Workers Act says that an employer cannot employ a foreigner without an employment permit from the Central Employment Board. The employer must first fill a vacancy from the pool of job applicants immediately available in the Netherlands. Subsequently it will be determined if applicants from other member states of the European Community are available. Only after these two applicant pools are exhausted can subjects from other countries be eligible for an employment permit. An employment permit can be sought only after a residence permit application (VTV) has been submitted. Applications for employment permits are available from the Regional Employment Office. Applications for employment permits are processed by the Employment Office only if the form has been completed, signed by both the employer and the employee, and all required material has been attached.

◗ **Requirements:** College Degree, experience and a TESOL/TESL Certificate

◗ **Cost of Living:** The Netherlands is an expensive place to live.

◗ **Currency:** £1 = € 1.49  $1 = € 0.76

◗ **Salaries/Taxes:** Qualified teachers can earn £8-12 per lesson. Tax is payable at around 30%.

◗ **Accommodation:** Accommodation in the Amsterdam area is extremely expensive and a studio apartment could cost you over £200 a month. Also bear in mind that a place will also be very hard to find.

◗ **Health advice:** If you are a taxpayer then you will be entitled to medical coverage under the 'Ziekenfonds' system. But you will still have to pay a premium to the health insurance company of between £6 - 12 a month.

### Schools in The Netherlands (+31)

**All-English Institute**
Iepenlaan 96, 2061 GN Bloemendaal (Haarlem area)
**Tel:** 023-5277394

**Arcus Contracting B.V.**
Diepenbrockstraat 15, 6411 TJ Heerlen **Tel:** 045-5609070

**Berlitz Language Centre**
Rokin 87-89, 1012 Kl Amsterdam **Tel:** 020-6221375

**British Language Training Centre**
NZ Voorburgwal 328, 1012 RW Amsterdam **Tel:** 020-6223634

**The British School in the Netherlands**
ELC, Vlaskamp 19, 2592 AA Den Haag **Tel:** 070-3338130

**CBE - Centre for British English**
Bergsingel 89-A, 3037 GA Rotterdam **Tel:** 010-4678705

**C J Korrel**
Schinkelhavenstraat 13 hs, 1075 VN Amsterdam **Tel:** 020-6627441

**Communications in English**
Piet Heinstraat 101, 2518 CE Den Haag **Tel:** 070-3466314

**Delftse Volksuniversiteit**
Ruys de Beerenbrouckstraat 31, 2613 AS Delft **Tel:** 015-2570130

**De Taaltrainers**
Burg. Raaymaekerslaan153, 5361 KL Grave **Tel:** 0486-421230

**Double Dutch**
Beringstraat 18, 7532 CP Enschede **Tel:** 053-4615822

**Dutchess English Language Centre**
Schoutenstraat 86, 1623 RZ Hoorn **Tel:** 0229-210581

**Engelse Taalcursussen**
IJsselsteinseweg 63, 3435 PB Nieuwegein **Tel:** 030-6035506

**English Language Institute**
Berkenweg 46, 3741 BZ Baarn **Tel:** 035-5424725

**Fontys Hogeschool**
Oude Markt 5, 6131 EN Sittard **Tel:** 046-4599579

**Fontys Hogeschool Talencentrum**
Rachelsmolen 1, 5600 AH Eindhoven **Tel:** 040-2454972

**Franglais**
Molenstraat 15, 2513 BH Den Haag **Tel:** 070-3611703

**HES/O & O**
K.P. van der Mandelelaan 22, 3062 MB Rotterdam **Tel:** 010-4532451

**Int. Studiecentrum v/d Vrouw**
Concertgebouwplein 17, 1071 LM Amsterdam **Tel:** 020-6761437

**Instituut De Wester**
Ruusbroechof 37, 1813 BC Alkmaar **Tel:** 072-5400920

**Instituut Taaltip**
Floralaan 19, 1211 JT Hilversum **Tel:** 035-7720211

**Instituut Uithoorn**
Postbus 238, 1420 AE Uithoorn **Tel:** 020-4823482

**Instituut Verschoor**
Piet Heinlaan 8, 3941 VG Doorn **Tel:** 0343-413319

**Instituut voor Taalhantering**
Postbus 368, 8000 AJ Zwolle **Tel:** 038-4449263

**The Language Academy**
Spuistraat 134, 1012 VB Amsterdam **Tel:** 020-5254637

**Leidse Volksuniversiteit K & O**
Oude Vest 45, 2312 XS Leiden **Tel:** 071-5141141

**LOI Tel: correspondentie cursussen**
Postbus 4200, 2350 CA Leiderdorp **Tel:** 071-5451888

**Onderwijsinstituut Netty Post**
Haverstraat 2, 1446 CE Purmerend **Tel:** 0299-641416

**P.C.I. Talen**
Bachlaan 43, 1817 GH Alkmaar **Tel:** 072-5156518

**RIVO**
Dorpstraat 3, 2902 BC Capelle a/d IJssel **Tel:** 010-4519464

**ROC Albeda Contract Groep**
Heemraadsingel 178, 3021 DL Rotterdam **Tel:** 010-4255333

**ROC Da Vinci College**
Groenedijk 49, Dordrecht **Tel:** 078-6572657

**ROC Instituut De Factoor**
Postbus 1, 8000 AA Zwolle **Tel:** 038-8508026

**ROC Joke Smit School**
R Vinkeleskade 62, 1071 SX Amsterdam **Tel:** 020-6647401

**ROC Koning Willem I College**
Vlijmenseweg 2, 5223 GW 'sHertogenbosch **Tel:** 073-6249624

**Schoevers Opleidingen**
Bezuidenhoutseweg 273, 2594 AN Den Haag **Tel:** 070-3491499

**Schoevers Opleidingen**
Eendrachtskade/Zuidzijde 12 Groningen **Tel:** 050-3182202

**Schoevers Opleidingen**
Javastraat 16-18, 6524 MB Nijmegen **Tel:** 024-3229742/024-3787602

**Schoevers Opleidingen**
Karel Doormanstraat 331, 3012 GH Rotterdam **Tel:** 010-4117855

**Schoevers Opleidingen**
Kromme Nieuwe Gracht 3, 3512 HC Utrecht **Tel:** 030-2368152

**Schoevers Opleidingen**
Markt 17, 5611 EB Eindhoven **Tel:** 040-2442832

**Schoevers Opleidingen**
Stadhouderskade 60, 1072 AC Amsterdam **Tel:** 020-6627156

**Schoevers Opleidingen**
Tuinstraat 1, 5000 JL Tilburg **Tel:** 013-5424128

**Schoevers Opleidingen**
Utrechtsestraat 35, 6811 LT Arnhem **Tel:** 026-4453641

**The School of English**
1e Wormerweg 238, 7331 MT Apeldoorn **Tel:** 055-5336769

**Secradesk**
Postbus 545, 7500 AM Enschede **Tel:** 053-4836420

**Stichting Holtland Contract**
Lammenschanspark 2, 2381 JK Leiden **Tel:** 071-5321952

**Stichting IVIO**
De Schans 1802, 8231 KA Lelystad **Tel:** 0320-229948

**Stichting Rotterdamse Volksuniv.**
Heemraadsingel 275, 3023 BE Rotterdam **Tel:** 010-4761200

**Suitcase**
Divertimentostraat 55, 1312 EB Almere **Tel:** 036-5367482

**Taalcursussen Doorn**
W. Alexanderweg 117, 3945 CH Cothen **Tel:** 0343-561617

**Taaltrainingscentrum Barendrecht**
Maasstraat 9, 2991 AD Barendrecht **Tel:** 0180-615410

**Talenlaboratorium**
Rijksuniversiteit Leiden, Postbus 9515, 2300 RA Leiden **Tel:** 071-5272332

**Taleninstituut Bogaers**
Groenstraat 139-155, 5021 LL Tilburg **Tel:** 013-5362101

**Talenpracticum Twente B.V.**
Ariënsplein 2, 7511 JX Enschede **Tel:** 053-4317842

**Universitair Talencentrum Nijmegen**
Erasmusplein 1, 6525 HT Nijmegen **Tel:** 024-612159

**Utrechtse Volksuniversiteit**
Nieuwe Gracht 41, 3512 LE Utrecht **Tel:** 030-2313395

**Van Beers & Kooijmans vof**
Rigelhof 14, 3318 CZ Dordrecht **Tel:** 078-6183998

**Volksuniversiteit Amersfoort**
Korte Bergstraat 5, 3811 ML Amersfoort **Tel:** 033-4656640

**Volksuniversiteit Amstelland**
Burg. Haspelslaan 2, 1181 NB Amstelveen **Tel:** 020-6457506

**Volksuniversiteit Amsterdam**
Rapenburgerstraat 73, 1011 VK Amsterdam **Tel:** 020-6261626

**Volksuniversiteit Bodengraven**
Groene Zoom 149, 2411 SP Bodegraven **Tel:** 0172-616924

**Volksuniversiteit Enschede**
Molenstraat 27, 7514 DJ Enschede **Tel:**053-4323304

**Volksuniversiteit Groningen**
Oude Boteringestraat 21, 9712 GC Groningen **Tel:** 050-3126555

**Volksuniversiteit Haarlem**
Leidsevaart 220, 2014 HE Haarlem **Tel:** 023-5329453

**Volksuniversiteit**
Havensingel 24, 5211 TX 's Hertogenbosch **Tel:** 073-6141120

**Volksuniversiteit Hilversum**
Arena 301, 1213 NZ Hilversum **Tel:**035-6892051/035-6892000

**Volksuniversiteit Soest/Soesterberg**
Di Lassostraat 65, 3766 EB Soest **Tel:**035-6022195

**The Workshop**
Rostocklaan 38, 7315 HM Apeldoorn **Tel:** 055-5216736

**Zeeuwse Volksuniversiteit**
Postbus 724, 4330 AS Middelburg **Tel:** 0118-634800

## NORWAY

There is often a shortage of English language teachers in Norway but it is hard to get a job unless you are qualified and have some experience. For non-EU teachers, it is almost impossible to find a job teaching English unless you are a Norwegian citizen or you are married to one!

**Embassy in UK:**
25 Belgrave Square, London SW1X 8QD
**Tel:** 020 7591 5500
www.norway.org.uk

**Embassy in USA:**
2720 34th Street NW, Washington DC 20008
**Tel:** 202 333 6000
www.norway.org/embassy

**British Council office:**
Fridtjof Nansens Plass 5, 0160 Oslo
Tel +47 (22) 396 190
www.britishcouncil.no

➲   **Visas/Work Permits:** A valid passport is required. U.S. citizens may enter Norway for tourist or general business purposes without a visa for up to 90 days. Tourists who have stayed in Norway for more than 90 days without a visa are usually not permitted to re-enter the country until six months have passed. Tourists who enter without a visa cannot usually change status in Norway in order to reside or work. Travellers planning a long-term stay, marriage or employment in Norway should seek the appropriate visa before departing the United States.

➲ **Requirements:** College Degree and a TESOL/TESL Certificate

➲ **Currency:** £1 = 12.18 / $1 = 6.23 Kroner

➲ **Cost of Living:** very expensive country to live in but the social welfare system is excellent.

➲ **Health advice:** Medical facilities are widely available and of high quality, but may be limited outside the larger urban areas. The remote and sparse populations in northern Norway, and the dependency on ferries to cross fjords of western Norway, may affect transportation and access to medical facilities.

## Schools in Norway (+47)

**Det Internasjonale Spraksenter**
Dronningensgenst 32, 0154 Oslo. **Tel:** 22 33 15 20. **Fax:** 22 33 69 30.

**Norsk Sprachinsitut**
Korgengst. 9, 0153 Oslo: **Tel:** 23 10 01 10. **Fax:** 23 10 01 27.

**Sprakskolen As**
Karl Johansgat 8, 0154 Oslo. **Tel:** 22 42 00 87. **Fax:** 22 42 32 94.

## PORTUGAL

Over the last few years it has become more difficult for non-EU passport holders to find teaching jobs in Portugal. But Americans and Canadians do find work, especially in Lisbon where some schools are willing to employ unqualified native-speaking tourists.

**Embassy in UK:**
11 Belgrave Square, London SW1X 8PP
**Tel:** 020 7235 5331

**Embassy in USA:**
2125 Kalorama Road NW, Washington DC 20008
**Tel:** 202 328 8610

**British Council office:**
Rua Lui Fernandes 1-3, 1249-062 Lisbon
**Tel:** +351 21 321 4500
www.pt.britishcouncil.org

➲ **Visa/Permits:** If you are lucky enough to get work before you leave (which is advisable), your paperwork should be sorted out in advance. A visa is not required for tourist or business stays of up to 60 days.

➲ **Requirements:** College Degree and a TESOL/TESL Certificate

➲ **Cost of Living:** Reasonable compared to the UK and USA

➲ **Currency:** £1 = € 1.49 $1 = € 0.76

➲ **Salaries/Taxes:** Annual income for a teacher ranges from £8,000 to £10,000. Tax is about 20% of your gross salary.

➲ **Accommodation:** Accommodation may be provided by the institute. You will pay at least £400 per month for accommodation in Lisbon.

➲ **English Language Media:** The News (weekly)

## Schools in Portugal (+351)

**American Language Institute**
Rua José Falcao 15-5° Esq, 4050 Oporto. **Tel:** 2 318 127, **Fax:** 2 208 5287.

**Berlitz**
Av Conde Valbom 6-4, 1000 Lisbon.

**Big Ben School**
Rua Moinho Fanares 4-1, 2725 Mem Martins.

**Bristol School Group**
Trav. Dr Carlos Felgueiras, 12-3°, 4470 Maia. **Tel:** 2 948 8803, **Fax:** 2 948 6460.

**British Council**
Rua De Sao Marcal 174, 1294 Lisbon Codex. **Tel:** 347 6141.

**British Council**
Rua Do Breyner 155, 4050 Oporto. **Tel:** 200 5577.

**Cambridge School**
Avenida da Liberdade 173-4, 1200 Lisbon. **Tel:** 352 7474, **Fax:** 353 4729.

**Casa de Inglaterra**
Rua Alexandre Herculano 134, 3000 Coimbra.

**CENA-Cent.**
Est. Norte Americanos, Rua Remedios 62 c/v, 1200 Lisbon.

**Centro de Estudos IPFEL**
Rua Edith Cavell 8, 1900 Lisbon.

**Centro de Instrucao Tecnica**
Rua Da Estefania 32-10 Dto, 1000 Lisbon.

**Centro Internacional Linguas**
Av Fontes P de Melo 25-1Dto, 1000 Lisbon.

**Centro de Linguas de Alvide**
Rua Fonte Nino, Viv Pe Americo 1, Alvide, 2750 Cascais.

**Centro de Linguas Estrangeiras de Cascais**
Av Marginal Bl A-30, 2750 Cascais.

**Centro de Linguas Intergarb**
Tv da Liberdade 13-1, 8200 Albufeira.

**Centro de Linguas de Quarteira**
Rua Proj 25 de Abril 12, 8125 Quartiera.

**Centro de Linguas de Queluz**
Av Dr Miguel Bombarda 62-1E, 2745 Queluz.

**Centro de Linguas de Santarem**
Lg Pe Francisco N Silva, 2000 Santarem.

**CIAL-Centro De Linguas**
Av Republica 14-20, 1000 Lisbon. **Tel:** 3533733

**Class**
Rua Gen Humberto Delgado 40-1, 7540 Santiago Do Cacem.

**Clube Conversacao Inglesa 3M**
Rua Rodrigues Sampaio 18-3, 1100 Lisbon.

**Communicate Language Institute**
Praceta Joao Villaret 12B, 2675 Povoa de Sto. Adriao.

**Curso de Linguas Estrangeiras**
Rua Dr Miguel Bombarda 271-1, 2600 Vila Franca De Xira.

**Ecubal**
Lombos, Barros Brancos, Porches, 8400 Lagoa.

**ELTA**
Av Jose E Garcia 55-3, 2745 Queluz.

**Encounter English**
Av Fernao De Magalha, 4300 Porto. **Tel:** 567916.

**English at PLC**
Praca Luis de Camoes 26, Apartado 73, 5001 Vila Real.

**English Institute Setubal**
Av 22 Dezembro 88, 2900 Setubal.

**The English Language Centre**
Rua Calouste Gulbenkian 22-r/c C, 3080 Figueira Da Foz.

**The English School of Coruche**
Rua Guerreiros 11, 2100 Coruche.

**Escola de Linguas de Agueda**
Rua Jose G Pimenta, 3750 Agueda

**Escola de Linguas de Ovar**
Rua Ferreira de Castro 124-1 A/B, 3880 Ovar.

**Eurocentre Instituto de Linguas**
Av de Bons Amigos 4-1, 2735 Cacem.

**Gab Tecnico de Linguas**
Rua Hermenegildo Capelo 2-2, 2400 Leiria.

**GEDI**
Pq Miraflores Lt 18-lA/B, 1495 Alges.

**Greenwich Instituto de Linguas**
Rua 25 de Abril 560, S Cosme, 4420 Gondomar.
**Tel/Fax:** 2 483 6429.

**IF - Ingles Funcional**
Rua Afonso Albuquerque 73-A, 2460 Alcobaca.

**IF Ingles Funcional**
Rua Com Almeida Henriques 32, 2400 Leiria.

**IF Ingles Funcional**
Ap 303, 2430 Marinha Grande. **Tel:** 44 568351

**INESP**
Rua Dr Alberto Souto 20-2, 3800 Aveiro.

**INLINGUA**
Campo Grande 30-1A, 1700 Lisbon.

**INPR**
Bernardo Lima 5, 1100 Lisbon.

**Instituto Britanico**
Rua Conselheiro Januario 119/21, 4700 Braga. **Tel:** 53 23898.

**Instituto Britanico**
Rua Municipio Lt B - 1 C, 2400 Leiria.

**Instituto Britanico**
Rua Dr Ferreira Carmo, 4990 Ponte De Lima.

**Instituto Franco-Britanico**
Rua 5 de Outubro 10-1Dto, 2700 Amadora.

**Instituto Inlas do Porto**
Rua S da Bandeira 522-1, 4000 Porto.

**Instituto de Linguas**
Rua Valverde 1, 2350 Torres Novas.

**Instituto de Linguas do Castelo Branco**
Av 1 Maio, 39 S - l E, 6000 Castelo Branco.

**Instituto de Linguas de Faro**
Av 5 de Outubro, 8000 Faro.

**Instituto de Linguas do Fundao**
Urb Rebordao Lt 17-r/c, 6230 Fundao.

**Instituto de Linguas de Oeiras**
Rua Infante D Pedro 1 e 3-r/c, 2780 Oeiras.

**Instituto de Linguas de Paredes**
Av Republica, Casteloes Cepeda, 4580 Paredes.

**Instituto Nacional de Administracao**
Centro de Linguas, Palacio Marquus de Oeiras, 2780 Oeiras.

**Instituto Sintrense de Linguas**
Rua Dr Almeida Guerra 26, 2710 Sintra.

**Interlingua**
Lg 1 de Dezembro 28, 8500 Portimao.

**Interlingu**
Rua Dr Joaquim Telo 32-1E, 8600 Lagos.

**International House Braga**
Rua dos Chaos 168, 4710 Braga. **Tel:** 53 215250, **Fax:** 53 61228.

**International House Lisbon**
Rua Marques Sa Da Bandeira 16, 1000 Lisbon

**International Language School**
Av Rep Guine Bissau, 26-A, 2900 Setubal.

**ISLA**
Bo S Jo de Brito, 5300 Bragan A, Manitoba,C Com Premar, l 72, 4490 Povoa De Varzim.

**Know-How**
Av Alvares Cabral 5-300, 1200 Lisbon.

**Lancaster College**
Rua C Civico, Ed A Seguradora 2, 6200 Covilha.

**Lancaster College**
Pta 25 Abril 35-1E, 4400 Vila Nova De Gaia. **Tel:** 2 306 495.

**Language School**
Rua Alm Candido Reis 98, 2870 Montijo.

**Linguacoop**
Av. Manuel da Maia 46-10 D, 1000 Lisbon.

**Linguacultura**
Rua Dr Joaquim Jacinto 110, 2300 Tomar.

**Linguacultura**
Lg Sto Antonio 6-1 Esq, 2200 Abrantes.

**Lisbon Language Learners**
Rua Conde Redondo 33-r/cE, 1100 Lisbon.

**Mundilingua**
Rua Dr Tefilo Braga, Ed Rubi-1, 8500 Portimao.

**Mundilinguas**
Rua Miguel Bombarda 34-1, 2000 Santarem.

**The New Institute of Languages**
Urb Portela Lt 197-5B-C, 2685 Sacavem. **Tel:** 1 943 5238.

**Novo Instituto de Linguas**
Rua Cordeiro Ferreira 19 C-1D, 1700 Lisbon.

**PEC**
Rua SA Bandeira 5385, 4000 Oporto. **Tel:** 200 5077.

**PROLINGUAS**
Rua Saraiva Carvalho, 84 - Pt2, 1200 Lisbon.

**Royal School of Languages**
Av Dr Lourenco Peixinho 92-2, 3800 Aveiro. **Tel:** 34 2956, **Fax:** 34 382870.

**Tell School**
Rua Soc Farmaceutica 30-1, 1100 Lisbon.

**Tjaereborg Studio**
Av Liberdade 166-4F, 1200 Lisbon.

**Wall Street Institutes Avenidas**
Av Praia de Vitoria, 71 3rd, 1000 Lisbon. **Tel:** 316 0810, **Fax:** 316 0553.

**Wall Street Institutes Oporto**
Rua do Campo Alegre 231, 3°, 4100 Oporto. **Tel/Fax:** 2 600 9875.

**Weltsprachen-Institut**
Qta Carreira 37 r/c, 2765 Sao Joao do Estoril. **Tel:** 4684032.

**Whyte Institute**
Lg das Almas 10-2E/F, 4900 Viana Do Castelo.

**World Trade Centre - Lisbon**
Av Brasil 1-5e8, 1700 Lisbon.

## SPAIN

Spanish English language schools have been hit recently with economic problems and some of the major chains have closed down. However, there are still jobs available, especially to qualified native-speakers from the UK.

The best time to arrive is in September when schools are recruiting teachers for the academic year ahead.

Native English language speakers can find teaching jobs in Spain without any qualifications beyond their degrees but it will make your professional life much easier if you have some training under your belt! The maximum number of teaching hours per week allowed by law is 33, but contracted teachers can expect a challenging schedule with close to this number of hours and often at inconvenient times. You might consider working privately as an option because it is better paid than working in schools. If you're in Madrid, try putting an ad for your services in the Segundamano newspaper.

Although it is difficult for non-EU citizens to work legally in Spain, the reality is that thousands of Americans, Canadians and Australians are employed as English language teachers throughout the country.

**Embassy in UK:**
39 Chesham Place, London SW1X 8SB
**Tel:** 020 7235 5555

**Embassy in USA:**
2375 Pennsylvania Ave NW, Washington DC 20037
**Tel:** 202 452 0100

www.spainemb.org

**British Council office:**
Paseo del General Martinez, Campos 31, 28010
Madrid
**Tel** +34 (91) 337 3500
www.britishcouncil.es

⊃ **Tip:** Dress formally for your interview. If you get the job, you can ask later if casual attire is acceptable while working.

⊃ **Visa/Permits:** Officially, non-EU citizens require a work visa if they are staying over three months. In reality most work without contracts at least initially as work visas are difficult to get. Those wishing to stay in the long term usually apply for a work visa, involving documentation from their employer and from the US, and a return trip, a lengthy process

⊃ **Requirements:** College Degree and a TESOL/TESL Certificate

⊃ **Cost of Living:** Urban life in Spain is expensive but if you are selective about where you stay, then savings can be made.

⊃ **Currency:**£1 = € 1.49  $1 = € 0.76

⊃ **Salaries/Taxes:** A minimum monthly salary in the big cities is around £300 / $550 a month. Private sector schools pay approximately £4.50 / $8 per hour in Catalonia. Freelancers can earn around £6.50 / $12 per hour in the Valencia region and from £7 / $13 to £15 / $30 in Catalonia. Residents pay 15% tax in arrears and an additional 6% in social security payments. If you work cash in hand (which is often the case for non-EU teachers) then you should not pay any taxes.

⊃ **Accommodation:** Rents often take up more than a quarter of a teacher's salary, especially in the major cities, although lower salaries in smaller towns might include accommodation. Expect to pay a minimum of £200 / $380 a month if you want to live on your own. For shared accommodation, standard rents are around £100 / $190 per month. Up to two months' deposit is payable in advance.

⊃ **Health advice:** As you will probably be working as a freelancer you must have your own insurance.

⊃ **English Language Media:** Barcelona Metropolitan, Costa Blanca News, Sur

---

## Schools in Spain (+34)

**Academia Andaluza de Idiomas**
Crta El Punto 9, Conil, Cadiz, **Tel:** 956 44 0552.

**Academia Britanica**
Rodriguez Sanchez 15, 14003 Cordoba.

**Academia Saint Patricks**
Calle Caracuel 1, 17402 Girona.

**Academia Wellington House**
Guiposcoa 79, 08020 Barcelona.

**Acento - The Language Company**
Ruiz De Alarcon 7, 21, 41007 Sevilla.

**Afoban**
Alfonso Xii 30, 41002 Sevilla.**Tel:** 95 421 8974

**AHIZKE/CIM**
Loramendi 7, Apartado 191, Mondragon Guipuzcoa.

**Alce Idiomas**
Nogales 2, 33006 Oviedo. **Tel:** 85 254543.

**Aljarafe Language Academy**
Crta Castilleja-Tomares 83, Tomares, Sevilla.

**American Institute**
El Bachiller 13, 46010 Valencia.

**Apple Idiomas**
Aben al Abbar 6, 46021 Valencia. **Tel:** 362 25 45.

**Audio Jeam**
Pza Ayuntamiento 2, 46002 Valencia.

**Augusta Idiomas**
Via. Augusta 128, 08006 Barcelona.

**Aupi**
Jesus 43, 46007 Valencia.

**Avila Centre of English**
Bajada de Don Alonso 1, 05003 Avila. **Tel:** 18 213719, **Fax**: 213631.

**Berlitz**
Gran Via 80, 4º, 28013 Madrid. **Tel:** 1 542 3586, **Fax**: 1 541 2765.

**Berlitz**
Edif Forum 1 Mod, 3 Av Luis Morales, S/N 41018 Sevilla.

**Big Ben College**
Plaza Quintiliano 13, Calahorra 26500 La Rioja.

**Brighton**
Rambla Catalunya 66, 08007 Barcelona.

**Bristol English School**
Fundacion Jado 10 Bis 6, 48950 Erlandio, Vizacaya. **Tel:** 467 6332.

**Britannia School of English**
s 9, Bl 2 41010 Sevilla.

**Britannia School**
Leopoldo Lugones 3-1B, 33420 Lugones, Asturias. **Tel:** 85 26 2800.

**Britannia School**
Raset 22, Barcelona 08021. **Tel:** 3 200 0100

**British Council**
Bravo Murillo 25, 35003 Las Palmas De Gran Canaria.
**Tel:** 28 36 83 00.

**British Council**
General San Martin 7, 46003 Valencia. **Tel:** 6 351 8818.

**British Language Centre**
C/Bravo Murillo 377, 28020 Madrid. **Tel:** 1 733 07 39.

**Business & United Schools**
Genova 4, 1D 41010 Sevilla. **Tel:** 427 3183

**Callan Method School of English**
Calle Alfredo Vicenti 6 bajo, 15004 La Coruna.

**Cambridge School**
Placa Manel Montanya, 4, 08400 Granollers. **Tel:** 3 870 2001.

**Centro Atlantico**
Villanueva 2 apdo, 28001 Madrid. **Tel:** 1 435 3661, **Fax:** 1 578 1435.

**Centro Britanico**
Republica De El Salvador 26-10m, (Edificio Simago), 15701 Santiago De Compostela, La Coruna. **Tel:** 81 59 7490.

**Centro Britannico**
Alfereces Provisionoles 1 1°B, 23007 Jaen.**Tel/Fax:** 53 22 21 08.

**Centro Cooperativo de Idiomas**
Clavel 2, 11300 La Linea, Cadiz.

**Centro Estudios Norteamericanos**
Aparisi y Guijarro 5, 46005 Valencia.

**Centro de Estudios de Ingles**
Garrigues 2, 46001 Valencia. **Tel:** 352 21 02.

**Centro De Idiomas Liverpool**
Libreros 11-1°, 28801 Alcala de Henares, Madrid. **Tel:** 1 881 3184, **Fax:** 1 881 3584.

**Centro De Ingles**
Tejon Y Marin, S/N 14003 Cordoba.

**Centro de Ingles Luz**
Passage Luz 8bajo, 46010 Valencia. **Tel:** 361 40 74.

**Centro Linguistico del Maresme**
Virgen De Montserrat. **Tel:** 35 55 5403.

**Centro Superior de Idiomas**
Tuset 26, 08006 Barcelona.

**Chatterbox Language Centre**
Verge de l'Assumpcio 21, Barbera del Valles.

**CLIC (Centro de Lenguas e Intercambio Cultural)**
Santa Ana, 1141002, Sevilla. **Tel:** 34-5-437 4500/438 6007, **Fax:** 437 18 06.

**Collegium Palatinum**
Calle de Rodriguez San Pedro 10, 28015 Madrid. **Tel:** 1 446 2349, **Fax:** 1 593 4446.

**The English Academy**
Cruz 15, 11370 Los Barrios, Cadiz.

**English Activity Centre**
Pedro Frances 22a, 07800 Ibiza. **Tel:** 7131 5828.

**The English Centre**
Apdo de Correos 85, 11500 El Puerto De Santa Maria, Cadiz. **Tel:** 34 56 850560, **Fax:** 873804.

**English Institute**
Carrer La Mar 38, 03700 Denia. **Tel:** 6 781026.

**English Language Centre**
Jesus Maria 9-1d, 14003 Cordoba.

**English Studies**
SA Avenida de Arteijo 8-1, 15004 La Coruna.

**English Way**
Platero 30, San Juan De Aznalfarache, Sevilla.

**Epicentre**
Niebla 13, 41011 Sevilla.

**Eurocentre**
Puerta De Jerez 3-1, 41001 Sevilla.

**Eurolingua**
San Felipe 3, 14003 Cordoba.

**European Language Schools**
Regueiro 2, 36211 Vigo. **Tel/Fax:** 86 291748.

**European Language Studies**
Edificio Edimburgo, Plaza Nina, 21003 Huelva. **Tel:** 34 59 263821, **Fax:** 34 59 280778.

**Fiac School**
Mayor 19, 08221 Terrassa, Barcelona.

**FLAC**
Escola De Idiomes Moderns Les Valls, 10 2/0, 08201 Sabadell, Barcelona.

**Glossa English Language Centre**
Rambla De Cataluna 9, 78 20 2A, 08008 Barcelona.

**Idiomas Blazek**
Llinas 2, 07014 Palma de Mallorca. **Tel:** 71 457260.

**Idiomas Oxford**
Calvo Sotelo 8-1, 26003 Logrono.**Tel:** 4124 41332.

**Idiomas Progreso**
Plaza Progreso 12, 07013 Palma De Mallorca. **Tel:** 7123 8036.

**Idiomaster**
Los Maristas, 2 Lucena, Cordoba.

**inlingua Idiomas**
C/o Greforio Fernandez 6, 47006 Valladolid.

**inlingua Idiomas**
Maestro Falla 5, 2,12, Puerto del Rosario, 35600
Fuerteventura, Canary Islands.

**inlingua Idiomas**
Tomas Morales 28, 35003 Las Palmas de Gran
Canaria. **Tel:** 2836 0671.

**Inlingua Madrid SL**
Calle Arenal 24, 28013 Madrid. **Tel:** 1 541 3246, **Fax:**
1 542 8296.

**The Institute of English**
Santiago Garcia 8, 46100 Burjasot.

**Interlang**
Pl Padre Jean de Mariana 3-2, 45002 Toledo.

**International House**
Trafalgar 14 Entlo, 08010 Barcelona. **Tel:** 3 268 4511.

**International House**
Calle Zurbano 8, 28010 Madrid. **Tel:** 1 310 13 14,
**Fax:** 1 308 53 21 **Email:** ih_madrid@mad.servicom.es

**International House**
C/Hernan Cortes 1, 21001 Huelva. **Tel:** 959 246529.

**International House**
Pascual y Genis 16, 46002 Valencia. **Tel:** 352 06 42.

**John Atkinson School of English**
Isaac Peral 11 y 13, 11100 San Fernando.

**Kensington Centros de Idiomas**
Avda Pedro Mururuza 8, 20870 Elgoibar. **Tel/Fax:** 43
740236.

**Language Study Centre**
Corredera Baja 15 Bajo, Chiclana De La Frontera,
Cadiz.

**Lawton School**
Cura Sama 7, 33202 Gijon, Asturias. **Tel:** 8534 9609.

**Lexis**
Avenida de la Constitucion 34, 18012 Granada.

**Linguasec**
Malaga 1, 14003 Cordoba.

**London House**
Baron de S Petrillo 23 bajo, 46020 Benimaclet.

**Manchester School**
San Bernado 81, 33201 Gijon, Alicante. **Tel:** 8535
8619. **Fax:** 8535 6932.

**Modern School**
Gerona 11, 41003 Sevilla.

**Nelson English School**
Jorge Manrique 1, Santa Cruz, Tenerife.

**Ten Centro de Ingles**
Caracuel 24, Jerez de la Frontera.

**The New School**
Calle Sant Joan 2, 2a Reus Tarragona.**Tel:** 77 330775

**Number Nine English Language Centre**
Sant Onofre 1, 07760 Ciudadella De Menorca,
Baleares. **Tel:** 7138 4058.

**Onoba Idiomas**
Rasco 19-2, 21001 Huelva.

**Oxford Centre**
Alvaro de Bazan 16, 46010 Valencia.

**Oxford House**
San Jeronimo 9-11, Granada.

**The Oxford School**
Maron Feria 4, 41800 Sanlúcar La Mayor, Sevilla.

**Piccadilly English Institute**
Los Chopos 8, 14006 Cordoba.

**Preston English Centre**
Edif El Carmen Chapineria 3, Jerez De La Frontera,
Cadiz.

**Principal English Centre**
Aptdo 85, Puerto De Santa Maria, Cadiz.

**SALT Idiomes**
Prat De La Riba, 86, 08222 Terrassa (Barcelona). **Tel:**
3 735 80 35.

**San Roque School**
Plaza San Roque 1, Guadalajara.

**Skills**
Trinidad 94, 12002 Castellon. **Tel:** 6424 2668.

**Stanton School of English**
Colon 26, 03001 Alicante. **Tel:** 65207581.

**St Patrick's Caracuel**
1 Jerez De La Frontera, Cadiz.

**TELC**
Av Andalucia 8, 6°, 11006 Cadiz. **Tel:** 56 271097.

**The Tolkien Academy**
Juan Bautista Erro 9, 20140 Andoain.

**Trafalgar Idiomas**
Avda Castilla 12, 33203 Gijon, Asturias. **Tel:** 85
332361.

**Trinity School SL**
C/ Golondrina (Plaza Jardines) 17 Bajo, 11500 Puerto
De Santa Maria, Cadiz. **Tel:** 9 56 871926.

**Wall Street Institute**
Gutenberg 3-13, 1° 8a, 08224 Terrassa (Barcelona).
**Tel:** 3 788 8566, **Fax:** 3 788 8538.

## Wall Street Institute
Centro Comercial Cuesta Blanca, Local 12, 2° Planta, la Moralega, Alcobendas, 28100 Madrid. **Tel:** 1 650 7602, **Fax:** 1 650 8246.

## Wall Street Institute
Av República Argentina 24 P12 D, 41011 Sevilla.

## Warwick House Centro Linguistico Cultural
Lopez Gomez 18-2, Valladolid 47002.

## Westfalia
Chapineria 3, Edificio El Carmen, Modulo 310, 11403 Jerez de la Frontera.

## William Halstead School of English
Camilo Jose Cela 12, 11160 Barbate de Franco.

## Windsor School of English
Virgen De Loreto 19-1, 41011 Sevilla.

## York House
English Language Centre, Muntaner 479, 08021 Barcelona. **Tel:** 32 113200.

## SWEDEN

There are opportunities for teaching EFL in Sweden but you need to be already living or studying there. Many teachers start out at adult education centres (studieförbund) such as Folkuniveristet, Studiefrämjandet, Medborgarskolan, TBV, ABF and Vuxenskolan. Unfortunately, most of these institutions are reluctant to hire teachers on a full-time basis since their student populations fluctuate from term to term There is rarely employment available during the summer months. Opportunities may exist in private language schools such as Berlitz. Many of these schools contract to teach groups or individuals at companies such as Ericsson, Volvo and Sony.

### Embassy in UK:
11 Montagu Place, London W1H 2AL
**Tel:** 020 7917 6400
www.swedish-embassy.org.uk

### Embassy in USA:
1501 M Street NW, Washington DC 20005
**Tel:** 202 467 2600
www.swedish-embassy.org

### British Council office:
PO Box 27819, S-115 93 Stockholm
**Tel** +46 (8) 671 3110
Www.britishcouncil.se

◆ **Visa/Work Permits:** If you want to teach in Sweden and are not an EU citizen you must be studying there or be married to somebody working there to qualify for a work permit.

◆ **Requirements:** College Degree and a TESOL/TESL Certificate

◆ **Cost of Living:** It is very expensive to live in Sweden but the standards of living are very high. A meal for two at an inexpensive café or restaurant can range from £10-20. A bottle of strong beer in a bar costs around £3. Transportation is expensive.

◆ **Currency:** £1 = 13.49 / $1 = 6.90  Swedish Krona.(SK)

◆ **Salaries/Taxes:** Annual income can be anywhere between £10,000-20,000. This often includes four weeks paid winter and summer vacation. Salaries really depend on the teaching situation and your qualifications and experience. Studieförbund generally pay less. State & private schools pay fairly well and offer some stability. Taxation runs at 30-35% of your salary.

◆ **Accommodation:** You can expect to pay between £150-£300 or more for a one-bedroom apartment in a large city. ESOL teachers usually live in single rental apartments or shared apartments.

◆ **Health advice:** If your contract is for less than a year you will not be covered by Sweden's socialized medical programmes even though you will be paying for them through your taxes.

### Schools in Sweden (+46)

### ABC Engelsk o. Amerikanska Sprakundervisning
Safflegatan 7, 123 44 Farsta.

### British Institute
Hagatan 3, 511348 Stockholm.. **Tel:** 8 341200, **Fax:** 8 344192.

### Folkuniversitetet
Box 26152, 100 41 Stockholm. **Tel:** 8 679 2950, **Fax:** 8 678 1544.

## SWITZERLAND

Tight immigration laws mean that Switzerland is a difficult place to find a teaching job on spec. School have to prove that no Swiss person could do the job which means that only highly qualified teachers stand a chance of getting a job here. If you do decide that Switzerland is the place for you, you could approach the various international schools in the country to see if they need teachers. You'll need at least two years' experience in teaching before they will consider you for employment. January and February are good months to look for jobs. Another possibility is to find work at a summer camp.

### Embassy in UK:
16-18 Montagu Place, London W1H 2BQ
**Tel:** 020 7616 6000

### Embassy in USA:
2900 Cathedral Ave NW, Washington DC 20008
**Tel:** 202 745 7900
www.swissemb.org

### British Council office:
Sennweg 2, PO Box 532, CH 3000 Berne 9
**Tel** +41 (31) 301 1473
www.britishcouncil.org/switzerland

➲ **Visa/Work Permits:** You need a work permit to teach in Switzerland. Permis A allows you to work seasonally, when the local workforce is considered too small to cope with the demand. Permis B can be granted for a specific one-year contract but the employer must guarantee a minimum number of hours and prove that no Swiss national could do the job.

➲ **Requirements:** College Degree and a TESOL/TESL Certificate

➲ **Cost of Living:** Most things are expensive in Switzerland.

➲ **Currency:** £1 = 2.38 / $1 = 1.22 Swiss Francs

➲ **Salaries/Taxes:** SFR 40-70 per hour in a private language school. Tax is around 15%.

➲ **Accommodation:**Schools often help in finding accommodation, but as with everything in Switzerland – it's expensive!

➲ **Health advice:** Many international schools will take care of your health insurance.

### Schools in Switzerland (+41)

### The American School in Switzerland
Summer Language Programmes, 6926 Montagnola-Lugano. **Tel:** 91 993 1647.

### Basilingua Sprachschule
Birsigstrasse 2, 4054 Basel. **Tel:** 61 281 3954.

### Bell Language School
12 Chemin des Colombettes, 1202 Geneva. **Tel:** 00 41 22 740 20.

### Berlitz
14 rue De L'Ancien-Port, 1202 Geneva. **Tel:** 22 738 3200.

### Berlitz
Munzgasse 3, 4001 Basel. **Tel:** 61 261 6360, **Fax:** 61 261 6405.

### Institute Le Rosey
Camp d'Eté, Route des Quatre Communes, CH-1180 Rolle.

### Leysin American School
CH-1854 Leysin. **Tel:** 24 493 37 7, **Fax:** 24 494 1585.

### Markus Frei Sprachenschulen
Neugasse 6, 6300 Zug. **Tel:** 710 4240, **Fax:** 710 4525.

### Village Camps
1296 Coppet. **Tel:** 22 776 2059, **Fax**: 22 776 2060.

## UNITED KINGDOM

British English native-speakers will have few problems in the UK since teachers are expected to teach British English; Americans will find it hard to get a job, however, for Canadians, Australian and New Zealand citizens, the prospects are much better. You will need an EU passport if you want to teach English in the UK

### Embassy in USA:
3100 Massachusetts Ave, Washington DC 20008
**Tel:** +1 202 588 6500
www.britainusa.com

### British Council main office:
10 Spring Gardens, London SW1A 2BN
**Tel** +44 (0) 20 7930 8466
www.britishcouncil.org

➲ **Visas/Work permits:** A work permit is extremely difficult for a non-EU citizen to obtain. You must find an employer who will apply on your behalf before you enter the country.

➲ **Requirements:** College Degree and a TESOL/TESL Certificate

➲ **Cost of Living:** The UK is an expensive country.

➲ **Currency:** US$1 = approx £0.51

➲ **Salaries/Taxes:** London salaries are not particularly good although schools in Oxford and Cambridge pay well.

➲ **Accommodation:** The cost of accommodation in London is steadily rising and public transportation is expensive and unreliable. In the centre of London expect to pay a minimum of £100 / $200 a week. In the suburbs anything from £60 / $110 - £70 / $130 is standard. Outside of London accommodation is usually a lot cheaper, especially in student towns, but a lot of schools will arrange accommodation for you often with host families.

➲ **Health advice:** While good medical services are widely available, free care under the National Health System is allowed only to EU citizens.

## Schools in the UK (+44)

*There are over 1000 ELT schools in the UK – we could fill this entire book (in fact, there are books just for the UK ELT market). The best way to find schools is to use one of the professional associations of schools – or the British Council. These offer accreditation to schools that meet various criteria, with over 500 accredited schools in the UK and some 5-600 schools concentrating just on teaching in the summer holidays (see Finding a Job), it is a vast market. Try some of these major schools and organisations of schools who can provide help and lists of contacts. See also the website directory, pages 60 and 272 for online search engines that will find schools in the UK*

### Organisations of Schools

**ARELS**
56 Buckingham Place, London SW1E 6AG. **Tel:** 020 7802-9200, **Fax:** 020 7630-9824.
www.arels.org.uk
*Note: ARELS and BASELT have merged into EnglishUK, however both offices and websites still operate as before.*

**BALEAP**
English Language Centre, University of Bath, Claverton Down, Bath BA2 7AY. **Tel:** (01225) 826 191, **Fax:** (01225) 323135.
www.baleap.org.uk

**BASELT**
Cheltenham and Gloucester College of Higher Education, Francis Close Hall, Swindon Road, Cheltenham, Glos GL50 4AZ. **Tel:** 01242 227099, **Fax:** 01242 227055.
www.baselt.org.uk
*Note: ARELS and BASELT have merged into EnglishUK, however both offices and websites still operate as before.*

**BATQI**
35 Barclay Square, Bristol BS8 1JA. **Fax:** 0117 925 1537.

### British Council
10 Spring Gardens, London SW1A 2BN, **Tel:** +44 (0)20 7389 4931, **Fax:** +44 (0)20 7389 4140
www.britishcouncil.org

### Central Bureau for Educational Visits and Exchanges (CBEVE)
The British Council, 10 Spring Gardens, London SW1A 2BN. **Tel:** 020 7389 4004, **Fax:** 020 7389 4426.

### Department for Education and Employment (DfEE)
Mowden Hall, Darlington DL3 9BG. **Tel:** 01325 460155, **Fax:** 01325 392695

### IATEFL
3 Kingsdown Chambers, Whitstable, Kent CT5 2FL **Tel:** 01227 276528, **Fax:** 01227 274415
www.iatefl.org

### School Groups

**Bell Language Schools**
The Personnel Department, Hillscross, Red Cross Lane, Cambridge CB2 2QX. **Tel:** 01223 246644, **Fax:** 01223 414080.

**Berlitz**
9-13 Grosvenor Street, London W1A 3BZ. **Tel:** 020 7915-0909, **Fax:** 020 7915-0222.

**EF**
36-38 St Aubyns, Hove, East Sussex BN3 2TD, **Tel:** 01273 201431, **Fax:** 01273 746742
www.englishfirst.com

**Inlingua**
Rodney Lodge, Rodney Road, Cheltenham, Gloucs. GL50 1JF. **Tel:** 01242 253171, **Fax:** 01242 253181.

**International House**
106 Piccadilly, London W1V 9FL. **Tel:** 020 7491-2598, **Fax:** 020 7409-0959
www.ihlondon.com

**Linguarama**
Oceanic House, 89 High Street, Alton, Hants GU34 1LG. **Tel:** 01420 80899, **Fax:** 01420 80856.

**St Giles**
154 Southampton Row, London WC1B 5JX, **Tel:** 020 7837 0404, **Fax:** 020 7837 4099
www.stgiles.co.uk

**Saxoncourt (UK) Ltd.**
59 South Molton Street, London W1Y 1HH. **Tel:** 020 7491 1911, www.sgvenglish.com

# Eastern and Central Europe

European countries outside of the European Union (EU) are very good places to look for work, and in these countries British and North American teachers are often on a level playing field (unlike Western Europe, where it's easier for British teachers to find work). American culture is a major influence in the former Soviet Bloc, learning English is big business in the region.

Some countries even offer similar salaries to those being offered in Western Europe now–amazing, considering that the cost of living is so much lower. However, times have changed since the post-communist honeymoon, when any young American, Canadian, Australian or Brit would be offered a teaching job on the street and then would spend their time partying rather than teaching. Now schools are looking for more dedicated and qualified teachers.

Some of these countries (in particular, Bulgaria and Romania) are about to join the European Union, which will eventually make it more difficult for non-EU citizens to work. However, for the time being, governments are focusing on bringing stability to their economies. This coupled with recent growth in tourism means that these are increasingly popular teaching destinations in spite of the occasionally difficult living and teaching conditions.

Competition means that qualifications may be necessary, especially in the major cities. A number of Central and East European countries are served by voluntary and cultural organizations, including the Peace Corps and the Soros Foundation. These organizations usually offer teachers salaries at local rates along with supplements, accommodation and other benefits.

There is considerable voluntary, as well as some commercial, English language teaching activity in the Ukraine, Uzbekistan and Kazakhstan, but standards of living can be modest and conditions harsh. Opportunities can be found also in the Baltic states, especially Lithuania and Estonia, which have been progressive in implementing policies promoting free enterprise.

## AZERBAIJAN

A former Soviet republic, Azerbaijan became independent in 1991. The capital, Baku, is relatively safe, although attacks on foreigners can occur, but the southern parts of the country along the border with Iran, and the western region (Nagorno-Karabakh) are not safe for travellers. The climate is generally quite warm, except in the mountains

**Embassy in UK:**
4 Kensington Court, London W8 5DL
**Tel:** 020 7938 5482
www.president.az

**Embassy in USA:**
927, 15th St NW, Suite 700, Washington DC 20035
**Tel:** (202) 842 0001
www.azembassy.com

**British Council office:**
1 Vali Mammadov Street, Ichari Shahar, Baku 370004
**Tel** +994 (12) 971 593
www.britishcouncil.org/azerbaijan

⊃ **Visas/Work Permits:** You need to obtain a visa from an embassy before you enter the country, if you are intending to work, and a letter of introductrion from your employer is required.

⊃ **Requirements:** College Degree and a TESOL/TESL Certificate

⊃ **Currency:** £1 = 8041 / $1 = 4884 manats

⊃ **Cost of Living:** Quite cheap by Western standards, but everything has to be paid in local currency. Credit cards are not generally accepted

⊃ **Health advice:** there are good medical facilities in Baku, but none elsewhere. It is better to get medical insurance before you travel. Immunization against typhoid is recommmended. All water should be boiled

⊃ **English language media:** Baku Sun, Baku Today, Caspian Business News

### Schools in Azerbaijan (+994)

**The British Council Training Centre**
1 Vali Mammadov St, Baku
**Tel:** 994 12 972 013
**Fax:** 994 12 989 236
**Email:** enquiries@britishcouncil.az

**International House Baku**
Khagani 20/20, Baku 370001
**Tel:** 994 12 97 15 85
**Email:** intellect@azerin.com

**Webb Academy**
148 Vidadi St, Baku 37000
**Tel & Fax:** 994 12 973 047

## BELARUS

Belarus is a destination only for the brave and adventurous. Economic and political reform in Belarus has stalled under the current government. Tourist facilities are not highly developed, and many of the goods and services taken for granted in other countries are not yet available. However, there is considerable demand for English, so it's quite easy to find a job. You need to contact a school or a University directly, that's the easiest and the quickest way. If you want to work in the private sector, there are a couple of schools in Minsk.

⊃ **Visas/Work Permits:** A visa must be obtained before entering Belarus.

⊃ **Requirements:** College Degree and a TESOL/TESL Certificate

⊃ **Currency:** £1 = 4014 / $1 = 2170 rubles.

⊃ **Salaries/Taxes:** A school teacher's average salary is about $200 per year after tax. University teachers are paid slightly more.

⊃ **Accommodation:** If you work for a University, they will offer you free accommodation at a student hostel. It is easy to rent an apartment, but it will cost about £30 per month.

⊃ **Cost of Living:** The cost of living is quite low. Local food is very cheap, but imported goods are expensive.

⊃ **Health advice:** Belarus requires all foreign nationals entering the country to purchase medical insurance at the port-of-entry regardless of any other insurance one might have. Costs for this insurance will vary according to the length of stay. You will then be entitled to receive health care, but medical care in Belarus is limited. There is a severe shortage of basic medical supplies, including anesthetics, vaccines and antibiotics. Insurance with evacuation cover is recommended.

⊃ **English Language Newspapers:** Minsk News

### Schools in Belarus (+375)

**The British Council**
ul. Zakharova, 21, Minsk 220662. **Tel:** 17 236 79 53, **Fax**: 17 236 40 47, **Email:** Natasha.Naida@britishcouncil. org.by

### International House Minsk
Room 306, Gykalo 9, Minsk 220071. **Tel:** 17 238 47 12, **Fax:** 17 231 60 07, **Email:** ih@user.unibel.by

---

# BULGARIA

Bulgaria has been slower than most of its neighbours to embrace the West and the elected government is Communist, so most teaching opportunities are in the public sector. Bulgarians take education very seriously and, in spite of economic and political troubles, there is a surprisingly developed English language teaching structure. Secondary schools recruit foreign language teachers on yearly, renewable contracts. Apply to: Bulgarian Ministry of Education & Science, 2A Knjaz Dondoukov, 1000 Sofia, Tel: 2 988 0494. In the private sector, teaching loads are notoriously great with some having to travel between two or three schools to deliver 30 contact hours per week, often in the evenings and on Saturday mornings. In the state sector, a week's teaching is likely to consist of about twenty 40-minute lessons. Because many students make great sacrifices to pay for their courses, a Bulgarian teaching experience can be very inspiring and rewarding. On the negative side expect food shortages, power failures, transport strikes and food rationing, especially in winter.

### Embassy in UK:
186-188 Queen's Gate, London SW7 5HL
**Tel:** 020 7584 9400
www.bulgarianembassy.org.uk

### Embassy in USA:
1621 22nd St. NW, Washington DC 20008
**Tel:** 202 387 0174
www.bulgaria-embassy.org

### British Council office:
7 Krakra Street, 1504 Sofia
Tel  +359 (2) 942 4344
www.britishcouncil.org/bulgaria

◐  **Visas/Work Permits:** All non-Bulgarian citizens need an entry visa, which can be obtained from the Bulgarian Consular Service in any country. Your school should help you to organize your work permit once you are in the country.

◐  **Requirements:** College Degree, experience and a TESOL/TESL Certificate

◐  **Currency:** £1 = 2.91 / $1 = 1.49 Bulgarian Leva.

◐  **Salaries/Taxes:**

Most contracted teachers are paid at local rates the equivalent of £100-200 per month. Paid airfares, furnished accommodation and holiday are generally included and there might also be a supplement paid in pounds or dollars. A highly paid Bulgarian teacher might be paid the equivalent of £90 per month. Tax deductions amount to 30-40%.

◐  **Cost of Living:** Very cheap in the provinces, reaching western levels in Sofia, but conditions are still extremely tough.

◐  **Accommodation:** Very basic accommodation is usually provided by employers.

◐  **Health advice:** Insurance is provided by state employers but it should be supplemented with a private policy.

◐  **English language media:** The Sofia Echo.

---

## Schools in Bulgaria (+359)

### Alliance for Teaching of Foreign Languages
3 Slaveikov Square, 1000 Sofia. **Tel:** 2 880238, **Fax:** 2 882 349.

### American College
Tsar Osvobodital Blvd, Sofia.

### Avo-3 School of English
House of Culture Sredets, 2a Krakra Street, Sofia.

### ANDRA
1 Ch Smirnenski Blvd, Sofia 1421.

### BELS & BELIN Centre
PO Box 37, 1421 Sofia.

### British Council
7 Tulovo Street, 1504 Sofia. **Tel:** 2 946 0098.

### Bulgarian Dutch College for Commerce
Trudovets Botebgrad, Sofia.

### Business Private High School
Kosta Lulchev Street, Sofia.

### Centre for Language Qualification
National Palace of Culture, Administrative Bldg, 2nd Floor, Room 131, Sofia.

### ELIT
14 GM Dimitrov Boulevard, Sofia.

### ELS
PO Box 16, Sofia 1404.

### ESPA
Darwin Street, Sofia.

### First Private English Language Medium School
Stara Planina Street, Sofia.

### ICO Intellect
Kostur Street, 1618 Sofia.

### Institute of Tourism
Park Ezero, 8000 Bourgas.

### Language High School
64 Tsar Shishman St., 6000 Stara Zagora. **Tel:** 42 52975, **Fax:** 42 40188.

### Language Schools of Europe
82 Tsar Simeon St., entr 3, fl 3, Sofia 1000.

### MEL
First Primary School, 24 Vessela Street, Plovdiv 4000.

### Meridian
22 Alabin Street, Sofia 1000.

### Meridian
Macedonia Boulevard, Sofia 1606.

### New School of English
13 Serdika Street, Sofia.

### Pharos Ltd
2 S.Vrachanski Street, Vasrazhdane Square, Sofia.

### Private High School for Law & Management
D Dimov Street, Sofia.

### Private High School for Management & Business Admin
Raiko Alexiev Street, Complex Iztok, Sofia.

### Private School for Banking and Business
83 Bogomil Street, Plovdiv

### Yanev School
bl 147 ap 38, Complex Liulin, Sofia.

## CROATIA

Croatia is being rapidly integrated into mainstream Europe and English is very much in demand in this former Yugoslav republic. With private schools operating in Zagreb, Karlovac and Varazdin, there are plenty of opportunities for teachers, especially native speakers, who are in short supply. Because there is an established English language industry, schools are reluctant to employ unqualified teachers. Jobs are often advertised abroad, but it's also possible to job-hunt on arrival. Full-time contracts are the norm and there are opportunities for private lessons.

### British Council office:
Illica 12, PP 55, 10001 Zagreb
**Tel** +385 (1) 489 9500
www.britishcouncil.hr

⊃ **Visas/Work Permits:** Anyone who intends to teach will need a work visa. This can be secured in advance when you present your contract to your local embassy, then a labour permit can be sent from an employer in Croatia.

⊃ **Requirements:** College Degree, experience and a TESOL/TESL Certificate

⊃ **Currency:** £1 = 10.97 / $1 = 5.61 Kuna.

⊃ **Salaries and taxes:** Salaries are usually paid in German marks with tax deducted by the employer. The average rate is between £500-1100 per month, while experienced teachers can earn more.

⊃ **Accommodation:** Accommodation is quite reasonable. An apartment with two or three rooms will cost around £300 per month.

⊃ **Cost of Living:** Food and basic living costs are cheap, but price are higher in tourist resorts.

⊃ **Health advice:** Insurance is advisable, as state facilities are under considerable strain. There are plenty of private doctors and dentists.

## Schools in Croatia (+385)

### Centar za strane jezike
Vodnikova 12, 4100 Zagreb *and* Trg republike 2, 58000 Split.

### Class
Jankomirska 1, 41000 Zagreb.

### The English Workshop
Medulinska 61, 52000 Pula.

### Interlang
Krisaniceva 7, 51000 Rijeka

### Lancon
Kumiciceva 10, 10000 Zagreb. **Tel:** 1 485 4985, **Fax:** 1 485 4984. **Email: lmo@lancon.hr**

### Linguar Centar
Miroslava Krleze 4c, 47000 Karlovac. **Tel/Fax:** 47 621900.

### Linguae
Radiceva 4, 51000 Rijeka.

### Linguapax Language School
B.Jelacica 1 32100 Vinkovci. **Tel:** 32 334 827, **Fax:** 32 334 827.

### LS Lukavec
Skolska 27, 41409 Donja Lomnica.

### Narodno sveuciliste
Skola za strane jezike, Trg Matice Hrvatske 3, 41430 Samobor.

**Octopus**
Savska 13, 41000 Zagreb.

**Radnicko sveuciliste**
Bozidar Maslaric, 5400 Osijek.

**Skola Stranih Jezika**
Cesarceva 10, 42000 Varazdin. **Tel**: 42 215055, **Fax**: 42 215036.

**Svjetski jezici**
Varsavska 13, 41000 Zagreb.

**Verba**
M. Gorkog 5, 51000 Rijeka.

**Vern Lingua**
Senoina 28, 10000 Zagreb. **Tel/Fax**: 1 428 548.

## CYPRUS

The Mediterranean island of Cyprus is divided into two sectors: Greek and Turkish. In the Greek sector of Cyprus, English is the second language. Here, it is very hard for foreigners to find teaching positions because local teachers fill most of the demand and the authorities are very strict about allowing non-Cypriots to work. In the Turkish sector, there are a number of private universities that hire native English speakers to teach in language departments.

**British Council office:**
3 Museum Street, CY- 1097 Nicosia
**Tel** +357 (22) 585 000
www.britishcouncil.org.cy

### Schools in Cyprus - Greek Sector (+357)

**American Academy**
PO Box 112, Larnaca. **Tel**: 4 652046, **Fax**: 4 651046.

**American Academy**
Despinas Pattichi Street, PO Box 1867, Limassol. **Tel**: 5 337054, **Fax**: 5 387488.

**American Academy**
3A Michalaki Paridi Street, Nicosia. **Tel**: 2 462886, **Fax**: 2-466290.

**Centre of Higher Studies**
PO Box 545, 2 Evagorou Street, floor 6, Nicosia. **Tel**: 2 445970, **Fax**: 2 369171.

**The English School**
PO Box 3575, Nicosia. **Tel**: 2 422274.

**Forum Language centre**
PO Box 5567, Nicosia 1310. **Tel**: 2497766, **Email**: forum1@cytanet.com.cy

**The Grammar School**
Katinas Paxious Street, PO Box 1340, Limassol. **Tel**: 5 727933, **Fax**: 5 727818.

**The Grammar School**
PO Box 2262, Nicosia. **Tel**: 2 621744, **Fax**: 2623044

**International Language Institute (ILI)**
12 Richard & Verengaria Street, Limmassol. **Tel**: 371017, **Fax**: 371018.

**Pascal English School**
3 Costaki Panteli Street, PO Box 4746, Nicosia. **Tel**: 2 450900, **Fax**: 2 367214.

**Terra Santa College**
12 Lycourgos Street, PO Box 1546, Nicosia. **Tel**: 2 421100, **Fax**: 2 466767.

### Turkish Sector (+90)

**Cyprus International University**
Ortakoy, Lefkosa, KKTC. **Tel**: 392 223 49 00. **Fax**: 392 223 49 01.

**Eastern Mediterranean University**
Famagusta, North Cyprus. **Tel**: 392 366 6588. **Fax**: 392 366 1317. **Email**: webmaster@salamis.emu.edu.tr

**Girne American University**
Yeni Liman Yolu, Girne, North Cyprus. **Tel**: 392 815 53 12. **Fax**: 392 815 11 33.

**International American University**
P.O.Box. 292, Kyrenia, North Cyprus. **Tel**: 392 815 6791 **Fax**: 392 815 6790.

**Near East University**
P.O. Box: 670, Nicosia, North Cyprus. **Tel**: 392 223 64 64. **Fax**: 392 223 64 61.

## CZECH REPUBLIC

This country in the heart of Europe has long been a magnet for English language teachers (particularly from the USA and Canada). It is estimated that there are as many as 60,000 Americans in Prague alone, many drawn here by its reputation as a "party" town. But the Czech authorities have tightened up regulations recently and it is difficult to find a teaching job unless you have some kind of qualification. Although most teaching jobs are in the private sector, the Ministry of Education recruits qualified teachers (who should have at least a certificate qualification and a BA in English) for elementary, middle and high schools. The main advantage of a governmental teaching contract is that it is worth the paper it's printed on and you will probably be eligible for health insurance coverage. In the private sector, alas! This is not the case. There are disreputable schools out there that will employ teachers illegally and then take advantage of them. If you are unhappy with your school, just pick up your last salary cheque and move on – there are plenty of good schools.

## Embassy in UK:

26-30 Kensington Palace Gardens, London W8 4QY
**Tel:** 020 7243 1115
www.czechembassy.org.uk

## Embassy in USA:

3900 Spring of Freedom St NW, Washington DC 20008
**Tel:** 202 274 9100
www.czechembassy.org

## British Council office:

Bredovsky dvur, Politickych Veznu 13, 110 00 Prague 1
**Tel** +420 (0)2 2199 1111
www.britishcouncil.cz

⮑ **Visas/Work Permits:** In January 2000, a major revision of the Czech law regarding residency permits for foreign nationals came into force. In the old days, teachers could arrive on tourist visas (good for up to 90 days) and then apply for a residency permit. Now, American citizens must apply for a residency permit before they travel. You can still apply for a work permit while you are in the country but your employer must prove you are not taking a job that a Czech national could do.

⮑ **Requirements:** College Degree, experience and a TESOL/TESL Certificate

⮑ **Currency:** £1 = 41.29 / $1 = 21.12 Koruny.

⮑ **Salaries/Taxes:** Teachers working in state schools earn about £180-250 per month after tax and accommodation is usually provided. You can earn more at a private language school (£300-400) as long as you are given the hours. Private tuition can be very lucrative; some business people are prepared to pay upwards of £20 an hour to learn English with a qualified and experienced tutor. The tax rate is around 30% for those working legally.

⮑ **Accommodation:** It's difficult to find a room in Prague. Ask the school to provide you with accommodation. If that doesn't work, try and find people who will share with you. Check out the notices at The Globe bookstore (where you might run into another teacher in the same predicament!) or at Radnost, a popular coffee shop. If you're very lucky you might pick up a cheap apartment for around £90 a month but you'll probably have to pay at least £150 so it's a good idea to share.

⮑ **Cost of Living:**If you eat fruit and vegetables that are locally produced and develop a taste for heavy Czech fare, then life will not be too expensive. Czech beer is very strong and very cheap!

⮑ **Health advice:**In Prague medical facilities are good but try not to be sick in a remote region. Better still, get a job with a school that provides medical coverage for its teachers.

⮑ **English language media:** The Prague Post.

## Schools in the Czech Republic (+420)

### Academic Information Agency (Public Sector Recruitment)
Dum zahranicnich sluzeb MSMT, Senovazne nam. 26, 111 21 Prague 1. **Tel:** 2 2422 9698, **Fax:** 2 2422 9697, **Email: aia@dzs.cz**

### Agency Unitour
Libor Kivana, Senovazne 21, 110 00 Prague 1. **Tel:** 2 35 9917, **Fax:** 786 2153.

### Agentura Educo
Veletrzni 24, 170 00 Prague 7. **Tel:** 2 333 70 163, **Fax:** 2 203 97 310.

### Anglictina Expres
Korunni 2, 12000 Prague 2. **Tel:** 2 2423 8186, **Email: anexpres@vol.cz**

### Bell School
Nedvezska 29, 100 00 Prague 10. **Tel:** 2 781 5342, **Fax:** 2 782 2961.

### British Council
Narodni 10, 12501 Prague 1. **Tel:** 2 203 751.

### Caledonian School
Vitavska 24, 150 00 Prague 5. **Tel:** 2 573 13650, **Email:** jobs@caledonianschool.com

### California Sun School
Na Bojisti 2, Prague 2. **Tel:** 2 294 817, **Fax:** 2 822 271.

### Cheb Free School
Kubelikova C.4, Cheb 350 02.

### Encounter English
Azalkova 12, 100 00 Prague 10-Hostivar. **Tel:** 2 758 773.

### Eminenc Language School
Vodikova 26, 110 00 Prague 1. **Tel:** 2 96226141-3, **Fax:** 2 96226144.

### English House
Vysedhradska 2, 128 00 Prague 2. **Tel/Fax:** 2 29 31 41.

### Et Cetera Language School
Dusni 17, 110 00 Prague 1. **Tel:** 2 231 3062, **Fax:** 2 894 484.

### Euro contact - Hulesovice
Jankovskeho 52, 7 Hulesovice. **Tel:** 801 527.

### European Management Institute (TEMI)
Na Truhlarce 3, 180 00 Prague 8. **Tel/Fax:** 2 68 88 052.

### Foundation for a Civil Society
Jeleni 200/3, 118 00 Prague 1. **Tel:** 2 24 51 08 73, **Fax:** 2 24 51 08 75.

### GEJA
Seifertova 37, Prague 3. **Tel:** 2 225 3750.

### Hampson CS Ltd
Zelezna 107, Mlada Boleslav 293 01. **Tel:** 326 732732, **Fax:** 326 732732.

### International House (ILC) Brno
Sokolska 1, 602 00 Brno. **Tel:** 5 41 24 0493, **Fax:** 5 41 24 59 54, **Email:** ihbrno@sky.cz

### International House Prague - Akcent
Bitovska 3, 140 00 Prague 4. **Tel:** 2 420 595, **Fax:** 2 422 845, **Email:** info.accent@akcent.cz.

### International Training Solutions Ltd
Thamova 24, 186 00 Prague 8. **Tel/Fax:** 2 238 0545.

### Intertext Servis Karel Narvatil
Anglicka 24, 360 09 Karlovy Vary. **Tel/Fax:** 17 323 0436.

### Languages at Work
Na Florenci 35, 110 000 Prague 1. **Tel/fax:** 2 248 11379, **Email:** employment@mbox.vol.cz

### London School of Modern Languages
Francouzska Ulice 30, 120 00 Prague 2. **Tel:** 2 242 53 437, **Fax:** 2 242 54 259.

### Prague 8 Language School
Buresova 1130, 18 000 Prague 8. **Tel:** 2 858 8028.

### Pro English 90
Mala Strana, 5 Helichova (4th floor), Prague 1. **Tel:** 534 551.

### St. James Language centre
Namesti Miru 15, 12000 Prague 2. **Tel.:** 2 2251 7869, **Fax:** 2 2251 7870.

### Spusa Education centre
Navratilova 2, 110 00 Prague 1. **Tel:** 2 22 23 17 02, **Fax:** 2 22 23 25 30.

### Statni Jazykova Skola
Skolsa 15, 116 72 Prague 1. **Tel:** 2 222 32 237, **Fax:** 2 222 32 236, **Email:** sjs@sjs.cz

## ESTONIA

Estonia is a rapidly developing Baltic state that has experienced significant success in reforming its political and economic institutions since regaining independence in 1991. With about 30 universities and private schools in Estonia, there are many opportunities for teachers. Students tend to be highly motivated although they can be a little shy at first.

### Embassy in UK:
16 Hyde Park Gate, London SW7 5DG
**Tel:** 020 7589 3428
www.estonia.gov.uk

### Embassy in USA:
Suite 503, 1730 M Street NW, Washington DC20036
**Tel:** 202 588 0101
www.estemb.org

### British Council office:
Vana Posti 7, Tallinn 10146
**Tel** +372 (6) 257 788
www.britishcouncil.ee

⮑ **Visas/Work Permits:** No visas are required for stays up to 90 days. It's not too difficult to obtain a work permit once you have found a job, although the paperwork can be confusing.

⮑ **Requirements:** College Degree, experience and a TESOL/TESL Certificate

⮑ **Currency:** £1 = 23.34 / $1 = 11.94 Kroon

⮑ **Salaries/Taxes:** After tax (around 26%) you should be able to take home £300-500 a month.

⮑ **Accommodation:** The average rent for a two-bedroom apartment in Tallinn's suburbs is around £200. Hopefully, your school will include accommodation in the package they offer you.

⮑ **Cost of Living:** Estonia is much cheaper than the UK and U.S.A. so even if you are only earning a few hundred dollars a month it should go a long way.

⮑ **Health advice:** The quality of medical care in Estonia is good but can fall short of UK and USA standards. Estonia has many highly trained medical professionals, but hospitals and clinics still suffer from a lack of equipment and resources. Your school may give you a medical card entitling you to free treatment but health insurance is a good idea.

## Schools in Estonia (+372)

**ALF Training centre**
Ravala pst. 4, Tallinn EE0001

**Concordia International University**
Kaluri tee 3, Viimsivald, Harjumaa EE3006. **Tel:** 6090077, **Fax**: 6090216

**International House Tallinn**
Pikk 69, Tallinn 10133. **Tel:** 64 10 607, **Fax**: 64 10 607, **Email:** ihte@online.ee

**International Language Services**
Pikk 9, Tallinn EE 0001. **Tel:** 646 4258, **Fax**: 641 2476, **Email:** ilsinfo@online.ee

**Tallinn Pedagogical University**
Language centre, Narva mnt. 29, Tallinn EE0101

# GEORGIA

This Caucasian republic (birthplace of Josef Stalin) has a long and fascinating history. There is a shortage of native English-speaking teachers in Georgia so intrepid travellers should not have a problem finding work here, either in a private school or even with one of the big energy companies that have offices in Tbilisi.

**British Council office:**
34 Rustaveli Avenue, Tblisi 380008
**Tel** +995 (32) 250 407 988014
www.britishcouncil.org.ge

➲ **Visas/Work Permits** Tourist visas are available on entry at Tbilisi Airport. The Georgian authorities are generous with work visas.

➲ **Requirements:** College Degree and a TESOL/TESL Certificate

➲ **Currency:** £1 = 3.36 / $1 = 1.82 Lari

➲ **Salaries/Taxes:** You can expect to earn around £200 a month in a private language school. If you land a teaching job with an oil company you can make a lot more money.

➲ **Accommodation:** A bedroom in a shared apartment costs around £90-100 per month.

➲ **Cost of Living:** Locally grown products are cheap and delicious. Georgian cuisine enjoys a high reputation.

➲ **Health advice:** Medical care in Georgia is limited. There is a severe shortage of basic medical supplies, including disposable needles, anesthetics, and antibiotics. Uninsured travellers who require medical care overseas may face extreme difficulties. The U.S. Embassy advises American citizens to avoid travel to the separatist-controlled region of Abkhazia.

## Schools in Georgia (+995)

**Byron School of Tbilisi**
2 Griboedov Street, Tbilisi 380008. **Tel:** 32 93 1578.

**The English Language Centre**
10 Shevchenko Street, Tbilisi 380018. **Tel/Fax:** 32 933999

**International House Tbilisi**
centre for Language Studies, 2, 26 May Square, Tbilisi 380015. **Tel:** 32 940 515, **Fax**: 32 001 127, **Email:** schoolih@access.sanet.ge

**International Language Academy**
17 Chavchavadze Ave., Tbilisi 380079. **Tel:** 32 22 0504, **Email:** ila@caucasus.net

**Professional Training Group**
82 Paliashvili Street, Second floor, III entrance, Tbilisi **Tel:** 32 294482/ 253547.

**Public Service Language** centre
8 Rustaveli Street, Tbilisi.

**Tbilisi Central School of English**
8 Jambuli Street, Tbilisi 380008. **Tel:** 32 92 3454.

# HUNGARY

The demand for native-speaking English language teachers has slowed in recent years. Reports suggest that competition for teaching jobs in Budapest has become pretty fierce. There are numerous tales of unscrupulous school owners operating in the Hungarian capital. Better opportunities for TEFL teachers lie in the provincial centres such as Gyor, Szeged and Pecs. September is a good time to come and look for a job.

**Embassy in UK:**
35 Eaton Place, London SW1X 8BY
**Tel:** 020 7235 5218
www.huemblon.org.uk

**Embassy in USA:**
3910 Shoemaker St NW, Washington DC 20008
**Tel:** 202 362 6730
www.huembwas.org

**British Council office:**
Benczúr u. 26, 1068 Budapest
**Tel** +36 (1) 478 4700
www.britishcouncil.hu

➲ **Visas/Work Permits:** You do not need a visa for a period of up to 90 days. Hungary is very strict about work permits and everybody needs to apply for one if they are going to teach in the country. Permits must be arranged before leaving your country of residence and the applicant has to produce a labour permit sent from the employer in Hungary, stating that no Hungarian is available to do the job.

⮕ **Requirements:** College Degree, experience and a TESOL/TESL Certificate

⮕ **Currency:** £1 = 377 / $1 = 193 Forint

⮕ **Salaries/Taxes:** Expect to earn between £3-5 an hour at a private language school which is pretty good by local standards. Taxation is very high – up to 50 % of your income. Many school owners prefer to pay foreign teachers under the table to avoid red tape. In the public sector, teachers make around the same as in the private schools (c. £180-200 per month) but accommodation is usually included.

⮕ **Accommodation:** You can find an apartment for around £90-100 a month in Budapest

⮕ **Cost of Living:** A decent dinner costs around £2. Annual inflation runs around 10% and salaries do not always rise to match this. Many teachers find it hard to get by on their salaries.

⮕ **Health advice:** Local health insurance is available but it doesn't cover repatriation, however, healthcare facilities are good, particularly compared to other countries of central Europe.

⮕ **English language media:** Budapest Sun, Budapest Week, Budapest Business Week Journal.

## Schools in Hungary (+36)

### American International School of Budapest
Kakukk u.1-3, 1121 Budapest. **Tel:** 396 2176.

### Atalanta Business and Language School
Visegradi u.9, 1132 Budapest. **Tel:** 1 131 4954, **Fax:** 1 339 8549, **Email:** atalanta.marketing@atalanta.datanet.hu

### Avalon '92 Agency
Erzsebet Krt 15, 1/19, 1073 Budapest. **Tel/Fax:** 342 6355.

### Babilon Nyelvstudio
Karoly krt. 3/a IV.em, 1075 Budapest. **Tel:** 1 269 5531, **Fax:** 1 322 6023, **Email:** bab@mail.datanet.hu

### Bell Iskolak
Tulipan u. 8, 1022 Budapest. **Tel:** 1 326 8457, **Fax:** 1 326 5033, **Email:** bellisk@mail.matav.hu

### Belvarosi Tanoda Foundation
Molnar u.9, 1056 Budapest. **Tel:** 118 6769.

### Britannica International School
Villanya ut 11-13, 1114 Budapest. **Tel:** 166 6306.

### Buda Drawing School
Marvany u. 23, 1126 Budapest. **Tel/Fax:** 155 0341.

### Budenz Jozsef High School Foundation
Budenz ut 20-22, 1021 Budapest. **Tel:** 176 3177.

### Budapest Pedagogical Institute
Horveth Mihaly Ter 8, Budapest 8.

### Business Polytechnic
Vendel u. 3/b, 1096 Budapest. **Tel:** 1 215 4900, **Fax:** 1 215 4906, **Email: titkar@mail.poli.hu**

### English Teachers' Association of the National Pedagogical Institute
Bolyai u.14, 1023 Budapest.

### Europai Nyelvek Studioja
Muzeum Krt. 39, 1053 Budapest. **Tel:** 1 317 1302 **Fax:** 1 266 3889, **Email: els@mail.datanet.edu**

### Helle Studio
Deri Miksa u. 18, 1084 Budapest. **Tel:** 1 114 0128.

### IHH A Nyelviskola
Teleki u. 18, 9022 Gyor. **Tel:** 96 315444/30 363195 **Fax:** 96 315665.

### Interclub
Hungarian Language School, Szent Janos u. 16, 1039 Budapest. **Tel** 250 4640.

### International Business School Budapest
Etele u. 68, 1115 Budapest. **Tel:** 203 0351.

### International House Budapest
Bimbó út 7, 1022 Budapest. **Tel:** 1 212 4010, **Fax:** 1 316 2491, **Email: bp@ih.hu**

### International House Eger
Mecset utca. 3, 3300 Eger. **Tel:** 36 413 770; 36 411 313, **Fax:** 36 413 770, **Email: eger@ih.hu**

### IS Prospero Language School
Sas u. 25, 1051 Budapest. **Tel:** 1 331 6779, **Fax:** 1 331 2150, **Email: isprospero@mail.matav.hu**

### Karinthy Frigyes Gimnazium
Thokoly utca 7, Pestlorinc, 1183 Budapest. **Tel:** 1 290 4316, **Fax:** 1 291 2367, **Email: ba@karinthy.hu**

### Kulvarosi Tankor
Dregelyvar u. 6, 1158 Budapest. **Tel:** 272 2604.

### Living Language Seminar
Fejer Gyorgy u 8-10, 1053 Budapest. **Tel:** 1 326 3251, **Fax:** 1 317 9655.

### London Studio
Villanyi ut. 27, 1114 Budapest. **Tel:** 1 385 0177.

### Mentor Nyelviskola
Ferenc krt. 37, 1094 Budapest. **Tel:** 216 0765.

### Novoschool Nyelviskola
Ulloi ut 63, 1091 Budapest. **Tel:** 1 215 5480, **Fax:** 1 215 5488, **Email:** novoschool@mail.matav.hu

### Oxford Nyelviskola
Ikva u. 52, Gyor. **Tel:** 96 429 882.

### Vaci Street Development centre
Terez Krt. 47, 1067 Budapest. **Tel:** 1 302 2214, **Fax:** 1 353 3274, **Email:** bruce@mail.inext.hu

### Western Maryland College Budapest
Villanyi ut 11-13, 1114 Budapest. **Tel:** 1 66 7366.

## LATVIA

Many teachers report that Latvia is a great place to live and work in although you must like cold weather to survive here! Students are keen to learn English and really appreciate being taught by a native speaker. You won't make a lot of money in Latvia but you will feel you are making a worthwhile contribution to society.

### Embassy in UK:
45 Nottingham Place, London W1M 3FE
**Tel:** 020 7312 0040

### Embassy in USA:
4325 17th Street NW, Washington DC 20011
**Tel:** 202 726 8213
www.latvia-usa.org

### British Council office:
5a Blaumana iela, Riga LV-1011
**Tel** +371 728 1730
www.britishcouncil.org/latvia

➲ **Visas/Work Permits:** No visa is required for travellers remaining up to 90 days in a half-calendar year (from January to June and from July to December). If you stay in Latvia for more than 90 days, including 180-day periods that cross over two half-calendar years, you must apply for temporary residence. Teachers who plan to remain in Latvia for more than 90 days must apply for an "educational work" visa or in-country for temporary residence.

➲ **Requirements:** College Degree and a TESOL/TESL Certificate

➲ **Currency:** £1 = 0.96 / $1 = 0.52 Lat.

➲ **Cost of Living:** Basic foods & clothing are very cheap, but specialist goods can be expensive.

➲ **Salaries/Taxes:** Pay is low – around £2-3 an hour in the private language schools.

➲ **Accommodation:** Expect very basic living conditions. Many buildings were constructed during the Soviet era and are of poor quality.

➲ **Health advice:** Foreign aid agencies and private employers sometimes provide medical insurance. Medical care in Latvia is steadily improving but remains limited.

➲ **English language media:** The Baltic Times

## Schools in Latvia (+371)

### Alna IT
K.Valdemara 149 - 600, Riga LV-1013. **Tel:** 7377142, **Email:** info@alnait.lv

### English Language Centre Satva
Office 8, Dzirnavu Str. 79/85, Riga LV-1011. **Tel:** 7226641

### Lingva Tev
Brivibas 87, Riga LV-1001. **Tel:** 7377734, **Email:** lintev@binet.lv

### Mirte
Culture and Education centre, Raina bulvaris 23, k.2 Riga LV-1050. **Tel:** 7223837, **Email:** info@mirte.lv

### Socialo tehnologiju augstskola
Balta 10 , Riga LV-1055. **Tel:** 2461001 **Email:** sti@mail.junik.lv

### Spade un Mikelsons
Barristers' Bureau, Aspazijas bulvaris 24 - 305, Riga LV-1050. **Tel:** 7228519, **Email:** spade@mail.bkc.lv

### Staltbriedis
Dzelzavas 74 - 507, Riga LV-1082. **Tel:** 2572676, **Email:** staltbriedis@mail.lv

### Strombus
Kalku 24 - 4.st., Riga LV-1050. **Tel:** 7224376, **Email:** strombus@com.latnet.lv

### T.U.I.
K.Barona 28, Riga LV-1011. **Tel:** 7242429, **Email:** tui@parks.lv

### Valodu macibu centres
Smilsu 1/3 - 3.st., Riga LV-1050. **Tel:** 7212251, **Email:** vmc@latnet.lv

## LITHUANIA

Lithuania is a country undergoing political and economic change. Tourist facilities are improving. Many goods and services are now available in the major cities, but may not be fully comparable to Western standards.

Most teachers who come here have very good experiences, as long as they are aware of the economics of teaching here before they arrive. Lithuanian schools are very keen to recruit native speakers, qualified or not, so graduates should have no problem finding a position either by contacting the Lithuanian embassy or by contacting the *Ministry of Education*, Dept. of Foreign Relations, Volvano Gatve 2/7, 2691 Vilnius, Tel: 2 622 483, Fax: 2 612 077. For US teachers, the main placement organization is the *American Partnership for Lithuanian Education*, PO Box 617, Durham, CT 06422, USA, Tel: (203) 347 7095, Fax: (203) 327 5837.

**Embassy in UK:**
84 Gloucester Place, London W1U 6AU
**Tel:** 020 7486 6401

**Embassy in USA:**
2622 16th Street NW, Washington DC 20009
**Tel:** 202 234 5860
www.ltembassyus.org

**British Council office:**
Business Centre 2000, Jogailos 4, 2001 Vilnius
**Tel** +370 (5) 264 4890
www.britishcouncil.lt

◐ **Visas/Work Permits:** You do not normally need Lithuanian visas for stays of 90 days or less. For most nationalities the procedure to obtain work permits is relatively straightforward once a position has been secured.

◐ **Requirements:** College Degree and a TESOL/TESL Certificate

◐ **Currency:** £1 = 4.84 / $1 = 2.64 Lati

◐ **Salaries/Taxes:** Salaries can be as low as £60 per month, so most teachers supplement their income with private lessons. The main private schools can pay up to £300 a month or about £5 an hour.

◐ **Accommodation:** Usually provided free with jobs arranged through the Ministry of Education. About £60 a month for an apartment in the suburbs, but cheap accommodation is difficult to find. Living with a family is the cheapest way and very easy to arrange.

◐ **Cost of Living:** Relatively low, but salaries will cover basic living costs only.

◐ **Health advice:** Insurance with evacuation cover is advised. Medical care in Lithuania is improving. Most medical supplies are now widely available.

◐ **English language media:** Baltic Times, also *Vilnius/Kaunas/Klaipeda in your pocket* are useful guides to living in these places.

## Schools in Lithuania (+370)
**American English School**
Pylimo 20, 2001 Vilnius. **Tel/Fax**: 2 791011.
**EF**
Kosciuskos g.11, 2000 Vilnius. **Tel:** 2 791616, **Fax**: 2 791646.
**Klaipeda International School of Languages**
Zveju g. 2, 5800 Klaipeda. **Tel:** 6 311190, **Fax:** 6 311190, **Email: mark.uribe@klaipeda.omnitel.net**
**Klaipeda Tourist School**
Taikos pr. 69, Klaipeda. **Tel:** 34 10 83, **Fax**: 34 02 46.
**Public Service Language Centre**
Vilniaus St 39/6, 2000 Vilnius. **Tel:** 2 220384, **Fax**: 2 220370, **Email: lora@vlkc.vno.osf.lt**
**Soros International House**
Ukmerges 41, korp A, 2662 Vilnius. **Tel:** 2 72 48 79, Fax: 2 72 48 39, **Email: daiva@ihouse.osf.lt**
**Siauliai Pedagogical Institute**
P. Visinskio 25, 5400 Siauliai. **Tel/Fax:** 1 432592, **Email: spi@siauliai.omnitel.net**

## MOLDOVA

Demand for English is very high in this tiny republic sandwiched between Romania and the Ukraine that only gained independence in 1991.

◐ **Visas/Work Permits:** U.S. citizens will need a tourist visa. The school will advise you regarding work permits. Teachers report that the rules do not seem to be enforced very strongly.

◐ **Requirements:** College Degree and a TESOL/TESL Certificate

◐ **Currency:** £1 = 22.85 / $1 = 12.35 Leu

◐ **Salaries/Taxes:** An average wage is £3 an hour, which, locally, is quite a good rate.

◐ **Cost of Living:** Very reasonable. Be aware that Moldova is basically a "cash-only" society. Credit cards are not used here very much.

◐ **Health advice:** Medical care in Moldova is limited, with severe shortages of basic medical supplies.

## Schools in Moldova (+373)

**ACTR-ACCELS**
Stefan cel Mare Blvd. 162, oficiul 1506, Chisinau, MD-2004. **Tel:** 2 248012, **Fax**: 2 238389, **Email: accels@dnt.md**

**Linguata**
Stefan cel Mare 64, office 175, Chisinau. **Tel:** 2 277779 **Email: linguata@ch.moldpac.md**

**Pro Didactica**
13 Armeneasca St., Chisinau, MD-2012. **Tel:** 2 541994, **Email: lschool@cepd.soros.md**

**Travel Teach Group**
Str. P. Rares 39, Chisinau MD-2074. **Tel:** 2 294067, **Fax**: 2 321817.

# POLAND

There is probably more demand for English in Poland than any other European country, due to two factors. Poland will soon become a member of the EU and is keen to attract foreign investment from the West. Secondly, the economy has been growing rapidly due to a steady process of liberalization, which has helped the export sector, which in turn increases the demand for English. In particular, the government administers English Proficiency exams, which are very important for young Poles who want to go into business. Many teachers head towards the big university cities such as Warsaw and Lodz. Most work in the private schools and supplement their income through individual private lessons. There are plenty of opportunities for English language teachers in both the public and private sectors. Public sector English teachers are placed in schools, teacher training colleges (NKJOs) and universities. Private schools are usually Polish-owned and very welcoming to native speaker teachers. They pay well and will assist with housing, health insurance and other matters.

**Embassy in UK:**
47 Portland Place, London W1B 1JH
**Tel:** 0870 7742700

**Embassy in USA:**
2640 16th Street NW, Washington DC 20009
**Tel:** 202 234 3800
www.polandembassy.org

**British Council office:**
Al Jerozolimskie 59, 00 697 Warsaw
**Tel** +48 (22) 695 5900
www.britishcouncil.pl

⮕ **Visas/Work Permits:** You should not require visas for stays up to 90 days for tourist, business, or transit purposes. Americans should ensure that their passports are date-stamped upon entry. Persons planning to stay in Poland for longer than 90 days or who will be employed in Poland must obtain a visa before they arrive in the country. Polish law requires every traveller to be able to show means of support, if asked. For persons above 16 years of age, this has been defined as 100 Polish zloty per day. Regulations have been tightened up recently. All teachers need to apply for a work permit before arriving in the country. Your notarized degree, TEFL certificate (if appropriate) and promissory permit from your prospective employer should be presented to your local Polish consulate. You cannot obtain a work permit while you are in Poland.

⮕ **Requirements:** College Degree, experience and a TESOL/TESL Certificate

⮕ **Currency:** £1 = 5.65 / $1 = 2.89 Zlotych

⮕ **Salaries/Taxes:** The average salary is around £200 per month in the state sector and at least £300 in the private sector. Some schools may offer overtime at £6-8 per hour. If you teach full-time and throw in a few private lessons you should be able to make over £600 a month which is very good money by Polish standards. The basic tax rate is 18%.

⮕ **Accommodation:** A one-bedroom apartment in the centre of Warsaw will cost £200-300 per month. Studios cost £200-250. You will have to pay at least a month's rent as deposit in advance to the landlord and you might have to pay the same amount to the agent who located your apartment. It's a good idea to arrive in July or August with some spare cash and beat the September rush for accommodation. January is also a good time. Some schools offer free accommodation.

⮕ **Cost of Living:** If you use public transport and adopt the local diet you can live on £5 a day including three good meals.

⮕ **Health advice:** The hospitals are of variable quality. Private doctors and clinics are very cheap, as are dentists. Your school may offer you health insurance as part of your employment package. Whatever deal you have, make sure you have comprehensive coverage.

⮕ **English language media:** The Warsaw Voice.

## Schools in Poland (+48)

**ABC**
Uslugi Jezykowe, ul ZWM 6 m 29, Warsaw.

**AJM**
ul Klaudyny 30 m 100, 01-684 Warsaw.

**American English School**
PO Box 3, 00-991 Warsaw 44. **Tel/Fax:** 22 272654.

**Angloschool**
ul Elblaska 65/84, Warsaw.

**AS**
Studio Jezykow Obcych, ul M L Kinga 13, 75-016 Koszalin.

**Bakalarz**
Prywatne Studium Jezykowe, ul Rakowiecka 45/25, 02-528 Warsaw. **Tel:** 489 889.

**Best**
ul. Pestalozziego 11/13, 80-445 Gdansk. **Tel/Fax:** 58 41 2902.

**Beyond 2000**
Szkola Jezykow Obcych, ul Szuberta 39/5, 02-408 Warsaw.

**British Council Warsaw Studium**
Warsaw Technical University, ul. Filtowa 2, 00-611 Warsaw. **Tel/Fax:** 22 25 82 87.

**Business and Educational English**
ul Conrada 10 m 57, 01-922 Warsaw.

**Centre of English Language Training**
Konarskiego 2, 30-049 Krakow. **Tel:** 12 15 17 32.

**Compact School of English**
Spolka Cywilna, Nowogrodzka 78/24, 02-018 Warsaw.

**Cosmopolitan Private Language School**
Ul. Katowicka 39, 45-061 Opole. **Tel/Fax:** 77 54 87 73.

**Discovery**
Osrodek Nauczania Jezykow Obcych, Klub WAT-u, ul Kaliskiego 25a, 01-489 Warsaw.

**The Eagle English Centre**
Al Stanow Zjednoczonych 26 m 25, 03-965 Warsaw.

**Elan**
Mokotowska 9 m 6, Warsaw. **Tel:** 25 19 91.

**Elite Language School**
ul Dunikowskiego 10 m 56, 02-784 Warsaw.

**English House**
AWF Przedszkole, ul. Marymoncka 34, Bielany.

**English House**
"Domino" ul. Boguslawskiego 6a Lingwista, ul. Reymonta 25, Bielany. **Tel:** 663 5569.

**English is Fun**
Warchalowskiego 2/13, Warsaw.

**English Language Academy**
ul Narbutta 9 m 3, 02-564 Warsaw.

**English Language Centre**
University of Silesia, Plac Sejmu Slaskiego 1, 40-032 Katowice. **Tel:** 32 156 1269, **Fax:** 32 155 2245.

**English Language Studio**
ul Jadzwingow 1 m 34, 02-692 Warsaw.

**English Unlimited**
Podmlynska 10, 80-885 Gdansk. **Tel/Fax:** 58 31 33 73, **Email:** info@eu.com.pl.

**Falaland**
Osrodek Nauczania Jez Obcych, Margerytki 52, 04-908 Warsaw.

**Fast**
Firma Prywatna, Jezyk Angielski-Lektoraty, Ewa Maszonska-Pazdro, ul. Mickiewicza 74/58, 01-650 Warsaw.

**Gama-Bell School of English**
ul. sw. Krzza 16, 31-023 Krakow. **Tel:** 12 21 97 55, **Fax:** 12 21 73 79.

**Greenwich School of English Poland**
ul Zakroczymska 6, 00-225 Warsaw.

**Human**
Agencja Jezykow Obcych, ul Swietokrzyshka 20 pok 317, 00-002 Warsaw.

**International House Bielsko Biala**
ul. Krasinskiego 24, Bielsko Biala 43-300. **Tel:** 33 811 79 27/811 02 29, **Email:** ihbb@silesia.top.pl

**International House Bydgoszcz**
ul. Dworcowa 81, Bydgoszcz 85-009. **Tel:** 52 322 3515/322 3444, **Fax:** 52 322 3515, **Email:** bydgoszcz@inthouse.pl

**International House Katowice**
ul. Sokolska 78/80, Katowice 40-128. **Tel:** 32 58 68 96, 599 997, **Fax:** 32 253 88 33, **Email:** ihih@silesia.top.pl

**International House Kielce**
ul. Wesola 33, Kielce 25-353. **Tel:** 41 34 30 258/34 30 430, **Fax:** 41 34 30 261, **Email:** kielce@ih.pl

**International House Koszalin**
ul. Zwyciestwa 7/9, Koszalin 75-728. **Tel:** 94 3410 196, **Fax:** 94 3410 180, **Email:** hubbard.koszalin@inthouse.pl

**International House Krakow**
ul. Pilsudskiego 6, lp, 31-109 Krakow. **Tel:** 12 21 94 40, **Fax:** 12 21 86 52. **Email:** admin@ih.pl

**International House Lodz**
ul. Zielona 15, Lodz 90-601. **Tel:** 42 630 00 26, **Fax:** 42 630 00 28, **Email:** lodz@ih.pl

**International House Opole**
ul. Kosciuszki 17, Opole 45-062. **Tel/Fax:** 77 454 66655, **Email:** sekret@pol.pl

**International House Poznan**
ul. Sw. Marcin 66/72, Poznan 61 807. **Tel:** 61 851 6171, **Fax:** 61 851 61 71, **Email:** Lektor_international_house@poczta.fm

**International House Torun**
Ul. Legionow 15, Torun 87-100. **Tel:** 56 655 40 83, **Fax:** 56 622 50 81, **Email:** torun@inthouse.pl

**International House Wroclaw**
ul. Leszczynskiego 3, Wroclaw 50-078. **Tel:** 71 781 72 90, **Fax:** 71 781 72 93, **Email:** wrocdos@id.pl

**International House Warsaw**
ul. S. Noakowskiego 3, Warsaw 00-664. **Tel:** 22 660 71 01, **Fax:** 22 660 71 05, **Email:** monika_s@ihwarsaw.com.pl

**International Language School**
ul. Krakowska 51, 45-075 Opole. **Tel/Fax:** 77 53 15 97.

**Junior Art-Language Studio**
ul Gwardzistow 8 m 5, 00-422 Warsaw.

**Kajman**
ul Felinskiego 15, 1 LO pokoj 57 (parter), 01-513 Warsaw.

**Konwersatorium**
Jezykow Obcych, Grojecka 40a m 13, 02-320 Warsaw.

**Kozlowski I Rejman**
Kusocinskiego 2, 31-300 Mielec.

**Langhelp**
Al Jerozolimskie 23/34, Warsaw. **Tel:** 21 44 34.

**Lektor Prywatna Firma Jezykowa**
ul. Olawska 2, 50-123 Wroclaw. **Tel/Fax:** 71 343 25 99.

**Lexis College of Foreign Languages**
ul Danilowiczowska 11m 18, Warsaw.

**Lingua**
Studium Jezykow Obcych, ul Moniuszki 4a, Lodz.

**Lingwista**
ul Saska 59, 03-958 Warsaw, *and* Janowskiego 50, 02-784 Warsaw.

**Mosak**
ul Bonifacego 83/85 m 87, Warsaw.

**MTA Language Centre**
Pl. Teatrainy 6, Wroclaw. **Tel:** 71 72 13 34.

**NKJO - Krakow**
ul. Kanonicza 14, 31-002 Krakow. **Tel:** 12 22 79 55, **Fax:** 12 22 63 06.

**Omnibus - Poznan**
Pl Wolnosci 5, 61-738 Poznan. **Tel:** 52 79 08.

**The Orlik Language Centre**
ul Rogalskiego 2 m 49, 03-982 Warsaw.

**Perfect**
Naucanie Jezykow Obcych, ul Wolnosci 2 bl 13 m 14, Maciej Musiala, Zielonka.

**Perfekts**
Firma Oswiatowa, ul J Kaden-Bandrowskiego 2/16, 01-494 Warsaw.

**Polanglo**
Szkola Jezykow Obcych, ul Nowowiejska 1/3, 00-643 Warsaw. **Tel/Fax:** 22 25 37 47.

**Poliglota**
Biuro Jezykowych, Dzialdowska 6, 01-184 Warsaw.

**Prima**
Osrodek Nauczania Jezykow Obcych, ul Rozana 7 m 3, 15-669 Bialystock.

**Program-Bell**
ul Fredry 7, Poznan. **Tel:** 61 53 69 72.

**Promotor**
Szkola Jezykow Obcych, Agencja Oswiatowa, Kraszewskiego 32a, 05-800 Pruszkow.

**Prymus**
ul Jasna 2/4 pok 209, 00-950 Warsaw.

**Pygmalion**
Szkola Jezyka Angielskiego, ul Saska 78, Warsaw.

**Studio Troll**
Wrzeciono 1/22, Warsaw.

**Studium Jezydow Obcych Project**
ul Szwolezerow 5B/10, 66-400 Gorzow Wlkp. **Tel:** 95 32 05 59.

**Success**
ul Agawy 5/9, 01-158 Warsaw. **Tel:** 22 623 39 40, **Fax:** 22 20 55 03.

**Surrey Business and Language Centres**
ul Gwardzistow 20, 00-422 Warsaw.

**Szansa**
Prywatny Zaklad Oswiatowy, ul Agawy 5/9, 01-158 Warsaw. **Tel:** 22 623 39 40, **Fax:** 22 20 55 03.

**Target**
ul. Dziatwy 6/ róg Modolinska, Bialoleka. **Tel:** 660 7028, 660 7029

**University of Szczecin**
Al. Piastow 40B, 71-065 Szczecin. **Tel:** 91 33 31 61,
**Fax**: 91 34 29 92.

**Urszula**
Biuro Organizacji Kursow, Dworcowa 1 pok 13,
10-431 Olsztyn

**Warsaw School of Commerce**
Kursy Handlowe, al Chlodna 9, Warsaw.

**Warsaw Study Centre**
Osrodek Jezykowo-Szkoleniowy, ul Raszynska 22,
02-026 Warsaw.

**World**
ul Basztowa 17, 31-143 Krakow. **Tel:** 22 91 61.

**Worldwide English School**
ul Stoleczna 21 paw 24, 01-530 Warsaw.

**YES**
ul Reformacka 8, 35-026 Rzeszow. **Tel/Fax:** 17 52 07
20.

---

## Schools in Warsaw and its suburbs:

**Mokotów ABC**
ul. Wita Stwosza 57, **Tel:** 682-86-19

**Columbus**
ul. Kazimierzowska 16, **Tel:** 841-38-04

**Greenwich**
ul. Zakrzewska 25, **Tel:** 825-29-53

**K i D**
Osrodek Nauczania Jezyków Obcychul. Barcelonska 8,
**Tel:** 39-52-04, 0-90-20-48-20

**Lingwista agencja**
ul. Rózana 22/24, **Tel:** 845-05-71

**Lingua Nova**
ul. Basniowa 3, **Tel:** 825-80-86, 668-76-74

**Lingwista agencja**
ul. Filtrowa 75, **Tel:** 659-50-01

**Ochota English Language Centre**
ul. Filtrowa 2, **Tel:** 660-55-71

**Osrodek Kultury Ochoty Kursy Jezyków Obcych**
ul. Grójecka 75, **Tel:** 822-48-70, 822-74-37

**TARGET**
ul. Bagatela 13, **Tel:** 660 70 28

**Warsaw Study Centre**
ul. Raszynska 22, **Tel/fax:** 822-14-12, **Tel:** 822-46-18

**Praga Poludnie English House**
Grochów-Kamionek, S.P. 60, ul. Zbarska 3

**English House**
Saska Kepa, ul. Kryniczna 12/14

**Lingwista**
Saska Kepa, ul. Saska, **Tel:** 617-85-83

**Lingwista**
ul. Miedzyborska 70, **Tel:** 810-22-01

**TARGET**
Saska Kepa, ul. Obronców 31, **Tel:** 660 70 28

**Sródmiescie ABILITY**
ul. Mazowiecka 12, **Tel:** 827-20-29

**Academia de la Lengua (Language Mega Centre)**
ul. Nowy Swiat 21A, **Tel:** 625-71-02, 828-10-21,
828-41-39, 646-09-20

**ALBION**
ul. Noakowskiego 26 m.26, **Tel/fax:** 628-89-92

**BOKANO SCHOOL**
ul. Chmielna 24/2, **Tel:** 826-31-17

**Cambridge School of English**
ul. Zakroczymska 6, **Tel:** 831-09-55

**Context Language** centre
ul. Hoza 61/1, **Tel:** 622 58 60

**Didier Szkola Jezyka Obcych**
ul. Kopernika 28 lok. 16, **Tel/fax:** 827-24-78

**EMPiK Szkola Jezyków Obcych**
ul. Marszalkowska 104/122, **Tel:** 826-79-17/18,
551-44-55/56/57, 826-71-04

**EMPiK Szkola Jezyków Obcych**
ul. Foksal 11, **Tel:** 826-79-17/18, 551-44-55/56/57,
826-71-04

**EMPiK Szkola Jezyków Obcych**
ul. Trebacka 3, **Tel:** 826-79-17/18, 551-44-55/56/57,
826-71-04

**English Language College "Metodysci"**
ul. Mokotowska 12, **Tel:** 628-53-48

**Infor**
ul. Sniadeckich 17, **Tel:** 629-77-90

**International House**
ul. Noakowskiego 3, **Tel:** 660-71-01

**Greenwich**
ul. Nowowiejska 5, **Tel:** 825-29-53

**Konwersatorium**
ul. Sempolowskiej 4, **Tel:** 622-61-62

**Lang LTC**
Al. Niepodleglosci, **Tel:** 825-39-40

**Language Mega Centre (Academia de la Lengua)**
ul. Nowy Swiat 21A, **Tel:** 625-71-02, 828-10-21, 828-41-39, 646-09-20

**Lexis**
Al. Marszalkowska 60 lok. 34, **Tel:** 625-53-86, 625-72-98, 622-25-23

**Lingua Nova**
ul. Nowowiejska 37A, **Tel**: 825-80-86, 668-76-74

**Lingwista**
ul. Kopernika 6, **Tel:** 827-86-85

**Lingwista**
ul. Ujazdowskie 37, **Tel:** 629-25-88

**Lingwista**
ul. Smolna 30 (Liceum/Szkola Podst.), **Tel:** 827-89-55

**Loyd**
pl. Powstanców Warszawy, Hotel Warsaw, **Tel:** 827 51 37.

**Maart**
ul. Nowy Swiat 1, **Tel:** 621-11-71

**Peritia**
ul. Bednarska 2/4, **Tel:** 826-95-30

**PolAnglo**
ul. Nowowiejska 1/3, **Tel:** 825-21-56

**TARGET**
ul. Polna 50, **Tel:** 660 70 28

**TFLS**
ul. Krucza 47 A, **Tel:** 622-20-58

**Tower Language Institute**
ul. Szpitalna 5 lok.16, **Tel:** 846-22-26, 828-36-99

**Towarzystwo Wiedzy Powszechnej**
pl. Defilad 1, Palac Kultury i Nauki, **Tel:** 656 61 75

**Twins/English Conversation**
ul. Krucza 17 lok. 3, **Tel:** 0604817817

**Warszawskie Centrum Studenckiego Ruchu Naukowego**
ul. Mokotowska 48, **Tel:** 628-82-81

**Wola Cambridge School of English**
ul. Bema 70, **Tel:** 632-78-86

**Focus Language School**
ul. Smocza 21, **Tel:** 636-44-31, 654-13-11

**Lingwista**
ul. Ksiecia Janusza 45/47, **Tel:** 36-17-71

**Poliglota**
ul. Dzialdowska 6, **Tel:** 632-02-08

**Zoliborz English House**
SDK, ul. Próchnika 8a, Teatr Komedia

**Greenwich**
ul. Gdanska 2/3, **Tel:** 833-24-31

**Lingwista**
ul. Gen. Zajaczka 7, **Tel:** 39-25-85

**TARGET**
ul. Kochanowskiego 8, **Tel:** 660 70 28

**Twins/English Conversation**
ul. Dyminska 6A/146 **Tel**: 39 25 84

**Cambridge School of English**
ul. Wasilkowskiego 6, **Tel:** 644-63-06

**English House**
Lasek Brzozowy 2 (Klub przez Lasku)

**Lingwista**
ul. Janowskiego 50, **Tel:** 643-72-79

## ROMANIA

Romania is a fascinating country but teachers who come here must be prepared to live in a society that is still coming to terms with its post-Communist phase. Life can be very harsh here, especially in big industrial cities. The demand for English is not as strong in Romania as it is in other countries but a determined teacher should be able to find work without too many problems.

**Embassy in UK:**
Arundel House, 4 Palace Green, London W8 4QD
**Tel:** 020 7937 9666

**Embassy in USA:**
1607 23rd Street NW, Washington DC 20008
**Tel:** 202 332 4848
www.roembus.org

**British Council office:**
Calea Dorobantilor 14, 71132 Bucharest
**Tel** +40 (21) 307 9600
www.britishcouncil.ro

⮥ **Visas/Work Permits:** You need a visa for a stay of longer than 30 days. You can hunt for jobs while visiting the country as a tourist. Your employer will apply for permits. Do not remain in Romania without a valid visa because the fines for overstaying are very high.

⮥ **Requirements:** College Degree, experience and a TESOL/TESL Certificate

⮥ **Currency:** £1 = 5.08 / $1 = 2.60 New Lei.

⮥ **Salaries/Taxes:** A typical package for a native-speaking teacher is £200 per month with accommodation provided by the school.

⮩ **Accommodation:** One of the major headaches of living in Romania is finding affordable and decent housing. Most buildings were poorly constructed and rents are very expensive.

⮩ **Cost of Living:** Food and locally made products are very cheap.

⮩ **Health advice:** Medical care in Romania is limited. Basic medical supplies are scarce. Doctors and hospitals often expect immediate cash payment for health services.

⮩ **English language media:** Bucuresti, Nine O'Clock, In Review, Romanian Business News.

## Schools in Romania (+40)

### ACCESS Language Centre
Str. Tebei nr. 21, 3400 Cluj. **Tel:** 064 420480 ext 128, **Fax**: 064-420476 **Email:** ovidiu@access.soroscj.ro

### Best
Colegiul I.L.Caragiale, Calea Dorobantilor 163, Sector 1 Bucharest. **Tel:** 01-322 6744.

### Calepinus Foundation - Foreign Language Institute
Piata Bernady 3, 4300 Târgu Mures. **Tel:** 065-216514

### Cambridge Study Centre
Liceul Vasile Alecsandri Str., N.Balcescu 41, 6200 Galati. Centrul de limbi straine FIDES, Str.Vasile Conta 7-9, sc.E, et.7, ap.168, 70139 Bucharest. **Tel:** 01-313 8080 ext.160

### CLASS (Constanta Language Association)
Bd. Mircea cel Batran nr. 103, 8700 Constanta. **Tel/Fax:** 041-612877.

### Computer Academy
Sala Mare A Palatului, Bucharest. **Tel:** 01-615 9710 Ext. 745/742.

### Daniel - Centrul De Limba Engleza
Str. Cosminului 10, 4300 Târgu Mures. **Tel:** 065-216950.

### International House Language Centre
Bd. Republicii nr. 9, 1900 Timisoara. **Tel/Fax:** 056-190593 **Email:** rodica@ihlctim.sorostm.ro

### International Language Centre
Str. Moara de Foc nr. 35 et. 8, 6600 Iasi. **Tel:** 032-252850 / 252870. **Fax:** 032-252902. **Email:** acolib@ilc.iasi.osf.ro

### Lexis Bucuresti
Piata Pache Protopopescu 96, Sector 2, Bucharest. **Tel:** 01-310 2629.

### Linguarama
Str. Delea Veche 51, Bl.46, Et.9, Sector 2, Bucharest. **Tel:** 01-320 6156.

### Open Doors School of English
Michelle Penta, str. L. Blaga nr. 4, 1900 Timisoara. **Tel/Fax:** 056- 194252.

### PROSPER-ASE Language Centre
Calea Grivitei 2-2A et.2 s.4211, Bucharest. **Tel/Fax:** 01-2117800, **Tel:** 01-6505456, **Email:** prosper1@rolink.iiruc.ro

### PROSPER-Transilvania Language Centre
c/o Bd.Valea Cetatii 6, bl.B2, sc.B, ap.6, 2200 Brasov **Tel:** 068-319908, **Email:** g.cusen@unitbv.ro

### RALEX Linguistic Centre
Str. Buna Vestire nr. 35, 1000 Ramnicu Valcea, **Tel/Fax:** 050-740032

### Soros Educational Centre Miercurea-Ciuc
Str. Florilor 9, et.3, 4100 Miercurea-Ciuc. **Tel/Fax:** 066-171799, **Email:** office@cemc.topnet.ro

### 'YES' Language Centre
Colegiul Pedagogic Andrei Saguna, Str. Gen. Magheru 34, 2400 Sibiu. **Tel:** 069-430809 / 434002

## RUSSIA

The Western media tends to paint a distorted view of life in Russia. Although there are hardships, most teachers report that their experiences in Russia were positive and that people actually enjoy themselves quite a lot here! There is a great demand for English lessons throughout Russia at present. This demand is not confined to the major cities like Moscow and St. Petersburg. Private language schools are springing up across the country – some more reputable than others. Russians are fascinated by all things American and you will be the centre of much attention, especially in the smaller towns. But a word of warning: if your grammar and spelling are weak, you better brush up on these areas before you go. Russians are precise and thorough in their language learning and they are not impressed by teachers who do not know how to use the English language correctly. Many teachers start off by working for a school, then pick up some private lessons as the word gets around, and finally going completely freelance.

### Embassy in UK:
13 Kensington Palace Gardens, London W8 4QX
**Tel:** 020 7229 8027
www.russianembassy.net

**Embassy in USA:**
2650 Winsconsin Ave. NW, Washington DC 20007
**Tel:** 202 298 5700
www.russianembassy.org

**British Council office:**
Ulitsa Nikoloyamskaya 1, Moscow 109189
**Tel** +7 095 782 0200
www.britishcouncil.ru

⮊ **Visas/Work Permits:** A Russian visa is considered as a permission to enter and exit the country. To obtain a visa, you must be sponsored by an organization such as a school or a tour company. Only the sponsor can extend or change your visa. It is a good idea to apply for a three-month visa. After that, the school can arrange your paperwork but you will have to have an AIDS test. Be careful that the school does not decide to keep you longer than you want to stay! Be prepared for a lot of red tape as far as visas are concerned. There is no such thing as a work permit in Russia.

⮊ **Requirements:** College Degree, experience and a TESOL/TESL Certificate

⮊ **Currency:** £1 = 51.57 / $1 = 26.39 Rubles

⮊ **Salaries/Taxes:** Russia operates on a dual currency system with both rubles and dollars in circulation. You can earn around £3500-4000 per month and as much as £30 an hour for private lessons in Moscow and St. Petersburg. These rates are lower in the provincial centres.

⮊ **Accommodation:** You can find an apartment in Moscow from around £100 a month.

⮊ **Cost of Living:** Moscow has a reputation as an expensive city but you will be earning far more than most people do there. If you indulge in imported western goods, then life will be expensive. Carry cash (US$) – credit cards are useless unless you plan to spend your time at expensive hotels.

⮊ **Health advice:** Teachers thinking of going to Russia should be in good physical condition. It's not a good idea to entrust your health to a badly paid doctor operating in poor facilities. Get shots for rabies, diphtheria, cholera, hepatitis A and B and encephalitis before you go.

⮊ **English language media:** Moscow Times, Moscow Tribune, Moscow News, St. Petersburg Press, Neva News, The Vladivostok Times.

## Schools in the Russian Federation (+7)

**Anglo-American School**
Penkovaya ui. 5, St. Petersburg.

**Benedict School**
Chapligina 92, Novosibirsk 630099. **Tel:** 3832 23 24 33, **Fax:** 3832 23 59 97.

**Centre for Intensive Foreign Language Instruction**
Sparrow Hills, Building 2, Moscow 119899.

**Go West Department of Foreign Languages**
2/1 Spartakovskaya Street, Moscow. **Tel:** 95 267 4700, **Fax:** 95 267 4700.

**Language Link Schools**
Novoslobod-skaya ul. 5 bld.2, 101030 Moscow. **Tel/Fax:** 95 973 2154.

**Link School of Languages**
15/81 pl Lenina, 394000 Voronezh. **Tel:** 732 55 23 31.

**LK Varioline**
12-12, Klyutchevskaya St., Ekaterinburg 620109. **Tel/Fax:** 3432 46 91 39.

**Marina Anglo-American School**
Leninsky Prospekt 39a, Moscow 117313.

**Moscow-Cambridge Project Management**
Academy of National Economy, 82 Vernadsky Prospect, Moscow 117571. **Tel:** 502 234 3873, **Fax:** 95 434 6030.

**Moscow International School**
2nd Ulitsa Maryinoy Roshchi 2a, Moscow.

**Moscow MV Lomonosov University**
Sparrow Hills, Moscow 117234.

**NevaLingua International Study Centre**
Malaya Morskaya Str. 11, office 315, St. Petersburg 191186. **Tel:** 812 3128129, **Fax:** 812 3126211.

**Polyglot International School**
22 Volkov Pereulok, Flat 56, Moscow.

**ProBa Language Centre**
Professora Popova 5, St.Petersburg 197376. (Mail: P.O. Box 109, Lappeenranta FIN-53101 Finland.) **Tel:** 812 3252618. **Fax:** 812 3462758

**Pushkin Language Centre**
Pushkin. (**Contact:** Leipziger Strasse 27, 09648 Mittweida, Germany.) **Tel:** +49-3727-976228

**RISC Language School**
Ulitsa Dekabristov 23a, Moscow

**Russian-American Centre**
Tomsk Polytechnic University, Room 319, Lenin Ave 30, 634004 Tomsk. **Tel:** 3822 22 45 48, **Fax:** 3822 22 46 07.

**St Petersburg University**
Universitetskaya, Naberezhnaya 7/9 B-164, St
Petersburg, 199164.

**St Petersburg University of Humanities &
Social Sciences**
Dept. of Foreign Languages, 15 Fuchika St., St
Petersburg 192238. **Tel:** 812 269 1925.

**Sunny School**
PO Box 23, Moscow 125057. **Tel:** 95 151 2500.

**System-3 Language & Communication**
Arnold Rubinstein, Kantemirovskaya Street 16 #531,
Moscow 115522. **Tel:** 9210141, **Fax**: 3204035.

**World Language Club**
1106e Panfilovsky Prosp., Zelenograd 103460. **Tel:** 95
532 9121, **Fax**: 95 530 9646.

# Spelling It Out in Siberia

## Professor Yuri Tambovtsev explains what intrepid EFL teachers might expect to find if they come to work in the Siberian city of Novosibirsk.

Novosibirsk is situated on the great Siberian River, Ob. It is quite a young city, founded in 1893 when a crossing for the Trans-Siberian railway was built over the river. Until 1925, Novosibirsk was known as Novonikolaevsk, named after the last Russian tsar, Nicholas II. In the 1920s, the city grew rapidly as it became an important industrial and transport centre between the coalfields to the southeast and the mineral deposits in the Ural Mountains to the west. In 1930s the building of the Turko-Siberian railway south from Novosibirsk to Almaty in Kazakhstan made the city a crucial transport link between Russia and Central Asia.

Now a city of 1.5 million people, Novosibirsk is a major industrial, scientific, cultural and educational centre. One in three of the city's residents is a student. Many Russians have realized how important it is to be able to talk English because it is the language of international communication. Every Russian pupil begins learning English in the 1st grade. The pupils usually have two lessons a week. However, there are some schools which give six lessons a week. At the universities, students normally have English once a week for two years. The communicative method of teaching English is now in fashion. It is also called the "rapid" method of teaching. The pupils at schools and the students at universities are asked to talk in English during the entire lesson. A native-speaking teacher is required to talk English all the time without resorting to Russian. Although having a degree, certificate or diploma in teaching EFL/ESL will help you as a teacher, the universities and colleges will hire unqualified native speakers of English if they can prove they are able to conduct an English lesson well.

I think one problem with English teaching here in Russia is that we do not teach the students correct English phonetics. The special lessons devoted to teaching only English sounds have been abolished. Now, the students just substitute English sounds with similar Russian ones. Younger teachers of English and their students speak with a stronger Russian accent than the older teachers of English, who had a special course of practical and theoretical phonetics every day for one year of their degree course. The English language textbooks are usually British or American, so the teacher does what is in the textbook.

The salaries of young native-speaking teachers are usually 5-10 times higher than those of Russian teachers of English. Native speakers can earn £30-60 a month. One can live very well on this salary: A kilogram of meat is £2 and one can buy 4 kilograms of potatoes for under £1. There are no problems buying food, as the shops are full of goods. It is cheaper to buy food at the street markets, but you can't be sure if the food is fresh or safe to eat. Although the city is rather gray and functional, its residents are very proud of it since it has the biggest railway station, the biggest library and the biggest airport in Siberia. The local ballet company is said to be the best after Bolshoi and Mariinsky companies of Moscow and St. Petersburg respectively. The Art Gallery in Novosibirsk is certainly worth seeing as it contains original works of Shishkin, Rerickh, Repin, and Surikov. Opera, ballet and theatre tickets cost from £2-4. Universities can provide a native speaker of English with a room in a dormitory for £6-12 a month. The dormitory has showers with hot water, and places to wash clothes and a communal kitchen for cooking. Elsewhere in the city, a one-room apartment costs about £30 a month; with two rooms – £50. One can easily hire a car, but it is cheaper to use public buses or trams: 12 rides cost under £1.

During your summer vacation, you can travel by boat along the Ob river to the North to visit the Finno-Ugric aboriginal peoples of Siberia: Mansi (Voguls), Hanty (Ostjaks), and Nenets (Samoyeds). You can also visit the Altai Mountains and meet the Turkic aboriginal peoples: Altai-Kizh, Kumandin, Telengits, and Teleuts, the latter being remnants of Genghis Khan's Tatar-Mongolian hordes.

*Professor Yuri Tambovtsev teaches at the Department of English and Linguistics, SIM, Novosibirsk, Russia.*

## SLOVAKIA

There is a shortage of English language teachers in Slovakia and native speakers with qualifications can land jobs here without problems. Many schools start recruiting in the spring for a September start but if you arrive in July or early August, you'll probably find work. If you want to teach in the state sector, you'll have to approach the Ministry of Education or one of the cultural organizations. There are fewer westerners here than in neighbouring countries.

**Embassy in UK:**
25 Kensington Palace Gardens, London W8 4QY
**Tel:** 020 7243 0803
www.slovakembassy.co.uk

**Embassy in USA:**
3523 International Court NW, Washington DC20008
**Tel:** 202 237 1054
www.slovakembassy-us.org

**British Council office:**
Panska 17 - P.O. Box 68, 814 99 Bratislava

**Tel:** +421 (2) 5443 1074
Www.britishcouncil.sk

⊃ **Visas/Work Permits:** You do not need a visa for a stay of less than 30 days so you can look for a job during this time. Your employer should arrange all the necessary paperwork but you will have to take a rather unpleasant medical exam.

⊃ **Requirements:** College Degree and a TESOL/TESL Certificate

⊃ **Currency:** £1 = 52 / $1 = 26 Koruny.

⊃ **Salaries/Taxes:** You will be paid at local rates–around £180-200 per month for a 25-hour week plus some overtime. You can earn better money with private lessons but these are hard to come by.

⊃ **Accommodation:** This is usually supplied by the school who should also pay for the utilities.

⊃ **Cost of Living:** Although Slovakia is cheap in dollar terms, you will be paid at local rates so basic items like shampoo and other toiletries are actually expensive. Credit cards are not used much here.

➲ **Health advice:** There are decent medical facilities but few doctors speak English. Some schools will provide you with medical coverage.

➲ **English language media:** Slovak Spectator.

## Schools in Slovak Republic (+421)

**Academia Vzdelavania**
Gorkeho 10, 815 17 Bratislava. **Tel:** 7 367 580, **Fax:** 7 321 661.

**American Language Institute**
Drienova 34, PO Box 78, 820 09 Bratislava.

**Foundation for a Civil Society**
V Zahradach 29A, 811 03 Bratislava. **Tel:** 7 580 2491, **Fax:** 7 531 1622.

**VSMU**
Katedra Jazykov, Venturska 3, 813 01 Bratislava.

# SLOVENIA

There are lots of opportunities for English language teachers in Slovenia. The country is more "western" than others in the region. Native-speaking teachers are usually assigned to the more advanced learners. It's easier to come here and find a job rather than applying from outside the country.

**British Council office:**
Cankarjevo nabrezje 27, Ljubljana 1000
**Tel** +386 (0) 1 200 0130
**Email:** info@britishcouncil.si

➲ **Visas/Work Permits:** You can stay for up to 90 days without a visa. Most teachers just stay on although some do overcome the red tape and acquire work permits. The authorities don't worry about foreign teachers unless they are perceived (rightly or wrongly) as troublemakers.

➲ **Requirements:** College Degree and a TESOL/TESL Certificate

➲ **Currency:** £1 = 357 / $1 = 182 Tolar

➲ **Salaries/Taxes:** Expect to earn $9-12 per 45-minute teaching "hour". Most teachers are paid in tolars

➲ **Accommodation:** A nice one-bedroom apartment costs around £150-200 per month or you can share a place for about £60.

➲ **Cost of Living:** You should be able to live well off your salary here.

➲ **Health advice:** Schools will not offer medical coverage so you should have your own policy. Medical care in Slovenia is of a high quality and many doctors speak English.

## Schools in Slovenia (+386)

**Accent On Language d.o.o.**
Ljubljanska c. 36, 1230 Domzale. **Tel:** 61 712 658, **Fax:** 61 712 658.

**Ambra d.o.o.**
Pobeska 18, 6000 Koper. **Tel:** 66 33 128.

**AS Asistent d.o.o.**
Glavni trg 17 B, 2000 Maribor. **Tel:** 62 226 442, **Fax:** 62 224 432.

**Athena d.o.o.**
Kolodvorska c. 17, 6230 Postojna. **Tel:** 67 23 907, **Fax:** 67 23 907.

**Bled**
Sola za Tuje Jezike, Breda Vukelj s.p., Kajuhova c. 11, 4260 Bled. **Tel:** 64 741 780, **Fax:** 64 741 780.

**Candor Dominko k.d.**
Turnovse 19, 1360 Vrhnika. **Tel:** 61 756 032, **Fax:** 61 756 032.

**Cenca p.o.**
Masarykova c. 18, Ribnisko selo, 2000 Maribor. **Tel:** 62 306 479.

**D and A Ita d.o.o.**
Japljeva ul. 4, 1241 Kamnik.

**Dialog d.o.o**
Jezikovna Sola, Terceva ul. 39, 2000 Maribor. **Tel:** 62 24 779, **Fax:** 62 227 866.

**Dude d.o.o**
English Language centre, Slamnikarska 1, 1230 Domzale. **Tel:** 61 716 913

**Euro**centre
Lilijana Durdevic s.p., Kidriceva ul. 46, 6000 Koper. **Tel:** 66 272 336, **Fax:** 66 281 653.

**Europa Bled, d.o.o.**
Alpska 7, 4260 Bled. **Tel:** 64 741 563, **Fax:** 64 741 563 **Email:** evropabl@perfech.si

**Ekocept d.o.o**
Sola za Tuje Jezike, Prezihova 8, 2230 Lenart v Slovenskih Goricah. **Tel:** 62 724 064, **Fax:** 62 724 064.

**Flamingo d.o.o.**
Pod Gonjami 44, 2391 Prevalje. **Tel:** 602 31 455.

**Forum centre d.o.o.**
Markova pot 8, 5290 Sempeter pri Gorici, **Tel:** 65 31 205, **Fax:** 65 31 205.

**G.A.P.**
Belokriska 22, 6320 Portoroz. **Tel:** 66 75 894 .

**Hello Sempeter d.o.o**
Sempeter v Savinjski dolini 34, 3311 Sempeter v Savinjski dolini. **Tel:** 63 701 795, **Fax:** 63 701 795.

**ISCG Domzale**
Kolodvorska c. 6, 1230 Domzale. **Tel:** 61 711 082, **Fax:** 61 712 278.

**Jezikovna Sola Tabula Rasa**
Trg svobode 12, 3325 Sostanj. **Tel:** 63 892 291.

**Jezikovni biro Lindic**
Cankarjeva ul. 10, 2000 Maribor. **Tel:** 62 221 629.

**Jezikovni Studio Kotar Sonja, s.p.**
Cesta na Svetino 10, 3270 Lasko, **Tel:** 63 731 105.

**Kamnik**
Altera d.n.o., Kettejeva 23, 1241 Kamnik. **Tel:** 61 831 117.

**Lingua**
Carman Cilka, s.p., Cesta Zasavskega bataljona 27, 1270 Litija. **Tel:** 61 882 137

**Lingva d.o.o.**
Ograde 7, 1386 Stari trg pri Lozu, Cerknica. **Tel:** 61 708 017.

**Lingva p.o**
Zavod za Opravljanje Izobrazevalnih in Organizacijskih Storitev, Vetrinjska ul. 16, 2000 Maribor. **Tel:** 62 24 795, **Fax:** 62 301 071.

**Little England Club d.o.o.**
Medvedova ul. 6, 1241 Kamnik . **Tel:** 61 832 865, **Fax:** 61 832 865.

**Ljudska Univerza Celje**
Cankarjeva ul. 1, 3000 Celje. **Tel:** 63 484 320, **Fax:** 63 443 181.

**Ljudska Univerza Dodatno Izobrazevanje**
Maistrova ul. 5, 2000 Maribor. **Tel:** 62 226 441, **Fax:** 225 017.

**Ljudska Univerza Koper**
Cankarjeva ul. 33, 6000 Koper. **Tel:** 64 271 258, **Fax:** 64 271 291.

**Ljudska Univerza Kranj**
Cesta Staneta Zagarja 1, 4000 Kranj. **Tel:** 64 222 226, **Fax:** 64 222 226.

**Ljudska Univerza Nova Gorica**
Cankarjeva ul 8, 5000 Nova Gorica. **Tel:** 65 22 302, **Fax:** 65 21 291.

**Ljudska Univerza Ptuj**
Mestni trg 2, 2250 Ptuj. **Tel:** 62 771 539, **Fax:** 62 779 849.

**Ljudska Univerza Ravne Na Koroskem**
Prezihova ul. 24, 2390 Ravne na Koroskem. **Tel:** 602 22 296.

**Ljudska Univerza Sezana**
Bazoviska c. 9, 6210 Sezana. **Tel:** 67 73 428, **Fax:** 67 32 046.

**Ljudska Univerza Skofja Loka**
Podlubnik 1b, 4220 Skofja Loka. **Tel:** 64 621 865.

**Most d.o.o.**
Kovinarska ul. 9, 8270 Krsko. **Tel:** 608 22 397, **Fax:** 608 22 397.

**Multilingua d.o.o.**
Ulica bratov Hvalic 16, 5000 Nova Gorica. **Tel:** 65 24 292, **Fax:** 65 24 292

**New College d.o.o.**
Med ogradami 11A, 5000 Nova Gorica. **Tel:** 65 23 733, **Fax:** 65 23 733.

**Niansa Jezikovna Sola**
Cesta talcev 4, 1230 Domzale. **Tel:** 61 712 012, **Fax:** 61 712 230.

**Nista Language School**
Smarska cesta 5d, 6000 Koper. **Tel:** 66 250 400, **Fax:** 66 258 440, **Email:** nista@siol.net

**Ontario d.o.o.**
Miklosiceva ul. 5, 2250 Ptuj. **Tel:** 62 779 108, **Fax:** 62 779 108.

**Poliglot d.o.o.**
Ljubljanska c. 110, 1230 Domzale. **Tel:** 61 723 089, **Fax:** 61 723 089.

**Pharmagan d.o.o.**
Straziska ul. 7, 4000 Kranj. **Tel:** 64 311 463, **Fax:** 64 311 463.

**Prevajanje s.p.**
Kalinskova ul. 31, 4000 Kranj. **Tel:** 64 340 010, **Fax:** 64 340 011.

**Progress Jezikovni Tecaji d.o.o.**
Seljakovo n. 33, 4000 Kranj, **Tel:** 64 310 644.

**Rossana d.o.o.**
Trzaska c. 30, 1370 Logatec. **Tel:** 61 743 104, **Fax:** 61 742 910.

**Samba d.n.o.**
Bresterniska ul. 225, 2351 Kamnica. **Tel:** 62 621 905.

**Selih Kozelj d.n.o.**
Studio za Ucenje, Miklosiceva 9, 3000 Celje. **Tel:** 63 24 236, **Fax:** 63 24 326.

**Sibon**
centre za Tuje Jezike, Ljubljanska c. 76 II, 1230
Domzale. **Tel**: 61 722 901, **Fax**: 61 722 928.

**Speak It**
Heintzman and Heintzman, Trubarjeva ul. 4, 1230
Domzale. **Tel**: 61 712 312, **Fax**: 61 712 312.

**Spektra Jameks d.o.o.**
Malgajeva 10, 3000 Celje. **Tel**: 63 443 192, **Fax**: 63
443 191.

**Sports Life Pevc d.o.o.**
Cesta talcev 6, 4220 Skofja Loka. **Tel**: 64 622 335,
**Fax**: 64 623 121.

**Studiom d.o.o.**
Radvanjska c. 74, 2106 Maribor. **Tel**: 62 35 481.

**Tecaj d.o.o.**
Kraigherjeva ul. 19A, 2230 Lenart v Slovenskih
Goricah. **Tel**: 62 723 224, **Fax**: 62 723 224.

**Tonson Posrednistvo in Storitve d.o.o.**
Velike Brusnice 13, 8321 Brusnice. **Tel**: 68 85 882,
**Fax**: 68 85 882.

**Unique d.o.o.**
Jezikovno izobrazevanje, Gabrsko 69, 1420 Trbovlje.
**Tel**: 601 27 442, **Fax**: 601 27 442.

**Vox Vidrih Trebnje k.d.**
Sola Tujih Jezikov, Simonciceva ul. 10, 8210 Trebnje.
**Tel**: 68 45 158, **Fax**: 68 45 158.

**Yurena d.o.o.**
Ulica Marjana Kozine 49A, 8000 Novo Mesto. **Tel**: 68
341 434, **Fax**: 68 341 434.

**Zavod za Izobrazevanje BAS**
Grajski trg 1, 2000 Maribor. **Tel**: 62 223 344, **Fax**: 62
223 344.

**Zavod za Izobrazevanje**
Kopitarjeva 5, 2000 Maribor. **Tel**: 62 214 273, **Fax**: 62
225 003.

## UKRAINE

There are two sides to the Ukraine: the western part is
mostly Catholic and looks to Poland while the east is
Orthodox. There is also the Crimea, a fascinating
region on the Black Sea heavily populated by Tatars.
There is a lot of interest in English language learning
in the Ukraine and many schools have opened in last
five years. The economic situation is still precarious
and outside of Kiev, you may find daily life difficult to
cope with, as food shortages still happen. It is probably
better to arrange a job before arriving here.

**British Council:**
4/12 Vul. Hryhoriya Skovorody, Kyiv 04070
**Tel** +380 (44) 490 5600
Www.britishcouncil.org/ukraine

➲ **Visas/Work Permits:** To obtain a visa, you need
an invitation to visit Ukraine either from a company or
an individual. Once you find a job, your employer
should take care of all the paperwork. Some teachers
work illegally but this is not advisable and it is very
hard to change your visa status from tourist to worker
while in the country.

➲ **Requirements:** College Degree and a
TESOL/TESL Certificate

➲ **Currency:** £1 = 9.8 / $1 = 5.33 Hyvrnia.

➲ **Salaries/Taxes:** Salaries range anywhere from
£300-600 a month, which is good by local standards.

➲ **Accommodation:** Housing is usually provided by
the school but you can find apartments from £100-200
pm in the suburbs and a lot more in the city centre.

➲ **Cost of Living:** Food and transport costs are very
reasonable.

➲ **Health advice:** Medical facilities are limited.
Insurance is essential.

➲ **English language media:** The Kiev Post, The
Odessa Post.

### Schools in the Ukraine (+380)

**American Academy of Foreign Languages**
89 Chervonoarmeyska, Office 9, 2520006 Kiev.
**Tel/Fax:** 44 268 5095.

**London School of English**
PO Box B 158, 2420001 Kiev. **Tel/Fax:** 44 2418654.
**Email: admin@lse.kiev.ua**

**Odessa English Language Study** centre
Pereulok Onilovoy 26/28, 270027 Odessa. **Tel/Fax:** 44
82 344 000.

**Ukrainian-American Humanitarian Institute**
9 Pyrogov St., 252030 Kiev. **Tel/Fax:** 44 216 0666.

**Union Forum**
10 Ternopiliska St., P.O. Box 10722, 290034 L'viv.
**Tel/Fax:** 322 759 488.

# Middle East & North Africa

O ver the past decade, many of the oil-rich Gulf States offered some the best employment packages for English language teachers anywhere in the world. However, with continuing tensions and war-zones, the Middle East it is often viewed as a dangerous region - some countries are certainly too dangerous to visit, but others are still as friendly and welcoming to travellers and teachers: Arab hospitality is legendary. Although the region was dominated by Great Britain in the earlier part of the 20th century, there is a growing preference for teachers with American and Canadian accents, particularly in the Gulf. Possible drawbacks include cultural differences, and, in certain countries, restrictions on the lifestyles of female teachers. But the region, birthplace to the three great monotheistic religions (Judaism, Christianity, and Islam), is as compelling as it is complex in terms of its history and its people. Teachers willing to overcome preconceptions will be rewarded by experiences that will open their eyes to the realities of a region rich in tradition and humanity. However, the current war zones and continuing tensions involving Iraq, Iran and some other neighboring countries means this is potentially a *very* dangerous region and you should check before travelling to any of the countries in this region. Visit www.fco.gov.uk for the UK-government's advice for travellers.

The overwhelming majority of teaching positions overseas are offered by private schools–including the American-sponsored international schools in Asia and Middle East. A graduate degree is a standard requirement for employment, including the UAE, Bahrain, Lebanon, Jordan, Syria, and others.

North Africa: Morocco and Tunisia are attractive prospects for English language teachers as both countries are shaking off their Francophone past by embracing English as a working language. Algeria and Libya are basically off limits to American teachers although oil companies in Libya do employ teachers. Recent reports suggest that Canadian teachers are welcome in Tripoli although only the truly intrepid should attempt to teach in Libya.

Two good sources of information on this region are: *TESOL Arabia* website - http://tesolarabia.uaeu.ac.ae and *AMIDEAST* - www.amideast.org

## BAHRAIN

A small island situated in the Arabian Gulf, Bahrain is quite liberal and women are welcome in the classroom. Employment should be arranged in advance and the only opportunities are for qualified teachers.

### Embassy in UK:
30 Belgrave Square, London SW1X 8QB
**Tel:** 020 7201 9170

### Embassy in USA:
3502 International Drive NW, Washington DC 20008
**Tel:** 202 342 0741
www.bahrainembassy.org

### British Council office:
AMA Centre (PO Box 452), 146 Shaikh Salman Highway, Manama 356
**Tel** +973 261 555
www.britishcouncil.org/bahrain

➲ **Visas/Work Permits:** Passports and visas are required. Three-day and seven-day visas may be obtained upon arrival at the airport in Manama, but obtaining visas before travel is recommended. Work permits are also required. Your employer should make arrangements to provide you with one soon after your arrival.

➲ **Requirements:** College Degree, experience and a TESOL/TESL Certificate

➲ **Currency:** £1 = 0.695 / $1 = 0.377 Dinar

➲ **Salaries/Taxes:** Monthly salaries range from BHD 600-750 for teachers with certificates and BHD 600-700 for those with diplomas. Part-time teachers earn around BHD 10 per hour. There is no personal income tax.

➲ **Accommodation:** A small apartment will cost BHD 200-500 per month. There is no deposit but three months' rent is required in advance.

➲ **Cost of Living:** More expensive than other Gulf States and salaries are often lower.

➲ **Health advice:** Essential: health insurance can be obtained locally at competitive rates. Vaccinations: Hepatitis A, Polio, Typhoid.

➲ **English Language Media:** Bahrain Tribune, Gulf Daily News.

➲ **Tip:** There has been some unrest from time to time in Bahrain. Although Americans have not to date been subject to attacks, it is wise to exercise caution at all times.

## Schools in Bahrain (+973)

**Al Maalem** centre
PO Box 20649, Manama. **Tel:** 553808. **Fax:** 554240.

**Al Rawasi Academy**
Mina Salman, Bahrain. **Tel:** 727442. **Fax:** 725442.

**Awal Training Institute**
PO Box 82110, Riffa. **Tel:** 773445. **Fax:** 771909.

**Bahrain Computer & Management Institute**
PO Box 26176, Manama. **Tel:** 293493.

**Bahrain Training Institute**
PO Box 323333, Essa Town. **Tel/Fax:** 683416.

**BCMI**
PO Box 26176, Manama. **Tel:** 293493. **Fax:** 290358.

**The British Council**
AMA Centre, (PO Box 452), Manama 356. **Tel:** 261555.

**The Cambridge School of English**
PO Box 20646, Manama. **Tel:** 532838.

**Capital Institute**
PO Box 22521, Manama. **Tel:** 740744/740088, **Fax:** 720060.

**Child Development**
PO Box 20284, Manama. **Tel:** 728000, **Fax:** 722636.

**Daar al Merifa**
PO Box 3174, Manama **Tel:** 722183, **Fax:** 722283.

**Delmon Academy**
PO Box 10362, Manama. **Tel:** 294400, **Fax:** 292010.

**Global Institute**
PO Box 11148, Manama. **Tel:** 740940, **Fax:** 720030.

**Gulf Academy**
PO Box 10333, Manama. **Tel:** 721700, **Fax:** 722636.

**Gulf School of Languages**
PO Box 20236, Manama. **Tel:** 290209, **Fax:** 290069.

**Pitman IPE**
PO Box 26222, Manama. **Tel:** 290028, **Fax:** 292006.

**Polyglot School**
PO Box 596, Manama. **Tel:** 271722, **Fax:** 722636.

**University of Bahrain**
PO Box 32038, Sakhir-Bahrain. **Fax:** 973 4496603.

## EGYPT

English language teaching in Egypt suffers from the usual catalogue of third-world woes such as overcrowded classrooms and inadequate resources. English is nevertheless well established as the primary foreign language, and most people want to learn it and work hard at doing so. There is great enthusiasm for improving programmes in the teaching of English by means of better teacher training and the development of better methods and materials for teachers to work with. More and more schools in Egypt are starting to go online although connections are not always reliable. Foreigners will have no problem in finding a teaching job in a private language school here, especially if they are prepared to work with young learners. Employers usually recruit teachers in the spring to begin work in September. Some teachers survive on a freelance basis through advertising and contacts.

### Embassy in UK:
26 South Street, London W1Y 6DD
**Tel:** 020 7499 2401

### Embassy in USA:
3521 International Drive NW, Washington DC20008
**Tel:** 202 895 5400

### British Council office:
192 El Nil Street, Agouza, Cairo
**Tel** +20 (2) 303 1514
www.britishcouncil.eg

⮑ **Tip:** When teaching in Egypt, it is a good idea to keep in mind that most people come from an oral culture and do not have a tradition of reading, even in their own language, let alone English.

⮑ **Visas/Work Permits:** American and Canadian citizens can obtain visitor's visas from the airport upon their arrival in Cairo. Go to one of the bank counters before the immigration windows and buy the visa stamps for your passport. They cost £10 ($19) and it is best to pay in U.S. dollars. These visas are good for one month. When they are close to expiration, you can easily get a six-month or one-year's extension. The schools obtain residency and work permits, which take around two months to process, while the teacher is working on a visitor's visa. A blood test is necessary.

⮑ **Requirements:** College Degree and a TESOL/TESL Certificate

⮑ **Currency:** £1 = 11.18 / $1 = 5.72 Pound

⮑ **Salaries/Taxes:** Most teachers earn around £5-10 per hour in a school, Rates for private lessons range from £10-20. Monthly salaries start around EGP 2,000 and go up to EGP 7,500 depending on your qualifications and experience, and the prestige of the school. Tax is 5-7%.

⮑ **Accommodation:** Do not expect Western standards of comfort and plumbing. Expect to pay around £300 a month for basic accommodations in Cairo and less elsewhere.

⮑ **Cost of Living:** Imported (American) items are expensive although locally made versions of most products (varying in quality) are available at a reasonable price. Fruit and vegetables are plentiful, inexpensive, and are fresh and delicious.

⮑ **Health advice:** Most foreign teachers are ill within a few weeks of arrival in Egypt although the majority of them recover. Hepatitis is a concern. Schistosomiasis, a parasitic infection, is found in fresh water in the region, including the Nile River. Do not swim in fresh water (except in well-chlorinated swimming pools.) Malaria is a risk limited to the El Faiyum area. Vaccinations: Hepatitis A, Polio, Typhoid, Malaria, Yellow Fever (if coming from an infected area).

⮑ **English Language Media:** Al Ahram Weekly, Cairo Today, Egyptian Gazette, Middle East Times.

⮑ **Information for Women:** You may find yourself the centre of attention as you walk down the street and the object of rude comments or occasional unwanted touching. Dress modestly and avoid public transportation (or, if taking the Cairo subway, ride the first car which is reserved for women.) Violent crime is rare.

## Schools in Egypt (+20)

### American Cultural centre
3 El Pharana Street, Alexandria. **Tel:** 3 483 1922

### The American University in Cairo
CACE, ESD P.O. Box 2511, Cairo. **Tel:** 2 357 6870.

### AMIDEAST
3 El Pharana Street, Alexandria. **Tel:** 3 483 1922.

### El Manar School
Amin Fikry Street, Ramleh Station, Cairo. **Tel:** 2 4823813.

### El Nasr Boys' College (EBC)
Chatby. **Tel:** 2 5976812.

### El Nasr Girls' College (ECC)
Chatby. **Tel:** 2 597 1752.

### El Pharaana School
El Pharaana Street, Bab Sharki. **Tel:** 2 4822229.

### Heliopolis
Cairo. **Tel:** 2 4155003, **Fax:** 2 2900552.

### IELP
6 Mostafa El Sherei Street, Dokki 12311, Cairo. **Tel:** 2 3365898, **Fax:** 2 3384780.

### International Language Institute
2, Mohamed Bayoumi St. Off Merghany St., Heliopolis, Cairo. **Tel:** 2 291 2218.

**International Language Learning Institute**
34 Talaat Harb Street, 5th Floor, Cairo. **Tel:** 2 748355.

**Kawmeya International School**
Horreya Avenue, Bab Sharki. **Tel:** 2 4938670.

**Lycee El Horreya**
English Dept., Chatby. **Tel:** 2 5976968.

**Port Said School**
7, Taha Hussein Street, Zamalek. **Tel:** 2 3403435.

**Ragab Language School**
Chatby. **Tel:** 2 5976968.

**Sacred Heart School**
Syria School, Roushdy. **Tel:** 2 840228.

**Sakkara Language School**
Block #3 Zahraa El-Maadi, Maadi, Cairo. **Tel:** 2 516-5205 **Fax:** 2 516-5204.

## ISRAEL & PALESTINIAN AUTHORITY

There is little demand for foreign teachers and it is difficult to find employment unless you are Jewish and are claiming your right of abode (which makes you liable for military service.) Be warned that an Israeli stamp in your passport may make travel to certain other countries in the Middle East impossible. You can ask for the stamps to be placed on removable pages. Except during periods of heightened security restrictions, most U.S. citizens may enter and exit Gaza and the West Bank on a U.S. passport with an Israeli entry stamp. It is not necessary to obtain a visitor's permit from the Palestinian Authority.

**British Council office:**
Crystal House, 12 Hahilazon St, Ramat Gan, 52136
**Tel** +972 (03) 611 3600
www.britishcouncil.org.il

➲  **Currency:** £1 = 8.18 / $1 = 4.18 New Shekels
➲  **Cost of Living:** Israel is an expensive country that has suffered frequent bouts of hyperinflation.
➲  **Salaries/Taxes:** £15-30 an hour in Israel. Taxation can go as high as 40%.
➲  **Accommodation:** Very expensive in Tel Aviv and Jerusalem, but less so in Gaza City where a comfortable apartment can be had for around £150 per month.
➲  **Health advice:** In Israel, take the same health precautions as you would at home. Note that national insurance is not available for non-Jews.

➲  **English Language Media:** Jerusalem Post, Palestine Report.

### Schools in Israel & Palestinian Authority (+972)

**AMIDEAST**
Ahmad Abd al-Aziz Street, behind Al-Karmel High School, PO Box 1247, Gaza City, Gaza. **Tel:** 7 2824635 **Fax:** 7-286-9338. **Email:** westbank-gaza@amideast.org

**AMIDEAST**
1 Anata Street, Shu'fat, PO Box 19665, Jerusalem. **Tel:** 2 5811962. **Fax:** 2 5328564. **Email:** westbank-gaza@amideast.org

**Anglican School**
P.O. Box 191, Jerusalem 91001. **Tel:** 2 38 5220.

**Arab American University**
P.O. Box 239/240, Jenin, West Bank. **Tel:** 6 43 6056.

**Ben Gurion University of the Negev**
342 Madison Avenue, Ste 1224, NY 10173, USA.

**British Council**
140 Hayarkon Street, (PO Box 3302), Tel Aviv 61032. **Tel:** 3 5222194.

**Walworth Barbour American International School**
P.O. Box 9005, Kfar Shmaryahu, Tel Aviv. **Tel:** 9 584 255

## JORDAN

Jordan is a fascinating country but teaching opportunities are limited. Many schools employ Jordanians who have qualified to teach EFL/ESL. The American Language Center employs qualified teachers on a part-time basis.

**Embassy in UK:**
6 Upper Phillimore Gardens, London W8 7HB
**Tel:** 020 7937 3685
www.jordanembassyuk.org

**Embassy in USA:**
3504 International Drive NW, Washington DC20008
**Tel:** 202 966 2664
www.jordanembassyus.org

**British Council office:**
Rainbow Street – off first circle, PO Box 634, Amman 11118
**Tel** +962 (6) 4636147
www.britishcouncil.org/jordan

⮑ **Visas/Work Permits:** Employers of teachers on full-time contracts will arrange for the necessary papers. Part-time teachers must pay around £500 a year for a permit.

⮑ **Requirements:** College Degree, experience and a TESOL/TESL Certificate

⮑ **Currency:** £1 = 1.29 / $1 = 0.70 Dinar

⮑ **Salaries/Taxes:** Salaries are generally lower than those in the Gulf States.

⮑ **Health advice:** Although Jordan is malaria-free, take sensible precautions with drinking water and food. Vaccinations: Hepatitis A, Typhoid, Polio, Yellow Fever (if coming from an infected area).

⮑ **English Language Media:** BYTE Middle East, Issues, Jordan Times The Star.

⮑ **Cost of Living:** Prices of imported goods are high but food and travel costs are reasonable.

⮑ **Salaries and taxes:** A full-time teacher at a private language school can expect to earn around £6,000 a year.

⮑ **Accommodation:** Expensive. Some landlords ask for a year's rent in advance which can amount to as much as £4,500.

⮑ **Tip:** Bars are few and far between in Amman. Expect to pay at least £4 for a beer in a high-class hotel.

## Schools in Jordan (+962)

### Al-Manhal International School
Iskan Al-Jami'a, P.O. Box 278, Jubaiha, Amman 11941. **Tel:** 6 60 3751.

### American Community School
Box 310, Dahiat Al-Amir Rashid, Amman, 11831.**Tel:** 6 5813944, **Fax:** 6 5823357. **Email:** school@acsamman.edu.jo

### American Language Center
Amman. **Tel:** 6 5859102/3, **Fax:** 6 5859101. **Email:** info@alc.edu.jo

### Amman Baccalaureate School
PO Box 441, Sweileh, Amman, 11910. **Tel:** 6 5411572, **Fax:** 541 2603. **Email:** abs@go.com.jo

### Modern American School
P.O. Box: 851819, Amman 11185. **Tel:** 6 5816861. **Fax:** 6 5816860. **Email:** **admin@ModernAmericanSchool.com**

### Yarmouk Cultural centre
PO Box 960312, Amman. **Tel:** 6 671447.

### Yarmouk University Language Center
P.O. Box 566, Irbid. **Tel:** 2 84 2700.

## KUWAIT

Kuwait was rapidly rebuilt after the Gulf War although there are not as many English language schools these days. Some teachers say that Kuwait is a good place to earn and save money because there is not that much on offer as far as nightlife is concerned.

Others claim that Kuwait is a "party town" because it's so easy to make friends with the locals and other nationalities working in the country! There are both public and private English language schools but you will need to be qualified if you want to teach English here. Opportunities do exist to find teaching jobs after your arrival in Kuwait. Check out local newspapers when you arrive.

**Embassy in UK:**
2 Albert Gate, London SW1X 7JU
**Tel:** 020 7 590 3400

**Embassy in USA:**
2940 Tilden Street NW, Washington DC 20008
**Tel:** 202 966 0702

**British Council office:**
2 Al Arabi Street, Block 2, PO Box 345, 13004 Safat
Mansouriya, Kuwait City
**Tel** +965 252 0067
www.britishcouncil.org/kuwait

⮑ **Visas/Work Permits:** Entry visas are required for all visitors. Work permits are difficult to obtain and involve testing for AIDS and tuberculosis. You can find private lessons although you are supposed to have a work permit before you start teaching.

⮑ **Requirements:** College Degree and a TESOL/TESL Certificate

⮑ **Currency:** £1 = 0.53 / $1 = 0.29 Dinar

⮑ **Salaries/Taxes:** Annual salaries start at around £20,000, which usually involves a full-time post with about 24 contact hours per week. There is no income tax.

⮑ **Accommodation:** Most schools find and pay for accommodation because it is expensive. Average rent is £400-600. Usually, one month's rent is required as a deposit.

⮑ **Health advice:** Unexploded bombs, mines, booby traps, and other items remain in open areas and beaches throughout Kuwait. Vaccinations: Hepatitis A, Polio, Typhoid.

➲ **English Language Media:** Kuwait Times.

➲ **Other Information:** Only limited public transport exists and taxis are very expensive. Women are permitted to drive.

## Schools in Kuwait (+965)

### Al-Bayan Bilingual School
PO Box 24472, Safat. **Tel:** 5315125, **Fax:** 5332836
**Email:** bbs@ncc.moc.kw

### American International School
Block 11, Uhud Street, Salmiya. **Tel:** 5645083/7, **Fax:** 5645089.

### American School of Kuwait
Block 7, Al-Muthanna Street and 4th Ring Road, Hawalli. **Tel:** 2664341/2655172, **Fax:** 2650438.
**Email: askkwt@kuwait.net**

### College of Business Studies
P.O. Box 43197, Hawalli, 32046. **Tel:** 261 4962

### ELS School of Languages
PO Box 5104, Salmiya 20062. **Tel:** 5722522/2558, 5710610. **Fax:** 5733005.

### ELU
The Kuwait Institute of Banking Studies, PO Box 1080, Safat 13011.

### Fahaheel English School
PO Box 7209, Fahaheel 64003. **Tel:** 3711070, **Fax:** 965 371 5458.

### Institute For Private Education
P.O. Box 6320, 32038 Hawalli. **Tel:** 573 7811, **Fax:** 574 2924.

### Language centre
Kuwait University, PO Box 2575, Safat. **Tel:** 481 0325, **Fax:** 484 3824.

## LEBANON

The UK and US governments continue to list Lebanon as a country you should not visit due to the rising tensions (which include kidnappings, violence and attacks). You should read the latest reports on www.fco.gov.uk for details of the current situation and whether it is safe to visit or travel to this otherwise beautiful country. In previous, safer times, English language teachers were in great demand and schools were advertising in the U.S. and Canada for qualified staff. Canadian citizens interested in volunteer work teaching English to Palestinian refugees in Lebanon should contact CEPAL by email at info@cepal.ca or call (613) 238-0410.

**Embassy in UK:**
21 Kensington Palace Gardens, London W8 4QM
**Tel:** 020 7727 6696

**Embassy in USA:**
2560 28th Street NW, Washington DC 20008
**Tel:** 202 939 6300

**British Council office:**
Sidani Street, Azar Building, Beirut
**Tel** +961 (1) 739 459
www.britishcouncil.org/lebanon

➲ **Currency:** £1 = 2776 / $1 = 1501 Pounds

➲ **Health advice:** Most hospitals in Beirut have modern facilities.

➲ **English Language Media:** Beirut Times, Lebanon Daily Star, Monday Morning.

## Schools in Lebanon (+961)

### American University of Beirut
Division of Education Programmes, 850 Third Avenue, 18th Floor New York, NY 10022-6297.

### AMIDEAST
P.O. Box 70-744, Antelias. **Tel:** 4 410438/19341/2/3. **Fax:** 4 419341. **Email:** lebanon@amideast.org

### AMIDEAST
Ras Beirut centre Building, 4th Floor, Surati Street, Hamra Area, Beirut. **Tel:** 1 345341, 340137. **Email:** lebanon@amideast.org

### Beirut International School
Bchamoun, Beirut. **Tel:** 3 215489. **Email:** bis@bis.edu.lb

### Beirut Modern School
Bir Hassan area between Golf Club & Airport Highway, Beirut. **Tel:** 1 823616. **Email:** bms95@cyberia.net.lb

### British Council
Sadat/Sidani Street, Azar Building, Beirut. **Tel:** 1 740123/4/5. **Fax:** 1 739461

### International College
P.O. Box 11-0236, Beirut. **Tel:** 1 867252. **Fax:** 1 362500/1

### Lebanese American University
Beirut Campus, P.O. Box 13-5053, Beirut. **Tel:** 1 786456/786464. **Fax:** 1 867098.

**Lebanese American University**
Byblos Campus, P.O. Box 36, Byblos. **Tel:** 9
547254/547262 **Fax**: 9 944851.

**Lebanese American University**
Sidon Campus, P.O. Box 267, Sidon. **Tel:** 7 728724,
728725 **Fax**: 7 728726.

## MALTA

A culturally diverse island in the Mediterranean, with a
beautiful climate. English is one of the official
languages

**High Commission in UK:**
Malta House, 36-38 Piccadilly, London W1V 0PQ
**Tel:** 020 7292 4800

**Embassy in USA:**
2017, Connecticut Avenue NW , Washington DC
20008
**Tel:** (202) 462 3611

**British Council office:**
Whitehall Mansions, Ta'Xbiex Seafront, Malta
**Tel** +356 23 23 2403
www.britishcouncil.org/malta

➲ **Visas/Work Permits:** no visas required for
tourists or for stays of less than 3 months
➲ **Requirements:** College Degree and a
TESOL/TESL Certificate
➲ Visas
➲ **Currency:** £1 = 0.61 / $1 = 0.33 liri
➲ **Health advice:** Medical care is good, and
available in either public or private hospitals. It is
advisable to get insurance before travelling
➲ **English language media:** Malta Independent,
Malta Star, Malta Today, Sunday Circle, Malta
Financial and Business Times

### Schools in Malta (+356)

**Academy Magister**
L-Arkati Menaija Street, St Julian's

**Alpha School of English**
Arznell Street, St Paul's Bay, SPB 03

**AM Language Studio**
299 Manuel Dimech Street, Sliema, SLM

**Bell Language Centre**
Elija Zammit Street, St Julian's STJ 02

**Bell Valletta**
10 Sur Santa Barabara, Valletta, Vlt 06
**Tel:** 21 25 25 30 **Fax:** 21 25 25 29

**BELS**
Triq Ta'Doti, Kercem, Gozo, VCT 113

**Berlitz Language Centre**
Draonara Street, St Julian's

**Britannia College**
124, Melita Street, Valletta

**Burlington English Language School**
Burlington Court, Dragonara Street, St Julian's, STJ 06

**Club Class Language School**
1 Chealsea Court, Triq L-Imghazel, Swieqi, St
Andrews

**Easy School of Languages**
331, St. Paul's Street, Valletta VLT 01

**EC Malta**
Language House, New Street off Sant Andrija Street,
St Julian's, STJ 02

**Education English Culture**
Villa Monaco, Sliema Road, Kappara, SGN 06

**EF International Language School**
Lower St. Augustine Street, St Julian's

**Ef Language Travel**
San Michel, St George'S Road, St Julians Stj 10

**Elanguest**
Keating House, Ross Street, Sliema, STJ 10

**English Communication School**
10 St Pius Street, Sliema SLM 06

**English Language Academy**
9 Tower Lane, Sliema, SLM 15

**European Centre of English**
Paolo Court, G.Cali Street, Ta'Xbiex, MSD 14

**European School of English**
Edgar Bernard Street, Gzira, GZR 06

**Gateway International School of English**
1, Triq il-Jonju, The Village, San Gwann

**GEOS Malta**
Level 5, The Plaza, Bisazza Str Commercial Centre,
Sliema, SLM 15

**In House Malta**
"Ogygia Foresteria", San Dimitri Street, Birbuba, l/o
Gharb, Gozo

**inLingua School**
9 Guze Fava Street, Tower Road, Sliema, SLM 15

**Institute of English Language**
Parisio Street, Gzira, GZR 04

**International House Malta**
11 Birbuba St, Gharb 4020
**Tel**: 21 5504 90 **Fax**: 21 55004 90
**Email: academyblc@mail.com**

**Kalypso Academy of English**
University of Malta, Mgarr Road, Xewkija

**La Salle Institute**
105 St Thomas Street, Floriana, VLT 14

**Lingua Time**
243E Tower Road, Sliema, SLM 05

**Link School of English**
Villa Petite Fleur, 88/90 Triq it-Tiben, Swieqi

**Mediterranean English Language Academy**
Mountbatten Street, Blata l-Bajda, Hamrun

**Melita Language School**
CAK s-Sommier Street, B'Kara

**MSD School of English**
Josmar Triq il - Paguni, Balzan

**MUT - Capital Language School**
213 Republic Street, Valletta VLT 03

**Nsts English Language Institute**
220 St Paul Street, Valletta Vlt 07

**Skylark Mediterranean School of English**
29 Victor Denaro Street, Msida MSD 04

**Sprachcaffe Languages**
Srachcaffe Club Village, Pembroke, STJ 14

**Students Travel School**
c/o Mimosa Valetta Road, Attard

**The Academy of English and Culture**
13, Mattew Pulis Street, Sliema

**The British Council**
Whitehall Mansions, Ta'Xbiex Seafront

**The Chamber College**
Edgar Bernard Street, Gzira

**The Leonardo Da Vinci Global Village**
Villa Rosa, St George's Bay

**Think English Language School**
100, Paola Square, Paola

**Unilang International School of Languages**
Workers Memorial Building, South Street, Valletta
VLT 11

**Universal Language Services**
Upper Ross Street, St Julian's

**Voice School of English**
PO Box 60, Msida, MSD 01

**World Wide Languages Academy**
128, Triq is-Sirk, Swieqi

## MOROCCO

Morocco has been a magnet for travellers for centuries. Everyone from Winston Churchill to William Burroughs has ended up spending some time in this intriguing country. Moroccans are tolerant people: teachers with qualifications are welcome although conditions do vary from school to school. American Language Centers (www.aca.org.ma) operates English language schools in most major Moroccan cities. Knowledge of French is helpful but not essential. Note that institutions must ensure that at least 50% of the teachers are Moroccan.

**Embassy in UK:**
49 Queen's Gate Gardens, London SW7 5NE
**Tel:** 020 7581 5001

**Embassy in USA:**
1601 21st Street NW, Washington DC 20009
**Tel:** 202 462 7979

**British Council office:**
36 Rue de Tanger, BP 427, Rabat
**Tel** +212 (37) 760 836
www.britishcouncil.org.morocco

➲ **Visas/Work Permits:** Paper-work will be taken care of by the school after you have agreed on a contract. Be patient: It can take up to three months for your papers to come through. You will need original copies of your birth certificate, degree and teaching qualification.

➲ **Requirements:** College Degree and a TESOL/TESL Certificate

➲ **Currency:** £1 = 15.70 / $1 = 8.49 Dirham

➲ **Cost of Living:** Prices are reasonable in Morocco although a meal at a sophisticated restaurant will be expensive.

➲ **Salaries/Taxes:** 8,0000-9,000 dirhams a month is an average salary. Getting paid in dollars will help compensate for the effects of inflation.

➲ **Accommodation:** 3,000 dirhams for pleasant 2-bedroom apartment in Casablanca. Rabat is cheaper.

➲ **Health advice:** There is a small risk of malaria in Morocco. Take adequate precautions. Vaccinations: Hepatitis A, Polio, Typhoid.

➲ **English Language Media:** Morocco Times.

## Schools in Morocco (+212)

**American Language Center**
Rue des Nations-Unies, Cité Suisse, Agadir. **Tel**: 8 821589. **Fax**: 8 848272. **Email: alcagad@marocnet**

**American Language Center**
2, Boulevard Mohamed V, Mohammedia. **Tel/Fax:** 3 326870.

**American Language Center**
4 Zankat Tanja, Rabat 10000. **Tel**: 7 761269

**American Language Center**
2, Rue Ahmed Hiba, BP 2136, Fes. **Tel**: 5 624850. **Fax**: 5 931608.

**American Language Center**
1, Place de la Fraternité, 20000 Casablanca. **Tel**: 2 277765. **Fax**: 2 207457.

**American Language Center**
3 Impasse du Moulin de Gueliz, Marrakesh. **Tel**: 4 447259.

**American Language Center**
1 rue M'sallah, Tangier. **Tel**: 9 933616.

**American Language Center**
2 Blvd. El Kadissa, Kenitra. **Tel**: 7 366884.

**American Language Center**
4bis, rue de Menton, BP 382, Meknes. **Tel**: 5 523636. **Fax**: 7 516464.

**American Language** centre
1, rue Maarakate Zalaka, Tetuan. **Tel**: 9 963308.

**Benedict School of English**
124 Ave. Hassan II, Ben Slimane. **Tel**: 3 290957. **Fax**: 3 328472.

**British Centre**
3, rue Brahim el Amraoui, Casablanca. **Tel**: 2 267019. **Fax**: 2 267043.

**British Council**
36 rue de Tanger, B.P. 427, Rabat. **Tel**: 7 76 0836, **Fax**: 7 760850.

**Business & Professional English Centre (BPEC)**
74 rue Jean Jaurès, Casablanca. **Tel**: 2 22.47.02.79. **Fax**: 2 22.29.68.61.

**EF**
20 rue du Marché, Casablanca. 2 255174. **Fax**: 2 296861.

**Institut Cegis**
23 Boulevard Ibnou Majid Al Bahhar, Casablanca. **Tel**: 2 308410.

**International Language Centre**
2 rue Tihama, Rabat. **Tel**: 7 709718.

**London School of English**
10 Ave. des FAR, Casablanca. **Tel**: 26 89 32.

# OMAN

Oman is one of the most relaxed of the Gulf States. Alcohol is freely available and single women have an easier time here than in other Islamic countries. There are many archaeological sites to visit and the country is beautiful.

Demand is high throughout the Sultanate amongst private language institutes and higher educational establishments. Teachers should go through the Yellow Pages, approach schools directly or look at the local newspapers where jobs are occasionally advertised. Teachers with Master's degrees in TESL/TEFL are in demand. CELTA-qualified teachers can usually find hourly paid work. Opportunities for work at the more reputable end of the market for inexperienced teachers are limited. The best time to search for jobs is the early summer through to September when summer schools are always on the lookout for more teachers. The government does restrict the number of permits granted to tourists so you may have to wait until the right opportunity to teach in Oman presents itself.

**Embassy in UK:**
167 Queen's Gate, London SW7 5HE
**Tel**: 020 7225 0001

**Embassy in USA:**
2535 Belmont Road NW, Washington DC 20008
**Tel**: 202 387 1980

**British Council office:**
Road One, Madinat al Sultan, Qaboos West, Muscat
P.O. Box 73 Postal Code 115
**Tel** +968 600 548
www.britishcouncil.org/oman

➲ **Visas/Work Permits:** Your employer must sponsor you (a no-objection certificate) and the paperwork is extensive. On arrival in Oman, your employer may ask you for your passport. Although this is customary, you are not legally obliged to hand it over. Surrendering your passport could seriously affect your ability to leave the country whenever you want.
➲ **Requirements:** College Degree and a TESOL/TESL Certificate
➲ **Currency:** £1 = 0.75 / $1 = 0.348 Rial
➲ **Salaries/Taxes:** Rates of pay vary according to nationality and qualifications. You can earn about RO

3-10 per hour in institutes. Monthly: Anything from RO 500-850 at the top end. There is no tax.

⮞ **Cost of Living:** The cost is living is higher than that elsewhere in the Gulf, including the UAE. Food and clothing is often imported and taxed at 17%. Supermarket costs are fairly comparable with the west overall, although imported Western luxury foods are very pricey. Petrol is cheap and you can also purchase cars at very competitive prices.

⮞ **Accommodation:** In most cases, the school will arrange this for you. If you are going to work at a teacher training college you will be expected to find your own lodging. It's not difficult to find an apartment. Many teachers use an agent. Apartments cost RO 150-275 a month and utilities are RO 25-45.

⮞ **Health advice:** Local medical treatment varies in quality, and it can be inadequate. While hospital emergency treatment is available, there is no ambulance service in Oman. Malaria is a concern in the interior and on the Batinah Coast. Doctors and hospitals often expect immediate cash payment for health services. Vaccinations: Yellow Fever (if coming from an infected area), Malaria.

⮞ **English Language Media:** Oman Daily Observer, Times of Oman.

⮞ **Tip:** Try to buy a car. You will miss much of the country if you have to rely on public transport. Visitors in possession of an international or American driver's licence may drive rental vehicles, but residents must have an Omani driver's licence. Visitors hiring rental cars are urged to ensure that the vehicle they are renting is adequately insured against loss or damage.

⮞ **Other Information:** As is the case in many countries, labour laws are strictly enforced in Oman. You may be contractually obliged to work for six months or more before you qualify for a holiday. Also, don't be surprised to find that you cannot work for another employer once your original contract has expired.

## Schools in Oman (+968)

**American-British Academy**
PO Box 372, Medinat Al Sultan Qaboos, Muscat. **Tel:** 605287/603 646. **Fax:** 603544. **Email:** abaad@gto.net.om

**American International School**
PO Box 202, Muscat 115. **Tel:** 600374. **Fax:** 697916.

**British Council**
PO Box 73, Medinat Al Sultan Qaboos, Muscat 115. **Tel:** 600548. **Fax:** 698018.

**Polyglot Institute**
PO Box 221, Ruwi. **Tel:** 701261, **Fax:** 794602.

**Sultan Qaboos University**
PO Box 50, Muscat 123. **Tel:** 513333. **Fax:** 514 455.

# QATAR

Qatar is a little-known Gulf emirate. It enjoys a high standard of living and is very modern. Most schools are very well-equipped boasting the latest in teaching gadgetry. Recruitment usually starts in February, interviews take place in the spring, and teachers arrive in August to start work in September. The weather can be surprisingly cold in the winter so remember to pack a couple of sweaters.

**British Council office:**
93 Al Sadd Street, PO Box 2992, Doha
**Tel** +974 442 6193 / 4
www.britishcouncil.org/qatar

⮞ **Requirements:** College Degree and a TESOL/TESL Certificate

⮞ **Currency:** £1 = 7.12 / $1 = 3.64 Riyal

⮞ **Health advice:** Basic modern medical care and medicines are available in the government-run Hamad General Hospital in Qatar. Serious medical problems could cost you thousands of dollars. Check with your insurer to see if you are covered in Qatar.

⮞ **English Language Media:** Gulf Times.

⮞ **Tip:** The British Council has a very good lending library.

⮞ **Information for Women:** Qatar is very safe and you will not be hassled by guys as is the case in certain other Middle Eastern countries. Bare arms and legs in public do not cause a negative reaction but draw the line at walking down the street in a bikini. Women driving alone are sometimes tailed by male drivers.

## Schools in Qatar (974)

**Arizona English Language School**
PO Box 7949, Doha.

**ELS Language centres**
P.O. Box 22678, 56 Jaber bin Ghaith, Doha.**Tel:** 699223. **Fax:** 685519. **Email:** elsdoha@qatar.net.qa

**English Modern School**
Al Naijah, 44 Najma Street, 44 Hamad bin Zaidoun St.

**Qatar International School**
P.O. Box 5697, Doha. **Tel:** 469 0552 , **Fax:** 469 0557. **Email:** info@qis.org

## SAUDI ARABIA

Saudi Arabia is one of the few countries where ESL/EFL teachers can expect to be rewarded with a good salary. Rates of pay may not be rising as fast as they did ten years ago but if you want to make good money in an English language teaching job, KSA (Kingdom of Saudi Arabia) is the place to be – teachers can earn upwards of £30,000 a year. And that's tax-free.

Try to get a job in one of the big cities (Jeddah or Riyadh, for example.) Life can get a little lonely in a one-camel town although the lack of any social life might do wonders for your bank balance. Ex-pat life in the big cities can be a lot of fun if you're prepared to get involved. So, the bottom line is simple: If you're not sure you can handle new experiences (good and bad) then don't go. Most teaching contracts are for one year so take some time to check out prospective employers and find out as much as you can about them and the job you will be doing. The majority of horror stories coming from teachers in KSA come from those unfortunate enough to have worked for "cowboy" operations.

**Embassy in UK:**
30 Charles Street, London W1X 7PM
**Tel:** 020 7917 3000
www.saudiembassy.org.uk

**Embassy in USA:**
601 New Hampshire Ave NW, Washington DC 20037
**Tel:** 202 337 4076
www.saudiembassy.net

**British Council office:**
Tower B, 2nd floor, Al Mousa Centre, Olaya Street
P.O. Box 58012, Riyadh 11594
**Tel** +966 (1) 462 1818
www.britishcouncil.org/saudiarabia

⊃ **Visas/Work Permits:** You must be sponsored by an employer to work in Saudi Arabia. You cannot travel to Saudi Arabia as a tourist unless you travel as part of a government-approved group. Visitors to Saudi Arabia generally obtain a meningitis vaccination prior to arrival. A medical report or physical examination is required to obtain work and residence permits. The sponsor (normally the employer) obtains work and residence permits for the employee. Residents working in Saudi Arabia generally must surrender their passports while in the Kingdom and carry a Saudi residence permit ("iqama") for identification in place of their passports.

⊃ **Requirements:** College Degree and a TESOL/TESL Certificate
⊃ **Currency:** £1 = 6.93 / $1 = 3.75 Riyal (SAR)
⊃ **Salaries/Taxes:** Starting c. £25,000 (it can be less in the smaller towns) going up to £30,000 and more. No tax. If you are offered a salary less than £15k you should think twice.
⊃ **Accommodation:** Your employer should provide accommodation and it's kismet whether you land up in a resort with pools and tennis court or sharing a trailer with four fellow teachers. If you strike out on your own, unfurnished apartments in Jeddah start around 12,000 SAR per year. Sizes range from one big room with a separate bath, up to a three-bedroom apartment, depending on where you go. The cheapest compound starts around 30,000 SAR per year and offers security.
⊃ **Cost of Living:** Salaries are so high and things are so cheap you can come back with a new car and lots of other goodies. Residents in Saudi Arabia may not leave the country without obtaining an exit permit prior to leaving and an exit/reentry permit if they intend to return to Saudi Arabia. The Saudi sponsor's approval is required for exit permits. Note that it is illegal for a Saudi employer to sell the approval (known as a Certificate of No Objection) to an employee.
⊃ **Health advice:** Malaria is endemic to the low-lying coastal plains of southwest Saudi Arabia, primarily in the Jizan region extending up the coast to the rural area surrounding Jeddah. Take precautions to avoid being bitten by mosquitoes if you're going to be in this area.. There are reports of cases of Rift Valley fever in southwestern Saudi Arabia (near the town of Jizan.) The virus is transmitted primarily by infected mosquitoes and by direct contact with the blood or body fluids of infected animals. Prevention of Rift Valley fever should focus on personal protective measures to limit contact with infected mosquitoes. The best prevention is appropriate use of an insect repellent containing DEET (N,N -diethylmetatoluamide) and wearing long sleeves and trousers. Vaccinations: Hepatitis A, Polio, Typhoid, Malaria, Meningitis, Yellow Fever (if coming from an infected area).
⊃ **Other Information:** Alcohol, women driving, men and women intermingling – are prohibited. Experienced Saudi hands have found ways to get around these restrictions but you risk punishment (even a public beating) if you are caught doing something illegal. Married couples usually stay longer in Saudi than straight singles. There is a large and active gay teaching community in KSA.

⮕ **English Language Media:** Arab News, Saudi Gazette, Riyadh Daily.

## Schools in Saudi Arabia

**The British Council**
Al Moajil Building, 5th Floor, Dhahran Street, Mohamed Street, PO Box 8387, Daman. **Tel:** 834 3484.

**Girls' College of Arts**
General Presidency for Female Institute for Languages and Translation, c/o King Saud University, PO Box 2465, Riyadh 11451.

**King Abdulaziz University**
Jeddah. **Tel:** 966 2 695 2468, **Fax:** 966 2 695 2471.

**King Fahd University of Petroleum and Minerals**
English Language centre, Dhahran 31261. **Tel:** 3 860 2393, **Fax:** 3 860 2340.

**Riyadh Military Hospital-Training Division**
PO Box 7897, Riyadh 11159. Saudi Airlines, PO Box 167, Jeddah 21231.

**Saudi Language Institute**
PO Box 6760, Riyadh 11575.

**SCECO - East Central Training Institute**
PO Box 5190, Damman 31422.

**Yanbu Industrial College**
PO Box 30436, Yanbu Al Sinaiyah 21477.

## SYRIAN ARAB REPUBLIC

Syrian civilization is ancient: Damascus is the oldest continually occupied city in the world and there is much to explore in this friendly country. As Syria shakes off years of Russian influence, English language teachers are in great demand but the opportunities are restricted to those who are qualified. Teachers cannot expect to be hired from abroad. Teachers must come to Syria then look into teaching options. AMIDEAST offers teaching jobs but cannot provide long-term residency. The American Language Center (ALC) does too, and offers residency. Even if regular jobs are not available it is easy to find work tutoring.

**Embassy in UK:**
8 Belgrave Square, London SW1X 8PH
**Tel:** 020 7245 9012

**Embassy in USA:**
2215 Wyoming Ave NW, Washington DC 20008

**Tel:** 202 238 6313
**British Council office:**
Maysaloun Street, Shalaan, P O Box 33105, Damascus
**Tel** +963 (11) 331 0631
www.britishcouncil.org/syria

⮕ **Visas/Work Permits:** You will need an entrance visa, which can be obtained from the Syrian embassy in your country. If you decide to stay 15 days or more you must register with Syrian Immigration by your 15th day in Syria. You can then extend the permit for two-week periods every two weeks. This is not a difficult process but you will need to take an AIDS test at a government-approved facility. If a teacher obtains regular work, he or she may obtain residency for up to one year. Be aware that you cannot enter Syria with an Israeli stamp in your passport.

⮕ **Requirements:** College Degree and a TESOL/TESL Certificate

⮕ **Currency:** £1 = 96 / $1 = 52 Pound

⮕ **Cost of Living:** Food is very cheap and the quality is excellent. Small restaurants offer great "shawarma" (meat, vegetables and yogurt wrapped in pita bread) and the seafood is top-notch too. Most teachers find it is cheaper to eat out than to cook.

⮕ **Salaries/Taxes:** ALC and AMIDEAST pay around £6 an hour; Syrian-owned schools pay less. Native speakers may tutor and receive upwards of £6 an hour. Foreign teachers do not have to pay taxes.

⮕ **Accommodation:** A basic apartment in Damascus costs around £120 a month.

⮕ **Health advice:** Basic medical care and medicines are available in the principal cities of Syria, but not necessarily in outlying areas.

⮕ **English Language Media:** Syria Times.

## Schools in Syria (+963)

**Al Kindi English Language Centre**
29 May Street, Damascus.

**Al Kudssi Institute**
PO Box 5296, Aleppo.

**Al Razi English Language Centre**
PO Box 2533, Damascus. **Tel:** 11 457301.

**Alson**
Damascus. **Tel:** 11 2227236.

**American Language Center**
PO Box 29, Rawda Circle, Damascus. **Tel:** 11 3327236. **Fax:** 11 3319327.

**AMIDEAST**
Wahab Bin Saad Street, Abou Roummaneh, Damascus. **Tel:** 11 3332804/3314420. **Fax:** 11-333-2804. **Email:** Syria@amideast.org

**Damascus Language Center**
PO Box 249, Damascus.

## TUNISIA

English is replacing French as the language of business in Tunisia so there is a growing demand for EFL teachers. Teachers often find they are the first native speaker their students have ever encountered. It is best to apply to schools in Tunisia before leaving home; a little knowledge of French will help you settle in.

**Embassy in UK:**
29 Prince's Gate, London SW7 1QG
**Tel:** 020 7584 8117

**Embassy in USA:**
1515 Massachusetts Ave NW, Washington DC20005
**Tel:** 202 862 1850

**British Council office:**
5 Place de la Victoire, BP 229, Tunis 1015 RP
**Tel** +216 71 259 053
www.britishcouncil.org/tunisia

➲ **Visas/Work Permits:** You should receive a temporary work permit or a letter from your employer allowing you to work until your permit is processed. Photocopies of your degree and birth certificates will not be accepted.

➲ **Requirements:** College Degree and a TESOL/TESL Certificate

➲ **Currency:** £1 = 2.54 / $1 = 1.30 Dinar

➲ **Cost of Living:** Tunisia is a cheap country to live in unless you insist on buying imported products.

➲ **Salaries/Taxes:** Private lessons earn teachers around 15 dinars an hour. At the top end, you can expect to earn a minimum of 13,000 dinars per year. The tax rate is around 20 percent.

➲ **Accommodation:** It's easy to find somewhere to live. Expect to pay 3-400 Tunisian dinars per month, with at least one month's rent as a deposit. Accommodation is largely unfurnished.

➲ **Health advice:** Essential vaccinations: Hepatitis A, Polio, Typhoid, Yellow Fever (if coming from an infected area).

➲ **English Language Media:** Tunisia News.

➲ **Tip:** Life is pretty free and easy for an Islamic country but there's not much in the way of nightlife unless you head out to tourist areas like the island of Jerba.

### Schools in Tunisia (+216)

**AMIDEAST**
22 rue Al Amine Al Abassi, Cité Jardins, 1002 Tunis. **Tel:** 1 790559, 790563. **Fax:** 1 791913.

**English Language Training Centre**
British Council, 47 Avenue Habib Bourguiba, Tunis.

**Institut Bourguiba des Languages Vivantes (IBLV)**
47 Avenue de la Liberté, Tunis. **Tel:** 1 282418. **Fax:** 1 780389.

## TURKEY

Turkey is a unique country straddling both Europe and Asia. Although its people are Muslims, there is a secular constitution. The Turkish language is written in the Latin alphabet (like English) not in the flowing Arabic script.

Turkey represents a big market for English language teachers. Government officials estimate that there is a need for 30,000 more English language teachers in the nation's public schools. English is taught from fourth grade in the public schools. In private schools, children start learning English in kindergarten. Needs for EFL teachers extend through middle and high schools to colleges and universities.

Native English speakers are in huge demand and there are plenty of opportunities for unqualified teachers who want to work in Turkey, although their salaries will not be as high as those of qualified teachers. University programmes prefer to recruit teachers with MAs in TESOL/TEFL.

Opinions about teaching English in Turkey are mixed: some teachers love it while others hate it. A lot depends on your attitude: If you expect things to be done the same way as at home then you probably won't want to come here. But that's a shame because you'll be missing out on the opportunity to live in an amazing country, which has been at the crossroads of civilizations for centuries.

Caution: be aware before you travel to Turkey that many English language teachers leave their jobs here disillusioned by working conditions and the attitudes of their employers. Unfortunately, in some schools, the directors are not concerned about the welfare of teachers, so choose carefully before you take up an offer of a job. A lot of foreigners regard teaching English in Turkey as a paid vacation. Alcohol is freely available and a few too many teachers drink to excess and are unable to carry out their duties. So you can't always blame school directors for their negative attitudes towards potential staff members.

Although your employer may not be willing to put anything down on paper, try to get something in writing from the person that you will be working for at the school. It's no guarantee that your "contract" will be honored but waving the paper around during a dispute may help your cause. Make sure that the agreement is hammered out between you and the owner of the school. A third party probably has no authority to make any agreements involving your work. Don't rely on assurances that accommodation, medical insurance or even salary have been settled. Discuss them before you sign a contract. Promises that you will be paid in American dollars may not always be kept. Important: you can always walk out of your job and find something that suits you better. Just make sure you have some backup cash.

[Note: Although a small part of the country and its major city, Istanbul, is in Europe, Turkish culture and society is Middle Eastern – with some interesting twists!]

## Embassy in UK:
43 Belgrave Square, London SW1X 8PA
**Tel:** 020 7393 0202

## Embassy in USA:
2525 Massachusetts Ave NW, Washington DC20008
**Tel:** 202 612 6700

## British Council office:
Esat Caddesi No: 41, Kucukesat, 06660 Ankara
**Tel** +90 (312) 424 1644, www.britishcouncil.org.tr

➲ **Tip:** Before you agree to work at a school, ask if you can sit in on a few lessons and watch other teachers at work. A reputable organization will allow you to do this and will appreciate your commitment. A school that refuses this reasonable request probably has something to hide.

➲ **Visas/Work Permits:** If you want to work in Turkey, you must apply for a work visa. You are not supposed to arrive as a tourist and then find a job. But some schools do employ teachers on tourist visas and send them to Greece every three months to get their visas renewed. Okay, this works for most of the time but if the authorities get suspicious, they may fine you. Keep your passport with you at all times: Teachers

have spent a night in prison for failing to present their documents to the police on demand.

➲ **Requirements:** College Degree and a TESOL/TESL Certificate

➲ **Currency:** £1 = 2.78 / $1 = 1.42 New Lir

➲ **Salaries/Taxes:** Wages and conditions vary depending on the location of the school and the level you are teaching at. Rates can range anywhere from £300-500 per month at private language institutes up to £600-1200 paid monthly by the elite colleges, plus air fares and other benefits.

➲ **Accommodation:** Usually, the school arranges for your housing. Unmarried teachers will often find themselves sharing an apartment with other foreign colleagues. Some schools will pay your rent, other will not. Furniture will be basic and beds may be army-style cots. Be warned that furnished apartments are often hard to find and are expensive. Many landlords are suspicious of single men. Single females will have an easier time but they may be asked to promise not to entertain male visitors. Expect a deduction of 25% from your salary for taxes.

➲ **Cost of Living:** There is a high rate of inflation in Turkey but salaries pegged to the dollar keep pace. The cost of living is low and it should be easy to save some money.

➲ **Health advice:** In the southeastern city of Diyarbakir, there are recurring outbreaks of dysentery, typhoid fever, meningitis and other contagious diseases. Malaria is still a risk in the eastern part of the country. Turkey is one of the most dangerous countries in the world as far as traffic accidents are concerned. Vaccinations: Hepatitis A, Polio, Typhoid.

➲ **English Language Media:** Turkish Daily News.

## Schools in Turkey (+90)

### Active English
Ataturk Bulvari 127/701, Secan Han. Bakanlikar, 06640, Ankara. **Tel:** 312 418 7973. **Fax:** 312 4258235.

### Akademi School of English
PK 234, 21001 Bahar Sokar No 2, Diyarbakir. **Tel:** 412 2242297. **Fax:** 412 2288020.

### Ankara University
Rektorlugu, Beslevler, Ankara. **Tel:** 312 41234361.

### Best English
Bayinder Sokak No. 53, Kizilay, Ankara. **Tel:** 312 4172536. **Fax:** 312 4176808. **Email:** bestenf@alnet.net

**Beykent University**
Beykent Belikdirisu, 34900, Istanbul. **Tel:** 212 8726432. **Fax:** 212 8722489.

**Bilkent University**
06533 Bilkent, Ankara. **Tel:** 312 2902746/2664390. **Fax:** 312 2664934.

**Cambridge English**
Kazim Ozalp Sok. No. 15, Kat. 4, Saskinbakkal, Istanbul. **Tel:** 216 3858431. **Fax:** 216 369 7891.

**Cinar School of English**
860 Sokak No. 1, Kat. 4, Konak, Izmir. **Tel:** 238 4837273. **Fax:** 238 441 1113.

**CTS Language Center**
Tayyareci Cemal Sk. 24/4 Sisli, Istanbul. **Tel:** 212 2660043. **Fax:** 212 2331931. **Email:** cts_language_centre@yahoo.com

**Cukurova University Center for Foreign Languages**
Balcali, Adana. **Tel:** 322 3386084 x2921.

**Dilko English Centres**
Hatboyo Caddesi No. 16, 34720 Bakirkoy, Istanbul. **Tel:** 212 5701270. **Fax:** 212 543 6123.

**Dilmer LTC**
Unlu Cad. 7, Keykel, Bursa. **Tel:** 224 2224673. **Fax:** 224 2231163.

**Elissa English**
Ihsaniye Mah 41, Sokak 48, Bandirma, Balikesir.

**The English Academy**
1374 Sokak No. 18/4, Selvili Is Hz. Izmir. **Tel:** 238 4462520. **Fax:** 238 4253042.

**The English Centre**
Rumeli Caddesi. 92, Zeki Bey Apt. 4, Osmanbey, Istanbul. **Tel:** 212 247 0983.

**English Fast**
Burhaniye Mah. Resmi Efendi Sok. No. 4, Beylerbeyi, Istanbul. **Tel:** 216 3187018. **Fax:** 216 318 7021.

**Evrim**
Cengiz Topel Caddesi 8, Camlibel, 33010 Mersin. **Tel:** 324 2339541, **Fax:** 324 2370862.

**Eyuboglu Kisesi**
Namik Kemal Mah., Dr. Rustem Eyuboglu Sok. 1, Umraniye 81240, Istanbul. **Tel:** 216 3291614. **Fax:** 216 3357198.

**Gediz College**
Seyrek Beldesi, Menemen, Izmir. **Tel:** 238 8447444. **Fax:** 238 8447441. **Email:** baysoy@gediz.kiz.tr

**Genctur**
Istiklal Cd. Zamabk Sok. 15/5, Taksom 80080, Istanbul. **Tel:** 212 249215. **Fax:** 212 2492554. **Email:** workcamps@genctur.com.tr

**Inkur ELI**
Ankara Caddesi, Yalihamam Sokak No. 8, Izmi, Kocaeli. **Tel:** 262 321 5325. **Fax:** 238 3225391.

**Interlang**
Russell Baulk, Zuhtu Pasa Mah, Recep Peker Cd, Sefikbey Sok No 17, Kiziltoprak, Istanbul. **Tel:** 216 4183910. **Fax:** 216 4182796.

**International School**
Eser Apt.A Blok Kasap, Sokak 1617, Esentepe, Istanbul.

**Isik Universitesi**
Buyukdere Cad., Maslak, Istanbul.

**Istanbul University**
Rektorlugu Beyarzit, Istanbul. **Tel:** 212 5221489.

**Kent English Ankara**
Mithatpasa Caddesi No. 46 Kat. 3/4/5, 06420 Kizilay, Ankara. **Tel:** 312 4343833. **Fax:** 312 4357334.

**Kumlu Dersanerleri**
Bursa Merkez, Basak Caddesi, Bursa. **Tel:** 224 24120465.

**London Language International**
Abide-i Hurriyet Caddesi, Kat. 1, Mecidiyekoy, Istanbul. **Tel:** 212 211 7445. **Fax:** 212 211 7441.

**Ozel Ortadogu Lisesi**
Spor Caddesi 26, Yakacik, Istanbul. **Tel:** 216 3772501. **Fax:** 216 3772502.

**Ozel Tan Lisesi**
Yeni Yalova Yolu 12km., 16335 Bursa. **Tel:** 224 2670072. **Fax:** 224 2670071.

**Sistem English**
Afiye Mah. Kibris Sehitleri Cad. 18/1, Eskisehir. **Tel:** 222 2312266. **Fax:** 222 2308681.

**Swissotel Training** centre
Suite Tower, Bayildim Cad. No. 2, Macka 80680, Istanbul. **Tel:** 212 259 0790. **Fax:** 212 259 0240.

# UNITED ARAB EMIRATES

In many ways, the United Arab Emirates (UAE) represents what most people imagine when they think of the Gulf States. In Dubai and Abu Dhabi, vast four-wheel drive jeeps fly along well-paved freeways while the passengers stay cool in the air-conditioning. In other parts of the UAE, you can still see fishermen setting out on their boats, negotiating their way past the offshore oil derricks, and coming back with their catch. Dubai is now one of the major destination cities in the world with spectacular hotels, developments and, of course, the famous horse-racing! These contrasts add up to an unforgettable experience and many foreigners decide to stay in the UAE on a long-term basis.

Teachers of English as a second or foreign language can expect only the very best here in as far as pay and accommodation are concerned.

**Embassy in UK:**
30 Prince's Gate, London SW7 1PT
**Tel:** 020 7581 1281

**Embassy in USA:**
Suite 700, 1255 22nd Street NW, Washington DC20037
**Tel:** 202 243 2400

**British Council office:**
Villa no. 7, Al Nasr Street, Khalidiya, Abu Dhabi
P.O. Box 46523
**Tel** +971 (2) 665 9300
www.britishcouncil.org/uae

➲ **Visas/Work Permits:** Tourist visas issued readily. To live and work in the UAE, you need a sponsor employer unless you are the spouse of someone already working there. Rules about visas change at short notice, so contact your local UAE embassy before departure.

➲ **Requirements:** College Degree and a TESOL/TESL Certificate

➲ **Currency:** £1 = 6.7 / $1 = 3.6 Dirham

➲ **Salaries/Taxes:** Around £2,000-3,000 per month for teachers with a Master's degree and experience. There is no tax for foreign teachers.

➲ **Accommodation:** Usually provided, otherwise expensive. A single apartment costs 30-40,000 dirhams per year, a double 50,000-75,000.

➲ **Cost of Living:** Dubai is being touted as the "new Hong Kong." Electrical goods are very reasonable and you should try to cash in on the some of the bargains available. Tailor-made clothing is also a great buy. Food is cheap and wonderful especially if you like curries. Western food items are widely available.

➲ **Health advice:** A Health Card costs about 300 dirhams. Vaccinations: Hepatitis A, Polio, Typhoid, Malaria (in some areas).

➲ **English Language Newspapers:** Emirates News, Gulf News, Gulf Today, Khaleej Times.

➲ **Other useful information:** With the growth of tourism, there has been an increasing demand for both male and female teachers. Although the percentage of women in the UAE labour force is still low, both Abu Dhabi and Dubai are cosmopolitan, relaxed cities, without the restrictions normally associated with the Gulf.

➲ **Tip:** Don't miss out on a trip to the Indian Ocean coast: Dibbah has the best beaches and Fujairah is a charming town. There are also the mangroves to visit at Kalba.

## Schools in UAE (+971)

**Al Farabi Language Center**
PO Box 3794, Dubai. **Tel:** 2 212556.

**Al-Worood School**
P.O. Box 46673, Abu Dhabi. **Tel:** 2 448855, **Fax:** 2 449732.

**American University of Sharjah**
College of Arts and Sciences, PO Box 26666, Sharjah. **Tel:** 6585067.

**Arabic Language Center**
(Dubai World Trade Centre), PO Box 9292, Dubai. **Tel:** 3086036. **Fax:** 3064089.

**Dar Al Ilm School of Languages**
PO Box 2550, Dubai. **Tel:** 447572, **Fax:** 4 91915.

**Dubai Aviation College**
PO Box 53044, Dubai. **Tel:** 824000, **Fax:** 824222.

**Dubai Cultural and Scientific Institute**
PO Box 8751, Dubai. **Tel:** 347747/377004, **Fax:** 347369.

**ELS Language centres**
P.O. Box 1496, Al Jimy Area, Al Ain. **Tel:** 3 623468. **Fax:** 3 623865 **Email:** elsaa@emirates.net.ae

**ELS Language centres**
Al Baten, Al Khaleej Al Arabi Street, Villa #4, P.O. Box 3079, Abu Dhabi. **Tel:** 2 669225. **Fax:** 2 653165. **Email: elsiauh@ns2.emirates.net.ae**

**ELS Language centres**
P.O. Box 2380, Al Garhoud Area, Villa #14, Street #20 , Dubai. **Tel:** 4 827616. **Fax:** 4 827861.**Email:** dbxels@emirates.net.ae

**Institute of Australian Studies**
PO Box 20183, Dubai. **Tel:** 4 666400, **Fax:** 4 623500.

**International Education Institute**
PO Box 524714. **Tel:** 360635, **Fax:** 348209.

**International Language Institute**
(Language Specialists Institute), PO Box 3253, Sharjah. **Tel:** 6 377257. **Fax**: 6 363427.

**International Training Solutions**
Lynne Haboubi, PO Box 4234, Dubai. **Tel/Fax:** 16 363249,

**Polyglot School**
PO Box 1093, Dubai. **Tel:** 223429, **Fax:** 217284.

# YEMEN

Yemen is the land of fables—the Queen of Sheba came from here and for centuries Yemen was the world's source of frankincense. By all accounts, people in Yemen are keen to learn English and are very receptive to qualified and experienced language teachers.

Petroleum companies operating in Yemen employ staff to teach English to local workers. Most teachers are paid by the hour. Check out some industry websites like Canadian Occidental (www.cdnoxy.com.ye) for positions on offer. Working for a foreign company may help you overcome some of the red tape that can arise when working for a Yemeni agency. If you get a job with an oil company be sure to clue up on industry-related terminology before you start teaching.

There are a number of institutes in the country—AMIDEAST operates offices in Sana'a and Aden. However, salary rates and visa processing requirements (see below) serve as disincentives. As a result of the relative difficulty in processing expatriate teachers and the seemingly low salary rates, most teachers are not recruited from abroad, but are rather language students or spouses of expatriates or Yemenis residing in Yemen.

Teachers thinking of working in Yemen should be aware that there have been a number of kidnappings of foreigners by tribesmen hostile to the government. Most of these incidents have occurred in the lawless northern region of the country although two American tourists were abducted in southern Yemen in 1998. Teachers should travel with an armed escort between cities if they choose not to fly.

**Embassy in UK:**
57 Cromwell Road, London SW7 2ED
**Tel:** 020 7584 6607

**Embassy in USA:**
Suite 705, 2600 Virginia Ave NW, Washington DC20037
**Tel:** 202 965 4760

**British Council office:**
3rd Floor, Administrative Tower, Sana'a Trade Centre Algiers Street, PO Box 2157, Sana'a
**Tel** +967 1448 356/7
www.britishcouncil.org/yemen

➲ **Visas/Work Permits:** EFL teachers from America can only obtain a one-month tourist visa (£20). The organization hiring the teacher must then convert the tourist visa into a work permit—an expensive and time-consuming procedure. All individuals wishing to obtain a work permit must have an HIV test performed in Yemen. External test results will not be accepted.

➲ **Requirements:** College Degree and a TESOL/TESL Certificate

➲ **Currency:** £1 = 344 / $1 = 186 Rial (YER)

➲ **Salaries/Taxes:** Salaries are generally paid per hour. An average salary for native speakers is around £6/hour, which is quite good because Yemen is an inexpensive country and the average monthly income is less than £60. Foreigners do not have to pay any local tax.

➲ **Accommodation:** Rents range from £30/month to £1000/month. An average rate for a furnished, one bedroom apartment in good condition is around £100 per month. Additionally, some language institutes offer housing to expatriate teachers.

➲ **Cost of Living:** Prices in Yemen are very reasonable and you can pick up exquisitely made handicrafts at bargain rates.

➲ **Health advice:** Cases of malaria are on the rise in Yemen especially along the coasts. You should take a course of chloroquine-resistant malaria suppressants before you travel to these areas. The altitude of Sana'a (7,200 feet) and lack of adequate medical facilities can cause problems for some visitors. Doctors and hospitals often expect immediate cash payment for health services. Vaccinations: Hepatitis A, Typhoid, Polio, Yellow Fever (if coming from an infected area).

➲ **English Language Media:** Yemen Times, Yemen Observer.

➲ **Tip:** Yemeni social life revolves around chewing the leaf known as "qat" that produces a mild euphoria among users.

## Schools in Yemen (+967)

**Al Farouq Institute**
PO Box 16927, Sana'a. **Tel:** 1 209721. **Fax:** 1 209721.

**The American School**
PO Box 16003, Sana'a. **Tel:** 1 417119. **Fax:** 1 415355.

**AMIDEAST**
162 Miswat Street, Khormaksar, Aden. **Tel:** 2 238345.
**Fax**: 2 238345. **Email: aden@amideast.org**

**AMIDEAST**
Algiers Street 66, P.O. Box 15508, Sana'a. **Tel:** 1
206222. **Fax:** 1 206942. **Email:** yemen@amideast.org

**The British Council**
PO Box 2157, Sana'a. **Tel:** 1 244 121. **Fax:** 1 244120.

**English Language** centre
PO Box 8984, Sana'a. **Tel:** 1 248090.

**Faculty of Art, English Department**
PO Box 6014, Aden. **Tel:** 2 32350.

**Faculty of Art**
English Department, Sana'a. **Tel:** 1 200515/6.

**Faculty of Education**
English Department, Sana'a. **Tel:** 1 250513.

**Faculty of Education**
English Department, PO Box 6480, Taiz. **Tel:** 4
212191/2, **Fax:** 4 219378.

**MALI**
PO Box 16003, Sana'a. **Tel:** 1 241561. **Fax:** 1 414348.

**Madina Institute of Technology (MIT)**
Aden. **Tel**: 2 251453.

**The Modern Yemen School**
PO Box 13335, Sana'a. **Tel:** 1 206548.

**Mohammed Ali Othman School**
PO Box 5713, Taiz. **Tel:** 4 211248/9.

**National Institute for Administrative Science**
PO Box 102, Sana'a. **Fax:** 1 251161.

**Pakistani School**
Sana'a. **Tel:** 1 247830/247838.

**The Pioneer School**
Sana'a. **Tel:** 1 210311.

**Sabaa University**
PO Box 14400, Sana'a. **Tel/Fax:** 1 205749.

**Sam Yemen International School**
PO Box 19390, Sana'a. **Tel:** 2 69648/63303. **Fax:** 2
69649.

**Sana'a International School**
PO Box 2002, Sana'a. **Tel:** 1 234437. **Fax:** 1 234438.

**Spectra Institute**
PO Box 16101, Sana'a. **Tel:** 1 414623. **Fax:** 1 414739.

**University of Science Technology**
PO Box 15201, Sana'a. **Tel:** 1 207026. **Fax:** 1 207027.

**Yemen-American Language Institute**
c/o USIA, American Embassy, Sana'a. **Tel:** 1 203251.
**Fax:** 1 203364. **Email:** info@yali.org.ye

**Yemen Language centre**
PO Box 1691, Sana'a. **Tel:** 1 285125. **Fax:** 1 289249.

**Yemen Sudanese Language centre**
PO Box 13187, Sana'a. **Fax:** 1 275407.

# Africa

For many countries in Africa, the English language is part of the legacy left to them by the colonialists. In these countries, English is often taught from a young age in the state schools and people use it to communicate if there are several tribal languages spoken in one nation. Other African countries are former French or Belgian colonies, so a working knowledge of French is useful.

Most English language teachers work in Africa as volunteers but there are some jobs available at university and college institutes although you may end up earning more as a volunteer than as a "salaried" teacher. Female teachers thinking of coming to Africa should be aware that societies are much more traditional here when it comes to the role of men and women. You may find that, in a staff meeting, men sit on one side of the room and women on the other.

A number of countries within Africa are currently too dangerous to visit - due to war, violence or unrest. This includes the whole of Chad, Ivory Coast, and Somalia; and parts of CAR, Burundi, Cameroon, Congo, Ethiopia, Nigeria, Sudan, Uganda. You can find out the latest status of which country is safe to visit at www.fco.gov.uk.

Teachers who want to work as volunteers can contact *Teachers for Africa,* an organization that places experienced teachers in Malawi, Namibia, Nigeria, Ethiopia, Ghana, Guinea and Benin. Web: www.ifesh.org, Email: teachers@ifesh.org.

*Note: African countries on the Mediterranean Coast are dealt with in the Middle East section.*

## BENIN

Benin is one of smaller West African states. Its capital city is Porto Novo; however, the city of Cotonou is the main port and largest city. There are interesting sites to visit in Benin including Ouidah, an ancient port where slaves were sent around the world, Abomey, the "royal" city, and Allada, known as the "cradle" of the voodoo religion. There is a very high demand for English language teachers in Benin. The best way to find a job here is to enter the country on a tourist visa and then start hunting around. You could also contact the *Syndicat National de l'Enseignement Primaire Public du Bénin*, SNEP, B.P. 69, Cotonou, Bénin. **Tel:** +229-303.613 **Fax:** +229-303.613.

➲ **Visas/Work Permits:** Tourist visas are valid for a 15- ($45) or 30-day ($60) period within three months of date of issue.

➲ **Requirements:** College Degree and a TESOL/TESL Certificate

➲ **Currency:** £1 = 922 / $1 = 501 CFA Franc.

➲ **Salaries/Taxes:** 4,500 CFA per hour. Foreigners do not have to pay tax unless they are registered with the OBSS – the Office of Social Security.

➲ **Accommodation:** Flats cost from 80,000 to 800,000 CFA per month.

➲ **Health advice:** Medical facilities in Benin are limited and not all medicines are available. A yellow fever certificate must be presented on entry to Benin. Cholera is a serious risk in this country and precautions are essential. Malaria is also a risk as is rabies. Health insurance is recommended.

### Schools in Benin (+229)

**American Cultural centre**
B.P. 2012, Cotonou. **Tel:** 304553. **Fax:** 301439. **Email:** vreeland@micronet.net

**Brilliant Stars International School**
04 B.P. 919 Cadjehoun, Cotonou. **Tel:** 302079, **Fax:** 313701/313809.

## BURKINA FASO

Although this landlocked country is one of Africa's poorest nations, there is a vibrant culture evident among its people. The Pan African Film and Television Festival of Ouagadougou (the capital city) is the largest event of its kind in Africa and draws over 100,000 visitors. Volunteers in urban and rural settings teach secondary school and university English. You can also contact the national teacher's association: Syndicat National des Enseignants du Secondaire et du Supérieur (SNESS), 01 B.P. 113, Ouagadougou 01, Burkina Faso. **Tel:** +226-362.362, **Fax:** +226-362.362.

➲ **Visas/Work Permits:** You will need both. Your employer will help you obtain them.

➲ **Currency:** £1 = 922 / $1 = 501 CFA Franc.

➲ **Health advice:** Medical facilities in Burkina Faso are limited. A Yellow fever certificate is required. Precautions against cholera, malaria and rabies are recommended.

### Schools in Burkina Faso (+226)

**American Language centre**
01 B.P. 539, Ouagadougou-01, Burkina Faso. **Tel:** 306360/308903. **Fax:** 31 5273. **Email: alcouaga@fasonet.bf**

**International School of Ouagadougou**
01 B.P. 35, c/o US Embassy, Ouagadougou. **Tel:** 362143. **Fax:** 362228. **Email:** issoua@fasonet.bf

## CAMEROON

There are occasional opportunities for experienced EFL teachers in Cameroon, an enchanting and spectacular country with mountains and a coastline to explore. Volunteers with VSO (see p.62) work to improve the quality of English language teaching in rural schools that have little or no resources. Unfortunately, teachers report that the security situation in Cameroon is getting worse and that foreigners should be very careful when travelling.

**British Council office:**
Immeuble Christo, Avenue Charles de Gaulle, BP 818, Yaoundé
**Tel** +237 2 21 16 96/20 31 72
www.britishcouncil.org/cameroon

➲ **Visas/Work Permits:** Visas are granted for up to 12 months. You will also need a residence permit, which costs £500.

➲ **Requirements:** College Degree and a TESOL/TESL Certificate

➲ **Currency:** £1 = 926 / $1 = 501 CFA Franc.

➲ **Salaries/Taxes:** Teachers can earn £550-800 a month with a housing and transport allowance.

➲ **Health advice:** Medical facilities in Cameroon are limited. Sanitation levels are low, even in the best hospitals. Not all medicines are available. Travellers are advised to bring their own supplies. Malaria prophylaxis and vaccination against hepatitis A and B, tetanus, diphtheria, polio, typhoid, and meningococcal meningitis are recommended.

## Schools in Cameroon (+237)

### American School of Douala
BP 1909, Douala. **Tel:** 421437. **Fax:** 421437. **Email:** adminasd@camnet.cm

### American School of Yaoundé
Dept of State, 2520 Yaounde Place, Washington DC, 20521-2520, USA. **Tel:** 230421. **Fax:** 236011. **Email:** asoy@camnet.cm

### The British Council
Immeuble Christo, Rue Drouot, B.P 12,801 Douala. **Tel:** 425145. **Fax:** 425170. **Email:** ELC.Douala@bc-douala.douala1.com

### The British Council
Immeuble Soms, Avenue Charles de Gaulle, B.P 818 Yaoundé. **Tel:** 211696. **Fax:** 215691. **Email:** ELC.Yaounde@bc-yaounde.iccnet.cm

### Ministry of Higher Education
2, Avenue du 20 Mai, Yaoundé. **Tel:** 22 13 70

## CENTRAL AFRICAN REPUBLIC

The CAR, as it known, is a developing country that it is full of potential. Interesting places to visit include the Dzanga-Sangha National Park, a primeval rain forest in the southwestern region of the country. There is a very strong demand for English language teaching in the CAR. Experienced teachers will have no problems in finding a job but they should apply from outside the country to avoid disappointment. Unfortunately, the political and social situation deters most teachers from working here and it can be a very dangerous country that features high on the list of countries to avoid at www.fco.gov.uk

⮞ **Visas/Work Permits:** As rules change so quickly, it is best to check with the embassy.

⮞ **Currency:** £1 = 926 / $1 = 501 CFA Franc.

⮞ **Salaries/Taxes:** Expect to be paid $150-300 a month but there are problems with getting paid in government contracts in a country where civil servants haven't had any money for almost two years.

⮞ **Accommodation:** An apartment in the capital, Bangui, will cost anywhere between £150-300 a month.

⮞ **Cost of Living:** Very cheap

⮞ **Health advice:** Medical facilities are limited, and the quality of acute care is unreliable. Sanitation levels are low. Many medicines are not available. Travellers are advised to bring their own properly-labeled supplies.

## Schools in Central African Republic (+236)

### Martin Luther King Cultural centre
c/o American Embassy, Avenue David Dacko, PO Box 924, Bangui. **Tel:** (236) 610200. **Fax:** 614494. **Email:** gazembetig@hotmail.com

## DEM. REPUBLIC OF CONGO

The situation in this country (formerly known as Zaire) has been improving as it recovers from civil war. However, it is still a dangerous country and features on the list of countries to avoid at www.fco.gov.uk

## Schools in Dem. Rep. Congo (+243)

### American School of Kinshasa
c/o American Embassy, Kinshasa, APO AE 09828. **Tel:** 88 46619.

### Congo-American Language Institute (CALI)
B.P. 8622, Kinshasa 1. **Tel:** 8843979. **Fax:** 88 46592.

## ERITREA

Eritrea is recovering from a recent war with neighbouring Ethiopia and conditions are very harsh. Many programmes have had to be suspended at various times because of instability in the region; it is still a dangerous country and features on the list of countries to avoid at www.fco.gov.uk

### British Council office:
Lorenzo Tazaz Street No 23, PO Box 997, Asmara **Tel** +291 (1) 123 415 www.britishcouncil.org/eritrea

⮞ **Salaries/Taxes:** Rates of pay are very low and may be supplemented by your agency.

⮞ **Accommodation:** Housing will be provided by your employer.

## Schools in Eritrea (+291)

### Asmara International Community School
PO Box 4941, Asmara, Eritrea **Tel:** 1 161705. **Fax:** 1 161705 **Email:** aics@eol.com.er

## The British Council

Lorenzo Ta'azaz Street, No. 23, PO Box 997, Asmara, **Tel**. 1 23415. **Email:** britcoun@eol.com.er

# ETHIOPIA

It is not easy to find a job teaching English in Ethiopia. Most private language schools employ Ethiopians who can speak English. A number of western aid organizations work in the country and it may be possible to land a job through one of them. Volunteers need to have had at least two years' teaching experience as well as a certificate or an MA. VSO Canada sends teachers to mainstream educational programmes and technical training institutions aiming to improve the standard of English (the medium of instruction) of the students. However, be aware that this is still a dangerous country and features on the list of countries to avoid at www.fco.gov.uk

## Embassy in UK:

17 Princes Gate, London SW7 1PZ
**Tel:** 020 7589 7212

## Embassy in USA:

3506 International Drive NW, Washington DC20008
**Tel:** 202 364 1200

## British Council office:

PO Box 1043, Artistic Building, Adwa Avenue, Addis Ababa
**Tel** +251 (1) 550 022
www.britishcouncil.org/ethiopia

⊃ **Visas/Work Permits:** You have to get a single-entry visa and you must get an exit visa each time you leave the country, which makes travel difficult.

### Schools in Ethiopia (+251)

## The British Council

Adwa Avenue, Artistic Building, PO Box 1043, Addis Ababa. **Tel:** 1 55 00 22. **Fax**: 251-1-55 25 44. **Email: Solomon.Hailu @bc-addis.bcouncil.org**

## International Community School

P.O. Box 70282, Addis Ababa.

## Sandford English Community School

P.O. Box 30056 MA, Addis Ababa. **Tel:** 1 55 2275. **Fax**: 1 55 1945.

## University of Addis Ababa

P.O. Box 1176, Addis Ababa.

# GHANA

There is much to explore in Ghana from the coastal slave forts recalling a tragic period in the country's history to the rainforests of the interior. Depending on which level you intend to teach you could get in touch with the educational authorities. Try: The General Secretary, Ghana National Association Of Teachers, GNAT Headquarters, P.O. Box 209, Accra, Ghana. Tel: +233-21-221.515 / 221.576, Fax:+233-21-224.877 for more information. For volunteer teaching opportunities in Ghana, see page 62. More limited openings can be found at a handful of language institutes affiliated with colleges and universities. To teach in Ghana you have to be a certified teacher, or serving with a volunteer organization, or a tenured lecturer.

## High Commission in UK:

13 Belgrave Square, London SW1X 8PN
**Tel**: 020 7235 4142

## Embassy in USA:

3512 International Drive NW, Washington DC20008
**Tel**: 202 686 4520

## British Council office:

11 Liberia Road, PO Box GP 771, Accra
**Tel** +233 (21) 683 068
www.britishcouncil.org/ghana

⊃ **Visas/Work Permits:** The school will take care of this for you.

⊃ **Currency:** £1 = 16551 / $1 = 8947 Cedi

⊃ **Salaries/Taxes:** Volunteers can expect to earn around £30-200 a month. Teachers at universities or language institutes can earn anywhere from £1000-2000.

⊃ **Health advice:** Facilities are limited, particularly outside Accra. Be aware that evidence of and/or assurances from insurance companies will not be accepted as settlement of medical expenses.

⊃ **English Language Media:** Ghanaian Chronicle, Ghanaian Times, Graphic.

### Schools in Ghana (+233)

## Centre of Language and Professional Studies

P.O. Box 4501, Accra.

## Institute of Languages

P.O. Box M67, Accra. **Tel:** 21 221052.

## The Language Centre

University of Ghana, Legon. **Tel:** 21 500381.

## KENYA

English is the working language of Kenyan schools and there is a shortage of qualified and experienced teachers. Although you won't make a lot of money here, it is a beautiful country with much to see and do.

**High Commission in UK:**
45 Portland Place, London W1N 3AS
**Tel:** 020 7636 2371

**Embassy in USA:**
2249 R Street NW, Washington DC 20008
**Tel:** 202 387 6101

**British Council office:**
ICEA Building, Kenyatta Avenue, PO Box 40751 Nairobi
**Tel** +254 (2) 334 855/6
www.britishcouncil.org/kenya

⮑ **Visas/Work Permits:** You are supposed to have a work permit before you arrive but teachers have picked up casual work while on tourist visas.
⮑ **Requirements:** College Degree and a TESOL/TESL Certificate
⮑ **Currency:** £1 = 136 / $1 = 69 Shillings
⮑ **Salaries/Taxes:** Teachers are usually paid at local rates, which allows for a simple lifestyle.
⮑ **Accommodation:** Outside Nairobi, housing can be very basic.

### Schools in Kenya (+254)

**American Universities Preparation & Learning centre**
P.O. Box 14842, Nairobi. **Tel:** 2 741764. **Fax:** 2 741690.

**The Language centre**
P.O. Box 14245, Ndemi Close, off Ngong Road, Nairobi. **Tel:** 2 569531. **Fax:** 2 568207.

## MADAGASCAR

Madagascar is a large island situated in the Indian Ocean. Many unique species of animals are threatened with extinction here as sapphire mining and other destructive activities go unchecked.
Teachers interested in working at the English Teaching programme in Antananarivo should contact the programme upon arrival in the city. Please do not send applications in advance.

⮑ **Visas/Work Permits:** Visas should be obtained in advance, although airport visas are available in Antananarivo, the capital.
⮑ **Currency:** £1 = 3233 / $1 = 1748 Ariary
⮑ **Health advice:** The hospital infrastructure is minimal and does not meet basic sanitary norms.

### Schools in Madagascar (+261)

**American School of Antananarivo**
US Dept of State/Antananarivo, Washington DC 20521-2040, USA. **Tel:** 202242039. **Fax**: 202234539.

**English Teaching Program**
4 Lalana Dr., Razafindratandra Ambohidahy, Antananarivo. **Tel:** 22220238. **Fax:** 221397.

## MALI

Mali is a vast land of savannas, steppes, and deserts. For the most of the last four millennia, it was one of the great centres of African civilization. During the middle ages, the Malian empire was famous throughout much of Africa and Europe; Timbuktu was a centre of Islamic study and its library was one of the largest in the world. The Peace Corps has been active in Mali for over 30 years and it enjoys a high reputation among the people of Mali.

### Schools in Mali (+223)

**American International School of Bamako**
Dept of State - Bamako, Washington DC, 20521-2050, USA. **Tel:** 224738. **Fax**: 220853.

## MOZAMBIQUE

For many years, Mozambique was in the grip of a bloody civil war. Although the situation has improved a lot since then, teachers should be warned that parts of country and the capital, Maputo, are unsafe. The civil war has severely disrupted education: The overall literacy rate is estimated at 30-40% and only 40% of school-age children actually attend school. Volunteers with VSO Canada are involved in English language teaching in rural elementary schools where there are sometimes more than 50 children in a classroom. Teachers report that life outside the capital is much more relaxed and that the weekends are worth waiting for because there are miles of empty beaches and fascinating countryside to explore. You will need to speak some Portuguese.

**British Council office:**
Rua John Issa, 226, P.O. Box 4178, Maputo
**Tel** +258 (1) 310 921
www.britishcouncil.org/mozambique

➲ **Visas/Work Permits:** You will need a visa, which must be obtained in advance. Travellers arriving without a visa are subject to a fine of £300. The authorities will impose a fine of £60 per day for each day travellers overstay their visas. Once your contract has been agreed, the school will apply for a work permit, which will take about four months to process. You are not supposed to work for the school during this period although this rule is commonly ignored.

➲ **Currency:** £1 = 33932 / $1 = 18342 Metical.

➲ **Salaries/Taxes:** Approximately £10 / $19 an hour. Tax is about 17%.

➲ **Accommodation:** Rents are expensive in Maputo. Typical rates are £600 / $1100 per month shared among three teachers. The upside is that the accommodation is clean and modern.

➲ **Cost of Living:** Mozambique is an expensive country where you might be able to save only a little of your salary – if you're not keen on going out and partying every night.

➲ **Health advice:**Facilities are minimal and many medicines are unavailable. Maputo's Sommerschield Clinic, which requires payment in hard currency, can provide general, non-emergency services. Many rural health centres were forced to close during the conflict with the MNR rebels. Yellow fever vaccination certificate is required. Cholera is a serious risk and precautions are essential. Malaria and rabies are risks.

## Schools in Mozambique (+258)

**Brumag**
Av. Mártires Mueda 563, Maputo. **Tel:** 496199.

**Contacto**
R. Tchamba 64, Maputo. **Tel:** 492479.

**Oikos**
R. General Pereira D'Eca, Maputo. **Tel**; 497850.

**Instituto De Linguas**
Av. Ahmed Sekou Touré, **Tel:** 425684.

**Lynden Language School**
PO Box 456, 1746 Rua de Resistencia 3rd floor, Maputo. **Tel:** 417569.

**Maputo International School**
Rua de Nachingwea, CP 4152, 389, Maputo. **Tel:** 492131/492195. **Fax:** 492382.

## SENEGAL

EFL teachers can find work on a casual basis in Senegal but there are no private language schools as such. If you want to work in the public sector, you could try the national teachers' union: *Syndicat des Professeurs du Sénégal* (SYPROS), Bourse du Travail CNTS, 7 Avenue du Président Lamine Guèye, B.P. 937, Dakar, Sénégal. **Tel:** +221-821.8381 / 821.0491, **Fax:** +221-821.7771).

**Embassy in UK:**
39 Marloes Road, London W8 6LA
**Tel:** 020 7937 723

**Embassy in USA:**
2112 Wyoming Ave NW, Washington DC 20008
**Tel:** 202 234 0540

**British Council office:**
34-36 Boulevard de la République, Immeuble Sonatel
BP 6238, Dakar
**Tel:** +221 822 2015/822 2048
www.britishcouncil.org/senegal

## Schools in Senegal (+221)

**American English Language** programme **(AELP)**
c/o USIS, B.P. 49, Dakar. **Tel:** 211634. **Fax:** 222345.

**The British Council**
34-36 Bd de la République, Dakar.**Tel:** 822 20 15 / 822 20 48. **Fax:** 821 81 36.

## SOUTH AFRICA

The demand for English language instruction is very strong in post-apartheid South Africa. There are many private language institutes, especially in and around Cape Town that cater to an international student market. In rural South Africa, the Peace Corps operates a programme where volunteers advise local elementary school teachers on English language lesson planning. Qualified teachers are welcomed here but you will be competing for jobs with South African citizens who do not require work permits.

**High Commission in UK:**
South Africa House, Trafalgar Square, London WC2N 5DP
**Tel:** 020 7451 7299
www.southafricahouse.com

**Embassy in USA:**
3051 Massachusetts Ave NW, Washington DC 20008

**Tel:** 202 238 4400

**British Council office:**
Ground Floor, Forum 1, Braampark, 33 Hoofd Street,
Braamfontein, Johannesburg 2001
Tel +27 (11) 718 4300
www.britishcouncil.org/southafrica

➲ **Visas/Work Permits:** Teachers need a work
permit, which costs around £90. Your employer must
be able to prove that the position was made available to
South Africans before a foreign national took up the
offer.

➲ **Requirements:** College Degree and a
TESOL/TESL Certificate

➲ **Currency:** £1 = 13.65 / $1 = 6.98 Rand

➲ **Salaries/Taxes:** Teachers earn from £5-10 an
hour and taxation ranges from 20-30%.

➲ **Accommodation:** There is a high standard of
accommodation in South Africa and rents are
expensive if you are earning a local salary.

➲ **English Language Media:** The Star, Weekly
Mail.

## Schools in South Africa (+27)

**Cape Communication Centre**
37 Riebeck Street, Cape Town 8001. **Tel:** 21 419 1967

**Cape Studies Language School**
100 Main Road Seapoint, P.O.Box 4425, Cape Town
8000. **Tel:** 21 439 0999. **Fax:** 21 439 3130

**Cape Town School of International Languages**
66 Main Rd, Claremont, Cape Town 7708. **Tel:** 21 674
4117.

**Good Hope Studies**
4 Mount Road, Rondebosch, Cape Town 7700. **Tel:** 21
686 0060. **Fax:** 21 686 0061.

**inlingua Language Training Centre**
Kinellan House, 14 Portswood Rd., Cape Town 8000.
**Tel:** 21 4190494. **Fax:** 21 4190725.

**INTERLINK School of Languages**
P.O. Box 694, Seapoint, Cape Town 8060. **Tel:** 21
4399 834 **Fax:** 21 4343 267.

**Language & Travel**
Mail: P.O. Box 868, Green Point, Cape Town 8051, 2
Braemar Road, Green Point 8005. **Tel:** 21 439 3101.
**Fax:** 21 439-0616.

**Language Lab International House**
4th Floor Aspern House, 54 De Korte Street,
Braamfontein, Johannesburg 2001. **Tel:** 11 339 1051.
**Fax:** 11 403 1759.

**One World Language School**
P. O. Box 7888, Roggebaai, Cape Town 8012.
**Tel/Fax:** 21 4231833.

**Table Mountain Language Centre**
7 Mountain Road, Claremont, Cape Town 7700. **Tel:**
21 674 49 14. **Fax:** 21 671 09 97.

**Tygerberg Language and Leisure Centre**
P.O. Box 2483, Bellville 7530. **Tel:** 21 948 3460.

## TANZANIA

You can find work as a volunteer teacher and there are
sometimes opportunities in colleges and universities.

**British Council office:**
Samora Avenue / Ohio Street, PO Box 9100, Dar Es
Salaam
Tel +255 (22) 211 6574
www.britishcouncil.org/tanzania

➲ **Visas/Work Permits:**Employers make the
necessary arrangements.

## Schools in Tanzania (+51)

**International Languages Orientation Services**
Oysterbay, Karume Road, P.O. Box 6995, Dar es
Salaam. **Tel:** 667159. **Fax:** 112752.

## TOGO

There are limited opportunities for EFL teachers in this
small West African nation. Contact the teachers'
union: Fédération des Syndicats de l'Education
Nationale, Tel: +228-222.547

## Schools in Togo (+228)

**English Language Program**
Centre Culturel Américain, Rues Pelletier et Vauban,
B.P. 852, Lomé. **Tel:** 212166.

# Australia & New Zealand

O ver the past few years, the prospects in both Australia and New Zealand have changed. Many English language schools have closed down and it is no longer quite as easy to get a job as it used to be. These ups and downs in the local ELT industry began when, in Australia, the recession has eased and the government introduced new 12-month visitor visas (allowing temporary work) giving young teachers the perfect excuse to travel around this fabulous country ... and earn money teaching. New Zealand, too, has had a change in government policy that impacted on English language teachers: the rules for immigration have been relaxed, resulting in an influx of immigrants – all keen to learn English. As a result, New Zealand is suffering something of a shortage of teachers. Only US citizens will find a problem with either country: they cannot take advantage of the 12-month young traveller visa and report that finding work (and a school willing to sponsor them through a work visa) is very tough.

# AUSTRALIA

There are good job prospects for teachers in Australia, with a good increase in the numbers of (mostly Asian, due to its location) students visiting Australia to learn English. The majority of the language schools are in Sydney (which has over 70 schools); around two-thirds of the schools are accredited and prefer teachers with experience and a recognised certificate (visit the accreditation website, www.neasaccred.com for more details).

Australia has changed its visa policy to around a dozen countries, allowing young (18-30) teachers to stay for 12 months and teach in temporary jobs. US citizens report that it is hard to get a job without a work permit which is difficult for US citizens to obtain (however, Canadians are included in the 12-month working-holiday visa scheme).

**High Commission in UK:**
Australia House, Strand, London WC2B 4LA
**Tel:** 020 7379 4334
www.australia.org.uk

**Embassy in USA:**
1601 Massachusetts Ave NW, Washington DC20036
**Tel:** 202 797 3000
www.austemb.org

**British Council office:**
PO Box 88, Edgecliff, Sydney NSW 2027
**Tel**: (2) 9326 2022
www.britishcouncil.org/au.htm

➲ **Visas:** British, American and Canadian citizens require visas before they can enter Australia as tourists, students or workers. Tourists need a tourist visa (now generally replaced by the Electronic Travel Authority, issued by major travel agents). All other work visas are assessed by the high commission or embassy – the basic reasoning is that any job opportunity must be made available to Australian citizens, so you will have to show that your work cannot be carried out by an existing resident.

➲ **Requirements:** College Degree and a TESOL/TESL Certificate

➲ **Currency:** £1 = 2.49 / $1 = 1.27 Dollars

➲ **Health:** Health-care standards are very high and if you are granted a resident permit for more than six months, you can join the national medical and hospital service, Medicare.

➲ **Tax:** all employees must register for tax – find out how at www.ato.gov.au

## Schools In Australia (+61)

**acl (Australian Centre for Languages)**
157-161 Gloucester Street, The Rocks, New South Wales 2000, **Tel:** +61 2 9252 3788, **Fax:** +61 2 9252 3799, **Email:** enquiry@acl.edu.au , **Web:** www.acl.edu.au

**Adelaide Institute of TAFE English Language Centre**
120 Currie Street, Adelaide, South Australia 5000, **Tel**: +61 8 8207 8279, **Fax:** +61 8 8207 8283,**Web:** www.tafe.sa.edu.au

**Anutech Education Centre at the Australian National University**
Cnr Barry Drive and North Road, Canberra, Australian Capital Territory 2601, **Tel:** +61 2 6125 5000, **Fax:** +61 2 6125 5664, **Email:** edu.enquiries@anutech.com.au, **Web:** www.anutech.com.au/ELC

**ASPECT ILA Sydney**
98-104 Goulburn Street, Sydney, New South Wales 2000, **Tel:** +61 2 9283 8055, **Fax:** +61 2 9283 9055, **Email:** aspectsydney@educate.com , **Web:** www.aspectworld.com

**Australian College of English**
Level 1, 237 Oxford Street, Bondi Junction, New South Wales 2022, **Tel**: +61 2 9389 0133, **Fax:** +61 2 9389 6880, **Email:** info@ace.edu.au, **Web:** www.ace.edu.au

**Australian Pacific College**
189 Kent Street, Sydney, New South Wales 2000, **Tel:** +61 2 9251 7000, **Fax:** +61 2 9251 7575, **Email:** info@apc.edu.au, **Web:** www.apc.edu.au

**Billy Blue English School**
Level 9, Northpoint, 100 Miller Street, North Sydney, New South Wales 2060, **Tel:** +61 2 9955 1122, **Fax**: +61 2 9957 1811, **Email:** info@billyblue.com.au **Web:** www.billyblue.com.au

**Cambridge English Language Centre**
Level 3, 4 Cross Street, Hurstville, New South Wales 2220, **Tel**: +61 2 9579 6244, **Fax:** +61 2 9570 9565, **Email:** cambridgecollege@tpg.com.au **Web:** www.camb.aust.com

**Central Queensland University Language Centre**
Bruce Highway, North Rockhampton, Queensland 4702, **Tel:** +61 7 4930 6577, **Fax:** +61 7 4930 6321 **Web:** www.language.cqu.edu.au

**Centre for English Teaching**
University of Sydney, 88 Mallett Street, Camperdown, New South Wales 2006, **Tel**: +61 2 9351 0706, **Fax:**

+61 2 9351 0710, **Email:** info@cet.usyd.edu.au, **Web:** www.usyd.edu.au/cet

### Centre for English Language Teaching
35 Stirling Highway, Crawley, West Australia 6009, **Tel:** +61 8 9380 3539, **Fax:** +61 8 9380 1077, **Email:** celt@ecel.uwa.edu.au, **Web:** www.celt.uwa.edu.au

### EF International Language Schools
Sydney, 5-7 Young Street, Sydney, New South Wales 2000, **Tel:** +61 2 9247 7668, **Fax:** +61 2 9247 7691, **Email:** ils.sydney@ef.com, **Web:** www.ef.com

### ELICOS
University of Canberra, University Drive, Bruce, Australian Capital Territory 2601, **Tel:** +61 2 6201 2102, **Fax:** +61 2 6201 5089, **Web:** www.slie.canberra.edu.au

### ELS Language Centres
Charles Sturt University, Boorooma Street, Wagga Wagga, New South Wales 2678, **Tel:** +61 2 6933 2602, **Fax:** +61 2 6933 4018, www.csu.edu.au/division/internat/els/index.htm

### Embassy CES Brisbane
119 Charlotte Street, Brisbane, Queensland 4000, **Tel:** +61 7 3238 1500, **Fax:** +61 7 3238 1670, **Email:** w.day@sga.edu.au, **Web:** www.embassyces.com

### Embassy CES Melbourne
399 Lonsdale Street, Melbourne, Victoria 3000, **Tel:** +61 3 9670 3788, **Fax:** +61 3 9670 9356, **Email:** info@taylorscollege.com, **Web:** www.embassyces.com

### International House Sydney
(Waratah Education Centre), 22 Darley Road, Manly, New South Wales 2095, **Tel:** +61 2 9976 2422, **Fax:** +61 2 9976 2433, **Web:** www.ihsydney.com

### International House Queensland English Language College
130 Mcleod Street, Cairns, Queensland 4870, **Tel:** +61 7 4031 3466, **Fax:** +61 7 4031 3464, **Email:** admin@ihqld.com, **Web:** www.ihqld.com

### Northern Territory University Centre for Access and ESL
Ellengowan Drive, Casuariana, Northern Territory 0909, **Tel:** +61 8 8946 6160, **Fax:** +61 8 8946 7144, **Email:** uni-info@ntu.edu.au, **Web:** http://mindil.ntu.edu.au

### Shane Global Village Sydney
Level 12, 222 Pitt Street, Sydney, NSW 2000 **Tel:** +61 (2) 9283 1088 **Fax:** +61 (2) 9283 1760 **Web:** www.sgvenglish.com

### TAFE English Language Centre, Northern Sydney
213 Pacific Highway, St Leonards, New South Wales 2065, **Tel:** +61 2 9942 0086, **Fax:** +61 2 9906 7423, **Email:** Telc@tafensw.edu.au , **Web:** www.tafensw.edu.au

### TAFE International Education Centre, Liverpool
Cnr Bigge and Moore Streets, Liverpool, New South Wales 2170, **Tel:** +61 2 9827 5197, **Fax:** +61 2 9827 5198, **Web:** www.tafensw.edu.au/swsit/

### Universal English College
Level 12, 222 Pitt Street, Sydney, New South Wales 2000, **Tel:** +61 2 9283 1088, **Fax:** +61 2 9283 1760, **Email:** enquiries@uec.edu.au, **Web:** www.uec.edu.au

### University of NSW Institute of Languages
22 King Street, Randwick, New South Wales 2031, **Tel:** +61 2 9385 0339, **Fax:** +61 2 9399 5420, **Email:** Institute.Languages@unsw.edu.au, **Web:** www.lang.unsw.edu.au/elicos/

### University of Western Sydney English Language Centre
Building 16, Room 7, Campbelltown Campus, Campbelltown, New South Wales 2560, **Tel:** +61 2 4620 3028, **Fax:** +61 2 4620 3782, **Email:** l.simon@uws.edu.au, **Web:** http://uwselc.uws.edu.au

### Victoria University English Language Institute
Level 5, 301 Flinders Lane, Melbourne, Victoria 3000, **Tel:** +61 3 9248 1175, **Fax:** +61 3 9248 1298, **Email:** eli@vu.edu.au, **Web:** www.vu.edu.au/eli/

## NEW ZEALAND

New Zealand is experiencing a good demand for English teachers – thanks to a rush of immigrants who want to learn English (tempted by the favourable exchange rate and easing of immigration requirements). There are not enough teachers and schools currently will offer to help visitors get a work visa; schools prefer teachers with a CELTA or Trinity certificate and at least one year's experience.

Auckland and Christchurch are the two main centres for schools and the bulk of students are from China, Korea and Japan. The only drawback is for US citizens hoping to teach in New Zealand – like Australia, it's hard for US citizens to get a work permit. A good source for jobs are the websites www.english-schools.co.nz and www.teachnz.gov.nz

**High Commission in UK:**
New Zealand House, 80 Haymarket, London SW1Y 4TQ
**Tel:** 020 7930 8422
www.nzembassy.com

**Embassy in USA:**
37 Observatory Circle NW, Washington DC20008
**Tel:** 202 328 4800
www.nzemb.org

**British Council office:**
44 Hill Street, PO Box 1812, Wellington 1
**Tel** (4) 495 0897
www.britishcouncil.org.nz

➲ **Visas:** British citizens can enter NZ without a visa and can stay in the country for up to six months, if they can prove that they have enough money and a return ticket. UK, Irish, Canadian, and Japanese citizens aged 18-30 can use the Working Holiday visa scheme to take temporary work whilst they stay in NZ for up to 12months. US citizens can stay for up to 90 days without a visa.

➲ **Requirements:** College Degree and a TESOL/TESL Certificate

➲ **Currency:** £1 = 2.82 / $1 = 1.44 Dollars

## Schools in New Zealand (+ 64)

**Auckland English Academy**
PO Box 11 241, Ellerslie, Auckland, New Zealand, **Tel**: +64 9-3793777, **Fax**: +64 9-358-3383, **Email:** learn@english.co.nz, **Web:** www.english.co.nz

**Auckland Institute of Studies**
PO Box 2995, Auckland, New Zealand, **Tel**: +64 9-815 3772, **Fax**: +64 9-815 1802, **Web:**www.ais.ac.nz

**Canterbury Language Institute**
PO Box 4425, Christchurch, New Zealand, **Tel**: +64 3-365 1920, **Fax**: +64 3-365 2296, **Email:** can.lancol@xtra.co.nz

**Dynaspeak English**
12 O'Connell Street, PO Box 106-052, Auckland 1001, New Zealand, **Tel**: +64 9 377 2434, **Fax**: +64 9 377 2811, **Web:** www.dynaspeak.co.nz

**Edenz Colleges**
Ideal House, 17 Eden St, Newmarket. Auckland, **Tel**: +64 9 815 3772, **Fax**: +64 9 522 1211, **Email:** edenz@edenz.com, **Web:** www.edenz.com

**ILA South Pacific - Auckland**
PO Box 9107, Auckland, New Zealand, **Tel**: +64 9 307 6507, **Fax**: +64 9 379 5749, **Email:** principal@ila.co.nz, **Web:**www.ila.co.nz

**ILA South Pacific - Christchurch**
PO Box 25170, Christchurch, New Zealand, **Tel**: +64 3 379 5452, **Fax**: +64 3 379 5957, **Email:** ilachch@ila.co.nz, **Web:**www.ila.co.nz

**LSNZ Christchurch & Queeenstown**
PO Box 911, Queenstown, New Zealand, **Tel**: +64 3 442 6625, **Fax**: +64 3 442 6676, **Web:**www.languageschool.co.nz

**Modern Age English Language School**
PO Box 2137, Tauranga, New Zealand, **Tel**: +64 7-576 8831, **Fax**: +64 7-578 5883, **Web:**www.modernage.co.nz

**New Horizon College of English**
PO Box 66, Napier, New Zealand, **Tel**: +64 6-835 6423, **Fax**: +64 6-835 6523, **Email:** office@nhce.ac.nz, **Web:** www.nhce.ac.nz

**Shane Global Village English Centre**
Level 2, 138 Queen Street. PO Box 105-347, Auckland., **Tel**:+64 (9) 309 2201, **Email:** auckland@sgvenglish.com, **Web:** www.sgvenglish.com

**Shore English School of Language New Zealand**
PO Box 33-614, Takapuna, Auckland, **Tel**: +64 9-486 1896, **Fax**: +64 9-486 0648, **Email:** shoreng@nznet.gen.nz, **Web:**www.shore-english.co.nz

**Southern Lakes English School**
PO Box 405, Queenstown, New Zealand, **Tel**: +64 3 442-7810, **Fax**: +64 3 442-7815, **Email:** slec@xtra.co.nz, **Web:** www.slec.co.nz

**Wellington College of Languages**
PO Box 9546, Wellington, New Zealand, **Tel**: +64 4 382 8938, **Fax**: +64 4 385 1518, **Email:** wcl@xtra.co.nz, **Web:** www.wcl.co.nz

**Worldwide School of English**
PO Box 1802, Auckland, New Zealand, **Tel**: +64 9 302 5288, **Fax**: +64 9 302 5299, **Email:** info@wwse.co.nz, **Web:** www.wwse.co.nz

# Asia

The English language is in great demand in Asia, particularly in China (including Hong Kong), Korea, Japan, Taiwan, and Thailand. In some countries in South East Asia (notably Singapore) the local government has introduced legislation to teach core subjects in English – students must learn maths and science in English.

China has seen an explosion of English language schools over the past few years - with native Chinese speakers learning English and learning to teach English with equal enthusiasm. Korea also offers a fast-changing EFL landscape, but is mostly dominanted by American-English language schools; by comparison, Japan and Thailand offer established school chains, networks for teachers and associations to help teachers.

The region has, mostly, recovered from the Asian economic crisis at the start of the 2000s; money has returned for education, and proficiency in English is widely regarded as essential for a successful career. For EFL teachers, levels of pay, the cost of living and working conditions vary considerably between the developed nations and the developing countries. Some teachers work long hours to live well and save a lot of money, whereas others supplement their income with their savings and use their spare time to travel. Whatever your goals, there is no doubt that you will have the experience of a lifetime should you choose to teach in Asia.

## BANGLADESH

Bangladesh is one of the most impoverished countries in the world. There are opportunities for EFL teachers here, mostly volunteer work with aid organizations and the Peace Corps.

### Schools in Bangladesh (+880)

**The British Council Teaching Centre**
754b Satmasjid Road, Dhanmondi, Dhaka 1205. **Tel:** 9116171/9116545. **Fax:** 8116554. **Email:** dto@TheBritishCouncil.net

**Regional Resources Centre**
SESDC Building, Teachers Training College, Bakulia, Chittagong. **Fax:** 031 612307.

## CAMBODIA

Cambodia is for the adventurous EFL teacher who enjoys getting off the beaten track. The country is still rebuilding after a long civil war and some areas are not safe, including the capital, Phnom Penh, where a number of teachers from Oklahoma were kidnapped and later released. Crime waves are sporadic so take the same precautions as you would in any major western city. Salaries are low when compared to the richer Asian nations. The better language schools (offering better rates of pay!) will want to see evidence of TESL certification but there are street corner schools who will take on an unqualified native speaker. Most schools employ teachers on a term-to-term basis so you are only guaranteed work for 10 weeks at a time. There is a lot of demand for English in Cambodia as the country slowly integrates with its neighbours. Few Cambodians can afford private lessons.

⮑ **Visas/Work Permits:** You can arrive in Cambodia and purchase a one-month working visa for £14 / $30. The working visa can be renewed without leaving the country. You don't have to prove you are actually working for someone when you arrive. Your school will not reimburse you for the cost of your visa.

⮑ **Requirements:** High School Diploma and a TESOL/TESL Certificate

⮑ **Requirements:** High School Diploma and a TESOL/TESL Certificate

⮑ **Currency:** £1 = 7455 / $1 = 4030 Riel

⮑ **Salaries/Taxes:** Schools pay around £6-10 / $10-20 an hour if you are qualified. Tax is 6%.

⮑ **Accommodation:** Rents have been forced up artificially high as Phnom Penh plays host to large groups of overpaid foreign aid workers. Flats are difficult to find and cost anywhere from £100-170 / $190-320 a month.

⮑ **Cost of Living:** The presence of well-paid foreign aid workers means that prices are sky-high in Phnom Penh. You can live on £6-10 / $11-20 a day if you rule out drinking at a smart hotel with the UN gang. Personal cheques and credit cards are not widely accepted within Cambodia, although a number of banks in Phnom Penh accept Visa cards for cash advances. Use dollars and/or Thai baht.

⮑ **Health advice:** The Cambodian medical system was virtually wiped out during the Khmer Rouge period, 1975-1979, and is being rebuilt slowly. Medical facilities and services in Cambodia are not up to western standards. Get shots for Hepatitis A, Malaria, Typhoid, and Polio. Make sure you have medical insurance that will guarantee and pay for evacuation in the case of an emergency.

⮑ **English Language Media:** The Cambodia Daily, Phnom Penh Post.

### Schools in Cambodia (+855)

**ACE**
46 Street 214, Sangkat Boeung Raing, Khan Daun Penh, Phnom Penh. **Email:** ace.idpcam@bigpond.com.kh

**ACE Battembang**
Rumcheak Village, Khum Ratanak, Svay Po, Battembang. **Tel:** 012-833602.

**ACE Siem Reap**
House 0675, Group 20, Wat Bo Village, Siem Reap, **Tel:** 012-833601.

**ACE Kompong Cham**
House 034, Group 1, Village 7, Sangkat Kompong Cham. **Tel:** 012-833600.

## CHINA

There is a huge demand for native-speaking English language teachers (both American and British English speakers), especially in the enterprise zones near Hong Kong. The demand for teachers is led both by private schools in China and by companies eager to take advantage of new international business opportunities. There is a need for ESP teachers, such as English for business, for tourism, for medical purposes and for law, the latter because many foreign firms regard cultural and legal differences between Chinese and external cultures as a major cause of failed western investments. Another area that is booming is teaching English for young learners but these positions are usually advertised by word of mouth and require an extrovert personality and infinite patience. Unqualified EFL teachers can find work here but given the demands of teaching in China a TESL certificate is highly recommended. Also, holders of more advanced qualifications like an MA in TESOL will be paid at higher rates because they are classified as Foreign Experts rather than Foreign Teachers who are usually under 25 and have a BA. Job seekers can contact the nearest Chinese embassy or State Bureau of Foreign Experts, Friendship Hotel, 3 Bai Shi Qiao Rd., 100873 Beijing. Tel: +86 10-849-888, x 83500, fax: +86 10-831-5832 for more information and should also check out the TEFLChina Teahouse site: www.teflchina.com– an excellent source of information about teaching English in China. There is also a listing of teaching jobs in China at www.teach-in-china.com

## Embassy in UK:
49 Portland Place, London W1N 4JL
**Tel:** 020 7631 1430
www.chinese-embassy.org.uk

## Embassy in USA:
2300 Connecticut Ave NW, Washington DC 20008
**Tel:** 202 328 2500
www.china-embassy.org

## British Council office:
4/f Landmark Building Tower 1, 8 North Dongsanhuan Road, Chaoyang District, 100004 Beijing
**Tel** +86 (10) 6590 6903
www.britishcouncil.cn

⮑ **Visas/Work Permits:** If you negotiate your job from home, then your employer or the agency will take care of the necessary paperwork. It is possible to go to China on a tourist visa and then start job hunting. Once you have a job, the school will send you to the Public Security Bureau (PSB) so that your visa can be changed. To obtain a visa, negative HIV test results are required for teachers who plan to stay nine months or more. Some teachers go to Hong Kong and secure six-month multiple entry visas from there.

⮑ **Requirements:** College Degree and a TESOL/TESL Certificate

⮑ **Currency:** £1 = 15.29 / $1 = 8.27 Yuan Renminbi (RMB)

⮑ **Salaries/Taxes:** Minimum salaries are RMB 2,500 per month for bachelors' degree holders and RMB 3,000 per month for masters' degree holders. Private tutors can charge around RMB 150-200 an hour in the big cities. There is no tax.

⮑ **Accommodation:** Your housing should be provided by the employer. Conditions can be harsh by Western standards although foreign teachers usually receive the best accommodation that the institution can offer.

⮑ **Cost of Living:** It is cheaper in the North than the South, excluding Beijing.

⮑ **Health advice:** Although most schools provide health insurance, which covers 80% of the cost, you should have your own insurance. The quality of medical care in China varies. Competent, trained doctors and nurses are available in major metropolitan centres, but many do not speak English. Hospital accommodation is spartan, and medical technology is not up-to-date. Doctors and hospitals often expect immediate cash payment for health services and may not accept cheques or credit cards.

⮑ **English Language Media:** Beijing Scene, China Daily, Shanghai Daily Star.

## Schools in China (+86)

### AES
102 Chang Jiang Liu, Dalian, 116001. **Tel:** (411) 281-7932. **Fax:** (411) 281-3318. **Email:** future@mail.dlptt.ln.cn

### American International School of Guangzhou
Box 212, Ti Yu Dong Post Office, 510620 Guangzhou. **Tel:** (20) 3881.0001/2711/2712,2713; **Fax:** (20) 3881.1102; **Email:** asg@gitic.com.cn; **Website:** www.concept.se/user/aisg/ aisg.html

### ASM Overseas Corp.
Asian Games Garden, Building No.2-6A. No.12 Xiaoying Lu, Chao Yang Dist., Beijing 100101. **Tel:** (10) 6497 4451. **Fax:** (10) 6497 4872.

### Capital Language School
101 Dong Yuan Lu, Zhongshan 528400.**Tel:** (760) 8335067. **Fax:** (760) 8335067.

### CDI Career Development Institute
110 Bloor Street West, Suite 202, Toronto, Ontario M5S 2W7, Canada. **Tel:** 1 416 964 6707, **Fax:** 1 416 964 0520.

### China International Education League
Suite C 4th floor, Zao Fong World-trade Building, Jiangsu Road 369, Shanghai 200050. **Tel:** (21) 52400111 **Fax:** (21) 52400101.

## China Teaching Program
Western Washington University, Old Main 530A, Bellingham, WA 98225-9047. **Tel:** (360) 650-3753, **Fax:** (360) 650-3753.

## Chinese Education Association for International Exchange
37 Damucang Hutong, Beijing 100816. **Tel:** (10) 660-20-731, **Fax:** (10) 660-16-56.

## Colorado China Council
4556 Apple Way, Boulder, CO 80301. **Tel:** (303) 443 1108, **Fax:** (303) 443-1107.

## Concordia International School Shanghai
Plot S2, Huang Yang Rd., P.O. Box 206-005, Pudong, 201206 Shanghai; **Tel:** (21) 5899.0380; **Fax:** (21) 5899.1685; **Email:** sandras@ciss.com.cn; **Website:** www.ciss.com.cn

## Fountain School
Ji Da Guo Mao, Zhuhai, Guangdong 519015. **Email:** wuvoka@mailcity.com

## The International School of Beijing
c/o American Embassy Beijing, PSC461, Box 50, FPO AP 96521-0002; **Tel:** (10) 6437.7119; **Fax:** (10) 6437.6989; **Email:** isb-info@isb.bj.edu.cn; **Website:** www.isb.bj.edu.cn

## New China Education Foundation
1587 Montalban Drive, San Jose, CA 95120. **Tel:** (408) 268 0418.

## Qingdao International School
Middle Sector Song Ling Rd., Stone Old Man National Tourism Spot, Qingdao, 266101. **Tel:** (532) 889-1000; **Fax:** (532) 889-8950l; **Email:** gbapk@hotmail.com **Website:** www.qischina.com

## Shanda International House
29-3 South Road Shanda, Jinan 250100, Shandong Province.**Tel:** +61 7 40 313466, **Fax:** +61 7 40 313 464.

## Shanghai American School
50 Ji Di Lu, Zhudi, Minhang, 201107 Shanghai. **Tel:** (21) 6221.1445 **Fax:** (21) 6221.1269. **Email:** info@saschina.org; **Website:** www.saschina.org

## Shanghai Changning International School
Jiangsu Lu 155, Shanghai 200050. **Tel:** (21) 6252-3688; **Fax:** 21-6212-2330; **Email:** scis@uninet.com.cn, **Website:** www.uninet.com.cn/ userhome/scis/index.htm

## Shekou International School
c/o Arco China, Inc., P.O. Box 260888, Plano, TX 75026-0888. **Tel:** (755) 669.3669; **Fax:** (755) 667.4099; **Email:** szejones@public.szptt.net.cn

## TEDA International School
Tianjin; 6 Mu Nan Dao, 300050 Tianjin; **Tel:** (22) 2311.4772. **Fax:** (22) 2331.2263; **Email:** tist@public1.tpt.tj.cn

## Tianjin International School
Xing Guo School, Xi Yuan Road, Ti Yuan Bei, He Xi District, 300061 Tianjin. **Tel:** (22) 283.53200. **Fax:** (22) 283.52455. **Email:** tmis@public1.tpt.tj.cn

## Western Academy of Beijing
P.O. Box 8547, 7A Bei Si Huan Dong Lu, Chao Yang Qu, Beijing 100102. **Tel:** (10) 6437.5935. **Fax:** (10) 6437.5936. **Email:** wabinfo@ns.wab.senet.gov.cn

## Wuhan Guanghua School
Jiangxia District, Wuhan, Hubei 430205. **Tel:** (27) 8794-4154, **Fax:** (27) 8794-5564. **Email:** doralei@netease.com

## Wuhan International School
c/o Holiday Inn Tian An Wuhan 868 Jie Fang Da Dao Wuhan 430022. **Tel:** (27) 8576-8863; **Fax:** (27) 8584-5353. **Email:** wis@teacher.com

## Xiamen International School
Jiu Tian Hu, Xinglin District, 361022 Xiamen; **Tel:** (592) 625.6581 **Fax:** (592) 625.6584. **Email:** JDFisch47@yahoo.com

## Yang-En University
Quanzhou, Fujian 362014. **Tel:** (595) 208 7600, Ext. 202. **Fax:** (595) 208 2017. **Email:** yeu@yeu.qz.fj.cn

## Yew Chung Shanghai International School (SIS)
11 Shui Cheng Road, 200336 Shanghai; **Tel:** (21) 6242.3243; **Fax:** (21) 6242.7331; **Email:** ycsis@public.sta.net.cn

## Yunnan Institute of the Nationalities
Foreign Affairs Office, Kunming 650031, Yunnan. **Tel:** (871) 515 4308.

## HONG KONG

The former British colony is now a Special Administrative Region within China. There are plenty of well-paid jobs here for EFL teachers although it is more difficult to obtain a working visa than it was in the past. The NET (Native-speaker English Teacher) program, operated by the Hong Kong Department of Education, allows qualified native speaker teachers to teach English in the public schools for 12 months. The scheme pays teachers anywhere from £1300-3500 / $2400-6500 per month plus a 15% gratuity payable on the completion of the contract. For more information about NET on the web, visit www.info.gov.hk/ed/english/teacher/native_eng_teach er/home.htm but be sure to confirm pay and other benefits before you decide to go.

## Embassy information:
*see China*

### British Council office:
3 Supreme Court Road, Admiralty, Hong Kong
**Tel** +852 291 35100
www.britishcouncil.org.hk

⮑ **Visas/Work Permits:** U.S. citizens can obtain tourist visas for stays of up to 90 days. To get a work permit, you need to be sponsored by an employer. One way to do this is to arrive in Hong Kong, land a job, and then leave the country while your application is being processed. If you work illegally, be aware that teachers have been deported in the past for overstaying their visas.

⮑ **Requirements:** College Degree and a TESOL/TESL Certificate

⮑ **Currency:** £1 = 15.18 / $1 = 7.77 HK Dollars

⮑ **Salaries/Taxes:** Teachers earn anywhere from HK$12,000 and up per month in the public schools to HK$50,000 at the top end in the private sector. Freelancers make from HK$300-750 or more per hour for private tuition.

⮑ **Accommodation:** Expensive if you are staying in Hong Kong itself, less so if you live on one of the other islands like Lamma, where a shared apartment costs around HK$2,500-3,000 a month.

⮑ **Cost of Living:** Expensive, until you learn where the best deals are.

⮑ **Health advice:** Medical facilities are excellent. Your employer should provide medical coverage for you.

⮑ **English Language Media:** Hong Kong Magazine, Hong Kong Standard, South China Morning Post.

### Schools in Hong Kong (+852)

#### Berlitz
1 Pacific Place, Central. **Tel:** 2826 9223, **Fax**: 2 525 9757.

#### English Language Club
Ka Nin Wah Commercial Building, Hennessy Road. **Tel:** 2 838 0036.

#### First Class Language Centre
22a Bank Tower, 351-353 King's Road, North Point. **Tel**: 5 887 7555.

#### Hong Kong English Club
Ground floor, 41 Carnarvon Road, Tsimshatsui, Kowloon. **Tel**: 2 366 6961.

#### HK Institute of Languages
Rm 501 30-32 D'Aguliar St, Central. **Tel**: 2 877 6160.

#### Island International High School
20 Borrett Road, Hong Kong.

#### Pasona Education
2/F One Hysan Ave, Causeway Bay. **Tel**: 2 577 8002.

#### The British Council
English Language Centre, 3 Supreme Court Road, Admiralty. **Tel**: 2 913 5100, **Fax**: 2 913 5102.

#### The Centre for Professional and Business English
7th Floor, Core B, Hong Kong Polytechnic University, T.S.T. **Tel**: 2 766 5111.

#### Venture Living Languages Ltd
1A 163 Hennessy Road, Hong Kong. **Tel**: 2 507 4985, **Fax**: 2 858 1764.

## INDONESIA

Indonesia is undergoing economic and political turmoil at present and the country is not as stable as it used to be. EFL teachers report that although life goes on as usual, especially in the big cities like Jakarta, Surabaya and Medan, demand for English lessons is slowing due to financial instability. If you decide to go to Indonesia, try getting a job with one of the larger and more reputable schools. Do not go unless you are offered a work visa, otherwise you will be working illegally and the authorities deal very harshly with offenders. For US teachers, anti-American sentiment is running high in some areas and caution should be exercised if you are travelling in Indonesia.

### British Council office:
S. Widjojo Centre, Jalan Jenderal Sudirman Kav 71, Jakarta 12190
**Tel** +62 (21) 252 4115
www.britishcouncil.or.id

⮑ **Visas/Work Permits:** Tourist visas are granted for up to two months. Some teachers do "visa runs" to Singapore or Darwin, Australia, when their visas run out but these trips are expensive, especially now that the rupiah is worth so little. Your school should arrange a work permit for you. Vacation time is usually given at Christmas and one week at the end of Ramadan.

◆ **Requirements:** High School Diploma and a TESOL/TESL Certificate

◆ **Currency:** £1 = 17706 / $1 = 9063 Rupiah.

◆ **Salaries/Taxes:** Teachers are paid in rupiah. Your contract should guarantee that you are paid between 6-8 million rupiah a month. If the amount is less than that, you will find it difficult to live in Indonesia. There is a mandatory tax of £90 / $170 each month imposed on all foreigners.

◆ **Accommodation:** You should receive free or subsidized housing as part of your employment package. Rents are generally cheaper outside of Jakarta.

◆ **Cost of Living:** Food, clothing and other basics are reasonable.

◆ **Health advice:** Make sure your school offers you insurance coverage that offers protection against sickness and that will evacuate you in the event of full scale rioting.

◆ **English Language Media:** Indonesian Times, Indonesian Observer, Jakarta Post.

---

### Schools in Indonesia (+62)

**American English Language Training (AELT)**
Jalan R.S. Fatmawati 42a, Keb Baru, Jakarta Selatan 12430. **Tel:** 21 769 1001, **Fax:** 21 751 3304.

**American Language** centre
Jl. Panglima Polim Raya No. 101, Kebayoran Baru, Jakarta 12160. **Tel:** (21) 722-8957, **Fax:** (21) 722-8960.

**Centre for Language Training (CLT)**
Soegijapranata Catholic University, Jl. Menteri Supeno 35, Semarang 50241. **Tel:** 24 316028, **Fax:** 24 415429.

**English Education Centre (EEC)**
Jalan Let. Jend S.Parman 68, Slipi, Jakarta 11410. **Tel:** 21 532 3176, **Fax:** 21 532 3178.

**Executive English Programmes (EEP)**
Jalan Wijaya VIII 4, Kebayoran Baru, Jakarta Selatan 12160. **Tel:** 21 720 1896.

**ELS International**
Jalan Tanjung Karang 7 c-d, Jakarta Pusat. **Tel:** 21 323 211.

**English First Bogor**
Jl. Raya Pajajaran No.8, Bogor 16151.**Tel:** 251 324374, **Fax:** 251 379296.

**EF English First Kelapa Gading**
Jl.Raya Bulevar Barat Blok LA 1 no 8 - 9 Kelapa Gading Permai Jakarta 14240. **Tel:** 21 451 5858. **Fax:** : 21 451 5959.

**EF English First Lampung**
Jl. Diponegoro No. 146, Bandar Lampung 35127. **Tel:** 721 263154, **Fax:** 721 263154.

**EF English First (Ujung Pandang)**
Jl. Slt. Hasanuddin 27, Ujung Pandang 90113. **Tel:** 411 315288, **Fax:** 411 315251.

**English Language Training International (ELTI)**
Complex Wijaya Grand Centre, Blok F 84A & B, Jalan Wijaya II, Jakarta Selatan 12160. **Tel:** 21 720 6653, **Fax:** 21 720 6654.

**Indonesia-Australia Language Foundation (IALF)**
Wisma Budi, Suite 503, Jalan HR Rasuna Said Kav c-6, Kuningan, Jakarta Selatan 12940. **Tel:** 521 3350.

**International Language Programmes (ILP)**
Jalan Raya Pasar Minggu No. 39A, Jakarta 12780. **Tel:** 21 798 5210, **Fax:** 21 798 5212.

**International Language Studies (ILS)**
Jalan Ngemplak 30, Arbengan Plaza B-34, Surabaya 60272. **Tel:** 31 531 9644, **Fax:** 31 531 9645.

**I-Pro International Programmes**
Jl Ngagel 179 -183, K1, Surabaya 60245. **Tel:** 31 566 2914/5, **Fax:** 31 566 7979.

**Logo Education Centre (LEC)**
Jelan H.Z. Arifin 208A, Medan, Sumatra Utara. **Tel:** 61 534991, **Fax:** 61 552385.

**Maple Leaf English Language Centre**
Jl. Raya Darmo Permai II / 32, Surubaya. **Tel:** 31 710722. **Fax:** (031) 725476

**Oxford Course Indonesia (OCI)**
Jalan Cempaka Putih Tengah 33C-2, Jakarta Pusat 10510. **Tel:** 21 424 3224, **Fax:** 21 425 4041.

**Professional Training Services (PTS)**
Wisma BII, Jalan Permuda No. 60-70, Surabaya 60271. **Tel/Fax:** 31 531 0006.

**School for International Communication**
Jalan Taman Pahlawan 194, Purwakarta. **Tel:** 264 201204.

**School for International Training (SIT)**
Jalan Sunda 3, Menteng, Jakarta Pusat 10350. **Tel:** 21 390 6920, **Fax:** 21 335671.

**Strive International**
Setiabudi 1 Building, Jalan HR Rasuna Said, Jakarta 12920. **Tel:** 21 521 0690, **Fax:** 21 521 0692.

**The British Institute (TBI)**
Plaza Setiabudi 2, Jalan HR Rasuna Said, Jakarta
12920. **Tel:** 21 525 6750, **Fax:** 21 520 7574.

**Triad English Centre**
Jalan Purnawarman 76 Bandung- 40116. **Tel:** 62 22
431309, **Fax:** 22 431149.

## JAPAN

Despite the recent economic crisis, Japan is still a
popular destination for English teachers, qualified or
not, because of the number of jobs available and the
favourable salaries. Japan's commitment to learning
English was recently demonstrated in very clear terms
by Prime Minister Keizo Obuchi's recent statement
that, "Achieving world-class excellence demands that
all Japanese acquire a working knowledge of English."
But it must be noted that the standard pay of 250,000
yen per month for an EFL teacher has hardly changed
in the last few years despite rising inflation so teaching
contracts in Japan are not as lucrative as they once
were.

After-hours schools where students cram for
exams, including English language, are known as juku.
An eikaiwa is an English conversation school.
Unqualified teachers can find work in private schools
giving conversation classes or through Japan's
Exchange and Teaching (JET) programme (see below).
There are also chains of schools, such as AEON,
GEOS and NOVA employing thousands of trained and
untrained teachers. The best time to come to Japan and
look for a job is in March just before the start of the
school year on April 1. The big chains of schools
recruit teachers year-round. If you negotiate your
employment with a recruiter outside of Japan
remember that the agreement you make is not binding.
It is the contract with the school in Japan that governs
the terms of your employment. Also, be aware that you
may run into problems if you decide to go off and
work for another school once you are in Japan. Your
first employer may not be happy that you are leaving
after so much of the school's money and time has been
invested in you. If you work outside of Tokyo, you
may need an International Drivers' Licence if the
school provides you with a car. It can take up to six
months to get acclimatized to Japan. Prepare yourself
before you go: look at the ELT News website for
regularly updated information about teaching in Japan
(www.eltnews.com).

**The JET Program**
The Japan Exchange and Teaching programme is a
Japanese government scheme aimed at improving
English language teaching and international relations
in schools. Although 34 countries are involved in the
program, the majority of the almost 6,000 participants
are from the US. Anyone under 35, with a degree and
an interest in Japan, can apply. The salary and
conditions are excellent – you get about £20,000 /
$38,000 for the year, free return airfare, 3-day
orientation and you work in conjunction with a
Japanese teacher – one participant described it as the
best job in the world! Applications must be in by early
December for the following summer.
**Contact:** www.jetprogramme.org

**Embassy in UK:**
101-104 Piccadilly, London W1V 9FN
**Tel:** 020 7465 6500
www.embjapan.org.uk

**Embassy in USA:**
2520 Massachusetts Ave NW, Washington DC20008
**Tel:** 202 238 6700

**British Council office:**
1-2 Kagurazaka, Shinjuku-ku, Tokyo 162-0825
**Tel** +81 (3) 3235 8031
www.britishcouncil.org/japan

➲ **Visas/Work Permits:** The opportunity to obtain a
working visa to teach in Japan is generally available to
native English speakers with a valid college diploma in
any field. The sponsoring employer in Japan must first
obtain a "Certificate of Eligibility" from the Japanese
Ministry of Justice, Immigration Bureau, for the
prospective teacher. With this certificate, you can
apply for a work visa at the Japanese Embassy (or at a
Japanese Consulate) prior to entering Japan. If you try
to enter into Japan as a tourist under the 90-day visa
waiver programme to work, you may be denied entry,
but you can enter to look for work. If you enter Japan
as a tourist and subsequently obtain an offer to teach,
you must leave the country, taking the "Certificate of
Eligibility" to a Japanese Embassy/Consulate in the
U.S. or a neighbouring country (usually Korea), to
obtain a work visa, and then re-enter Japan on the
correct visa. If you are from Canada, Australia or New
Zealand, you can teach in Japan on a working holiday
visa, which can be obtained in your own country. You
must be between the ages of 18-30 to go on the
working holiday programme. The visa is for six
months, renewable only once. After that you have to

find a sponsor or a legal visa to continue working in Japan.

◗ **Requirements:** College Degree and a TESOL/TESL Certificate

◗ **Currency:** £1 = 230 / $1 = 118 Yen.

◗ **Salaries/Taxes:** Salaries begin at around 250,000 yen per month with airfares and end-of-contract bonuses offered to more qualified candidates. If you are teaching privately, expect to earn 3,000-6,000 yen per lesson. Salaries are usually based on an hourly wage with a guarantee of a certain minimum number of hours per month. Many teachers hold side jobs as private tutors outside of their classroom workplaces. Income tax in Japan is approximately 10% of your gross income. Watch out for deductions by employers for accommodation and other expenses, which, if you are not careful, can leave you with about half your salary left to live on. It should be possible for you to save a fair amount of money after living in Japan for a few months.

◗ **Accommodation:** Many schools provide free or subsidized housing as part of the employment package. If a school is taking a large percentage of your pay packet (more than 25%) then you should question the contract. If you try to rent on your own you should be aware that housing is much smaller, more expensive and complicated to rent than in the west. Rents range from 60,000-100,000 Yen per month in Tokyo, but in smaller towns you can pay a quarter of that. Landlords can be reluctant to rent to foreigners, so it's worth getting somebody to help. There are agents who can do this, otherwise you might have to pay as much as £3000 / $5,700 in advance as a security deposit ('key money'). Schools that recruit overseas often include accommodation assistance as a benefit.

◗ **Cost of Living:** The cost of living, especially in cities, is very high. Don't be surprised if a simple night out with some friends costs you $100 or more! Supporting a family in Japan, according to middle class American standards, is well beyond the reach of most English teachers. However, salaries are high. It is possible to save money, especially outside Tokyo.

◗ **Health advice:** Most teachers are covered by the Japanese national health insurance plan, which does not pay for treatment outside of Japan. While recently on the rise, health care costs remain relatively low in Japan. The self-employed, employees of small businesses, and others not covered by employer plans can apply to the government for low-cost National Health Insurance, which provides coverage similar to workplace-based insurance. Teachers should obtain private, supplemental health insurance that includes worldwide medical evacuation and care. Vaccinations recommended are Polio and Typhoid.

◗ **English Language Media:** Japan Times, Kansai Time Out, The Asahi Evening News, The Daily Mainichi.

## Schools in Japan (+82)

### A Ring English Conversation
3-9-12-304 Nishi Shinagawa, Shinagawa-ku, Tokyo, **Tel:** 0120-750510.

### Academy of Language Arts
Tobundo Bldg. No.2 5F, 2-16 Agebacho, Shinjuku-ku, Tokyo. **Tel:** 03-3235-0071. **Fax:** 03-3235-0004. **Website:** www.kbic.ardour.co.jp /~newgenji/ala/

### ACE English School
6-6-22 Hachimancho, Takahmashi Aichiken, 444-1302. **Tel:** 566 52 3235. **Fax:** 566 52 3235.

### AEON Inter-Cultural
Shinjuku I-Land Tower Bldg. 12F, 6-5-1 Nishishinjuku, Shinjuku-ku, Tokyo 163-1377. **Tel:** 03-5381-1500. **Fax:** 03-5381-1501. **Email:** aejedu@corp.aeonet.co.jp)

### Ai Language Studio
Hiroo Stone Bldg. 5F, 1-3-17 Hiroo, Shibuya-ku, Tokyo. **Tel:** 03-5421-3572. **Fax:** 03-5421-3573. **Website:** http://plaza24.mbn.or.jp/~als/ **Email:**tokim@bd.mbn.or.jp

### AIT Foreign Language Centre
3-20-1-401, Tamagawa, Setagaya-ku, Tokyo. **Tel:** 03-3700-8110. **Fax:** 03-3700-8889. **Website:** www2.tky.3web.ne.jp/~ai **Email:** aitcorp@tky2.3web.ne.jp

### Alpha Language School
3-4-11 Mita, Minato-ku, Tokyo. **Tel:** 03-3769-4945. **Fax:** 03-3769-4946. **Email:**ala@a2.mbn.or.jp

### American Academy
4-1-3 Kudan Kita Chiyoda-Ku, Tokyo 102.

### America Eiko Gakuin
Misono-cho 5-2-21, Wakayama City 640.

### American School of Business
1-17-4 Higashi Ikebukuro, Toshima-Ku, Tokyo 170.

### Azabu Academy
401 Shuwa-Roppongi Building, 3-14-12 Roppongi, Minato-ku, Tokyo 106.

### Berlitz Schools of Languages (Japan) Inc.
Kowa Bldg. 1,5f, 11-41, Alasaka 1-chome, Minato-ku, Tokyo 107.

**Bernard Group**
2-8-11 Takezono, Tsukuba City, Ibaraki-Ken, 305.

**CA English Academy**
2nd Floor Kotohira Building, 9-14 Kakuozan-dori, Chikusa-ku, Nagoya.

**Cambridge English School**
Dogenzaka 225 Building, 2-23-14 Dogenzaka, Shibuya-ku,Tokyo 150.

**Cambridge School of English**
Kikumura 91 Building1-41-20 Higashi, Ikebukuro Toshima-ku, Tokyo 170.

**Canadian School of Languages**
3-9-7-202 Kameari, Katsushika-ku, Tokyo. **Tel:** 03-3601-7648.

**Canning**
The, 2-9 Kanda Surugadai, Chiyoda-ku, Tokyo. **Tel:** 03-3295-5500

**CEC Foreign Language centre**
Takahashi Bldg. 3F, 1-44-3 Fuda, Chofu City, Tokyo. **Tel:** 0424-87-3623. **Fax:** 0424-87-3664.

**Celc English School**
1-3-5 Mejirodai, Hachioji City, Tokyo. **Tel:** 0426-66-5041 **Fax:** 0426-66-5042. **Website:** http://member.nifty.ne.jp/celc/index.html

**CIC English Schools**
Kawamoto Building, Imadegawaagaru Nishigawa Karasuma-dori, Kamigyo-ku, Kyoto.

**Cosmopolitan Language Institute**
1-8-9 Yaesu, Chou-ku, Tokyo. **Tel:** 03-3273-7878. **Fax:** 03-3273-7870.

**Cosmopolitan Language Institute**
Yashima B Building 4f, 1-8-9 Yesu Chuo-ku,Tokyo 104.

**Daigakushorin International Language Academy**
AM Bldg., 9 Rokubancho, Chiyoda-ku, Tokyo. **Tel:** 03-3264-2131. **Fax:** 03-3264-2133.

**David English House**
2-3f Nakano Building, 1-5-17 Kamiyacho, Naka-ku, Hiroshima 730.

**Den House International Language School**
Meguro Ekimae School, Tamagawa Bldg. 3F, 2-16-5 Kami Osaki, Shinagawa-ku, Tokyo. **Tel:** 03-3280-4255.

**Den House International Language School**
Tsukahara Bldg. 2F, 7-19-9 Okusawa, Setagaya-ku, Tokyo. **Tel:** 03-3704-7636. **Fax:** 03-3704-7696.

**Dual International School**
ILYA Bldg. 3F, 1-1 Yotsuya-dori, Chikusa-ku, Nagoya, 464-0819. **Tel:** 052-783-3031. **Fax:** 052-783-3035. **Email:** dual6@spice.or.jp

**Educational Information Institute**
Level 7, 2-15-22 Shinjuku, Shinjuku-ku, Tokyo. **Tel:** 03-5366-7201. **Fax:** 03-5366-7203. **Email:** eiijabli@mx2.ttcn.ne.jp

**EEC Foreign Languages Institute**
Shikata Building 2f, 4-43 Nakazald-Nishi 2-chrome, Kita-ku, Osaka 530.

**EII Educational Information Institute**
S2 Bldg. 7F, 2-15-22 Shinjuku, Shinjuku-ku, Tokyo. **Tel:** 03-3352-5280. **Fax:** 03-3352-5871

**ELEC Eigo Kenkyujo (The English Language Education Council)**
3-8 Kanda Jimbo-cho, Chiyoda-ku,Tokyo 101.

**English Plus**
Bell Maison Minami Azabu 1F, 1-3-17 Minami Azabu, Minato-ku, Tokyo. **Tel:** 03-5238-0111. **Fax:** 03-5238-0300.

**English Studio**
Meguro School, 5-12-2 Shimo Meguro, Meguro-ku, Tokyo. **Tel:** 03-3712-3313. **Fax:** 03-3710-3386. **Email:**e-studio@tkc.att.ne.jp

**English Studio**
Mita School, 4-2-14 Mita, Minato-ku, Tokyo. **Tel:** 03-3798-5829. **Fax:** 03-3769-9397. **Email:** e-studio@tkc.att.ne.jp

**English Studio**
Setagaya School, 2-31-11 Oyamadai, Setagaya-ku, Tokyo. **Tel:** 03-5758-2491. **Fax:** 03-5758-2492. **Email:** e-studio@tkc.att.ne.jp

**English Telephone Club**
1-19-28 Minami Oizumi, Nerima-ku, Tokyo. **Tel:** 03-3924-3853. **Fax:** 03-3978-0990. **Website:** www.aoki.com/job/etc

**Eurocentres Japan**
2-12 Kanda Surugadai, Chiyoda-ku, Tokyo. **Tel:** 03-3295-5441. **Fax:** 03-3295-5443. **Email:** euro-tyo@orange.ifnet.or.jp

**Evergreen Language School**
1-21-18 Yutenji, Meguro-ku, Tokyo. **Tel:** 03-3713-4958. **Fax:** 03-3719-4383. **Website:** www.evergreen.gr.jp

**Executive Gogaku Centre (Executive Language Centre)**
1 Kasumigaseki Building, 12F, 3-2-5 Kasumigaseki, Chiyoda-ku,Tokyo 100.

**English Circles/EC Inc.**
President Building 3rd Floor, South-1, Chuo-Ku, Sapporo 060. **Tel:** 011 221 0279.

**FCC (Fukuoka Communication Centre)**
Dai Roku Okabe Building, 5f, Hakata Eki Higashi, 2-4-17 Hakata-ku, Fukuoka 812.

**F L Centre (Foreign Language Centre)**
1 Iwasaki Building, 3f, 2-19-20 Shibuya-ku,Tokyo 150.

**Four Seasons Language School**
Aoyamashorin 2F, 4-32-11 Sanarudai, Hamamatsu-shi 432. **Tel:** 534 48 1501.

**Fukuoka International School**
3-18-50 Momochi, Sawara-ku, 814-0006 Fukuoka. **Tel:** 92- 841.7601, **Fax:** 92-841-7602, **Email:** adminfis@fka.att.ne.jp

**Galaxy Language Academy**
Noda Bldg., 2-12-1 Kami Osaki, Shinagawa-ku, Tokyo. **Tel:** 03-3473-3251. **Fax:** 03-3473-3334. **Website:** www.jade.dti.ne.jp/~galaxy **Email:** galaxy@jade.dti.ne.jp

**Gateway Gakuin Rokko**
Atelier House, 3-1-15 Yamada-cho, Nada-ku, Kobe.

**GEOS Language System**
Shin Osaki Bldg. 4F, 1-6-4 Osaki, Shinagawa-ku, Tokyo. **Tel:** 03-5434-0200.

**Global English School**
1887-86 Kubo-cho, Matsusaka, Mie 515-0044. **Tel:** 598-60-0873. **Fax:** 598-29-8730. **Email:** recruit@ges-hiro.co.jp

**Gregg Int'l School of Language**
1-14-16 Jiyugaoka, Meguro-ku, Tokyo. **Tel:** 03-3718-0552.

**Gunma Language** centre **& Language Academy**
840, Munadaka, Gunma 370-3521. **Tel:** 273-732310. **Fax:** 273-730846. **Email:** glc@mail.wind.co.jp

**Hearts English School**
2146-3 Shido, Shido-cho, Okawa-gun, Kagawa 769-21. **Tel:** 878 943557, **Fax:** 947227.

**Hiroshima International School**
3-49-1, Kurakake, Asakita-ku, 739-1743 Hiroshima. **Tel:** 82-843-4111, **Fax:** 82-843-6399, **Email:** hisadmin@orange.ocn.ne.jp

**ICA Kokusai Kaiwa Gakuin (International Conversation Academy)**
1 Mikasa 2 Building, 1-16-10 Nishi.

**IF Foreign Language Institute**
7f Shin Nakashima Building, 1-9-20 Nishi Nakashima, Yodogawa-ku, Osaka.

**inlingua School of Languages**
Kyodo Bldg. 9F, 2-4-2 Nihombashi Muromachi, Chuo-ku, Tokyo. **Tel:** 03-3231-0167. **Fax:** 03-3245-0086. **Email:** inlingua@fa.mbn.or.jp

**INTECO Business English School**
4-2-25 Akasaka, Minato-ku, Tokyo. **Tel:** 03-5570-2821 **Fax:** 03-5570-4323 **Website:** www2.gol.com/users/inteco/ **Email:** inteco@gol.com

**Jelly Beans English School**
16-908 Shinyashiki cho, Kagoshima City 892-0838. **Tel:** 90-2511-9733. **Fax:** 81-99-224-7595.

**Kains English School in Gakko**
1-5-2 Ohtemon Chuo-ku, Fukuoka 810.

**KICC English and Computer School**
1-8-13 Horai, Shingu, Wakayama 647. **Tel:** 735-28-2230. **Fax:** 735-28-2234. **Email:** kiccjob@kiccworld.com

**King's Road School of English**
Akasaka 4-3-9, Takaike Bldg 3F, Minato-ku, Tokyo 107. **Tel:** 03 3589 8666, **Fax:** 03 3589 7868.

**Kyoto English Centre**
Sumitomo Seimei Building, Shijo-Karasuma Nishi-iru Shimogyo-ku, Kyoto.

**Kobe Language Centre**
3-18 Wakinoharnacho, 1-chome, Chuo-ku, Kobe 651. **Tel:** 78 2614316.

**Language Education Centre**
7-32 chome Ohtemachi Nakaku, Hiroshima-shi 730.

**London Study Centre**
1-1 Tamanuki, Ohyama, Ohtama, Fukushima 969-1301. **Tel:** 0243 48 4286. **Fax:** 0243 48 4286. **Email:** londoneigakuin@hotmail.com

**Luna International**
1-2-9 Asahi, Matsumoto-shi 390-0802. **Tel:** 263-34-4481. **Fax:** 263-34-4481.

**Matty's School of English**
3-15-9 Shonan-takatori, Yokosuka 234. **Tel:** 468 658717.

**Michigan English School**
Enya Bld. 2F, 7-34 Sanae-cho, Gifu-city, Gifu, 500-8304. **Tel:** 058 251 9421. **Fax:** 058 251 9850. **Email:** michigan@ktroad.ne.jp

**MIL Language Centre**
3.4F Eguchi Bldg, 1-6-2 Katsutadai, Yachiyo-shi, Chiba-ken 276. **Tel:** 474 857555.

**Miyazaki College**
2520-88, Hongo-kitakata, Miyazaki 880-0925. **Tel:** 985-52-7568. **Fax:** 985-52-7568.

### Mobara English Institute
618-1 Takashi, Mobara-shi, Chiba-ken 297. **Tel:** 475 224785.

### Mukogawa Women's University
Edagawa-cho 4-16, Nishinomiya-city, Hyogo-ken 545-0002. **Tel:** 0798-47-6436. **Fax:** 06-6719-2093.

### NOVA Group
Harajuku Carillon Bldg. 4F, 1-8-9 Jingumae, Shibuya-ku, Tokyo 150-0001. **Tel:** 03-3478-3475. **Fax:** 03-3478-3665.)

### Op-Net English Institute
Torinose 222-1, Iwata-shi, Shizuoka-ken 438-0072. **Tel:** 0538 34 8686. **Fax:** 0538 36 1217. **Email:** opnet1@peace.ne.jp

### Ph.D. Language centre
743 Aramaki-machi, Maebashi-shi, Gunma-ken 371-0044. **Tel:** 027 233 8442. **Fax:** 027 233 8442.

### Plus Alpha
2-25-20 Denenchofu, Ota-Ku, Tokyo 145.

### Queens School of English
3f Yuzuki Bldg, 4-7-14 Minamiyawata, Ichikawa 272.

### Pegasus Language Services
Sankei Building, 1-7-2 Otemachi Chiyoda-ku, Tokyo 100.

### REC School of Foreign Language
Nijojo-mae Ebisugawasagaru Higashihorikawa-dori, Nakagyo-ku, Kyoto.

### Royal English Language Centre
4-31-3-2 Chyo Hakata-ku, Fukuoka 82.

### Seido Language Institute
12-6 Funado-cho, Ashiya-shi, Kyoto.

### Stanton School of English
12 Gobancho Chiyoda-ku, Tokyo 102.

### Sumikin-Intercom, Inc
Andrew Vaughan, 7-28 Kitahama 4-Chome, Chou-ku, Osaka 541 **Tel:** 06 220 5500, **Fax:** 06 220 5713.

### Sun Eikaiwa School
6f Cherisu Hachoubori Building, 6-7 Hachoubori Naka-ku, Hiroshima-shi 730.

### Toefl Academy
1-12-4 Kundankita, Chiyoda-ku, Tokyo 102. **Tel:** (3) 2303500.

### Tokyo English Centre
(TEC) 7-9 Uguisudai-cho, Shibuyaku, Tokyo 150.

### Tokyo Language Centre
Tatsunama Building, 1-2-19 Yaesu, Chuo-Ku, Tokyo 103.

### Tokyo YMCA College of English
7 Kanda Mitoshiro-Cho, Chiyoda-ku, Tokyo T-101.

### Trident School of Languages
1-5-31 Imaike, Chikusa-ku, Nagoya 464.

### Westgate HR Department
1173-1 Hagiwara, Gotemba Shizuoka 412-0042. **Fax:** 550-84-0770

### World Language School Inc
Tokiwa Soga Ginko Building 4f 1-22-8 Jinnan, Shibuya-ku, Tokyo 171.

## KOREA (SOUTH)

A favourite destination for teachers of English over the last 15 years, South Korea has witnessed rapid economic growth and foreign investment, and even if the economic situation is not as favourable as in the past, there are still many opportunities. Korean is the major language, but some Mandarin Chinese is spoken. English is not widely spoken but is much sought after. Crime is not a major problem but be aware that nationalist sentiments are on the increase, particularly in view of recent economic difficulties and sales to foreign companies. As the number of teachers applying to go to Korea has decreased you should be able to find a job easily and, with the right qualifications, you can secure some very favourable terms and conditions. Many teachers are able to build up significant savings while working in Korea.

In the past, many travellers took casual teaching jobs on tourist visas. However, the government has cracked down on illegal workers. Anyone found working without a work permit will be deported and any companies found employing illegal workers risk being closed down.

One popular type of school is known as the hagwon. These are privately-run schools where Koreans learn English, usually on a daily basis before they go to work in the morning or in the evenings. If you teach in one of these schools, you'll be expected to teach 20-30 hours a week and you'll have free time during the day. Finding a job in a hagwon should not be a problem. Try and get a reference from a teacher already working at the hagwon you are thinking of working for. Also, if you can have a Korean-speaker help you go through your contract, it may help you in the event of a dispute—the Korean language contract takes precedence over the English language version and the two do not always match up. Another place to find a teaching job in Korea is in a chaebol. These are the large corporations that dominate business in Korea (like Hyundai). Many run their own in-house English language programmes. Expect to work at least 30 hours a week from early morning until late at night. If you have an MA in TESOL you could look for a job in a university language institute. The institutes offer better pay and conditions than hagwons or the chaebol – so the staff turnover is low. Do not confuse working in a university foreign language institute with teaching in a university department. Departmental teaching involves conversational English classes with large numbers of university students for about 10-15 hours a week. Private lessons offer teachers the chance to supplement their incomes but you should know that working for another school other than your official employer or teaching privately is illegal. Some teachers have been imprisoned and/or deported for giving private lessons. If you do teach private students insist on payment in advance for the lessons.

In 1995, the Korean government started the EPIK (English programme in Korea) program, which sends English language instructors to work in Korean middle and high schools. EPIK participants are paid according to their qualifications anywhere from 1.6-2 million won a month. Airfares and accommodation are included in the package. In 2000, 392 teachers took part in the programme. Reactions from participants have been mixed — some teachers were unhappy at being placed in rural schools far from the big cities and contact with other foreigners. But most old Korea hands agree that it is a good way to be introduced to the country's culture and people. Contact your closest Korean consulate or embassy for more information. The website is http://cc.knue.ac.kr/~epik/off.htm

**Embassy in UK:**
60 Buckingham Gate, London SW1E 6AJ
**Tel:** 020 7227 5505

**Embassy in USA:**
2450 Massachusetts Avenue NW, Washington DC20008
**Tel:** 202 939 5600

**British Council office:**
Joongwhoo Building, 61-21 Taepyungro 1 Ka, Choong-ku, Seoul, Korea100-101
**Tel** +82 (2) 3702 0600
www.britishcouncil.or.kr

➲ **Visas/Work Permits:** In order to work legally in Korea, one must first obtain the appropriate employment visa. The Korean government tightly controls employment visas and sometimes teachers have been unable to obtain visas. A person who wishes to work in Korea must obtain the visa outside Korea. One can, however, come to Korea on a tourist visa, obtain sponsorship documents, and apply for the visa in a nearby country. Depending on the job and other factors, it can take between one week and two months to obtain the appropriate visa. A teacher arriving in Korea with a teaching visa must register with Korean Immigration and obtain a residence certificate and re-entry permit within 90 days of entry. Most English instructors are granted an E-2 visa (conversation instructor), an E-1 visa (professor at educational institution higher than a junior college), or an E-5 visa (professional employment with a public relations firm or corporation). Once you have your permit, do not allow your employer to keep your passport even if he or she says that you are obliged to do so – you are not!

➲ **Requirements:** College Degree and a TESOL/TESL Certificate

➲ **Currency:** £1 = 1806 / $1 = 925 Won.

➲ **Salaries/Taxes:** The average salary at a hagwon is equivalent to about £1,000 / $1,900 per month. You can earn £1,200 / $2,200 or more at a chaebol. University departments pay c. £1,000 / $1,900 per month while the foreign language institutes pay the highest salaries. It is possible to earn £30 / $57 per hour with private tuition. Taxation rates depend on how much you are actually making – they range from 10-40% of your income. There is also a residency tax of 7.5%. If your employer tries to deduct a "security deposit" from your wages for any reason, refuse (politely but firmly).

➲ **Accommodation:** Your employer should meet your accommodation needs otherwise renting an apartment is an expensive and complicated process. You will probably find yourself sharing a small apartment with some fellow teachers. Apartments vary in quality.

➲ **Cost of Living:** Korea is not a cheap place to live in — especially if you are fond of sampling the nightlife. This the reason why so many teachers risk deportation lured by the extra cash of private lessons.

➲ **Health advice:** Your employer should cover your insurance costs.

➲ **English Language Media:** Korea Herald, Korea Times.

## Schools in South Korea (+81)

**All Nations Community Church**
Yuksamdong Youngdong APT 28-105, Yuksamdong 765, Seoul 135-082. **Tel:** (02) 555-0691.

**ANC Language Institute**
2nd Fl., Taeyoung Bldg., Daechi-dong, Kangnam-gu, Seoul. **Tel:** (02) 508-0081.

**ANS Recruiters**
Seocho-gu, Seocho-dong 1575-2, Soryong Bldg. 5th Fl. Seoul, Korea 137-070. **Tel:** (02) 3472-0020. **Fax:** (02) 3472-2173.

**ARC Language Education**
636-1 Shinsa-dong, Kangnam-gu, Seoul. **Tel:** (02) 511-9311.

**BCM Institute (Konkuk University)**
3nd Fl. Daeyang Bldg., 8-3 Noyu 1-dong, Kwangjin-gu, Seoul. **Tel:** (02) 499-0515. **Fax:** (02) 464-0516.

**BCM Institute (Kuro)**
1123-3 Kuro 3-dong, Kuro-gu, Seoul. **Tel:** (02) 830-2121. **Fax:** (02) 830-2124.

**BCM Institute (Pundang)**
4th Fl. Kwangrim Praza, Sohyon-dong, Pundang-gu, Kyonggi-do. **Tel:** (031) 708-9090. **Fax:** (031) 708-3161.

**BCM Institute (Sanggye)**
6th Fl. Kyongwon Bldg., Sanggye-dong, Nowon-gu, Seoul. **Tel:** (02) 933-8656. **Fax:** (02) 933-4525.

**BCM Institute (Songpa)**
11th Fl. Taemun Bldg., 174-2 Sokchon-dong, Songpa-gu, Seoul. **Tel:** (02) 412-2335. **Fax:** (02) 412-2350.

**Berlitz Korea company**
2nd Fl., Sungwoo Academy Bldg., 1316-17 Socho-dong, Socho-gu, Seoul. **Tel:** (02) 3481-5324.

**Berlitz Language Centre (Ulchiro)**
16th Fl. Ileun Jungkwon Bldg., 198 Ulchiro 2-ga, Chung-gu, Seoul. **Tel:** (02) 775-1441. **Fax:** (02) 775-8088.

**Chungmoon Language Institute**
18-4 Kwanchol-dong, Chongno-gu, Seoul. **Tel:** (02) 738-5151.**Fax:** (02) 738-6150.

**CPI Foreign Language Academy**
#2-24, Mullae-dong, Yongdungpo-gu, Seoul. **Tel:** (02) 723-8882. **Fax:** (02) 2631-0928. **Email:** sscyber@sscyber.com

**Daewon Language School**
3nd Fl. Hyundae Chonghap Sangga, 615 Shinsa-dong, Kangnam-gu, Seoul. **Tel:** (02) 3445-7221. **Fax:** (02) 3445-7791.

**Ding Ding Dang English School**
1275-3 Bummul-dong Soosung-gu, Taegu 706-100. **Fax:** (53) 782-6434. **Email:** dings@thrunet.com

**E2 Foreign Language Institute**
1F Lotte Hagwon Sangga, 63 Yong Ho Dong, Changwon, Kyungnam, 641-041. **Tel:** (55) 261-0888 **Fax:** (55) 261-0797 **Email:** mcleod@chollian.dacom.co.kr

**ESS Language Institute**
38-1, 1-ka Kwangbok-dong, Jung-ku, Pusan 600-131. **Tel:** (51) 246-3251. **Fax:** (51) 241-1988.

**FSFA Institute of Junior English**
Gu-wol Plaza 2F, 342-256, Gu-wol dong, Nam-dong Gu, Inchon. **Tel:** (32) 472-8636. **Fax:** (32) 472-8637. **Email:** DarrenFSFA2000@yahoo.com

**Global Christian School**
243-5 Pogwang-dong, Yongsan-gu, Seoul. **Tel:** (02) 797-0234. **Fax:** (02) 797-0401.

**Good Teacher's Centre**
271-19, Dong In-3Ga, Jung-Gu, Taegu 700-423. **Tel:** (53) 427-8291. **Fax:** (53) 427-8295. **Email:** gta@chollian.dacom.co.kr

**JS Language School**
1-190, Munwha-dong, Jung-ku, Daejon. **Tel:** (42) 252-3500. **Fax:** (42) 254-6452. **Email:** js@englishcampus.com

**Jungjin Language Institute 1**
5th Fl., Kyungdong Bldg., 130-1 Hyehyun 1-ga, Chung-gu, Seoul. **Tel:** (02) 753-5243.

**Kangrung High School**
886 Kyo-1 Dong, Kangrung City 210-101. **Tel:** (016) 297-2095. **Fax:** (031) 641-5118.

**Kid's College**
261-2 Yangjae-dong Seocho-gu, Seoul 137-130. **Tel:** (2) 529-3831. **Fax:** (2) 529-7809. **Email:** kidscollege@hotmail.com

**Korea Foreign Language Institute**
16-1 Kwanchol-dong, Chongno-gu, Seoul. **Tel:** (02) 739-8000. **Fax:** (02) 739-0602.

**Korea Herald Institute (Hoehyondong)**
9th Fl. Korea Herald Bldg., 1-12 Hoehyon-dong 3-ga, Chung-gu, Seoul. **Tel:** (02) 727-0271. **Fax:** (02) 727-0668.

**Korea Herald Institute (Suhadong)**
65-1 Suha-dong, Chung-gu, Seoul. **Tel:** (02) 757-0419. **Fax:** (02) 319-3936.

**Latt**
3nd Fl. Shinwon Bldg., Chungjongno 3-ga, Sodaemun-gu, Seoul. **Tel:** (02) 363-3291. **Fax:** (02) 313-5620.

**L.A. Wilshire Language School Korea**
4th Fl., Kyewon Bldg., 32-7 Kwanchol-dong, Chongno-gu, Seoul. **Tel:** (02)723-6600.

## LovEnglish
Duckhwa Building, Room 401, 444-17, Seogyo-dong, Mapo-gu, Seoul 121-210. **Tel:** (02) 3141-3766. **Fax:** (2) 332-2245. **Email:** mhkim@lovenglish.com

## Mido Foreign Language School
Mido Sang-Ga Bldg., 3rd Floor, 311, Dae-Chi Chong, Kang-nam Ku, Seoul 135-280. **Tel:** (2) 562-6714. **Fax:** (2) 563-1205. **Email:** mido1@uriel.net

## Mokdong SLP
7F Whasung Plaza BL 909-5, Mok-dong Yangchun-ku, Seoul. **Tel:** (2) 654-7331. **Fax:** (2) 654-7335. **Email:** perryr@nuri.net

## Naeja English Academy
19-2 Hyoja-dong, Chunchon City, Kangwon Province. **Tel:** (361) 242-0505. **Fax:** (361) 251-0594. **Email:**naeja@hanmail.net

## Oedae Junior English Institute
4th Fl. 286 Wolpyong-dong, So-gu, Taejon. **Tel:** (042) 487-0545. **Fax:** (042) 487-0572.

## Pagoda Foreign Language Institute (Abgujung)
2nd Fl. Dongwon Bldg., 598 Shinsa-dong, Kangnam-gu, Seoul. **Tel:** (02) 3442-4000. **Fax:** (02) 515-4030.

## Pagoda Foreign Language Institute (Chongno)
56-6 Chongno 2-ga, Chongno-gu, Seoul. **Tel:** (02) 2274-4000. **Fax:** (02) 2278-7538.

## Pagoda Foreign Language Institute (Kangnam)
816 Yoksam-dong, Kangnam-gu, Seoul. **Tel:** (02) 501-4002. **Fax:** (02) 3452-0203.

## Pusan Foreign School
1492-8, Chung-Dong, Haeundae-Gu, Pusan 612-010. **Tel:** (51) 747-7199. **Fax:** : (51) 747-9196. **Email:** pfs@chollian.net

## Seoul Academy
Young dong P.O. Box 85, Seoul 135-600. **Tel :** (02) 555-2475.

## Sisa English Institute
19-23 Kwanchol-dong, Chongno-gu, Seoul. **Tel:** (02) 734-2442. **Fax:** (02) 720-4931.

## Sisa Language Institute
1099-1 Sanpon, Kunpo-dong, Kyonggi-do. **Tel:** (031) 398-6445.

## Sogang University
1-1 Sinsu-dong, Mapo-gu, Seoul 121-742. **Tel:** (2) 716-1230. **Fax:** (2) 705-8733. **Email:** johng@ccs.sogang.ac.kr

## Space Corporation
2nd floor, 656-502, 1Dong, 1Ga, Sung Su-Dong Sung Dong-Gu, Seoul 133-821. **Tel:** (2) 2205-0213. **Fax:** (2) 2205-0382.

## World Language School
19-16 Kumnaro-1 ka, Dung-ku, Kwangju 501-021. **Tel:** (62) 228-1723. **Fax:** (62) 226-3562. **Email:** worldedu@hotmail.com

## YBM
Sisa Yongasa 5-3 Kwanchul-dong, Chongno-gu, Seoul. **Tel:** (02) 2276-0509. **Fax:** (02) 2271-0172.

## YES English School
Daewon Bldg., 5th Fl., Daechi-dong 599, Kangnam-gu, Seoul 135-281. **Tel:** (2) 553-8880. **Fax:** (2) 553-5764. **Email:** yescho@nuri.net

## LAOS

Unlike other southeastern Asian countries, Laos is only just starting to open up to the West. As a recently joined member of the Association of Southeast Asian Nations (ASEAN), which uses English as the language of communication, the Lao P.D.R. government has made the study of English a national priority. The national curriculum was recently rewritten to include an emphasis on English learning, and members of the government are eager to study English. Most English language teaching is done by volunteers but there are limited opportunities for teachers at private language schools in Vientiane and possibility of work at universities.

◗ **Visas/Work Permits:** You can obtain a tourist visa (good for two weeks) at the border or at the airport in Vientiane. A one-month visa offered by a sponsor can be extended. Work permits are hard to acquire and the government is strict about illegal workers.

◗ **Requirements:** College Degree and a TESOL/TESL Certificate

◗ **Currency:** £1 = 19147 / $1 = 10350 Kip

◗ **Salaries/Taxes:** You can make anywhere from $1,200-2,000 a month less income tax of 10%.

◗ **Accommodation:** The school should assist you with accommodation.

◗ **Cost of Living:** Laos is much cheaper than neighbouring Thailand to live in but some basic items are hard to find.

◗ **Health advice:** Medical facilities and services are severely limited and do not meet Western standards. The blood supply is not screened for HIV or AIDS.

Visitors should be aware that there have been a number of bombings in public places and to be vigilant at all times.

## Schools In Laos (+856)

**Lao American Language Centre**
152 Sisangvone Road, Saysettha, Ban Naxay, P.O. Box 327, Vientiane. **Tel:**21 41 4321, **Fax:** 21 41 3760.

**National University of Laos**
Dept. of English, Dong Dok Campus, Vientiane.

**Vientiane International School**
P.O. Box 3180, Vientiane. **Tel:** 21-313606, **Fax**: 21-315008, **Email: VIS@panlaos.net.la**

**Vientiane University College**
P.O. Box 4144, Vientiane. **Tel:** 21 414873, **Fax**: 21 414 346.

## MALAYSIA

Malaysia offers a relatively high standard of living, a stunning natural environment, and easy access to many of the other countries in the region. It is difficult for foreign teachers to find a job here because of strict labour laws and current economic problems. English is widely spoken throughout the country.

**British Council office:**
PO Box 10539, 50916 Kuala Lumpur
**Tel** +60 (3) 2723 7900
www.britishcouncil.org/malaysia

⮑ **Visas/Work Permits:** Most teachers go to Malaysia on a tourist visa (Valid for 90 days) and then look for jobs. The number of work permits allocated to foreigners are limited: teachers have to have an MA, teaching experience and be between 26-55 years old to qualify for one. Be prepared to spend up to a year doing "visa runs" to Singapore, Thailand or Indonesia if you are working without a permit.

⮑ **Requirements:** High School Diploma and a TESOL/TESL Certificate

⮑ **Currency:** £1 = 6.9 / $1 = 3.5 Malaysian ringgit.

⮑ **Salaries/Taxes:** Local salaries are reasonable if you are not planning to send money home. Teachers earn around 2,500-4,000 ringgits per month. Income tax is 5% (once you have a permit) but the rate leaps to 30% if you spend less than 165 consecutive days in the country.

⮑ **Accommodation:** Rents are very high for Asia. Expect to share accommodation with others.

⮑ **Cost of Living:** Reasonable with lots of products available in Kuala Lumpur.

⮑ **Health advice:** The standard of medical care is very high in the major cities where credit cards are usually accepted.

⮑ **English Language Media:** The Borneo Post (Sabah and Sarawak), The Daily Express (Sabah), The New Straits Times, The Malay Mail, The Sarawak Tribune, The Star, The Sun.

## Schools in Malaysia (+60)

**Bangsar English Language Centre**
60-1 Jalan Ma'arof Bangsar Baru, 59100 Kuala Lumpur. **Tel:** 3 282 3166/68, **Fax:** 3 282 5578.

**Centre for Language and Communications Studies**
University Malaysia Sarawak, 94300 Kota Samarahan, Samarahan, Sarawak.

**Centre for Promoting Language and Knowledge**
University Malaysia Sabah, Temporary Campus Likas Bay, Locked bag 2073, 88999 Kota Kinabalu, Sabah.

**The English Language Centre**
1st Floor, Lot 2067, Block 10, K.C.L.D., Jalan Keretapi, PO Box 253, 93150 Kuching, Sarawak.

**International Tuition School**
PO Box 3062, 93760 Kuching, Sarawak. **Tel:** 82 480780, **Fax**: 82 416250.

**IPOH Learning and Training Institute**
6 Jalan Tambun, 30350 Ipoh, Perak. **Tel:** 5 255 3067, **Fax**: 5 255 7136.

**Kinabulu Commercial College**
3rd & 4th Floors, Wisma Sabah, Kota Kinabulu, Sabah.

**Kinabulu International School**
PO Box 12080, 88822 Kota Kinabalu, Sabah.

**Lodge Preparatory School**
Jalan Tabuan Jaya, 93550 Kuching, Sarawak.

**University Malaysia - Sarawak**
94300 Kota Samarahan, Sarawak. **Tel:** 82 671000, **Fax**: 82 672315.

## MONGOLIA

Teachers who have experienced Mongolia report that the country has a harsh but fascinating beauty. The capital, Ulaanbaatar, suffers from pollution but visiting the surrounding steppes is a must do. There are many opportunities to teach English here, including volunteer workers (notably the Peace Corps). Most of the teaching involves young learners in the public schools system. Flights to and from Mongolia should be arranged by your organization.

⮑ **Visas/Work Permits:** It is common practice for a school to reimburse you for the cost of your visa when you have completed your contract. Visas may be obtained at the international airport in Ulaanbaatar and at train stations on the Russian and Chinese borders. Two photographs and a $50 processing fee are required.

⮑ **Requirements:** College Degree and a TESOL/TESL Certificate

⮑ **Currency:** £1 = 2360 / $1 = 1280 Tugrik.

⮑ **Salaries/Taxes:** Some schools in Ulaanbaatar pay around $3.50 for a 45-minute lesson based on 20-24 teaching hours per week. At other schools, like those in smaller cities like Erdenet, expect around $100 a month, which is more than adequate to live on.

⮑ **Accommodation:** Simple accommodation (including utilities) should be provided by your employer.

⮑ **Cost of Living:** Very reasonable if you develop a taste for yak's milk!

⮑ **Health advice:** Medical facilities in Mongolia are very limited, and some medicines are unavailable. Infectious diseases, such as plague and meningococcal meningitis, are present at various times of the year. Your school should provide medical cover.

## Schools in Mongolia (+976)

**Battsetseg Namnansuren**
Box-346, Central Post Office, Ulaanbaatar-13. **Tel:** 9611-5597. **Fax:** 1-459732.

**Eagle English Language School**
Erdenet 976-35. **Tel:** 9935-1450. **Fax:** 35-73978. **Email:** rinchin@erdnet.mn

**International School of Ulaanbaatar**
P.O. Box 49/564, Ulaanbaatar. **Tel:** 1-452-959. **Fax:** 1-358-375. **Email:** inschool@magicnet.mn

**Mongol Caravan, Inc.**
P.O. Box 191, Clifton, NJ 07011. **Tel:** (973) 594-0655. **Fax:** (209) 729-4674. **Email:** mc@mongolcaravan.com

**Santis Educational Services**
P.O. Box 1174, Ulaanbaatar 210657. **Fax:** 32-3276. **Email:** santis@magicnet.mnw

## MYANMAR

The current government restrictions on foreigners make it very difficult to find a teaching job in Myanmar (formerly Burma). Access to the Internet is strictly monitored by the present regime. The U.S. government has forbidden American companies to make new investments in the country while human rights abuses continue in Myanmar. General dissatisfaction with public universities has led to the opening of large numbers of private schools, many of which teach English. If the political situation improves, Myanmar could develop into a leading destination for EFL teachers.

⮑ **Visas/Work Permits:** A single entry visa is good for a stay of 28 days.

⮑ **Requirements:** College Degree and a TESOL/TESL Certificate

⮑ **Health advice:** Medical facilities in Myanmar are inadequate for even routine medical care. There are few trained medical personnel because the universities were closed for several years and have recently reopened.

## Schools in Myanmar (+951)

**The British Council**
78 Kanna Road, P.O. Box 638, Yangon. **Tel:** (951) 254658. **Fax:** 245345 **Email:** malcolm.jardine@bc-burma. bcouncil.org

## NEPAL

Nepal is an impoverished country with great educational needs: the adult literacy rate in Nepal in 1995 was just 41% for men and a meagre 14% for women. It is possible to land a job teaching English at a private language school in Kathmandu, the backpacking capital of the world, but most teachers will not make enough money to survive unless they have funds of their own to fall back on.

There are aid agencies and Christian groups working with schools throughout and you might find a job in Nepal by taking this route.

**British Council office:**
PO Box 640, Lainchaur, Kathmandu

**Tel** +977 (1) 410 798
www.britishcouncil.org/nepal

⮑ **Visas/Work Permits:** A tourist visa is extendible to a maximum period of 150 days in one visa year (January to December). Working for a school will allow you to remain in the country for up to a year.

⮑ **Currency:** £1 = 129 / $1 = 70 Rupees

⮑ **Salaries/Taxes:** You can earn around £60 / $110 a month in a private language school but remember that Nepal is a very poor country — you are not here for the money!

⮑ **Accommodation:** You can find a small apartment for $150-200 per month. Volunteers will have housing provided for them.

⮑ **Cost of Living:** Estimate £300-350 / $570-650 per month as a comfortable amount.

⮑ **Health advice:** Medical care is extremely limited and is generally not up to Western standards. Serious illnesses often require evacuation to the nearest adequate medical facility (in Singapore, Bangkok or New Delhi). Illnesses and injuries suffered while on trek in remote areas often require rescue by helicopter. The cost is typically £1,800 - 6,000 / $3,300 - 11,000. Medical insurance is essential.

⮑ **English Language Media:** Kathmandu Post, The Rising Nepal.

## Schools in Nepal (+977)

**Debbie's English Language Institute**
Jamal, Kathmandu. **Tel:** 1-248140.

**Friendship Club Nepal**
P.O. Box 11276, Maharajgunj, Kathmandu. **Tel:** 1-427406. **Email:** fcn@ccsl.com.np

**Grahung Kalika**
(Walling Village Development Committee), Bartung, Ward 2, Syngja. **Fax:** 1-262878.

**Insight Nepal**
P.O. Box 489, Zero K.M. Pokhara, Kaski. **Email:** insight@clcexp.mos.com.np

**Universal Language & Computer Institute**
Putalisadak, Kathmandu. **Tel:** 1-419443.

## PAKISTAN

It is best to arrange a job before coming to Pakistan, as there are few private language schools in the country. There is a small demand for TEFL teachers although most children learn English in the public schools. Do not take on private lessons unless your contract stipulates that you may do so. The authorities will not be pleased if you are caught working illegally.

**High Commission in UK:**
935 Lowndes Square, London SW1X 9JN
**Tel:** 020 76649220

**Embassy in USA:**
2315 Massachusetts Avenue, Washington DC20008
**Tel:** 202 939 6200

**British Council office:**
House 1, Street 61, F-6/3, P.O. Box 1135, Islamabad
**Tel** +92 (51) 111 424 424
www.britishcouncil.org/pk

⮑ **Visas/Work Permits:** paperwork will be taken care of by your employer.

⮑ **Requirements:** College Degree and a TESOL/TESL Certificate

⮑ **Salaries/Taxes:** A TEFL teacher can earn £10,000-12,000 / $19,000-22,000 a year.

⮑ **Accommodation:** This should be provided by your employer.

⮑ **Health advice:** Adequate medical care is available in major cities in Pakistan, but is limited in rural areas. Your employer should provide you with medical insurance.

## Schools in Pakistan (+92)

**Pakistan American Cultural Center (PACC)**
Head Office, 11 Fatima Jinnah Road, Karachi. **Tel:** 5670516/5670513/515305.

**Pakistan American Cultural Center (PACC)**
Hyderabad centre, Hospital Road, Hyderabad. **Tel:** (0221) 619854/618854.

**Pakistan American Cultural Center (PACC)**
Karimabad centre, 54-C, Block 8, Federal B Area, Karimabad. **Tel:** 6363277.

**Pakistan American Cultural Center (PACC)**
Lahore centre, 25 E-3, Gulberg III, Lahore. **Tel:** (042) 5756438 / 5763644.

**Pakistan American Cultural Center (PACC)**
Peshawar centre, c/o St. John's School, 1, Sir Syed Rd., Peshawar. **Tel:** (0521) 279734.

**Pakistan American Cultural Center (PACC)**
Quetta centre, Sadiq Shaheed Park, Arbab Mohammad Khair Road, Mali Bagh, Quetta. **Tel:** (081) 826970 / 830889.

## SINGAPORE

This wealthy city-state is popular with British and Australian EFL teachers. The demand here is for well-qualified teachers with a lot of experience and it is harder to find a job here than in other Asian countries.

**High Commission in UK:**
9 Wilton Crescent, London SW1X 8SP
**Tel:** 020 7235 8315
www.mfa.gov.sg/london

**Embassy in USA:**
3501 International Place, Washington DC20008
**Tel:** 202 537 3100

**British Council office:**
30 Napier Road, 258509
Tel +65 6473 1111
www.britishcouncil.org/singapore

➲ **Visas/Work Permits:** U.S. citizens can stay for 90 days without a visa.

➲ **Requirements:** College Degree and a TESOL/TESL Certificate

➲ **Currency:** £1 = 3.01 / $1 = 1.54 Dollar (S$).

➲ **Salaries/Taxes:** An average salary in Singapore is S$2,500 a month.

➲ **Accommodation:** Apartments start at around S$1,200 a month.

➲ **Cost of Living:** You can get by on S$2,000 a month.

➲ **English Language Media:** Straits Times.

### Schools in Singapore (+65)

**Advanced Training Techniques (ATT)**
Tanglin Shopping Centre, 19 Tanglin Road, Singapore 247909. **Tel:** 235 5222, **Fax:** 738 1257.

**American College**
25 Paterson Road, Singapore 0923. **Tel:** 235 9537.

**Canadian International School**
5 Toh Tuck Road, Singapore 2159. **Tel:** 467 1732.

**Coleman Commercial and Language Centre**
Peninsula Plaza, Singapore. **Tel:** 336 3462.

**Corrine Private School**
Selegie Complex 04-277, Selegie Road, Singapore 188350. **Tel:** 339 5564.

**Dimensions Language Centre**
50 East Coast Road, Singapore 0238.

**Dover Court Preparatory School**
Dover Road, Singapore 0513. **Tel:** 775 7664.

**ILC Language and Business Training Centre**
545 Orchard Road, 11-07 Far East Shopping Centre, Singapore 238882. **Tel:** 338 5415.

**inlingua School of Languages**
1 Grange Road, 04-01 Orchard Building, Singapore 239693. **Tel:** 737 6666.

**International School**
21 Preston Road, Singapore 0410. **Tel:** 475 4188.

**Language Teaching Institute of Singapore**
30 Orange Grove Road, Singapore 258352. **Tel:** 737 9044.

**Linguamedia**
230 Orchard Road, 04-230 Faber House, Singapore, 238854. **Tel:** 235 2620. **Fax:** 235 2080.

**Morris Allen Study Centre**
1 Newton Road 02-47/49, Goldhill Plaza, Singapore 307943. **Tel:** 253 5737.

**St. Francis Methodist School**
11 Mount Sophia, Singapore 228461. **Tel** 334 8944. **Fax:** 337 1825. **Email:** stfrancm@mbox5.signet.com.sg

## TAIWAN

Prospects for English language teachers are very good in Taiwan, especially for native speakers of American English. Private schools (bushibans) pay well and jobs are easy to find. Unqualified travellers can find work here as long as they have a degree. The school year begins on August 1 and the winter semester starts on February 1. Local papers start carrying ads for English language teaching jobs in the spring. You should bring between £750-1500 / $1,300-$2,200 to cover you for about five weeks until you get your first full salary cheque. If you pre-arrange a teaching job before you travel to Taiwan, you may find that you are making less money than fellow teachers who arrived here and then found a job. But remember that you will not have to go through all the hassles of getting the right permits which can be very complicated since the authorities in Taiwan cracked down on freelance teachers working without the correct papers.

**British Council office:**
Education and Cultural Section, 7F-1, Fu Key Building, No 99 Jen Ai Road, Section 2, Taipei 100
Tel  +886 (2) 2192 7050
www.britishcouncil.org.tw

⊃ **Visas/Work Permits:** Most teachers go to Taiwan on a tourist visa. Try to get a 60-day visa, as your paperwork will take 3-6 weeks to process: If your visa runs out before your paperwork is processed you will have to leave the country to obtain another resident visa. Many teachers go to Hong Kong, Singapore or Thailand to do this. If you enroll for Chinese language lessons at a government-recognized school, you can renew your visa without having to leave the country. To teach legally in Taiwan, the government requires that all foreign teachers obtain a Work Permit and an Alien Resident Certificate. To be eligible for these, you must: possess a bachelor's degree or higher, a contract of employment and a health certificate from a government-approved hospital. You will be expected to pay for the health exam and the processing fees.

⊃ **Requirements:** College Degree and a TESOL/TESL Certificate

⊃ **Currency:** £1 = 63 / $1 = 33 New Dollar (NT$)

⊃ **Salaries/Taxes:** Monthly wages for teachers in language schools usually average between NT$30,000 and NT$70,000 net depending on the number of classes taught, and the number of students in each class. An entry-level salary for an assistant professor is about NT$73,000 per month (including a $10,000/month bonus for those with PhDs); for a lecturer, the figure is about NT$52,000 per month. Taxes are 20% until you have worked in Taiwan for 183 days in the same calendar year. The rate then drops to 10%. If you have been in the country for more than 183 days you are eligible for a tax refund in the next year.

⊃ **Cost of Living:** A quick lunch costs NT$100.

⊃ **Health advice:** Teachers working for the larger and more reputable schools are usually covered under group plans where they might make a contribution (around 30%) from their pay packets. Medical insurance is essential for freelancers unless you have a residency permit in which case you will be covered under the state system.

⊃ **English Language Media:** China News, China Post.

## Schools in Taiwan (+886)

**American Children School**
Chung Shan North Road, Sec. 6, #34, Taipei. **Tel:** 2-2831-6664.

**American Culture University**
Hsu Chang Street, #40, 7F, Taipei. **Tel:** 2-2311-8889.

**Bao Bei Yuan English School**
Jian Guo South Road, Sec. 1, Lane 270, #28, Taipei.. **Tel:** 2-2754-8066.

**Bei Song Language School**
Chung Hsiao East Road, Sec. 6, #436, Taipei. **Tel:** 2-2788-7778.

**Big Bird English**
Hsin Yi Road, Sec. 4, #181, 2F, Taipei. **Tel:** 2-2754-8405.

**Big Byte English School**
Hsin Hai Road, Sec. 2, #35, Taipei. **Tel:** 2-2369-2868.

**Canadian-American Language Schools**
2 Chien Hua Street, 2nd Floor, Hsinchu, 300. **Tel:** 3-562-0535. **Fax:** 3-561-6905. **Email:** employment@can-am.org

**Chang Chun English**
Ji Long Road, Sec. 2, #260, 2F, Taipei. **Tel:** 2-2735-2617.

**Cheng Dan Language Centre**
Hang Chou Road, Sec. 1, Lane 71, #9, Taipei. **Tel:** 2-2381-5147.

**Ching Shan English**
Hsin Sheng South Road, Sec. 3, #98, 3F, Taipei. **Tel:** 2-2366-1855.

**David's English Centre**
Nan Jing East Road, Sec. 2, #100, 3F, Taipei. **Tel:** 2-2522-4004.

**Disney English**
Hoping East Road, Sec. 2, Lane 96, Taipei. **Tel:** 2-2732-8969.

**Dong Han English**
Hoping East Road, Sec. 2, #100, 4F, Taipei. **Tel:** 2-2732-2771.

**English Bridge School**
Ching Hsing Road, Lane 202, No. 8, 2F, Taipei. **Tel:** 2-2933-5118.

**Everyday English**
Chung Hsiao East Road, Sec. 4, #177, 4F, Taipei. **Tel:** 2-2741-8989.

**Gauden Language School**
48 Jing Shiou East Road, Yuan Lin, Changhwa, 510. **Tel:** No: 4- 8368176. **Fax:** 4-8350431. **Email:** gauden@ms11.hinet.net

**Giraffe English Centre**
Shi Pai Road, Sec. 1, #160, 1F, Taipei. **Tel:** 2-2822-5815.

### Gram English Centre
4th fl., 116 Yung Ho Rd., Sec. 2, Yung Ho City 234, Taipei County. **Tel**: 2-2927-2478. **Fax**: 2-2926-2183. **Email:** gram@ms7.hinet.net

### Great Time English
Min Chuan East Road, Sec. 3, Lane 60, #10, Taipei. **Tel:** 2-2506-3033.

### Han Bang Language School
Chung Yuan Road, #17, 2F, Taipei. **Tel**: 2-2531-6835.

### He Jing Language School
Dun Hua South Road, Sec. 1, Lane 100, Alley 5, #37, 2F, Taipei. **Tel:** 2-2731-2822.

### Hers English School
Wo Long Street, #1, 11F-2, Taipei. **Tel:** 2-2378-0186.

### Hess Educational Organization
English Human Resources Department, 419 Chung Shan Rd., Section 2, Chung-Ho City 235, Taipei County. **Tel:** 2-3234-6188 ext. 1053/ 1052. **Fax:** 2-2222-9499. **Email:** hesswork@hess.com.tw

### Jya Ying English
Jwang Jing Road, Lane 325, #37, Taipei. **Tel**: 2-2723-5259.

### Kid Castle
Min Chuan Rd., No.98, 8F, Taipei. **Tel:** 2-2218-5996 ext.319/341.

### Lang Wen English Centre
Jin Jou Street, #16, 3F, Taipei. **Tel:** 2-2551-8956.

### Lian Hsin English
Fu Hsing North Road, #92, 7F, Taipei. **Tel:** 2-2773-6161.

### Little Forest
4th Floor 121-5 Da Chang 2nd Rd., Kaohsiung. **Tel:** 7-395-6736. **Fax:** 7-733-4288. **Email:** jyy@usa.net

### Melody English centre
San Min Area, Bei Ping 2nd Street, #6, 6F, Kaohsiung. **Tel:** 7-322-7492.

### Min Sheng English School
Min Sheng East Road, Sec. 5, #226-1, Taipei. **Tel**: 2-2769-9243.

### Ming Tai Language School
Chung Hua Road, Sec. 1, #178, Taipei. **Tel:** 2-2311-0712.

### Pai Han Language School
Bo Ai Road 1st Road, #43, Kaohsiung. **Tel:** 7-316-1518.

### Sen Yuan Language Centre
Jian Guo Road, #258, Kaohsiung. **Tel:** 7-395-6736.

### Timothy Language Institute
Cheng Kung Road, Lane 213, No. 97. Tainan County, Jiali. **Tel:** 6- 723-2819.

### Tom's English
Shwun Hsing Road, #95, Hualien. **Tel:** 38-822-2059.

### Wen Tzao English
Yong Fu Road, Sec. 2, #83, 7F, Tainan. **Tel:** 6-228-2818.

### Woodpecker English School
Bo Ai Road, #282, Pingtung. **Tel:** 8-733-8691.

### Ya Ya
Chwei Yang Road, #199, 2F, Chiayi. **Tel:** 5-223-0358.

### Twinkle Language Centre
66 Hsyn Hai Road, Tso Ying District 813, Kaohsiung. **Tel:** 7-557-1883. **Email:** twinklelanguagecentre@yahoo.com

## THAILAND

There are many opportunities to teach English in Thailand, particularly in the universities. Most teachers find work in Bangkok, which is the economic, cultural and educational hub of the country. Although there was a slump in English language teaching because of the Asian economic crisis, the situation is improving. English language schools are looking for qualified teachers — the market for native-speaking beach bums has dried up.

**Embassy in UK:**
29 Queens Gate, London SW7 5JB
**Tel:** 020 7589 2944

**Embassy in USA:**
1024 Wisconsin Avenue, Suite 401, Washington DC20007
**Tel:** 202 944 3600

**British Council office:**
254 Chulalongkorn Soi 64, Siam Square, Phayathai Road, Pathumwan, Bangkok 10330
**Tel** +66 (2) 252 5480
www.britishcouncil.org/th

➲ **Visas/Work Permits:** In order to get a work permit you need at least a bachelors' degree and some form of TEFL certification. Before you can apply for a work permit you need a Non-Immigrant 'B' visa. These are three-month visas that initially allow you to be employed in Thailand. To get the visa, you need a copy of a letter from your prospective employer clearly stating that you have been offered a job. For private companies you need a copy of the said company's registration documents, if you're working for a government establishment this isn't required, and two passport sized photos. Embassies usually take two days to process the visa. Most Thai embassies work on the system that you apply for visas in the morning and collect them the next afternoon. Once you have found a job and can prove to the Immigration officials that you are applying for a work permit you can extend the three-month visa for another nine months.

➲ **Requirements:** College Degree and a TESOL/TESL Certificate

➲ **Currency:** £1 = 68 / $1 = 35 Baht

➲ **Salaries/Taxes:** There is a wide range of salaries for teaching English in Thailand. Working a typical 20-25 hour week can earn you anywhere from as little as 10,000 baht a month for an unqualified teacher in a small provincial school to 60,000 baht or more for a TEFL teaching professional in a well-established school or college in Bangkok or another large city. Teachers at language schools pay around 25-35,000 baht per month in tax. Income earned by a U.S. resident from teaching in Thailand is exempt from income tax if the following conditions are met: (1) The teacher is a resident of the U.S.A. before he/she comes to teach in Thailand; (2) The teacher teaches in a university, college or other recognized educational institution in Thailand; (3) It must be his/her first visit for teaching in Thailand; and (4) He/she does not teach in Thailand for more than two years.

➲ **Accommodation:** In most cases, teachers are expected to find their own accommodation. Studios in Bangkok cost around 5,000 baht a month while a one-bedroom apartment is anywhere from 8-18,000 baht.

➲ **Cost of Living:** You can get a three-course meal for two people without alcohol for under 100 baht. If you can't do without imported items you will spend a lot of money because they are heavily taxed.

➲ **Health advice:** Basic coverage for a single teacher will cost you at least 15,000 baht.

➲ **English Language Media:** Bangkok Post, The Nation.

## Schools in Thailand (+66)

**Adanac Community Language Centre**
Suite 605 Bangkok Tower, 2170 New Petchburi Rd., Bangkok 10320. **Tel/Fax:** 3080787-90

**American University Alumni (AUA) Language Center**
24 Rajadamnern Road, Chiang Mai 50200. **Tel:** 53-211-973. **Fax:** 53-211-973. **Email:** aualanna@loxinfo.co.th

**Anna's Language School & Travel Services**
116 Phisitgaranee Road, Patong Beach, Phuket 83150. **Tel:** 296372. Fax: 296423 **Email:** annatran@samart.co.th

**Arundel Language Institute (A.L.I.)**
61/67 Soi 10/3 Pechkasem Rd, Hat Yai, Songkla, 90110. **Tel:** 74 345 341-2. **Fax:** 74 345 342. **Email:** ali@loxinfo.co.th

**Asia Institute of English**
59 Sukhumvit 56, Bangchak , Prakanong, Bangkok 10250. **Tel:** 741- 5970-2. **Email:** AIE@a-net.net.th

**Bangkok Patana School**
2/38 Soi Lasalle, Sukhumvit 105, 10260 Bangkok. **Tel:** 2 398 0200. **Fax:** 2 399 3179. **Email:** patanarc@loxinfo.co.th/patreg@loxinfo.co.th

**The Bell Educational Trust Thailand**
204/1 Ranong 1 Road, Samsen, Dusit, Bangkok 10300. **Tel:** 2 241 0356. **Fax:** 2 668 2124. **Email:** gbradd@loxinfo.co.th

**Berlitz Silom**
191 Silom Complex Building, 22F Silom Road, Bangkok 10500. **Tel:** 2 231 3652. **Fax:** 2 231 3656.

**Berlitz Sukhumvit**
Times Square Bldg, 14F, 2246 Sukhumvit Road, Bangkok 10110. **Tel:** 2 250 0950. **Fax:** 2 250 0907.

**Bright Future Language Centre**
7th floor, Room 107, Sibunruang 2 Building, 1/7 Convent Road, Silom, Bangkok 10500. **Tel:** 2 631 0497. **Fax:** 2 631 0498. **Email:** bright@idn.co.th

**Cambridge World International English Language Schools**
296-300 Sukhumvit Road, Paknam.

**Charansanitwong School of Business (CSB)**
Charansanitwong Soi 41 Charansanitwong Rd.,

**Bangkoknoi**
Bangkok 10700. **Tel:** 8824676 **Fax:** 4333647. **Email:** NewCambridge@excite.com

**Company English Language Centre of Excellence**
Prince of Songkla University Wichitsongraram Rd, A. Kathu Phuket 83120. **Tel:** 202556 / 7. **Fax:** 202558 **Email:** h&t@ratree.psu.ac.th

### English and Computer College (ECC)
430/17-24 Chula Soi 64, Siam Square, Bangkok 10330. **Tel:** 2-253-3312; **Email:** eccthai@comnet3.th.

### EF - English First
Suite 701, 7th Fl. Sibunruang 2 Bldg. 1/7 Convent Rd., Silom, Bangrak, Bangkok 10500. **Tel:** 2-631-0497/8. **Fax:** 2-631-0499. **Email:** teach@efenglish.com

### English Language Centre
Assumption University, Ramkhamhaeng 24 Road, Huamark, Bangkapi, Bangkok 10240. **Fax:** 2 318 7159. **Email:** elc@au.edu

### English Language Instructors
PO Box 604 Amphur Muang, Phuket 83000. **Tel:** 282230.

### Fun English Language Programme
Pichaya Suksa School, Pakkret, Nonthaburi. **Tel:** 1-313-8319. **Fax:** 2-373-8938. **Email:** ayatan@mozart.inet.co.th

### Fun English Language Programme
Yamsaard School, Lard-Praow Road, Bangkok. **Tel:** 1-313-8319. **Fax:** 2-373-8938. **Email:** ayatan@mozart.inet.co.th

### In Company Ltd.
206/1 Nawanakorn, Pathumthani 12120. **Tel:** 2 909 1569. **Email:** patricks@samart.co.th

### inlingua International School of Languages
Central Chidlom Tower, 22 Ploenchit Road, Patumwan, 10330 Bangkok. **Tel:** 2 254 7028-30. **Fax:** 2 254 7098. **Email:** inlingua.bkk@inlingua.com

### International Community School
72 Soi Prong Jai, Sathorn, 10120 Bangkok. **Tel:** 2 679 7175. **Fax:** 2 287 4530. **Email:** icsbkk@loxinfo.co.th

### International School Bangkok
39/7 Soi Nichada Thani, Samakee Road, 11120 Pakkret. **Tel:** 2 583 5401-19. **Fax:** 2 583 5431-2. **Email:** reyadik@isb.ac.th

### Kaplan
Bangkok Bank Siam 5th floor, 394 Rama 1 Road, Siam Square Soi 5, Bangkok 10330. **Tel:** 2 658-3991 / 2. **Fax:** 2 658-4354.

### NAVA Language School
183/105-106 Phang-Nga Rd, A. Muang, Phuket 83000. **Tel:** 238398/9 **Fax:** 238397. **Email:** nava@phuket.a-net.net.th

### NAVA Language Schools
34 Yosawadi Bldg, Ground floor, Paholyothin 7 Road (Soi Aree) Samsen-nai, Payathai, Bangkok. **Tel:** 617 1390-3. **Email:** nava3@navaed.co.th

### PEP Kindergarten
973 Ladproaw 48, Bangkok 10310. **Tel:** 2 277 8170. **Fax:** 2 276 2916. **Email:** maes2@hotmail.com

### P.E.T.S.
160/1-2 Praram 6 Muang Trang 92000. **Tel:** 075 215556. **Email:** ffracs@hotmail.com

### Rajabhat Institute Surin
186 Surin-Prasart Road, Muang District, Surin 32000. **Tel:** 44 511 604. **Fax:** 44 511 631. **Email:** intanin@risurin.nepnet.ac.th

### St. Stephen's International School
107 Viphavadi Rangsit Road, Ladyao Chatuchak, Bangkok 10900. **Tel:** 2 513 0270. **Fax:** 2 513 0265. **Email:** richard@ocean.co.th

### Sarasas Witaed Suksa School
300 Moo 10 Pracha Utid Rd., Naiklongbangplakot, Samut Prakarn,Bangkok 10270. **Tel:** 2 815 7540. **Fax:** 2 815 7541. **Email:** saraswitaed@hotmail.com

### Siam Computer & Language School
2 Soi 7, Phang-Nga Road Amphur Muang, Phuket 83000. **Tel:** 219914/5.

### Taiyo Co. Ltd.
3F, Prasarnmit Plaza, Sukhumvit Road, Soi 23Klong Toey, Bangkok 10110. **Tel:** 2 6641630-2. **Fax:** 2 6641630. **Email:** taiyobkk@yahoo.com

### Training Creativity Development (TCD)
399/7 Soi Thongloh 21, Sukhumvit Soi 55, Bangkok 10110. **Tel/Fax:** 2 391 5670.

### Universal International School
49 Moo 4, Thanarat Road, Tambol Nongnamdaeng, Amphur Pak Chong, Nakorn Ratchasima 30130. **Tel:** 44 328 334. **Fax:** 44 313 519.

## Teaching in Thailand

Well, how about Thailand? You may well have seen the TV and print ads extolling the virtues of Thailand, 'The Land of Smiles', and Bangkok, 'The City of Angels'. New Year's Resolution No. 1 "I Really Want To Teach Somewhere Hot & Sunny". But is life as an English language teacher as idyllic as these slogans suggest? Well, I've been here for three and a half years so it can't be too bad. Hopefully the following article will equip you with enough basic information to ascertain whether you are ready for Thailand and whether Thailand is ready for you.

Thailand has never been colonized, unlike most South East Asian countries. While Thais are justifiably proud of this fact, there is actually a long history of English teaching in Thailand and an English teaching methodology has developed over a long period of time. Indeed, in the majority of Thai schools and colleges, English is taught in the same manner as every other subject–learning by rote.

Average students in Malaysia, Singapore and the Philippines usually have a much higher standard of English than their peers in Thailand. In an effort to correct this imbalance and make up lost ground on fellow ASEAN countries, the government has recently introduced new legislation to try to replace the old "chalk and talk" teaching methods with student centred activities. Although this idea is commendable, schools and individual teachers have been rather too quick to point out obstacles rather than channelling their thoughts constructively. As with many good ideas, implementation is often delayed indefinitely and/or the original proposal/law altered beyond all recognition or scrapped entirely. According to the local press, the Education Reform Bill 2000 appears, unfortunately, to be heading for oblivion.

With respect to the availability of jobs in Thailand, teaching in Thailand equates to teaching in Bangkok. I'd estimate that over 90% of the foreign teachers working in Thailand are working in Bangkok. It's best to think of Bangkok and the rest of Thailand as two separate entities when it comes to teaching opportunities, salaries, job prospects, standard of living and so on.

If you have a notion of coming to Thailand, heading down to the beaches of Phuket or Samui or up to the hills in the North and getting a job teaching to finance your stay in paradise – forget it. Job vacancies and opportunities are very limited in these areas.

It is possible to find work if you have the right connections but, if you're reading this and not already there doing the job, then you don't have the right connections. If you prefer the quieter life, then both Chiang Mai, in the north and Hat Yai in the south offer some possibilities – however the competition, particularly in Chiang Mai can be fierce, and the pay is often much lower than in Bangkok.

My first impressions of Bangkok? It's a sprawling, polluted, overcrowded city with one foot in the past and another, attempting, to stride into the future. But once you've been here a while you discover that the city does have quite a few redeeming qualities: It's much safer than any western city – it's very rare to hear of any muggings or see any fights. Friendly people – Thais are more willing that most to make you feel at home in their country. Their natural, relaxed lifestyle makes life here less hectic and stressful than say Japan, Taiwan or Hong Kong.

Cheap food: 20 to 30 baht will buy you a simple meal at a roadside food stall – of which there are thousands in Bangkok. Dining out is a way of life here – very few people cook their evening meals, preferring to eat with their friends after work or to buy something on the way home.

The Skytrain, an elevated electric railway opened in December 1999 and, although underused by Thais, is very popular amongst the teaching community. If you're lucky enough to live and teach on or near either of the two lines your commuting time will be measured in minutes rather than hours.

Nightlife: Let's be honest, one of the big attractions of Bangkok is its well-known and varied nightlife. For many teachers this is the deciding factor in the choice whether to come to Bangkok or go elsewhere. There's something for everyone from arty, stylish bars and bistros to the delights of Patpong and Nana Plaza.

Phillip Williams, Academic Director at the Asia Institute of English, sums up life in the City of Angels, "Bangkok is just about as teacher-friendly as a city can be. It offers a relatively low cost of living, affordable entertainment and, most importantly teachers are always in great demand."

The vast majority of Thai students have been taught by using the rote learning method. Anything the teacher writes on the board is automatically copied into your book. The information passes straight from the eye to the hand, bypassing the brain entirely. Students rarely question the teacher, that's tantamount to having doubts about the teacher's knowledge and, as we all know, what your teacher says is always correct. This results in the average Thai student being able to cope with a multiple choice exam, which requires the memorization of facts, but having a great deal of difficulty with any exam that requires a written answer, especially one requiring a personal opinion or giving a reason why something happens.

Historically the Thai people are farmers and the economy largely based on agriculture. During labour intensive periods, planting and harvest time, families will pool their resources to help their neighbours. Nowadays, the attitude on lending a helping hand is carried over into schools, colleges and the workplace. Weaker students are given a lot of encouragement (usually in the form of the correct answers) by their classmates. Teachers give students every opportunity to pass an exam; this manifests itself in the form of multiple retakes until the student passes. Work colleagues help each other produce reports for their bosses to ensure that even those staff who would be considered a liability stay in a job. Therefore, if you are teaching a class, never expect Thai students to work on their own, everything must be done in pairs or groups. If you specify that a certain report or piece of homework must be done individually, you could count on at least 70% still being done as a group effort.

By now you may feel that I am being very negative about Thai students, but that's not so. I'm just trying to make you aware of the differences between western students and Thai students. Knowing about these differences before you start teaching will save you a great deal of head shaking and hand wringing. On the plus side the students respect their teachers, Thais are talkative but you won't have any verbal or physical abuse from any students. As I said earlier, your students will enjoy a laugh and a joke; they won't expect you to be serious.

From an academic point of view, teaching ability isn't really valued or regarded as high as it should be. There are many well-qualified TEFL/ESL teachers who have left Thailand in despair. The reason being is that their abilities aren't recognized by fellow Thai teachers and/or their students. Succeeding in Thailand isn't a matter of having a list of academic qualifications as long as your arm. What is important is that you can understand your students and know what they expect from you. For many career teachers, especially those used to teaching more dedicated students in, say, Japan, this aspect of Thai life can be particularly frustrating.

Anyone who is governed by absolute obedience to rules and regulations, timetables, strict adherence to contracts, the need to be involved in decisions that affect you and the belief that displays of anger will get conflicts resolved won't enjoy their time here.

Get used to "going with the flow," "rolling with it" and any number of similar phrases that could be used to describe the notion that if something goes to plan then that's an unexpected bonus and not something to be taken for granted.

Thai students want to be entertained as well as educated. Therefore the successful teacher has to bear in mind what I like to call the 4 "Ss" of Thai society. These are:

1. Sanook (Fun): If it's not sanook then why do it? Makes sense really, doesn't it. Listening to a teacher drone on, copying from a board, mindless choral repetition and so on aren't considered fun activities. First thing to remember then is to make your lessons fun, include a couple of games and keep things moving along – don't get bogged down – it's not sanook.

2. Suay (Beautiful): All the best things in life are suay. Outward appearance is of the utmost importance to Thais, especially personal appearance. While teachers in the west may be used to teaching classes in jeans and a t-shirt, that kind of attire is frowned upon here. Get a haircut; you'll need to wear a shirt, tie, trousers and polished shoes. Female teachers should stick to knee length skirts and non-revealing blouses. Suay carries over into any homework or reports you'll give your students. Style is always placed above substance, trying to convince your students otherwise will result in a look of disbelief upon their faces.

3. Suparb (Politeness): This covers everything from the way you dress and speak to having respect for your elders. Everyone knows their place in the social structure and people address each other accordingly. Elders are addressed as pee: those younger than you as nong. Elders, bosses, teachers and monks are all wai'd (use the traditional Thai greeting with them – hold your hands as though praying and bow your head slightly.) This is just the tip of the politeness iceberg. A couple of things for teachers new to Thailand should remember are: (1) never perch on the edge of a desk (as I remember my old high school math teacher doing every lesson) and (2) don't touch your students, especially if you're a male teacher and have female students.

4. Serious – Okay, it's an English word but all Thais know it. This is something you shouldn't be. It's almost as bad as being boring. God help you if you are boring and serious because no one else will. In a practical sense, try to treat everything with the same lack of importance, for example if someone doesn't do their homework, give them more time, if they copy – no problem so long as they only copy a little bit. You'll find your students are only serious around exam time – and then for only a very brief period.

In a nutshell, dress the part, clean, smart and professional – if you look like a teacher Thais will treat you like a teacher (i.e., with respect.) Be friendly and polite, stay calm, don't raise your voice, have fun, laugh at yourself and laugh with your students. This isn't a licence to spend all class playing games but it does allow you to be creative and not be ruled by the constraints of a rather dull course book.

You've read some background information (I hope!), now ask yourself this question: "Why do I want to go to Thailand to teach English as a foreign language? Here are three possible scenarios:

(1) You plan on backpacking around the world and you need to earn some cash during your trip. The large language schools are always looking for teachers, qualified or not. This fact, coupled with the reality that Thai students are fun loving and pretty forgiving towards their teachers means that it's not hard to get work, even if you only plan to stay a few months. You will be on a relatively low hourly rate but a couple of months work will enable you to save enough to pay for a month chilling out on Koh Pa Ngan.

(2) You've finished university and it's time to take a year out before starting life as a corporate slave. Ideally you'd like to spend a year experiencing life in a country with a different culture and climate from what you're used to. However you also have the reality of a student loan to face, so you need to make sure that your overseas experience pays it's way and doesn't drain your bank account further. If you have the presence of mind to, at least, read a couple of books on TEFL, then armed with a copy of your degree, you should have no trouble in finding work once you arrive. A better scenario would be if you took some form of TEFL course before you arrived, it doesn't have to be a Cambridge or Trinity College course – which are quite expensive. Any evidence that you had the presence of mind to take a TEFL qualification will show employers that you are serious about teaching and will ensure a better rate of pay and more job opportunities than if you'd arrived totally unprepared.

(3) You are an experienced teacher. If you're financially minded then you will probably want to avoid Thailand. Sure, there are well paying jobs available at international schools and private universities, but on the whole the availability of these jobs is pretty limited. Even if you worked as the Director of Studies at a language school you might find that your 10+ years of experience only results in a salary a few thousand Baht higher than a new teacher with little or no experience. In general, teaching experience isn't well rewarded financially. However, if you're looking for a less stressful atmosphere than say, Japan or Korea (where experience is more prized), then Thailand offers the chance to earn a decent salary in a more easy going atmosphere.

A recent report concluded that the market for English language teaching was far from saturated and would continue to grow. The demand for both qualified and unqualified teachers would therefore remain high for the foreseeable future. But what about the conditions for teachers in language schools? Back to Phillip Williams, who, having been here for over 10 years, has noticed the impact the Internet is having on the standard of teaching and the attitude of schools towards their teachers. "What is very worrying for the poor quality schools is the number of times their name gets dragged through the mud on the Internet. Their dirty laundry is hung out for all to see."

Schools now realize that they are being held accountable for their actions. Phillip continues, "Many schools are waking up to the fact that proper teachers want proper jobs. They want a competitive salary, access to modern teaching materials, a worthwhile training programme and an employer who values their contribution to the education of Thailand's new generation."

So, what are you waiting for . . . . ?

*Ian McNamara teaches EFL at Assumption College, Bangkok and, when time allows, is also the webmaster of Ajarn – for those interested in life in Bangkok (www.ajarn.com).*

# VIETNAM

After the first flush of foreign investors rushing to do business in Vietnam, the atmosphere is more cautious as people realize that the country cannot embrace capitalism overnight. There is a lot of bureaucracy in Vietnam and this extends into the English language teaching market. Demand for English fluctuates from year to year: early in 2000, EFL teachers reported a big downturn in student numbers enrolling in established schools in Ho Chi Minh City (Saigon). Students were moving to cheaper schools that had just opened and competition among EFL schools was intensifying. Although unqualified travellers can find jobs here, they will be paid very badly. It's much better to apply for jobs in Vietnam as a qualified EFL teacher.

### British Council office:

40 Cat Linh Street, Dong Da, Hanoi
**Tel** +84 (4) 843 6780
www.britishcouncil.org/vietnam

➲ **Visas/Work Permits:** A tourist visa is valid for 30 days. This can be extended three more times for one-month periods. After this time, you have to leave Vietnam. Some teachers apply for six-month, multiple-entry extendable business visas through travel agencies, which should charge no more than $60-80 for the service. You then have to leave the country and pick up your business visa at the Vietnamese embassy in the country you choose to go to — usually Cambodia.

➲ **Requirements:** High School Diploma and a TESOL/TESL Certificate

➲ **Currency:** £1 = 31400 / $1 = 16100 Dong

➲ **Salary:** £520-750 / $950-1400 per calendar month, depending on the school and your experience. Be prepared to work longer hours in Vietnam (30 or more hours a week) than in other Asian countries. Overtime rates are around £7.50-10 / $12-18 per hour.

➲ **Accommodation:** You can get nice "shophouse" accommodation in Ho Chi Minh City for £120-240 / $220-450 a month. Hanoi is more expensive. Make sure your landlord has a permit to rent to foreigners or you could face eviction.

➲ **Cost of Living:** There are two sets of prices in Vietnam: one for locals and another (higher) for foreigners. Teachers who have lived for some time in the country still expect to pay 20-30% more than the Vietnamese. But remember that foreign English language teachers are paid far more than the average Vietnamese worker. You can live well on $500 a month. Sharpen your bargaining skills – it's expected of you to haggle over prices.

➲ **Health advice:** Avoid local hospitals if you can help it. Membership of a foreign-run medical service costs around £100 / $190 a year. You can get evacuation insurance for about £300 / $570 a year.

➲ **English Language Media:** Vietnam News.

## Schools in Vietnam (+84)

### American English School
357 Dien Bien Phu, District 3, Ho Chi Minh City. **Tel**: 8 8324226. **Fax**: 8342484.

### Apollo Education Centre
67 Le Van Huu, Hanoi. **Tel**: 4-9432051. **Fax**: 4-9432052.

### Duong Minh Language School
132c Phan Dang Luu, Phu Nhuan District, Ho Chi Minh City.

### English 2000
70 Ding Tien Hoang, District 1, Ho Chi Minh City.

### ELT Lotus
8 Nguyen Van Trang, District 1, Ho Chi Minh City.

### Hanoi ELTE
10 Hang Chao St, Hanoi. **Fax**: 4 7332300.

### Hollywood English centre
87B Tran Din Xu, District 1, Ho Chi Minh City.

### Interaction Language School
59 Dinh Tien Hoang, District 1, Ho Chi Minh City.

### New Star ELT centre
217 Doi Can Street, Cong Vi, Ba Dinh, Hanoi. **Tel**: 4 762 6696. **Fax**: 4 762 6699.

### T.E.S.T. International
552 Dien Bien Phu, District 10, Ho Chi Minh City. **Tel**: 8 8334676.

### Top Globis Training centre
3-7 P. Tan Phu, District 7, Ho Chi Minh City.

### VATC (Vietnamese American Training College)
44 Truong Dinh St, District 3, Ho Chi Minh City. **Tel**: 8 8293971.

# Latin America

Central and South American countries are attractive destinations for many American and Canadian language teachers, simply because a majority of these countries are not too far away and there are plenty of job opportunities.

Although teachers in some countries like Brazil, Mexico and Argentina can earn a good salary dollars, Latin America is not really a good destination for graduates trying to pay off their loans. However, teaching English in Latin America gives foreigners the opportunity to experience life in a vibrant and fascinating culture.

Mexico is probably the easiest place to find a job, and there are also well-paid positions in Brazil, Argentina, Colombia and Brazil. There are fewer opportunities in Peru, Chile, Venezuela, Uruguay, Ecuador and Bolivia, but even in these countries, there are prestigious schools, willing to pay the premium for native speakers. Even unqualified teachers will find jobs in most of these countries however; to get the better jobs you will need to have either a TESOL-related MA or a recognized certificate. Opportunities in Belize, Dominican Republic, the eastern Caribbean, Guatemala, Guyana, Haiti, Honduras, Nicaragua and Panama are mainly for qualified teachers through aid programmes. Salaries are usually paid in local currency and might not cover living costs, but some include supplements paid in foreign currency.

In South America, the best time of year to find a job is just before the beginning of the academic year in January or February, although many institutes operate year-round and are happy to recruit teachers at any time. In addition to jobs at universities, English-medium schools, bi-national centres and language schools, companies encourage their employees to learn and often employ in-company teachers.

Only the larger schools with an international presence recruit overseas, mainly because work permits require so much paperwork, so most teachers find work by approaching schools in places they want to stay in. It also helps if you send your CV beforehand and dress professionally when you go looking for work: you can usually revert to jeans and a t-shirt after you've got the job.

## ARGENTINA

Following the economic and political uncertainties caused by the massive devaluation of the local currency, Argentine schools cannot pay much for teachers – but, what you are paid covers local costs (food and accommodation) since these too have been re-valued. Unqualified teachers are having a harder time finding work. Nowadays, there is plenty of competition for jobs teaching English from local English language graduates and English-speaking immigrants.

Nevertheless, a qualified teacher should have no problem finding a job here. October is a good time to start writing to potential employers who will want teachers who can start work in the following spring. Teachers who want to pick up a job while they're in the country should arrive in January. If you don't like big cities, consider Mendoza or Cordoba as alternatives to Buenos Aires. You could even travel out to Patagonia and chance your luck there.

### Embassy in UK:
65 Brook Street, London W1Y 1YE
**Tel:** 020 7318 1300
www.argentine-embassy-uk.org

### Embassy in USA:
1600 New Hampshire Ave NW, Washington DC20009
**Tel:** 202 238 6400
www.embajadaargentina-usa.org

### British Council office:
Marcelo T de Alvear 590 4th Floor, C1058AAF, Buenos Aires
**Tel** +54 (11) 4311 9814/7519
www.britishcouncil.org.ar

⊃ **Visas/Work Permits:** Most teachers work on tourist visas, which they renew every three months. For a longer-term contract, you need a work permit, which is arranged by your employer. Securing the correct permit can take up to eight months, so plan ahead.

⊃ **Requirements:** TESOL/TESL Certificate

⊃ **Currency:** £1 = 5.9 / $1 = 3.1 Pesos.

⊃ **Salaries/Taxes:** Institutes pay on an hourly basis

⊃ **Accommodation:** If you are paying for accommodation yourself, a one-bedroom apartment can cost £300 / $600 per month. Teachers often live in simple, family-owned hotels until they have saved some deposit money.

⊃ **English Language Media:** Buenos Aires Herald.

⊃ **Tip:** Many institutes expect teachers to provide their own supplies including copies of materials, blank tapes, videos, a tape player and books.

⊃ **Health advice:** Local medical care is expensive, so private insurance is recommended. You should be protected against Hepatitis A; in some northern areas Malaria and Yellow Fever occur.

### Schools in Argentina (+54)

**ALICANA**
San Martin 2293, 3000 Sanata Fe. **Tel:** 42 53 7567, **Fax**: 42 55 2026

**American English Institute**
Córdoba 392 3ºD, Buenos Aires. **Tel:** 4312-8646, **Fax**: 4312-8462

**American English Institute**
Gral.M. Belgrano 179, Paraná, Entre Rios. **Tel:** 0343 431-5018

**American Training Co.**
Viamonte577, Piso 7, 1053 Buenos Aires. **Tel:** 1 311 3699, **Fax**: 1 315 3573

**AMICANA**
Chile 985, 5500 Mendoza. **Tel:** 61 23 6271, **Fax**: 61 29 8702, **Email:** amicana@impsat.com.ar

**ARICANA**
Buenos Aires 934, 2000 Rosario. **Tel:** 41 21 7664, **Fax**: 41 21 9179, **Email:** aricana@interactive.com.ar

**Asociacion Comodoro Rivadavia de Intercambio Cultural Argentino Norteamericano (ACRICANA)**
Escalada 1567, 9000 Comodoro Rivadavia. **Tel:** 0297 446-6311. **Fax:** 0297 447-3956. **Email:** acricana@infovia.com.ar

**Asociacion Mendocina de Intercambio Cultural Argentino Norteamericano (AMICANA)**
Chile 987, 5500 Mendoza. **Tel**: 0261 423-6271. **Fax:** 0261 429-8702. **Email:** amicana2@impsat1.com.ar

**Asociacion Paranense de Intercambio Cultural Argentino Norteamericano (APICANA)**
Córdoba 256, 3100 Parana. **Tel/Fax:** 0343 431-9678. **Email:** apicana@arnet.com.ar

**Asociacion Rosarina de Intercambio Cultural Argentino Norteamericano (ARICANA)**
Buenos Aires 934, 2000 Rosario . **Tel:** 0341 421-7664. **Fax:** 0341 421-9179. **Email:** aricana@arnet.com.ar

## Instituto Cultural Argentino Norteamericano (ICANA)
Maipú 672, 1006 Buenos Aires. **Tel:** 011 4322-3855/4557. **Fax:** 011 4322-2106. **Email:** secretaria@bcl.edu.ar

## Instituto Dean Funes de Intercambio Cultural Argentino Norteamericano (IDFICANA)
9 de Julio 177, 5200 Dean Funes, Córdoba. **Tel:** 03521 420-738. **Fax:** 03521 421-001/20899

## Instituto de Intercambio Cultural Argentino Norteamericano (IICANA)
Dean Funes 726, 5000 Cordoba. **Tel:** 0351 421-4026/425-4216/426-3941. **Fax:** 0351 423-7858. **Email:** IICANA@onenet.com.ar

## ATICANA
Salta 581, 4000 San Miguel de Tucuman. **Tel:** 81 31 0616, **Fax:** 81 30 3070, **Email:** aticana@starnet.net.ar

## Berlitz
Av. de Mayo 847, 1er Piso, 1084 Buenos Aires. **Tel:** 11 4342 0202 **Email:** info@berlitz.com.ar

## Berlitz
Av. Del Libertador 15231, 1640 Acassuso. **Tel**: 11 4747 1871 **Fax**: 11 4732 3096, **Email:** info@berlitz.com.ar

## British Council
Marcalo T De Alvera 590 (4th Floor), 1058 Buenos Aires. **Tel:** 54 1 311 9814.

## Brooklyn Bridge
Reconquista 715, 6 C y D, 1003 CF, Buenos Aires. **Tel**: 1 313 1652

## CAIT
Maipú 863 3°C, Buenos Aires. **Tel/Fax:**4311-44/4314-2583

## Centum Servicios de Idiomas
Bartlome Mitre, Piso 4, 1036 Buenos Aires. **Fax:** 1 328 5150/2385

## English Studies
Catalina Hansen, Rodriguez Pena 238 40 A - 1020, CF, Buenos Aires. **Tel:** 1 371 5352, **Fax:** (21) 720393.

## ICANA
Maipu 672, 1006 Buenos Aires. **Tel:** 1 322 3855, **Fax**: 1 322 2106, **Email:** icana@bcl.edu.ar

## IELI
Alberti 6444, San Jose de la Esquina, Santa Fe 2185.

## Instituto Cultural Argentino-Britanico
Calle 12, No 1900, La Plata.

## Instituto ELT
Isabel Gonzalez Bueno, Soler 458 (1714) Ituzaingo, Buenos Aires. **Tel/Fax:** (541) 624 0148.

## International House
IH Belgrano, Arcos 1830, 1428 CF, Buenos Aires. **Tel:** 541 785 4425.

## Landmark
Marcelo T. de Alvear 2331 1°D, Buenos Aires. **Tel/Fax:** 4825-3806, **Email:** landmark@arnet.com.ar

## Language Network
Billinghurst 2476 piso 2, Buenos Aires. **Tel:** 4805-6586, **Fax:** 4805-8452.

## Liceo Superior de Cultura Inglesa
Italia 830, Tandil, 7000 Pica de Buenos Aires.

## Northside School of English
G W Seminario, Velez Sarsfield 56, 1640, Martinez, Buenos Aires. **Tel/Fax:** 798 5150/793 5469.

## St John's School
Recta Martinoli 3452, V Belgrano 5417 Cordoba, Pica de Cordoba.

## TOKEN
Av.de Mayo 1260-5°Q, Capital Federal. **Tel:** 4383-0751/15-4979-3929 **Email:** houses@infovia.com.ar

## BOLIVIA

Bolivia is currently enjoying a rare period of political and economic stability although there has been a recent increase in street protests because of popular dissatisfaction with government policies. Bolivians are keen to learn English and travelling teachers are attracted here because it is cheap to stay and culturally fascinating.

### Embassy in UK:
106 Eaton Square, London SW1W 9AD
**Tel:** 020 7235 4248

### Embassy in USA:
3014 Massachusetts Ave NW, Washington,DC20008
**Tel:** 202 483 4410

### British Council office:
Avenida Arce 2708 (esq.Campos), Casilla 15047, La Paz
**Tel:** +591 (2) 2431 240
www.britishcouncil.org/bolivia

➲ **Visas/Work Permits:** All nationalities need a tourist visa to enter. Work permits are obtained by employers for contracts of at least one year in duration. They cost around £240 / $450 and you may be asked to make a small payment (around £12-30 / $22-57) towards the cost.

- **Requirements:** TESOL/TESL Certificate
- **Currency:** £1 = 14.91 / $1 = 8.06 Bolivianos
- **Salaries and taxes:** As low as £2 / $4 per hour in a language school or £6/ $11 per hour for private classes.
- **Accommodation:** Cheap and easy to find. Some schools will supply accommodation.
- **Cost of Living:** Bolivia is an inexpensive country to live in.
- **Health advice:** La Paz is situated 13,000 feet above sea level and many teachers report that it takes a while to become acclimatized to the altitude. Medical facilities, even in La Paz, are not adequate to handle serious medical conditions, such as cardiac problems. You should be vaccinated against Hepatitis A, Malaria, and Yellow Fever.

## School in Bolivia (+591)

**Centro Boliviano Americano**
Calle 25 de Mayo N-0365, Casilla 1399, Cochabamba. **Tel**: 42 21288, 22518. **Fax**: 42 51225. **Email:** suarezmj@llajta. nrc.bolnet.bo

**Centro Boliviano Americano**
Parque Iturralde Zenon 121, Casilla 12024, La Paz. **Tel:** 2 430107 **Fax:** 2 431342. **Email:** cbalp@datacom-bo.net

**Centro Boliviano Americano**
c/ Cochabamba 66, Casilla 510, Santa Cruz de la Sierra. **Tel:** 3 342299 **Fax:** 3 350188 **Email:** cbascz@datacom.bo.net

**Centro Boliviano Americano**
Calle Calvo No. 331, Casilla No. 380, Sucre, Chuquisaca. **Tel:** 64 41608. **Fax:** 64 41608. **Email:** cba@nch.bolnet.bo

**Colegio Ingles Saint Andrews**
Av. Las Relamas, La Florida, La Paz. **Tel:** 2 792484.

**Colegio San Calixto**
C/Jenaro Sanjines 701, La Paz. **Tel:** 2 35 5278.

**Colegio San Ignacio**
Av. Hugo Ernest 7050, Seguencoma, La Paz. **Tel:** 2 783720.

**Pan American English Centre**
Edificio Avenida, Avenida 16 de Julio 1490, 7º piso, Casillo 5244, La Paz. **Tel/Fax:** 2 340796.

**Tito's Place**
P.O. Box 3112, Cochabamba. **Tel:** 4 289308, **Fax**: 4 288836. **Email:** mahergar@comteco.entelnet.bo

## BRAZIL

English language teaching is booming in Brazil and it is still quite easy to find a job here. Many parents are keen to send their children to private schools to learn English. There are around 60 bi-national centres specifically catering for Brazilians who want to learn English.

**Embassy in UK:**
32 Green Street, London W1Y 4AT
**Tel:** 020 7499 0877
www.brazil.org.uk

**Embassy in USA:**
3006 Massachusetts Ave NW, Washington DC20008
**Tel:** 202 238 2700
www.brasilemb.org

**British Council office (see also appendix):**
Ed.Centro Empresarial Varig, SCN Quadra 04 Bloco B Torre Oeste Conjunto 202, Brasilia – DF, 70710-926
**Tel** +55 (0) 61 327 7230
www.britishcouncil.org/brazil

- **Visas/Work Permits:** It is very difficult to obtain a work visa so some schools are willing to hire teachers who are in the country on a tourist visa although this is illegal. It is your responsibility to arrange for a work visa, which can take up to two months to get. You need to be qualified and have at least two years' experience to qualify. It is possible to arrive, find a job, apply for a visa and pick it up in a neighbouring country, although this is not popular with the bureaucrats. Otherwise, the process should be initiated through the Brazilian consulate at home.
- **Requirements:** TESOL/TESL Certificate
- **Currency:** £1 = 4.19 / $1 = 2.14 Reals.
- **Salaries/Taxes:** Teachers are paid for 13 months and salaries are higher in cities. Full-time salaries start at around £220 / $400 a month, plus basic accommodation. Incomes can be supplemented with private classes starting at £6 / $11 per hour. Experienced teachers with a Masters degree can earn up to £1500 / $2700 a month. Tax varies from 13-25% and there is a statutory social security deduction.
- **Accommodation:** Better schools will either provide lodging for free or offer a subsidy. Otherwise, expect to pay between a third and half of your salary. Apartments are unlikely to be furnished.
- **Cost of Living:** Food is cheap but rent is moderately expensive.

⮌ **Health advice:** Insurance can be taken out locally but it does not cover dental treatment.

⮌ **English Language Media:** Brazil Herald.

## Schools in Brazil (+55)

**Britannia Schools**
Rua Garcia D'Avila 58, Ipanema, Rio De Janeiro RJ 22421-010. **Tel:** 21 511 0143, **Fax:** 21 511 0893.

**Britannia Special English Studies**
Rua Dr Timoteo, 752 Moinhos De Vent, Porto Alegre RS.

**Britannia Juniors**
Rua. Barao da Torre 599 - Rio de Janeiro, CEP 22411-003, RJ. **Tel:** 21 239-8044, **Fax:** 21 259 6197.

**Britannia Executive School**
Rua Barao De Lucena 61, Botofogo, Rio de Janeiro 22260.

**Britannic International House**
Rua Hermogenes de Morais 178, Recife PE 50610-160. **Tel:** 81 445 5564, **Fax:** 81 445 5481.

**British House**
Rua Tiradentes 2258, Centro, Pelotas RS 96060-160. **Tel:** 532 27 3139, **Fax:** 532 27 5604.

**Cambridge Sociedade Brasileira de Cultura Inglesa**
Rua Piaui 1234, Londrina 86020-320 PR. **Tel:** 43 324 1092, **Fax:** 324 0314.

**Casa Branca**
Rua Ma-chado De Assis 37, Boqueirao, Santos SP. **Tel/Fax:** 13 233 5258.

**CEBEU**
Av Marechal Rondon, 745, Centro, Ji-Paraná RO. **Tel:** 69 422 3100, **Fax:** 69 422 3100.

**CEL-LEP**
Av. dos Tajuras 212, Sao Paulo SP 05670-000. **Tel:** 11 212 6183, **Fax:** 11 210 0698.

**CEMID**
Rua Santa Luzia, 799 conj. 401, Rio de Janeiro - RJ 20030-040. **Tel:** (21) 262-1793 **Fax:** (21) 240-9271

**Centro Britanico**
Rua Joao Ramalho 344, Sao Paulo SP 05008-011. **Tel:** 11 622984, **Fax:** 11 872 9483.

**Centro Cultural Brasil Estados Unidos**
Avenida T 5, No. 441, 74230-040 Goiania GO. **Tel:** 62 833 1313, **Fax:** 62 833 1308.

**Centro Cultural Brasil-Estados Unidos**
Avenida Julio de Mesquita, 606 13025-061 Campinas – SP. **Tel:** 192 51-3664/52-6668. **Fax:** 192 52-6888

**Centro Cultural Brasil-Estados Unidos**
Rua Amintas de Barros, 99, Edifico Itatiaia Centro Caixa Postal 3328, 80060-200 Curitiba – PR. **Tel:** 41 320-4777. **Fax:** 41 238-2822

**Centro de Enseñanza PLI**
Rua de Octubro, 1234 Conj 4, Porto Alegre, RS 90000.

**Centro De Cultura Inglesa**
Av Guapore 2.236, Cacoal RO, CEP 78 975-000. **Tel:** (69) 441-2833, **Fax:** 441-5346.

**Cultura Inglesa**
Rua do Progresso 239, Recife PE 50070-002. **Tel:** 81 423 6266, **Fax:** 81 231 2318.

**Cultura Inglesa**
Av. 17 de Agosto 233, Recife PE 52060-090. **Tel:** 81 268 6938, **Fax:** 81 268 6787.

**Cultura Inglesa**
Rua Visconde Albuquerque 205, Recife PE 50610-090. **Tel:** 81 228 6649, **Fax:** 81 228 6649.

**Cultura Inglesa**
Rua Visconde de Inhauma 980, Ribeirao Preto SP 14010-100. **Tel:** 16 610 6616, **Fax:** 16 610 9868.

**Cultura Inglesa**
Rua Paul Pompeia 231, Rio de Janeiro RJ 22080-000. **Tel:** 21 287 0990, **Fax:** 21 267 6474.

**Cultura Inglesa**
R. Plinio Moscoso 945, Salvador BA 40155-020. **Tel:** 71 247 9788, **Fax:** 71 245 3287.

**Cultura Inglesa**
Av. Sao Sebastiao 848, Santarem PA 68005-090. **Tel:** 91 522 7247.

**Cultura Inglesa**
Rua Sao Sebastiao 1530, Sao Carlos SP 13560-230. **Tel:** 16 272 2276, **Fax:** 16 272 9875.

**Cultura Inglesa**
Av. Tiradentes 670, Sao Joao del Rei MG 36300-000. **Tel:** 32 371 7035, **Fax:** 32 371 2764.

**Cultura Inglesa**
Av. Brig. Faria Lima 2000, Sao Paulo SP 01452-002. **Tel:** 11 870 4955, **Fax:** 11 813 1945.

**Cultura Inglesa**
R. Joao Pinheiro 808, Uberlandia MG 38400-58. **Tel:** 34 235 2786, **Fax:** 34 236 9250.

**Cultura Inglesa**
Praca Rosalvo Ribeiro 110, Maceio AL 57021-57. **Tel:** 82 221 8055, **Fax:** 82 223 3785.

**Cultura Inglesa**
R. Eng Mario de Gusmao 603, Maceio AL 57035-000, **Tel:** 82 231 8687. **Fax:** 82 231 8132.

**Cultura Inglesa**
Rua Natal 553, Manaus AM 69005-000. **Tel:** 92 611 1635, **Fax:** 92 611 1635.

**Cultura Inglesa**
Av. Rio Branco 741, Maringa PR 87015-380. **Tel/Fax:** 44 225 1518.

**Cultura Inglesa**
Rua Acu 495, Natal RN 59020-110. **Tel:** 84 211 6070, **Fax:** 84 211 4559.

**Cultura Inglesa**
R. Silvio Henrique Braune 15, Nova Friburgo RJ 28625-050. **Tel:** 245 22 5392, **Fax:** 245 22 5392.

**Cultura Inglesa**
R. Eduardo de Moraes 147, Olinda PE 53030-250. **Tel/Fax:** 81 429 2281.

**Cultura Inglesa**
Av. Bernardo Vieira de Melo 2101, Jaboatao dos Guararapes PE 54 410-010. **Tel:** 81 361 3458, **Fax:** 813610467.

**Cultura Inglesa**
Rua Paula Xavier 501, Ponta Grossa PR 84010-430. **Tel/Fax:** 42 223 2735.

**Cultura Inglesa**
Rua Quintino Bocaiuva 1447, Porto Alegre RS 90570-010. **Tel/Fax:** 51 333 4033.

**Cultura Inglesa**
Rua Mamanguape 411, Recife PE 51020-50. **Tel:** 81 326 1908, **Fax:** 81 326 7618.

**Cultura Inglesa**
Alameda Julia da Costa 1500, Curitiba PR 80730-070. **Tel:** 41 222 7339, **Fax:** 41 224 1024.

**Cultura Inglesa**
Rua Ponto Grossa 1565, Dourados MS 79824-160. **Tel:** 67 421 7147, **Fax:** 67 421 5753.

**Cultura Inglesa**
Rua Conde de Porto Alegre 59, Buque de Caxias RJ 25070-350. **Tel:** 21 671 2543, **Fax:** 21 671 4346.

**Cultura Inglesa**
Rua Rafael Bandeira 335, Florianapolis SC 88015-450. **Tel/Fax:** 48 224 2696.

**Cultura Inglesa**
Rua Ana Bilhar 171, Fortaleza CE 60160-110. **Tel:** 85 244 3784, **Fax:** 85 224 4665.

**Cultura Inglesa**
Rua Marechal Deodoro 1326, Franca SP 14400-440. **Tel/Fax:** 16 722 0011

**Cultura Inglesa**
Rua 86 No. 7, Golania GO 74083-330. **Tel:** 62 241 4516, **Fax:** 62 241 2582.

**Cultura Inglesa**
Rua 20 778, Ituiutaba MG 38300-000. **Tel:** 34 268 1681, **Fax:** 34 261 5975.

**Cultura Inglesa**
Av. Rio Grande do Sul 1411, Joao Pessoa PB 58030-021. **Tel:** 83 224 7005, **Fax:** 83 224 9479.

**Cultura Inglesa**
Rua Dr. Joao Colin 559, Joinville SC 89204-004. **Tel:** 47 433 7603, **Fax:** 47 433 4512.

**Cultura Inglesa**
Av. dos Andras 536, Juiz de Fora MG 36036-000. **Tel:** 32 215 5169, **Fax:** 32 215 9659.

**Cultura Inglesa**
Av. Barao de Maruim 761, Aracaju SE 49015-020. **Tel/Fax:** 79 224 7360.

**Cultura Inglesa**
Rua Almeida Campos 215, Araxa MG 38180-00. **Tel/Fax:** 34 661 3275.

**Cultura Inglesa**
Rua Virgilio Malta 1427, Bauru SP 17040-440. **Tel/Fax:** 142 23 3016.

**Cultura Inglesa**
R. Fernandes Tourinho 538, Belo Horizonte MG 30112-011. **Tel:** 31 221 6770, **Fax:** 31 225 1791.

**Cultura Inglesa**
Rua Mal. Floriano Peixoto 433, Blumenau SC 89010-000. **Tel/Fax:** 47 326 7272.

**Cultura Inglesa**
SEPS 709/908 Conjunto B DF 70390-89. **Tel:** 61 244 5650, **Fax:** 61 244 8571.

**Cultura Inglesa**
Av. Guapore 2236, Cacoal RO 78975-000. **Tel:** 69 441 2833. **Fax:** 69 441 4547.

**Cultura Inglesa**
Rua Lino Gomes da Silva 53, Campina Grande PB 58107-613. **Tel/Fax:** 83 322 4658.

**Cultura Inglesa**
R. Humberto de Campos 419, Campo Grande MS 79020-060. **Tel:** 67 751 0272, **Fax:** 67 751 0570.

**Cultura Inglesa**
Av. Agamenon Magalhaes 634, Caruaru PE 55000-000. **Tel/Fax:** 81 721 4749.

**Cultura Inglesa**
Rua Antonio Ataide 515, Vila Velha ES 29100-290. **Tel:** 27 229 5194, **Fax:** 27 229 3206.

### Cultura Inglesa
Av Tiradentes 670, 36300 Sao Joao Del Rei MG. **Tel**: 32 371-4377, **Fax**: 32 371-4377.

### Cultura Inglesa de Londrina
Rua Goias 1507, Centro, Londrina PR 86020-340. **Tel/Fax**: 43 323 7700.

### ELC
Rua Sa e Souza 655, Boa Viagem, Recife PE, 51030-350. **Tel**: 81 342 0351.

### English Forever
Rua Rio Grande Do Sul 356, Pituba, Salvador-BA 41830-140. **Tel**: 71 240 2255, **Fax**: 71 248 8706, **Email**: forever@svn.com.br

### George Otto
Av. Vereador de Campo 525, Sala 4, Ibiuna - SP 18150-000. **Tel**: (15) 249-1159 **Fax**: (15) 249-1159

### Global Team
Caixa Postal 6504, Campinas - SP 13084-970. **Tel**: (19) 287-4427 **Fax**: (19) 287-4427

### Independent British Institute
SHCGN 703 Area Especial, s/no Brasilia DF 70730-700. **Tel**: 61 322 8373, **Fax**: 323 5524, **Email**: ibi@nutecnet.com.br

### Instituto Britanico
Rua Deputado Carvalho Deda 640, 49025-070 Salgado Filho, Aracaju SE, Brazil. **Tel**: 79 23 2791, **Fax**: 79 27 2645.

### Instituto da Lingua Inglesa
Av. do CPA 157, Cuiaba MT 78008-000. **Tel/Fax**: 65 624 1197.

### International House-Matriz
The School House, Rua 4, 80, Goiania GO 74110-140, Goais, SE.

### International House Goiania
Rua 04 n° 80, Setor Oeste, Goiania GO 74110-140. **Tel**: 62 224 0478, Fax: 62 223 1846.

### Liberty English Centre
Rua Amintas De Barros 1059, Curitiba PR. **Tel**: 41 263 3586, **Fax**: 41 262 1738.

### New Vision English
Av. Ibirapuera, 2249 São Paulo - SP 01248-001. **Tel**: (11) 241-4199 **Fax**: (11) 241-4199 **Email**: newvision@newvision.com.br

### PBF - Pink and Blue – Freedom
Rua Santos, 54 Joinville - SC 89202-46. **Tel**: (47) 433-1471 **Fax**: (47) 433-1471 **Email**: pbfjlle@netville.com.br

### Sharing English
Rua Souza de Andrade 56, Recife PE 52050-300. **Tel/Fax**: 81 421 2286.

### Schütz & Kanomata
Rua Galvão Costa, 85 Santa Cruz do Sul – RS. **Tel**: (51) 711-2248 **Fax**: (51) 715-3366 **Email**: english@viavale.com.br

### Skill
Av. Indianópolis, 3356 São Paulo - SP 04062-003. **Tel**: (11) 5589-9535 **Fax**: (11) 5589-9447 **Email**: fruggie@ibm.net

### Sky Cursos e Traduções SC Ltda
Av. Senador Virgílio Távora, 867 - Meireles Fortaleza - CE 60170.250. **Tel**: (85) 224-7879 **Fax**: (85) 224-7879 **Email**: sky@fortalnet.com.br

### Soc Bras de Cultura Inglesa
Rua Fernandes Tourinho, 538 - Savassi BH-MG 30112.000, **Tel**: 031 221 6770.

### System 2000
Rua Deputado Jose Lajes 491, Ponta Verde, Maceio AL 57035-330. **Tel**: 82 231 7808, **Fax**: 82 327 4946.

### St. Peter's English School
Rua Berilo Guimaraes, 182 Centro Itabuna, Bahia.

### The English Office
Rua D. Eponina Afonseca, 116 São Paulo - SP 04720-010. **Tel**: (11) 546-0796 **Fax**: (11) 546-0796

### Universitas
Rua Goncalves Dias 858, Belo Horizonte MG 30140-091. **Tel**: 031 261 1477, **Fax**: 031 261 5138.

### UP Language Consultants
Av. Brig. Faria Lima, 1912, 18m, Jd. Paulistano, Calcerter Sao Paulo - SP 01451-907. **Tel**: (11) 211-9990 **Fax**: (11) 212-5366 **Email**: up@ensino.net

### Upper English
Rua 09 de Julho 2143, Sao Carlos SP 13560-590. **Tel**: 16 271 8146, **Fax**: 16 271 5431.

### Vision English Escola de Inglês S/C Ltda.
Av. Ibirapuera, 2249 São Paulo - SP 04029-100.**Tel**: (11) 241-4199 **Fax**: (11) 241-4199 **Email**: newvision@newvision.com.br

## CHILE

The government has placed improving Chile's school system and developing foreign export markets at the top of its economic agenda, so learning English is an educational priority.

Although it is impossible to work in state schools without a qualification from a Chilean university, there are many private schools and in-company opportunities, especially in Santiago.

Foreigners coming to Chile with the intention of teaching English should preferably have both qualifications and experience. Teachers are trained to a high standard in Chile and competition is tough.

**Embassy in UK:**
12 Devonshire Street, London W1N 2DS
**Tel:** 020 7580 1023

**Embassy in USA:**
1732 Massachusetts Ave NW, Washington DC20008
**Tel:** 202 785 1746
www.chile-usa.org

**British Council office:**
Eliodoro Yáñez 832, Providencia 6640356, Casilla 115 Correo 55, Santiago
**Tel** +56 (2) 410 6900
www.britcoun.cl

➲ **Visas/Work Permits:** Applications for visas and work permits should be made before arrival. It is possible to obtain a work permit after arrival but you have to show that you intend to stay for at least one year. Working on a tourist visa is possible although illegal.

➲ **Requirements:** (A degree is recommended) TESOL/TESL Certificate

➲ **Currency:** £1 = 1024 / $1 = 524 Pesos

➲ **Salaries/Taxes:** For contracted teaching positions, a minimum wage for overseas teachers is set by the government at £250 / $460 per month. Rates vary from £5-7 / $9-13 per hour for qualified teachers. Private lessons pay £10 / $19 an hour and up. The tax rate is around 10%

➲ **Accommodation:** Schools offer little help, but it's easy to stay in hostels, which offer long-term accommodation with good facilities. Rooms can cost as little as £80 / $150 per month but average around £150 / US$300. Apartments can cost up to £250 / US$470 per month and landlords expect a month's rent as deposit and a month in advance.

➲ **Cost of Living:** Low but higher than much of Latin America.

➲ **English Language Media:** News Review.

➲ **Health advice:** Medical care is generally good, but it may not meet western standards. Supplemental medical insurance, which includes specific overseas coverage, including provisions for medical evacuation, is highly recommended, as in-country medical

evacuations from outlying areas to Santiago cost £1,500 / $2,700 or more.

## Schools in Chile (+56)

**Abbey Road Cultural De Idiomas**
Gorostiaga 608 P. 2, Iquique. **Tel:** 57 428737 **Fax:** 57 427147 **Email:** Abbeyroa.Dcult001@chilnet.cl

**Acpen Academy**
Av. Lib. B. O'higgins 949 P. 21 Of. 2103, Santiago. **Tel:** 2 6724460 **Fax:** 2 6724460 **Email:** acpenaca.demy001@chilnet.cl

**American Language Institute**
Lord Cochrane 286, Santiago, **Tel:** 2 6955487 **Fax:** 2 6955487 **Email:** american.langu001@chilnet.cl

**Anglo-American International School**
San Sebastian 2975, Santiago. **Tel:** 231 1771.

**Antofagasta British School**
Pedro Leon Gallo 723, Casilla 1, Antofagasta. **Tel:** 241 368.

**Berlitz**
Padre Mariano 305, Santiago. **Tel:** 2 2361557 **Fax:** 2 2361563 **Email:** Berlitz_Chile@entelchile.net

**British Council**
Eliodora Yanez 832, Casilla 115-Correo 55, Santiago. **Tel:** 22361199.

**British School**
Waldo Seguel 454, Casilla 379, Punta Arenas. **Tel:** 223 381, **Fax:** 248 447.

**British High School**
Los Gladiolos 10281, Santiago. **Tel:** 217 2204.

**Burford Institute**
Av. Pedro De Valdivia 511, Santiago. **Tel:** 2 2744603 **Fax:** 2 2235944 **Email:** info@burford.cl

**Cie**
Orella 1089, Antofagasta. **Tel:** 55 268339 **Fax:** 55 268339 **Email:** Capacita.Cioni001@chilnet.cl

**Centro Chileno Canadiense Idiomas Ltda.**
Av. Luis Thayer Ojeda 0191 P. 6 Of. 601, Santiago. **Tel:** 2 3341090 **Fax:** 2 3341089 **Email:** centroch.ileno001@chilnet.cl

**Colegio Charles Darwin**
Manantiales 0314, Punta Arenas. **Tel:** 212 671.

**Colegio Dunalastair**
Av. Las Condes 11931, Santiago. **Tel:** 215 2666.

**Colegio Ingles George Chaytor**
Callejon Ingles 4B, Temuco. **Tel:** 211 301.

**Colegio Ingles De Talca**
12 Norte 5/6 Oriente, Talca. **Tel:** 226692.

**Colegio St George**
Av. Americo Vespucio Norte 5400, Santiago.

**Colegio Del Verbo Divinio**
Av. Presidente Errazuriz 4055, Santiago. **Tel:** 228 6076.

**Colegio Villa Maria Academy**
Av. Presidente Errazuriz 3753, Santiago. **Tel:** 228 3398.

**Computacion E Ingles Intercom Ltda.**
Av. Pedro Montt 2053, Valpo. **Tel:** 32 254436 **Fax:** 32 254436 **Email:** Intercom.Pescu001@chilnet.cl

**Craighouse**
El Rodeo 12525-La Dehesa, Casilla 20007-Correo 20, Santiago. **Tel:** 242 4011, **Fax:** 215 7400.

**Fischer English Institute**
Cirujano Guzman 49, Santiago, **Tel:** 2 2356667 **Fax:** 2 2359810 **Email:** Fischeri.Nstit001@chilnet.cl

**Grange School**
Av. Principe De Gales 6154, Casilla 51-Correo 12, Santiago. **Tel:** 277 1181, **Fax:** 277 0946.

**Greenhouse School**
Ines De Suarez 1500, Temuco. **Tel:** 240 840.

**Henry Renna Instituto**
Mark Twain 7241, Santiago. **Tel:** 2 2199044 **Fax:** 2 2193013 **Email:** Henryren.Nains002@chilnet.cl

**Instituto Chileno-Britanico De Cultura**
Baquedano 351, Casilla 653, Arica. **Tel:** 58 238399, **Fax:** 58 231960.

**Instituto Chileno-Britanico De Cultura**
3 Norte 824, Casilla, Vina Del Mar. 929. **Tel:** 32 971061, **Fax:** 32 686656.

**Instituto Chileno-Norteamericano De Cultura**
Moneda 1467, Santiago. **Tel:** 2 238 6107, **Fax:** 2 698 1175, **Email:** infocent@hood.ichn.cl

**Instituto Chileno Norteamericano**
Caupolican 315, Casilla 612, Concepcion. **Tel:** 41 248 589, **Fax:** 41 233 851 (Also In Antofagasta And Valparaiso.)

**Instituto De Ingles Impact S.A.**
Rosa O'higgins 259, Santiago. **Tel:** 2 2125609, **Fax:** 2 2116165

**Instituto De Ingles Lorbeth**
Cabo Arestey 2468 Of., Santiago. **Tel:** 2 6956018, **Fax:** 2 6956018,

**International Preparatory School**
Pastor Fernandez 16001, El Arrayan, Santiago. **Tel:** 215 1094.

**Iquique English College**
Jose Joaquin Perez 419, Iquique. **Tel:** 411 2409.

**Let's Do English**
Villa Vicencio 361, Office 109, Santiago.

**Lincoln International Academy**
Camino San Antonio 55- Las Condes, Santiago. **Tel:** 217 1907.

**Linguatec**
Av. Los Leones 439, Santiago. **Tel:** 2 2334356, **Fax:** 2 2341380, **Email:** Michelle@Linguatec.cl

**Lm Language** centre
Agustinas 853 Of. 301, Santiago. **Tel:** 2 6396419, **Fax:** 2 6396419

**Mackay School**
Vicuna Mackenna 700, Casilla 558, Vina Del Mar. **Tel:** 832 574 **Fax:** 832 419.

**Mayflower School**
Las Condes 12167, Santiago. **Tel:** 217 1085.

**Nido De Aquilas School**
Nido De Aquilas 14515, Casilla 16211-Providencia, Santiago. **Tel:** 216 6842.

**Polyglot**
Villavicencio 361 Of. 102, Santiago. **Tel:** 2 6398078, **Fax:** 2 6322485, **Email:** info@polyglot.cl

**Redland School**
Camino El Alba 11357, Las Condes, Santiago. **Tel:** 2 214 1265, **Fax:** 2 214 1020.

**St Gabriel's School**
Av. Bilbao 3070-Providencia, Santiago. **Tel:** 204 1915, **Fax:** 225 2136.

**St John's School**
Pedro De Valdivia 1783, Casilla 284, Concepcion. **Tel:** 331 670, **Fax:** 340 809.

**St Margaret's School**
5 Norte 1351, Casilla 392, Vina Del Mar. **Tel:** 977 000, **Fax:** 975 220.

**St Peter's School**
Calle Libertad 575, Vina Del Mar. **Tel:** 971 993.

**Santiago College**
Los Leones 584, Casilla 130-D, Santiago. **Tel:** 2 238 1813, **Fax:** 2 238 0755.

**Thewhla's English School**
Las Camelias 2854, Santiago.

**Tronwell**
Av. Apoquindo 4499 P. 1-2-3, Santiago. **Tel:** 2 2461040, **Fax:** 2 2289739, **Email:** tronwell.sa001@chilnet.cl

**Wenlock School**
Carlos Pena Otaegui 10880, La Foresta, Los Dominicos, Santiago. **Tel:** 212 8982, **Fax:** 212 9226.

**Wessex School**
Colo-Colo 222-Clasificador 43, Concepcion. **Tel:** 315436.

**Windsor School**
Av. Francia Esq. Simpson, Casilla 530, Valdivia.

## COLOMBIA

Although Colombia has a reputation for violence, the reality is that, except for a few "no-go" zones, the country is no more dangerous than others in the region. In fact, many teachers report that Bogota and even Medellin are fun cities to live and work in as long as you don't stray into the "bad" areas. Schools welcome native English speakers because Colombia's image has deterred many of them from travelling here to teach. There is a network of Colombian-American Cultural centres and many of the private schools are American-owned. Bilingual high schools offer good rates of pay and working conditions.

This means that most EFL teachers, including unqualified ones looking for short-term positions while travelling, can get a job pretty easily. However, you may have to settle for a low wage initially, and it might be only just enough to live on. If you want to stay more than a few months, it is advisable to get qualified first so that you can get a job in one of the more reputable schools and build up contacts to secure more lucrative private classes.

**Consulate in UK:**
15-19 Great Titchfield Street, London W1P 7FB
**Tel:** 020 7495 4233

**Embassy in USA:**
2118 Leroy Pl NW, Washington DC20008
**Tel:** 202 387 8338
www.colombiaemb.org

**British Council office:**
Calle 87 No 12 - 79, Bogota
**Tel** +57 (1) 618 7680
www.britishcouncil.org.co

⮞ **Visas/Work Permits:** Teachers must have a work permit before they travel and, unusually, a private language school cannot intervene directly with the Ministry of Foreign Affairs to secure this visa. Only those employed by approved institutions can secure the necessary work visa and the application process is associated with red tape, delays and expense, so make sure that your school is one of these institutions. If you want to insure that your visa is legal, your degrees and transcripts must be validated with a rubber stamp from the Colombian consulate.

⮞ **Requirements:** TESOL/TESL Certificate

⮞ **Currency:** £1 = 4436 / $1 = 2290 Pesos

⮞ **Salaries/Taxes:** Many schools offer no more than £2 / $4 per hour and unqualified teachers can expect to earn as little as £1.50 / $3. Average monthly salaries are £300 / $570 and it is possible to earn £525 / $950. Many institutions pay teachers 14 times per year and, with a normal work visa, teachers will pay tax of 10% or more. Private lessons can earn you up to £12 / $20 an hour or more.

⮞ **Accommodation:** Expensive. In Bogota and most other cities, a one-bedroom apartment in a safe area costs about £200 / $380 per month and administration fees are often charged on top.

⮞ **Cost of Living:** The cost of living is expensive as inflation is still high. However, once established, teachers can have a good standard of living.

⮞ **Health advice:** Travellers to Bogota may require some time to adjust to the altitude (8,600 feet), which can adversely affect blood pressure, digestion and energy levels

### Schools in Colombia (+57)

**Academia Ingles Para Niños**
Calle 106 No 16-26, Bogota.

**Advanced Learning Service**
Transversal 20 No 120-15, Bogota.

**American School Way**
Dg. 110 No. 42-96 Casa 4, Bogota. **Tel:** 1 6198356

**Aprender Ltda**
Calle 17 No 4-68 Ql. 501, Bogota.

**Aspect Language Schools Ltda.**
Cl. 90 No. 11-44 Of. 301, Bogota. **Tel:** 1 2569827

**BBC De Londres**
Calle 59 No 6-21, Bogota.

**Babel**
Avenida 15 No 124-49 Cf. 205, Bogota.

**Berlitz**
Tr. 26 No. 146-60 L. 201, Bogota. **Tel:** 1 6275294

**Berlitz de Colombia S.A.**
Tr. 26 No. 146-60 L. 201, Medellin. **Tel:** 4 6250554

**Best English Services Today**
Dg. 110 No. 42-85 Int. 2 Ap. 103, Bogota. **Tel:** 1 2156380

**Bi-Cultural Ltda.**
Cl. 98 No. 10-32, Bogota. **Tel:** 1 6231478

**Bi Cultural Institute**
Avenida 7 No 123-97 Of. 202, Bogota.

**Boston School of English Ltda**
Carrera 43 No 44-02, Barranquilla.

**Británico Americana**
Cr. 40 No. 105A-46, Bogota. **Tel:** 1 2180045

**The British Council**
Calle 87 No 12-79, Bogota.

**Business Language Centre Ltda.**
Carrera 49 No 15-85, Medellin.

**California English Institute**
Cl. 46 No. 8-10 P. 2, Bogota. **Tel:** 1 2456429

**California Institute Of English**
Carrera 51 No 80-130, Barranquilla.

**Carol Keeney**
Carrera 4 No 69-06, Bogota.

**Ceico**
Calle Siete Infantes, San Diego, Cartagena.

**Centro Anglo Frances**
Carrera 11 No 6-12, Neiva.

**Centro Audiovisual De Ingles Chelga**
Calle 137 No 25-26, Bogota.

**Centro Colombo Andino**
Calle 19 No 3-16 Of. 203, Bogota.

**Centro Colombo Americano**
Cr. 45 No. 53-24, Medellin. **Tel:** 4 513 4444

**Centro Cultural Colombo Americano**
Carrera 43, No. 51-95, Apt. Aereo 2097, Barranquilla.

**Centro de Idiomas Teachers Inc.**
Cr. 15 No. 75-35, Bogota. **Tel:** 1 5456712

**Centro de Inglés Lincoln**
Cl. 49 No. 9-37, Bogota **Tel:** 1 2852224

**Centro De Idiomas Winston Salem**
Calle 45 No 13-75, Bogota.

**Centro De Idiomas Winston Salem**
Transversal 74 No C2-33 Laureies, Medellin.

**Centro De Idiomas Winston Salem**
Ave-nida La Ceste No 10-27, Santa Teresita, Cali.

**Centro De Idiomas y Turismo De Cartagena**
Popa Calle 30 No 20- 177, Cartagena.

**Centro De Lengua Inglesa**
Calle 61 No 13-44 Of. 402, Bogota.

**Centro De Lenguas Modernas**
Carrera 38 No 69 C 65, Barranquilla.

**Centro Educativo Bilingüe English centre Envigado**
Cr. 40 No. 38 S-55 Int. 201-202-203, Medellin. **Tel:** 4 3312211

**Clever Training Corp**
Av. Cr. 15 No. 122-51 Of. 509-510, Bogota. **Tel:** 1 2143239

**Coningles Ltda**
Cl. 71 No. 13-56, Bogota. **Tel:** 1 3128646

**Darlitz English Institute Ltda.**
Cr. 11A No. 69-89, Bogota. **Tel:** 1 3101780

**Dynamic English**
Cl. 119 No. 13A-84, Bogota. **Tel:** 1 3102277

**Easy English**
Carrera 45 A No 34 Sur 29 Torre No 4, Portal Del Cerro , A. A. 80511, Envigado, Medellin.

**Eccles**
Cr. 13 No. 55-21 P. 3, Bogota. **Tel:** 1 2550552

**EF Educación Internacional**
Cr. 38 No. 10A-40, Bogota. **Tel:** 1 2664275

**EF Learn a Language**
Cl. 76 No. 9-66, Medellin. **Tel:** 4 3172180

**El Centro Inglés**
Cl. 11A No. 43D-14 P. 3, Medellin. **Tel:** 4 3114888

**El Centro Inglés**
El Poblado Carrera 10 A.No 36-39, Medellin.

**Elci**
Cr. 18 No. 89-16, Bogota. **Tel:** 1 2183535

**ELS Language centres**
Cl. 118 No. 25-52, Bogota. **Tel:** 1 6299774

**English For Infants (John Dewey)**
Diagonal 110 No 40-85, Bogota.

**English Hard Practice for School and Company Improvement**
Cl. 34 S No. 50-10, Bogota. **Tel:** 1 2701142

**English Language & Culture Institute (ELCI)**
Calle 90 No 10-51, Bogota.

**English Systems**
Cr. 13 No. 32-51 Of. 807, Bogota. **Tel:** 1 3381361

**English Zone Institute**
Cl. 70A No. 31-29, Bogota. **Tel:** 1 3108559

**Esquela De Inglés**
Calle 53 No 38-25, Barranquilla.

**Escuela De Idiomas Berlitz**
Calle 83 No 19-24, Bogota.

**Escuela Mundial del Idioma Inglés**
Cl. 34 No. 64A-11, Medellin. **Tel:** 4 2353266

**First Class English**
Cr. 12 No. 93-78 P. 4, Bogota. **Tel:** 1 6238380

**FLS Learning centres**
Cl. 106 No. 16-50, Bogota. **Tel:** 1 2140031

**Genelor International**
Avenida 78 No 20-49 Piso 20, Bogota.

**I.C.L.**
Calle 119 No 9a-25, Bogota.

**Idiomas-Munera-Cros Ltda**
Carrera 58 No 72-105, A.A. 52032, Barranquilla.

**Ingles Cantando Y Jugando**
Calle 106 No 16-26, Bogota.

**Inlingua**
Cr. 77B No. 47-70, Medellin. **Tel:** 4 2509746

**Instituto Anglo Americano De Idiomas**
Carrera 16a No 85-34 Of. 204, Bogota.

**Instituto Bridge Centro De Idiomas**
Carrera 65 No 49 A 09, Cali.

**Instituto De Inglés Thelma Tyzon**
Carrera 59 No 74-73, Barranquilla.

**Instituto De Lenguas Modernas**
Carrera 41 No 52-05, Baranquilla.

**Instituto Electronico De Idiomas**
Carrera 6 No 12-64 Piso, Bogota.

**Instituto Experimental De Atlantico**
"jos Celestino Mutis", Calle 70 No 38-08,
Barranquilla.

**Instituto Meyer**
Calle 17 No 10-16 Piso 80, Bogota.

**Interlingua**
Cr. 18 No. 90-38, Bogota. **Tel:** 1 2180942

**International Language Institute**
Carrera 5a No 21-35, Neiva.

**International Language Institute Ltda**
Carrera 11 No. 65-28 Piso 3, Bogota. **Tel:** 571
235-8152/72, **Fax**: 310-2892.

**International Language Institute Ltda**
Carrera 13 No 5-79 Castillogrande, Cartagena.

**International Study centre**
Cl. 116 No. 22-45 Of. 503, Bogota. **Tel:** 1 2165830

**International System**
Transversal 6 No 51 A 33, Bogota.

**K.O.E De Columbia**
Calle 101 A No 31-02, Bogota.

**Life Ltda.**
Transversal 19 No 100-52, Bogota.

**Lubigon English Academy**
Cl. 48D No. 67A-14 , Medellin. **Tel:** 4 2602840

**Oxford Centre**
A.A. 102420, Santate de Bogota.

**Royal English Club**
Tr. 42A No. 100-59, Bogota. **Tel:** 1 2718887

**Stanton School of English**
Cl. 57 No. 18-22 Of. 503, Bogota. **Tel:** 1 3479017

**The Better English centre**
Cr. 73B No. 5C-19, Bogota. **Tel:** 1 2640535

**The British Council**
Cl. 91 No. 21-55, Bogota. **Tel:** 1 6103077

**The British Council**
Cr. 42 No. 16A S-41, Medellin. **Tel:** 4 3131867

**Total English Solutions**
Cr. 36A No. 57A-15, Bogota. **Tel:** 1 2215233

**Wall Street Institute**
Cr. 9 No. 70-09, Bogota. **Tel:** 1 3460566

**Way's English School**
Calle 101 No 13 A 17, Bogota.

**Winston - Salem**
Cl. 45 No. 13-75, Bogota. **Tel:** 1 3128646

**World English** centre
Cr. 16 No. 53-46 P. 2, Bogota. **Tel:** 1 5471950

**Worldwide Languages**
Tr. 19A No. 123-49, Bogota. **Tel:** 1 6190762

## COSTA RICA

Costa Rica is one of the more stable of the Central
American republics and a favourite haunt of "gringo"
tourists. There are many private language schools,
especially in San José, an unattractive city of around
five million people. The rest of the country is beautiful
with volcanoes and beaches to explore.

**Consulate in UK:**
14 Lancaster Gate, London W2 3LH
**Tel:** 020 7706 8844

**Embassy in USA:**
2114 S Street NW, Washington DC 20008
**Tel:** 202 234 2945

➲ **Visas/Work Permits:** Work visas are very
difficult to obtain and teachers usually work on tourist
visas.

➲ **Currency:** £1 = 1011 / $1 = 517 Colon

⮞ **Salaries/Taxes:** Salaries are not high (c. £2.50-3 / $4-5 an hour for part-timers; £400-600 / $700-$1100 per month full-time is about average) but you can earn enough to get by. Private tutors can earn $15 an hour.

⮞ **Accommodation:** £180-250 / $350-460 a month for a shared apartment. Assistance is often provided by employers.

⮞ **Cost of Living:** One of the most expensive Central American countries, but prices are still low compared to the UK or USA.

⮞ **Health advice:** Medical facilities are available, but may be limited outside urban areas. Be aware that on both the Caribbean and Pacific coasts, currents are swift and dangerous. Several drownings occur each year, and there are no lifeguards.

## Schools in Costa Rica (+506)

### American International School
Bosques de Doña Rosa, Ciudad Cariari, Heredia. **Fax**: 239-0625.**Email:** brown@cra.ed.cr

### Berlitz
Santa Ana 2000, Edificio A, Planta Baja, Santa Ana, San José. **Tel**: 204 7555, **Fax**: 204 7444.

### Blue Valley School
P.O. Box 2050-1000, San José. **Fax**: 253-7708

### Centro Cultural Costarricense Norteamericano
Apt.1489-1000, San José, Calle Los Negritos, Barrio Dent. **Tel**: 225 6433, **Fax**: 224 1480, **Email:** centrcr@sol.racsa.co.cr

### Country Day School
P.O. Box 8-6170-1000, San José. **Fax**: 289-6798

### ELS International
Apt 6495-1000, San Jose. **Tel**: 261 4242, **Fax**: 261 3212, **Email:** acallen@uicr.ac.cr

### Escuela Britanica
P.O. Box 8184-1000, San José. **Fax**: 234-7833.

### Instituto Britanico
PO Box 8184-1000, San José. **Tel**: 256 0256, **Fax**: 253 1894

### Instituto de Inglés USA
Apt 418-1000 C1 A6, San José

### International Christian School
P.O. Box 3512-1000, San José. **Tel**: 236-7879. **Fax**: 235-1518.

### Lincoln School
P. O. Box 1919-1000, San José. **Tel**: 235 7733, **Fax**: 236-1706.

### Marian Baker School
P.O. Box 4269-1000, San José. **Fax**: 273-4609

### Monteverde Friends School
P.O. Box 10165-1000, San José. **Fax**: 645-5219.

### World Education Forum
PO Box 383-4005, San Antonio de Belén, Heredia. **Tel:** 239 2245, **Fax**: 239 2254.

## ECUADOR

Even though the current economic situation is very difficult and many Ecuadorians are leaving the country, there are hundreds of language schools in Ecuador, so it is easy for English teachers to find work, whether they are qualified or not. Until recently, Ecuador was generally considered the best starting point for teachers planning to work their way round South America. Although this may no longer be the case, it is more relaxed than many of its neighbours and still offers plenty of opportunities, especially in the main cities of Quito, Guayaquil and the beautiful Cuenca. Terms and conditions vary and most recruitment is done locally. Many expatriates have set up their own schools, but to find work in them it helps to have personal contacts and qualifications. Some private language schools will often take on native speakers with no qualifications.

⮞ **Visas/Work Permits:** It is illegal to work on a tourist visa but many teachers do so anyway. Visitors from the US and Canada are entitled to stay for up to 90 days on a tourist visa. To extend the visa, you have to prove that you have independent income not resulting from work in the country. If you intend to work legally, you have to produce a return air ticket. A tourist visa cannot be exchanged for any other kind of visa once in the country, so if you get a job while you are there, you have to go to neighbouring country, usually Colombia, to get the necessary paperwork. Most employers will help teachers to get a one-year cultural exchange visa, as long as they commit themselves to staying for a reasonable length of time.

⮞ **Requirements:**TESOL/TESL Certificate

⮞ **Currency:** £1 = 1.85 / $1 = 1 US Dollar

⮞ **Salaries/Taxes:** The monthly rate for unqualified teachers starts at about £215 / $370, rising to £300 / $570 in more reputable schools. The top schools pay about £500-600 / $950-1100 a month and only employ qualified teachers. Everyone is taxed at 5-8%, regardless of whether they are working legally or not.

◆ **Accommodation:** Wide range available. Expect to pay £150 / $220 a month for an apartment in Quito. The usual deposit is two months' rent.

◆ **Cost of Living:** Figure on basic living expenses of around £80 / $150 per month.

◆ **Health advice:** Malaria and dengue fever are prevalent in Guayaquil and the coastal region. Cases of cholera and yellow fever have also been reported. Medical care is available but it varies in quality and generally is below UK or U.S. standards.

◆ **English Language Media:** Q Magazine, Inside Ecuador.

## Schools in Ecuador (+593)

**American Language School**
Carchi 904 y Velez, Guayaquil. **Tel:** 452926.

**Benedict**
9 De Octubre 1515, Y Orellana, Quito.

**Benedict**
Datiles y La Primera, CC Urdesa, Guayaquil.

**Centro De Estudios Interamericanos**
Casilla 597, Cuenca.

**Centro Ecuatoriano NorteAmericano**
Luis Urdeneta y Cordoba, Guayaquil, **Tel:** 564536.

**Experimento De Convivencia International Del Ecuador**
Les Embleton, Hernando de la Cruz 218 y Mariana de Jesús, Quito. **Tel:** 2 551937/550179, **Fax:** 2 55 0228.

**Fulbright Commission**
Almagro 961 y Colon, Quito. **Tel:** 2 562999.

**International Benedict Schools of Languages**
PO Box 09-01-8916, Guayaquil. **Tel:** 4 444418, **Fax:** 4 441642.

**Lingua Franca**
Edificio Jerico, 12 De Octubre 2449 y Orellana, Casilla 17-2-68, Quito. **Tel:** 2 546075, **Fax:** 2 500734.

**Quito Language and Culture Centre**
Republica De El Salvador, 639 Y Portugal, Quito.

## EL SALVADOR

The country is slowly recovering from the long and bloody civil war. English lessons are very popular and experienced native speakers are genuinely respected here. Many English teachers are Salvadorans who have been deported from the States who are not teachers by profession. An MA in TESOL or a certificate will enhance your wage-earning capacity. You can live quite well on a tight budget in El Salvador and, unlike Costa Rica the country is not full of "gringos."

◆ **Visas/Work Permits:** You will be given a free tourist card on your flight in. This is good for 30-90 days after which you can pop across the border and then return. Each school has its own policy regarding work permits but most are not interested in red tape and will employ teachers on tourist visas.

◆ **Currency:** £1 = 16.37 / $1 = 8.75 Colon

◆ **Salaries/Taxes:** You can earn about £300 / $570 per month or £6 / $10 an hour if you freelance. Foreigners are liable for tax unless they are being paid "under the table."

◆ **Accommodation:** In San Salvador, you can pay anywhere from £30 / $60 a month for a two-bedroom house in a rough area to £600 / $1100 for an apartment in a tony neighbourhood. Utility bills are around £12-15 / $20-30 per month.

◆ **Health advice:** Dengue fever is a big problem. Medical care is limited. Emergency services, even in San Salvador, are very basic. Ambulance services are not staffed by trained personnel and lack life-saving necessities such as oxygen. Doctors in the major hospitals are generally well-trained, often in U.S. hospitals, but nursing and support staff are not up to UK or U.S. standards.

## Schools in El Salvador (+503)

**Academia Europea**
911 Ave Nte., San Salvador. **Tel:** 263 4355. **Fax:** 263 4430. **Email:** jobs@euroacad.edu.sv

**Escuela Superior De Idiomas**
Ave. La Campilla 226, Colonia San Benito, San Salvador. **Tel:** 264 1256.

## GUATEMALA

This is a popular destination for EFL teachers drawn here by the colourful indigenous culture. Some teachers recommend getting out of the capital city and working in Antigua or Quetzaltenango.

◆ **Visas/Work Permits:** Tourist visas are granted for 90 days. It is possible to obtain a work permit through the Guatemalan consulate in your country if you have a job offer, your last two bank statements showing you have funds to live on when you arrive and two photos. But most teachers just turn up and work on their tourist visas.

⊃ **Currency:** £1 = 14.39 / $1 = 7.78 Quetzal

⊃ **Salaries/Taxes:** Salaries are very low (around £3 / $5 an hour) and if you have a work permit, you will pay tax at around 30%.

⊃ **Health advice:** Health care facilities are good in Guatemala City but are more limited elsewhere.

## Schools in Guatemala (+502)

**American School of Guatemala**
Aptdo Postal 83, 01901 Guatemala City. **Tel:** 369 0791.

**Colegio Americano de Guatemala**
11 Calle 15-70, Zona 15, Vista Hermosa.

**Colegio Ingles Americano**
0 Calle 19-70, Zona 15, V.H. II , Guatemala City.

**Colegio Internacional Montessori**
Carr. el Salv. Km. 13.5 finca la Luz, Guatemala City. **Tel:** 2 3641921.

**Instituto Guatamelteco-Americano**
Ruta 1, 4-05, Aptdo. 691, Guatemala City. **Tel:** 331 0022, **Fax:** 332 3135

**Modern American English School**
c/ de los Nazarenos 16, Antigua. **Tel:** 932 3306, **Fax:** 932 0217.

## HONDURAS

Demand for native-speaking English teachers is high in Honduras both in private language schools and in the state colleges and universities. Students at bilingual school learn Spanish and English. The country is still recovering from the effects of Hurricane Mitch and many roads are washed out.

⊃ **Visas/Work Permits:** After you have a job offer, you must apply for a residency permit from outside Honduras although you can look for work as a tourist. The process can take anywhere from four to six months.

⊃ **Currency:** £1 = 34 / $1 = 18 Lempira

⊃ **Salaries/Taxes:** Rates of pay vary from £2-5 / $3-$8 an hour.

⊃ **Accommodation:** Your employer will probably offer you accommodation but be warned that many apartment blocks in the country are not finished and that you may be without water and electricity for periods of time.

⊃ **Cost of Living:** Cheap.

⊃ **Health advice:** Doctors are generally well trained; but support staff and facilities generally are not up to UK or U.S. standards, and facilities for certain surgical procedures are not available. Drink bottled water.

## Schools in Honduras (+504)

**American School**
c/o American Embassy-Tegucigalpa Honduras, Dept of State, Washington DC  20521-3480: **Tel:** 32 4696

**Centro Cultural Sampedrano**
3 Calle, entra 3A y 4A Avenida 20 , Apartado Postal 511, San Pedro Sula, Cortes.

**Escuela Anglo-Hondurena**
Colonia La Reforma, Edificio Club Arabe, Tegucigalpa. **Tel:** 236 8814.

**Harris Communications**
Ave. Circunvalación, Centro Comercial La Careta, San Pedro Sula **Tel/Fax:** 504 557-3416.

**Instituto Hondureno de Cultura Americana**
2 Avenida entre 5 y 6 Calles No. 520, Apartado 201, MDC Comayaguela , Tegucigalpa.

## JAMAICA

American teachers are sometimes employed in the public school system. There are limited opportunities in private EFL schools.

⊃ **Visas/Work Permits:** You can apply for a work permit when you are in Jamaica.

⊃ **Currency:** £1 = 130 / $1 = 67 Dollars

⊃ **Salaries/Taxes:** You can make J$150 an hour in a school and at least J$200 for private lessons. Income tax is 25%.

⊃ **Accommodation:** It is hard to find cheap accommodation in Kingston.

⊃ **Cost of Living:** Prices are quite high in Kingston but cheaper elsewhere.

⊃ **Health advice:** Ambulance service is limited both in the quality of emergency care, and in the availability of vehicles in remote parts of the country.

## Schools in Jamaica (+809)

**Language Training Centre Ltd**
24 Parkington Plaza, Kingston 10. **Tel:** 926 03756.

**Target English Associates**
9a Duquesnam Ave., Kingston 10. **Tel:** 929 2473.

# MEXICO

Mexico is a popular destination for all ELT teachers, particularly American ESL teachers – after all, they can always walk home if something goes wrong! Increasing trade with the U.S. and Canada means that more Mexican companies require their employees to speak (American) English. Teachers are usually recruited locally because schools are finding it increasingly difficult to pay recruitment costs, but it is possible to organize a job from outside the country.

## Embassy in UK:
8 Halkin Street, London SW1X 7DW
**Tel:** 020 7235 6393

## Embassy in USA:
1911 Pennsylvania Ave NW, Washington DC 20006
**Tel:** 202 728 1600
www.embassyofmexico.org

## British Council office:
Lope de Vega 316, Col. Chapultepec Morales, Mexico City, 11570 DF
**Tel** +52 (55) 5263 1900
www.britishcouncil.org.mx

⮕ **Visas/Work Permits:** Tourist visas are available for up to six months. Work permits are usually granted to American and Canadian teachers. Make sure your school provides you with all the necessary paperwork. There are reports of immigration inspectors posing as English students trying to catch out foreigners teaching on tourist visas. Keep your tourist card or other papers on you at all times in case an official asks to see them.

⮕ **Requirements:** TESOL/TESL Certificate

⮕ **Currency:** £1 = 21.1 / $1 = 10.7 New Peso

⮕ **Salaries/Taxes:** Teachers with an MA in TESOL can make £600 / $1100 a month or more, which is very good considering that Mexican teachers in the state system receive about £300 / $570. Tax is about 25%.

⮕ **Cost of Living:** It's quite expensive to live in Mexico City but much cheaper elsewhere. Meals can be anywhere from £1-£6 depending on where you go, Estimate spending about £20-£30 / $35-$60 a month on food if you eat out once or twice a week.

⮕ **Accommodation:** Rents vary across the country. Cheap rooms (£30 / $60 per month) can be found in most towns but they tend to be in noisy and sometimes dangerous areas. If you're lucky you may find a nice apartment for around £100 / $190 a month. Of course, you will pay a lot more in the big cities.

⮕ **Health advice:** Health facilities in Mexico City are excellent. Care in more remote areas is limited. Serious medical problems requiring hospitalization and/or medical evacuation home can be very costly so insurance is essential.

⮕ **English Language Media:** The Mexico City Times, The News.

---

## Schools in Mexico (Mexico City)

### Academia De Idiomas Tepeyac
Misterios 764 Col. Tepeyac Insurgentes C.P.07020, Ciudad De Mexico, Df. **Tel:** 5 7810046

### American Tem
Eduardo Molina 440 Col. Nueva Atzacoalco C.P.07420, Ciudad De Mexico, Df. **Tel:** 5 7531720

### Angloamericano
Campos Eliseos 111 Col. Polanco, C.P.11560, Ciudad De Mexico, Df. **Tel:** 5 6586700

### Aprendizaje Inst. A.C.
Montevideo 284 P-2 Col. Lindavista, C.P.07300, Ciudad De Mexico, Df. **Tel:** 5 5860196, 5 5861776

### Berlitz
Reforma 132 Col. Juarez C.P.06600, Ciudad De Mexico, Df. **Tel:** 5 7050832, 5 7056695

### Berlitz
Bosque Ciruelos 194, 2do. Piso Col. Bosques De Las Lomas C.P.11700 Ciudad De Mexico, Df. **Tel:** 5 5969190, 5 5969160

### Berlitz
Pafnucio Padilla #17 P-1, Plaza Satelite Col. Satelite C.P.53100 Ciudad De Mexico, Df. **Tel:** 5 5620190, 5 3934981 **Email:**Centro.Satelite@Berlitz.com.mx

### Berlitz
Sn Jeronimo 240 Col. Pedregal De San Angel C.P.01900 Ciudad De Mexico, Df. **Tel:** 5 6161953, 5 5504359

### Berlitz
Montevideo 365 Esq. Payta Col. Lindavista C.P.07300 Ciudad De Mexico, Df. **Tel:** 5 7521210, 5 7544025.

### Berlitz
Lomas Verdes 825 43 Col. Lomas Verdes Nauc C.P.53120 Ciudad De Mexico, Df. **Tel:** 5 3436497.

### Berlitz
Del Hueso 480 Loc 11 Col. Los Girasoles C.P.04920 Ciudad De Mexico, Df. **Tel:** 5 6797146, 5 6790438

**Berlitz**
Insurgentes Sur 1261 Col. Extrem-adura Insurgentes C.P.03740 Ciudad De Mexico, Df. **Tel:** 5 6117468, 5 6117551

**Britt Servicios Linguisticos**
Berlin 27 B Col. Juarez C.P.66000 Ciudad De Mexico, Df. **Tel:** 5 5466160

**Britt Servicios Linguisticos**
Luz Avi&On 2011 4 Col. Narvarte C.P.03020 Ciudad De Mexico, Df. **Tel:** 5 6873571

**Centro Cultural Benjamin Franklin Sc**
Parroquia 828 Col. Del Valle C.P.03100 Ciudad De Mexico, Df. **Tel:** 5 5347747

**Ef**
Alfredo Musset 228 Col. Polanco C.P.11550 Ciudad De Mexico, Df. **Tel:** 5 5143333, 55313156

**Endicott College**
Ibsen 43 P-8 Col. Polanco C.P.11560 Ciudad De Mexico, Df. **Tel:** 5 2801225

**English For Executives**
Viveros De Asis 19 Col. Viveros De La Loma C.P.54080 Ciudad De Mexico, Df. **Tel:** 5 3615234, 5 3979980

**English On Site**
Giotto 29, Col. Mixcoac C.P.04300 Ciudad De Mexico, Df. **Tel:** 5 6112761

**Harmon Hall**
San Luis Potosi 196 Col. Roma C.P.06700 Ciudad De Mexico, Df. **Tel:** 5 5847599

**Harmon Hall**
Puebla 319 0670 Col. Roma C.P.06700 Ciudad De Mexico, Df. **Tel:** 5 2118019, 5 2112020

**Harmon Hall**
Rojo Gomez 1457 Col. San Pablo C.P.09360 Ciudad De Mexico, Df. **Tel:** 5 6853258, 5 6852181

**Ingles Sin Barreras Sa De Cv**
Medellín 184, Col. Roma C.P.06700 Ciudad De Mexico, Df. **Tel:** 5 5649739

**Instituto Anglo Mexicano De Cultura Ac**
Av Insurgentes Sur 710 Col. Del Valle C.P.03100 Ciudad De Mexico, Df. **Tel:** 5 5360742, 55236641

**Instituto Anglo Mexicano De Cultura Ac**
Rio Nazas 116 Col. Cuauhtemoc C.P.54124 Ciudad De Mexico, Df. **Tel:** 5 2085640, 5 2085799, 5 7051866, 5 5116926

**Instituto Hamer Sharp**
M Avila Camacho 291 Loc-A-29-30-31 Col. Lomas De Sotelo C.P.11220 Ciudad De Mexico, Df. **Tel:** 5 5806834, 5 5800341, 5 5802676

**Instituto Mexico Norteamericano De Idiomas Sc**
Av Chapultepec 474 Col. Roma Nte C.P.06700 Ciudad De Mexico, Df. **Tel:** 5 2116758, 5 2867988

**Instituto Superior De Idiomas Sa**
Viena 71-301 Col. Del Carmen Coyoacan C.P.04100 Ciudad De Mexico, Df. **Tel:** 5 6593533

**Interlingua**
Montevideo 405 073 Col. Lindavista C.P.07300 Ciudad De Mexico, Df. **Tel:** 5 5864398, 5 5863275, 5 7541209

**Interlingua**
Medicos 3 Piso 2 Col. Zp Em Frac Cd Satelite C.P.53100 Ciudad De Mexico, Df. **Tel:** 55720697, 55623713

**Interlingua, Genova**
33 Piso 6 Col. Juarez C.P.06600 Ciudad De Mexico, Df. **Tel:** 5 2080737, 5 5336706, 5 2081919

**Interlingua**
J Balmes 11 D Piso 2 Mezzanine Col. Los Morales Polanco C.P.11510 Ciudad De Mexico, Df. **Tel:** 5 5572875

**Interlingua**
Av Insurgentes Sur 1971 L-280 Col. Guadalupe Inn C.P.01020 Ciudad De Mexico, Df. **Tel:** 5 6627208, 5 6627207, 5 6613787, 5 6614166

**La Villa English Academies**
Calz De Guadalupe 156-A Col. Ex-Hipodromo De Peralvill C.P.06220 Ciudad De Mexico, Df. **Tel:** 5 5176876, 5 5374401

**Prompt English**
Viveros De Asis 13-200 Col. Viveros De La Loma C.P.54080 Ciudad De Mexico, Df. **Tel:** 5 3628523

**Quick Learning**
Arellano 14 Piso 2 Col. Cd Satelite Edo De Me C.P.53100 Ciudad De Mexico, Df. **Tel:** 5 5626036, 5 5626852

**Quick Learning**
Av Division Del Norte 2646 Col. Churubusco Contry Club C.P.04210 Ciudad De Mexico, Df. **Tel:** 5 6055934

**Quick Learning**
Liverpool 143-102 Col. Juarez C.P.06600 Ciudad De Mexico, Df. **Tel:** 5 5330180

**Quick Learning**
Av Molina Enriquez 4231 P-1 Col. Viaducto Piedad C.P.08200 Ciudad De Mexico, Df. **Tel:** 5 7406466, 5 7406569, 5 7406576

## Quick Learning
Insurg Sur 586 601 Col. Del Valle C.P.03100 Ciudad De Mexico, Df. **Tel:** 5 6829970, 5 6829962

## Quick Learning
Rancho Toyocan 61 Loc 5 Y 6 - R Col. Los Girasoles C.P.04929 Ciudad De Mexico, Df. **Tel:** 5 6842021

## Quick Learning
Calle Sur 71 No 4231 Col. Viaducto Piedad C.P.08200 Ciudad De Mexico, Df. **Tel:** 5 7406677

## Quick Learning
Calendula 111 Piso 3 Col. Xotepingo C.P.04610 Ciudad De Mexico, Df. **Tel:** 5 6104246

## Quick Learning
Jinetes 18 Col. Las Arboledas C.P.53139 Ciudad De Mexico, Df. **Tel**: 5 3792054

## Schola
Lamartine 138 Col. Polanco C.P.11570 Ciudad De Mexico, Df. **Tel:** 5 5453804

## Servicio Linguistico Empresarial
Sn Fco 657 A Piso 12 - B Col. Del Valle C.P.03100 Ciudad De Mexico, Df. **Tel:** 5 6874449, 5 5236380, 5 6691066

## USA
Egipto 206 Loc-A Col. Claveria C.P.02080 Ciudad De Mexico, Df. **Tel:** 5 3410092, 5 3410211

## Wall Street Institute
Ipsen 4343 8 Piso Col. Polanco C.P.11580 Ciudad De Mexico, Df. **Tel:** 5 2800809

## Wave Comunicacion De Mexico
Insurg Cto 51 204 Col. San Rafael C.P.06470 Ciudad De Mexico, Df. **Tel:** 5 5350124

---

## Schools (on outskirts of Mexico City)

## Academia Comercial Linguistica
Montiel 205 Col. Lindavista C.P.07300 Ciudad De Mexico, Df. **Tel:** 5 5776380

## Active English Institute
Playa Langosta 311 Col. Reforma Ixtaccihuatl C.P.08840 Ciudad De Mexico, Df. **Tel:** 5 5322881

## American British English Sc
Londres 40-10 P-1 Col. Juarez C.P.06600 Ciudad De Mexico, Df. **Tel**: 5 5145856, 5 5143348

## Angloamericano De Satelite
Circunvala-cion Ote 8 Deps 308 Col. Satelite C.P.0 1030 Ciudad De Mexico, Df. **Tel:** 5 5721737

## Angloamericano Satelite
Vito Alessio Robres 233 Col. Florida C.P.01030 Ciudad De Mexico, Df. **Tel:** 5 5727838

## Centro Angloamericano Sur
Alessio Robles 233 Col. Florida C.P.01030 Ciudad De Mexico, Df. **Tel:** 5 6580889

## Centro De Aprendizaje Linguistico
M Escobedo 446 Col. Polanco Reforma C.P.11550 Ciudad De Mexico, Df. **Tel:** 5 2503851

## Centro De Capacitacion En Lenguas Extranjeras
Coru&A 201 P-1 Col. Viaducto Piedad C.P.08200 Ciudad De Mexico, Df. **Tel:** 5 5305050

## Centro De Convivencia Linguistica
O Del Ajusco 2 Col. Zp Em Frac Los Pirules C.P.54040 Ciudad De Mexico, Df. **Tel:** 5 3791310

## Centro De Idiomas Dinamicos
Luz Savi&On 13 - 902 Col. Del Valle C.P.03100 Ciudad De Mexico, Df. **Tel:** 5 5438280

## Centro De Idiomas Dinamicos
L Savi&On 13 301 Col. Del Valle C.P.03100 Ciudad De Mexico, Df. **Tel:** 5 5434534, 5 6692259, 5 6829805

## Centro De Idiomas Sn Angel
Insurgentes Sur 2047 P-A Col. Sn Angel C.P.01000 Ciudad De Mexico, Df. **Tel:** 5 6617422, 5 6617423

## Centro De Idiomas Tamesis
Plaza De La Constitucion Mz 10 Lt 44 Col. Plaza Aragon C.P.57139 Ciudad De Mexico, Df. **Tel:** 5 7104056

## Centro De Idiomas Y Diversificados
Nuevo Leon 253 305 Col. Escandon C.P.11800 Ciudad De Mexico, Df. **Tel:** 5 5163049

## Centro De Ingles Abraham Lincoln
Ermita Izt 326 Col. Cacama C.P.09080 Ciudad De Mexico, Df. **Tel:** 5 5814949

## Centro Especializado De Servicios Linguisticos
Cuitlahuac 2725 Col. Popular C.P.02840 Ciudad De Mexico, Df. **Tel:** 5 3412253

## Centro Linguistico De Ingles
Yucatan 189 Ph Col. Tizapan Sn Angel C.P.01090 Ciudad De Mexico, Df. **Tel:** 5 6164315

## Centro Linguistico Lucerna
Tulipan 40 Col. Ciudad Jardin C.P.04370 Ciudad De Mexico, Df. **Tel:** 5 5495846

## Centro Linguistico Valle Dorado
Atenas 137 Col. Valle Dorado C.P.54020 Ciudad De Mexico, Df. **Tel:** 5 3706808

## Centro Universitario De Idiomas
Dr Galvez 38 Col. San Angel C.P.01000 Ciudad De Mexico, Df. **Tel:** 5 5503808

**Chanor Company**
Bosques De Duraznos 65-205 Col. Bosques De Las Lomas C.P.11 700 Ciudad De Mexico, Df. **Tel:** 5 5964052

**Cima**
Saltillo 91-B Col. Hipodromo C.P.0 6100 Ciudad De Mexico, Df. **Tel:** 5 516 4605, 5 5165516, 5 5167138

**Comercio En Mexico Del Centro Internacional**
Ave Insurgentes Sur No 421 B-301 Col. H Condesa C.P.06140 Ciudad De Mexico, Df. **Tel**: 5 2643347

**Complete Language Services**
Barranca Del Muerto 525 P-6 Col. Merced Gomez C.P.01600 Ciudad De Mexico, Df. **Tel:** 5 6643622

**Converse International School Of Languages**
Melchor Ocampoloc-H4-6 193 Col. Veronica Anzures C.P.11590 Ciudad De Mexico, Df. **Tel:** 5 2609002

**Cosmo Educacion**
Insurg Sur 1694 Col. Florida C.P.01030 Ciudad De Mexico, Df. **Tel:** 5 6618367

**Cosmo**
Anatole France 13 Altos Col. Chapultepec Polanco C.P.11560 Ciudad De Mexico, Df. **Tel:** 5 2820380, 5 2821021, 5 2821279

**Desarrollo De Idiomas Empresariales**
Av Nuevo Leon 270 P-2 Col. Hipodromo C.P.06100 Ciudad De Mexico, Df. **Tel:** 5 2719024

**Easy English Institute**
Ave San Isidro 288-302 Col. San Isidro Cacahulton C.P.0 2720 Ciudad De Mexico, Df. **Tel:** 5 3523951

**EF Servicios En Educacion Internacional**
Londres No 188 Mezzanine Col. Juarez C.P.06600 Ciudad De Mexico, Df. **Tel:** 5 5251216

**Escuela Internacional De Idiomas**
Ailes 144 Col. Sn Mateo. C.P.53240 Ciudad De Mexico, Df. **Tel:** 5 3733951

**Escuela Mexicana Canadiense De Ingles**
Miguel A De Quevedo 928 - M Col. Parque Sn Andres C.P.04330 Ciudad De Mexico, Df. **Tel:** 5 6593252

**Escuela Mexicana Canadiense De Ingles**
M Angel De Quevedo 928 Col. Rosedal Coyoacan C.P.04330 Ciudad De Mexico, Df. **Tel:** 5 6594112

**Especialistas En Idiomas**
Arellano 14 P-1 Col. Cd Satelite C.P.53100 Ciudad De Mexico, Df. **Tel:** 5 3939271

**Focus On Language**
Colina De Aconitos 15 8 Col. Boulevares C.P.53140 Ciudad De Mexico, Df. **Tel:** 5 5723406

**Gpo Educativo Angloamericano**
Vito Alessio Robles 233 Col. Florida C.P.01030 Ciudad De Mexico, Df. **Tel:** 5 6589656, 5 6589540, 5 6589632

**Harmon Hall**
Eugenia No 106 Col. Narvarte C.P.03020 Ciudad De Mexico, Df. **Tel:** 5 5238359

**Harmon Hall Del Valle**
Eugenia 1606 Col. Narvarte C.P.03020 Ciudad De Mexico, Df. **Tel:** 5 6874987

**Harmon Hall Toreo**
Av Rodolfo Gadna No 6 5do Piso Col. Lomas De Sotelo C.P.53390 Ciudad De Mexico, Df. **Tel:** 5 3958300, 5 3958400

**Ibi Instituto Britanico**
Campos Eliseos 204 P-4 Col. Polanco C.P.11560 Ciudad De Mexico, Df. **Tel:** 5 2812465

**Idiomas Empresariales Marva**
Gante 15 P-2 Loc-213 Col. Centro C.P.06010 Ciudad De Mexico, Df. **Tel:** 5 5102997, 5 5129242

## Guadalajara

**American English centre**
Av Federalismo Sur 415 Col. Centro C.P.44100 Guadalajara, Jalisco. **Tel:** 3 6131667

**Ayusa Internacional Mexico**
Lopez Co-tilla 1713 202 Y 204 Col. Guadalajara C.P. 44140 Guadalajara, Jalisco. **Tel:** 3 6153688

**Berlitz**
Plabo Neruda #2914 Col. Providencia C.P.44630 Guadalajara, Jal-isco. **Tel:** 3 412074, 3 6414048, 3 641 2768.

**Berlitz**
Vallarta 1550 Loc. 1 Esq. Marsella Col. Sector Juarez C.P.44140 Guadalajara, Jalisco. **Tel:** 3 6303987

**Centro Cultural Linguistico**
Universo 746 Jardines Del Col. Jardines Del Bosque Guad C.P.44520 Guadalajara, Jalisco. **Tel:** 3 1216863

**Centro De Desarrollo Linguistico**
Mariano Otero No 3677 Col. La Calma C.P. 45070 Guadalajara, Jalisco. **Tel:** 3 6342713

**Centro Linguistico De Guad-Alajara**
S H C 68 Nº 46 Desp 201 Col. Santa Teresita C.P.44600 Guadalajara, Jalisco. **Tel:** 3 6166626

**Connections**
Francisco Frejes 222 Col. Rojas Ladron De Guevara C.P.44650 Guadalajara, Jalisco. **Tel:** 3 6160708, 3 6157451, 3 6161077

**EF**
Circun Agustin Ya&Ez 2559-2 Col. Arcos Del Sur
C.P.44100 Guadalajara, Jalisco. **Tel:** 3 6301835

**Harmon Hall**
Lopez Mateos Sur Esq Chimalhuacan Col. Cd Del Sol
C.P.45050 Guadalajara, Jalisco. **Tel:** 3 1212435

**Imac Ingles Total**
Donato Guerra 180 Col. Alcalde Barranquitas
C.P.44270 Guadalajara, Jalisco. **Tel:** 3 6132805

**Ingles Individual**
Agustin Ya&Ez 2583 Loc-106 Col. Barrera C.P.44150
Guadala-jara, Jalisco. **Tel:** 3 6165798, 3 6303393

**Instituto Anglo Mexicano De Cultura**
Av Americas No 1301 Col. Col Providencia Norte
C.P.05308 Guadalajara, Jalisco. **Tel:** 3 8170506

**Instituto Luis Silva**
Eje Pte 644 Col. El Santuario C.P.44200 Guadalajara,
Jalisco. **Tel:** 3 6134392

**Interlingua**
Mexico 3065 Piso 2 Col. Vallarta San Lucas Zp 6
C.P.44690 Guadalajara, Jalisco. **Tel:** 3 6150401

**International Language Design**
Madero 710 Col. Centro C.P.44100 Guadalajara,
Jalisco. **Tel:** 3 8251226

**Kaao Centro De Idiomas**
Av Lapizlazuli 2515 A Col. Residencial Victoria C.P.
44580 Guadalajara, Jalisco. **Tel:** 3 6327949

**Lenguaje World Institud**
Santuario 830 Col. Juan Diego C.P.44510 Guadalajara,
Jalisco. **Tel:** 3 1219833

**Linguas**
Patria 1398 Desp 203 Col. Villa Universitaria
C.P.45110 Guadalajara, Jalisco. **Tel:** 3 6402272

**USA English Institute**
Victoriano Aguer-os 1474 Col. Sect Juarez Cp 44150
C.P. 44150 Guadalajara, Jalisco. **Tel:** 3 6302255

**Vancouver Language Centre**
Avenida Vallarta 1151 Col. Americana C.P.44100
Guadalajara, Jalisco. **Tel:** 3 8254271

**Wall Street Institute**
Ave Vallarta 1530 Col. Centro C.P.44100 Guadalajara,
Jalisco. **Tel:** 3 6162803, 3 6166615, 3 6169124

**Aprendizaje Instantaneo Chap**
Av Del Sur 1974 Sj Col. Obrera Centro C.P.44140
Guadalajara, Jalisco. **Tel:** 3 8252059

**Centro Cultural Norteamericano**
Sjc 18 N 172 A S Col. Zp 1 Gua C.P.44100
Guadalajara, Jalisco. **Tel:** 3 6144416

**Idiomas SA**
Ave Mexico 3065 Piso 2 Col. Residencial San Jorge
C.P.44690 Guadalajara, Jalisco. **Tel:** 3 6152451

**Idiomas SA**
Shc 7 3065 Piso 2 Col. Residencial San Jorge
C.P.44690 Guadalajara, Jalisco. **Tel:** 3 6300118

**Instituto Cultural Mexicano Norteamericano
De Guadalajara**
Enrique Diaz De Leon 300 Col. Americana C.P.44170
Guadalajara, Jalisco. **Tel:** 3 8258834

**Instituto Anglo Mexicano De Cultura**
Manuel Acu&A 2674-102 Col. Lomas De Guevara
C.P.44680 Guadalajara, Jalisco. **Tel:** 3 6414017

**Instituto Anglo Mexicano De Cultura**
Manuel Acu&A 2674-102 Col. Lomas De Guevaraia
C.P.44680 Guadalajara, Jalisco. **Tel:** 3 6414009

**Universidad De Guadalajara**
Esc Superior De Lenguas Modernas, Apdo. Postal
2-416, 44280 Guadalajara, Jalisco.

## Monterrey

**Academia De Ingles Prof Gil Moreno**
Galeana Sur 418 Col. Centro C.P.64000 Monterrey,
Nl. **Tel:** 83 423844

**Berlitz**
Padre Mier Pte 241 Pte. Col. Centro C.P.64000
Monterrey, Nl. **Tel:** 83 441761, **Fax**: 83 455781

**Berlitz**
Rio Mississippi 101-B Col. Del Valle C.P.66220
Monterrey, Nl. **Tel:** 83 561605, 83 561612

**English Comunication System**
De Los Leones Po 2389 A Col. Las Cumbres
C.P.64610 Monterrey, Nl. **Tel:** 83 001878

**English Now**
Av Constitucion 1251 Pte Col. Centro C.P.67460
Monterrey, Nl **Tel:** 83 449175

**Harmon Hall**
Pablo Moncayo 117 Piso 2 Col. Col De San Jeronimo
C.P.64630 Monterrey, Nl. **Tel:** 83 477775, 83 477774

**Instituto Mexicano Norteamericano De
Relaciones Culturales**
Hidalgo Pte 768 Col. Centro C.P.64000 Monterrey, Nl.
**Tel:** 83 401583

**Ingles En Siete Semanas**
Washington 2910 Pte Col. Obispado C.P.64610
Monterrey, Nl. **Tel:** 83 477735

## Interlingua
Av Jose Vasconcelos Or 109 Col. Del Valle C.P.66220 Monterrey, Nl. **Tel**: 83 786222, 83 786500

## Quick Learning
Gonzalitos 916 Col. Mitras Centro C.P.64460 Monterrey, Nl. **Tel:** 83 468718

## Teaching Of International Languages
San Lorenzo 165 Col. Vista Hermosa C.P.64620 Monterrey, Nl. **Tel**: 83 465655

## Boston English Institute
Matamoros Pte 1174 Col. Centro C.P.64610 Monterrey, Nl. **Tel:** 83 401981

## British American School Sc
P Mier Pte 421 Col. Centro C.P.64000 Monterrey, Nl. **Tel:** 83 423887

## British American School Sc
Priv Rhin Y Priv Sevilla 651 Col. Centro C.P.64000 Monterrey, Nl. **Tel:** 83 401993

## Centro Educativo Bilingue La Paz Sc
Hidalgo Pte 380 Col., C.P. 64000 Monterrey, Nl. **Tel:** 83433406

## Cosmo Educacion
Rio Colorado Ote 240 Loc-10 Col. Del Valle C.P.66220 Monterrey, Nl. **Tel:** 83 562935, 83 562925, 83 359221

## Desarrollo De Ingles Rapido
Av Pino Suarez 853 Nte Col. Centro C.P.64000 Monterrey, Nl. **Tel:** 83 721222

## English Through The Arts
Av Jose Vascon-celos 1501 Pte Loc-5 Y 6 Col. San Pedro C.P.66220 Monterrey, Nl. **Tel:** 83 386713

## Harmon Hall Hermosillo A C
Av Eug-enio Garza Sada 3755 Col. Alfonso Reyes C.P.64730 Monterrey, Nl. **Tel:** 83 691924

## Interlingua
Av Jose Vasconcelos Or 109 Col. Del Valle C.P.66220 Monterrey, Nl. **Tel:** 83 786244

## Liceo Anglofrances De Monterrey
Rio De La Plata Ote 114 Col. Jardines Del Valle C.P.66220 Monterrey, Nl. **Tel:** 83 353576

## New English System
Dr Coss 843 Sur Loc-E Col. Centro C.P.64000 Monterrey, Nl. **Tel:** 83 421222

## Puebla

## Berlitz
39 Ote 3302 Loc 36, 37,38 Col. Centro C.P.72400 Puebla, Pue. **Tel:** 22 498838, 22 498850, **Fax**: 22 498 475, **Email:** Centro.Puebla@Berlitz.Com.Mx

## English Training centre
Calle 27 Sur 111 Col. Centro C.P.72000 Puebla, Pue. **Tel**: 22 303243, 22 313848

## Harmon Hall
Juarez 2108 Col. La Paz C.P. 72160 Puebla, Pue. **Tel**: 22 424160, 22 424158

## Harmon Hall
Calle 51 Pte 505 Loc 133 Col. Plza America C.P.72000 Puebla, Pue. **Tel:** 22 435701, 22 435487

## Personal English
9 Pte No 1308 1er Piso Col. Centro C.P.72000 Puebla, Pue. **Tel:** 22 465880

## Instituto Anglo Frances
Calle 25 Oriente 1020 Col. Bellavista C.P.72500 Puebla, Pue. **Tel:** 22 432748

## Instituto Anglo Mexicano De Cultura Ac
C Comercial Plaza Crystal Zona A Loc 9-1 Col. C.P.72440 Puebla, Pue. **Tel:** 22 405 122

## Instituto Angloamericano De Puebla
Clle 5 Pte No 1710 Col. Centro C.P.72000 Puebla, Pue. **Tel:** 22 328885

## Interlingua
Reforma Sur 231 R Col. La Paz Pue C.P.72160 Puebla, Pue. **Tel:** 22 493168

## Langtrac
Juarez 1905 Desp 10 Col. La Paz C.P.72160 Puebla, Pue. **Tel:** 22 329245, 22 420339

## Lewis & Lopez Language Services For Business
7 Poniente 309 Desp 201 Col. Col Centro C.P.72080 Puebla, Pue. **Tel:** 22 422116

## Quick Learning
Blvd 5 De Mayo Nº 2509 Col. Del Carmen C.P.72000 Puebla, Pue. **Tel:** 22 430075

## Total English
Av Juarez 1310 P-4 Col. Cen-tro C.P.72000 Puebla, Pue. **Tel:** 22 466020

## English Training centre
Calle 7 Pte 1905 7 Col. La Pue C.P.72000 Puebla, Pue. **Tel:** 22 323874

## Idiomas SA De Cv
Reforma Sur 231 R Col. La Paz Pue C.P.72160 Puebla, Pue. **Tel:** 22 49317

# PERU

Spanish is the first language in Peru, and there is a lot of interest in learning English. Many ELT teachers also take advantage of the Spanish schools to learn or improve their Spanish. The country has some of the world's most important archaeological remains, and people leaving the country may be searched to make sure they are not exporting illegal treasures.

**Embassy in UK:**
52 Sloane Street, London SW1X 9SP
**Tel:** 020 7838 9223
www.peruembassy-uk.com

**Embassy in USA:**
1700 Massachusetts Avenue NW, Washington DC 200036
**Tel: (**202) 833 9860
www.peruemb.org

**British Council Office:**
Torre Parque Mar (Floor 22)
Av Jose Larco 1301
Miraflores
**Tel:** 51 1 617 3060
www.britishcouncil.org.pe

➲ **Visas/Work Permits:** Visitors from the UK and US are entitled to stay for 90 days as tourists without a visa. If you intend to work it is necessary to obtain a visa before entering the country.
➲ **Requirements:** TESOL/TESL Certificate
➲ **Currency:** £1 = 6.27 / $1 = 3.21 nuevos soles
➲ **Health advice:** You should get vaccinations against yellow fever, smallpox and malaria if you are intending to visit the tropical north of the country

## Schools in Peru (+51)

**Cambridge School**
La Alameda de Los Molinos 730-28, La Encantada de Villa, Chorrillos, Lima 9
**Tel:** (1) 254 0163
**Fax**: (1) 254 0149
**Email:** camoff@amauta.rcp.net.pe

**Colegio Franklin Delano Roosevelt**
Av. La Palmeras 325, Urb. Camacho, La Molina, Lima 12
**Tel:** (1) 435 0890
**Fax:** (1) 436 0927
**Email:** fdr@amersol.edu.pe

**Colegio Peruano Britanico**
Av. Via Lactea 445, Monterrico
**Tel:** (1) 436 0151
**Fax**: (1) 436 1006
**Email:** postmast@copebrit.edu.pe

**Davy College**
Av. Hoyos Rubio 2684, Cajamarca
**Tel:** (44) 827 501
**Fax**: (44) 827 502
**Email:** postmaster@davycollege.edu.pe

**Hiram Bingham Scool**
Paseo La Castellana 919, Higuereta, Lima 33
**Tel:** (1) 448 1222
**Fax**: (1) 479 0430
**Email:** dpringle@hirambingham.edu.pe

**Markham College**
Augusto Angulo 291, Miraflores, Lima 18
**Tel:** (1) 241 7677
**Fax**: (1) 447 5295
**Email:** postmaster@markham.edu.pe

**Newton College**
Av. Elias Aparicio 240, Las Lagunas de La Molina, Lima 12
**Tel:** (1) 368 0163
**Fax**: (1) 479 0430
**Email:** college@newton.edu.pe

**San Silvestre School**
Av. Santa Cruz 1251, Miraflores, Lima 18
**Tel:** (1) 241 3334
**Fax**: (1) 445 5075
**Email:** postmaster@staff.sansil.edu.pe

**Sir Alexander Fleming School**
Av. America Sur 3701, Trujillo
**Tel:** (44) 280 395
**Fax**: (44) 284 440
**Email:** admissions@fleming.edu.pe

# URUGUAY

Rapidly developing economy, with few political problems. There is some street crime in Montevideo, and especially along the beach resorts

**Embassy in UK:**
140 Brompton Road, London SW3 1HY
**Tel:** 020 7589 8835

**Embassy in USA:**
2715 M St NW Washington DC 20007
**Tel:** (202) 331 1313
www.embassy.org/uruguay

⮑  **Visas/Work Permits:** no visas required for short stays, but you will need to show a return ticket; work permits needed if you are intending to work
⮑  **Currency:** £1 = 45.7 / $1 = 24.7 pesos
⮑  **Health advice:** Medical care is reasonable, but you should get insurance before travelling

## Schools in Uruguay (+598)

**London Institute (International House)**
Av. Brasil 2831, Montevideo 11300
**Tel:** (2) 709 6774
**Fax**: (2) 709 0297
**Email:** araz@netgate.com.uy

# VENEZUELA

Venezuela is a well-developed reasonably rich country, and life in the major cities is subject to urban crime like anywhere else

**Embassy in UK:**
1 Cromwell Rd, London SW7 2HR
**Tel:** 020 7584 4206
www.venezlon.demon.co.uk

**Embassy in USA:**
1099, 30th St NW, Washington DC 20007
**Tel:** (202) 342 2214
www.embavenez-us.org

**British Council office:**
Piso 3, Torre Credicard, Av Principal El Bosque, Caracas
**Tel**: +58 (212) 952 9965
www.britishcouncil.org.ve

⮑  **Visas/Work Permits:** you need to get a tourist entry card (on the plane) before you enter the country. You also need to show your return ticket. For a longer stay (up to 180 days) you will need a visa and a letter of introduction from your employer
⮑  **Currency:** £1 = 4194 / $1 = 2147 bolivares
⮑  **Health advice:** Medical care is good in the capital Caracas, but less good in country areas. You will probably have to pay cash to get treatment. Vaccinations against cholera and yellow fever are recommended

## Schools in Venezuela (+58)

**Wall Street Institute**
Avda. Francisco de Miranda, Torre Lido, Piso 11, Torre C, Ofic. 111C, 113C El Rosal, Caracas
**Tel:** (212) 953 7473
**Fax:** (212) 374 65 03
**Email:** wsiven@cantv.net

# North America

Finding a job in the USA is not as straight-forward as in other countries. If you are not a US-resident, you'll find that the Homeland Security laws introduced following the September-11 tragedy make it far harder to get a visa and work permit. In addition, in the USA, each state has its own requirements for teacher qualifications. The schools within a state must also be registered with their state education body – and each state, again, has its own requirements for schools operating in their area. To send out your CV, you need a a list of ESL schools (and there are hundreds in the US). The simplest route to getting a list is is to use the Internet. See p28 for job-websites. Alternatively, visit the state's main website for a listing of schools within that state. In Canada, each province has its own requirements for teacher qualification and certification; provinces also have their own requirements for any school operating in the area.

Job seekers in the field of teaching ESL have a number of resources to turn to help them in their search for work in the U.S. and Canada. *ESL Magazine* and *Language Magazine* often feature display advertisements for ESL teaching positions from schools, colleges and school districts in Canada and the U.S. Local newspapers usually carry advertisements for teaching jobs and *The Chronicle of Higher Education* usually contains positions in colleges and universities for ESL teachers. Try *Education Week* for jobs teaching young learners (the K-12 sector).

You can also find some U.S. and Canadian teaching jobs through the Placement E-Bulletin offered by the professional teachers' association, TESOL, Inc. (http://careers.tesol.org) – the service is free of charge to TESOL members. Jobseekers should also check out the annual TESOL convention where employers are often recruiting for new staff. Another cybersource for ESL jobs is the useful TESLJB-L listserv. Go to  http://lc.ust.hk/~teach/temployment.html for information on how to sign on.

On the Internet, visit Tom Riedmiller's site (www.uni.edu/riedmill) for a good overview of ESL job sites. The job listings at Dave's ESL Café site (www.eslcafe.com) sometimes contain positions in Canada and the U.S. although it's mostly adverts for other countries.

If you are interested in teaching in the K-12 sector (Kindergarten to 12th grade – young learners), you might try a search of a local school district's site: many of them feature a jobs section. Also, most universities and colleges offer a recruitment section although many of these are not regularly updated and the deadlines for job applications can be months or even years past due.

# Career Development

Teachers can also be learners! Career development is a natural progression if you want to expand your horizons within the profession or in related fields

### Diploma/Certificate Qualifications See p.178

Diploma courses usually take 8 weeks full-time or a year part-time. With this qualification, you can normally get a job anywhere round the world if you have one.

### Master's Degree Courses See p.193

Masters' programmes offer a way to study the more theoretical approach to English language teaching. In the US, they are not always post-experience qualifications, whereas outside the US applicants will be expected to have an undergraduate degree and two or more years experience.

### Specialist Qualifications See p.208

English as a second language is a field that continues to specialize as it matures as a discipline. This section covers Computer Assisted Language Learning and English for Specific Purposes.

### Doctorates See p.217

This is the ultimate academic qualification in English language teaching. A Ph.D. is generally research-based whereas the Ed.D. is often geared towards those who want to be a school administrator.

### Publishing See p.220

Teachers often find that they are creating their own materials for classroom use. Over the years, these materials are honed until they are fully developed. This is when you should consider getting these materials published.

### School Management / Ownership See p.226

As teachers work their way up the career ladder, some are drawn to school management. Others go on to be school owners.

# Diploma and Master's Courses

To further your career you will certainly need a higher qualification. One way to do this is to take a Diploma course such as those run by the University of Cambridge or Trinity College London, or a Master's degree.

There is an acute shortage of highly qualified teachers around the world, so having a Diploma under your belt means that you can be guaranteed a job anywhere. It proves that you have both a high level qualification and several years' experience in the classroom. Because the University of Cambridge and Trinity College London Diplomas have both theoretical exams and observed teaching practice, most schools prefer these.

The two best-known qualifications are: Diploma in English language teaching to adults (DELTA) from University of Cambridge ESOL and the Licentiate Diploma in Teaching English to speakers of other languages (LTCL.DipTESOL) from Trinity College London.

In order to enrol on a Cambridge DELTA course, you must have at least two years' post-qualification teaching practice The requirements for Trinity are similar. Each course takes eight weeks full-time, although there are part-time courses and many schools and colleges offer distance learning options for part of the course.

There are also university diploma courses which are usually one year in length. They are open to both native speakers and non-native speakers with at least one year's teaching experience. University diploma courses tend to be more theoretically oriented than the University of Cambridge ESOL or Trinity College London Diplomas.

# Diploma/Certificate Courses

This section lists Diploma courses from the main schools around the world. The main courses are: **DELTA** (Diploma in English Language Teaching to Adults, from University of Cambridge ESOL) and **LTCL DipTESOL** (Licentiate Diploma in TESOL, from Trinity College London). Many of the schools and universities listed provide the Diploma course by distance learning.

## ARGENTINA (+54)

**International House**
Pacheco De Melo 2555, 1425 Buenos Aires
**Tel:** 11 4805 6393
**Fax:** 11 4805 6393
**Email:** ihrecoleta@international-house.com.ar
**Website:** www.international-house.com.ar
Courses offered  DELTA

## AUSTRALIA (+61)

**Australian TESOL Training Centre (ATTC)**
PO Box 82, Bondi Junction, New South Wales 2022
**Tel:** 29389 0249
**Fax:** 29389 7788
**Email:** lynnev@ace.edu.au
**Website:** www.attc.nsw.edu.au
Courses offered  DELTA

**International House, Sydney**
Level 3, 89 York Street, Sydney, NSW 2000
**Tel**: 29279 0733
**Fax:** 0 29279 4544
**Email:** jtennant@ihsydney.com
**Website:** www.training.ihsydney.com
Courses offered  DELTA

**Phoenix English Language Academy**
223 Vincent Street, West Perth 6005
**Tel**: 89227 5538
**Fax:** 89227 5540

**Email:** pjones@phoenixela.com.au
**Website:** www.phoenixela.com.au
**Courses offered**  DELTA

**Australian TESOL Training Centre,**
PO Box 82, Bondi Junction NSW 2022.
**Tel:** 02 9389 0249.
**Fax:** 02 9389 7788.
**Courses Offered:** DELTA

## AUSTRIA (+43)

**Berufsförderungsinstitut Wien,**
Kinderspitalgasse 5, A-1090 Vienna.
**Tel:** 1 4043 5114.
**Fax:** 1 4043 5124.
**Email:** bfi.dion@bfi-wien.or.at
**Website:** www.bfi-wien.or.at/bfiwien/
**Courses Offered:** DELTA

## BAHRAIN (+973)

**The British Council**
P.O. Box 452, Manama 356.
**Tel:** 261555.
**Fax:** 258689.
**Courses Offered:** DELTA

## BULGARIA (+359)

**AV0-3 School Of English**
2a Krakra Street, 1504 Sofia
**Tel**: 2 944 3 032
**Fax**: 2 943 3 943
**Email:** binnie@avo-3.com
**Website:** www.avo-3.com
 **Courses offered**: DELTA

## BRAZIL (+55)

**SBCI, Sao Paulo**
Rua Ferreira de Araujo 741, 3° andar - Pinheiros, São
Paulo - SP, CEP 05428-002
**Tel:** 11 3039 0551
**Fax:** 11 3039 0562
**Website:** www.culturainglesasp.com.br
**Courses offered** DELTA

## CANADA (+1)

**Oxford Seminars**
131 Bloor Street West, Suite 200-390, Toronto,
Ontario M5S 1R8
**Tel:** 416-924-3240
**Toll Free**: 1-800-779-1779
**Email:** info@oxfordseminars.com
**Website:** www.oxfordseminars.com
**Courses Offered:** TESOL/TESL Certificate

**Oxford Seminars**
10405 Jasper Avenue, Suite 16-21, Edmonton, Alberta
T5J 3S2
**Tel:** 780 428 8700
**Toll Free**: 1-800-779-1779
**Email:** info@oxfordseminars.com
**Website:** www.oxfordseminars.com
**Courses Offered:** TESOL/TESL Certificate

**Shane Global Village English Centre**
Westcoast English Language Centre Ltd
888 Cambie Street, Vancouver BC, V6B 2P6
**Tel:** 604 684 2112
**Fax:** 604 648 2124
**Email: teachertraining_van@sgvenglish.com**
**Website:** www.sgvenglish.com
**Courses offered**: DELTA

## CYPRUS (+357)

**Forum Language Centre**
PO Box 25567, Nicosia 1310
**Tel:** 2 2317 029
**Fax:** 2 249 7766
**Email:** peterl@forum.ac.cy
**Website:** www.forum.ac.cy
**Courses offered** DELTA

## CZECH REPUBLIC (+42)

**Akcent International House**
Bítovská 3, 140 00 Praha 4
**Tel:** 02 6126 1675
**Fax:** 02 6126 1880
**Email:** dana@akcent.cz
**Website:** www.akcent.cz
**Courses offered** DELTA

## EGYPT (+20)

**The British Council**
192 Sharia El Nil, Agouza, Cairo
**Tel:** 2 301 8341
**Fax:** 2 344 3076
**Email:** Louise.Greenwood@britcoun.org.eg
**Website:** www.britishcouncil.org.eg
**Courses offered** DELTA

## GREECE (+30)

**Anglo-Hellenic Teacher Recruitment,**
PO Box 263, 201 00 Corinth.
**Tel:** 741 53511.
**Fax:** 741 86989.
**Courses Offered:** Lic. Dip.TESOL

**CELT Athens**
77 Academias Street, 106 78 Athens
**Tel:** 1 330 2406
**Fax:** 1 330 1455
**Email:** celtath@otenet.gr/celt@celt.gr
**Website:** www.celt.gr
**Courses offered** DELTA

**Profile**
Frantzi 4 and Kallirois Street, 117 45 Athens
**Tel:** 1 922 2065
**Email:** profile-educinst@ath.forthnet.gr
**Website:** www.profiletraining.net
**Courses offered** DELTA

## Study Space

Tsimiski 86, Thessaloniki 54622
**Tel:** 31 269 697
**Fax:** 31 269 697
**Email:** studyspa@compulink.gr
**Website:** www.compulink.gr/studyspa
**Courses offered** DELTA

## HUNGARY (+36)

## International House, Budapest

PO Box 92, 1276 Budapest
**Tel:** 1345 7046
**Fax:** 1 316 2491
**Email:** ttraining@ih.hu
**Website:** www.ih.hu
**Courses offered** DELTA

## IRELAND (+353)

## English in Dublin

Clifton House, Lower Fitzwilliam Street, Dublin, 2
**Email:** cliftonh@indigo.ie
**Tel:** 1 4732101
**Fax:** 1 661 5200
**Courses Offered:** LTCL.Dip.TESOL

## Language Centre

O'Rahilly Building, UCC, The National University of Ireland, Cork.
**Tel:** 3 21 4902043.
**Fax:** 3 21 4903223.
**Course Length:** 9 months' intensive
**Course Fees:** IEP1750.
**Start dates:** January / October
**Courses Offered:** DELTA.

## University College Cork

The Language Centre, College Road, Cork
**Tel:** 2 1490 2962 / 2043
**Fax:** 2 1490 3223
**Email:** rmasterson@langcent.ucc.ie
**Website:** www.ucc.ie
**Courses offered** DELTA

## ITALY (+39)

## British Council, Milan

Via Manzoni 38, 20121 Milano
**Tel:** 02 772221
**Fax:** 02 781119

**Email:** simon.creasy@britishcouncil.it
**Website:** www.britishcouncil.it/milan
**Courses offered** DELTA

## British Council, Naples

Via Morghen, 31, NAPLES 80129
**Email:** BCNaples@britishcouncil.it
**Courses Offered:** DELTA
**Course Length:** 6 months
**Start Dates:** June, September

## British Institute of Florence Language Centre

Palazzo Strozzino, Piazza Strozzi 2, 50123 Firenze
**Tel:** 055 267 782 05
**Fax:** 055 267 782 23
**Email:** sellis@britishinstitute.it
**Courses offered** DELTA

## The Cambridge School of English

Via Rosmini 6, 37123 Verona
**Tel:** 45 800 3154
**Fax:** 45 801 4900
**Email:** info@cambridgeschool.it
**Website: www.cambridgeschool.it**
**Courses offered:** DELTA

## International House

Via Jannozzi 6, 20097 S. Donato, Milan.
**Tel:** 02 527 9124.
**Fax:** 02 5560 0324.
**Courses Offered:** DELTA.

## International House, Rome

Via Marghera 22, ROMA 185
**Email:** tiziana.di.dedda@dilit.it
**Courses Offered:** DELTA
**Course Length:** FT:12 weeks; PT 4 months

## Lord Byron College

Via Sparano 102, 20121 Bari
**Tel:** 08 052 32 686
**Fax:** 08 052 41 349
**Email:** johncredico@lordbyroncollege.com
**Website:** www.lordbyroncollege.com
**Courses offered** DELTA

## JAPAN (+81)

## British Council, Tokyo

2-1 Kagurazaka, Shinjuku-ku, Tokyo 162-0825
**Tel:** 3 3235 8011
**Fax:** 3 3235 0049
**Email:** sheena.palmer@britishcouncil.or.jp

**Website:** www.uknow.or.jp
**Courses offered** DELTA

## KOREA (+82)

### Yonsei Institute Of Language Research & Education
Yonsei University, 134 Shinch'on-Dong
Sodaemun-Gu, Seoul 120-749.
**Tel:** 2 361 3462.
**Fax:** 2 393 4599.
**Courses Offered:** DELTA.

## MEXICO (+52)

### British Council, Mexico
Lope de Vega 316, Col. Chapultepec Morales
(Polanco), 11570 Mexico D.F.
**Tel:** 52 63 1900 (General) 1982 / 1965
**Fax:** 52 63 1960 / 1660
**Email:** bcmexico@britishcouncil.org.mx
**Website:** www.britishcouncil.org/mexico
**Courses offered** DELTA

### International House
Calle Montecito 38, Piso 20 Despacho 4, Colonia
Nápoles, 03810 Mexico DF
**Tel:** 5 448 0223
**Fax:** 5 488 0223
**Courses Offered:** DELTA

## NEW ZEALAND (+64)

### Capital Language Academy
PO Box 1100, Wellington.
**Tel:** 4 385 0600.
**Fax:** 4 385 6655.
**Courses Offered:** DELTA.

### Christchurch College of English
PO Box 31-212, Christchurch, New Zealand
**Tel:** 3 343 3790
**Fax:** 3 343 3791
**Email:** pauline.taylor@ccel.co.nz
**Website:** www.ccel.co.nz
**Courses:** DELTA

### EDENZ EDENZ College
PO Box 10-222 Dominion Road, Mt Eden, Auckland,
1030

**tel**: 0064 9 522 1211
**fax**: 0064 9 522 1511
**Courses Offered:** LTCL.Dip.TESOL.

### ILA South Pacific Limited
21 Kilmore Street, PO Box 25170, Christchurch.
**Tel:** 3 3795452.
**Fax:** 3 3795373.
**Courses Offered:** DELTA

### Languages International
PO Box 5293, Auckland 1036.
**Tel:** 9 309 0615.
**Fax:** 9 377 2806.
**Courses Offered:** DELTA
**Course Length:** 7 months
**Start dates:** April

### Unitec School Of Languages
Private Bag 92025, Auckland.
**Tel:** 9 849 4180.
**Fax:** 9 815 2906.
**Courses Offered:** DELTA

## POLAND (+48)

### ELS - Bell Gdansk
ul. Matejki 6, 80-238Gdansk
**Tel:** 58 344 7312
**Fax:** 58 344 0784
**Email:** ziolkowska@elsbell.pl
**Website:** www.bellschools.pl
**Courses offered** DELTA

### ELS - Bell (Warsaw)
ul. Nowy Swiat 2, 00-497 Warszawa
**Tel:** 58 344 7312
**Fax:** 58 344 0784
**Email:** ziolkowska@elsbell.com
**Website:** www.bellschools.pl
**Courses offered** DELTA

### International House, Katowice
ul. Leszczynskiego 3, 50-078 Wroclaw
**Tel:** 71 781 7290
**Fax:** 71 781 7290 ext 11
**Email:** ttcentre@ih.com.pl
**Website: www.ih.com.pl**
**Courses offered** DELTA

**International House, Kraków**
ul. Pitsudskiego 6, 31-109 Kraków
**Tel:** 12 422 6482
**Fax:** 12 430 1000
**Email:** admin@ih.pl
**Website:** www.ih.pl
**Courses offered** DELTA

**International House, Wroclaw**
ul. Leszczynskiego 3, 50-078 Wroclaw
**Tel:** 71 781 7290
**Fax:** 71 781 7290 ex. 111
**Email:** ttcentre@ih.com.pl
**Website:** www.ih.com.pl
**Courses offered** DELTA

**UEC Bell School Of English**
Plac Trzech Krzyzy 4/6, 00-499 Warsaw.
**Tel:** 22 625 4792.
**Fax:** 22 629 5865.
**Courses Offered:** DELTA

## PORTUGAL (+35)

**International House**
Rua Marquês Sá da Bandeira, 16, 1050-148 Lisbon.
**Tel:** 1 21 315 1496
**Fax:** 1 21 353 0081
**Email:** ttraining@ihlisbon.com
**Website:** www.international-house.com
**Courses offered** DELTA

## RUSSIA (+7)

**BKC - International House, Moscow**
ul. Tverskaya 9a, Building 4, 103009 Moscow
**Tel:** 095 234 0314
**Fax:** 095 234 0316
**Email:** t-training@bkc.ru
**Website:** www.bkc.ru
**Courses offered** DELTA

**Language Link**
Novoslobodskaya ul. 5/2, 103030 Moscow.
**Tel:** 095 238 0225.
**Fax:** 095 234 0703.
**Courses Offered:** DELTA.

## SEBIA (+381)

**Embassy CES / Rainbow School of English**
Kolo Srpskih Sestara 8, 21000 Novi Sad
**Tel**: 21 363
**Email:** infouk@embassyces.com
**Courses offered**: DELTA

## SOUTH AFRICA (+27)

**International House, Johannesburg**
4th Floor, Aspern House, 54 De Korte Street,
Braamfontein 2001, Johannesburg
**Tel:** 11 339 1051
**Fax:** 11 403 1759
**Email:** laurencek@ihjohannesburg.co.za
**Website:** www.ihjohannesburg.co.za
**Courses offered** DELTA

## SPAIN (+34)

**The British Council Examination Services**
P. del General Martinez Campos 31
Madrid, 28010
**Tel**: 91 337 3529
**Fax**: 91 337 3586
**Website: www.britishcouncil.org**
**Courses Offered:** LTCL.Dip.TESOL.

**British Language Centre**
Calle Bravo Murillo 377, 2°, 28020 Madrid
**Tel:** 91 733 0739
**Fax:** 91 314 5009
**Email:** ted@british-blc.com
**Website:** www.british-blc.com
**Courses offered** DELTA

**Campbell College**
Teacher Training Centre, Calle Pascual y Genís, 14 pta
4, 46002 Valencia
**Tel:** 96 352 4217
**Fax:** 96 351 5402
**Email:** campbell@cpsl.com
**Website:** www.cpsl.com/campbell
**Courses offered** DELTA

**International House, Barcelona**
Trafalgar 14
08010 Barcelona
**Tel:** 93 268 4511 / 93 268 3304

**Fax:** 93 268 0239
**Email:** training@bcn.ihes.com
**Website:** www.ihes.com/bcn
**Courses offered** DELTA

### International House, Madrid
Calle Zurbano 8, 28010 Madrid
**Tel:** 91 319 7224
**Fax:** 91 308 5321
**Email:** ttraining@ihmadrid.es
**Website:** www.ihmadrid.es
**Courses offered** DELTA

### International House, Seville
Calle Menez Nunez 7, 41001 Seville
**Tel:** 954 50 03 16
**Fax:** 954 50 08 36
**Email:** mike@clic.es
**Website:** www.clic.es
**Courses offered** DELTA

### Language Institute
Calle Oliva 11-20, Pontevedra, Galicia.
**Tel/Fax:** 986 871978.
**Courses Offered:** LTCL.Dip.TESOL.

### Oxford TEFL
Avda Diagonal 402 Principal , Barcelona, Spain 8037
**Tel**: 93 458 0111
**Fax**: 93 458 6638
**Website: www.oxfordtefl.com**
**Courses Offered:** LTCL.Dip.TESOL.

## SWITZERLAND (+41)

### Klubschule Migros
Bahnhofplatz 2, 9001 St. Gallen
**Tel:** 71 228 1609
**Fax:** 71 228 1601
**Email:** lee.walker@ksmos.ch
**Website:** www.klubschule.ch
**Courses offered** DELTA

## TURKEY (+90)

### Bilkent University
Teacher Training Unit, School of English Language,
06533 Bilkent, Ankara
**Tel:** 312 290 5190
**Fax:** 312 266 4320

**Email:** elif@bilkent.edu.tr
**Website:** www.bilkent.edu.tr/~busel
**Courses offered** DELTA

### Eastern Mediterranean University
School of Foreign Languages, Magosa, PO Box 95
Mersin 10
**Tel:** 392 630 2163
**Fax:** 392 365 0785
**Email:** stephen.pike@emu.edu.tr
**Website:** www.emu.edu.tr
**Courses offered** DELTA

### International Training Institute (I.T.I.)
Kallavi Sok 7-9 Kat: 4, Istiklal Cad, Galatasaray
Istanbul
**Tel:** 212 243 28 88
**Fax:** 212 245 31 63
**Email:** iti_ist@yahoo.com
**Website: www.itistanbul.org**
**Courses offered** DELTA

## UNITED ARAB EMIRATES (+971)

### Abu Dhabi Men's College
Higher College of Technology, P.O. Box 25035, Abu
Dhabi
**Tel:** 2 4048 353
**Fax:** 2 4048 367
**Email:** phil.quirke@hct.ac.ae
**Website:** www.admc.hct.ac.ae/admcinternet/
**Courses offered** DELTA

### Dubai Men's College
PO Box 15825, Dubai
**Tel:** 4 608 5502
**Fax:** 4 269 1369
**Email:** suzanne.McMahon@hct.ac.ae
**Website:** www.hct.ac.ae
**Courses offered** DELTA

### Higher Colleges of Technology - Al Ain
Al Ain Men's College, PO Box 17155, Al Ain
**Tel:** 382 0888
**Fax:** 782 0099
**Email:** norman.williams@hct.ac.ae
**Website:** www.hct.ac.ae
**Courses offered** DELTA

**Higher Colleges Of Technology - Abu Dhabi**
PO Box 25026, Abu Dhabi.
**Tel:** 2 681 4600 / 5654.
**Fax**: 2 681 5833 / 6579.
**Courses Offered:** DELTA.

**Higher Colleges of Technology - Sharjah**
Sharjah Men's College, PO Box 7946, S.A.I.F. Zone,
Sharjah
**Tel:** 6558 5222
**Fax:** 6558 5252
**Email:** lesley.dick@hct.ac.ae
**Website:** www.hct.ac.ae
**Courses offered** DELTA

## UNITED KINGDOM (+44)

**Aberdeen College**
Gallowgate Centre, Gallowgate, Aberdeen, AB25 1BN
**Website:** www.abcol.ac.uk
**Email:** b.ilett@abcol.ac.uk
**Tel:** 01224 612000
**Fax:** 01224 612001
**Courses Offered**: LTCL.Dip.TESOL

**Anglo-Continental School of English**
29-35 Wimborne Rd, Bournemouth, England BH1 4PT
**Tel:** 01202 557414
**Fax:** 01202 556156
**Website:** www.anglo-continental.com
**Courses Offered**: LTCL.Dip.TESOL

**Barnet College**
CELTA Courses, LBCE Department
Wood Street, Barnet, EN5 4AZ
**Tel:** 0208 275 2828
**Fax:** 0208 441 5236
**Email:** fran.linley@barnet.ac.uk
**Website:** www.barnet.ac.uk
**Courses offered** DELTA

**Bell Language School**
Bowthorpe Hall, Norwich, NR5 9AA
**Tel:** 01603 745615
**Fax:** 01603 747669
**Email:** info.norwich@bell-centres.com
**Website:** www.bell-centres.com
**Courses offered** DELTA

**Bell Language School**
South Road, Saffron Walden, CB11 3DP
**Tel:** 01799 582100
**Fax:** 01799 582199
**Email:** Bruce.Milne@bell-centres.com
**Website:** www.bell-schools.ac.uk
**Courses offered** DELTA

**Bournemouth & Poole College of FE**
Room 345, Lansdowne, Bournemouth, England BH1
3JJ
**Tel**: 01202 205851
**Website:** www.bpc.ac.uk
**Courses Offered**: LTCL.Dip.TESOL

**Brasshouse Language Centre**
50 Sheepcote Street, Birmingham, B16 8AJ
**Tel:** 0121 303 0114
**Fax:** 0121 303 4782
**Website:** www.birmingham.gov.uk/brasshouse
**Courses offered** DELTA

**City of Bristol College**
Department of Languages, Cabot House, Brunel
Centre, Ashley Down, Bristol, BS7 9BU
**Tel:** 0117 312 5163
**Fax:** 0117 312 5180
**Email:** emmanuel.raud@cityofbristol.ac.uk
**Website:** www.cityofbristol.ac.uk
**Courses offered**: DELTA

**Brooklands College**
Heath Road, Weybridge, KT13 8TT
**Website:** www.brooklands.ac.uk
**Email:** uover@brooklands.ac.uk
**Tel:** 01932 847029
**Fax:** 01932 797800
**Courses Offered**: LTCL.Dip.TESOL

**Canterbury Christ Church University College**
North Holmes Road, Canterbury, CT1 1QU
**Tel:** 01227 458459
**Email:** english@cant.ac.uk
**Website:** www.cant.ac.uk/io
**Courses Offered**: LTCL.Dip.TESOL

**Chester English College/English in Chester**
9-11 Stanley Place, Chester, CH1 2LU
**Tel:** 0 1244 318913
**Fax:** 0 1244 320091
**Email:** study@english-in-chester.co.uk

**Website:** www.english-in-chester.co.uk
**Courses offered** DELTA

### City of Bath College
Avon Street, Bath, BA1 1UP
**Tel:** 0 1225 312191
**Fax:** 0 1225 444213
**Email:** bulld@citybathcoll.ac.uk
**Website:** www.citybathcoll.ac.uk
**Courses offered** DELTA

### City College Manchester
Fielden Centre, 141 Barlow Moor Road, West
Didsbury, Manchester, M20 2PQ
**Website:** www.ccm.ac.uk
**Email:** aspencer@ccm.ac.uk
**Tel:** 0161 957 1660
**Fax:** 0161 434 0443
**Courses Offered**: LTCL.Dip.TESOL

### Ealing, Hammersmith, West London College
Gliddon Road, London W14 9BL
**Freephone:** 44 800 980 2175
**Fax:** 0 20 8563 8247
**Email:** cic@hwlc.ac.uk
**Website:** www.hwlc.ac.uk
**Courses offered** DELTA

### Eastbourne School of English
8 Trinity Trees, Eastbourne, BN21 3LD
**Tel:** 0 1323 721759
**Fax:** 0 1323 639271
**Email:** delta@esoe.co.uk
**Website:** www.esoe.co.uk
**Courses offered** DELTA

### Embassy CES
Palace Court, White Rock, Hastings, TN34 1JY
**Tel:** 0 1424 720100
**Fax:** 0 1424 720323
**Email:** training@embassyces.com
**Website:** www.embassyces.com
**Courses offered** DELTA

### English First - EF
26 Wilbraham Road, Manchester, England M14 6JX
**Tel**: 0161 256 1400
**Website:** www.ef.com
**Courses**: LTCL.Dip.TESOL

### English Language Centre
5 New Street, York, YO1 8RA
**Tel:** 0 1904 423594
**Fax:** 0 1904 672200
**Email:** english@btinternet.com
**Website:** www.elcyork.com
**Courses offered** DELTA

### English Language House
300 Saxon Gate West, Milton Keynes, MK9 2ES
**Tel:** 0 1908 694 357
**Fax:** 0 1908 694 355
**Email:** info@englishlanguagehouse.co.uk
**Website:** www.englishlanguagehouse.co.uk
**Courses offered** DELTA

### Golders Green Teacher Training Centre
11 Golders Green Road, London NW11 8DY
**Email:** teachertraining@ggcol.fsnet.co.uk
**Tel:** 020 8731 0963
**Fax:** 020 8455 6528
**Courses Offered**: LTCL.Dip.TESOL

### Guildford College Of Further & Higher Education
Stoke Park, Guildford, GU1 1EZ
**Tel:** 01483 448500
**Fax:** 01483 448600
**Courses Offered**: LTCL.Dip.TESOL

### inlingua
iTTR, Rodney Lodge, Rodney Road, Cheltenham,
GL50 1HX
**Tel**: 01242 253 171
**Email:** info@inlingua-cheltenham.co.uk
**Website:** www.inlingua-cheltenham.co.uk
**Courses**: LTCL.Dip.TESOL

### Institute for Applied Language Studies
Univ. of Edinburgh, 21 Hill Place, Edinburgh
EH8 9DP
**Tel:** 0 131 650 6200
**Fax:** 0 131 667 5927
**Email:** IALS.enquiries@ed.ac.uk
**Website:** www.ials.ed.ac.uk
**Courses offered** DELTA

### International House
106 Piccadilly, London W1J 7NL
**Tel:** 0 20 7518 6928
**Fax:** 0 20 7518 6921

**Email:** fernando.nonohay@ihlondon.co.uk
**Website:** www.ihlondon.com
**Courses offered** DELTA, also Distance-DELTA
(www.thedistancedelta.com)

## International House
14-18 Stowell Street, Newcastle upon Tyne, NE1 4XQ
**Tel:** 0 191 238 9551
**Fax:** 0 191 238 1126
**Email:** info@ihnewcastle.com
**Website:** www.ihnewcastle.com
**Courses offered** DELTA

## International House - The Distance DELTA
106 Piccadilly, London W1V 9FL
**Tel:** +44 (0) 20 7518 6999
**Fax:** +44 (0) 20 7518 6998
**Email:** admin@thedistancedelta.com
**Website:** www.thedistancedelta.com
**Courses offered** DELTA

## ITTC United Kingdom Ltd
Nortoft Road, Charminster, Bournemouth, BH8 8PY
**Tel:** 0 1202 397 721
**Fax:** 0 1202 309 662
**Email:** tefl@ittc.co.uk
**Website:** www.ittc.co.uk
**Courses offered** DELTA

## Kingston College
Kingston Hall Road, Kingston-upon-Thames, KT1 2AQ
**Website:** www.kingston-college.ac.uk
**Email:** kise@kingston-college.ac.uk
**Tel:** 020 8546 2151
**Fax:** 020 8268 2900
**Courses Offered**: LTCL.Dip.TESOL

## King's College English Language Teaching Centre
English Language Centre, King's College London, The Strand, London WC2R 2LS
**Tel:** 0 207 848 1604
**Fax:** 0 207 848 1601
**Email:** christopher.sciberas@kcl.ac.uk
**Website:** www.kcl.ac.uk
**Courses offered** DELTA

## Langside College
50 Prospecthill Road, Glasgow, G42 9LB
**Website:** www.langside.ac.uk

**Email:** tfoster@langside.ac.uk
**Tel:** 0141 649 4991
**Fax:** 0141 632 5252
**Courses Offered**: LTCL.Dip.TESOL

## Language Link
181 Earls Court Road, Earls Court, London SW5 9RB
**Tel:** 0 20 7370 4755
**Fax:** 0 20 7370 1123
**Email:** languagelink@compuserve.com
**Website:** www.languagelink.co.uk
**Courses offered** DELTA

## Language Project
27 Oakfield Road, Clifton, Bristol, BS8 2AT
**Website:** www.languageproject.co.uk
**Email:** info@languageproject.co.uk
**Tel:** 0117 9090911
**Fax:** 0117 907 7181
**Courses Offered**: LTCL.Dip.TESOL

## Languages Training and Development
Suite 2, Waterloo House , 58-60 High Street , Witney, OX28 6RJ
**Tel**: 01993 708 637
**Fax**: 01993 862791
**Website:** www.ltdoxford.com
**Courses Offered**: LTCL.Dip.TESOL

## Manchester Academy of English
St Margaret's Chambers, 5 Newton Street, Manchester, England M1 1HL
**Tel:** 0161 237 5619
**Fax:** 0161 237 9016
**Website: www.manacad.co.uk**
**Courses Offered**: LTCL.Dip.TESOL

## Northbrook College
Modern Languages Centre, Littlehampton Road, Goring-by-Sea, Worthing, BN12 6NU
**Website:** www.nbcol.ac.uk
**Email:** s.scowen@nbcol.ac.uk
**Tel:** 01903 606243
**Fax:** 01903 606207
**Courses Offered**: LTCL.Dip.TESOL

## Nottingham Trent University
Nottingham Language Centre, Newton Building, Room 519, Burton Street, Nottingham, NG1 4BU
**Tel:** 0 115 941 8418
**Fax:** 0 115 848 6513

**Email:** linda.taylor@ntu.ac.uk
**Website:** www.nlc.ntu.ac.uk
**Courses offered**   DELTA

## Oxford Cherwell College
Oxpens Road, Oxford, OX1 1SA
**Tel**: 01865 269268
**Fax**: 01865 269412
**Email:** Steven_Haysham@oxfordcollege.ac.uk
**Website:** www.oxfordcollege.ac.uk
**Courses offered**: DELTA

## Oxford College of Further Education
1 Oxpens Road, Oxford, OX1 1SA
**Tel**: 0 1865 269268
**Fax**: 0 1865 269412
**Email:** Steven_Haysham@oxfordcollege.ac.uk
**Website:** www.oxfordcollege.ac.uk
**Courses offered**   DELTA

## Oxford House College
28 Market Place, Oxford Circus, London W1W 8AW
**Tel:** 0 20 7580 9785
**Fax:** 0 20 7323 4582
**Email:** teachertraining@oxfordhouse.co.uk
**Website:** www.oxfordhousecollege.co.uk
**Courses offered**   DELTA

## Reading College
Crescent Road, Reading, RG1 5RQ
**Tel:**  0118 967 5442
**Fax:**  0118 967 5441
**Courses Offered**: LTCL.Dip.TESOL

## Reading College and School of Arts & Design
Crescent Road, Reading, RG1 5RQ
**Tel:** 0 118 967 5411
**Fax:** 0 118 967 5441
**Email:** baberm@reading-college.ac.uk
**Website:** www.reading-college.ac.uk
**Courses offered**   DELTA

## Regency School of English
Royal Crescent, Ramsgate, CT11 9PE
**Email:**  regency.school@btinternet.com
**Tel:** 01843 591212
**Fax:**  01843 850035
**Courses Offered**: LTCL.Dip.TESOL

## St George International
76 Mortimer Street, London W1N 7DE

**Website:** www.stgeorges.co.uk
**Email:**  teflenq@stgeorges.co.uk
**Tel:**  020 7299 1700
**Fax:**  020 7299 1711
**Courses Offered**: LTCL.Dip.TESOL

## St Giles College
51 Shepherds Hill, London, N6 5QP
**Tel:** 0208 340 0828
**Fax:** 0208 348 9389
**Email:** edtrust@stgiles.co.uk
**Website:** www.tefl-stgiles.com
**Courses offered**: CELTA, DELTA

## Sandwell College
Smethwick Campus, Crocketts Lane, Smethwick, B66 3BU
**Website:** www.sandwell.ac.uk
**Email:**  gill.clarke@sandwell.ac.uk
**Tel:**  0121 253 6238
**Fax:**  0121 253 6322
**Courses Offered**: LTCL.Dip.TESOL

## Saxoncourt Teacher Training
Nightingale House, 56-70 Queensway, Petts Wood Bromley, BR5 1DH
**Tel:** 01689 873 355
**Fax:** 01689 872 100
**Email:** jshepheard@sgvenglish.com
**Website:** www.sgvenglish.com
**Courses offered**   DELTA

## Shane English School
59 South Molton Street, London W1K 5SN
**Website:** www.sgvenglish.com
**Email:**  awhitehead@sgvenglish.com
**Tel:**  07491 1911
**Fax:**  07493 3657
**Courses Offered**: LTCL.Dip.TESOL

## Sheffield Hallam University, TESOL Centre
36 Collegiate Campus, Sheffield, S10 2BP
**Email:**  tesol@shu.ac.uk
**Tel:**  0114 225 2240
**Fax:**  0114 225 2280
**Website:** www.shu.ac.uk
**Courses Offered**: LTCL.Dip.TESOL

## Sidmouth International School
May Cottage, Sidmouth, EX10 8EN
**Email:**  efl@sidmouth-int.co.uk

**Tel:** 01395 516754
**Fax:** 01395 579270
**Website:** www.sidmouth-int.co.uk
**Courses Offered**: LTCL.Dip.TESOL

### Solihull College
Blossomfield Road, Solihull, Birmingham, B91 1SB
**Tel:** 0 121 678 7173
**Fax:** 0 121 678 7276
**Email:** pat.morris@Solihull.ac.uk
**Website:** www.solihull.ac.uk
**Courses offered**   DELTA

### Stanton Teacher Training Courses Ltd
Stanton House, 167 Queensway, London W2 4SB
**Tel:** 0 207 221 7259
**Fax:** 0 207 792 9047
**Email:** study@stanton-school.co.uk
**Website:** www.stanton-school.co.uk
**Courses offered**   DELTA

### TLI Ltd. Teacher Training
Jewel and Esk Valley College, 24 Milton Road East, Edinburgh, England EH15 2PP UK
**Tel:** +441316201163
**Website:** www.tlieurope.com
**Courses Offered**: LTCL.Dip.TESOL

### Universal Language Services
43 - 45 Cambridge Gardens, Hastings, TN34 1EN
**Website:** www.unversallanguageservices.com
**Email:** enquiries@universallanguageservices.com
**Tel:** 01424 438025
**Fax:** 01424 438050
**Courses Offered**: LTCL.Dip.TESOL

### University of Bath
English Language Centre, Claverton Down, Bath BA2 7AY,
**Tel:** 0 1225 323139
**Fax:** 0 1225 323135
**Email:** mlssfw@bath.ac.uk
**Website:** www.bath.ac.uk/elc/delta.htm
**Courses offered**   DELTA

### University of Durham
The Language Centre, Elvet Riverside, New Elvet, Durham, DH1 3JT
**Tel:** 0 191 374 3716
**Fax:** 0 191 374 7790
**Email:** CELTA.training@durham.ac.uk

**Website:** www.durham.ac.uk/language.centre
**Courses offered**   DELTA

### University College London (UCL)
Language Centre, 136 Gower Street, London, WC1 6BT
**Tel**: 0207 679 7722
**Fax:** 0207 383 3577
**Email:** a.salisbury@ucl.ac.uk
**Website:** www.ucl.ac.uk
**Courses offered**: DELTA

### Waltham Forest College
Forest Road, London E17 4JB
**Tel:** 0 208 501 8178
**Fax:** 0 208 501 8001
**Email:** lawlor@waltham.ac.uk
**Website:** www.waltham.ac.uk
**Courses offered**   DELTA

### Warwickshire College
Thornbank Centre, Warwick New Road, Leamington Spa, CV32 5JE
**Tel:** 0 1926 318 165
**Fax:** 0 1926 427 317
**Email:** bbuxton@warkscol.ac.uk
**Website:** www.warkscol.ac.uk
**Courses offered**   DELTA

### Westminster Kingsway College
Castle Lane, London SW1E 6DR
**Tel:** 0 207 963 8515
**Fax:** 0 207 233 8509
**Email:** annecandan@westking.ac.uk
**Courses offered**   DELTA

### Windsor Schools TEFL
21 Osborne Road, Windsor, SL4 1RU
**Website:** www.windsorschools.co.uk
**Email:** info@windsorschools.co.uk
**Tel:** 01753 858995
**Fax:** 01753 831726
**Courses Offered**: LTCL.Dip.TESOL

## USA (+1)

### Oxford Seminars
12335 Santa Monica Blvd, Suite 337, Los Angeles, California 90025
**Tel:** 310-820-2359

**Toll Free**: 1-800-779-1779
**Email:** info@oxfordseminars.com
**Website:** www.oxfordseminars.com
**Courses Offered:** TESOL/TESL Certificate

### Oxford Seminars

244 5th Avenue, Suite J262, New York, New York
10001-7406
**Tel:** 212-213-8978
**Toll Free**: 1-800-779-1779
**Email:** info@oxfordseminars.com
**Website:** www.oxfordseminars.com
**Courses Offered:** TESOL/TESL Certificate

### St. Giles Language Teaching Center

One Hallidie Plaza (Suite 350), San Francisco, CA
94102
**Tel**:1 415 788 3552
**Fax**:1 415 788 1923
**Email:** info@stgiles-usa.com
**Website:** www.stgiles-usa.com
**Courses offered:** DELTA

## VIETNAM (+84)

### International Language Academy (ILA) Vietnam

402 Nguyen Thi Minh Khai Street, District 3, Ho Chi
Minh City
**Tel**: 8 929 0100 (Ext. 124)
**Fax**: 8 929 0070
**Email:** andrew@ilavietnam.com
**Website:** www.ilavietnam.com
**Courses offered**: DELTA

# Master's Degree Courses

A Master's Degree in Teaching English as a Second or Foreign Language is, for many teachers, a key qualification for those who want to work to cover the theory of teaching – or work in schools and universities.

For many prospective teachers, the decision to embark on a Master's degree programme represents a crucial investment of time and money in the career of their choice. Studying for a postgraduate degree need not leave you in debt for the rest of your natural born days. Many students can earn money while they study by working as a Graduate Teaching Assistant. A number of universities and colleges offer the opportunity for students to earn their degrees on a part-time basis, so you can work while you study. Most institutions offer scholarships and grants: make it a point to inquire about when you contact a school or university.

Master's degree programmes vary in terms of admission requirements and length of the course. Prospective students whose first language is not English will need to submit their TOEFL score for consideration by the admission office of the institution where they hope to study. M.A. programmes are usually flexible and you can work at your own pace within the criteria for time set by the university or college: a programme can take anywhere from one to five years or more to complete.

There are many different titles for Master's degree programmes. These often reflect the historical development of the department with which they are associated. There are three main types of Master's degree in TESL/TEFL: (1) Master of Arts (M.A.), (2) Master of Science (M.Sc./M.S.) and (3) Master of Education (M.Ed.). In general there is little difference between all three degrees although earning a M.Ed., which is awarded by a School of Education, may not involve writing a thesis. A MAT (Master of Arts in Teaching) focuses more on the practical aspects of teaching than the other types of Master's degrees.

An Applied Linguistics degree is at the other end of the scale in that these programmes usually concentrate more directly on the theory of language acquisition.

The benefits associated with a Master's degree are numerous. Although there are institutions that will hire teachers who have not earned a postgraduate degree, the reality is that many employers, especially in higher education, insist that candidates have a Master's degree in TESL, TEFL, TESOL or Applied Linguistics. A teacher with a Master's degree usually enjoys a greater earning power than a colleague who lacks the qualification. Above all, embarking on a Master's programme reinforces a teacher's decision that he or she has made teaching English as a second or foreign language a serious career choice.

# Choosing a Master's Degree Course

If you plan to make teaching English as a second or foreign language your major career decision, then you should be looking at studying for a Master's Degree in TEFL / TESL or TESOL. The first thing to do when choosing a Master's programme that's right for you is to ask questions: What kinds of courses are offered in the programme? Are they more practical or theoretical in scope?

If you are interested in going directly into teaching after getting your master's degree, you should stick to a practical curriculum. If, on the other hand, if you are interested in pursuing a Ph.D., then look for a more theoretically based curriculum.

What do the faculty members specialize in? Ask the programme director for details on what the faculty is researching, what courses they teach, and even about possible internships or assistantships. This will give you an indication of what the focus of your studies will be. If your interests are similar to theirs, you have a good match.

If you are interested in teaching in the public school system, find out if the courses lead to or satisfy provincial certification (in Canada) or state certification (in the US), and if they satisfy the requirements in any other province or state where you are considering certification.

## General guidelines:

Ask for a reference or two from the programme director. Ask recent graduates if they are satisfied with the education they received and whether their courses have actually met the needs of their current jobs.

Examine the job placement record. What percentage of graduates get jobs after they receive their degrees? Does the school offer placement assistance or career counselling?

## English for Special Purposes Programmes

Other professions look to university TESOL master's programmes to develop instructors for teaching English for special purposes (ESP) in specialized fields such as medicine, law, computer science, engineering, and business. Master's programmes must provide their students with the expertise needed to teach a wide range of skills from basic English for those working at entry level jobs to accent reduction courses for professionals seeking to improve their oral communication skills. Additionally, ESP instructors need a familiarity with the content subject matter and the ability to collaborate with professors and other professionals in various disciplines.

Teaching English as a Foreign Language Master's programmes continue to fulfill their traditional role of providing teachers for positions overseas teaching English to college and university students, professional adults, and young learners. With the worldwide demand for English instruction, American students wishing to teach abroad and international students planning to teach English in their own countries seek out programmes in Teaching English as a Foreign language (TEFL).

These programmes feature methodology courses that address frequent concerns of English as a Foreign Language (EFL) teachers such as curriculum design for large class sizes, limited budget and materials, and resources for authentic language input and natural language acquisition.

## TESOL Doctoral Study

TESOL master's programmes are the training ground for prospective doctoral candidates who conduct research, design and implement university degree programmes, and teach at the master's and doctoral levels in institutions of higher education. To prepare students for these academic roles, TESOL master's programmes typically offer a combination of courses which cover the theory and practice of second language teaching, curriculum development, and the fundamentals of linguistics, second language acquisition, and research.

# Master's Degree Courses

There are opportunities to study for a Master's degree in a wide range of countries around the world. These selected schools and universities offer full-time intensive courses and, more often, distance or part-time study.

## AUSTRALIA (+61)

### Macquarie University
Sydney, NSW 2109.
**Tel:** 2 9850 9647.
**Fax:** 2 985 9352.
**Email:** lingpgo@ling.mq.edu.au
**Website:** www.ling.mq.edu.au/researchdegrees
**Start Dates:** March, July.
**Course length:** 2-3 semesters FT.
**Admission Requirements:** First degree + teaching experience.
**Programmes:** M.A. and PhD in Applied Linguistics.

### University of Melbourne
Department of Language, Literacy and Arts Education, Room 513, Doug McDonell Building, Victoria, 3010.
**Tel::** 3 9344 8377.
**Fax:** 3 8344 5104.
**Programmes:** Master of TESOL.

### Monash University
Normanby House, 100 Normanby Road, Clayton, Victoria 3168.
**Programmes:** M.A. TESOL.
**Course length:** 2 years FT; 4 years PT.

### Queensland University of Technology
School of Culture & Language Education, Kelvin Grove Campus, Victoria Park Road, Kelvin Grove, Brisbane, Queensland 4059.
**Tel:** 7 3864 3242.
**Fax:** 7 3864 3988.
**Programmes:** M.Ed. TESOL.

### University of South Australia
GPO Box 2471, Adelaide, South Australia 5001.
**Start Dates:** February.
**Tel:** 8 8302 6611.
**Fax:** 8 8302 2466.
**Programmes:** M.Ed. TESOL.

### Tasmania University
English Language Centre, P.O. Box 1214, Launceston, Tasmania 7250.
**Programmes:** M.Ed. TESOL.
**Course length:** 18 months FT.
**Admission Requirements:** Degree.

### Victoria University
PO Box 14428, Melbourne, Victoria, 8001.
**Tel:** 3 9688 4000.
**Fax:** 3 9689 4069.
**Programmes:** M.A. in TESOL and Literacy.

## CANADA (+1)

### Brock University
Graduate Studies Office, St. Catharines, Ontario L2S 3A1.
**Tel:** (905) 688-5550, x4467.
**Fax:** (905) 988-5488.
**Email:** ekoop@spartan.ac.brocku.ca
**Programmes:** M.Ed. TESL.
**Course length:** 1 year.
**Grant Availability**: Possible Teaching/Research Assistantships.
**Admission Requirements:** Undergraduate degree with an average of 75% in the last 10 credits.

## Carleton University
School of Linguistics and Applied Language Studies,1125 Colonel By Drive, Ottawa K1S 5B6.
**Tel:** (613) 520-2802.
**Fax:** (613) 520-6641.
**Email:** linguistics@carleton.ca
**Programmes:** M.A. Applied Language Studies.
**Course length:** Usually 4 terms FT depending on which option student decides to complete (thesis, research essay or all courses).
**Start Dates:** January, May, September.
**Admission Requirements:** Honors degree with a B - B+ average.

## Concordia University
School of Graduate Studies
Office of the Registrar, 1455 de Maisonneuve Boulevard West, Montreal, Quebec H3G 1M8
**Tel**: 1-514-848-2837
**Website**: www.concordia.ca
**Programmes**: M.A. - Applied Linguistics

## McGill University
Faculty of Graduate Studies, Second Language Education, Education Bldg., Rm. 431A, 3700 McTavish St. Montreal, Quebec H3A 1Y2
**Tel**: 1-514-398-6982
**Website**: www.education.mcgill.ca
**Programmes**: M.Ed.-Second Language Education

## Memorial University of Newfoundland
Faculty of Education, Teaching and Learning Studies, St. John's, Newfoundland, A1B 3X8
**Tel**: 1-709 -737 -8587
**Website**: www.mun.ca
**Programmes**: M.Ed.-Teaching and Learning Studies

## Trinity Western University
School of Graduate Studies, Teaching English as a Second or Other Language, 7600 Glover Road, Langley, BC V2Y 1Y1
**Tel**: 1-604-888-7511
**Website**: www.twu.ca
**Programmes**: M.A. - TESOL

## University of Calgary
Faculty of Graduate Studies, Graduate Division of Educational Research, Teaching English as a Second Language, Education Tower 940, 2500 University Drive, NW, Calgary, Alberta T2N 1N4
**Tel**: 1-403-220-5675
**Website**: www.ucalgary.edu
**Programmes**:  M.Ed

## York University
Room 544 South, Ross Building, 4700 Keele Street, Toronto, Ontario M3J 1P3.
**Tel:** (416) 736-2100 x88270.
**Fax:** (416) 736-5483.
**Email:** gradling@yorku.ca
**Programmes:** M.A. in Theoretical & Applied Linguistics.
**Course length:** 1 year FT.
**Grant Availability:** Teaching Assistantships, Graduate Assistantships, Scholarships.
**Start Dates:** September.

# CHINA (HONG KONG +852)

## Chinese University of Management
Tat Chee Avenue, Kowloon, Hong Kong.
**Tel:** 2788 9400.
**Fax:** 2788 9020.
**Programmes:** M.A. Degree in TESL.

## City University of Hong Kong School of Graduate Studies
5/F Cheng Yick Chi Building, Tat Chee Avenue, Kowloon.
**Tel:** 2788 9076.
**Fax:** 2788 9940.
**Programmes:** M.A. Degree in TESL.

# EGYPT (+20)

## The American University in Cairo
113 Sharia Kasr el-Aini - PO Box 2511, Cairo, 11511.
**Tel:** 2-357-5530.
**Fax:** 2-355-7565. (In the U.S.: **Tel:** (212) 730-8800.
**Fax:** (212) 730-1600)
**Programmes:** M.A. Degree in TEFL.
**Course length:** 2 years FT.
**Start Dates:** January, September.

# IRELAND (+353)

## The National University of Ireland Language Centre
O'Rahilly Building, UCC, Cork.
**Tel:** 21 4902043.
**Fax:** 21 4903223.
**Programmes:** M.A. Degree in Applied Linguistics.
**Course length:** FT 1 year.
**Start Dates:** October.

Admission Requirements: Relevant primary degree at Second Class Honors standard or equivalent, English to IELTS level 7.0 if not a native speaker.

## MALAYSIA (+60)

### Universiti Malaya Faculty of Languages and Linguistics Education
Pantai Valley, 59100 Kuala Lumpur.
Tel: 3 756-0022.
Fax: 3 755-2975.
Programmes: M.A. Degree in TESOL.

## MEXICO (+52)

### Universidad de las Américas
Departamento de Lenguas, Sta. Catarina Mártir, Puebla, 72820.
Tel: 22 29 31 05.
Fax: 22 29 31 05
Email: eckep@mail.udlap.mx
Programmes: M.A. in Applied Linguistics.
Course length: 2 years FT.
Aid Availability: A limited number of teaching assistantships is available in the Department of Languages. Mexican students can obtain financial aid from the Ministry of Public Education of Mexico, while participants from the United States are able to procure college loans from institutions in the U.S.

## PHILIPPINES (+63)

### University of the East
2219 C.M. Recto Avenue, 1008 Manila.
Tel: 2-741-95-01.
Programmes: M.A. Degree in Education (TESOL).

## SOUTH AFRICA (+27)

### Rhodes University
Faculty of Arts, P.O. Box 94, Grahamstown, 6140.
Tel: 461 318111.
Fax: 461 25049.
Programmes: M.A. TESOL.
Course length: 2 years.

## THAILAND (+66)

### Assumption University
A Building 3rd floor, Ramkhamhaeng Soi 24 Road Huamark, Bangkok 1.
Tel: 2-3004543-62.
Fax: 2-7191521.
Programmes: M.A. TESL.

### Chiang Mai University Graduate School
Chang Mai, 50200.
Tel: 53-221699.
Fax: 53-892231.
Programmes: M.A. TEFL.

### Payap University Graduate School
Chiang Mai, 50000.
Programmes: M.A. TEFL.

## UNITED KINGDOM (+44)

### Aston University
Aston Triangle, Birmingham B4 7ET.
Tel: 121 359 3611.
Fax: 121 359 6350.
Email: lsu@aston.ac.uk
Website: www.les.aston.ac.uk/tesol
Programmes: M.Sc./Diploma TESOL, M.Sc./Diploma Teaching ESP. Both distance learning

### Canterbury Christ Church University
North Holmes Road, Canterbury, Kent, CT1 1QU
Tel: 01227 458459
Fax: 01227 781558
Email: english@cant.ac.uk
Website: www.cant.ac.uk/io
Courses offered: MA TESOL

### Middlesex University
White Hart Lane, London N17 8HR
Tel: 020 8411 5898
Email: admissions@mdx.ac.uk
Website: www.ilrs.mdx.ac.uk/lang/eng_non.htm
Courses: MA TEFL with Applied Linguistics

### Norwich Institute of Language Education (NILE)
PO Box 2000, Norwich, NR2 1LE
Tel: 01603 664473
Fax: 01603 664493

**Email:** registrar@nile-elt.com
**Website:** www.nile-elt.com
**Courses offered:** MA language education, range of courses for professional development

## Oxford Brookes University

**Tel:** 01865 483874
**Fax:** 01865 484377
**Email: icels@brookes.ac.uk**
**Website: www.brookes.ac.uk/icels**
**Courses:** MA Applied Linguistics, MA ELT

## Sheffield Hallam University

TESOL Centre, School of Education, Collegiate Campus, Sheffield S10 2BP.
**Tel:** 114 225 2240.
**Fax:** 114 225 2280.
**Programmes:** M.A. TESOL.
**Course length:** 12 weeks DL phase, + 6 weeks intensive direct contact phase, + 32 weeks research phase.
**Admission Requirements:** PG diploma in TESOL or equivalent.
**Start Dates:** March or October each year for direct contact phase in June/July or January/February.

## University of Bath

English Language Centre, University of Bath, BA2 7AY
**Tel:** 01225 383024
**Fax:** 01225 383135
**Email:** english@bath.ac.uk
**Website:** www.bath.ac.uk/elc
**Courses offered:** MA in ELT

## University of Birmingham

CELS, University of Birmingham, Edgbaston, Birmingham, B15 2TT
**Tel:** 0121 414 3239
**Fax:** 0121 414 3298
**Email:** cels@bham.ac.uk
**Courses offered:** MA Applied Linguistics, MA ESP, MA TEFL/TESL,

## University of Bristol

Graduate School of Education, 35 Berkeley Square, Bristol BS8 1JA.
**Tel:** 117 9287040.
**Fax:** 0117 927250.
**Email:** janet.woolways@bristol.ac.uk

**Course length:** 12 months full-time; up to five years part-time; can also be done in term blocks: October to December or January to March.
**Start Dates:** October FT; January, October PT. Summer Session: Presessional available for those who have either been out of full-time education for many years, or who feel that one month of academic preparation would benefit them. Usually held throughout September.
**Admission Requirements:** First degree, at least one year fulltime teaching experience; preferably a professional qualification in TESL/TEFL.
**Specializations:** Specialist centre for Language in Education, including English as an additional language; off shore teaching can be provided for closed groups.
**Courses:** M.Ed. TEFL, EdD in TESOL, MPhil/PhD in TESOL

## University Of Durham

Department Of Linguistics And English Language, Elvet Riverside II, New Elvet, Durham DH1 3JT.
**Tel:** 191 374 2641.
**Fax:** 191 374 2685.
**Programmes:** M.A. Linguistics, M.A. Language Acquisition, M.A. Applied Linguistics, M.A. Applied Linguistics (ELT), M.A. Applied Linguistics, (ELT, CALL And Educational Technology), M.A. Applied Linguistics (ESP), M.A. Applied Linguistics (ESOL), M.A. Applied Linguistics (ELT And Materials Development), M.A. Applied Linguistics (FLT),M.A. Applied Linguistics (Translation).

## University of Edinburgh

Faculty of Education, Moray House, Holyrood Road, Edinburgh, EH8 8AQ, Scotland.
**Tel:** 131 651 6329.
**Fax:** 131 651 6409.
**Programmes:** M Ed (TESOL) (DL available).
**Course length:** 1 year FT; 6 years maximum DL.
**Start Dates:** October Full-time; Continuous DL.
**Admission Requirements:** Degree + 3 years' relevant experience.

## University of Exeter

School of Education and Lifelong Learning
**Tel:** 01392 264815
**Fax:** 01392 264902
**Email:** ed-cpd@exeter.ac.uk
**Website:** www.ex.ac.uk/sell
**Courses:** MPhil in TESOL, MEd in TESOL, EdD in TESOL, Pgcert in TESOL

## University of Leicester
21 University Road, Leicester, LE1 7RF.
**Tel:** 116 2523675.
**Fax:** 116 2523653.
**Programmes:** M.A. Applied Linguistics and TESOL (DL).

## University of London
Institute of Education, 20 Bedford Way, London WC1 0AL.
**Tel:** 020 7612 6536
**Fax:** 020 7612 6534.
**Course length:** 1 year FT; 2 years PT.
**Start Dates:** October.
**Admission Requirements:** A good Honours class degree, and at least two years teaching experience
**Programmes:** M.A. TESOL.

## University of Luton
Vicarage Street, Luton, LU1 3JU.
**Tel:** 1582 489019.
**Fax:** 1582 743466.
**Programmes:** M.A. Applied Linguistics (TEFL).
**Course length:** 1 year. **Start Dates:** October.

## University of Manchester
Faculty of Education, University of Manchester, Oxford Rd, Manchester, M13 9PL
**Tel:** 0161 275 3463
**Email**: education.enquiries@man.ac.uk
**Website:** www.man.ac.uk/langlit
**Courses offered**: MEd in ELT, MEd in Educational Technology and ELT

## University of Newcastle upon Tyne
Language Centre, Level 4, Old Library Bldg., Newcastle upon Tyne, NE1 7RU.
**Tel:** 191 222 5621
**Fax:** 191 222 5239
**Programmes:** M.A. in Media Technology for TEFL, M.A. in Linguistics for TESOL.
**Course length:** 12 months FT for both programmes, 24 months PT (Linguistics).
**Requirements:** 2 years FT teaching experience.
**Start Dates:** September.

## University of Sunderland
School of Humanities & Social Sciences, Forster Building, Chester Road, Sunderland SR1 3SD.
**Tel:** 191 515 2000.
**Programmes:** M.A. TESOL.

## University of Surrey
English Language Institute, Guildford, Surrey, GU2 5XH.
**Tel:** 1483 259910
**Fax:** 1483 259507.
**Programmes:** M.A. Linguistics (TESOL) (DL). M.Sc. English Language Teaching Management (DL).
**Course length:** 27 months.
**Start Dates:** March, October.
**Admission Requirements:** 1st degree and at least two years full time teaching experience.

## University of Warwick
CELTE, Coventry, CV4 7AL
**Tel**: 024 7652 3200
**Fax**: 024 7652 4318
**Email:** celte@warwick.ac.uk
**Website:** www.warwick.ac.uk/celte
**Courses offered**: MA in ELT, MA in ESP, Diploma in ELT and Administration, research degrees of PhD and EdD

## University of York
EFL Unit, York, Y010 5DD
**Tel**: 01904 432483
**Fax**: 01904 432481
**Email:** efl2@york.ac.uk
**Website**: www.york.ac.uk/ltc/efl
**Courses offered**: MA in teaching young learners (distance course)

## UNITED STATES OF AMERICA (+1)

## Adelphi University
1 South Avenue, Garden City, NY 11530
**Tel:** (516) 877-3000
**Website:** www.adelphi.edu/

## University of Alabama
UAB Station, Birmingham, AL 35294
**Website:** http://main.uab.edu/
**Courses:** MA TESOL

## American University
4400 Massachusetts Avenue NW, Washington DC 20016-8001
**Tel:** 202-885-6000
**Fax**: 202-885-1025
**Website:** www.american.edu/
**Email:** afa@american.edu

**Courses:** MA TESOL, MIP TESOL, w/Peace Corps., MAT in ESOL

## University of Arizona
Tucson, AZ 85721
**Tel:** (520) 621-2211
**Website:** www.arizona.edu
**Courses:** MA ESL

## Arizona State University
University Drive and Mill Avenue, Tempe, AZ 85287
**Tel:** (480) 965-9011
**Website:** www.asu.edu/
**Email:** information@asu.edu
**Courses:** MA TESL

## Azusa Pacific University
901 E. Alosta Ave.Azusa, CA 91702
**Tel:** (626) 969-3434
**Website:** www.apu.edu/
**Courses:** MA TESOL

## Ball State University
Muncie, IN 47306.
**Tel:** 1-800-482-4278.
**Website:** www.bsu.edu/
**Email:** ASKUS@bsu.edu.
**Courses:** MA in TESOL

## Biola University
13800 Biola Avenue, La Mirada, California 90639-0001
**Tel:** 1-800-OK-BIOLA 562-903-4752
**Website:** www.biola.edu/
**Courses:** MA TESOL

## Boston University
121 Bay State Road Boston, MA 02215
**Website:** www.bu.edu/
**Courses:** Med TESOL

## Bowling Green State University
Bowling Green, OH 43402
**Website:** www.bgsu.edu/
**Courses:** MATESL programme

## Brigham Young University
Provo, Utah 84602
**Tel:** (801) 378-INFO or (801) 378-4636
**Website:** www.byu.edu

**Courses:** TESOL MA

## University of California
One Shields Avenue, Davis, CA 95616
**Tel:** (530) 752-1011
**Website:** www.ucdavis.edu/
**Courses:** MA with concentration in applied linguistics.

## University of California, LA
405 Hilgard Avenue, Box 951361 Los Angeles, CA, 90095-1361
**Tel:** (310) 825-4321
**Website:** www.ucla.edu/
**Courses:** MA Applied Linguistics & TESL
**Course length:** 2 years full-time

## Cal. State Univ, Dominguez Hills
1000 E. Victoria Street, Carson, California 90747
**Tel:** (310) 243-3696
**Website:** www.csudh.edu/
**Courses:** MA English with TESL

## Cal. State Univ, Fresno
5241 N. Maple Avenue, Fresno, CA 93740-8027
**Tel:** (559) 278-4240
**Website:** www.csufresno.edu/
**Email:** webmaster@csufresno.edu
**Courses:** MA Linguistics/ESL Emphasis

## Cal. State Univ, Fullerton
P.O. Box 34080 Fullerton, CA 92834
**Tel:** (714) 278-2011
**Website:** www.fullerton.edu/
**Courses:** MS Education with TESOL
**Course length:** 30 semester units, full or part-time

## Cal. State Univ, Hayward
25800 Carlos Bee Blvd, Hayward, CA 94542
**Tel:** (510) 885-3000
**Website:** www.csuhayward.edu/
**Courses:** MA English – TESOL option.
**Course length:** 6 quarters, full or PT
Aid Availability: Grants and fellowships

## Cal. State Univ, Los Angeles
5151 State University Drive, Los Angeles, California 90032-4226
**Tel:** (323) 343-3000
**Website:** www.calstatela.edu/
**Courses:** MA TESOL
**Course length:** 45 quarter units, full or part-time

Aid Availability: Scholarships, assistantships, fee waivers
**Other:** Practical teacher-training programme. Also offered in Buenos Aires, Argentina.

### Cal. State Univ, Northridge
18111 Nordhoff Street, Northridge, California 91330
**Tel:** (818) 677-1200
**Website:** www.csun.edu/
**Courses:** MA Linguistics with TESOL

### Cal. State Univ, Sacramento
6000 J Street, Sacramento, CA 95819.
**Tel:** (916) 278-6011
**Website:** www.csus.edu/
**Courses:** MA TESOL
**Other**: Pedagogical focus. Joint programme with the Peace Corps is offered.

### Cardinal Stritch University
6801 N. Yates Rd., Milwaukee, WI 53217-3985.
**Tel:** (414) 410-4000
**Website:** www.stritch.edu/
**Courses:** MEd Professional Development with ESL

### Carson-Newman University
Jefferson City, TN, 37760.
**Tel:** (865) 475-9061
**Fax:** (865) 471-3502
**Website:** www.cn.edu/
**Courses:** MAT-ESL
**Course length:** 12-18 mths

### Central Connecticut St. University
1615 Stanley St., New Britain, CT 06050
**Tel:** 1-860-832-CCSU
**Website:** www.ccsu.edu/
**Courses:** M.S. in TESOL; Certification in TESOL.

### Central Michigan University
Mount Pleasant, Michigan 48859
**Tel:** (517) 774-4000
**Website:** www.cmich.edu/
**Courses:** MA TESOL
**Other**: Teaching practice at university language centre.

### Central Missouri State Universtiy
Department of Linguistics
P.O. Box 800, Warrensburg MO 64093
**Tel:** 1-800-SAY-CMSU (1-800-729-2678)

**Website:** www.cmsu.edu
**Courses:** MA-TESL, MA TESL

### Central Washington University
400 E. 8th Avenue, Ellensburg, WA 98926
**Tel:** (509) 963-1211
**Website:** www.cwu.edu/
**Courses:** MA English with TESL/TEFL

### University of Cincinnati
2624 Clifton Avenue, Cincinnati, OH 45221
**Tel:** (513) 556-6000
**Website:** www.uc.edu
**Courses:** MEd Literacy Education with TESL

### University of Colorado, Boulder
Boulder, CO 80309
**Tel:** (303) 492-1411
**Website:** www.colorado.edu
**Courses:** MA Linguistics
**Other**: Primarily an MA in linguistics with some TESL options.

### University of Colorado, Denver
P.O. Box 173364, Denver, CO 80217-3364
**Tel:** 303-556-2400
**Website:** www.cudenver.edu/
**Courses:** MA English/Applied Linguistics (ESL)
**Other**: Teaching practice available at the program's campuses in Beijing and Moscow.

### Colorado State University
Fort Collins, CO 80523
**Tel:** (970) 491-1101
**Website:** www.colostate.edu/
**Courses:** MA TESL

### Colombia Intl. University
**Website:** www.columbia.edu/
**Courses:** MA TEFL/Intercultural Studies

### University of Delaware
Newark, DE 19716
**Tel:** (302) 831-2000
**Website:** www.udel.edu/
**Courses:** MA ESL
**Other**: Teaching practice locally in ESL and bilingual classes, and option of teaching in Panama.

**East Carolina University**
East Fifth Street, Greenville, NC 27858-4353
**Tel:** (252) 328-6131
**Website:** www.ecu.edu/
**Courses:** MA English with TESL

**Eastern College**
521 Lancaster Avenue, Richmond, KY, 40475
**Tel:** (859) 622-1000
**Website:** www.eku.edu/
**Courses:** MA Multicultural Education.
**Other**: Strong spiritual emphasis.

**Eastern Mennonite University**
1200 Park Road, Harrisonburg, VA 22802-2462
**Tel:** (540) 432-4000
**Fax**: (540) 432-4444
**Website:** www.emu.edu/
**Courses:** MA Education, minor in TESL

**Eastern Michigan University**
Ypsilanti, MI, USA 48197
**Tel:** (734) 487-1849
**Website:** www.emich.edu/
**Courses:** MA in TESOL, Graduate Certificate in
TESL/Summer 2 Summer, Undergrad minor in
TESOL, K-12 Endorsement in TESL.

**Evergreen State College, WA**
2700 Evergreen Parkway NW, Olympia, WA 98505
**Tel:** (360) 866-6000
**Website:** www.evergreen.edu/
**Courses:** MA Teaching w/ Bilingual Education and
TESL.

**Fairfield University**
1073 North Benson Road, Fairfield, CT 06430
**Tel:** (203) 254-4000
**Website:** www.fairfield.edu/
**Courses:** MA TESOL

**Fairleigh Dickinson University**
Florham-Madison Campus, 285 Madison Avenue,
Madison, NJ 07940
**Tel:** (973) 443-8500
**Courses:** MAT ESL

**University of Findlay**
1000 North Main Street, Findlay, OH 45840-3695
**Tel:** (800) 472-9502  or (419) 422-8313

**Website:** www.findlay.edu/
**Courses:** MA TESOL and Bilingual Education

**Florida Atlantic University**
**Tel:** 1-800-299-4FAU
**Website:** www.fau.edu/about/campuses/
**Email:** admisweb@fau.edu
**Courses:** Master's In Curriculum and Instruction with
ESOL.

**Florida International University**
University Park Campus
11200 S.W. Eighth Street, Miami, FL 33199
**Tel:** 305-348-2000
**Website:** www.fiu.edu/
**Courses:** M.Sc TESOL.

**Florida State University**
Tallahassee, FL 32306
**Tel:** 850-644-2525.
**Website:** www.fsu.edu/
**Courses:** Multilingual/Multicultural Education

**Fordham University**
New York City
**Website:** www.fordham.edu/
**Courses:** MS Education.

**Fresno Pacific University**
**Tel:** 559-453-2039 Toll-Free: 1-800-660-6089
**Fax**: 559-453-2007
**Website:** www.fresno.edu/
**Email:** ugadmis@fresno.edu
**Courses:** TESOL M.A. and TESOL Certificate

**Georgetown University**
37th and O Street NW, Washington DC 20057
**Tel:**  (202) 687-0100
**Website:** www.georgetown.edu/
**Courses:** MAT TESL

**Grand Canyon University**
3300 West Camelback Road, Phoenix, AZ 85017
**Tel:** 1-800-800-9776
**Courses:** MA with TESL major

**University of Hawaii, Manoa**
2444 Dole Street, Honolulu, HI 96822
**Tel:** (808) 956-8111
**Website:** www.uhm.hawaii.edu/

**Courses:** MA ESL
**Other**: The first and largest Department of ESL at a US university.

## Hofstra University
Hempstead, NY 11549-1000
**Tel:** 1-800-HOFSTRA
**Website:** www.hofstra.edu/
**Courses:** MS Education: TESL, MEd TESL

## University of Houston
4800 Calhoun Rd, Houston, Texas 77204
**Tel:** (713) 743-2255
**Website:** www.uh.edu/
**Courses:** MA Applied English Linguistics

## University of Houston, Clear Lake
2700 Bay Area Blvd, Houston, TX 77058
**Tel:** (281) 283-7600
**Website:** www.cl.uh.edu/
**Courses:** MS Multicultural Studies with ESL endorsement

## Hunter College, City Univ, NY
**Website:** www.hunter.cuny.edu/
**Courses:** MA Education (TESOL)

## Univ. Illinois, Urbana-Champaign
1401 West Green Street, Urbana, IL 61801
**Tel:** ( 217) 333-1000
**Website:** www.uiuc.edu/
**Email:**iuforum@uiuc.edu
**Courses:** MA TESL

## Illinois State University
**Website:** www.uillinois.edu/
**Courses:** MA Writing with TESOL
**Other**: Can lead to an Illinois credential in TESOL. Teaching internships and jobs on offer in Korea and Thailand.

## Indiana State University
Terre Haute, IN 47809
**Tel:** (812) 237-6311
**Website:** www-isu.indstate.edu/
**Courses:** MA English with Applied Linguistics
**Other**: Exchange programmes with institutions in China and Japan.

## Indiana University
107 S. Indiana Ave, Bloomington, IN 47405-7000
**Tel:** (812) 855 4848
**Website:** www.indiana.edu/
**Courses:** MA Applied Linguistics with TESOL

## Indiana Univ. Of Pennsylvania
Indiana, PA 15705-0001.
**Tel:** (724) 357-2100.
**Website:** www.iup.edu/
**Courses:** MA English (TESOL)

## University of Iowa
107 Calvin Hall, Iowa City, Iowa 52242
**Tel:** 1-800-553-IOWA
**Courses:** MA Linguistics with TESL

## University of Kansas
Lawrence, KS 66045
**Tel:** 785/864-2700
**Website:** www.ukans.edu/
**Courses:** MA TESL

## Long Island University
700 Northern Boulevard, Brookville, New York 11548-1326
**Website:** www.liu.edu/
**Courses:** MS Education with TESL
**Course length:** 3 semesters, full or p/t

## Univ. of Maryland, Balt. County
1000 Hilltop Circle, Baltimore, MD 21250
**Tel:** (410) 455-1000
**Website:** www.umbc.edu/
**Courses:** MA ESOL/Bilingual Instructional Systems Development (w/ K-12 cert)

## Univ. of Maryland, College Park
College Park, MD 20742
**Tel:** (301) 405-1000
**Website:** www.umcp.umd.edu/
**Courses:** MEd TESOL

## Marymount University
2807 N. Glebe Road, Arlington, VA, 22207-4299
**Tel:** 703-522-5600 or 800-548-7638
**Website:** www.marymount.edu/
**Courses:** MEd ESL

**Univ. Massachusetts, Amherst**
Massachusetts, 01003.
**Tel:** (413) 545-0111
**Website:** www.umass.edu/
**Courses:** MEd with ESL

**Univ. Massachusetts, Boston**
100 Morrissey Boulevard, Boston, Ma 02125-3393
**Tel:** 617-287-5000
**Website:** www.umb.edu/
**Courses:** MA Bilingual or ESL Studies

**University of Memphis**
Office of Admissions, 229 Administration building,
Memphis, TN 38152-3370
**Tel:** 901 678-2169 or 800-669-2678
**Website:** www.memphis.edu/
**Courses:** MA English with ESL
**Other**: Summer programme in Czech Republic and
internships in China.

**Meredith College**
3800 Hillsborough Street, Raleigh, NC, 27607-5298
**Tel:** 919-760-8600  Fax: 919-760-2828
**Website:** www.meredith.edu/
**Courses:** MEd with ESL

**Michigan State University**
East Lansing, Michigan
**Tel:** 517-355-1855
**Website:** www.msu.edu/
**Courses:** MA TESOL

**University of Montana**
**Website:** www.umt.edu/
**Courses:** MA in TESOL

**Montclair University**
1 Normal Avenue, Upper Montclair, N.J. 07043
**Tel:** (973) 655-4000
**Website:** www.montclair.edu/
**Courses:** MA Applied Linguistics with TESL

**Monterey Int. Of Intl. Studies**
425 Van Buren Street, Monterey, CA 93940
**Tel:** (831) 647-4100
**Fax**: (831) 647-4199
**Website:** www.miis.edu/
**Courses:** MA in TESOL, MA in TFL (Teaching
Foreign Language), Peace Corps Masters' International

**Mount Vernon College**
800 Martinsburg Road, Mount Vernon, Ohio 43050
**Tel:**  (740) 397-9000 or (800) 782-2435
**Website:** www.mvnc.edu/
**Courses:** MA TESOL

**National-Louis University**
Chicago Campus, 122 S. Michigan Avenue, Chicago, IL
60603
**Tel:** 800-443-5522 (x 5151)
**Website:** www.nl.edu/
**Courses:** MEd with ESL

**University of Nevada, Reno**
Reno, Nevada  89557
**Tel:**  (775) 784-1110
**Website:** www.unr.edu/
**Courses:** M.A. in TESOL

**University of New Hampshire**
Durham, NH 03824
**Website:** www.unh.edu/
**Courses:** MA in English Language and Linguistics (with
ESL specialization), MAT w/TESL

**University of New Mexico**
Albuquerque, NM 87131
**Tel:** (505) 277-0111
**Website: www.unm.edu/**
**Courses:** MA Education with TESOL

**New Mexico State University**
Las Cruces, NM 88003-8001
**Tel:** 505-646-0111
**Website:** www.nmsu.edu/
**Courses:** MA Curriculum & Instruction with TESOL
**Other**: Teaching practice in Mexico

**College of New Rochelle, NY**
**Website:** http://cnr.edu/
**Courses:** MS TESOL

**New York State Univ., Albany**
1400 Washington Avenue, Albany, NY 12222
**Tel:** (518) 442-3300
**Website:** www.albany.edu/
**Courses:** MA TESOL

**New York State Univ., Buffalo**
15 Capen Hall, Buffalo, NY 14260-1660

**Tel:** 1-888-UB-ADMIT or (716) 645-6900
**Website:** www.buffalo.edu/
**Courses:** MEd TESOL

**New York State Univ., Stony Brook**
Stony Brook, NY 11794
**Website:** www.sunysb.edu/
**Courses:** MA TESOL

**New York University**
70 Washington Square South, New York, NY 10012
**Tel:** (212) 998-1212
**Website:** www.nyu.edu/
**Courses:** MA TESOL

**Univ. Of North Carolina, Charlotte**
9201 University City Blvd, Charlotte, NC 28223-0001
**Tel:** (704) 687-2000
**Website:** www.uncc.edu/
**Courses:** MEd

**University of North Texas**
PO Box 311277, Denton, TX 76203
**Tel:** (940) 565-2000 or (800) 735-2989
**Website:** www.unt.edu/
**Courses:** MA English with ESL

**Northeastern Illinois University**
5500 North St. Louis Avenue, Chicago, Illinois
**Tel:** 60625-4699, 773/583-4050
**Website:** www.neiu.edu/
**Courses:** MA Linguistics with TESL

**Northern Arizona University**
**Tel:** 1-888-MORE-NAU
**Website:** www.nau.edu/
**Courses:** MA TESL
**Programme length:** 4 semesters, full or p/t

**Northern Illinois University**
DeKalb, IL 60115
**Tel:** (815) 753-1000
**Website:** www.niu.edu/
**Courses:** MA English with TESOL
**Other**: Teaching opportunities in China.

**Northern Iowa University**
1227 West 27th Street, Cedar Falls, IA 50614
**Tel:** (319) 273-2311
**Website:** www.uni.edu/

**Courses:** MA TESOL
**Other**: International programme with internships in
Moscow and St. Petersburg, Russia.

**Notre Dame College**
1500 Ralston Avenue, Belmont, California
94002-1997
**Tel:** (650) 593-1601
**Fax**: (650) 508-3660
**Website:** www.cnd.edu/
**Courses:** MEd TESL

**Nova Southeastern University**
3301 College Avenue, Fort Lauderdale, Florida 33314
**Tel:** 800-541-6682
**Courses:** MS Education with TESOL

**Ohio State University**
Columbus, Ohio 43210
**Tel:** 614-292-OHIO
**Website:** www.ohio-state.edu/
**Courses:** MA TESOL

**Ohio University**
Department of Linguistics, Gordy Hall 383, Athens,
OH 45701-2979
**Tel:** (740) 593-4564
**Fax**: (740) 593-2967
**Website:** www.ohiou.edu/
**Email:** lingdept@ohio.edu
**Courses:** MA Applied Linguistics and TESOL

**Oklahoma State University**
Office of Academic Affairs, 101 Whitehurst,
Stillwater, OK 74078
**Tel:**(405) 744-5627
**Fax:** (405) 744-5495
**Website:** http://osu.okstate.edu/
**Courses:** MA English with TESL
**Programme length:** 4 semesters, full or p/t

**University of Oregon**
Eugene, OR 97403
**Tel:** (541) 346-1000
**Website:** www.uoregon.edu/
**Courses:** MA in Linguistics with concentration in
Applied Linguistics/SLA

**Our Lady of the Lake Univ., S.A.**
411 S.W. 24th Street, San Antonio, TX 78207-4689
**Tel:** 800-436-OLLU

**Website:** www.ollusa.edu/
**Courses:** MEd with ESL

**University of Pennsylvania**
3451 Walnut, Philadelphia PA 19104
**Tel:** 215-898-5000
**Website:** www.upenn.edu/
**Courses:** MSEd TESOL

**Pennsylvania State University**
201 Shields Building, Box 3000 , University Park, PA 16804-3000
**Tel:** (814) 865-5471
**Website:** www.psu.edu/
**Courses:** MA TESL

**University of Pittsburgh**
Pittsburgh, PA 15260
**Tel:** (412) 624-4141
**Website:** www.pitt.edu/
**Courses:** MA Linguistics with TESOL certificate

**Portland State University**
PO Box 751, Portland, Oregon 97207
**Tel:** (503) 725-3000
**Website:** www.pdx.edu/
**Courses:** MA TESOL

**University of Puerto Rico**
PO Box 364984, San Juan, PR  00936-4984
**Tel:** (787) 250-0000
**Website:** www.upr.clu.edu/
**Courses:** BA in TESS, MEd. in TESL,and ED.D. in Curriculum and Teaching in TESL

**Queen's College of City Univ, N.Y.**
65-30 Kissena Blvd,.Flushing, New York 11367
**Tel:**  (718) 997-5000
**Website:** www.qc.edu/
**Courses:** MA applied Linguistics, MS Education with TESOL

**Radford University**
East Norwood St., Radford, Va. 24142
**Tel:** 540- 831-5000
**Website:** www.runet.edu/
**Courses:** MS Education with curriculum/instruction and TESL

**Rhode Island College**
600 Mount Pleasant, Providence, RI 02908-1991
**Tel:** (401) 456-8000
**Website:** www.ric.edu/
**Courses:** MEd TESL

**Rhode Island University**
Kingston, RI 02881
**Tel:** 401-874-1000
**Website:** www.uri.edu/
**Courses:** MA TESL

**University of Rochester**
Rochester, New York 14627
**Tel:** (716) 275-2121
**Website:** www.rochester.edu/
**Courses:** MS TESOL

**State Michael's College**
1 Winooski Park, Colchester, VT 05439
**Tel:** 802-654-2000
**Website:** www.smcvt.edu/
**Courses:** MA TESL/TEFL

**Sam Houston State University**
1803 Ave I, Huntsville, TX 77341
**Tel:** (936) 294-1111
**Website:** www.shsu.edu/
**Courses:** MEd with Bilingual Education

**University of San Francisco**
2130 Fulton Street, San Francisco, CA 94117
**Tel:** 415-422-5555
**Website:** www.usfca.edu/
**Courses:** MA TESL

**San Francisco State University**
1600 Holloway Avenue, San Francisco, CA 94132
**Website:** www.sfsu.edu/
**Courses:** MA English with TESOL

**San Jose State University**
One Washington Square, San José, CA 95192
**Tel:** 408-924-1000
**Website:** www.sjsu.edu/
**Courses:** M.A. TESOL

**College of Santa Fe**
1600 St. Michael's Drive, Santa Fe NM 87505
**Tel:** 800-456-2673  or 505-473-6011

**Website:** www.csf.edu/
**Courses:** MA with TESL (focus on at-risk youth)

## School for International Training
Kipling Road, P.O. Box 676, Brattleboro, Vermont
05302-0676
**Tel:** (802) 257-7751
**Fax**: (802) 258-3248
**Website:** www.sit.edu/
**Email:** info@sit.edu
**Courses:** Master of Arts in Teaching (TESOL, French,
Spanish), U.S. Public School Certification option,
Bilingual-Multicultural Education Endorsement option,
also Master International programme with US Peace
Corps option., Master of Arts in Teaching
Concentrations : English to Speakers of Other
Languages (ESOL), Spanish, French
Further options available in the Academic Year MAT
Program: Vermont State Certification and
Bilingual-Multicultural Education Endorsement

## Seattle University
900 Broadway, Seattle WA 98122-4340
**Tel:** (206) 296-6000
**Website:** www.seattleu.edu/
**Courses:** MA/MEd TESOL
**Other**: Focus on teaching the adult learner

## Seattle Pacific University
3307 Third Avenue West, Seattle, WA 98119-1997
**Tel:** (206) 281-2000
**Website:** www.spu.edu/
**Courses:** MA TESOL

## Seton Hall University
400 South Orange Avenue, South Orange, New Jersey
07079
**Tel:** (973) 761-9000
**Website:** www.shu.edu/
**Courses:** MA ESL

## Shenandoah University
1460 University Drive, Winchester, VA 22601
**Tel:** 800-432-2266
**Website:** www.su.edu/
**Courses:** MSEd TESOL

## Simmons College
300 The Fenway, Boston, Massachusetts, 02115-5898
**Tel:** 617-521-2000 or 800-345-8468
**Fax**: 617-521-3190

**Website:** www.simmons.edu/
**Courses:** MATESL

## Soka University
California campus, 26800 West Mulholland Hwy,
Calabasas, California 91302
**Tel:** (818) 880-6400
**Fax**: (818) 880-9326
**Courses:** MA Second/Foreign Language Education
with TESOL
**Other**: Internships and post-graduation working
opportunities at affiliating university and high schools
in Japan.

## University of South Carolina
Columbia, South Carolina, 29208
**Tel:** (803) 777-7000
**Website:** www.sc.edu/
**Courses:** MA Linguistics

## University of South Florida
**Tel:** (813) 974-3350 or 1-877-USF-BULL
**Website:** www.usf.edu/
**Courses:** MA Applied Linguistics

## Southeast Missouri State Univ.
One University Plaza, Cape Girardeau, MO 63701
**Website:** www.semo.edu/
**Courses:** MA TESOL

## Southern Illinois Univ., Carbondale
Carbondale, Illinois 62901
**Tel:** 618.453.4381
**Website:** www.siuc.edu/
**Courses:** MA TESOL

## University of Southern Maine
P.O. Box 9300, Portland, ME 04104-9300,
**Tel:** (207) 780-4141 or 1-800-800-4USM
**Website:** www.usm.maine.edu/
**Courses:** MSEd Literacy Education with ESL

## University of Southern Mississippi
Multiple Campuses
**Website:** www.usm.edu/
**Courses:** MA Teaching of Languages (TESOL)

## Syracuse University
Syracuse, NY 13244
**Tel:** (315) 443-1870

**Website:** www.syr.edu/
**Courses:** MA Linguistics with ESL

**Teachers College, Columbia Univ.**
525 West 120th St. New York, 10027
**Tel:** 212-678-3000
**Website:** www.tc.columbia.edu/
**Courses:** MA TESOL

**Temple University**
1801 North Broad Street, Philadelphia, PA 19122
**Tel:** 215-204-7000
**Website:** www.temple.edu/
**Courses:** EdM TESOL, MEd TESOL

**University of Texas, Arlington**
701 South Nedderman Drive, Arlington, TX 76019
**Tel:** (817) 272-2222
**Website:** www.uta.edu/
**Courses:** MA Linguistics with TESOL

**University of Texas, Austin**
University of Texas at Austin, Austin, Texas 78712
**Tel:** (512) 475-7348.
**Website:** www.utexas.edu/
**Courses:** MA Foreign Language Education with TESL/TEFL

**University of Texas, El Paso**
500 West University Avenue, El Paso, Texas 79968
**Website:** www.utep.edu/
**Courses:** MA Linguistics with Applied or Hispanic Linguistics

**University of Texas, Pan American**
**Website:** www.panam.edu/
**Courses:** MA ESL

**University of Texas, San Antonio**
6900 N. Loop 1604 West, San Antonio, TX 78249
**Tel:** 210-458-4011
**Website:** www.utsa.edu/
**Courses:** MA with ESL
**Programme length:** 3-4 semesters, full or p/t

**Texas Tech University**
**Website:** www.ttu.edu/
**Courses:** MA Applied Linguistics
**Programme length:** 4 semesters, full or p/t

**Texas Woman's University**
304 Administration Dr., Denton, TX 76201
**Tel:** (940)TWU-2000
**Website:** www.twu.edu/
**Courses:** MEd with ESL
**Programme length:** 2 years, full or p/t

**University of Toledo**
Toledo, Ohio 43606-3390
**Tel:** (419) 530-4242
**Website:** www.utoledo.edu/
**Courses:** MA-Ed. in ESL; MA in English with Concentration in ESL (these are two different degrees; both are offered)

**U.S. International University**
Admissions Office, 10455 Pomerado Road, San Diego, CA 92131
**Website:** www.usiu.edu/
**Courses:** MEd with TESOL

**University of Utah**
Salt Lake City, UT 84112
**Tel:** (801) 581-7200
**Website:** www.utah.edu/
**Courses:** MA Bilingual Education

**University of Washington**
**Website:** www.washington.edu/
**Courses:** MA TESL

**Washington State Univ., Vancouver**
Vancouver, Canada
**Website:** www.vancouver.wsu.edu/
**Courses:** Master of Education programme with ESL Endorsement (K-12 emphasis)

**West Chester University**
West Chester, PA 19383
**Tel:** (610) 436-1000
**Website:** www.wcupa.edu/
**Courses:** Master's & Certificate in TESL (Teaching English as a Second Language)

**West Virginia University**
Morgantown, WV 26506
**Tel:** (304) 293-0111
**Website:** www.wvu.edu/
**Courses:** Master of Arts in Foreign Languages (TESOL area of emphasis)

## Western Kentucky University
1 Big Red Way, Bowling Green, KY 42101-3576
**Tel:** (270) 745-0111.
**Website:** www.wku.edu/
**Courses:** MA English with TESL

## Wheaton College
501 College Avenue, Wheaton, IL 60187
**Tel:** (630) 752-5000
**Website:** www.wheaton.edu/
**Courses:** MA Intercultural Studies with TESL
**Other**: Leads to an Illinois State credential in TESOL.
Teaching practice may be undertaken locally or at
universities in Russia, China, Korea or Romania.

## Wichita State University
1845 Fairmount, Wichita, Kansas, 67260.
**Website:** www.wichita.edu/
**Courses:** MA Curriculum and Instruction with TESOL
**Other**: Leads to Kansas State endorsement in TESOL.
Opportunities for fieldwork in Mexico and Cyprus.

## William Paterson University
300 Pompton Road, Wayne, NJ 07470
**Tel:** (973) 720-2000
**Website:** www.wpunj.edu/

**Courses:** MEd. in Education with a concentration in
Bilingual/ESL

## Wright State University
3640 Colonel Glenn Highway, Dayton, Ohio
45435-0001
**Tel:** (937) 775-3333
**Website:** www.wright.edu/
**Courses:** Undergraduate or graduate TESOL
certificate. Undergraduate BA in English – emphasis in
TESOL, MA in TESOL, Graduate endorsement in
TESOL

## Youngstown State University
One University Plaza, Youngstown, OH 44555
**Tel:**  877-GO-TO-YSU (877-468-6978)
**Website:** www.ysu.edu/
Courses: M.A. English, TESOL concentration

## VENEZUELA

## Universidad Central de Venezuela
Facultad de Humanidades y Educación, Ciudad
Universitaria, Los Chaguaramus, Caracas, 1050.
**Programmes:** M.A. Degree in TEFL.

# Learning to teach with CALL

Computer technology is now playing an increasingly influential role in education. Language education has been no exception to this trend and in recent years growing numbers of teachers are undertaking graduate level courses in the field of CALL. Mark Peterson examines the choices and courses for Computer Assisted Language Learning teaching qualifications

In the first part of this article, I will identify the major factors that teachers must consider before embarking on such a course of study. In the second part, a number of CALL courses in various countries will be examined in order to assist teachers in the task of selecting a course suitable to their needs and future career goals.

The number of CALL focused training programmes has increased rapidly in recent years. In contrast to a few years ago, teachers considering entering a CALL course are faced with a larger number of possible options. However before embarking on a course potential applicants should consider the following questions:

If your goal is to improve your knowledge of computer technology, ESL pedagogy and make you a better teacher then a CALL course may be for you. If you think that graduating from such a course will make you more marketable you may be disappointed. While it is certainly true that the demand for computer literate language teachers is increasing, the number of posts is limited. Moreover the financial returns from undertaking what is a demanding course of study may not justify for some, the high costs of such a programme.

Most Masters degree programmes in CALL will usually require applicants to hold a first degree and some previous teaching experience in the language teaching field. However there are exceptions and negotiation over entry requirements may be possible in some cases.

To many mid-career teachers or those with circumstances that make undertaking a residential based MA impossible, distance learning may be a possibility. However candidates should first ensure that any distance based course is accredited internationally. British universities appear to be taking the lead in this area of course provision; distance based MA's have been common in the UK for many years. However it is fair to say that suspicion regarding the validity of distance based degrees remains in some conservative quarters of academe.

Graduate programmes are expensive and CALL courses are no exception to this trend. Potential applicants should compare and contrast course fees and the cost of living in North America with the UK and Australia. Potential applicants should also note that the level of course fee is often determined by an applicant's nationality and residency status. For example, a British applicant for a Master degree resident in the UK usually qualifies for reduced rate "home" fees, while applicants from overseas are usually required to pay a higher "overseas" fee.

Various sources of financial help are available including competitive bursaries, home government support and grants from private charitable institutions.

Masters degrees generally take two years to complete. But in some cases it is certainly possible to finish in a shorter period of time. Burn out may be a factor in many accelerated MA programmes. Full time doctoral degrees generally take three or more years to complete. Part time doctoral degrees may take several years.

There is a great deal of variety in course content within CALL postgraduate degree programmes. In the author's view, a CALL degree should include a through grounding in applied linguistics, instructional design and practical computer skills. These skills should include the use of software tools and authoring packages. Other relevant areas of study would be hypermedia design; concordancing and computer mediated communication (CMC).

Any potential applicant to a masters programme would do well to find out as much as possible about the faculty who will teach them. CALL experts of long experience are still relatively rare so it pays to take the time to check if the faculty in your programme have the appropriate backgrounds in educational technology and applied linguistics.

Potential students with little or no background in computers may expect to experience a degree of technostress in the initial stages of the course. This may be alleviated to some degree, if applicants already possess basic computer skills including familiarity with the more popular word processing, email and web browser software. Being prepared may make the course more enjoyable and beneficial in the long term.

Assessment methods vary between degree programmes, but in most cases assessment is based on course work and examinations.

In the US most CALL based degrees are given the degree classification of MA whereas in the UK by contrast, many CALL degrees are classed as M.Sc. or M.Ed.

Although the job market in EFL is growing, finding a suitable post where CALL skills can be fully utilized isn't easy. One motivation for those taking CALL courses is that they provide transferable skills. Many graduates of CALL programmes have launched alternative careers in areas such as web design, instructional technology and software consultancy.

Embarking on an advanced degree is a major undertaking in terms of time and money. Selecting an appropriate course depends largely on an individuals needs and circumstances.

While obtaining a Master's degree in the CALL field does not guarantee employment, it does provide opportunities in what is an expanding and increasingly important area of language education.

*Mark Peterson holds an M.Sc. degree in TESOL and CALL and is currently a faculty member at Japan Advanced Institute of Science and Technology.*

# CALL courses

## M.Sc. in CALL and TESOL
### University of Stirling, Scotland
www.stir.ac.uk/celt/courses/MSC.HTM#CALL

This course was established in 1993 by John Higgins, one of the founders of CALL as a distinct discipline, and was the first CALL postgraduate programme to be launched in the UK. The programme combines a solid grounding in applied linguistics with the essential elements in CALL theory and methodology.

The M.Sc. may be completed in one year and is made up of the following components: Autumn Semester, Teaching of skills or Second Language, Acquisition, Syntax and Grammar, Classroom Observation (for those with no ELT experience), Introduction to CALL concepts and materials, CALL and communications. In addition to the above requirements, students must also complete a 12,000 to 15,000 word dissertation on an aspect of CALL research. A research based Ph.D. degree in CALL is also available at the same institution.

## M.Ed. (Master of education) course in educational technology and ELT
### University of Manchester
Centre for English Language Studies in Education
www. man.ac.uk/CELSE/centre/techELT.htm

This course is offered in two modes. Fully distance learning based or through a combination of distance learning and summer attendance. In order to graduate students are required to undertake a total of six course modules, three of which must be in the area of educational technology. In addition, students are required to submit a dissertation of between 12,000 and 20,000 words on a research topic of their choice.

## MA in Media Technology for Teaching English as a Foreign Language
### University of Newcastle upon Tyne
www.ncl.ac.uk/langcen/postgrad/media.html

This course provides students with a grounding in language teaching methodology, computer assisted language learning, video in ELT and media centre management. This course may be completed in 12 months of full-time study. Assessment is by course work.

## MA in Computer Assisted Language Learning
### University of Melbourne, Australia
www.hlc.unimelb.edu.au/callmast_ arts.htm

The above programme takes the form of a research based Masters degree. In order to graduate a candidate must submit a 30,000 word CALL based thesis by research. It may be undertaken on a full time or part-time basis. The University of Queensland Australia runs a Master's degree programme in applied linguistics, computers, technology and language learning (www.cltr.uq. edu.au/mactll.html). This programme is composed of the following courses: Structure of Language, Applied Linguistics and Language Teaching, Second Language Acquisition, Second Language Research, Second Language Teaching, Literacy or Issues in Language programme

Development, Portfolio and Synthesis, Principles of Computer-Enhanced Language Learning. This programme can be completed over 3 semesters full time or 6 semesters part time.

## MA in applied linguistics (includes a major CALL element)
### University of Waikato New Zealand
Department of General and Applied Linguistics

www.waikato.ac.nz/ling/

Some of the courses in this degree programme may be undertaken through distance learning. M.Phil. and Ph.D. courses in CALL are also available.

## MA in TESOL with a CALL specialization
### Iowa State University
www.engl.iastate.edu/tesling/ma.html

This programme is designed for those seeking training as a CALL specialist in an ESL programme. Core course requirements include the study of the following subjects: Sociolinguistics, Grammatical Analysis, Second Language Acquisition Methods for Teaching ESL, Second Language Testing Practicum in Teaching ESL or Seminar in Teaching English Composition, Computer Assisted Language Learning Instructional Technology.

In order to graduate, MA candidates must submit a research-based thesis. The University of South Florida runs a Ph.D. programme in interdisciplinary education (www.coedu.usf.edu/deptseced/forlanged/phdbro.html) with an emphasis on SLA and instructional technology. Core elements of this programme include courses in the areas of applied linguistics and SLA. In addition courses are available in the areas of educational technology described below: Authoring Systems and Languages, Programming Languages for Education, Applications for Computers as Educational Tools, Instructional Design for Computers, Interactive Media and Interactive Video, Telecommunications, Sound Processing and Animation. Candidates are also required to complete a dissertation. The State University of New York at Stony Brook has established a Doctor of Arts programme in Foreign Language Instruction (http://ccmail.sun- .edu/llrc//llrc3.html). Included in this programme are graduate level courses in educational technology with an emphasis on CALL and language centre management. Students on this course have access to the Language Learning and Research centre at Stony Brook.

## MA in teaching English as foreign language
### Ohio University in Athens Ohio
Department of Linguistics

http://cscwww. cats.ohiou.edu/linguistics/dept/

This degree programme is composed of courses in language teaching theory and methodology, curriculum development and evaluation. A practicum is also provided to give candidates supervised teaching experience.

Five CALL courses are available as part of the above degree programme. Entry requirements include a bachelor's degree with a minimum GPA of 3.0. This course requires two years of full time study.

# Teaching ESP (English for Specific Purposes)

Some EFL teachers find that their career becomes focused on teaching a particular aspect of English language skills geared to help learners in specific situations or jobs. Teachers of ESP (English for Specific Purposes) are usually in high demand, not only in schools in English-speaking countries but all over the world.

Teaching ESP (English for Specific Purposes) can be an interesting and lucrative career development. Much of the world's demand for English comes from the business sector: companies are prepared to pay top rates for training to ensure that their workforce is effective and competitive. In particular, company executives are almost universally required to know Business English, the world's working language. Other common areas of specialization in ESP are English for Law, English for Medical Purposes and English for Tourism. Less well studied in terms of student numbers but equally important areas are English for Engineering, English for Shipping, Aviation English, English for Engineering and English for the Military.

Teaching positions in the ESP require specialized knowledge of the key language used in the field and an understanding of the industries and professions that the language derives from. Some teachers come from a background (legal or medical, for example) that will enable them to tutor in a specialist field without too much trouble. Quite often, teachers with a specialist background like law are able to teach students from their homes. Other teachers find teaching ESP hard going especially when they have little confidence in their own knowledge of the industry or specialization they are teaching in. There are courses available for teachers who do not have experience in a particular field but who do want teach it.

Obtaining a job teaching ESP may require a little lateral thinking on your part. For example, if you'd like to work in the oil industry, why not contact some of the big oil companies and find out what their hiring practices are. If you want to teach English for Military Purposes, contact the relevant branch of the armed forces. Integration of commands within NATO means that the military are always on the lookout for a few good men (and women) to teach English.

Teaching ESP can be a fascinating and rewarding experience. Some ESP teachers have taught classes to oilrig workers on derricks in the Gulf of Siam. Others have worked with Russian cosmonauts in training in closed cities in Siberia. Be aware, however, that many teachers are turned off by the very thought of teaching anything with a commercial aspect. If you want to succeed as an ESP teacher, you must at least display a passing interest in your area of specialization.

# Business English

One of the most important areas of specialization in teaching English as a second or foreign language is Business English. Many students are interested in improving their English skills in the areas of conducting business meetings, making presentations, understanding discussions at formal meetings, reading technical journals, and receiving and interacting effectively with American and other English-speaking business people.

Some schools specialize in teaching Business English as a means of attracting better-paying clients. Teachers working with these classes often find they are dealing with mixed-ability students whose needs may not be all the same. After all, an accountant has to learn a different vocabulary than that required by a sales person. Of course, schools with larger numbers of Business English students can divide classes based on ability and needs. Another factor to be aware of when teaching Business English is that there are very few textbooks and published materials to rely on. Most major publishers feel that it is not worth investing in textbooks for teaching Business English (and ESP in general) because it is too small a market to be profitable. Business English teachers are often forced to create their own materials for use in the classroom using a variety of sources such as professional journal articles and college textbooks.

If you are employed in a corporate environment, remember that you will be expected to dress accordingly. You may find yourself discussing students' progress with managers, directors and human resources personnel so it pays to have a professional appearance and attitude.

There are a number of ESP examinations – mostly for students, but with one or two designed for teacher-training certification (from LCCIB). The following are the main developers of business English examinations:

## Cambridge ESOL (UCLES)

*Business English Certificates (BEC)*
*Certificate in English for International Business and Trade (CEIBT)*
University of Cambridge Local Examinations Syndicate
Syndicate Buildings, 1 Hills Road, Cambridge, CB1 2EU
**Tel**: 01223 553311
**Fax**: 01223 460278 / 553068
**Website**: www.ucles.org.uk

## The Chauncey Group (part of ETS)

*TOEIC (Test of English for International Communication)*
The Chauncey Group
664 Rosedale Road, Princeton, NJ 08540-2218 USA
**Tel**: +1 609.720.6500
**Fax**: +1 609.720.6550
**Email:** info@chauncey.com
**Website**: www.toeic.com

## LCCI Examinations Board

*English for Business (EFB)*
*Spoken English for Industry and Commerce (SEFIC)*
*Written English for Tourism (WEFT)*
*English for the Tourism Industry (EFTI) - Group Award (WEFT + SEFIC)*
*Practical Business English (PBE)*
*English for Commerce (EFC)*
LCCI Examinations Board
Athena House, 112 Station Road, SIDCUP, Kent DA15 7BJ, UK
**Tel**: +44 (0)20 8302 0261
**Fax**: +44 (0)20 8302 4169
**Website:** www.lccieb.com

## Pitman

*English for Business Communications*
*English for Office Skills*
Pitman Qualifications, 1 Giltspur Street, London EC1A 9DD
**Tel**: +44 (0)20 7294 3500
**Fax**: +44 (0)20 7294 2403
**Email:** info@pitmanqualifications.co.uk
**Website:** www.pitmanqualifications.com

# Certificates for Teachers of Business English

There are few specialist certificates for teachers who want to gain a qualification in this specialist field. The standard CELTA, Cert.TESOL or other certificate courses (see chapter 1) include sections on teaching business English, as do diplomas, MAs and Ph.Ds. The main two certificates for teachers are issued by LCCIEB (London Chamber of Commerce and Industry Examinations Board (below).

### LCCIEB: CertTEB (Certificate in Teaching English for Business)

Administered in conjunction with ARELS (www.arels.org.uk), this exam is aimed at teachers with little or no previous experience of teaching business English, and develops the basic practical skills for working in this area.

### FTBE (Further Certificate for Teachers of Business English)

A supplementary qualification for teachers of general English wishing to broaden their skills into teaching business English. The exam aims to develop management skills and understanding of business practice. LCCIEB has a worldwide network of centres.

**LCCI Examinations Board**

International House, Siskin Parkway East, Middlemarch Bus. Park, Coventry, CV3 4PE, UK
**Tel**: 08707 202909
**Fax**: +44 (0)24 76516505
**Website**: www.lccieb.com
**Email**: customerservice@ediplc.com

# English For Academic Purposes

Students whose first language is not English who are planning to study at a college or university where instruction is in English often require specialist help if they are going to succeed on their courses. In particular, these students need to learn how to write about academic subjects including all the relevant conventions of presentation and style that will be expected of them as they submit written work like essays and theses. Students taking EAP (English for Academic Purposes) classes often do so while taking part in an IEP (Intensive English Program) programme at the university they plan to graduate from. Specialist tutors, usually from an academic background themselves, are in demand to teach EAP on these courses. One of the easiest ways to find a position in teaching EAP is to apply through the university that you are studying at or have graduated from although you will probably need to have a Master's degree if your job application is to be considered seriously.

# Young Learners

Another area of teaching ESL/EFL that is becoming increasingly specialized is the teaching of English to young learners. Teachers have realized that approaches to the teaching of a second language to children requires specific training if they are to be successful. Teachers with an interest in this area may want to follow a course in order to qualify as a specialist. There are several certificate courses on offer and a Master's degree in Teaching English to Young Learners is offered on a two-year distance-based programme by the University of York in the UK. Teachers with a specialization in TEYL (Teaching English to Young Learners) are especially welcome in Asian countries like Korea and Japan where the teaching of young learners is considered a priority.

Many schools and colleges offer certificate-level courses that prepare teachers for the discipline of teaching young learners. The best-known international qualifications are the CELTYL (Certificate in ELT for Young Learners) from University of Cambridge ESOL and the Cert.TEYL (Certificate in Teaching English to Young Learners) from Trinity College, London. We list the schools and colleges offering these courses in the section on Certificate courses. These courses are normally taken as an add-on module to a standard CELTA or Cert.TESOL certificate course).

# Cultural Studies

In the U.S., the teaching of ESL can be just one component of an overall programme in "American Culture" or "American Studies." If you have a degree or qualification in sociology, cultural studies or a related field, you may be able to find a job on one of these programmes where both your language teaching skills and your specialist knowledge can be put to good use.

# Studying for a Doctorate

As the English language teaching field becomes more saturated with teachers who hold a Master's degree, many observers predict that doctorates will become a prerequisite for those who want to hold jobs on the top rungs of the professional ladder. Mary Ellen Butler-Pascoe evaluates TESOL doctoral programmes.

While there has been a continuous professional dialogue on various aspects of the TESOL master's programmes, similar attention has not been afforded to TESOL doctoral programmes. This in large part has been a result of the master's degree serving as a terminal degree for most ESL instructors and many directors and teacher trainers. Since the 1960s, when master's degrees in TESOL were rare, the TESOL profession has gained worldwide respect as the discipline continues to define and assert itself in local school districts and institutions of higher education. Master's programmes have proliferated over the past two decades with over 200 now being offered in Canada and the United States alone. Considerably fewer colleges and universities offer doctoral degrees in TESOL or related fields.

What are the characteristics of these doctoral programmes? Where are they located both geographically and institutionally? In what disciplines do they offer degrees? What courses does a typical curriculum include and most importantly in what areas can these programmes better meet the needs of TESOL practitioners? A recent study of these programmes sought to shed light on these questions.

Of the twenty-nine doctorate-granting institutions surveyed, the degree programmes were housed in seventeen different academic departments with the most frequent placement being in the Department of Linguistics, followed by the Departments of English and Education. Eighteen institutions granted Ph.D. degrees and six awarded Ed.D. degrees, indicating the research emphasis of the majority of the programmes. Three institutions provided a choice of either a Ph.D. or Ed.D. and two offered a Doctorate of Arts degree. Within the departments, degrees were granted in a wide range of disciplines with the greatest number in Linguistics followed closely by Education/ Curriculum and Instruction. Only three departments offered a degree major specifically in TESOL though several of the various other degrees offered TESOL/ESL as a concentration option. The standard admissions requirements included a master's degree with acceptable GPAs, letters of recommendation, the Graduate Record Exam (GRE) or in two cases the Miller's Analogy Test (MAT), and the TOEFL for non-native English-speaking applicants. Only two programmes specifically listed teaching experience as a prerequisite for admissions.

For degree completion, twenty-seven of the twenty-nine programmes required comprehensive exams and one required a qualifying paper; nineteen demanded knowledge of a foreign language, and twenty-three required a dissertation/thesis. Only six required practice teaching experience. The length of time for degree completion ranged from two to seven years with an average of 4.02 years of study. Interestingly, 45% of the graduates were non-native English speakers.

While there was a great variety in course nomenclature, for purposes of clarity, similar course titles were grouped together under common headings. Of the twenty-five different course types identified in the curriculum of the various universities, the one most frequently offered was first and/or second Language Acquisition. The second most prominent course was Teaching Methods with over three-fourths of the programmes listing courses specifically in TESOL Methodology/Teaching ESL. Others in the top five headings included Research Methodology focusing on research designs of both quantitative and qualitative methods, Linguistics, and Testing and Assessment.

Heading the list of least frequently provided courses was ESL Administration with only four programmes listing courses in any aspect of programme administration, design, or evaluation. Courses in Language Policy and Planning were similarly scarce, and only eight offered courses in technology media or allowed electives in technology. A typical programme profile incorporating the most common characteristics of all the doctoral programmes would be a Ph.D. degree programme in Linguistics administered by the Department of Linguistics. Students would be predominantly native-English speakers who would be required to have knowledge of a foreign language, pass comprehensive exams, conduct a research study and author a dissertation in order to complete a degree in approximately four years. The curriculum would include courses in second language acquisition and TESOL Methods with no student teaching required.

Fortunately, there are several combinations of location, degree, discipline, concentration, curriculum, and programme requirements from which students may choose a programme. But a review of the current programmes does raise questions as to how well they serve the needs of the ESL practitioners who are teaching in all types of educational settings and directing programmes around the world.

The TESOL profession has conducted a long campaign to establish ESL as a legitimate academic discipline. To this end it has established standards for ESL and teacher training programmes with the latest being the standards for the Intensive English Programmes. To a large extent the profession has overcome the notion that any native English speaker could intuitively teach ESL as evidenced by the now routine requirement of a master's degree for adult education, community college and university level ESL instruction, and teaching abroad. For the thousands of teachers who have obtained master's degrees in recent years, it would be a natural next step in their professional development and in the struggle to constantly enhance the status of the TESOL profession for more practitioners to seek a doctoral degree.

Many obstacles such as lack of time, financial resources, professional incentives and encouragement hinder aspirations for a doctorate, but there are additional negative factors influencing that decision that are within the control of TESOL faculties, university administrators, and even the prospective students themselves. One could start by looking at the doctoral curriculum.

An obvious group of candidates for doctoral study would be programme directors or directors of study in a school. "Doctorate in TESL or related field preferred" is commonly seen in job announcements for ESL director positions, yet only four universities listed doctoral courses in ESL programme design and implementation, programme evaluation, or administrative leadership. Despite the importance of language policy and planning to TESOL local and worldwide issues, just five programmes provided study in this area. Leaders in second language teaching need the knowledge and skills to infuse technology into the language curriculum and to manage the technology that is becoming an increasingly important part of the language learning process. While the role of English as the de facto language of the Internet means that the ESL/EFL field will continue to grow in prominence, it also suggests a need to study the impact the power of English and technology might have on languages in non-English-speaking societies. In what ways do our doctoral programmes assist students in gaining the expertise to use computer technology in language teaching? The answer does not appear to be in the curriculum of most TESOL doctoral programmes. Few programmes offered courses in the educational uses of technology and of those only four included courses specifically in technology for language teaching. Looking at recent journals, it is obvious that an area of great concern to the profession is the apparent dichotomy between classroom teaching and research. TESOL professionals have warned that too many classroom teachers view research as the domain of the university research community and fail to see its relevance to their own teaching. Stronger teacher-researcher ties through collaborations between university faculty and classroom teachers have been urged. The solution argued by the teacher-researcher movement is to recognize teachers as researchers with the advantages of insider perspective and applicability. Perhaps the simplest way to ensure connections between university research and classroom practice is for more classroom teachers to join the university research community as doctoral students. The crucial questions on teaching practices and the language learning process will not be answered until ESL teachers assume a more prominent role in the research process. TESOL doctoral programmes face the challenge of facilitating that outcome.

As TESOL continues to mature, more positions will demand a doctorate, therefore making it incumbent upon universities to analyze the needs not only of traditional doctoral students seeking a university teaching or research position, but also the needs of classroom teachers from a wide array of instructional settings.

# Getting Published

Dr. Lin Lougheed, the author of more than 40 English language teaching textbooks, offers his advice on becoming a successful writer in this market, highlighting the best ways to getting your lesson plans in print.

So you want to contribute to the overpublished field of ESL/EFL? Don't give up your day job teaching. You'll need it if you like to eat and if you want a good place to test your materials. A textbook is simply an organized set of daily lesson plans well printed and illustrated on good quality paper. You have these lesson plans, don't you? You've been repurposing textbooks for years and creating your own supplementary materials. Everyone loves them. Your students' proficiency rates have skyrocketed because of the quality of your exercises. Your lazy colleagues are always praising them as they photocopy them to use in their own classes.

The path to becoming an author is simple: have an idea; write it down; teach it; revise it; send it to a publisher. At that point, the process becomes more complicated so let's analyze the easy steps first.

## The idea

To publish your fabulous activities you'll need to convince someone in the publishing world that your materials have universal applicability and universal appeal. Universal is the key word. You don't want your materials to be unique. You want them to stand out, but you don't want them to be so different from everything else on the market that no one (especially the sales reps who will have to push your books) can understand how to use them.

## Write it down

You have a brilliant idea how to teach a particular grammar point or to reinforce vocabulary. You want to develop a lesson around this idea. Look at some of the books you are using. Most lessons have three parts: Warm Up, Teach, Review.

When you begin to put your idea on paper, think in terms of a class session. How will you prepare the students, teach the lesson, and review the material in 45 minutes?

As you refine your lesson, keep in the back of your mind how you plan to expand this one lesson into enough lessons to fill a book.

# Teach it

Actually, have someone else teach it. You have been experimenting with your materials in class. You know what will work or how to make it work. Let someone else interpret your perfect lesson. It would be ideal if you could observe your colleague teaching your materials. Then you can gauge the reactions of the students to the material and the way your colleague adapts the material to his or her teaching style.

# Revise it

Was your audience confused? Did they not follow your structure? Was the teacher supplementing the material with too many explanations? Or was it just perfect? Remember your materials have to work outside your own classroom. They will undoubtedly be used by total strangers in a variety of teaching situations. They must have universal appeal.

At this stage, you might even want to post your material on a teacher's bulletin board on the Web or email it to colleagues around the world. Don't worry about someone stealing your idea. I send entire manuscripts to teachers in countries that don't even have copyright protection agreements. What is important to me is their feedback. If they want to use some messy, unformatted materials in their classroom, they can be my guest. Remember there is very little that has not already been done in EFL/ESL publishing.

# Send it to a publisher

You have written, taught, revised, taught, and revised again your materials. You are now ready to have your work published. Your material can be published as a book to be downloaded from the Internet or can be published in book form and sold in bookstores. You can do either yourself or you can find a publisher to do it for you.

Whatever the method, you will have to do a market survey of your material. You should know—and your publisher will want to learn from you—why your book should be on the market.

You will put this explanation in a proposal that provides a brief description of your book, a list of the outstanding features, a survey of the competition, a discussion of the target audience, production considerations, and projected time frame for completing the book. You will also want to include a table of contents and a few of the completed chapters along with any reviewers' comments.

The survey of the competition is a very important part of your proposal. A publisher will need to know where your book fits and how it will be positioned. This detailed analysis will help the publisher see right away how your book can be set apart from the competition. You can't discuss the outstanding features of your book without pointing out the specific best selling titles that lack those features.

The survey of the competition will also help the publisher target the right market and determine whether it fills a hole in his or her publishing plan. A publisher might be desperate for a book on email correspondence for Japanese students in middle school with limited English proficiency or the publisher may feel that this topic would not be a good match for its marketing and sales force.

Production issues are also important to consider. Does your book require a lot of art work or photos? Would an audio CD or an on-line component be necessary? Any publisher has to look at the bottom line. What will it cost to produce this material? How much can I sell it for? How many copies can I sell? This information is also important to you. The cheaper it is, the better the sales; the better the sales, the larger the royalty cheque.

## Time is money. When are you going to finish this work?

Think about your own expenditure of time. Is it worth the year writing, the year revising, the year in production? Could you not do something more productive (i.e. earn more money) doing something else with your time?

That's a question I ask myself constantly. Is it worth it? I wrote my first book when I had a Fulbright scholarship to Sri Lanka. I remember a Sri Lankan professor asking me, "Aren't you a little young to be writing a book?" I wasn't too young to write it, but I was too naïve to publish it properly. I left it in the public domain. Similarly, my second book was written while I was on a Fulbright to Tunisia. That book too ended up in the public domain.

My third book, The Great Preposition Mystery, was also in the public domain. It's been licensed around the world and is still in print after 20 years. I don't get a dime, but I do have great name recognition in Angola.

These three books gave me a track record as an author and made it easier for me to get my manuscripts considered by publishers. Even after 20 years of writing EFL/ESL textbooks, the process for me is the same as for any potential author. I still start with an idea that I test and revise and test and revise. I still submit proposals and competition surveys. Once a book is published, I am still revising for subsequent printings and new editions.

It's difficult for me to find time to start new projects because the old ones are still demanding attention. They need to be revised to meet the demands and expectations of new users and to keep current users on their toes. Keeping my readers and myself interested is a challenge in itself and one that makes each day at the computer worthwhile. Besides, I always make time for something new.

*Dr.Lin Lougheed has written over 40 EFL/ESL textbooks and has produced a daily radio show in China, Dr. Lougheed's Business English. You can find out more about Lin's books at his website: www.lougheed.com.*

# Finding a Publisher

So you're trying to find a publisher interested in your work. What next? Andy Martin, Mona Scheraga, and Tina Carver explain the process.

You've done it in class. You've done it in more than one class. Your techniques work. The students are learning year after year and it's your material and your methods that are creating success. Now, how are you going to share it.

A great place to find publishers is at one of the big English language shows: the TESOL Convention in the USA, the TESL Canada conference, or the IATEFL show in the UK. If you can't get to a show, get as many publishers' catalogues as you can. Study them to see who is publishing the kind of material you have to offer. Talk to the salespeople from these publishing companies when they visit your institution. They know what your colleagues are asking for. Then make the transition from teacher's lesson plans to author's presentation. Write a prospectus–a brief summary of what you want to publish, including any research and/or experience that validates your premise. Include what market/target audience you have in mind, such as elementary, community college, etc.; the skills to be taught, the pedagogy involved, ancillary materials to be included, and reasons why your work is so necessary. Be sure to include a brief CV. Work up a Table of Contents and at least one chapter, including any exercises and an answer sheet so the publisher has an idea of the format you have in mind. Check the competition so you can discuss what makes your work different, special, and unique. Write up a competitive analysis indicating what the competition is, what its strengths and weaknesses are and how your work compares.

Finally, your sample package is ready, accompanied by your cover letter, which outlines what is included and together with your resume or bio data.

Get the name of the acquisitions editor at each publisher you submit your work to so you have a person to connect with. Talk to people in the field and get an idea of the marketing practices of different publishers; what kinds of royalties/flat fees are being paid; what kinds of materials sell best (series versus individual books, CD-ROMs, etc.). Get out to conferences and do as many workshops as possible presenting your materials so you can keep refining them.

You've got a publisher who's interested in your idea or manuscript and you've been assigned an acquisitions editor. Your editor receives the sample package. Now it's ready for review. The best reviewers are usually those who are currently teaching the equivalent course for which your project is designed and who are accustomed to evaluating materials, either as textbook committee members or as experienced publishers' reviewers. The editor sends along the review package and guide questionnaires that will give you feedback on your materials. This feedback will enable you and the editor to evaluate your sample and perhaps redirect the writing, or make major changes (for example, adding/eliminating units, changing exercise formats, redesigning the flow of lessons).

So, you've passed the trial by fire, the reviewing stage, discussed the reviews with your editor and have agreed on changes. It's time to publish your masterpiece! After the editor's supervisor approves the project, a contract is offered.

Negotiation is an important part of the process. Before you sign, read your contract carefully, suggesting any changes you'd like to make. Feel good about what you're doing and whom you're working with. The bottom line for contract negotiations is this: Is it fair to both you and the publisher? No publisher is out to "get" an author on a contract.

The financials of publishing are complex and royalties are figured as an expense of publishing the material, along with expenses of development, production, and publishing. It's important to understand that, as an author, if you receive 10%, the publisher's profit is not 90%. In fact, educational publishing survives on a very small margin of profit. Don't expect to get rich from an EFL textbook

Once the contract is signed, the work is yours to finish on time in a form appropriate for final review. When this work is complete, the editor can "accept" the manuscript. Now the fun begins.

In most publishing houses, the manuscript heads for development and you are assigned an editor (sometimes called a Development Editor or DE). It is the editor's job to work with you to look over the manuscript with an eagle eye. It has to be checked for consistency, that it ensures a variety of activities, that the exercises all work, that the tape script is accurate. Together, you must finalize the art and photo specs to get the manuscript in tip-top shape for the copy editor. The copy editor scrutinizes the manuscript for consistency, for punctuation, misspellings and for minute errors that have evaded detection. You will be sent the manuscript with copy edit queries and for approval of changes made.

Next step: Production. Here, your manuscript, art specification notes and sketches are thrown into the crucible. With the magic of computer programmes, art on CD ROMS, and the talents of the production editor, the whole hodgepodge becomes beautiful pages.

Your job is to review the pages and make corrections only–no changes at this stage, heaven forbid! It's necessary for you to meet schedules and support the production editor so the process of making the work on time and in an excellent fashion proceeds smoothly.

Voilà! After many sleepless nights, the work is in your hands. Your work, now your publication, is ready to move into the next phase, marketing and sales.

Now you've got a publisher, signed a contract, been through reviews, edits, production and design, but this means nothing if the book does not sell! Here's what's got to happen: the book has to be positioned, pre-sold, packaged, promoted and possibly piloted.... Hmmm, a lot of "p's" here. Then there's advertising, journal reviews, direct mail, following up on leads, and committee presentations. Sampling is critical, it can be done at your basic sales calls, telemarketing, book fairs, and convention presentations. We mustn't forget Internet sales, and if warranted, author tours, and in-service training. Yeah, there's a lot of stuff to be done. We don't usually cover all the bases, but there's always some combination of these sales and marketing elements. It all depends on the sales potential of the book. Basically marketing/sales can be split into pre- and post-publication activities. Let's take a peek...

- Positioning - what is the best potential market for the book?
- Sales forecasting - Estimating how many copies a book will sell and how much money it will bring in to the publishing company
- Packaging consulting - Working with editorial and design to come up with the most attractive cover for the book
- Pre-selling - Getting the word out to build excitement and interest about a book before it's published. Word-of-mouth, conferences, brochures, and marketing focus group can do this.
- Piloting - Having a teacher, or several, try-out the finished books in their classes in the hope that if they like it the whole school or district will adopt the text.
- Advertising - Promoting the book in the company catalogue, brochures and space ads in professional publications such as English Teaching Professional (www.etprofessional.com).
- Journal reviews - Mailing the new book to the review editors of professional ESL journals in the hope that they will have the book reviewed (positively) in their journal.
- Direct mail - Sending out a brochure by mail to all the English language professionals on a rented mailing list, or from the company's own database.
- Following up leads - Contacting professionals upon the recommendation of the author who provides a list of contacts in the field.
- Presenting to textbook committees - Meeting with committees at colleges or schools to convince them to adopt the new text.
- Sampling/Complimentary/Examination copies (perhaps the single most important selling technique) - Giving away free copies of the book to potential users to try out with their students.
- Calling on English language teachers/decision makers - Meeting with teachers, coordinators, chair people, etc., to present the book, let them know it's available and making sure they have a sample.
- Telemarketing - Calling potential customers on the phone to try to get them to agree to accept a sample book.
- Book fairs - Displaying the book along with other new and best selling titles at a meeting of all the ESL teachers in a school or department with the goal of leaving copies of the book behind as samples.
- Presenting at conventions - Conducting commercial presentations and giving away sample copies at local state, regional and national ESL conventions.
- The Internet - Promoting a book at the company website and soliciting sample requests and/or actual on-line sales.
- Author Tours - For really big books/series, sending the Author to different parts of the United States and/or other countries to present the book.
- In-service Training - When a book/series is adopted by a very large program, the publisher will provide free training of the English language teachers on how to use the book.

*Mona Scheraga (ESL author, freelance writer, reviewer, and trainer extraordinaire) wrote "Finding a Publisher." "Publishing the Book" was written by Tina Carver, ESL publisher, editorial director, and best-selling author. "Selling the Book" was written by Andy Martin.*

# Running a School

One of the many opportunities for teachers is the possibility of opening or running your own school. Here, Barbara Stipek discusses the possibility of doing just that – and the freedom of designing your own programmes.

Many of you who are teaching English, or will soon be teaching English, may also be wondering about possible areas of advancement within the field. The most common pathway is via promotion into administrative positions. Another possibility is to open a new school, design a programme or in some way test your entrepreneurial skills. Whichever path you choose, you are about to embark on a wonderful adventure with many rewards.

The best way to become a first-choice candidate for promotions is to show a high degree of interest in the programme where you are teaching. Make it known that you are available for extra work or special projects (paid or unpaid!) so that you can a) gain valuable administrative experience and b) show everyone how terrific you are.

I once hired a teacher who was so eager to advance into administration that the first time I asked him if he'd like to help out on a project, he said "yes!" before I even finished the question. He consistently made himself useful and showed a great willingness to learn. He was enthusiastic and performed competently, so when openings came available, he was the first person we thought of. Eventually, he was working full-time in administration.

Looking back on my early administrative positions, I realize this was a time of great personal and professional development for me. It was a time to solidify my skills in administration and management, and I found I had an insatiable appetite for learning what made a programme good. I spent a lot of time talking to other ESL administrators and studying criteria used by external agencies to judge strong programmes. I started finding many commonalties among programmes that I felt to be academically sound, such as:
- Participation of site directors and teachers in writing curricula and course descriptions that are shared throughout the school system.
- Centralization of financial, marketing, and business affairs so that site personnel can focus on academic matters.
- Establishment of clear forms of communication so that information can be shared between all of the sites and administrative offices.
- Participation in the greater ESL community through conference attendance, presentations, and board memberships.

The most important thing to remember is that you don't know everything. You can always learn something from others—even if it's what NOT to do. You can also find wonderful camaraderie with fellow administrators, which is important because, once you've been promoted out of teaching, the teachers you used to work with won't be your peer group any longer. You will be tested in your management skills as you learn to define your new role and keep the loyalty of your teaching staff.

If you find yourself as the director of the programme where you are currently teaching, there are a few important "don'ts" to keep in mind:

- Don't pretend to know something that you really don't—you'll miss wonderful opportunities to learn new things.
- Don't try to be "one of the guys" with your teaching staff—they know you are now responsible for their jobs, and they'll see through the act
- Don't be too surprised if there is some resentment among the staff—especially if you're supervising anyone who was passed over for your promotion

After I'd been in programme administration for awhile, I started recognizing my own entrepreneurial tendencies. While I thoroughly enjoyed the technical and managerial phases of my career—and would certainly feel comfortable in any teaching or administrative position—there was something particularly exhilarating about this period. I wanted to open new programmes and have the authority—and the responsibility— to do what needed to be done to be successful. I believe that there are certain qualities that indicate an "entrepreneurial bent", including:

- Higher than average risk tolerance.
- Ability to recognize talent around you and to empower it.
- Being able to listen to others and learn new things.
- Strong desire to see your vision become a reality.
- High level of comfort with change.

It is important to do some self-assessment to decide what type of person you are and what path is right for you. If security is an important issue for you, the entrepreneurial route is probably not the best way to go.

Clearly the English language field is filled with opportunities for teachers who wish to pursue administrative careers or entrepreneurial ventures. Keep your eyes and ears open, show enthusiasm and a willingness to learn, and most of all, follow your dreams.

*Barbara Stipek is the former owner of IEI, a group of ten intensive English programmes located on university campuses across the United States. In 1998, she sold the company to Sylvan Learning Systems, Inc.*

# School Management

Some teachers make their way up to management level. These positions require organizational and people skills – talents you will have developed during your teaching career.

It is not difficult to find teachers and former teachers who have taken over managerial roles at language schools all over the world. Some accept their new responsibilities with a pang of regret for their glory days in front of the blackboard. A manager with teaching experience should be sympathetic to the needs of staff members but will also be aware of the realities of what can go on both in and outside the classroom.

Many teachers find themselves becoming managers in an incremental process. When a teacher is appointed or chooses of his or her own free will to be in charge of examination matters or of materials procurement, the initial steps towards a managerial role have already been taken.

This role can develop as a teacher becomes involved with the creation and implementation of school or departmental policies, compliance with accreditation bodies, staff recruitment and teacher training programmes.

Some teachers naturally develop an interest in the commercial aspects of language teaching. It is not too difficult to understand that a school needs to recruit students in order to survive. Some of criteria normally associated with the private sector such as "customer satisfaction" and "performance" have even seeped into the current administrative thinking that governs the public schools system.

To be an effective manager, teachers need to be aware of basic business principles. Familiarity with the theory and practice of marketing methods is a definite asset as is managerial ability.

A head for figures and an acquaintance with accounting will also help the school or department manager deal with professionals such as bookkeepers and accountants, not that the manager has to be an expert in any of these fields.

If you decide to manage and/or own a school in a country that is not your homeland be sure that you are familiar with local laws regarding business operations and employment regulations. Although most schools operated by native English speakers run without major problems, there have been reports of foreign-owned institutions falling foul of local labour laws and other regulations and having to pay sometimes harsh penalties.

Teachers who are serious about a career in school management could consider taking one of the specialist courses that exist for managers. There is a M.Sc. degree course (taught by distance) in English Language Teaching Management offered by the University of Surrey. Core Modules include: ELT Management, Syllabus Design, Business and Financial Management in ELT, Human Resource Management, Language Teaching Methodology, Marketing Research Methods and Quantitative Techniques for Business Language Testing.

If you are interested in the issues that surround ESL/EFL school management, you may be interested in joining the ELT Management SIG (Special Interest Group) operated under the auspices of IATEFL.

*Further Reading:*

*Impey, G. and Underhill N. An ELT Manager's Handbook, Heinemann ELT, 1994, Oxford.*

*White R. V. et. al. Management in English Language Teaching, Cambridge University Press, 1991, Cambridge.*

# Appendix

Essential contacts to help you plan your travel, find a job, source ideas for your lessons, find a supplier, join an association, subscribe to a magazine or find a publisher

# Teacher Associations

New teachers have much to learn during their training periods. Developing professional bonds with other teachers and networking as much as you can will help you to stay informed early in your career.

## AsiaTEFL

Organisation with over 5000 members who work as ELT teachers in the countries within the asian region (mostly within south-east asia).
**Website:** www.asiatefl.org

## IATEFL

Based in the UK, but with regional offices and special-interest groups around the world., IATEFL (The International Association of Teachers of English as a Foreign Language) offers members an annual international conference with a programme of talks, workshops and exhibits as well as hundreds of regional meetings and SIG-sessions.

IATEFL
Darwin College, University of Kent
Canterbury, Kent
CT2 7NY, UK
**Website:** www.iatefl.org

## MLA

The MLA (Modern Language Association) serves the interests of teachers of language and literature.

Modern Language Association
26 Broadway, 3rd Floor
New York, NY 10004-1789
**Tel:** (646) 576-5000
**Fax:** (646) 458-0030
**Website:** www.mla.org

## NABE

NABE (National Association for Bilingual Education) is the only national organization exclusively concerned with the education of language-minority students in American schools. Many of these students are English language learners who need to preserve their first languages while they acquire a second one. NABE News, the Association's official news magazine, is published eight times annually and distributed free of charge to its members.

National Association for Bilingual Education
1220 L Street NW, Suite 605
Washington DC 20005-4018
**Tel:** (202) 898-1829
**Fax:** (202) 789-2866
**Website:** www.nabe.org

## NAFSA

NAFSA promotes the exchange of students and scholars to and from the United States. There is a professional section of NAFSA called ATESL (Administrators and Teachers in English as a Second Language). These international teachers have responsibilities in the teaching and/or management of programmes, which teach English to speakers of other languages.
NAFSA: Association of International Teachers
1307 New York Avenue NW, Eighth Floor,
Washington DC 20005-4701
**Tel:** (202) 737-3699
**Fax:** (202) 737-3657
**Website:** www.nafsa.org

## TESOL

The largest professional association of teachers of English as a second or foreign language is called TESOL: Teachers of English to Speakers of Other Languages, Inc. Based in Alexandria, Virginia, TESOL numbers some 16,500 members (Source: The World Almanac 2000). TESOL provides a variety of useful services to members including the bimonthly newsletter, TESOL Matters, which is included with the basic level of membership. Other benefits of TESOL membership include access to an insurance programme and the opportunity to apply for a number of awards and grants including the TESOL Professional Scholarships. During the summer months, the TESOL Academies are held at venues across the U.S. These events are designed to "increase your effectiveness as a teacher, administrator, curriculum planner, computer specialist, or ESL resource specialist." The annual TESOL Convention offers the prospect of workshops and lectures designed to inform and stimulate teachers. It is also the showcase of ESL/EFL teaching materials.

TESOL: Teachers of English to Speakers of Other Languages, Inc.
700 South Washington Street, Suite 200
Alexandria, VA 22314
**Tel**. 703-836-0774
**Fax:** 703-836-7864
**Website:** www.tesol.org

## TESOL Affiliates

Organized on a state or regional basis, the TESOL affiliates serve members on a local level. Some are larger than others (California-based CATESOL is the biggest) but all are active in the promotion of ESL teaching. Nearly all of them hold an annual convention where teachers can attend professional development seminars, join in networking groups and visit exhibits by ESL/EFL book publishers, software producers and other businesses. There are also international associations affiliated with TESOL such as MEXTESOL in Mexico and KOTESOL in Korea. If you want to know if there is a local TESOL affiliate in your area, go to www.tesol.org/isaffil/affil/index.html

## Country-specific Teacher Associations

Almost every country has its own teacher association (often with many regional groups and smaller special-interest groups too!). These all help to provide information, news, support and newsletters (with the latest job opportunities). There are 100s of country-specific assocations and 1000s of special interest groups, however most are affiliates of the two biggest worldwide groups: IATEFL and TESOL. Almost every association organises its own conferences, talks and shows – great places to learn

new techniques and find out about the latest materials on offer - the selection below is a good place to start but, if your country is not listed, find out more from www.iatefl.org or www.tesol.org.

**American Council on the Teaching of Foreign Languages (ACTFL)**
www.actfl.org

**Asociación De Profesores de Inglés de América Latina**
www.aplial.net

**Association for the Advancement of Computing in Education (AACE)**
www.aace.org

**Australian Council for TESOL Associations**
www.tesol.org.au

**Arizona-TESOL**
www.az-tesol.org

**BALEAP - British Association of Lecturers in English for Academic Purposes**
www.baleap.org.uk

**BASELT - British Association of State English Language Teaching**
www.baselt.org.uk/

**BC TEAL - British Columbia Teachers of English as an Additional Language**
www.vcn.bc.ca/bcteal/

**British Institute of English Language Teaching (BIELT)**
www.bielt.org

**Business English Special Interest Group of IATEFL**
www.besig.org

**California TESOL**
www.catesol.org

**Carolina TESOL**
www.intrex.net/cartesol/

**CASLT - Canadian Association of Second Language Teachers**
www.caslt.org

**English Language Teachers' Associations of Stuttgart and Frankfurt/Main, Germany**
www.eltas.de

**English Language Teachers Contacts Scheme (ELTECS)**
www.britishcouncil.org/english/eltecs/

**EUROCALL - European Association for Computer Assisted Language Learning**
www.hull.ac.uk/cti/eurocall.htm

**Fukuoka JALT**
www.kyushu.com/FukuokaJALT.html

**Georgia TESOL**
www.gatesol.org

**IATEFL - International Association of Teachers of English as a Foreign Language**
www.iatefl.org.uk

**IATEFL Greece**
www.iatefl.gr

**IATEFL Hungary**
www.iatefl.hu

**IATEFL Poland**
www.iatefl.pl

**Indiana TESOL**
www.intesol.org

**JALT (Japan association of language teachers)**
www.jalt.org

**JALT Testing & Evaluation Special Interest Group**
www.jalt.org/test/

**Japan Association of College English Teachers (JACET)**
www.jacet.org

**Japan Association of Language Teaching (JALT)**
www.jalt.org

**JETAA - The Japan Exchange and Teaching Alumni Association**
www.jet.org

**Korea Teachers of English to Speakers of Other Languages (KOTESOL)**
www.kotesol.org

**MIDITESOL - MidAmerica Teachers of English to Speakers of Other Languages**
www.midtesol.org

**Michigan TESOL**
www.mitesol.org

**NALDIC - National Association of language development in the curriculum**
www.naldic.org.uk

**NATECLA - National Association for Teaching English and other Community Languages to Adults**
www.natecla.org.uk

**Oregon TESOL**
www.ortesol.org

**TESOL - Teachers of English to Speakers of Other Languages**
www.tesol.edu

**TESOL Greece**
www.tesolgreece.com

**TESOL Spain**
www.tesol-spain.org

**TESOL Ukraine**
www.tesol-ua.org

**The Computer Assisted Language Instruction Consortium**
www.calico.org

**TESL Canada**
www.tesl.ca

**VATE - Victorian Association for Teaching of English**
www.vate.org.au

# Websites & Contacts

Plan your career, travel the world, get a job – just some of the uses of the mass of excellent websites on the Internet. You'll find the sites and contacts on the following pages help you get a visa, plan your classes, work out your teacher training, travel around the world and study the latest methodology.

## Good Places To Start

**Dave's ESL Café**
www.eslcafe.com

**EFLweb**
www.eflweb.com

**English Teaching Professional magazine**
www.etprofessional.com

**ESL Magazine**
www.eslmagazine.com

**IATEFL**
www.iatefl.org

**Internet TESL Journal**
www.aitech.ac.jp/~iteslj

**Linguistic Funland**
www.linguistic-funland.com

**Oxford Seminars**
www.oxfordseminars.com

**Randall's ESL Cyber Listening Lab**
www.esl-lab.com

**TESL**
www.tesl.com

**TESOL organisation**
www.tesol.org

## Web Directories

These sites include directories of useful websites – a good place to start looking for materials or other information online.

**Business English Links for ESL**
www.geocities.com/kurtracy/

**English as a Second Language Page**
www.rong-chang.com/

**English as a Second/Foreign Language for Kids**
www.eslkid.com/

**English Grammar Links for ESL Students**
www.gl.umbc.edu/~kpokoy1/grammar1.htm

**English Language Teaching Web (ELTWEB)**
www.eltweb.com/

**ESL Café's Web Guide**
www.eslcafe.com/search/index.html

**ESL Forum**
www.eslforum.net/

**ESLdirectory.com**
www.esldirectory.com/

**GlobalStudy**
www.globalstudy.com

**Internet TESL Journal web directory**
www.iteslj.org

**Australian TESOL Websites Page**
www.tesol.org.au/links.htm

**English Language Teaching & Learning Resources**
www.bernieh.com.ar/

**Bilingual and ESL Education Related Resources**
http://jan.ucc.nau.edu/~jar/BME.html

**Carnegie Library's ESL/EFL Links**
www.carnegielibrary.org/subject/education/esl.html

**CATESOL's ESL Resources**
www.catesol.org/resource.html

**Online Resources for ESL Students and Teachers**
www.clpccd.cc.ca.us/cc/maj/lahum/esl/resources.html

**Bilingual / ESL Resources**
www-rcf.usc.edu/~cmmr/BEResources.html

**General English Links**
www.englishnetlinks.homestead.com

**ESL Webring**
www.eslwebring.com

**ESL-EFLworld Directory**
www.esl-eflworld.com/

**ESLoop**
www.esloop.org/

**IATEFL's BEsig - Links Page**
www.besig.org/pages/links.htm

**JALT Web Links**
Http://jalt.org/jalt_e/main/materials_link/linkster.php

## Schools

The web provides almost too much information about schools: almost every school has a website and it can be hard to compare them. Use one of these directories to help select a school according to type of course, level, experience and location.

**ApplyESL.com**
www.applyesl.com

**Global Study**
www.globalstudy.com

**ESL Directory**
www.esldirectory.com

**Language Courses Comparison**
www.languagecourse.net

**eduPASS: US schools**
www.edupass.org/english

**Study in the USA**
www.studyusa.com

**Accredited schools in the UK**
www.101schools.co.uk

**Abracadebra ESL: Canadian schools**
www.abracadabraesl.com

**GotoEd - Study English Abroad (outside the US)**
www.gotoed.com

**Hyper Study: Australia and New Zealand**
www.hyperstudy.com

**American Cultural Exchange**
www.cultural.org/map.htm

**Canadian Association of Private Language Schools**
www.capls.com

**Directory of ESL Programme Websites Around the World**
www.globalstudy.com/esl/

**Education and Homestay in New Zealand**
www.studentstay.com

**EF Education: chain of schools around the world**
www.ef.com

**EFL Directory - EFL Courses**
www.europa-pages.co.uk/uk/tefl.html

**Study in the USA**
www.studyusa.com

**International Language Schools**
www.aspectworld.com

**Global Studies: UK schools**
www.globalstudies.co.uk

**go2study**
www.go2study.com/english/index.htm

**TESL courses in Thailand**
www.langserv.com

## Bookshops

**KEL (Argentina)**
www.ediciones-kel.com

**SBS (Argentina)**
www.sbs.com.ar

**Disal (Brazil)**
www.disal.com.br

**Liv. Martins Fontes (Brazil)**
www.martinsfontes.com.br

**Special Book Services (Brazil)**
www.sbs.com.br

**The English Centre (Canada)**
www.theenglishcentre.ca

**Books and Bits S.A. (Chile)**
www.booksandbits.cl

**SBS (Chile)**
www.sbs.cl

**Algoritam (Croatia)**
www.algoritam.hr

**Bohemian Ventures (Czech Rep.)**
www.venturesbooks.com

**Mega Books International (Czech Rep.)**
www.megabooks.cz

**Nakladatelstvi Fraus (Czech Rep.)**
www.fraus.cz

**English Center (Denmark)**
www.englishcenter.dk

**Middle East Observer (Egypt)**
www.meobserver.com.eg

**Accendo (Estonia)**
www.accendo.ee

**Allecto Bookshop (Estonia)**
www.allecto.ee

**The Academic Bookstore (Finland)**
www.akateeminen.com

**Attica (France)**
www.attica-langues.com

**Bookshop Stäheli Ltd. (Germany)**
www.staehelibooks.ch

**Kosmos Floras Bookshops (Greece)**
www.floras.gr

**International Books (Ireland)**
www.interbooksirl.com

**Overseas Book Service (Italy)**
www.overseasbookservice.com

**Nellie's Group (Japan)**
www.nellies.co.jp

**English Resource (Japan)**
www.englishresource.com

**Sanseido Bookstore (Japan)**
www.books-sanseido.co.jp

**Kyobo Book Centre (Korea)**
www.kyobobook.co.kr

**Kungman Book Center (Korea)**
www.kyobobook.co.kr

**Delti Bookstore (Mexico)**
www.delti.com.mx

**CenterCom (Russia)**
www.centercom.ru

**Slovak Ventures (Slovakia)**
www.venturesbooks.com

**DZS (Slovenia)**
www.dzs.si

**The English Book Centre (Sweden)**
www.engbookcen.se

**The Uppsala English Bookshop (Sweden)**
www.ueb.se

**Bergli Books (Switzerland)**
www.bergli.ch

**Staeheli (Switzerland)**
www.staehelibooks.ch

**Hans Stauffacher (Switzerland)**
www.stauffacher.ch

**Caves Educational Training (Taiwan)**
www.cettw.com

**BEBC (UK)**
www.bebc.co.uk

**Cambridge International Book Centre (UK)**
www.cibc.co.uk

**English Book Centre (UK)**
www.ebcoxford.co.uk

**English Language Bookshop (UK)**
www.elb-brighton.com

**KELTIC (UK)**
www.keltic.co.uk

**LCL International Bookshop (UK)**
www.lclib.com

**Alta Book Center Publishers (USA)**
www.altaesl.com

**Delta Systems Co. Inc. (USA)**
www.delta-systems.com

**World of Reading, Ltd. (USA)**
www.wor.com

## Magazines

Magazines and journals are a teacher's best friends; they can provide practical information, lesson-plans and photocopiable material as well as a forum for technical discussions and analysis of methodology.

**EL Gazette**
www.elgazette.com

**English Teaching Professional**
www.etprofessional.com

**ESL Magazine**
www.eslmag.com

**Hands-on English**
www.handsonenglish.com/

**IATEFL Newsletter**
www.iatefl.org

**IT's magazines**
www.its.com

**Language Magazine**
www.languagemag.com

**Mary Glasgow Magazines**
www.link2english.com

**Modern English Digest**
www.ModernEnglishDigest.net

**Modern English Teacher**
www.onlineMET.com

**Spotlight**
www.spotlight.de

**TESOL Journal**
www.tesol.org/pubs/magz/tj.html

**TESOL Quarterly**
www.tesol.org/pubs/magz/tq.html

## Publishers

**ABAX ELT Publishers**
www.abax.co.jp

**Adams & Austen Press Publishers**
www.aapress.com.au

**Alta Book Center Publishers**
www.altaesl.com

**Barron's**
www.barronseduc.com/english-language-arts.html

**Beaumont Publishing**
www.beaumont-publishing.com

**Cambridge University Press**
www.cup.cam.ac.uk

**Crown House Publishing**
www.crownhouse.co.uk

**Delta Publishing**
www.deltabooks.co.uk

**Dymon Publications**
www.dymonbooks.com

**DynED International**
www.dyned.com

**EFL Press**
www.EFLPress.com

**Encomium Publications, Inc.**
www.encomium.com

**Express Publishing ELT Books**
www.expresspublishing.co.uk

**Full Blast Productions**
www.fullblastproductions.com

**Garnet Education**
www.garneteducation.com

**Georgian Press**
www.georgianpress.co.uk

**Griffith Books**
www.griffith-books-ltd.sagenet.co.uk

**HarperCollins Publishers**
www.harpercollins.com

**Hodder and Stoughton**
www.madaboutbooks.com

**Houghton Mifflin**
www.hmco.com

**JAG Publications**
www.jagpublications-esl.com

**John Benjamins Publishing**
www.benjamins.com/jbp/index.html

**Keyways Publishing**
www.keywayspublishing.com

**Longman English language Teaching**
www.longman-elt.com

**Macmillan Heinemann English Language Teaching**
www.mhelt.com

**Marsall Cavendish ELT**
www.mcelt.com

**New Readers Press**
www.newreaderspress.com/main.html

**Oxford University Press**
www.oup.co.uk

**Pro Lingua Associates**
www.ProLinguaAssociates.com

**Publishing Choice**
www.publishingchoice.com

**Richmond Publishing**
www.richmondelt.com

**Summertown Publishing**
www.summertown.co.uk

**The McGraw-Hill Companies**
www.mhhe.com/catalogs/hss/esl/

**Heinle & Heinle Thomson Learning**
www.heinle.com

**Prentice Hall Regents**
www.phregents.com

**Addison-Wesley**
www.awl.com

## Conferences

There are thousands of conferences, shows and lectures around the world each year: the sister magazine of this yearbook, English Teaching Professional, holds its conference every year in Londo (www.etplive.com); every association has its own. the biggest are run by IATEFL (www.iatefl.org.uk) and TESOL (www.tesol.org). Use one of these sites that catalogues them all.

**ELT Events Calendar in Japan**
http://eltcalendar.com

**English Teaching Professional**
www.etprofessional.com

**ESL Magazine**
www.eslmag.com

**TESOL Online's Conference Calendar**
www.tesol.org/isaffil/calendar/

## Discussion and Mailing Lists

Discuss ideas and chat with colleagues and peers about materials, courses, schools or work – these discussion boards and emailing lists are dedicated to ELT.

**Sign-up for TESL Mailing Lists**
www.linguistic-funland.com/tesllist.html

**Bulletin Board for EFL teachers working in Germany**
http://pub95.ezboard.com/belt.html

**CALLNews mailing list**
http://listserv.cddc.vt.edu/mailman/listinfo/callnews

**ELTASIA-L mailing list for ESL teachers in Asia**
http://eltasia.com/

**English Teaching Professional - discussion forum**
www.etprofessional.com

**ESL Café's Discussion Center for Teachers**
www.eslcafe.com/discussion/#teacher

**JALTTALK - Japan**
www.jalt.org/jalt_e/main/jaltcall_main.shtml

**Discussion Forums for Teachers**
www.eslpartyland.com/tdisc.htm

**Modern English Teacher - discussion forum**
www.onlineMET.com

**NETEACH-L - using technology in the classroom**
www.ilc.cuhk.edu.hk/english/neteach/main.html

**TESL-L Discussion List**
www.hunter.cuny.edu/~tesl-l/

**The ESL/Language ChatBoard**
www.teachers.net/mentors/esl_language/

**Free-ESL Discussion Forums**
www.free-esl.com/teachers/forums/default.asp

## Lesson Plans

Lesson plans are an essential part of every teacher's kit – trying to make teaching academic subjects such as grammar interesting, relevant to the student and easy to understand. The web has masses of free lesson plans that you can download and use as a basis for your own work. Try these sites for ideas and free plans.

**EFL4U Lesson Plans**
www.efl4u.com

**ESLFLOW**
www.eslflow.com

**ESL Classroom Handouts**
www.englishclub.net/handouts

**Ideas for the ESL Classroom**
www.eslcafe.com/ideas

**ESL Teachers Guide**
http://humanities.byu.edu/elc/Teacher/TeacherGuideMain

**Karin's ESL PartyLand**
www.eslpartyland.com/teach3.htm

**askERIC Lesson Plans**
Http://ericir.syr.edu/Virtual/Lessons

**Games in ESL Classroom**
http://eslsv001.esl.sakuragaoka.ac.jp/teachers/BR/games/Games.html

**Free Instant Lessons**
www.english-to-go.com

**English Lessons**
www.nwrel.org/sky/

**PIZZAZ!**
http://darkwing.uoregon.edu/~leslieob/pizzaz.html

**TEFL Farm**
www.teflfarm.com

**TEFL.net**
www.tefl.net

**Lessons and Lesson Plans from The Internet TESL Journal**
http://iteslj.org/Lessons/

**Boggle's World ESL Lesson Plan Archive**
http://bogglesworld.com/lessons/archive.htm

**Bradley's Worksheets**
www.bradleys-english-school.com/worksheets/nfindex.html

**Free English Lessons**
www.cerbranetics.com/english.html

**Churchill House School of English Lanuage**
www.churchillhouse.com/english/downloads.html

**CNN Newsroom Daily Classroom Guide**
http://Learning.turner.com/newsroom/index.html

**Free Lesson**
www.english-to-go.com/english/

**ESL Games and Activities**
www.etanewsletter.com/games.htm

**Teachers Teaching Teachers**
www.etni.org.il/teacteac.htm

**Activities for Summer School ESL**
http://everythingesl.net/lessons/summerschool_esl.php?ty=print

**Classroom ESL Games**
http://genkienglish.net/games.htm

## Classroom Materials

**Wordsmyth Glossary Maker**
www.wordsmyth.net/foundry/glossary.html

**Wordsmyth Vocabulary Quiz Generator**
www.wordsmyth.net/foundry/vocabquiz.shtml

**Course for Adults**
http://iteslj.org/Lessons/Vorland-4units/

**Crosswords and Word Searches for Young Children**
http://abcteach.com/EasyPuzzles/kidsTOC.htm

**Boggle's World**
http://bogglesworld.com/

**Community ESOL**
www.communityesol.org.uk/

**EFL Club Resource Box**
www.eflclub.com/9resourcebox/resourcebox.html

**What's Wrong - Intensive Reading**
http://esl.about.com/homework/esl/library/lessons/nbl wrong.htm

**Grammar: Nature and Teaching**
www.gabrielatos.com/Grammar.htm

**Pronunciation: /r/ and /l/**
www.csulb.edu/~linguag/ali/r_and_l.html

**Word Search Factory**
www.schoolhousetech.com/wordsearch.html

**Classroom Materials Generators**
www.teach-nology.com/web_tools/materials/

**Free handouts for EFL teachers**
www.handoutsonline.com/

**Simple English Grammar Exercises**
www.theenglishprofessor.com/freeworksheets.htm

## Teaching Tips and Ideas

If you're faced with your first class or if you are stuck for ideas after teaching the same subject to the thousandth student, these sites can help with fresh ideas and tips.

**75 ESL Teaching Ideas**
http://iteslj.org/Techniques/Houston-TeachingIdeas.html

**Tips for Teachers**
http://2merediths.org/esl/teachertips.htm

**Conversation starters for students**
www.languageimpact.com/articles/rw/conv_starters.htm

**Teacher's Tips**
www.developingteachers.com/tips/currenttip.htm

**FAQ about Teaching ESL Students (For Mainstream Teachers)**
www.fis.edu/eslweb/esl/students/teanotes/

**Forty Helpful Hints & Tips**
www.handsonenglish.com/40tips.html

**Hints and Pointers**
http://genkienglish.net/general.htm

**Practical Teaching Ideas on ESL**
www.ncte.org/teach/esl.shtml

**Survival Guide for New Teachers**
www.ed.gov/pubs/survivalguide/

**Tips for Teaching Grammar**
www.ateg.org/grammar/tips.htm

## Travel advice

www.1000traveltips.org
www.canuckabroad.com
www.gapyear.com
www.goabroad.com
www.globetrotters.co.uk
www.journeywoman.com
www.lonelyplanet.com
www.roughguides.com
www.mapsworldwide.co.uk
www.timeout.com
www.vtourist.com
www.worldtimeserver.com

## Official travel advice

**British Foreign and Commonwealth office**
www.fco.gov.uk

**British passport enquiries**
www.ukpa.gov.uk

**Canadian Consular Affairs**
www.voyage.gc.ca

**US Department of State**
www.travel.state.gov

**NHS Direct**
www.knowhow.co.uk

## Visas

**Visas for Australia**
www.australia.org.uk

**Visas for Canada**
www.cic.gc.ca/english/visit/

**Visas for USA**
www.usembassy.org.uk

## Emailing & cybercafés

Cybercafes.com
Visit before you go to find your local cybercafé – you'll be able to keep in touch with friends and family cheaply and quickly by emailing them while you're away. This website contains a list of over 4,000 Internet cafés around the globe.

## Finances

**Mastercard**
www.mastercard.com/atm

**Visa**
www.visa.com/pd/atm

**American Express**
www.americanexpress.com

**Currency Conversion**
www.xe.com

**Western Union Money Transfer**
www.westernunion.com

## Travel health

**National Centre for Disease Control**
www.cdc.gov/travel

**Travel health**
www.tmvc.com.au/info10.html

**TripPrep**
www.tripprep.com

**World Health Organization**
www.who.int/ctd

## Travel Agencies

**Ebookers**
www.ebookers.com

**Expedia**
www.expedia.com

**STA Travel**
www.statravel.co.uk

**Trailfinders**
www.trailfinders.co.uk

**Intl Student Travel**
www.istc.org

**Studenttravel.com**
www.studenttravel.com

**Thomson travel**
www.austravel.com

## Ferry operators and ports

**Brittany Ferries**
www.brittanyferries.com

**Hoverspeed**
www.hoverspeed.co.uk

**P&O Stena Line**
www.posl.com

**Stena Line**
Www.stenaline.co.uk

## Bus

**Buslines (Australia)**
www.buslines.com.au

**Greyhound (USA)**
www.greyhound.com

**Ticabus (Central America)**
www.ticabus.com/Eindex/htm

## Train

**BudgetTravel**
www.budgettravel.com

**EuroRailways**
www.eurorailways.com

**Public Transport (in North America)**
www.geocities.com/capitolhill/5355/

**Australian Train Routes**
www.gsr.com.au

**RailServe**
www.railserve.com

**TrainWeb**
www.trainweb.com/indiarail

# British Council

The British Council network has offices in just about every country; these should be your first point of contact: the offices provide information on visas, grants, jobs and local economic conditions as well as English-language resources, contacts with local schools and advice for teachers hoping to get established in the country. Main Website: www.britishcouncil.org

## AFGHANISTAN

The British Council
15th Street Roundabout
Wazir Akbar Khan
P.O. Box 334
Kabul
**Tel:** +93 (0)70 102 302
**Fax:** +93 (0)70 102 250
**Email:** richard.weyers@britishcouncil.org

## ALBANIA

The British Council
Rruga Ded Gjo Luli 3/1
Tirana
**Tel:** +355 (4) 240856/40857
**Fax:** +355 (4) 240858
**Email:** info@britishcouncil.org.al
**Website:** www.britishcouncil.org.al

## ALGERIA , Algiers

The British Council
Hotel Hilton International 7th floor
Pins Maritimes, Palais des Expositions
El Mohammadia
Algiers
**Tel:** +213 (21) 230 068
**Fax:** +213 (21) 230 751
**Email:** rachida.benyahia@fco.gov.uk
**Website:** www.britishcouncil.org/algeria

## ARGENTINA, Buenos Aires

The British Council
Marcelo T de Alvear 590 4th Floor
C1058AAF
Buenos Aires
**Tel:** +54 (11) 4311 9814/7519
**Fax:** +54 (11) 4311 7747
**Email:** info@britishcouncil.org.ar
**Website:** www.britishcouncil.org.ar

## ARMENIA

The British Council
Baghramian Avenue 24, Yerevan, 375019
**Tel:** +374 (1) 55 99 23
**Fax:** +374 (1) 55 99 29
**Email:** info@britishcouncil.am
**Website:** www.britishcouncil.am

## AUSTRALIA, Sydney

The British Council
PO Box 88
Edgecliff, Sydney NSW 2027
**Tel:** +61 (2) 9326 2022
**Fax:** +61 (2) 9327 4868
**Email:** enquiries@britishcouncil.org.au
**Website:** www.britishcouncil.org/australia

## AUSTRIA, Vienna

The British Council
Schenkenstrabe 4
A -1010 Vienna
**Tel:** +43 (1) 533 2616

**Fax:** +43 (1) 533 261685
**Email:** bc.vienna@britishcouncil.at
**Website:** www.britishcouncil.at

## AZERBAIJAN, Baku

The British Council
1 Vali Mammadov Street
Ichari Sheher
Baku AZ1000
**Tel:** +994 (12) 971 593
**Fax:** +994 (12) 989 236
**Email:** enquiries@britishcouncil.az
**Website:** www.britishcouncil.org.az

## BAHRAIN , Manama

The British Council
AMA Centre (PO Box 452)
146 Shaikh Salman Highway
Manama 356
**Tel:** +973 261 555
**Fax:** +973 241 272
**Email:** bc.enquiries@britishcouncil.org.bh
**Website:** www.britishcouncil.org/bahrain

## BANGLADESH, Dhaka

The British Council
5 Fuller Road
PO Box 161, Dhaka 1000
**Tel:** +880 (2) 861 8905 – 7
**Fax:** +880 (2) 861 3375
**Email:** Dhaka.Enquiries@bd.britishcouncil.org
**Website:** www.britishcouncil.org/bangladesh

## Bangladesh, Chittagong

The British Council
77/A East Nasirabad
Chittagong
**Tel:** +880 (31) 657884
**Fax:** +880 (31) 657 881
**Email:** Chittagong.Enquiries@bd.britishcouncil.org

## BELGIUM, Brussels

The British Council
Leopold Plaza
Rue du Trône 108 / Troonstraat 108
1050 Brussels
**Tel:** +32 (2) 227 08 41
**Fax:** +32 (2) 227 08 49
**Email:** enquiries@britishcouncil.be
**Website:** www.britishcouncil.org/belgium

## BOLIVIA, La Paz

The British Council
Avenida Arce 2708 (esq.Campos)
Casilla 15047
La Paz
**Tel:** +591 (2) 2431 240
**Fax**+591 (2) 2431 377
**Email:** information@britishcouncil.org.bo
**Website:** www.britishcouncil.org/bolivia

## BOSNIA & HERZEGOVINA , Sarajevo

The British Council
Ljubljanska 9, Sarajevo 71 000
**Tel:** +387 (0) 33 250 220
**Fax:** +387 (0) 33 250 240
**Email:** British.Council@britishcouncil.ba
**Website:** www.britishcouncil.ba

## BOTSWANA, Gaborone

British High Commission Building
Queen's Road
The Mall
P.O Box 439, Gaborone
**Tel:** +267 395 3602
**Fax:** +267 395 6643
**Email:** general.enquiries@britishcouncil.org.bw
**Website:** www.britishcouncil.org/botswana

## BRAZIL, Brasilia

The British Council
Ed.Centro Empresarial Varig
SCN Quadra 04 Bloco B
Torre Oeste Conjunto 202
Brasilia – DF
70710-926
**Tel:** +55 (0) 61 2106 7500
**Fax:** +55 (0) 61 2106 7599
**Email:** brasilia@britishcouncil.org.br
**Website:** www.britishcouncil.org.br

## BRAZIL, Curitiba

The British Council
Rua Presidente Faria, 51
Conjunto 204
Curitiba  PR  80020-290
**Tel:** / **Fax:** +55 41 238 2912
**Email:** curitiba@britishcouncil.org.br

## BRAZIL, Recife

The British Council
Av. Domingos Ferreira, 4150
Boa Viagem
51021-040 Recife PE,
P.O. Box 4079
**Tel:** +55 81 2101 7500
**Fax:** +55 81 2101 7599
**Email:** recife@britishcouncil.org.br

## BRAZIL , Rio de Janeiro

The British Council
Rua Jardim Botanico, 518/1 andar
Jardim Botanico,
22461 – 000 Rio de Janeiro RJ
**Tel:** +55 21 2105 7500
**Fax:** +55 21 2105 7598
**Email:** riodejaneiro@britishcouncil.org.br
Regional Director  - Mr Sital Dhillon

## BRAZIL, Rio de Janeiro

The British Council
Management Centre
Av. Rio Branco 80/4 andar
Centro 20040-070
Rio de Janeiro – RJ
**Tel:** +55 (21) 2242 1223
**Fax:** +55 (21) 2221 0515

## BRAZIL , São Paulo

The British Council
Centro Brasileiro-Britanico
Rua Ferreira Araujo, 741 – 3 andar, Pinheiros
05428 002, Sao Paulo – SP
**Tel:** +55 (0) 112126 7500
**Fax:** +55 (0) 11 2126 7575
**Email:** saopaulo@britishcouncil.org.br

## BRUNEI DARUSSALAM, Bandar Seri Begawan

The British Council
Level 2, Block D,
Yayasan Sultan Haji Hassanal Bolkiah
Jalan Pretty, B.S.B.
Brunei Darussalam BS8711
**Tel:** +673 223 7742
**Fax:** +673 223 7392
**Email:** all.enquiries@bn.britishcouncil.org
**Website:** www.britishcouncil.org/brunei

## BULGARIA, Sofia

The British Council
7 Krakra Street
1504 Sofia
**Tel:** +359 (0) 2 942 4344
**Fax:** +359 (0) 2 942 4222
**Email:** bc.sofia@britishcouncil.bg
**Website:** www.britishcouncil.org/bulgaria

## BURMA, Myanmar

The British Council
78 Kanna Road,
(PO Box 638)
Yangon
Myanmar
**Tel:** €+ 95 (0)1 254658/256290
**Fax:** + 95 (0)1 245345
**Email:** enquiries@britishcouncil.org.mm
**Website:** www.britishcouncil.org/burma

## CAMEROON, Yaoundé

The British Council
Immeuble Christo
Avenue Charles de Gaulle BP 818
Yaoundé
**Tel:** +237 2 21 16 96/20 31 72
**Fax**: +237 2 21 56 91
**Email:** bc-yaounde@britishcouncil.cm
**Website:** www.britishcouncil.org/cameroon

## CAMEROON, Douala

The British Council
Rue Joffre, Akwa
BP 12801
Douala
**Tel:** +237 343 49 66
**Fax:** +237 342 51 70
**Email:** bc-douala@bc-douala.iccnet.cm

## CANADA, Ottawa

The British Council
80 Elgin Street
Ottawa
Ontario K1P 5K7
**Tel:** +1 613 364 6233
**Fax:** +1 613 569 1478
**Email:** ottawa.enquiries@ca.britishcouncil.org
**Website:** www.britishcouncil.org/canada

## CANADA, Montreal

The British Council
1000 ouest rue de La Gauchetiere
Bureau 4200
Montreal
Quebec H3B 4W5
**Tel:** +1 514 866 5863
**Fax:** +1 514 866 5322
**Email:** montreal.enquiries@ca.britishcouncil.org

## CHILE, Santiago

The British Council
Eliodoro Yáñez 832
Providencia 750-0651
Casilla 115 Correo 55
Santiago
**Tel:** +56 (2) 410 6900
**Fax:** +56 (2) 410 6929
**Email:** info@britishcouncil.cl
**Website:** www.britishcouncil.cl

## CHINA, Beijing

The British Council
4/f Landmark Building Tower 1
8 North Dongsanhuan Road
Chaoyang District,
100004
Beijing
**Tel:** +86 (10) 6590 6903
**Fax:** +86 (10) 6590 0977
**Email:** enquiry@britishcouncil.org.cn
**Website:** www.britishcouncil.org/china

## CHINA, Hong Kong

The British Council
3 Supreme Court Road
Admiralty
**Tel:** +852 291 35100
**Fax:** +852 291 35102
**Email:** info@britishcouncil.org.hk
**Website:** www.britishcouncil.org.hk

## CHINA, Shanghai

The British Council
1 Floor Pidemco Tower
318 Fu Zhou Lu
Shanghai 200001
**Tel:** +86 (21) 6391 2626
**Fax:** +86 (21) 6391 2121
**Email:** bc.shanghai@britishcouncil.org.cn

## CHINA, Chongqing

The British Council
Room 5-7 28 Floor Metropolitan Tower
No 68 Zou Rong Road
Yuzhong District
Chongqing 400010
**Tel:** +86 (23) 6373 6888
**Fax:** +86 (23) 6373 7898
**Email:** bc.chongqing@britishcouncil.org.cn

## CHINA, Guangzhou

The British Council
1001 Main Tower
Gungdong International Hotel
339 Huanshi Dong Lu
Guangzhou 510098
**Tel:** +86 (20) 8335 1316
**Fax:** +86 (20) 8335 1321
**Email:** bc.guangzhou@britishcouncil.org.cn

## COLOMBIA, Bogotá

The British Council
Calle 87 No 12 - 79
Bogota
**Tel:** +57 (1) 618 7680
**Fax:** +57 (1) 218 7754
**Email:** info@britishcouncil.org.co
**Website:** www.britishcouncil.org/colombia

## CROATIA , Zagreb

The British Council
Illica 12
PP 55
10001 Zagreb
**Tel:** +385 (0) 1 4899 500
**Fax:** +385 (0) 1 4833 955
**Email:** zagreb.info@britishcouncil.hr
**Website:** www.britishcouncil.hr

## CUBA, Havana

The British Council
Calle 34 no 702, esq.a 7ma Avenida,
Miramar,
La Habana
**Tel:** +53 (0) 7 204 1771/2
**Fax:** +53 (0) 7 204 9214
**Email:** information@cu.britishcouncil.org
**Website:** www.britishcouncil.org/cuba

## CYPRUS, Nicosia

The British Council
3 Museum Street
CY- 1097 Nicosia
**Tel:** +357 (22) 585000
**Fax:** +357 (22) 677 257
**Email:** enquiries@britishcouncil.org.cy
**Website:** www.britishcouncil.org.cy

## CZECH REPUBLIC, Prague

The British Council
Bredovsky dvur, Politickych veznu 13,
110 00 Prague 1
**Tel:** +420 221 991 111
**Fax:** +420 224 933 847
**Email:** info.praha@britishcouncil.cz
**Website:** www.britishcouncil.cz

## CZECH REPUBLIC, Brno

The British Council
Trida Kpt. Jarose 13
602 00 Brno
**Tel:** +420 545 210 174
**Fax:** +420 545 211 065
**Email:** info.brno@britishcouncil.cz

## CZECH REPUBLIC, Pilsen

The British Council
Purkynova 27
301 36 Plzen
**Tel:** +420 377 220 180
**Fax:** +420 377 220 181
**Email:** info.pilsen@britishcouncil.cz

## DENMARK, Copenhagen

The British Council
Gammel Mønt 12.3
1117 Copenhagen K
**Tel:** +45 (33) 369 400
**Fax:** +45 (33) 369 406
**Email:** british.council@britishcouncil.dk
**Website:** www.britishcouncil.org/denmark

## EGYPT, Cairo

The British Council
192 El Nil Street
Agouza, Cairo
**Tel:** +20 (2) 303 1514
**Fax:** +20 (2) 344 3076

**Email:** british.council@britishcouncil.org.eg
**Website:** www.britishcouncil.org/egypt

## EGYPT, Alexandria TC

The British Council
9 Batalsa Street
Bab Sharki
Alexandria
**Tel:** +20 (3) 486 0199
**Fax:** +20 (3) 484 6630
**Email:** british.council@britishcouncil.org.eg

## EGYPT, Heliopolis TC

The British Council
4 El Minya Street
Off Nazih Khalifa Street
Heliopolis
Tel: +20 (2) 452 3395-7
Fax: +20 (2) 258 3660
**Email:** british.council@britishcouncil.org.eg

## ERITREA, Asmara

The British Council
Lorenzo Tazaz Street No 23
PO Box 997 Asmara
**Tel:** +291 (1) 123 415/120 529
**Fax:** +291 (1) 127 230
**Email:** information@ britishcouncil.org.er
**Website:** www.britishcouncil.org/eritrea

## ESTONIA, Tallin

The British Council
Vana Posti 7
Tallinn 10146
**Tel:** +372 (0) 625 7788
**Fax:** +372 (0) 625 7799
**Email:** british.council@britishcouncil.ee
**Website:** www.britishcouncil.org/estonia

## ETHIOPIA, Addis Ababa

The British Council
PO Box 1043
Artistic Building
Adwa Avenue, Addis Ababa
**Tel:** +251 (1) 550 022
**Fax:** +251 (1) 552 544
**Email:** bc.addisababa@et.britishcouncil.org
**Website:** www.britishcouncil.org/ethiopia

## FINLAND, Helsinki

The British Council
Hakaniemenkatu 2
00530 Helsinki
**Tel:** +358 (9) 774 3330
**Fax:** +358 (9) 701 8725
**Email:** office@britishcouncil.fi
**Website:** www.britishcouncil.fi

## FRANCE, Paris

The British Council
9 rue de Constantine
75340 Paris cedex 07
**Tel:** +33 (1) 4955 7300
**Fax:** +33 (1) 4705 7702
**Email:** information@britishcouncil.fr
**Website:** www.britishcouncil.fr

## GEORGIA, Tbilisi

The British Council
34 Rustaveli Avenue, Tbilisi 380008
**Tel:** +995 32 250 407/988014
**Fax:** +995 32 989591
**Email:** office.bc@ge.britishcouncil.org
**Website:** www.britishcouncil.org.ge

## GERMANY, Berlin

The British Council
Hackescher Markt 1
10178 Berlin
**Tel:** +49 (0) 30 311 0990
**Fax:** +49 (0) 30 311 09920
**Email:** bc.berlin@britishcouncil.de
**Website:** www.britishcouncil.de

## GHANA, Accra

The British Council
11 Liberia Road
PO Box GP 771
Accra
**Tel:** +233 21 683 968
**Fax:** +233 21 683 062
**Email:** infoaccra@gh.britishcouncil.org
**Website:** www.britishcouncil.org/ghana

## GHANA, Kumasi

The British Council
Bank Road
PO Box KS 1996
Kumasi
**Tel:** +233 51 23462
**Fax:** +233 51 26725
**Email:** infokumasi@gh.britishcouncil.org

## GREECE, Athens

The British Council
17 Kolonaki Square
Plateia Philikis Etairias
10673 Athens
**Tel:** +30 210 369 2333
**Fax:** +30 210 363 4769
**Email:** customerservices@britishcouncil.gr
**Website:** www.britishcouncil.org/greece

## GREECE, Thessaloniki

The British Council
Ethnikis Amynis 9
P. O. Box 50007
54013 Thessaloniki
**Tel:** +30 2310 378 300
**Fax:** +30 2310 282 498
**Email:** general.enquiries@britishcouncil.gr

## HUNGARY, Budapest

The British Council
Benczúr u. 26
1068 Budapest
**Tel:** +36 (1) 478 4700
**Fax:** +36 (1) 342 5728
**Email:** information@britishcouncil.hu
**Website:** www.britishcouncil.hu

## INDIA, New Delhi

The British Council
17 Kasturba Gandhi Marg
New Delhi 110 001
**Tel:** +91 11 2-3711401
**Fax:** +91 11 2-3710717
**Email:** delhi.enquiry@in.britishcouncil.org
**Website:** www.britishcouncil.org/india

## INDONESIA, Jakarta

The British Council
S. Widjojo Centre
Jalan Jenderal Sudirman Kav 71
Jakarta 12190
**Tel:** +62 (21) 252 4115
**Fax:** +62 (21) 252 4129
**Email:** information@britishcouncil.or.id
**Website:** www.britishcouncil.org/indonesia

## INDONESIA, Surabaya

The British Council
Jalan Cokroaminoto 12A, 3rd Floor
Surabaya 60264
**Tel:** +62 (31) 568 9958
**Fax:** +62 (31) 568 9957
**Email:** tony.saputra@britishcouncil.or.id

## IRAN, Tehran

The British Council
Qolhak
Dr Shariati Avenue
Opposite Bonbaste Elahieh
19396 13661 Tehran
**Tel:** +98 (021) 200 1222
**Fax:** +98 (021) 200 7604
**Email:** enquiries@britishcouncil.org.ir
**Website:** www.britishcouncil.org/iran

## IRELAND, Dublin

The British Council
Newmount House
22/24 Lower Mount Street
Dublin 2
**Tel:** +3531 676 4088
**Fax:** +3531 676 6945
**Email:** tom.farrell@ie.britishcouncil.org
**Website:** www.britishcouncil.org/ireland

## ISRAEL, Tel Aviv

The British Council
12 Hahilazon Street, Ramat Gan, Tel Aviv 52136
**Tel:** +972 (0) 3 611 3600
**Fax:** +972 (0) 3 611 3640
**Email:** bcta@britishcouncil.org.il
**Website:** www.britishcouncil.org.il

## ISRAEL, Nazareth

The British Council
P O Box 2545
Nazareth 16121
**Tel:** +972 (0)4 657 9570
**Fax:** +972 (0)4 655 0436
**Email:** Jane.Shurrush@britishcouncil.org.il

## ISRAEL , West Jerusalem TC, i

The British Council
Hagmidal, Gan Ha'technologi
Jerusalem 96951
**Tel:** +972 (0)2 6403900

**Fax:** +972 (0)2 6403919
**Email:** bcwjlm@britishcouncil.org.il

## ITALY, Rome

The British Council
Via Quattro Fontane 20
00184 Rome
**Tel:** +39 (06) 478 141
**Fax:** +39 (06) 481 4296
**Email:** studyandcultureuk@britishcouncil.it
**Website:** www.britishcouncil.org/italy

## ITALY, Bologna TC

The British Council
Corte Isolani 8
Strada Maggiore 19
40125 Bologna
**Tel:** +39 (051) 225 142
**Fax:** +39 (051) 224 238
**Email:** enquiries.bologna@britishcouncil.it

## ITALY , Milan TC

The British Council
Via Manzoni 38
20121 Milan
**Tel:** +39 (02) 772 221
**Fax:** +39 (02) 781 119
**Email:** enquiries.milan@britishcouncil.it

## ITALY , Naples

The British Council
Via Morghen 36
80129 Naples
**Tel:** +39 (081) 578 5817
**Fax:** +39 (081) 556 2585
**Email:** enquiries.naples@britishcouncil.it

## JAMAICA, Kingston

The British Council
28 Trafalgar Road
Kingston 10
**Tel:** +1 876 929 7090
**Fax:** +1 876 960 3030
**Email:** bcjamaica@britishcouncil.org.jm
**Website:** www.britishcouncil.org/caribbean

## JAPAN, Tokyo

The British Council
1-2 Kagurazaka
Shinjuku-ku

Tokyo 162-0825
**Tel:** +81 (0) 3 3235 8031
**Fax:** +81 (0) 3 3235 8040
**Email:** enquiries@britishcouncil.or.jp
**Website:** www.britishcouncil.org/japan

## JAPAN, Kyoto TC

The British Council
Karasuma Chuo Building 8F
659 Tearaimizu-cho, Nishikikoji-agaru
Karasuma-dori
Nakagyo-ku, Kyoto 604-8152
**Tel:** +81 (0) 75 229 7151
**Fax:** +81 (0) 75 229 7154
**Email:** enquiries@britishcouncil.or.jp

## JAPAN, Nagoya

The British Council
NHK Nagoya Broadcasting Centre Building 6F
1-13-3, Higashi Sakura
Higashi-ku Nagoya-shi, Aichi 461-0005
**Tel:** +81 (0) 52 963 3671
**Fax:** +81 (0) 52 963 3670
**Email:** enquiries.nagoya@britishcouncil.or.jp

## JAPAN, Osaka

The British Council
Dojima Avanza 4F
1-6-20 Dojima, Kita-ku
Osaka-shi, Osaka 530-0003
**Tel:** +81 (0) 6 6342 5301
**Fax:** +81 (0) 6 6342 5311
**Email:** enquiries.osaka@britishcouncil.or.jp

## JORDAN, Amman

The British Council
First Circle , Jebel Amman
PO Box 634, Amman 11118
**Tel:** +962 6 4636147
**Fax:** +962 6 465 6413
**Email:** bcamman@britishcouncil.org.jo
**Website:** www.britishcouncil.org.jo

## KAZAKHSTAN, Almaty

The British Council
Republic Square 13, 480013 Almaty, Kazakhstan
**Tel:** +7 3272 72 0111
**Fax:** +7 3272 72 0113
**Email:** general@kz.britishcouncil.org
**Website:** www.britishcouncil.kz

## KAZAKHSTAN, Astana

The British Council
1st Floor, Renco Building
62 Cosmonaut Street, Chubary District
473000 Astana
**Tel:** +7 3172 971179
**Fax:** +7 3172 971180
**Email:** general@kzbritishcouncil.org

## KENYA , Nairobi

The British Council
ICEA Building
Kenyatta Avenue
PO Box 40751
Nairobi
**Tel:** +254 (0) 20 334 855
**Fax:** +254 (0) 20 339 854
**Email:** information@britishcouncil.or.ke
**Website:** www.britishcouncil.org/kenya

## KOREA, Seoul

The British Council
Hungkuk Life Insurance Building 4F
226 Shinmunro 1-ga
Jongro-gu, Seoul 110-786
**Tel:** +82 (0) 2 3702 0600
**Fax:** +82 (0) 2 3702 0660
**Email:** info@britishcouncil.or.kr
**Website:** www.bckorea.or.kr

## KUWAIT, Kuwait City

The British Council
2 Al Arabi Street, Block 2
PO Box 345, 13004 Safat
Mansouriya, Safat 13004
**Tel:** +965 251 5512
**Fax:** +965 252 0069
**Email:** bc.enquiries@kw.britishcouncil.org
**Website:** www.britishcouncil.org/kuwait

## LATVIA, Riga

The British Council
5a Blaumana iela
Riga LV-1011
**Tel:** +371 728 1730
**Fax:** +371 750 4100
**Email:** mail@britishcouncil.lv
**Website:** www.britishcouncil.lv

## LEBANON, Beirut

The British Council
Sidani Street
Azar Building
Beirut
**Tel:** +961 (1) 740 123
**Fax:** +961 (1) 739 461
**Email:** general.enquiries@lb.britishcouncil.org
**Website:** www.britishcouncil.org/lebanon

## LIBYA, Tripoli

The British Council
24th Floor,
Burj al Fatah,
PO Box 4206, Tripoli
**Tel:** + 218 21 335 1473/5
**Fax:** +218 21 335 1471
**Email:** info.libya@britishcouncil-ly.org
**Website:** www.britishcouncil.org/libya

## LITHUANIA, Vilnius

The British Council
Jogailos 4
LT - 2001 Vilnius
**Tel:** +370 5 264 4890
**Fax:** +370 5 264 4893
**Email:** mail@britishcouncil.lt
**Website:** www.britishcouncil.lt

## MACEDONIA, Skopje

The British Council
Bulevar Goce Delcev 6
P.O. Box 562
1000 Skopje
**Tel:** +389 2 313 5035
**Fax:** +389 2 313 5036
**Email:** info@britishcouncil.org.mk
**Website:** www.britishcouncil.org/macedonia

## MALAWI, Lilongwe

The British Council
Plot No 13/20 City Centre
P O Box 30222
Lilongwe 3
**Tel:** +265 (0) 1 773 244
**Fax:** +265 (0) 1 772 945
**Email:** Info@britishcouncil.org.mw
**Website:** www.britishcouncil.org/malawi

## MALAYSIA, Kuala Lumpur

The British Council
PO Box 10539
50916 Kuala Lumpur
**Tel:** +60 (0) 3 2723 7900
**Fax:** +60 (0) 3 2713 6599
**Email:** kualalumpur@britishcouncil.org.my
**Website:** www.britishcouncil.org.my

## MALAYSIA, Kota Kinabalu

The British Council
1st Floor EONCMG Building
1 Lorong Sagunting
88000 Kota Kinabalu
Sabah
**Tel:** +60 (88) 222 059
**Fax:** +60 (88) 238 059
**Email:** sabah@britishcouncil.org.my

## MALAYSIA, Penang TC

The British Council
3 Weld Quay
10300 Penang
Malaysia
**Tel:** +60 (4) 263 0330
**Fax:** +60 (4) 263 3262
**Email:** penang.info@britishcouncil.org.my

## MALTA, Valletta

The British Council
Whitehall Mansions, Ta'Xbiex Seafront
**Tel:** +356 23 238403
**Fax:** +356 23 238402
**Email:** information@britishcouncil.org.mt
**Website:** www.britishcouncil.org/malta

## MAURITIUS, Rose Hill

The British Council
Royal Road, PO Box 111, Rose Hill
**Tel:** +230 454 9550
**Fax:** +230 454 9553
**Email:** general.enquiries@mu. britishcouncil.org
**Website:** www.britishcouncil.org/mauritius

## MEXICO, Mexico City

The British Council
Lope de Vega 316
Col. Chapultepec Morales
Mexico City
11570 DF

**Tel:** +52 (55) 5263 1900
**Fax:** +52 (55) 5263 1940
**Email:** bcmexico@britishcouncil.org.mx
**Website:** www.britishcouncil.org/mexico

## MOROCCO, Rabat

The British Council
36 Rue de Tanger
BP 427, Rabat
**Tel:** +212 (37) 760 836
**Fax:** +212 (37) 760 850
**Email:** bc@britishcouncil.org.ma
**Website:** www.britishcouncil.org/morocco

## MOROCCO, Casablanca

The British Council
87 Boulevard Nador, Quartier Polo
20500 Casablanca
**Tel:** +212 (0)22 520990
**Fax:** +212 (0)22 520964
**Email:** casa.info@britishcouncil.org.ma

## MOZAMBIQUE, Maputo

The British Council
Rua John Issa, 226
P.O. Box 4178
Maputo
**Tel:** +258 (1) 355 000
**Fax:** +258 (1) 321 577
**Email:** General.enquiries@britishcouncil.org.mz
**Website:** www.britishcouncil.org/mozambique

## NAMIBIA, Windhoek

The British Council
1-5 Fidel Castro Street
Windhoek
**Tel:** +264 (61) 226 776
**Fax:** +264 (61) 227 530
**Email:** general.enquiries@britishcouncil.org.na
**Website:** www.britishcouncil.org/namibia

## NEPAL, Kathmandu

The British Council
PO Box 640
Lainchaur
Kathmandu
**Tel:** +977 1 4410 798
**Fax:** +977 1 4410 545
**Email:** general.enquiry@britishcouncil.org.np
**Website:** www.britishcouncil.org.np

## NETHERLANDS, Amsterdam

The British Council
Weteringschans 85A
1017 RZ Amsterdam
**Tel:** +31 (20) 550 6060
**Fax:** +31 (20) 620 7389
**Email:** information@britcoun.nl
**Website:** www.britishcouncil.org/netherlands

## NEW ZEALAND, Wellington

The British Council
44 Hill Street
PO Box 1812
Wellington 1
**Tel:** +64 (4) 924 2880
**Fax:** +64 (4) 473 6261
**Email:** enquiries@britishcouncil.org.nz
**Website:** www.britishcouncil.org/nz

## NEW ZEALAND, Auckland

The British Council
151 Queen Street
Private Bag 92014
Auckland
**Tel:** +64 (0) 9 373 4478
**Fax:** +64 (0) 9 373 4479
**Email:** enquiries@britishcouncil.org.nz

## NIGERIA, Abuja

The British Council
Plot 2935
IBB Way
Maitama
P.M.B. 550
Garki
Abuja, FCT
**Tel:** +234 (9) 413 7870-7
**Fax:** +234 (9) 413 0902
**Email:** maureen.ideozu@ng.britishcouncil.org
**Website:** www.britishcouncil.org/nigeria

## NIGERIA, Lagos

The British Council
11 Alfred Rewane Road
Ikoyi
PO Box 3702
Lagos
**Tel:** +234 (1) 269 2188
**Fax:** +234 (1) 269 2193
**Email:** yinka.ijabiyi@ng.britishcouncil.org

## NIGERIA, Kano

The British Council
10 Emir's Palace Road
(PMB 3003)
Kano
**Tel:** +234 (64) 646652
**Fax:** +234 (64) 632500
**Email:** Kano.info@ng.britishcouncil.org

## NORWAY, Oslo

The British Council
Fridtjof Nansens Plass 5
0160 Oslo
**Tel:** +47 (22) 396 190
**Fax:** +47 (22) 424 039
**Email:** british.council@britishcouncil.no
**Website:** www.britishcouncil.no

## OMAN, Muscat

The British Council
Road One
Madinat al Sultan, Qaboos West, Muscat
P.O. Box 73 Postal Code 115
**Tel:** +968 600 548
**Fax:** +968 699 163
**Email:** bc.muscat@om.britishcouncil.org
**Website:** www.britishcouncil.org/oman

## PAKISTAN, Islamabad

The British Council
House 1, Street 61, F-6/3
P.O. Box 1135
Islamabad
**Tel:** +92 (51) 111 424 424
**Fax:** +92 (51) 111 425 425
**Email:** info@britishcouncil.org.pk
**Website:** www.britishcouncil.org/pakistan

## PAKISTAN , Karachi

The British Council
20 Bleak House Road
P.O. Box 10410
Karachi 75530
**Tel:** +92 (21) 111 424 424
**Fax:** +92 (21) 111 425 425
**Email:** info@britishcouncil.org.pk

## PALESTINIAN TERRITORIES, East Jerusalem

The British Council
31 Nablus Road

PO Box 19136
East Jerusalem 97200
**Tel:** +972 (2) 628 7111
**Fax:** +972 (2) 628 3021
**Email:** british.council@ps.britishcouncil.org
**Website:** www.ps.britishcouncil.org

## PALESTINIAN TERRITORIES, Gaza

The British Council
Al-Nasra Street, Al-Rimal
Gaza City
PO Box 355
**Tel:** +972 (0)8 282 2274
**Fax:** +972 (0)8 282 0512
**Email:** british.council@ps.britishcouncil.org

## PERU, Lima

The British Council
Torre Parque Mar (Floor 22)
Av Jose Larco 1301
Miraflores
Lima 18
**Tel:** +51 (1) 617 3060
**Fax:** +51 (1) 617 3065
**Email:** bc.lima@britishcouncil.org.pe
**Website:** www.britishcouncil.org/peru

## PHILIPPINES, Manila

The British Council
10th Floor, Taipan Place
Emerald Avenue
Ortigas Centre
Pasig City 1605
**Tel:** +63 (2) 914 1011  - 14
**Fax:** +63 (2) 914 1020
**Email:** britishcouncil@britishcouncil.org.ph
**Website:** www.britishcouncil.org.ph

## POLAND, Warsaw

The British Council
Al Jerozolimskie 59
00 697 Warsaw
**Tel:** +48 (22) 695 5900
**Fax:** +48 (22) 621 9955
**Email:** bc.warsaw@britishcouncil.pl
**Website:** www.britishcouncil.org/poland

## POLAND, Krakow

The British Council
Rynek Glowny 26

31-007 Krakow
**Tel:** +48 (12) 428 5930
**Fax:** +48 (12) 428 5940
**Email:** bc.krakow@britishcouncil.pl

## PORTUGAL, Lisbon

The British Council
Rua Luis Fernandes 1-3
1249-062 Lisbon
**Tel:** +351 21 321 45 00
**Fax:** +351 21 347 61 51
**Email:** lisbon.enquiries@pt.britcoun.org
**Website:** www.pt.britishcouncil.org

## PORTUGAL, Coimbra

The British Council
Rua de Tomar 4
3000-401 Coimbra
**Tel:** +351 239 823 700
**Fax:** +351 239 836 705
**Email:** Coimbra.Enquiries@pt.britcoun.org

## PORTUGAL, Porto

The British Council
Rua do Breyner 155
4050-126 Porto
**Tel:** +351 22 207 3060
**Fax:** +351 22 207 3068
**Email:** Porto.Enquiries@pt.britcoun.org

## PORTUGAL, Parede

The British Council
Rua Dr Camilio Dionisio Alvares
Lote 6
2775-177 Parede
**Tel:** +351 21 458 7370
**Fax:** +351 21 457 9918
**Email:** parede.enquiries@pt.britcoun.org

## PORTUGAL, Cascais

The British Council
Edificio Sao Jose
1 Piso, Sala 102
Av Combatentes da Grande Guerra
2750-326 Cascais
**Tel:** +351 21 482 0714
**Fax:** +351 21 482 0722
**Email:** Cascais.Enquiries@pt.britcoun.org

## QATAR, Doha

The British Council
93 Al Sadd Street
PO Box 2992
Doha
**Tel:** +974 442 6193 / 4
**Fax:** +974 442 3315
**Email:** general.enquiries@qa.britishcouncil.org
**Website:** www.britishcouncil.org/qatar

## ROMANIA, Bucharest

The British Council
Calea Dorobantilor 14
010572 Bucharest
**Tel:** +40 21 307 9600
**Fax:** +40 21 307 96 01
**Email:** bc.romania@britishcouncil.ro
**Website:** www.britishcouncil.ro

## RUSSIA, Moscow

The British Council
Ulitsa Nikoloyamskaya 1
Moscow 109189
**Tel:** +7 095 782 0200
**Fax:** +7 095 782 0201
**Email:** bc.moscow@britishcouncil.ru
**Website:** www.britishcouncil.ru

## RUSSIA, St Petersburg

The British Council
46 Fontanka River Embankment
St Petersburg 191025
Tel: +7 812 118 5060
Fax: +7 812 118 5061
**Email:** bc.stpetersburg@britishcouncil.ru

## SAUDI ARABIA, Riyadh

The British Council
Tower B, 2nd floor
Al Mousa Centre, Olaya Street
P.O. Box 58012
Riyadh 11594
**Tel:** +966 (1) 462 1818
**Fax:** +966 (1) 462 0663
**Email:** Enquiry.riyadh@sa.britishcouncil.org
**Website:** www.britishcouncil.org/saudiarabia

## SAUDI ARABIA, Jeddah

The British Council
3rd Floor

Farsi Centre,
Waly Al Ahd St.
PO Box 3424, Jeddah 21471
**Tel:** +966 2 657 6200
**Fax:** + 966 2 657 6123
**Email:** enquiry.jeddah@sa.britishcouncil.org

## SAUDI ARABIA, Dammam

The British Council
2nd Floor, Al-Waha Mall
First Street
P.O. Box 8387, Dammam 31482
**Tel:** +966 3 826 9036 / 9831
**Fax:** +966 3 826 8753
**Email:** enquiry.dammam@sa.britishcouncil.org

## SENEGAL, Dakar

The British Council
34-36 Boulevard de la Republique
Immeuble Sonatel
BP 6238
Dakar
**Tel:** +221 822 2015/822 2048
**Fax:** +221 821 8136
**Email:** postmaster@britishcouncil.sn
**Website:** www.britishcouncil.org/senegal

## SERBIA, Belgrade

The British Council
Terazije 8/I, POB 248,
11000 Belgrade
**Tel:** + 381 (11) 3023 800
**Fax:** + 381 (11) 3023 898
**Email:** info@britishcouncil.org.yu
**Website:** www.britishcouncil.org/yugoslavia

## SIERRA LEONE, Freetown

The British Council
Tower Hill
PO Box 124
Freetown
**Tel:** +238 (22) 222 223
**Fax:** +238 (22) 224 123
**Email:** enquiry@sl.britishcouncil.org
**Website:** www.britishcouncil.org/sierraleone

## SINGAPORE, Singapore

The British Council
30 Napier Road
258509 Singapore

**Tel:** +65 6473 1111
**Fax:** +65 6472 1010
**Email:** enquiries@britishcouncil.org.sg
**Website:** www.britishcouncil.org.sg

## SLOVAKIA, Bratislava

The British Council
Panska 17 - P.O. Box 68
814 99 Bratislava
**Tel:** +421 (2) 5443 1074 / 5443 1185
**Fax:** +421 (2) 5443 4705
**Email:** info.bratislava@britishcouncil.sk
**Website:** www.britishcouncil.org/slovakia

## SLOVENIA, Ljubljana

The British Council
Tivloi Center, Tivolska 30
Ljubljana 1000
**Tel:** +386 (0) 1 300 2030
**Fax:** +386 (0) 1 300 2044
**Email:** info@britishcouncil.si
**Website:** www.britishcouncil.si

## SOUTH AFRICA, Pretoria

The British Council
Suite 1, Sanlam Gables
1209 Schoeman Street
Hatfield, Pretoria 0083
**Tel:** +27 (12) 431 2400
**Fax:** +27 (12) 431 2415
**Email:** information@britishcouncil.org.za
**Website:** www.britishcouncil.org/southafrica

## SOUTH AFRICA, Johannesburg

The British Council
Ground Floor
Forum 1, Braampark
33 Hoofd Street
Braamfontein
Johannesburg 2001
**Tel:** +27 (11) 718 4300
**Fax:** +27 (11) 718 4400
**Email:** information@britishcouncil.org.za

## SPAIN, Madrid

The British Council
Paseo del General Martinez
Campos 31
28010 Madrid
**Tel:** +34 91 337 3500

Fax: +34 91 337 3573
Email: Madrid@britishcouncil.es
Website: www.britishcouncil.es

## SPAIN, Barcelona

The British Council
Calle Amigo 83
08021 Barcelona
Tel: +34 93 241 9700
Fax: +34 93 202 3168
Email: barcelona@britishcouncil.es

## SPAIN, Bilbao

The British Council
Avenida Lehendakari Aguirre 29 - 2º
Deusto
48014 Bilbao
Tel: +34 94 476 3650
Fax: +34 94 476 2016
Email: bilbao@britishcouncil.es

## SPAIN, Segovia

The British Council
Avenida Padre Claret 3
40003 Segovia
Tel: +34 921 43 48 13
Fax: +34 921 43 48 13
Email: aoife.buckley@britishcouncil.es

## SPAIN, Valencia

The British Council
Avinguda de Catalunya, 9
46020 Valencia
Tel: +34 96 339 29 80
Fax: +34 96 369 13 89
Email: Valencia@britishcouncil.es

## SRI LANKA, Colombo

The British Council
49 Alfred House Gardens
PO Box 753
Colombo 3
Tel: +94 (0)11 2581171
Fax: +94 (0)11 2587 079
Email: enquiries@britishcouncil.lk
Website: www.britishcouncil.lk

## SUDAN, Khartoum

The British Council
14 Abu Sin Street

PO Box 1253
Central Khartoum
Tel: +249 183 780 817 / 777310
Fax: +249 183 774 935
Email: info@sd.britishcouncil.org
Website: www.britishcouncil.org/sudan

## SWEDEN, Stockholm

The British Council
PO Box 27819
S-115 93 Stockholm
Tel: +46 (8) 671 3110
Fax: +46 (8) 663 7271
Email: info@britishcouncil.se
Website: www.britishcouncil.org/sweden

## SWITZERLAND, Berne

The British Council
Sennweg 2
PO Box 532
CH 3000 Berne 9
Tel: +41 (31) 301 1473
Fax: +41 (31) 301 1459
Email: britishcouncil@britishcouncil.ch
Website: www.britishcouncil.ch

## SYRIA , Damascus

The British Council
Maysaloun Street
Shalaan
P O Box 33105
Damascus
Tel: +963 (11) 331 0631
Fax: +963 (11) 332 1467
Email: general.enquiries@sy.britishcouncil.org
Website: www.britishcouncil.org/syria

## TAIWAN, Taipei

British Council
2F-1, 106 XinYi Rd
Section 5
Taipei 110
Tel: +886 (0) 2 8722 1000
Fax: +886 (0) 2 8786 0985
Email: enquiries@britishcouncil.org.tw
Website: www.britishcouncil.org/taiwan

## TANZANIA, Dar Es Salaam

The British Council
Samora Avenue / Ohio Street

PO Box 9100
Dar Es Salaam
**Tel:** +255 (22) 211 6574
**Fax:** +255 (22) 211 2669
**Email:** info@britishcouncil.or.tz
**Website:** www.britishcouncil.org/tanzania

## THAILAND, Bangkok

The British Council
254 Chulalongkorn Soi 64
Siam Square
Phayathai Road
Pathumwan
Bangkok 10330
**Tel:** +66 (2) 252 5480
**Fax:** +66 (2) 253 5312
**Email:** info@britishcouncil.or.th
**Website:** www.britishcouncil.or.th

## THAILAND, Chiang Mai

The British Council
198 Bumrungraj Road
Chiang Mai 50000
**Tel:** +66 (53) 242 103
**Fax:** +66 (53) 244 781
**Email: info@britishcouncil.or.th**

## TRINIDAD (Caribbean), Port of Spain

The British Council
19 St Clair Avenue,
St Clair, PO Box 778
Port of Spain, Trinidad
**Tel:** +1 868 628 0565
Fax: +1 868 622 2853
**Email:** candice.fabien@britishcouncil.org.tt
**Website:** www.britishcouncil.org/caribbean

## TUNISIA, Tunis

The British Council
c/o British Embassy
5 Place de la Victoire
BP 229
Tunis 1015 RP
**Tel:** +216 71 259 053 / 351 754
**Fax:** +216 71 353 411
**Email:** info@tn.britishcouncil.org
**Website:** www.britishcouncil.org.tn

## TURKEY, Ankara

The British Council
Karum Is Merkesi
C Blok No 437 Kat 5
Kavaklidere/ Ankara
**Tel:** +90 312 455 3600
**Fax:** +90 312 455 3636
**Email:** bc.ankara@britishcouncil.org.tr
**Website:** www.britishcouncil.org.tr

## TURKEY, Istanbul

The British Council
PO Box 16
81690 Besiktas
Istanbul
**Tel:** +90 212 355 5657
**Fax:** +90 212 355 5658
**Email:** bc.istanbul@britishcouncil.org.tr

## TURKEY, Izmir

The British Council
C/o Izmir Ekonomi Universitesi
Ismet Kaptan Mahallesi
Sakarya cad. No 156
Balçova 35330 Izmir
**Tel:** +90 238 295 00 52
**Fax:** +90 238 295 00 27
**Email:** bc.izmir@britishcouncil.org.tr

## UGANDA , Kampala

The British Council
Rwenzori Courts
Plot 2 and 4a
Nakasero Road
PO Box 7070
Kampala
**Tel:** +256 (0)41 234 725/730
**Fax:** +256 (0)41 254 853
**Email:** info@britishcouncil.or.ug
**Website:** www.britishcouncil.org/uganda

## UK, London

The British Council
10 Spring Gardens
London SW1A 2BN
**Tel:** +44 (0) 20 7930 8466
**Fax:** +44 (0) 20 7839 6347
**Email:** firstname.surname@britishcouncil.org
**Website:** www.britishcouncil.org

## UKRAINE, Kyiv

The British Council
4/12 Vul. Hryhoriya Skovorody
Kyiv 04070
**Tel:** +380 (44) 490 5600
**Fax:** +380 (44) 490 5605
**Email:** enquiry@britishcouncil.org.ua
**Website:** www.britishcouncil.org.ua

## UNITED ARAB EMIRATES, Abu Dhabi

The British Council
Villa no. 7, Al Nasr Street
Khalidiya
Abu Dhabi
P.O. Box 46523
**Tel:** +9712 665 9300
**Fax:** +9712 666 4340
**Email:** information@ae.britishcouncil.org
**Website:** www.britishcouncil.org/uae

## UNITED ARAB EMIRATES, Dubai

The British Council
Tariq bin Zaid Street
(near Rashid Hospital)
P.O. Box 1636
Dubai
**Tel:** +9714 337 0109
**Fax:** +9714 337 0703
**Email:** information@ae.britishcouncil.org

## USA, Washington

British Embassy
3100 Massachusetts Avenue NW
Washington DC 20008-3600
**Tel:** +1 202 588 6500 / 7830
**Fax:** +1 202 588 7918
**Email:** studyintheuk@us.britishcouncil.org
**Website:** www.britishcouncil-usa.org

## UZBEKISTAN, Tashkent

British Council Information Centre
11 Kounaev Street
Tashkent 700031
**Tel:** +998 (71) 120 6752
**Fax:** +998 (71) 120 6371
**Email:** bc-tashkent@britishcouncil.uz
**Website:** www.britishcouncil.org/uzbekistan

## VENEZUELA, Caracas

The British Council
Piso 3, Torre Credicard
Av. Principal El Bosque
Chacaito, Caracas
**Tel:** +58 (212) 952 9965
**Fax:** +58 (212) 952 9691
**Email:** bc-venezuela@britishcouncil.org.ve
**Website:** www.britishcouncil.org.ve

## VIETNAM, Hanoi

The British Council
40 Cat Linh Street
Dong Da
Hanoi
**Tel:** +84 (0)4 843 6780
**Fax:** +84 (0)4 843 4962
**Email:** bchanoi@britishcouncil.org.vn
**Website:** www.britishcouncil.org/vietnam

## VIETNAM, Ho Chi Minh City

The British Council
25 Le Duan
District 1
Ho Chi Minh City
**Tel:** +84 (0)8 823 2862
**Fax:** +84 (0)8 823 2861
**Email:** bchcmc@britishcouncil.org.vn

## YEMEN, Sana'a

The British Council
3rd Floor, Administrative Tower
Sana'a Trade Centre
Algiers Street
PO Box 2157
Sana'a
**Tel:** +967 1448 356/7
**Fax:** +967 1448 360
**Email:** britishcouncil@ye.britishcouncil.org
**Website:** www.britishcouncil.org/yemen

## ZAMBIA, Lusaka

The British Council
Heroes Place
Cairo Road, (PO Box 34571)
Lusaka
**Tel:** +260 (1) 223 602 / 228 332
**Fax:** +260 (1) 224 122
**Email:** info@britishcouncil.org.zm
**Website:** www.britishcouncil.org/zambia

## ZIMBABWE, Harare

The British Council
Corner House, Samora Machel Avenue
P. O. Box 664
Harare
**Tel:** +263 4 775 313/4
**Fax:** +263 4 756 661
**Email:** general.enquiries@britishcouncil.org.zw
**Website:** www.britishcouncil.org.zw

# Canadian Embassies

When preparing to teach and travel overseas it is vital to contact the your local embassy or consulate within the country you are planning to visit to find out information on visas, restrictions and a variety of other information.

## Afghanistan

Embassy of Canada
Address: Street No. 15, House No. 256, Wazir Akbar Khan, Kabul, Afghanistan
**Tel:** 93 (0) 799 742 800
**Fax:** 93 (0) 799 742 805
**Email:** kabul@international.gc.ca
**Website:** www.canada-afghanistan.gc.ca

## Albania

Consulate of Canada
Address: Rruga "Dervish Hima," Kulla, No. 2, Apt. 22, Tirana, Albania
Tel: 355 (4) 257 274 / 25 7275 / 355 (68) 20 29364
**Fax:** 355 (4) 257 273
**Email:** canadalb@canada.gov.al

## Algeria

Embassy of Canada
Address: 18, rue Mustapha-Khalef, Ben Aknoun, Alger, Algeria
Postal Address: P.O. Box 48, Alger-Gare, 16000 Alger, Algeria
**Tel:** 213 (0) 70-08-30-00
**Fax:** 213 (0) 70-08-30-70
**Email:** alger@international.gc.ca
**Website:** www.algeria.gc.ca

## Angola

Consulate of Canada
Address: Rua Rei Katyavala 113, Luanda, Angola
**Tel:** 244 (222) 448-371,- 377, -366
**Fax:** 244 (2) 449-494
**Email:** consul.can@angonet.org

## Argentina

Embassy of Canada
Address: 2828 Tagle, C1425EEH Buenos Aires, Argentina
Postal Address: P.O. Box 1598, C1000WAP, Buenos Aires, C1000WAP Correo Central, Argentina
**Tel:** 54 (11) 4808-1000
**Fax:** 54 (11) 4808-1012
**Email:** bairs@international.gc.ca
**Website:** www.dfait-maeci.gc.ca/bairs

## Armenia

Consulate of Canada
Address: 1 Amirian Street, Hotel Marriott, Suite 306, Yerevan, Armenia
**Tel:** 374 (10) 56-79-90
**Fax:** 374 (10) 56-79-90

## Australia

High Commission of Canada
Address: Commonwealth Avenue, Canberra ACT 2600, Australia
**Tel:** 61 (2) 6270-4000
**Emergency toll-free to Ottawa:** 0011-800-2326-6831
**Fax:** 61 (2) 6270-4081
**Email:** cnbra@international.gc.ca
**Website:** www.dfait-maeci.gc.ca/australia

Consulate of Canada
Address: Level 50, 101 Collins Street, Melbourne, Victoria 3000, Australia
**Tel:** 61 (3) 9653-9674
**Emergency toll-free to Ottawa:** 0011-800-2326-6831

Consulate of Canada
Address: 3rd Floor, 267 St. George's Terrace, Perth, Western Australia 6000, Australia
**Tel:** 61 (8) 9322-7930
Emergency toll-free to Ottawa: 0011-800-2326-6831
**Fax:** 61 (8) 9261-7706

Consulate General of Canada
Address: Level 5, Quay West, 111 Harrington Street, Sydney, New South Wales 2000, Australia
**Tel:** 61 (2) 9364-3000
Emergency toll-free to Ottawa: 0011-800-2326-6831
**Fax:** 61 (2) 9364-3098
**Email:** sydny@international.gc.ca

## Austria

Embassy of Canada
Address: Laurenzerberg 2, 1010 Vienna, Austria
**Tel:** 43 (1) 531-38-3000
Emergency toll-free to Ottawa: 00-800-2326-6831
**Fax:** 43 (1) 531-38-3905
**Email:** vienn@international.gc.ca
**Website:** www.kanada.at

## Bahamas

Consulate of Canada
Address: Shirley Street Shopping Plaza, Nassau, Bahamas
Postal Address: P.O. Box SS-6371, Nassau, Bahamas
**Tel:** 1 (242) 393-2123, -2124
Emergency toll-free to Ottawa: 1-881-949-9993
**Fax:** 1 (242) 393-1305
**Email:** cdncon@batelnet.bs

## Bahrain

Consulate of Canada
Address: Al Jasrah Tower, 12th Floor, Building No. 95, Road 1702, Block 317, Diplomatic Area, Manama, Kingdom of Bahrain
Postal Address: P.O. Box 2397, Manama, Bahrain
**Tel:** (973) 17 536270
Emergency toll-free to Ottawa: 800-00-732
**Fax:** (973) 17 532520
**Email:** canadabh@batelco.com.bh

## Bangladesh

High Commission of Canada
Address: House CWN 16/A, Road 48, Gulshan, Dhaka, Bangladesh
Postal Address: P.O. Box 569, Dhaka, 1000, Bangladesh
**Tel:** 880 (2) 988-7091/2/3/4/5/6/7
**Fax:** 880 (2) 882-3043
**Email:** dhaka@international.gc.ca
**Website:** www.bangladesh.gc.ca

## Barbados

High Commission of Canada
Address: Bishop's Court Hill, St. Michael, Barbados
Postal Address: P.O. Box 404, Bridgetown, Barbados
**Tel:** 1 (246) 429-3550
Emergency toll-free to Ottawa: 1-888-949-9993
**Fax:** 1 (246) 437-7436
**Email:** bdgtn@international.gc.ca
**Website:** www.bridgetown.gc.ca

## Belgium

Consulate of Canada
Address: Sint Pietersvliet, 15, B-2000 Anvers, Belgium
**Tel:** 32 (03) 220-0211
Emergency toll-free to Ottawa: 00-800-2326-6831
**Fax:** 32 (03) 220-0204

Embassy of Canada
Address: 2, avenue de Tervueren, 1040 Brussels, Belgium
**Tel:** 32 (02) 741-0611
Emergency toll-free to Ottawa: 00-800-2326-6831
**Fax:** 32 (02) 741-0619
**Email:** bru@international.gc.ca
**Website:** www.ambassade-canada.be

## Belize

Consulate of Canada
Address: 80 Princess Margaret Drive, Belize City, Belize
Postal Address: P.O. Box 610, Belize City, Belize
**Tel:** 501 223-1060
**Fax:** 501 223-0060
**Email:** cdncon.bze@btl.net

## Benin

Canadian Cooperation Support Unit
Address: behind the postal triage at the airport, Lot 2371, Zone Djomèhountin, Cotonou, Benin
Postal Address: P.O. Box 04-1124, Cotonou, Benin
**Tel:** 229 21-30-24-79
**Fax:** 229 21-30-05-32
**Email:** secretariat@uapbenin.net

## Bhutan

Canadian Cooperation Office
Address:
Postal Address: P.O. Box 201, Thimphu, Bhutan
**Tel:** 975 (2) 322-109 or 332-615
Tel. after hours: 975 17110040
**Fax:** 975 (2) 332-614
**Email:** canada@druknet.net.bt

## Bolivia

Consulate of Canada
Address: Calle Victor Sanjinez 2678, Edificio
Barcelona, 2nd Floor, Plaza España (Sopocachí), La
Paz, Bolivia
**Tel:** 591 (2) 241-5141, 5021,4517
**Fax:** 591 (2) 241-4453
**Email:** lapaz@international.gc.ca

## Bosnia and Herzegovina

Embassy of Canada
Address: 4, Grbavicka 71 000, Sarajevo, Bosnia and
Herzegovina
**Tel:** 387 (33) 222-033
**Fax:** 387 (33) 222-044
**Email:** sjevo@international.gc.ca

## Botswana

Consulate of Canada
Address: Vision Hire Building, Queens Road, Plot 182,
Gaborone, Botswana
Postal Address: P.O. Box 882, Gaborone, Botswana
**Tel:** 267 30-4411
**Fax:** 267 30-44-11
**Email:** canada.consul@info.bw

## Brazil

Consulate of Canada
Address: Rua Rio Grande do Norte, 1164-conj. 502,
Belo Horizonte, Minas Gerais, 30130-131, Brazil
**Tel:** 55 (31) 3261-1017
Emergency toll-free to Ottawa: 0-800-891-6614
**Fax:** 55 (31) 3261-1071

Embassy of Canada
Address: Setor de Embaixadas Sul, Avenida das
Naçoes lote 16, 70410-900 Brasilia D.F., Brazil
Postal Address: P.O. Box 00961, Brasilia D.F,
70359-900, Brazil
**Tel:** 55 (61) 3424-5400
Emergency toll-free to Ottawa: 0-800-891-6614

**Fax:** 55 (61) 3424-5490
**Email:** brsla@international.gc.ca
**Website:** www.dfait-maeci.gc.ca/brazil

Consulate of Canada
Address: Av. Atlântica 1130, 4th Floor, Copacabana,
22021-000 Rio de Janeiro,
**Tel:** 55 (21) 2543-3004
**Emergency toll-free to Ottawa:** 0-800-891-6614
**Fax:** 55 (21) 3873-4843, 2275-2195
**Email:** rio@international.gc.ca
**Website:** www.dfait-maeci.gc.ca/brazil

Consulate General of Canada
Address: Centro Empresarial Nações Unidas - Torre
Norte, 16th floor, Avenida Nações Unidas, 12901 São
Paulo, SP, Brazil
Postal Address: P.O. Box CEP 04578-000, São Paulo,
**Tel:** 55 (11) 5509-4321
**Emergency toll-free to Ottawa:** 0-800-891-6614
**Fax:** 55 (11) 5509-4260
**Email:** spalo@international.gc.ca
**Website:** www.dfait-maeci.gc.ca/brazil

## Brunei Darussalam

High Commission of Canada
Address: 5th Floor, Jalan McArthur Building, No. 1,
Jalan McArthur, Bandar Seri Begawan, Brunei
Darussalam
**Tel:** 673 (2) 22-00-43
**Fax:** 673 (2) 22-00-40
**Email:** bsbgn@international.gc.ca
**Website:** www.dfait-maeci.gc.ca/Brunei

## Bulgaria

Consulate of Canada
Address: 9 Moskovska Street, 1000 Sofia, Bulgaria
**Tel:** 359 (2) 969-9710
**Fax:** 359 (2) 981-6081
**Email:** consular@canada-bg.org

## Burkina Faso

Embassy of Canada
Address: rue Agostino Néto, Ouagadougou, Burkina
Faso
Postal Address: P.O. Box 548, Ouagadougou 01,
Province du Kadiogo, Burkina Faso
**Tel:** 226 50-31-18-94
**Fax:** 226 50-31-19-00
**Email:** ouaga@international.gc.ca
**Website:** www.ouagadougou.gc.ca

## Burma

Australian Embassy
Address: 88 Strand Road, Rangoon, Burma (Myanmar)
Tel: 95 (1) 251810
Fax: 95 (1) 246159, 246160

## Burundi

Consulate of Canada
Address: 4708, Boulevard de l'UPRONA, Bujumbura
Postal Address: P.O. Box 7112, Bujumbura, Burundi
Tel: 257 24-58-98
Fax: 257 24-58-99
Email: consulat.canada@usan-bu.net

## Cambodia

Australian Embassy
Address: Villa 11, RV Senei Vannavaut Oum (Street 254), Daun Penh District, Phnom Penh, Cambodia
Tel: 855 (23) 213 470
Fax: 855 (23) 213 413
Email: pnmpn@international.gc.ca
Website: www.phnompenh.gc.ca

## Cameroon - Douala

Consulate of Canada
Address: a/s PRO-PME, 1726, avenue Charles de Gaulle, Douala, Cameroon
Postal Address: P.O. Box 2373, Douala, Cameroon
Tel: 237 343-2934
Fax: 237 342-31-09

## Cameroon - Yaoundé

High Commission of Canada
Address: Immeuble Stamatiades, Place de l'Hôtel de Ville, Yaoundé, Cameroon
Postal Address: P.O. Box 572, Yaoundé, Cameroon
Tel: 237 223-2311
Fax: 237 222-1090
Email: yunde@international.gc.ca

## Cayman Islands

Consulate of Canada
Address: 24 Huldah Avenue, George Town, Cayman Islands
Postal Address: P.O. Box 10102 SMB, George Town, Cayman Islands
Tel: (345) 949-9400
Emergency toll-free to Ottawa: 1-888-949-9993
Fax: (345) 949-9405
Email: cdncon.cayman@candw.ky

## Central African Republic

Consulate of Canada
Address: Cabinet ARC
Postal Address: P.O. Box 514, Bangui, Central African Republic
Tel: 236 61-30-39
Email: consulatbangui@yahoo.fr

## Chad

Consulate of Canada
Address: Rue 5041, Porte 964, Quartier Moursal, N'Djamena, Chad
Postal Address: P.O. Box 6013, N'Djamena, Chad
Tel: 235 53-42-80
Tel. after hours: 235 27-30-27
Email: honconca@intnet.td
Email: nigel.whiteho@intnet.td

## Chile

Consulate of Canada
Address: José Toribio Medina 146, Apt. 601, Antofagasta, Chile
Tel: 56 (55) 24-7652
Emergency toll-free to Ottawa: 800-201-670
Fax: (2) 652-3916
Email: ca.consul.antofa@emol.com

Consulate of Canada
Address: Caupolicán 245, Chiguayante, Concepción, Chile
Postal Address: P.O. Box Casilla 425, Concepción, Chile
Tel: 56 (41) 236-97-05
Emergency toll-free to Ottawa: 800-201-670
Fax: 56 (41) 236-81-85
Email: ca.consul.concep@emol.com

Embassy of Canada
Address: Nueva Tajamar 481, Torre Norte, 12th Floor, Las Condes, Santiago, Chile
Postal Address: P.O. Box Casilla 139, Correo 10, Chile, Chile
Tel: 56 (2) 652-3800
Emergency toll-free to Ottawa: 800-201-670
Fax: 56 (2) 652-3916
Email: stago@international.gc.ca
Website: www.santiago.gc.ca

## China

Embassy of Canada
Address: 19 Dong Zhi Men Wai Street, Chao Yang
District, Beijing 100600, People's Republic of China
Tel: 86 (10) 6532-3536
Emergency toll-free to Ottawa: 10800-1400125;
00800-2326-6831
Fax: 86 (10) 6532-5544
Email: bejing-cs@international.gc.ca
Website: www.beijing.gc.ca

Consulate of Canada
Address: Room 1705, Metropolitan Tower, Wu Yi Lu,
Yu Zhong District, Chongqing 400010, People's
Republic of China
Tel: 86 (23) 6373-8007
Emergency toll-free to Ottawa: 10800-1400125;
00800-2326-6831
Fax: 86 (23) 6373-8026
Email: chonq@international.gc.ca
Website: www.chongqing.gc.ca

Consulate General of Canada
Address: Suite 801, China Hotel Office Tower, Liu
Hua Lu, Guangzhou 510015, People's Republic of
China
Tel: 86 (20) 8666-0569
Emergency toll-free to Ottawa: 10800-1400125;
00800-2326-6831
Fax: 86 (20) 8667-0267
Email: ganzu@international.gc.ca
Website: www.guangzhou.gc.ca

Consulate General of Canada
Address: 14th Floor, One Exchange Square, Central,
Hong Kong SAR, People's Republic of China
Postal Address: P.O. Box 11142, Central, Hong Kong
SAR, China
Tel: 85 (2) 2810-4321
Emergency toll-free to Ottawa: 001-800-2326-6831
Fax: 85 (2) 2810-6736
Email: hkong@international.gc.ca
Website: www.dfait-maeci.gc.ca/hongkong/

Consulate General of Canada
Address: American International Centre, West Tower,
Suite 604, 1376 Nanjing Xi Lu, Shanghai 200040,
People's Republic of China
Tel: 86 (21) 6279-8400
Emergency toll-free to Ottawa: 10800-1400125;
00800-2326-6831
Fax: 86 (21) 6279-8401

Email: shngi@international.gc.ca
Website: www.shanghai.gc.ca

## Colombia

Embassy of Canada
Address: Cra. 7, No. 115-33, Bogotá, Colombia
Postal Address: P.O. Box 110067, Bogotá, Colombia
Tel: 57 (1) 657-9800
Emergency toll-free to Ottawa: 01-800-919-0114
Fax: 57 (1) 657-9912
Email: bgota@international.gc.ca
Website: www.dfait-maeci.gc.ca/bogota

Consulate of Canada
Address: Edificio Centro Ejecutivo Bocagrande,
Carrera 3, No. 8-129, Oficina No. 1103, Cartagena,
Colombia
Tel: 57 (5) 665-5838
Emergency toll-free to Ottawa: 01-800-919-0114
Fax: 57 (5) 665-5837
Email: honcartagena@enred.com

## Costa Rica

Embassy of Canada
Address: La Sabana Executive Business Centre,
Building No. 5, 3rd Floor, behind the Contraloría
General de la República, San José, Costa Rica
Postal Address: P.O. Box 351-1007, San José, Costa
Rica
Tel: 506 242-4400
Emergency toll-free to Ottawa: 0-800-015-1161
Fax: 506 242-4410
Email: sjcra@international.gc.ca
Website: www.dfait-maeci.gc.ca/sanjose

## Côte d'Ivoire

Embassy of Canada
Address: Immeuble Trade Center, 23, avenue Noguès,
Le Plateau, Abidjan, Côte d'Ivoire
Postal Address: P.O. Box 4104, Abidjan 01, Côte
d'Ivoire
Tel: 225 20-30-07-00
Fax: 225 20-30-07-20
Email: abdjn@international.gc.ca
Website: www.dfait-maeci.gc.ca/abidjan

## Croatia

Embassy of Canada
Address: Prilaz Gjure Dezelica 4,10000 Zagreb,
Croatia
Tel: 385 (1) 488-1200,1211

**Fax:** 385 (1) 488-1230
**Email:** zagrb@international.gc.ca
**Website:** www.dfait-maeci.gc.ca/canadaeuropa/croatia

## Cuba

Consulate of Canada
Address: Hotel Atlantico, Suite # 1, Guardalavaca,
Holguín, Cuba
**Tel:** 53 (24) 30-320
**Fax:** 53 (24) 30-290
**Email:** honconcanada.hog@enet.cu

Embassy of Canada
Address: Calle 30, n° 518, Esquina a7a, Miramar,
Havana, Cuba
**Tel:** 53 (7) 204 2516
**Fax:** 53 (7) 204 2004
**Email:** havan@international.gc.ca
**Website:** www.havana.gc.ca

Consulate of Canada
Address: Calle 13E, Avenida Primera y Camino del
Mar, Varadero, Mantanzas, Cuba
**Tel:** 53 (45) 61-2078
**Fax:** 53 (45) 66-7395
**Email:** vra.honcon@enet.cu

## Curaçao

Consulate of Canada
Address: Maduro and Curiel's Bank, N.V., Plaza Jojo
Correa 2-4, Willemstad (Punda), Curaçao, Netherlands
Antilles
Postal Address: P.O. Box 305, Willemstad, Curaçao
**Tel:** 599 (9) 466-1115, 466-1121
**Fax:** 599 (9) 466-1122, 466-1130

## Cyprus

Consulate of Canada
Address: 1 Lambousa Street, 1095 Nicosia, Cyprus
Postal Address: P.O. Box 22115-1517, Nicosia, Cyprus
**Tel:** 357 (2) 2775-508
**Emergency toll-free to Ottawa:** 8009-6082
**Fax:** 357 (2) 2779-905
**Email:** info@consulcanada.com.cy

## Czech Republic

Embassy of Canada
Address: Muchova 6, 160 00 Prague 6, Czech Republic
**Tel:** 420 27210-1800
**Fax:** 420 27210-1890
**Email:** prgue@international.gc.ca

**Website:** www.dfait-maeci.gc.ca/prague

## Democratic Republic of Congo

Embassy of Canada
Address: 17, Pumbu Avenue, Commune de Gombe,
Kinshasa, Democratic Republic of Congo
Postal Address: P.O. Box 8341, Kinshasa 1,
Democratic Republic of Congo
**Tel:** 243 895-0310/0311/0312
**Tel. after hours:** (243) 81-700-5188
**Fax:** 243-997-5403 / 243-81-301-6515
**Email:** kinshasa@international.gc.ca
**Website:** www.congo.gc.ca

## Denmark

Embassy of Canada
Address: Kr. Bernikowsgade 1, 1105 Copenhagen K,
Denmark
**Tel:** 45 33 48 32 00
**Fax:** 45 33 48 32 20
**Email:** copen@international.gc.ca
**Website:** www.canada.dk

Consulate of Canada
Address: Air Greenland, Nuuk Airport, 3900 Nuuk,
Greenland
Postal Address: P.O. Box 1012, Nuuk, 3900, Denmark
**Tel:** 299 31-16-47
**Fax:** 299 32-02-88
**Email:** gohtsh@greenlandair.gl

## Djibouti

Consulate of Canada
Address: Place Lagarde, Djibouti, Djibouti
Postal Address: P.O. Box 1188, Djibouti, Djibouti
**Tel:** 25 (3) 35-38-59, 35-59-50
**Fax:** 25 (3) 35-00-14
**Email:** georgalis@intnet.dj

## Dominican Republic

Consulate of Canada
Address: Calle Virginia E. Ortea, Edificio Isabel de
Torres, Suite 311-C,
Puerto Plata, Dominican Republic
**Tel:** (809) 586-5761
**Emergency toll-free to Ottawa:** 1-888-156-3102
**Fax:** (809) 586-5762
**Email:** pplat.canada@verizon.net.do

Embassy of Canada
Address: Capitán Eugenio de Marchena No. 39, La Esperilla, Santo Domingo, Dominican Republic
Postal Address: P.O. Box 2054, Santo Domingo 1
Tel: (809) 685-1136; 1-200-0012 (toll-free within Dominican Republic - service sans frais en République dominicaine)
Emergency toll-free to Ottawa: 1-888-156-3102
Fax: (809) 682-2691
Email: sdmgo@international.gc.ca
Website: www.santodomingo.gc.ca

## Ecuador

Consulate of Canada
Address: 810 Avenida General Córdova and Victor Manuel Rendón, Edificio Torres de la Merced, 21st Floor, Guayaquil, Ecuador
Tel: 593 (4) 256-3580, 231-4561
Fax: 593 (4) 231-4562
Email: consulc1@gye.satnet.net

Embassy of Canada
Address: Avenida 6 de diciembre, No. 2816, and Paul Rivet, Josueth Gonzalez Building, 4th Floor, Quito, Ecuador
Postal Address: P.O. Box 17-11-6512 (CC1), Quito, Ecuador
Tel: 593 (2) 250-6162, 223-2114
Fax: 593 (2) 250-3108
Email: quito@international.gc.ca
Website: www.quito.gc.ca

## Egypt

Embassy of Canada
Address: 26 Kamel El Shenawy Street, Garden City, Cairo, Egypt
Postal Address: P.O. Box 1667, Cairo, Egypt
Tel: 20 (2) 791-8700
Fax: 20 (2) 791-8862
Email: cairo@international.gc.ca
Website: www.cairo.gc.ca

## El Salvador

Embassy of Canada
Address: Centro Financiero Gigante, Torre A, Lobby 2, Alameda Roosevelt y 63 Ave. Sur, Colonia Escalón, San Salvador, El Salvador
Tel: 503 2279-4655, -4657, -4659
Fax: 503 2279-0765
Email: ssal@international.gc.ca
Website: www.sansalvador.gc.ca

## Eritrea

Consulate of Canada
Address: Abeneh Street 745, House No. 152/154, Tiravolo, Eritrea
Postal Address: P.O. Box 3962, Asmara, Eritrea
Tel: 291 (1) 18-64-90, 18-19-40
Fax: 291 (1) 18-64-88
Email: mkcca1@yahoo.com

## Estonia

Office of the Embassy of Canada
Address: Toom Kooli 13, 2nd Floor, 10130 Tallinn, Estonia
Tel: 372 627 3310; -3311
Fax: 372 627 3312
Email: allinn@canada.ee
Website: www.dfait-maeci.gc.ca/dfait/missions/baltiks/

## Ethiopia

Embassy of Canada
Address: Old Airport Area, Nifas Silk Lafto K.K. Kebele 4, House #122
Addis Ababa, Ethiopia
Postal Address: P.O. Box 1130, Addis Ababa, Ethiopia
Tel: 251 (0) 11-371-3022
Fax: 251 (0) 11-371-3033
Email: addis@international.gc.ca
Website: www.dfait-maeci.gc.ca/world/embassies/ethiopia/

## Fiji

Consulate of Canada
Address:
Postal Address: P.O. Box 10690, Nadi Airport, Nadi
Tel: (679) 6722-400
Tel. after hours: (679) 9924 999 (mobile)
Fax: (679) 672 1936; 679 672 4489
Email: vyases@connect.com.fj

## Finland

Embassy of Canada
Address: Pohjoisesplanadi 25B, 00100 Helsinki
Postal Address: P.O. Box 779, Helsinki, 00101
Tel: 358 (9) 228-530
Emergency toll-free to Ottawa: 990-800-2326-6831; +800-2326-6831
Fax: 358 (9) 601-060
Email: hsnki@international.gc.ca
Website: www.canada.fi

## France

Embassy of Canada
Address: 35, avenue Montaigne, 75008 Paris, France
**Tel:** 33 1-44-43-29-00
**Emergency toll-free to Ottawa:** 00-800-2326-6831
**Fax:** 33 1-44-43-29-86
**Email:** paris@international.gc.ca
**Website:** www.amb-canada.fr

Consulate of Canada
Address: 30, avenue Émile Zola, 59800 Lille, France
**Tel:** 33 3-20-14-05-78
**Emergency toll-free to Ottawa:** 00-800-2326-6831
**Fax:** 33 3-20-14-36-96
**Email:** consulatcanadalille@wanadoo.fr

Consulate of Canada
Address: 21, rue Bourgelat, 69002 Lyon, France
**Tel:** 33 4-72-77-64-07
**Fax:** 33 4-72-77-65-09
**Email:** consulatcanadalyon@wanadoo.fr

Consulate of Canada
Address: 10, rue Lamartine, 06000 Nice, France
**Tel:** 33 4-93-92-93-22
**Fax:** 33 4-93-92-55-51
**Email:** cancons.nce@club-Website.fr

Consulate of Canada
Address: 16, rue Jacques Debon, Saint-Pierre,
Saint-Pierre et Miquelon, France
Postal Address: P.O. Box 4370, 97500, Saint-Pierre,
Saint-Pierre et Miquelon, 97500, France
**Tel:** 508 41-55-10
**Fax:** 508 41-55-10
**Email:** consulat.canada@cheznoo.com

Consulate of Canada
Address: 10, Jules de Rességuier, 31000 Toulouse,
France
**Tel:** 33 5-61-52-19-06
**Fax:** 33 5-61-55-40-32
**Email:** consulat.canada.toulouse@wanadoo.fr

## French Polynesia

Consulate of Australia
Address: Service Mobil, Motu Uta
Postal Address: P.O. Box 9068, Papeete (Tahiti),
98715, French Polynesia
**Tel:** (689) 46 88 06
**Fax:** (689) 43 39 26

## Gabon

Consulate of Canada
Address: Résidence Saint-Georges, Pont de Gué-Gué
Postal Address: P.O. Box 4037, Libreville, Gabon
**Tel:** 241-44 29 65
**Fax:** 241-44-29-64
**Email:** conhongab@gmail.com

## Germany

Embassy of Canada
Address: Leipziger Platz 17, 10117 Berlin, Germany
**Tel:** 49 (30) 20 31 20
**Emergency toll-free to Ottawa:** 00-800-2326-6831
**Fax:** 49 (30) 20 31 24 57
**Email:** brlin-cs@international.gc.ca
**Website:** www.berlin.gc.ca

Consulate of Canada
Address: Benrather Strasse 8, 40213 Düsseldorf,
Germany
**Tel:** 49 (211) 17 21 70
**Fax:** 49 (211) 35 91 65
**Email:** ddorf@international.gc.ca

Consulate of Canada
Address: Ballindamm 35, 5th Floor, 20095 Hamburg,
Germany
**Tel:** 49 (40) 46 00 27 0
**Fax:** 49 (40) 46 00 27 20
**Email:** hmbrg@international.gc.ca

Consulate of Canada
Address: Tal 29, 80331 Munich, Germany
**Tel:** 49 (89) 21 99 57 0
**Fax:** 49 (89) 21 99 57 57
**Email:** munic@international.gc.ca

Consulate of Canada
Address: Lange Strasse 51, 70174 Stuttgart, Germany
**Tel:** 49 (711) 22 39 67 8
**Fax:** 49 (711) 22 39 67 9
**Email:** hcons.stuttgart@consulates-canada.de

## Ghana

High Commission of Canada
Address: 42 Independence Avenue, Accra, Ghana
Postal Address: P.O. Box 1639, Accra, Ghana
**Tel:** 233 (21) 21-15-21; 22-85-55
**Fax:** 233 (21) 21-15-23; 77-37-92
**Email:** accra@international.gc.ca
**Website:** www.accra.gc.ca

## Greece

Embassy of Canada
Address: 4 Ioannou Ghennadiou Street, 115 21 Athens,
Greece
**Tel:** 30 (210) 727-3400
**Fax:** 30 (210) 727-3480
**Email:** athns@international.gc.ca
**Website:** www.athens.gc.ca

Consulate of Canada
Address: c/o Hotel Palace, 12 Tsimiski Street, 546 24
Thessaloniki, Greece
**Tel:** 30 (2310) 256-350
**Fax:** 30 (2310) 256-351
**Email:** yakoumis_canada@profinet.gr

## Guatemala

Embassy of Canada
Address: Edyma Plaza Building, 8th Floor, 13 Calle
8-44, Zona 10, Guatemala City, Guatemala
Postal Address: P.O. Box 400, Guatemala City,
Guatemala
**Tel:** 502 2363-4348
**Fax:** 502 2365-1216
**Email:** gtmla@international.gc.ca
**Website:** www.guatemala.gc.ca

## Guyana

High Commission of Canada
Address: High and Young Streets, Georgetown,
Guyana
Postal Address: P.O. Box 10880, Georgetown, Guyana
**Tel:** 592 227-2081/2/3/4/5
**Fax:** 592 225-8380
**Email:** grgtn@international.gc.ca
**Website:** www.georgetown.gc.ca

## Haiti

Embassy of Canada
Address: Delmas Road, between Delmas 75 and 71,
Port-au-Prince, Haiti
Postal Address: P.O. Box 826, Port-au-Prince, Haiti
**Tel:** 509 249-9000
**Tel. after hours:** 558-0479
**Fax:** 509 249-9920, 249-9921, 249-9922, 249-9928
**Email:** prnce@international.gc.ca
**Website:** www.port-au-prince.gc.ca

## Holy See (Vatican City)

Canadian Embassy to the Holy See
Address: Via della Conciliazione 4/D, 00193 Rome
**Tel:** 39 (06) 6830-7316, 7386, 7398
**Fax:** 39 (06) 6880-6283
**Email:** vatcn@international.gc.ca
**Website:** www.vatican.gc.ca

## Honduras

Office of the Embassy of Canada
Address: Centro Financiero BANCO UNO, 3rd Floor,
Boulevard San Juan Bosco, Colonia Payaquí,
Tegucigalpa, Honduras
Postal Address: P.O. Box 3552, Tegucigalpa
**Tel:** 504 232-4551
**Fax:** 504 239-7767
**Email:** tglpa@international.gc.ca

## Hungary

Embassy of Canada
Address: Budapest 1027, Ganz utca 12-14,
**Tel:** 36 (1) 392-3360
**Fax:** 36 (1) 392-3390
**Email:** bpest@international.gc.ca
**Website:** www.budapest.gc.ca

## Iceland

Embassy of Canada
Address: 14 Tungata, 101 Reykjavik, Iceland
Postal Address: P.O. Box 1510, 121 Reykjavik
**Tel:** 354 575-6500
**Fax:** 354 575-6501
**Email:** rkjvk@international.gc.ca
**Website:** www.reykjavik.gc.ca

## India

Consulate General of Canada
Address: SCO 54-56, Sector 17A, Chandigarh 160
017, India
**Tel:** 91 (172) 505-0300
**Fax:** 91 (172) 505-0323
**Email:** CHADG-G@international.gc.ca

Consulate of Canada
Address: 18 (Old 24), 3rd floor YAFA Tower, Khader
Nawaz Khan Road, Nungambakkam, Chennai, 600
034
**Tel:** 91 (44) 2833-0888
**Fax:** 91 (44) 5215-9393
**Email:** cheni@gocindia.org

Consulate of Canada
Address: c/o RPG Enterprises, Duncan House, 31,
Netaji Subhas Road, Calcutta 700 001, West Bengal,
India
**Tel:** 91 (33) 2242-6820
**Fax:** 91 (33) 2242-6828
**Email:** ccklkta@rpg.in

Consulate General of Canada
Address: 6th floor, Fort House, 221 Dr. D.N. Road,
Mumbai, 400 001
**Tel:** 91 (22) 6749 4444
**Fax:** 91 (22) 6749 4454
**Email:** mmbai@international.gc.ca

High Commission of Canada
Address: 7/8 Shantipath, Chanakyapuri, New Delhi
110021, India
Postal Address: P.O. Box 5207, New Delhi, India
**Tel:** 91 (11) 4178-2000, -2100
**Fax:** 91 (11) 4178-2023
**Email:** delhi.consular@international.gc.ca
**Website:** www.india.gc.ca

## Indonesia

Consulate General of Australia
Address: Jalan Hayam Wuruk, No. 88B, Tanjung
Bungkak, Denpasar, Bali, Indonesia
Postal Address: P.O. Box 3243, Denpasar, Bali,
Indonesia
**Tel:** 62 (361) 283-011, 283-241
**Emergency toll-free to Ottawa:** 008-800-105-171
**Fax:** 62 (361) 282-281

Embassy of Canada
Address: World Trade Centre, 6th Floor, Jl. Jend
Sudirman, Kav. 29, Jakarta 12920, Indonesia
Postal Address: P.O. Box 8324/JKS.MP, Jakarta,
12084, Indonesia
**Tel:** 62 (21) 2550-7800
**Fax:** 62 (21) 2550-7811
**Email:** jkrta@international.gc.ca
**Website:** www.jakarta.gc.ca

Consulate of Canada
Address: c/o Wisma Dharmala, 2nd Floor Suite 2, Jl.
Panglima Sudirman 101-103, Surabaya 60271
**Tel:** 62 (31) 546-3419
**Fax:** 62 (31) 546-3420
**Email:** canada@sby.prima.net.id

## Iran

Embassy of Canada
Address: 57 Shahid Javad-e-Sarfaraz (Darya-E-Noor),
Ostad Motahari Avenue, Tehran, Iran
Postal Address: P.O. Box 11365-4647, Tehran, Iran
**Tel:** 98 (21) 8873-2623, -2624, -2625, -2626
**Fax:** 98 (21) 8873-3202
**Email:** teran@international.gc.ca
**Website:** www.iran.gc.ca

## Ireland

Embassy of Canada
Address: 65 St. Stephen's Green, Dublin 2, Ireland
**Tel:** 353 (1) 417-4100
Tel. after hours: 353 (1) 478-1476
**Fax:** 353 (1) 417-4101
**Email:** dubln@international.gc.ca
**Website:** www.dublin.gc.ca

## Israel, the West Bank and Gaza - Ramallah

Representative Office of Canada
Address: 12 Mahfal Street, Ramallah, West Bank
P.O. Box 2286, Ramallah, West Bank
P.O. Box 18604, Jerusalem 91184
**Tel:** 972 (2) 295-8604
**Fax:** 972 (2) 295-8606
**Email:** rmlah@international.gc.ca

Embassy of Canada
Address: 3/5 Nirim Street, Tel Aviv 67060, Israel
P.O. Box 9442, Tel Aviv, 67060, Israel
**Tel:** 972 (3) 636-3300
**Fax:** 972 (3) 636-3383
**Email:** taviv@international.gc.ca
**Website:** www.telaviv.gc.ca

## Italy

Embassy of Canada
Address: Via Zara 30, Rome, Italy 00198
**Tel:** 39 (06) 85 444 2911
**Fax:** 39 (06) 85 444 2912
**Email:** rome.citizenservices@international.gc.ca
**Website:** www.rome.gc.ca

Consulate General of Canada
Address: Via Vittor Pisani 19, Milan, Italy 20124
**Tel:** 39 (02) 6758-1
Emergency toll-free to Ottawa: 00-800-2326-6831
**Fax:** 39 (02) 6758-3900
**Email:** milan@international.gc.ca

Consulate of Canada
Address: Via Carducci 29, Naples, Italy 80121
**Tel:** 39 (081) 401-338
**Fax:** 39 (081) 410-4210
**Email:** cancons.nap@tiscali.it

Consulate of Canada
Address: Riviera Ruzzante 25, Padova, Italy 35123
**Tel:** 39 (049) 876-4833
**Fax:** 39 (049) 878-1147
**Email:** consolato.padova@canada.it

Consulate of Canada
Address: Via Panfilo Mazara 26, Sulmona (Aquila),
Italy 67039
**Tel:** 39 (0864) 212-341
**Fax:** 39 (0864) 210-158
**Email:** consolato.canadese@tin.it

## Jamaica

High Commission of Canada
Address: 3 West Kings House Road, Kingston, 10,
Jamaica
Postal Address: P.O. Box 1500, Kingston, 10, Jamaica
**Tel:** (876) 926-1500
**Fax:** (876) 511-3493
**Email:** kngtn@international.gc.ca
**Website:** www.kingston.gc.ca

Consulate of Canada
Address: 29 Gloucester Street, Montego Bay, Jamaica
**Tel:** (876) 952-6198
**Fax:** (876) 952-3953
**Email:** cancon@cwjamaica.com

## Japan

Consulate of Canada
Address: FT Building, 9F, 4-8-28 Watanabe-Dori,
Chuo-ku, Fukuoka-shi, Fukuoka-ken 810-0004, Japan
**Tel:** 81 (92) 752-6055
**Fax:** 81 (92) 752-6077
**Email:** fkoka@international.gc.ca
**Website:**
www.dfait-maeci.gc.ca/ni-ka/contacts/fukuoka

Consulate of Canada
Address: c/o Chugoku Electric Power Co. Inc., 4-33
Komachi, Naka-ku, Hiroshima-shi, Hiroshima-ken
730-8701, Japan
**Tel:** 81 (82) 246-0057
**Fax:** 81 (82) 246-0057

Consulate of Canada
Address: Nakato Marunouchi Building, 6F, 3-17-6
Marunouchi, Naka-ku, Nagoya-shi, Aichi-ken
460-0002, Japan
**Tel:** 81 (52) 972-0450
**Fax:** 81 (52) 972-0453
**Email:** ngoya@international.gc.ca
**Website:**
www.dfait-maeci.gc.ca/ni-ka/contacts/nagoya

Consulate of Canada
Address: Daisan Shoho Building, 12th Floor, 2-2-3,
Nishi-Shinsaibashi, Chuo-ku, Osaka 542-0086, Japan
**Tel:** 81 (6) 6212-4910
**Fax:** 81 (6) 6212-4914
**Email:** osaka@international.gc.ca
**Website:** www.dfait-maeci.gc.ca/ni-ka/contacts/osaka

Consulate of Canada
Address: Tokyo Tatemono Sapporo Building 2F, 20
Kita-7 Nishi-2, Kita-ku, Sapporo 060-0807, Japan
**Tel:** 81 (11) 726-2863
**Fax:** 81 (11) 726-2863

Embassy of Canada
Address: 3-38 Akasaka 7-chome, Minato-ku, Tokyo
107-8503, Japan
**Tel:** 81 (3) 5412-6200
**Fax:** 81 (3) 5412-6289
**Email:** tokyo@international.gc.ca
**Website:** www.tokyo.gc.ca

## Jordan

Embassy of Canada
Address: Pearl of Shmeisani Building, Shmeisani,
Amman, Jordan
Postal Address: P.O. Box 815403, Amman, 11180,
Jordan
**Tel:** 962 (6) 520-3300
**Fax:** 962 (6) 520-3396
**Email:** amman@international.gc.ca
**Website:** www.amman.gc.ca

## Kazakhstan

Embassy of Canada
Address: 34 Karasai Batir Street (Vinogradov Street),
Almaty, 480100, Kazakhstan
**Tel:** 7 (3272) 501151, 501153
**Fax:** 7 (3272) 582493
**Email:** almat@international.gc.ca
**Website:**
www.dfait-maeci.gc.ca/canadaeuropa/kazakhstan

## Kenya

High Commission of Canada
Address: Limuru Road, Gigiri, Nairobi, Kenya
Postal Address: P.O. Box 1013, 00621, Nairobi, Kenya
Tel: 254 (20) 366-3000
Fax: 254 (20) 366 3900
Email: nrobi@international.gc.ca
Website: www.nairobi.gc.ca

## Kiribati

Australian High Commission
Address: Bairiki, Tarawa, Kiribati
Postal Address: P.O. Box 77, Tarawa, Kiribati
Tel: 686 21-184
Fax: 686 21-904

## Kuwait

Embassy of Canada
Address: 24, Al Mutawakel Street, Block 4, Da'aiyah, Kuwait City, Kuwait
Postal Address: P.O. Box 25281, Safat, Kuwait City, 13113, Kuwait
Tel: 965 256-3025
Fax: 965 256-0173
Email: kwait@international.gc.ca
Website: www.kuwait.gc.ca

## Kyrgyz Republic

Consulate of Canada
Address: 189 Moskovskaya Avenue, 720010 Bishkek, Kyrgyz Republic
Tel: 996 (312) 65-05-06
Fax: 996 (312) 65-01-01
Email: canada_honcon@infotel.kg

## Laos

Australian Embassy
Address: J. Nehru Street, Phone Xay, Vientiane, Laos
Postal Address: P.O. Box 292, Vientiane, Laos
Tel: 856 (21) 413 600
Fax: 856 (21) 413 601

## Latvia

Embassy of Canada
Address: 20/22 Baznicas St, 6th Floor, Riga, Latvia, LV-1010
Tel: 371 781-3945
Fax: 371 781-3960
Email: canembr@bkc.lv
Email: riga@international.gc.ca

Website: www.dfait-maeci.gc.ca/canadaeuropa/baltics

## Lebanon

Embassy of Canada
Address: 43 Jal El Dib Highway, 1st Floor, Coolrite Building, Jal El Dib, Beirut, Lebanon
Postal Address: P.O. Box 60163, Jal El Dib, Lebanon
Tel: 961 (4) 713-900
Fax: 961 (4) 710-595
Email: berut@international.gc.ca
Website: www.beirut.gc.ca

## Lesotho

Consulate of Canada
Address: c/o Sechaba Consultants, 3 Orpen Road, Maseru, Lesotho
Postal Address: P.O. Box 1191, Maseru, 100, Lesotho
Tel: 266 (22) 316-555
Fax: 266 (22) 310-437
Email: canada@lesoff.co.za

## Libya

Embassy of Canada
Address: Great Al-Fateh Tower Building, Tower 1, 7th Floor, Tripoli, Libya
Postal Address: P.O. Box 93392, Al-Fateh Tower Post Office, Tripoli, Libya
Tel: 218 (21) 335-1633
Fax: 218 (21) 335-1630
Email: trpli@international.gc.ca
Website: www.libya.gc.ca

## Lithuania

Office of the Embassy of Canada
Address: Jogailos St. 4, 7th Floor, Vilnius 11116
Tel: 370 (5) 249-0950
Fax: 370 (5) 249-7865
Email: vilnius@canada.lt
Website:
www.dfait-maeci.gc.ca/canadaeuropa/baltics/

## Luxembourg

Consulate of Canada
Address: 15, rue Guillaume Schneider, L-2522 Luxembourg, G.D. Luxembourg
Tel: 352 2627-0570
Emergency toll-free to Ottawa: 800-23679
Fax: 352 2627-0670
Email: canada@pt.lu
Website: www.canada.lu

## Macedonia, Former Yugoslav Republic of

Consulate of Canada
Address: Partizanska odredi 17-a, 1st Floor, 1000
Skopje, Former Yugoslav Republic of Macedonia
**Tel:** 389 (2) 3225-630
**Fax:** 389 (2) 3220-596
**Email:** honcon@unet.com.mk

## Madagascar

Consulate of Canada
Address: c/o QIT Madagascar Minerals Ltd., Villa 3H,
Lot II J 169, Ivandry, Antananarivo Madagascar
Postal Address: P.O. Box 4003, Antananarivo, 101,
Madagascar
**Tel:** 261 (20) 22-425-59, 22-423-22
**Fax:** 261 (20) 22-425-06
**Email:** consulat.canada@wanadoo.mg

## Malawi

Consulate of Canada
Address: Accord Centre, M Chipembere Highway,
Blantyre-Limbe, Malawi
Postal Address: P.O. Box 51146, Blantyre-Limbe
**Tel:** 265-(1) 645-441, 641-612, 643-277
**Fax:** 265-1 643-446
**Email:** kokhai@malawibiz.com

## Malaysia

High Commission of Canada
Address: 17th Floor, Menara Tan & Tan, 207 Jalan
Tun Razak, 50400 Kuala Lumpur, Malaysia
Postal Address: P.O. Box 10990, Kuala Lumpur,
50732, Malaysia
**Tel:** 6 (03) 2718-3333
**Fax:** 6 (03) 2718-3399
**Email:** klmpr-cs@international.gc.ca
**Website:** www.kualalumpur.gc.ca

Consulate of Canada
Address: 3007 Tingkat Perusahaan 5, Prai Industrial
Park, 13600 Prai, Penang, Malaysia
**Tel:** 6 (04) 390-6000
**Fax:** 6 (04) 390-6000
**Email:** tyt@lbsb.com

## Mali

Embassy of Canada
Address: Immeuble Séméga, Route de Koulikoro,
Bamako, Mali
Postal Address: P.O. Box 198, Bamako, Mali
**Tel:** 223 221-2236
**Fax:** 223 221-4362
**Email:** bmako@international.gc.ca
**Website:** www.bamako.gc.ca

## Malta

Consulate of Canada
Address: Demajo House, 103 Archbishop Street,
Valletta, Malta
**Tel:** 356 2552-3233
**Fax:** 356 2552-3233
**Email:** canhcon@demajo.com

## Mauritania

Consulate of Canada
Address: Centre Commercial Abass, avenue Charles de
Gaulle, îlot "O", n 34, 1 étage, bureau 2, Nouakchott,
Mauritania
Postal Address: P.O. Box 428, Nouakchott, Mauritania
**Tel:** (222) 529 26 97/8
**Fax:** (222) 292-698
**Email:** j.taya@mr.refer.org

## Mauritius

Consulate of Canada
Address: 18 Jules Koenig Street, c/o Blanche Birger
Co. Ltd., Port Louis, Mauritius
Postal Address: P.O. Box 209, Port Louis, Mauritius
**Tel:** 230 212-5500
**Fax:** 230 208-3391
**Email:** canada@intnet.mu

## Mexico

Consulate of Canada
Address: Centro Comercial Marbella, local 23.
Prolongación Farallón s/n, Esq. Miguel Alemán,
39690, Acapulco, Guerrero México
**Tel:** 52 (744) 484-1305, 481-1349
Emergency toll-free to Ottawa: 001-800-514-0129
**Fax:** 52 (744) 484-1306
**Email:** acapulco@canada.org.mx

Consulate of Canada
Address: Plaza Caracol II, 3er piso, Local 330,
Boulevard Kukulcán km 8.5, Zona Hotelera, 77500
Cancún, Quintana Roo, Mexico
**Tel:** 52 (998) 883-3360/1
**Fax:** 52 (998) 883-3232
**Email:** cancun@canada.org.mx

Consulate of Canada
Address: Hotel Fiesta Americana, Local 31, Aurelio Aceves 225, Colonia Vallarta Poniente, 44100 Guadalajara, Jalisco, Mexico
Tel: 52 (33) 3615-6270, 6215, 6266, 3616-5642
Emergency toll-free to Ottawa: 001-800-514-0129
Fax: 52 (33) 3615-8665
Email: mxicogjara@international.gc.ca

Consulate of Canada
Address: De la Colina # 567, Fracc. El Cid, Mazatlan, Sinaloa 82110, Mexico
Postal Address: P.O. Box 614, Mazatlán, Sinaloa, 82110, Mexico
Tel: 52 (669) 913-73-20
Fax: 52 (669) 914-66-55
Email: mazatlan@canada.org.mx

Embassy of Canada
Address: Calle Schiller No. 529 (Rincón del Bosque), Colonia Bosque de Chapultepec, 11580, Mexico, D.F., Mexico
Postal Address: P.O. Box 105-05, Mexico, Distrito Federal, 11580, Mexico
Tel: 52 (55) 5724-7900 Ext.: 3322
Tel. after hours: 01-800-706-2900
Fax: 52 (55) 5724-7943
Email: mxico@international.gc.ca
Website: www.mexico.gc.ca

Consulate General of Canada
Address: Edificio Kalos, Piso C-1, Local 108-A, Zaragoza 1300 Sur y Constitución, 64000 Monterrey, Nuevo Léon, Mexico
Tel: 52 (81) 8344-32-00, 27-53,29-06, 29-61, 8345-9105, 9045
Fax: 52 (81) 8344-30-48
Email: mxicomntry@international.gc.ca

Consulate of Canada
Address: Pino Suarez 700, Local 11B, Multiplaza Brena, Colonia Centro, 68000 Oaxaca, Oaxaca
Postal Address: P.O. Box Apartado Postal 29, Succ C,, Oaxaca, 68050 Oaxaca, Mexico
Tel: 52 (951) 513-3777
Fax: 52 (951) 515-2147
Email: oaxaca@canada.org.mx

Consulate of Canada
Address: Edificio Obelisco Local 108, Avenida Francisco Medina Ascencio No. 1951, Zona Hotelera Las Glorias, Puerto Vallarta, Jalisco, Mexico

Postal Address: P.O. Box 48300, Mexico
Tel: 52 (322) 293-0098/9
Fax: 52 (322) 293-2894
Email: vallarta@canada.org.mx

Consulate of Canada
Address: Plaza José Green, Local 9, Boulevard Mijares s/n, Colonia Centro, 23400 San José del Cabo, Baja California Sur, Mexico
Tel: 52 (624) 142-4333
Fax: 52 (624) 142-4262
Email: loscabos@canada.org.mx

Consulate of Canada
Address: Germán Gedovius No. 10411-101, Condominio del Parque, Zona Río, 22320 Tijuana, Baja California Norte, Mexico
Tel: 52 (664) 684-04-61
Fax: 52 (664) 684-03-01
Email: tijuana@canada.org.mx

## Micronesia

Australian Embassy
Address: H&E Enterprises Building, Kolonia, Pohnpei, Micronesia
Postal Address: P.O. Box S, Kolonia, Pohnpei, Micronesia
Tel: 691 320-5448
Fax: 691 320-5449

## Monaco

Consulate of Canada
Address: Palais de la Scala, 1, avenue Henry Dunant, bureau 1178, 98000 Monaco
Tel: 377 97 70 62 42
Fax: 377 97 70 62 52
Email: consul-canada@monte-carlo.mc

## Mongolia

Consulate of Canada
Address: Bodi Tower, 7th floor, Sukhbataar Square, Sukhbaatar District, Ulaanbaatar, Mongolia
Postal Address: P.O. Box 1028, Central Post Office, Ulaanbaatar-13, Mongolia
Tel: 976 (11) 328-285
Fax: 976 (11) 328-289
Email: can_honcon@mongolnet.mn

## Morocco

Embassy of Canada
Address: 13 bis, rue Jaafar Assadik, Agdal-Rabat,
Morocco
Postal Address: P.O. Box 709, Agdal-Rabat, Morocco
**Tel:** 212 (37) 68 74 00
**Fax:** 212 (37) 68 74 30
**Email:** rabat@international.gc.ca
**Website:** www.rabat.gc.ca

## Mozambique

High Commission of Canada
Address: 1138 Kenneth Kaunda Avenue, Maputo,
Mozambique
Postal Address: P.O. Box 1578, Maputo, Mozambique
**Tel:** 258 (21) 492-623
**Fax:** 258 (21) 492-667
**Email:** mputo@international.gc.ca
**Website:** www.maputo.gc.ca

## Namibia

Consulate of Canada
Address: Suite 1118, Sanlam Centre, Independence
Ave, Windhoek, Namibia
**Tel:** 264 (61) 251 254
**Fax:** 264 (61) 251 686
**Email:** canada@mweb.com.na

## Nepal

Canadian Cooperation Office
Address: Lazimpat, Nepal
Postal Address: P.O. Box 4574, Kathmandu, Nepal
**Tel:** 977 (1) 4415-193, -389, -391, -861, 4426-885,
4425-669
**Fax:** 977 (1) 4410-422
**Email:** cco@canadanepal.org

## Netherlands

Embassy of Canada
Address: Sophialaan 7, 2500 GV, The Hague, The
Netherlands
Postal Address: P.O. Box 30820, The Hague,
Netherlands
**Tel:** 31 (70) 311-1600
**Fax:** 31 (70) 311-1620
**Email:** hague@international.gc.ca
**Website:** www.canada.nl

## New Caledonia

Australian Consulate General
Address: Immeuble Foch, 7th Floor, 19 Avenue du
Maréchal Foch, Nouméa, New Caledonia
Postal Address: P.O. Box 22, Nouméa, 98845, New
Caledonia
**Tel:** 687 272-414
**Fax:** 687 278-001

## New Zealand

High Commission of Canada
Address: Level 11, 125 The Terrace, Wellington
Postal Address: P.O. Box 8047, Wellington
**Tel:** 64 (4) 473-9577
**Fax:** 64 (4) 471-2082
**Email:** wlgtn@international.gc.ca
**Website:** www.wellington.gc.ca

## Nicaragua

Office of the Embassy of Canada
Address: De los Pipitos, 2 blocks west 25, Nogal
Street,Bolonia, Managua, Nicaragua
Postal Address: P.O. Box 25, Managua, Nicaragua
**Tel:** 505 (2) 68-0433,-3323
**Fax:** 505 (2) 68-0437
**Email:** mngua@international.gc.ca

## Niger

Office of the Embassy of Canada
Address: Sonara II Building, 8th Floor, Avenue du
Premier Pont, Niamey, Niger
Postal Address: P.O. Box 362, Niamey, Niger
**Tel:** 227 75-36-86, -87
**Fax:** 227 75-31-07
**Email:** niamy@international.gc.ca

## Nigeria

High Commission of Canada
Address: 15 Bobo Street, Maitama, Abuja, Nigeria
**Tel:** 234 (9) 413-9910
**Fax:** 234 (9) 413-9932
**Email:** abuja@international.gc.ca
**Website:** www.nigeria.gc.ca

Deputy High Commission of Canada
Address: 4 Anifowoshe Street, Victoria Island, Lagos
**Tel:** 234 (1) 262-2512, -2513, -2515
**Fax:** 234 (1) 262-2517
**Email:** lagos@international.gc.ca
**Website:** www.nigeria.gc.ca

Consulate of Canada
Address: 15 Ahoada Street, Rumuibekwe Housing
Estate, Port Harcourt, Nigeria
**Tel:** 234 (8) 461-0434; 461-1601
**Fax:** 234 (8) 461-0899
**Email:** phconsul2004@yahoo.com

## North Korea

Swedish Embassy
Address: Munsudong, Daehak Street, Taedonggang
District, Pyongyang, Democratic People's Republic of
Korea
**Tel:** 850 (2) 381-7908
**Fax:** 850 (2) 381-7663
**Email:** ambassaden.pyongyang@foreign.ministry.se
**Website:**
www.sweden.gov.se/sb/d/4189/l/en/pd/4189/e/3647

## Norway

Consulate of Canada
Postal Address: P.O. Box 2439, Solheimsviken, 5824,
Bergen Norway, Bergen, 5824, Norway
**Tel:** 47 55-29-71-30
Emergency toll-free to Ottawa: 00-800-2326-6831
**Fax:** 47 55-29-71-31
**Email:** honconbergen@canada.no

Embassy of Canada
Address: Wergelandsveien 7, 0244 Oslo, Norway
**Tel:** 47 22-99-53-00
Emergency toll-free to Ottawa: 00-800-2326-6831
**Fax:** 47 22-99-53-01
**Email:** oslo@international.gc.ca
**Website:** www.canada.no

## Pakistan

High Commission of Canada
Address: Diplomatic Enclave, Sector G-5, Islamabad
Postal Address: P.O. Box 1042, Islamabad, Pakistan
**Tel:** 92 (51) 227-9100, 208-6000
Tel. after hours: 92 (51) 227-9113
**Fax:** 92 (51) 227-9110
**Email:** isbad@international.gc.ca
**Website:** www.islamabad.gc.ca

Consulate of Canada
Address: c/o Beach Luxury Hotel, Room 120, Moulvi
Tamiz Uddin Khan Road, Karachi 0227, Pakistan
**Tel:** 92 (21) 561-0685, 1031/2/3/4/5/6/7
**Fax:** 92 (21) 561-0673/4
**Email:** honcon@khi.comsats.net.pk

Consulate of Canada
Address: 102-A Siddiq Trade Centre, 1st floor, 72
Main Boulevard, Gulberg, Lahore, Pakistan
**Tel:** 92 (42) 578-1763, -1966
**Email:** canconlhr@yahoo.com
**Email:** canconlhr@brain.net.pk

## Panama

Embassy of Canada
Address: World Trade Center, Calle 53E, Marbella,
Galería Comercial, Piso 1, Panama City, Panama
Postal Address: P.O. Box Apartado 0832-2446,
Estafeta World Trade Center, Panama City, Panama
**Tel:** 507 264-9731, 7115
**Fax:** 507 263-8083
**Email:** panam@international.gc.ca
**Website:** www.panama.gc.ca

## Papua New Guinea

Australian High Commission
Address: Godwit Road, Waigani, NCD, Port Moresby,
Papua New Guinea
**Tel:** 675 325-9333
**Fax:** 675 325-9239

## Paraguay

Consulate of Canada
Address: Prof. Ramírez No. 3 at Juan de Salazar
(between Perú and Padre Pucheu), Asunción, Paraguay
**Tel:** 595 (21) 227-207
**Fax:** 595 (21) 227-208
**Email:** honconpy@telesurf.com.py

## Peru

Embassy of Canada
Address: Calle Libertad 130, Miraflores, Lima 18, Peru
Postal Address: P.O. Box 18-1126, Miraflores Post
Office, Lima, 18, Peru
**Tel:** 51 (1) 444-4015
**Fax:** 51 (1) 242-4050
**Email:** lima@international.gc.ca
**Website:** www.lima.gc.ca

## Philippines

Consulate of Canada
Address: 45-L Andres Abellana Street, Cebu City
6000, Philippines
**Tel:** 63 (32) 256-3320
**Fax:** 63 (32) 255-3068
**Email:** canada-consulate-cebu@mozcom.com

Embassy of Canada
Address: 6th, 7th, and 8th Floors, RCBC Plaza Tower 2, 6819 Ayala Ave., 1200 Makati City, Manila,
**Tel:** 63 (2) 857-9000, 857-9001
**Fax:** 63 (2) 843-1082, 810-4299
**Email:** manil@international.gc.ca
**Website:** www.manila.gc.ca

## Poland

Embassy of Canada
Address: ul. Matejki 1/5, 00-481 Warsaw, Poland
**Tel:** 48 (22) 584-3100
**Fax:** 48 (22) 584-3192, 584-3101
**Email:** wsaw@international.gc.ca
**Website:** www.dfait-maeci.gc.ca/warsaw

## Portugal

Consulate of Canada
Address: Rua Frei Lourenço de Santa Maria No. 1, 1st Floor, Faro, Portugal
Postal Address: P.O. Box 79, Faro, 8001-957, Portugal
**Tel:** 351 289-80-3757
Emergency toll-free to Ottawa: 800-819-826
**Fax:** 351 289-88-0888
**Email:** consul.faro.canada@mail.net4b.pt

Embassy of Canada
Address: Avenida da Liberdade 196-200, 3rd Floor, 1269-121 Lisbon, Portugal
**Tel:** 351 21316-4600
**Fax:** 351 21316-4693
**Email:** lsbon@international.gc.ca
**Website:** www.portugal.gc.ca

Consulate of Canada
Address: Rua Antonio Jose de Almeida, No. 27, 1st Floor, 9500-053 Ponta Delgada, Sao Miguel, Azores
**Tel:** 351 296-281488
**Fax:** 351 296-281489
**Email:** canadapdl@mail.telepac.pt

## Romania

Embassy of Canada
Address: 1-3, Tuberozelor St. 011411, Bucharest, sector 1, Romania
Postal Address: P.O. Box 117, Post Office No. 22, Bucharest, Romania
**Tel:** 40 (21) 307-5000
**Fax:** 40 (21) 307-5010
**Email:** bucst@international.gc.ca
**Website:** www.bucharest.gc.ca

## Russia

Embassy of Canada
Address: 23 Starokonyushenny Pereulok, Moscow, 119002 Russia
**Tel:** 7 (495) 105-6000
**Fax:** 7 (495) 105-6004
**Email:** mosco@international.gc.ca
**Website:** www.moscow.gc.ca

Consulate General of Canada
Address: 32B Malodetskoselski Prospekt, St. Petersburg, 198013 Russia
**Tel:** 7 (812) 325-8448
**Fax:** 7 (812) 325-8393
**Email:** spurg@international.gc.ca

Consulate of Canada
Address: 306-46 Verhneportovaya street, Vladivostok 600003, Russia
**Tel:** 7 (4232) 49-11-88
**Fax:** 7 (4232) 49-11-88
**Email:** cbcrfe@mail.ru
**Email:** cbcrfe@rambler.ru

## Rwanda

Office of the Embassy of Canada
Address: 1534 Akagera Street, Kigali, Rwanda
Postal Address: P.O. Box 1177, Kigali, Rwanda
**Tel:** 250 5 73210
**Fax:** 250 5 72719
**Email:** kgali@international.gc.ca

## Saint Martin/Sint Maarten

Consulate of Canada
Address: 11A Green Star Shell Road, Dawn Beach, Sint Maarten
**Tel:** (599) 543-6261
**Tel. after hours:** (599) 520-5202
**Fax:** (599) 543-6291
**Email:** canadacon@caribserve.net

## Saint Vincent and the Grenadines

Address:
Emergency toll-free to Ottawa: 1-881-949-9993
See: Barbados

## Samoa

Australian High Commission
Address: Fen Gai Ma Leata Building, Beach Road, Tamaligi, Apia, Samoa

Postal Address: P.O. Box 704, Apia, Samoa
**Tel:** 68 (5) 234-11, 236-13, 252-32
**Fax:** 68 (5) 231-59

## Saudi Arabia

Consulate of Canada
Address: Madina Road, Ali Reza Tower, 11th Floor,
Jeddah, Saudi Arabia
Postal Address: P.O. Box 9484, Jeddah, 21413, Saudi
Arabia
**Tel:** 966 (2) 653-0597, 653-0434
**Fax:** 966 (2) 653-0538
**Email:** canada.consulate.jeddah@nazergroup.com

Embassy of Canada
Address: Diplomatic Quarter, Riyadh, Saudi Arabia
Postal Address: P.O. Box 94321, Riyadh, 11693, Saudi
Arabia
**Tel:** 966 (1) 488-2288
**Fax:** 966 (1) 488-1997
**Email:** ryadh@international.gc.ca

## Senegal

Embassy of Canada
Address: corner of Galliéni and Brière-de-l'Isle Streets,
Dakar, Senegal
Postal Address: P.O. Box 3373, Dakar, Senegal
**Tel:** 221 889-47-00
**Fax:** 221 889-47-20
**Email:** dakar@international.gc.ca
**Website:** www.dakar.gc.ca

## Serbia

Embassy of Canada
Address: Kneza Milosa 75, 11000 Belgrade, Serbia
**Tel:** 381 (11) 306-3000
**Tel. after hours:** 381 (11) 306-3050
**Fax:** 381 (11) 306-3042
**Email:** bgrad@international.gc.ca
**Website:**
www.dfait-maeci.gc.ca/canada-europa/serbia/

## Singapore

High Commission of Canada
Address: One George Street, #11-01Singapore 049145
Postal Address: P.O. Box 845, Robinson Road,
Singapore, 901645, Singapore
**Tel:** 65 6854-5900
**Fax:** 65 6854-5912
**Email:** spore@international.gc.ca
**Website:** www.singapore.gc.ca

## Slovakia

Office of the Embassy of Canada
Address: Carlton Court Yard & Savoy Buildings,
Mostova 2, 811 02 Bratislava, Slovakia
**Tel:** 421 (2) 5920-4031
**Fax:** 421 (2) 5443-4227
**Email:** brtsv@international.gc.ca

## Slovenia

Consulate of Canada
Address: Maple Leaf, c/o Slovenijales Business
Centre, Dunajska 22, 1511 Ljubljana, Slovenia
**Tel:** 386 (1) 430-3570
**Fax:** 386 (1) 430-3575
**Email:** canada.consul.ljubljana@siol.net

## Solomon Islands

Australian High Commission
Address: Corner Hibiscus Avenue and Mud Alley,
Honiara, Solomon Islands
**Tel:** 677 21561
**Fax:** 677 23691

## South Africa

High Commission of Canada
Address: 19th Floor, South African Reserve Bank
Building, 60 St. George's Mall, Cape Town 8001
Postal Address: P.O. Box 683, Cape Town, 8000,
South Africa
**Tel:** 27 (21) 423-5240
**Fax:** 27 (21) 423-4893
**Email:** cptwn@international.gc.ca
**Website:** www.dfait-maeci.gc.ca/southafrica

Consulate of Canada
Address: 25/27 Cypress Avenue, Stamfordhill, Durban
4001, South Africa
Postal Address: P.O. Box 712, Durban, 4000
**Tel:** 27 (31) 303-9695
**Fax:** 27 (31) 303-9694
**Email:** vnaidu@trematon.co.za
**Website:** www.dfait-maeci.gc.ca/southafrica

High Comission of Canada Trade Office
Address: Cradock Place, 1st Floor, 10 Arnold Road,
off Cradock Avenue, Rosebank, Johannesburg 2196
Postal Address: P.O. Box 1394, Parklands,
Johannesburg, 2121, South Africa
**Tel:** 27 (11) 442-3130
**Fax:** 27 (11) 442-3325
**Email:** jobrg@international.gc.ca

High Commission of Canada
Address: 1103 Arcadia Street, Hatfield, Pretoria 0083
Postal Address: P.O. Box Private Bag X13, Hatfield,
Pretoria, 0028, South Africa
Tel: 27 (12) 422-3000
Fax: 27 (12) 422-3052
Email: pret@international.gc.ca
Website: www.pretoria.gc.ca

## South Korea

Consulate of Canada
Address: c/o Dongsung Chemical Corporation, 472
Shin Pyung-dong, Saha-gu, Busan 604-721, South
Korea
Tel: 82 (51) 204-5581
Emergency toll-free to Ottawa: 001-800-2326-6831;
008-800-2326-6831; 002-800-2326-6831
Fax: 82 (51) 204-5580

Embassy of Canada
Address: 10th and 11th Floors, Kolon Building, 45
Mugyo-Dong, Chung-Ku,
Seoul 100-170, Korea
Postal Address: P.O. Box 6299, Seoul, 100-662, South
Korea
Tel: 82 (2) 3455-6000
Fax: 82 (2) 755-0686, 3455-6123
Email: seoul@international.gc.ca
Website: www.seoul.gc.ca

## Spain

Consulate of Canada
Address: Elisenda de Pinos, 10, 08034 Barcelona,
Tel: 34 (93) 204-2700
Fax: 34 (93) 204-2701
Email: bcncon@sefes.es

Embassy of Canada
Address: Goya Building, 35 Nuñez de Balboa, 28001
Madrid, Spain
Postal Address: P.O. Box 587, Madrid, 28080, Spain
Tel: 34 (91) 423-3250
Emergency toll-free to Ottawa: 00-800-2326-6831
Fax: 34 (91) 423-3251
Email: mdrid@international.gc.ca
Website: www.canada-es.org

Consulate of Canada
Address: Horizonte Building, Plaza de la Malagueta 2,
1st Floor, 29016, Málaga, Spain
Postal Address: P.O. Box 99, Málaga, 29080, Spain
Tel: 34 (95) 222-3346

Emergency toll-free to Ottawa: 00-800-2326-6831
Fax: 34 (95) 222-9533
Email: cancon@microcad.es

## Sri Lanka

High Commission of Canada
Address: 6 Gregory's Road, Cinnamon Gardens,
Colombo 7, Sri Lanka
Postal Address: P.O. Box 1006, Colombo, 7, Sri Lanka
Tel: 94 (11) 522-6232 (5-CANADA), 532-6232
Fax: 94 (11) 522-6299
Email: clmbo-cs@international.gc.ca
Website: www.srilanka.gc.ca

## Sudan

Embassy of Canada
Address: 29 Africa Road, Block 56, Khartoum 1,
Sudan
Tel: 249 (183) 56 36 70/72/73/74
Fax: 249 (183) 56 36 71
Email: khrtm@international.gc.ca

## Suriname

Consulate of Canada
Address: Wagenwegstraat 50, boven, Paramaribo
Postal Address: P.O. Box 1449, Paramaribo, Suriname
Tel: 59 (7) 424-527, -575
Fax: 59 (7) 425-962
Email: cantim@sr.net

## Sweden

Consulate of Canada
Address: Marieholmsgatan 1, 415 02, Gothenburg
Tel: 46 (31) 707 4288
Emergency toll-free to Ottawa: 00-800-2326-6831
Fax: 46 (31) 154 099
Email: got@canadianconsulate.se

Consulate of Canada
Address: Canadian Oil Co. AB, Verkstadsgatan 4, 233
51 Svedala, Sweden
Tel: 46 (40) 40 23 51
Emergency toll-free to Ottawa: 00-800-2326-6831
Fax: 46 (40) 40 31 12

Embassy of Canada
Address: Tegelbacken 4, 7th Floor, Stockholm,
Sweden
Postal Address: P.O. Box 16129, Stockholm, 10323,
Sweden
Tel: 46 (8) 453-3000

Emergency toll-free to Ottawa: 00-800-2326-6831
**Fax:** 46 (8) 453-3016
**Email:** stkhm@international.gc.ca
**Website:** www.stockholm.gc.ca

## Switzerland

Embassy of Canada
Address: Kirchenfeldstrasse 88, 3005 Bern, Switzerland
Postal Address: P.O. Box 3000, Bern, 6, Switzerland
**Tel:** 41 (31) 357-3200
**Fax:** 41 (31) 357-3210
**Email:** bern@international.gc.ca
**Website:** www.bern.gc.ca

Permanent Mission of Canada to the Office of the United Nations, Consular Section
Address: 5, avenue de l'Ariana, 1202 Geneva, Switzerland
**Tel:** 41 (22) 919-9200
**Fax:** 41 (22) 919-9233
**Email:** genev@international.gc.ca

## Syria

Consulate of Canada
Address: Al Sabil Street No. 2, Al Rabat Avenue, Sector 12, Aleppo, Syria
Postal Address: P.O. Box 1250, Aleppo, Syria
**Tel:** 963 (21) 268-4160
**Fax:** 963 (21) 268-4100
**Email:** mhismail@net.sy

Embassy of Canada
Address: Lot 12, Mezzeh Autostrade, Damascus, Syria

Postal Address: P.O. Box 3394, Damascus, Syria
**Tel:** 963 (11) 611-6692, 611-6851
**Fax:** 963 (11) 611-4000
**Email:** dmcus@international.gc.ca
**Website:** www.damascus.gc.ca

## Taiwan

Trade Office of Canada
Address: 13th Floor, 365 Fu Hsing North Road, Taipei, 105, Taiwan,
**Tel:** 886 (2) 2544-3000
Emergency toll-free to Ottawa: 00-800-2326-6831
**Fax:** 886 (2) 2544-3590
**Email:** tapei@international.gc.ca
**Website:** www.canada.org.tw

## Tanzania

High Commission of Canada
Address: 38 Mirambo Street, Corner Garden Avenue, Dar es Salaam, Tanzania
Postal Address: P.O. Box 1022, Dar es Salaam, Tanzania
**Tel:** 255 (22) 216 3300
**Fax:** 255 (22) 211 6897
**Email:** dslam@international.gc.ca
**Website:** www.daressalaam.gc.ca

## Thailand

Embassy of Canada
Address: 15th Floor, Abdulrahim Place, 990 Rama IV, Bangrak, Bangkok 10500, Thailand
Postal Address: P.O. Box 2090, Bangkok, 10501
**Tel:** 66 (2) 636-0540
**Fax:** 66 (2) 636-0555
**Email:** bngkk@international.gc.ca
**Website:** www.dfait-maeci.gc.ca/bangkok

Consulate of Canada
Address: 151 Super Highway, Tambon Tahsala, Muang, Chiang Mai 50000, Thailand
**Tel:** 66 (53) 850-147, 242-292
**Fax:** 66 (53) 850-147, 850-332
**Email:** cancon@loxinfo.co.th

## Timor-Leste (East Timor) - Dili

Australian Embassy
Address: Avenida dos Martires da Patria, Dili, East Timor
**Tel:** 670 332-2111
**Fax:** 670 332-2247

## Tonga

Australian High Commission
Address: Salote Road, Nuku'Alofa, Tonga
**Tel:** 676 23-244
**Fax:** 676 23-243

## Trinidad and Tobago

High Commission of Canada
Address: Maple House, 3-3A Sweet Briar Road, St. Clair, Port of Spain, Trinidad and Tobago
Postal Address: P.O. Box 1246, Port of Spain, Trinidad and Tobago
**Tel:** 1 (868) 622-6232 (6-CANADA)
Emergency toll-free to Ottawa: 1-800-387-3124
**Fax:** 1 (868) 628-2581

**Email:** pspan@international.gc.ca
**Website:** www.portofspain.gc.ca

## Tunisia

Embassy of Canada
Address: 3, rue du Sénégal, Place d'Afrique,
Tunis-Belvédère, Tunisia
Postal Address: P.O. Box 31, Tunis-Belvédère, 1002,
Tunisia
**Tel:** 216 71-104-000
**Fax:** 216 71-104-191
**Email:** tunis@international.gc.ca
**Website:** www.tunis.gc.ca

## Turkey

Embassy of Canada
Address: Cinnah Caddesi No. 58, Çankaya 06690,
Ankara, Turkey
**Tel:** 90 (312) 409-2700
Emergency toll-free to Ottawa: 00800-14-220-0149
**Fax:** 90 (312) 409-2712
**Email:** ankra@international.gc.ca
**Website:** www.dfait-maeci.gc.ca/ankara

Consulate of Canada
Address: Istiklal Caddesi No 373/5, Beyoglu, 80050
Istanbul, Turkey
**Tel:** 90 (212) 251-9838
Emergency toll-free to Ottawa: 00800-14-220-0149
**Fax:** 90 (212) 251-9888

## Uganda

Consulate of Canada
Address: Jubilee Insurance Centre, 14 Parliament
Avenue, Kampala, Uganda
Postal Address: P.O. Box 20115, Kampala, Uganda
**Tel:** 256 (41) 258-141, 256 (31) 260-511
**Fax:** 256 (41) 349-484
**Email:** canada.consulate@utlonline.co.ug

## Ukraine

Embassy of Canada
Address: 31 Yaroslaviv Val Street, Kyiv 01901,
Ukraine
**Tel:** 380 (44) 590-3100
**Fax:** 380 (44) 590-3134
**Email:** kyiv@international.gc.ca
**Website:** www.kyiv.gc.ca

Consulate of Canada

Address: 2 Bohomoltsa Street, Suite 4, Lviv 79005,
Ukraine
**Tel:** 380 (322) 97-1772
**Fax:** 380 (322) 97-8154
**Email:** oksmyr@link.lviv.ua

## United Arab Emirates

Embassy of Canada
Address: Abu Dhabi Trade Towers (Abu Dhabi Mall),
West Tower, 9th Floor
Postal Address: P.O. Box 6970, Abu Dhabi, United
Arab Emirates
**Tel:** 971 (2) 694-0300
Emergency toll-free to Ottawa: 800-014-0145
**Fax:** 971 (2) 694-0399
**Email:** abdbi@international.gc.ca
**Website:** www.abudhabi.gc.ca

Consulate of Canada
Address: Bank Street Building, Suite 701, Bur Dubai,
United Arab Emirates
Postal Address: P.O. Box 52472, Dubai, United Arab
Emirates
**Tel:** 971 (4) 314-5555
Emergency toll-free to Ottawa: 800-014-0145
**Fax:** 971 (4) 314-5556/5557
**Email:** dubai@international.gc.ca

## United Kingdom

Consulate of Canada
Address: Unit 3, Ormeau Business Park, 8, Cromac
Avenue, Belfast, Northern Ireland BT7 2JA, United
Kingdom
Postal Address: P.O. Box 405, Belfast, BT9 5BL,
United Kingdom
**Tel:** 44 (2891) 272060

Consulate of Canada
Address: 55 Colmore Row, Birmingham, B3 2AS,
England, U.K.
**Tel:** 44 (121) 236-6474
Emergency toll-free to Ottawa: 00-800-2326-6831
**Fax:** 44 (121) 214-1099

Consulate of Canada
Address: c/o St John Cymru Wales, Beignon Close,
Ocean Way, Cardiff, Wales, CF24 5PB, United
Kingdom
**Tel:** 44 (0) 2920- 449635
Emergency toll-free to Ottawa: 00-800-2326-6831
**Fax:** 44 (0) 2920-449645
**Email:** dan.clayton-jones@talk21.com

Consulate of Canada
Address: Burness, 50 Lothian Road, Festival Square, Edinburgh, United Kingdom, EG3 9WJ
Tel: 44 (131) 473 6320
Emergency toll-free to Ottawa: 00-800-2326-6831
Fax: 44 (131) 473 6321
Email: canada.consul@burness.co.uk

High Commission of Canada
Address: Canada House, Consular Services, Trafalgar Square, London, SW1Y 5BJ, England, U.K.
Tel: 44 (20) 7258-6600
Emergency toll-free to Ottawa: 00-800-2326-6831
Fax: 44 (20) 7258-6533
Email: LDN@international.gc.ca
Website: www.london.gc.ca

## United States of America

Consulate General of Canada
Address: 1175 Peachtree Street N.E., 100 Colony Square, Suite 1700, Atlanta, Georgia 30361-6205, U.S.A.
Tel: (404) 532-2000
Emergency toll-free to Ottawa: 1-888-949-9993
Fax: (404) 532-2050
Email: atnta@international.gc.ca
Website: www.atlanta.gc.ca

Consulate General of Canada
Address: 3 Copley Place, Suite 400, Boston, Massachusetts 02116, U.S.A.
Tel: (617) 262-3760
Emergency toll-free to Ottawa: 1-888-949-9993
Fax: (617) 262-3415
Email: bostn@international.gc.ca
Website: www.boston.gc.ca

Consulate General of Canada
Address: 1 HSBC Center, Suite 3000, Buffalo, New York 14203-2884, U.S.A.
Tel: (716) 858-9500
Emergency toll-free to Ottawa: 1-888-949-9993
Fax: (716) 852-4340
Email: bfalo@international.gc.ca
Website: www.buffalo.gc.ca

Consulate General of Canada
Address: Two Prudential Plaza, 180 North Stetson Avenue, Suite 2400, Chicago, Illinois 60601, U.S.A.
Tel: (312) 616-1860
Emergency toll-free to Ottawa: 1-888-949-9993
Fax: (312) 616-1877

Email: chcgo@international.gc.ca
Website: www.chicago.gc.ca

Consulate General of Canada
Address: St. Paul Place, 750 North St. Paul Street, Suite 1700, Dallas, Texas 75201-3247, U.S.A.
Tel: (214) 922-9806
Emergency toll-free to Ottawa: 1-888-949-9993
Fax: (214) 922-9815
Email: dalas@international.gc.ca
Website: www.dallas.gc.ca

Consulate General of Canada
Address: World Trade Center, 1625 Broadway, Suite 2600, Denver, CO 80202, U.S.A.
Tel: (303) 626-0640
Emergency toll-free to Ottawa: 1-888-949-9993
Fax: (303) 572-1158
Email: denvr-g@international.gc.ca
Website: www.denver.gc.ca

Consulate General of Canada
Address: 600 Renaissance Center, Suite 1100, Detroit, Michigan 48243-1798, U.S.A.
Tel: (313) 446-4747
Emergency toll-free to Ottawa: 1-888-949-9993
Fax: (313) 567-2164
Email: dtrot@international.gc.ca
Website: www.detroit.gc.ca

Consulate General of Canada
Address: 550 South Hope Street, 9th Floor, Los Angeles, California 90071-2327, U.S.A.
Tel: (213) 346-2700
Emergency toll-free to Ottawa: 1-888-949-9993
Fax: (213) 620-8827
Email: lngls@international.gc.ca
Website: www.losangeles.gc.ca

Consulate General of Canada
Address: 200 South Biscayne Boulevard, Suite 1600, Miami, Florida 33131, U.S.A.
Tel: (305) 579-1600
Emergency toll-free to Ottawa: 1-888-949-9993
Fax: (305) 374-6774
Email: miami@international.gc.ca
Website: www.miami.gc.ca

Consulate General of Canada
Address: 701 Fourth Avenue South, Suite 900, Minneapolis, Minnesota 55415-1899, U.S.A.
Tel: (612) 333-4641

Emergency toll-free to Ottawa: 1-888-949-9993
**Fax:** (612) 332-4061
**Email:** mnpls@international.gc.ca
**Website:** www.minneapolis.gc.ca

Consulate General of Canada
Address: 1251 Avenue of the Americas, Concourse
Level, New York, New York 10020-1175, U.S.A.
**Tel:** (212) 596-1628
Emergency toll-free to Ottawa: 1-888-949-9993
**Fax:** (212) 596-1666/1790
**Email:** cngny@international.gc.ca
**Website:** www.newyork.gc.ca

Consulate of Canada
Address: Home Mortgage Plaza, 268 Ponce de Leon,
Suite 802, San Juan, Puerto Rico 00918, U.S.A.
**Tel:** (787) 759-6629
Emergency toll-free to Ottawa: 1-866-600-0184
**Fax:** (787) 294-1205

Consulate of Canada
Address: 402 W.Broadway, 4th Floor, San Diego, CA
92101, U.S.A.
**Tel:** (619)-615-4286
Emergency toll-free to Ottawa: 1-888-949-9993
**Fax:** (619) 615-4287
**Website:** www.dfait-maeci.gc.ca/can-am/san_diego

Consulate General of Canada
Address: 580 California Street, 14th floor, San
Francisco, CA 94104, U.S.A.
**Tel:** (415) 834-3180
Emergency toll-free to Ottawa: 1-888-949-9993
**Fax:** (415) 834-3189
**Email:** sfran@international.gc.ca
**Website:** www.dfait-maeci.gc.ca/san_francisco

Consulate General of Canada
Address: 1501-4th Ave, Suite 600, Seattle, Washington
98101, U.S.A.
**Tel:** (206) 443-1777
Emergency toll-free to Ottawa: 1-888-949-9993
**Fax:** (206) 443-9662
**Email:** seatl@international.gc.ca
**Website:** www.seattle.gc.ca

Embassy of Canada
Address: 501 Pennsylvania Avenue N.W.,
Washington, D.C. 20001, U.S.A.
**Tel:** (202) 682-1740
Emergency toll-free to Ottawa: 1-888-949-9993

**Fax:** (202) 682-7738
**Email:** wshdc-outpack@international.gc.ca
**Website:** www.washington.gc.ca

## Uruguay

Embassy of Canada
Address: 749 Plaza Independencia, app.102,
Montevideo, Uruguay
**Tel:** 598 (2) 902-2030
**Fax:** 598 (2) 902-2029
**Email:** mvdeo@international.gc.ca
**Website:** www.montevideo.gc.ca

## Uzbekistan

Consulate of Canada
Address: 56, U. Nasir Street, Apt. 39-40, 100100,
Tashkent, Uzbekistan
**Tel:** 998 (71) 362-9205
**Fax:** 998 (71) 120-7270
**Email:** antal@rol.uz

## Vanuatu

Australian High Commission
Address: KPMG House, Port Vila, Vanuatu
**Tel:** 678 22-777
**Fax:** 678 23-948

## Venezuela

Embassy of Canada
Address: Consular Section, Avenida Francisco de
Miranda con Avenida Sur Altamira, Altamira, Caracas
Postal Address: P.O. Box 62-302, Caracas, 1060-A
**Tel:** 58 (212) 600-3000, 3042, 3043
**Fax:** 58 (212) 263-4981
**Email:** crcas@international.gc.ca
**Website:** www.caracas.gc.ca

Consulate of Canada
Address: Calle Ortega, Edificio Monseratto, #12-100,
apartment 2-B, Porlamar, Estado Nueva Esparta
**Tel:** 58 (295) 264-1684
**Fax:** 58 (295) 249-1071

## Vietnam

Embassy of Canada
Address: 31 Hung Vuong Street, Hanoi, Vietnam
**Tel:** 84 (4) 734 5000
**Fax:** 84 (4) 734 5049
**Email:** hanoi@international.gc.ca
**Website:** www.hanoi.gc.ca

Consulate General of Canada
Address: 10th Floor, The Metropolitan, 235 Dong Khoi Street, District 1, Ho Chi Minh City, Vietnam
**Tel:** 84 (8) 827-9899
**Fax:** 84 (8) 827-9936
**Email:** hochi@international.gc.ca

## Yemen

Consulate of Canada
Address: Yemen Computer Co. Ltd., Building 4, 11th Street off Haddah Street, Sanaa, Yemen
Postal Address: P.O. Box 340, Sanaa, Yemen
**Tel:** 967 (1) 20 88 14
**Fax:** 967 (1) 20 95 23
**Email:** canconsulye@hotmail.com

## Zambia

High Commission of Canada
Address: 5199 United Nations Avenue, Lusaka

Postal Address: P.O. Box 31313, Lusaka, Zambia
**Tel:** 260 (1) 25 08 33
**Fax:** 260 (1) 25 41 76
**Email:** lsaka@international.gc.ca
**Website:** www.zambia.gc.ca

## Zimbabwe

Embassy of Canada
Address: 45 Baines Avenue, Harare, Zimbabwe
Postal Address: P.O. Box 1430, Harare, Zimbabwe
**Tel:** 263 (4) 252-181/2/3/4/5
**Fax:** 263 (4) 252-186/7
**Email:** hrare@international.gc.ca
**Website:** www.harare.gc.ca

# US Embassies

When preparing to teach and travel overseas it is vital to contact the embassy of the country, or the U.S. embassy within the country, you are planning to visit to find out information on visas, restrictions and a variety of other information.

## Afghanistan

Embassy
The Great Masoud Road, Kabul
**Tel:** 93 2 2300436
**Fax:** 93 2 2301364

## Albania

Embassy
Rr Elbasanit 103, Tirana
**Tel:** +355 4247285
**Fax:** +355 423 2222

## Angola

Embassy
Rua Houari Boumeddienne #32
Luanda, Angola
C.P. 6468
**Tel:** 244-2-445-481
**Fax:** 244-2-446-924

Consulate
Rua Major Kanhangulo #132-136
Luanda, Angola
C.P. 6468
**Tel:** 244-2-371645
**Fax:** 244-2-390-515
**Email:** luandaconsular@yahoo.com

## Argentina

Embassy
Avenida Colombia 4300
1425 Buenos Aires

**Tel:** 54-11-5777-4533
**Fax:** 54-11-5777-4240

## Armenia

Embassy
18 Baghramyan Avenue, Yerevan. 375019
**Tel:** (3741) 52-0791
**Fax:** (3741) 52-0800
**Email:** usinfo@uas.am

## Australia

Embassy
Moonah Place, Yarralumla, Canberra, ACT 2600
**Tel:** (02)-6214-5600
**Fax:** (02) 6214-5970
**Email:** info@usembassy-australia.state.gov

Sydney Consulate
MLC Centre, Level 59
19-29 Martin Place
Sydney NSW 2000
**Tel:** (612) 9373-9200

Melbourne Consulate
U.S. Consulate General, 553 St Kilda Road, VIC 3004
**Tel:** (03) 9526-5900

Perth Consulate- General
16 St. George's Terrace, 13th Floor, Perth, WA 6000
**Tel:** (08) 9202 1224

## Austria

Embassy
Boltzmanngasse 16
A-1090 Vienna
**Tel:** +43 (1) 31339-0
**Fax:** +43 (1) 310-0682
**Email:** embassy@usembassy.at

Consular Agency Salzburg
Alter Markt 1
A-5020 Salzburg
**Tel:** (0662)848 776
**Fax:** (0662) 849 777

## Azerbaijan

Embassy
83 Azadlyg Prospecti, AZ 1007 Baku
**Tel:** (994-12) 980 335
**Fax:** (994-12) 656 671

## Bahrain

Embassy
Manama, Bahrain, Bldg 979, Road 3119, Block 321, Zinj.
**Tel:** (973) 273 300.

## Bangladesh

Embassy
Madani Avenue
Dhaka 1212, Bangladesh
**Tel:** [880] (2) 885 55 00
**Fax:** [880] (2) 882 37 44
**Email:** dhaka@pd.state.gov

## Barbados

Embassy
P.O. Box 302
Bridgetown, Barbados, W.I.

From the U.S.:
(Department Name)
CMR 1014
APO AA 34055

**Tel:** (246) 436-4950
**Fax:** (246) 429-5246
**Consular Tel:** (246) 431-0225
**Consular Fax:** (246) 431-0179

## Belarus

Embassy
46 Starovilenskaya Street, Minsk 220002
**Tel:** +375-17 210 1283
**Fax:** +375-17 234 7853

## Belgium

Embassy
Regentlaan 27 / Boulevard du Régent
B-1000 Brussels
**Tel:** +32-2-508-2111
**Fax:** +32-2-511-2725

## Bolivia

Embassy
Avenida Arce 2780,
Casilla 425
**Tel:** (591) 2 216 8000
**Fax:** (591) 2 216 8111
**Email:** Ipzirc@state.gov

## Bosnia & Herzegovina

Embassy
Alipasina 43, 71000 Sarajevo
**Tel:** +387-33 445-700
**Fax:** +387-33 659-722
**Email:** bhopa@state.gov

## Botswana

Embassy
PO Box 90 Gaborone
**Tel:** (267) 395 3982
**Fax**. (267) 395 6947
**Email:** consulargaboro@state.gov

## Brazil

Rio de Janeiro Consulate
Avenida Presidente Wilson, 147
20030-020 Rio de Janeiro,RJ
**Tel**.: 55 21 2292-7117
**Fax:** 55 21 2262-1820

São Paulo Consulate
Rua Henry Dunant, 700
Chacara Santo Antonio
04709-110 São Paulo - SP
**Tel:** 55 11 5186 7000
**Fax:** 55 11 5186 7199

## Bulgaria

Embassy
Consular Section: 1 Kapitan Andreev Street, Sofia
1421
**Tel:** (359) (2) 963 2022
**Email:** irc@usembassy.bg

## Burkina Faso

Mailing from the U.S.A.:
AmEmbassy Ouagadougou
Department of State
2440 Ouagadougou Place
Washington DC 20521-2440

International Mailing:
Ambassade des Etats-Unis d'Amérique
01 B.P. 35 Ouagadougou 01
Burkina Faso

**Tel:** (226) 50-30-67-23
**Fax:** (226) 50-31-23-68
**Email:** amembouaga@state.gov

## Burundi

Embassy
BP 1720 Ave des Etats-Unis, Bujumbura
**Tel:** (257) 22-34-54
**Fax:** (257) 22-29-26

## Cambodia

Embassy
16, Street 228 (between streets 51 and 63)
Phnom Penh, Cambodia
**Tel:** (855-23) 216 436
**Fax:** (855-23) 216 437

## Cameroon

Embassy
Rue Nachtigal
P.O. Box 817, Yaoundé, Cameroon
**Tel:** (237) 223-40-14
**Fax:** (237) 223-07-53

Embassy Branch Office in Douala
**Tel:** (237) 342-53-31; (237) 342-03-03
**Fax:** (237) 342-77-90

## Canada

Embassy
490 Sussex Drive
Ottawa, Ontario K1N 1G8
**Tel:** 613.238.5335

Consular Service
490 Sussex Drive
Ottawa, Ontario K1N 1G8
**Tel:** 613 238 5335
**Fax:** 613 688 3082

Halifax Consulate
1969 Upper Water Street
Purdy's Wharf Tower II, suite 904
Halifax, Nova Scotia, B3J 3R7
**Tel:** 902 429-2485

Montréal Consulate
1155 St. Alexandre Street, Montréal, Québec, H3B
1Z1
**Tel:** 514 398-9695

Mailing address:
PO Box 65, Station Desjardins, Montréal, Québec
H5B 1G1

Québec City Consulate
2 Place Terrasse Dufferin, B.P. 939
Québec City, Québec, G1R 4T9
**Tel:** 418 692-2095

Toronto Consulate
360 University Avenue, Toronto, Ontario
M5G 1S4
**Tel:** : 416 595-1700

Calgary Consulate
615 Macleod Trail SE, Calgary, Alberta
T2G 4T8
**Tel:** 403 266-8962

Vancouver Consulate
1095 West Pender Street, Vancouver, British
Columbia, V6E 2M6
**Tel:** 604/685-4311

Winnipeg Consulate
860-201 Portage Avenue, Winnipeg, Manitoba
R3B 3K6
**Tel:** 204 940 1800

## Chad

Embassy
BP 413 Ave Felix Eboué, N'Djamena

**Tel:** (235) 51 70 09
**Fax:** (235) 51 56 54

## Chile

Embassy
Andres Bello 2800, Las Condes,
Santiago, Chile
**Tel:** (56-2) 238-2600
**Fax:** (56-2) 330-3710

## China

Embassy
3 Xiu Shui Bei Jie, Beijing, China 100600
**Tel:** (86-10) 6532-3431

Shenyang (Consulate)
No.52, 14 Wei Road, Heping District, Shenyang,
Liaoning, P.R.C 110003
**Tel:** (86-24) 2382-1198
**Fax:** (86-24) 2382-2374

Shanghai (Consulate)
1469 Huai Hai Zhong Lu, Shanghai 200031
**Tel:** (86-20) 6433-6880
**Fax:** (86-20) 6433-4122

Guangzhou (Consulate)
1 Shamian South Street, Guangzhou 510133
**Tel:** (86-20) 8121-8000
**Fax:** (86-20) 8121-9001

## Colombia

Embassy
Calle 22D-Bis # 47-51
Bogotá, Colombia
**Tel:** (571) 315-0811
**Fax:** (571) 315-2197

## Democratic Republic of Congo

Embassy
310 Ave des Aviateurs, Kinshasa
**Tel:** (243) 81 225 5872
**Fax:** (243) 88 43467

## Costa Rica

Embassy
Calle 120 Avenida O
Pavas, San José, Costa Rica
**Tel:** (506) 519-2000
**Fax:** (506) 519-2305

## Côte d'Ivoire

Embassy
Rue Jesse Owens,
B.P. 1712,
Abidjan 01, République de Côte d'Ivoire
**Tel:** (225) 20-21-09-79
**Fax:** (225) 20-22-32-59

## Croatia

Embassy
Thomasa Jeffersona 2, 10010, Zagreb
**Tel:** 385 (1) 661 2200

## Cuba

US Interests Section
U.S. Interests Section of the Embassy of Switzerland,
Havana, Cuba
Calzada between L & M Streets, Vedado, Havana
**Tel:** (53-7) 33-3551/59
**Fax:** (53-7) 833 33-1084

## Cyprus

Embassy
P.O.Box  24536,
Metochiou & Ploutarchou Street, Engomi, 2407
Nicosia, Cyprus
**Tel:** 357-22-393939
**Fax:**  357-22-780944

## Czech Republic

Embassy
Trziste 15, 118 01 Praha 1, Czech Republic
**Tel:** (420-2) 5753-0663

## Denmark

Embassy
Dag Hammarskjölds Allé 24,
2100 København Ø.
**Tel**. +45 35 55 31 44
**Fax:** +45 35 43 02 23

## Dominican Republic

Embassy
César Nicolás Penson esquina Máximo Gomez
**Tel:** (809) 221-2171
**Fax:** (809) 685-6959

## Ecuador

Embassy
Av. Patria and Av. 12 de Octubre,
Quito, Ecuador
**Tel:** (593) 22 562 890
**Fax:** (593) 22 502 052

## Egypt

Embassy
5 Latin America Street, Garden City, Cairo, Egypt
**Tel:** [20] 2-795-7371
**Fax:** [20] 2-797-3200

## El Salvador

Embassy
Final Boulevard Santa Elena, Antiguo Cuscatlán, La
Libertad, El Salvador
**Tel:** (011) [503] 278-4444
**Consular Fax:** (011) [503] 278-5522

## Estonia

Embassy
Kentmanni 20, 15099 Tallinn
**Tel:** (372) 668 8100
**Fax:** (372) 668 8134,
**Email:** USASaatkond@state.gov

**Consular Fax:** (372) 668 8267
**Email:** visaTallinn@state.gov

## Ethiopia

Embassy
P.O.Box 1014 , Addis Ababa , Ethiopia
Tel. 251-1-174000
**Fax:** 251-1-174001
**Email:** usemaddis@state.gov

## European Union

U.S. Mission to the European Union
27, Boulevard du Régent, B-1000 Brussels, Belgium
**Tel:** 32-2-508-2774
**Fax:** 32-2-512-5720

## Finland

Embassy
Itäinen Puistotie 14 B,
FIN-00140, Helsinki
**Tel:** +358-9-616 250
**Email:** webmaster@usembassy.fi

## France

Embassy
2, ave Gabriel, 75008 Paris
Cedex 08
**Tel:** (33) 1- 43 12 22 22
**Fax:** (33) 1- 42 66 97 83

## Gabon

Embassy
Blvd. Du Bord de Mer B.P. 4000
Libreville, Gabon
**Tel:** (241) 76.20.03
**Fax:** (241) 74.55.07

## Georgia

Embassy
25 Atoneli Street, Tbilisi, 0105
**Tel:** (995-32) 98-99-67
**Fax:** (995-32) 93-37-59

## Germany

Embassy
Neustädtische Kirchstr. 4-5
10117 Berlin
**Tel:** (49) (030) 8305-0

Düsseldorf (Consulate General)
Willi-Becker-Allee 10, 40227,
Düsseldorf
**Tel:** (0211) 788 – 8927
**Fax:** (0211) 788-8938

Frankfurt (Consulate General)
Siesmayerstraße 21
60323 Frankfurt
**Tel:** (49) (69) 7535-0
**Fax:** (49) (69) 7535-2277

Hamburg (Consulate General)
Alsterufer 27/28
20354 Hamburg
**Tel:** (040) 411 71-100
**Fax:** (040) 4132 7933

Leipzig (Consulate General)
Wilhelm-Seyfferth-Straße 4
04107 Leipzig
**Tel:** (49) (341) 213-84-0

Munich (Consulate General)
Königinstraße 5

80539 Munich
**Tel:** (49)(89) 2888-0
**Fax:** (49)(89) 280-9998

## Ghana

Embassy
PO Box 194, Accra
**Tel:** (233) 21-775348
**Fax:** (233) 21-776008
**Email:**accracon@ghana.com

## Greece

Embassy
91 Vassilissis Sophias Avenue,
101 60 Athens
**Tel:** (30-210) 721-2951
Public Affairs Section
8 Makedonon Street, 115 21 Athens,
**Tel:** (30-210) 363 8114
**Fax:** (30-210) 364 2986

Thessaloniki (Consulate General)
43 Tsimiski , 7th Floor
546 23 Thessaloniki
**Tel:** (0030) 2310 242 905
**Email:** amcongen@compulink.gr

## Guatemala

Embassy
Avenida Reforma 7-01, Zona 10
Guatemala Ciudad
**Tel:** (502) 2331-1541/55
**Fax:** (502) 2334-8477

## Haiti

Embassy
5, Boulevard Harry S Truman
Port-au-Prince, Republic of Haiti
**Tel**. (509) 222-0200
**Fax**. (509) 223-9038

## Honduras

Embassy
Avenida La Paz
Apartado Postal No. 3453
Tegucigalpa, Honduras
**Tel:** (504) 236-9320
**Fax:** (504) 236-9037

## Hong Kong

Hong Kong (Consulate-General)
26 Garden Road, Hong Kong
**Tel:** (852) 2523-9011
**Fax:** (852) 2845-1598

## Hungary

Embassy
Szabadság tér 12., H-1054
Budapest
**Tel:** (36-1) 475-4400
**Fax:** (36-1) 475-4764

## Iceland

Embassy
Laufásvegur 21, Reykjavik
**Tel:** : (354) 562-9100
**Consular Fax:** (354) 562-9110

## India

Embassy
Shantipath, Chanakyapuri
New Delhi 110021
**Tel:**(11) 419-8000
**Fax:**(11) 419-0017
8:30am-5:30pm Monday-Friday

Calcutta (Consulate)
U.S. Mission Calcutta
5/1 Ho Chi Minh Sarani,
Calcutta 700-071
**Tel:** 91-33-2282-3611;
**Fax:** 91-33-2282-2335.

## Indonesia

Embassy
Jl. Merdeka Selatan 4-5, Jakarta 10110, Indonesia
**Tel:** (62-21) 3435 9000
**Fax:** (62-21) 3436-9922

## Ireland

Embassy
42 Elgin Road, Ballsbridge, Dublin 4
**Tel:** 353-1-668-8777
**Fax:** 353-1-668-9946

## Israel

Embassy
1 Ben Yehuda Street,
Tel Aviv, Israel

**Tel:** (972) 3 510 3822
**Fax:** (972) 3 510 3828

## Italy

Embassy
Via Vittorio Veneto 119/A - 00187
Roma
**Tel:** (+39) 06.4674.1
**Fax:** (+39) 06.4882.672

Milan Consulate General
Via Principe Amedeo 2/10
20121 Milano
**Tel:** 39 02 290 351
**Fax:** 39 02 2900 1165

Florence Consulate General
Lungarno Vespucci 38
50123 Firenze
**Tel:** 39 055 266 951
**Fax:** 39 055 284 088

Naples Consulate General
Piazza della Republica
80122 Napoli
**Tel:** 39 081 583 8111
**Fax:** 39 081 7611 869

## Jamaica

Embassy
2 Oxford Road
Kingston 5
Jamaica, West Indies
**Tel:** (876) 935 6053
**Fax:** (876) 929 3637
**Email:** opakgn@state.gov

## Japan

Embassy
1-10-5 Akasaka, Minato-ku, Tokyo 107-8420
**Tel:** (03)3224-5000
**Fax:** (03)3505-1862

Consulate General Osaka
11-5 Nishitenma 2-chome,
Kita-ku, Osaka 530-8543
**Tel:** (06)6315-5900
**Fax:** (06)6315-5914

Consulate General Naha
2564 Nishihara,

Urasoe-shi, Okinawa 901-2101
**Tel:** (098)876-4211
**Fax:** (098)876-4243

Consulate General Sapporo
Kita 1-jo, Nishi 28-chome,
Chuo-ku, Sapporo 064-0821
**Tel:** (011)641-1115
**Fax:** (011)643-1283

Consulate Fukuoka
5-26 Ohori 2-chome,
Chuo-ku, Fukuoka 810-0052
**Tel:** (092)751-9331
**Fax:** (092)713-9222

Consulate Nagoya
Nishiki SIS Bldg. 6F, 10-33, Nishiki
3-chome, Naka-ku,
Nagoya 460-0003
**Tel:** (052)203-4011
**Fax:** (052)201-4612

## Jordan

Embassy
P.O. Box 354, Amman 11118
Jordan
**Tel:** 962-6-592-0101
**Fax:** 962-6-592-0121

## Kazakhstan

Embassy
99/97 Furmanova Street at the Corner of Aiteke Bi and
Furmanova, Almaty
**Tel:** +7 (3272) 63-39-21
**Fax:** +7 (3272) 50-62-69

## Kenya

Embassy
United Nations Avenue
P.O. Box 606
00621 Nairobi
**Tel:** 254-2-3636000
**Fax:** 254-2-537810

## Korea

Embassy
32 Sejongno, Jongno-gu
Seoul 110-710
**American Citizen Services Fax:** 82-2-397-4101

## Kuwait

Embassy
Bayan, Al-Masjed Al-Aqssa St.
PO Box 77, Safat, 13001Kuwait
**Tel:** 539-5307/8
**Fax:** 538 0282

## Laos

Embassy
19 Rue Bartholonie, Vientiane, Lao P.D.R
**Tel:** (856) 21-212966
**Fax:** (856) 21-213045

## Latvia

Embassy
7 Raina Blvd.,
Riga LV1510, Latvia
**Tel:** +371-7036 200
**Fax:** +371-7820 047

## Lebanon

Embassy
Awkar, P.O. Box: 70-840
Beirut – Lebanon
**Tel:** (04) 542600
**Fax:** (04) 544136

## Lithuania

Embassy
Akmenu 6
2600 Vilnius, Lithuania
**Tel**.: (370-5) 266 5500
**Fax:** (370-5) 266 5510
Monday-to-Friday: 8:30 a.m. - 5:30 p.m.

## Macedonia

Embassy
Consular Section
Bul.Ilinden B.B.
1000 Skopje
**Tel:** 389-2 31 16 180
**Fax:** 389-2 31 17 103

## Madagascar

Embassy
14, Rue Rainitovo, Antsahavola, Antananarivo 101
B.P. 620, Antsahavola
**Tel:** (261-20) 22-212-57
**Fax:** (261-20) 22-345-39

## Malaysia

Embassy
376 Jalan Tun Razak, 50400 Kuala Lumpur.
**Tel:** 603-2168-5000
**Fax:** 603-2142-2207

## Mali

Embassy
Rue Rochester NY, Bamako
**Tel:** (223) 222 5470
**Fax:** (223) 222 3712

## Malta

Embassy
Development House, 3rd Floor
St. Anne Street, Floriana, Malta. VLT 01
**Tel:** (356) 2561 4000
**Fax:** (356) 2124 3229

## Mauritius

Embassy
4th Floor, Rogers House, John Kennedy Ave
Port Louis, Mauritius
**Tel:** (230) 202 4400
**Fax:** (230) 208 9534
**Email:** usembass@intnet.mu

## Mexico

Embassy
Paseo de la Reforma 305
Col. Cuauhtémoc
06500 Mexico, D.F.

Mail from the U.S.
American Embassy Mexico
P.O. Box 9000
Brownsville, TX 78520-9000

**Tel. From the U.S.**: (011-52) 55-5080-2000
**Tel. From Mexico:** (01) 55-5080-2000
**Fax From the U.S.**: (011-52) 55-5511-9980
**Fax From Mexico:** (01) 55-5511-9980

Guadalajara (Consulate)
Progreso 175, Guadalajara, Jalisco C.P. 44100
**Tel:** (33) 3268 2100
**Fax:** (33) 3826-6549

Juarez (Consulate)
Av. Lopez Mateos 924 Nte.

Ciudad Juarez, Mexico
U.S. Mailing Address:
P.O. Box 10545
El Paso, Tx. 79995
**Tel:** (52) (656) 611-3000
**Fax**: (52) (656) 616-9056

Monterrey (Consulate)
Ave. Constitucion 411 Pte.
Monterrey NL 64000 Mexico
**Tel:** (8) 345-2120
Office Hours: Monday-Friday 08:00am-5:00pm

Tijuana (Consulate)
Tapachula No. 96
Colonia Hipódromo
22420 Tijuana, B.C., México
**Tel:** (664) 622-7400
**Fax:** (664) 622 7625

## Micronesia

Embassy
P.O. Box 1286
Kolonia, Pohnpei , FSM 96941
**Tel:** (691) 320-2187
**Fax**. (691) 320-2186
**Email:** usembassy@mail.fm

## Moldova

Embassy
103 Mateevici Street,
Chisinau MD-2009
**Tel:** 373-2-233772
**Fax**: 373-2-233044

## Mongolia

Embassy
P.O. Box 1021
Ulaanbaatar-13
**Tel:**  976-11-329095
**Fax**: 976-11-320776

## Morocco

Embassy
2 Avenue de Mohamed El Fassi
Rabat, Morocco
**Tel:** (212)(7)-76-22-65
**Fax**: (212)(7)-76-56-61

## Mozambique

Embassy
Av. Kenneth Kaunda, 193; P.O. Box 783, Maputo
**Tel:** (258 1) 492797
**Fax:** (258 1) 490114

## Namibia

Embassy
14 Lossen Street, Private Bag 12029,
Windhoek
**Tel:** 264 61 221601
**Fax:** 264 61 229792
**Email:** HealyKC@state.gov

## Netherlands

Embassy
Lange Voorhout 102
2514 EJ The Hague
The Netherlands
**Tel:** +31 70 310-9209
**Fax:** +31 70 361-4688
**Website:** www.usemb.nl

Amsterdam (Consulate)
Museumplein 19
1071 DJ Amsterdam
**Tel:** 020-575 5309
**Fax:** 020-575 5310

## Netherlands Antilles

Consulate-General
J B Gorsiraweg #1, Willemstad AN, Curacao
Netherlands Antilles
**Tel:** (011) 59-99 461-3066
**Fax:** (011) 59-99 461-6489
**Email:** info@amcongencuracao.an

## New Zealand

Embassy
29 Fitzherbert Terrace, Thorndon
(Or P.O. Box 1190)
Wellington, New Zealand
**Tel:** 644 462 6000
**Fax:** 644 499 0490

Auckland (Consulate)
3rd Floor Citibank Building
23 Customs Street
Auckland, New Zealand
*Or* Private Bag 92022

Auckland
**Tel:** (649)303-2724
**Fax**: (649)366-0870

## Nicaragua

Embassy
Apartado Postal 327
Kilometro 4 ½ Carretera Sur
Managua, Nicaragua
**Tel:** 505-268-0123
**Fax:** 505-268-9943

## Niger

Embassy
BP 11201, rue des Ambassades
Niamey, Niger
West Africa
**Tel**. (227) 73-31-69
**Fax:** (227) 73-55-60
**Email:** NiameyPASN@state.gov

## Nigeria

Embassy
7 Mambilla Street, Abuja
**Tel:** (234) 9 523 0916
**Fax:** (234) 9 523 0353
**Email:** usabuja@state.gov

Consulate
2, Walter Carrington Crescent, Victoria Island, Lagos
**Tel:** (234) 1 261-0050
**Fax:** (234) 1 261-9856
**Email:** uslagos@state.gov

## Norway

Embassy
Drammensveien 18
0244 Oslo, Norway
**Tel:** (+47) 22 44 85 50
**Email:** oslo@usa.no

## Oman

Embassy
P.O. Box 202, Code 115
Madinat Al-Sultan Qaboos, Muscat
Sultanate of Oman
**Tel:** (968) 698-98
**Fax:** (968) 699-18
**Email:** aemctira@omantel.net.om

## Pakistan

Embassy
Diplomatic Enclave, Ramna 5
Islamabad, Pakistan
**Tel:** (92) 51-2080-0000
**Fax:** (92) 51-2276427

Lahore (Consulate)
50, Empress Road
Lahore, Pakistan
**Tel:** (92) 42-6365530
**Fax:** (92) 42-6365177

Karachi (Consulate)
8, Abdullah Haroon Road
Karachi, Pakistan
**Tel:** (92) 21-5685170
**Fax:** (92) 21-5683089

Peshawar (Consulate)
11, Hospital Road
Peshawar, Pakistan
**Tel:** (92) 91-279801-3
**Fax**: (92) 91-276712

## Panama

Embassy
Apartado 0816-02561
Zona 5 Panama
**Tel:** (507) 207 7000
**Fax:** (507) 227 1964
**Email:** panamaweb@pd.state.gov

## Paraguay

Embassy
1776 Mariscal Lopez Ave.
Asunción
**Tel:** (595) 21 213-715
**Fax:** (515) 21 213-728

## Peru

Embassy
Avenida La Encalada cdra. 17 s/n
Surco, Lima 33, Peru
**Tel:** (51-1) 434-3000
**Fax:** (51-1) 618 2397

## Philippines

Embassy
1201 Roxas Boulevard, Ermita 1000, Manila
**Tel:** (63-2) 528 6300
**Fax:** (63-2) 522 4361

## Poland

Embassy
Al. Ujazdowskie 29-31, 07-00-540 Warsaw
**Tel.:** +48-22 504 2000
**Fax:** +48-22 504 2688

## Portugal

Embassy
Av. das Forças Armadas
1600-081 LISBOA
Apartado 4258
1507 LISBOA CODEX
**Tel:** 351-21-727-3300
**Fax:** 351-21-727-9109

## Qatar

Embassy
PO Box 2399
Doha, Qatar
**Tel:** 488-4101
**Fax:** 488 4298
**Email:** usembdoh@qatar.net.qa

## Romania

Embassy
Tudor Arghezi, 7-9,
Bucharest, Romania
**Tel:** (40-21) 210-4042
**Fax:** (40-21) 210-0395

## Russia

Embassy
Bolshoy Deviatinsky Pereulok, 8
Moscow, 121099 Russia
**Tel:** 7 095 728 5000
**Fax:** 7 095 738 5090

St. Petersburg (Consulate)
Furshtadtskaya ul., 15
191028 St. Petersburg, Russia
**Tel:** (812) 331 2600
**Fax:** (812) 331 2852

## Saudi Arabia

Embassy
P.O. Box 94309
Riyadh 11693
Saudi Arabia
**Tel:** (966-1) 488-3800
**Fax:** (966-1) 488-7360

Jeddah (Consulate)
P.O. Box 149, Jeddah 21411
Jeddah - Saudi Arabia
**Tel:** (966-2) 667-0080
**Fax:** (966-2) 660-2567

Dhahran (Consulate)
P.O. Box 38955, Dhahran Airport 31942
Saudi Arabia
**Tel:** (966-3) 330-3200
**Fax:** (966-3) 330-0464

## Senegal

Embassy
Ave. Jean XXIII x Rue Kleber
BP. 49 Dakar, Senegal
**Tel:** (221) 823.42.96
**Fax:** (221) 822.29.91
**Email:** usadakar@state.gov

## Singapore

Embassy
27 Napier Road
Singapore 258508
**Tel:** (65)-6476 9100
**Fax:** (65)-6476 9340

## Slovak Republic

Embassy
PO Box 309, 814 99 Bratislava
**Tel:** +421-5443 3338
**Fax:** +421-5443 0096

## Slovenia

Embassy
Presernova 31
1000 Ljubljana,
Slovenia
**Tel:** +386 (1) 200-5500
**Fax:** +386 (1) 200-5555

## South Africa

Embassy
PO Box 9536
Pretoria 0001
877 Pretorius St
Pretoria
**Tel:** (27-12) 431-4000
**Fax:** (27-12) 342-2299

## Spain

Embassy
Serrano, 75, 28006 Madrid, Spain
**Tel:** (34) 91587 2200
**Fax:** (34) 91587 2303

Barcelona (Consulate)
Paseo Reina Elisenda de Montcada, 23
08034 Barcelona, Spain
**Tel:** (34) 93280 2227
**Fax:** (34) 93280 6175

## Sri Lanka

Embassy
210, Galle Road,
Colombo 3, Sri Lanka
**Tel:** (94-1) 448-007
**Fax**: (94-1) 437-345

## Sweden

Embassy
Dag Hammarskjölds Väg 31,
SE-115 89 Stockholm
**Tel:** (46) 8 783 5300

## Switzerland

Embassy
Jubiläumsstrasse 93, 3001 , Bern
**Tel.**: 031/357-7011
**Fax:** 031/357-7344

## Tanzania

Embassy
PO Box 9123, 686 Old Bagamoyo Road
Msasani, Dar-es-Salaam
**Tel:** 255 22 266 8001
**Fax:** 255 22 266 8238
**Email:** embassyd@state.gov

## Thailand

Embassy
120/22 Wireless Road
Bangkok 10330
**Tel:** (66) 2 205-4000
**Fax:** (66) 2 254-1171

Chiang Mai (Consulate)
387 Wichayanond Road,
Chiang Mai 50300, Thailand
**Tel:** (66-53) 252-629
**Fax:** (66-53) 252-633

## Togo

Embassy
Angle Rue Kouenou et Rue 15 Béniglato
B.P. 852, Lomé
**Tel:** (228) 221 2994
**Fax**: (228) 221 79 52

## Trinidad & Tobago

Embassy
15 Queen's Park West
Port of Spain, Trinidad & Tobago
**Tel:** (868) 622-6371/6
**Fax:** (868) 628-5462

## Turkey

Embassy
Public Affairs Section
Paris Caddesi 32 Kavaklidere
06540 Ankara, Turkey
**Tel:** (90-312) 468-6102
**Fax:** (90-312) 468-6145

Istanbul (Consulate)
Kaplicalar Mevkii Sokak No 2
Istinye 34460, Istanbul,
**Tel:** 212 335 9000

## Turkmenistan

Embassy
9 1984 Street, Ashgabat, Turkmenistan
744000
**Tel:** (99312) 35 0045
**Fax:** (993-12) 39 2614

## Ukraine

Embassy
Yuriya Kotsubinskoho 10,
Kyiv 04053, Ukraine.
**Tel:** (380) 44 490 4000
**Fax:** (380) 44 490 4085
**Consular Fax:** (380) 44 216 3393

## United Arab Emirates

Embassy
P.O. Box 4009, Abu Dhabi,
United Arab Emirates
**Tel:** 9712 443 6691

## United Kingdom

Embassy
24 Grosvenor Square
London W1A 1AE
United Kingdom
**Tel:** 020 7499-9000

## Uruguay

Embassy
Lauro Muller 1776
Montevideo 11200
**Tel:** (598-2) 418-7777
**Fax:** (598-2) 418-8611

## Uzbekistan

Embassy
82, Chilanzarskaya Street
Tashkent, 700115, Uzbekistan
**Tel:**(+998-71)120-54-44
**Fax:**(+998-71)120-63-35
**Email:** consul_tashkent@yahoo.com

## Venezuela

Embassy
Calle F con Calle Suapure
Urb. Colinas de Valle Arriba
Caracas 1080, Venezuela
**Tel:** (58-212) 975-6411
**Email:** consularcaracas@state.gov

## Vietnam

Embassy
7 Lang Ha Street

Ba Dinh District
Hanoi, Vietnam
**Tel:** (844) 7721 500
**Fax:** (844) 7721 510
**Email:** hanoicons@fpt.vn

Ho Chi Minh City (Consulate)
4 Le Duan Blvd., District 1,
Ho Chi Minh City
**Tel:** (84-8) 822 9433
**Fax:** (84-8) 824 5571

## Yemen

Embassy
Sa'awan Street
PO Box 22347, Sana'a, Yemen
**Tel:** 967-1-303155

## Zambia

Embassy
Public Affairs Section
COMESA Building, Ben Bella Road,
PO Box 32053
Lusaka
**Tel:** (260-1) 227 993
**Fax:** (260-1) 226 523
**Email:** paslib@zamnet.zm

## Zimbabwe

Embassy
172 Herbert Chitepo Avenue, Harare
**Tel:** 263- 4-703169/378/478
**Fax:** 263- 4-796488
**Email:** consularharare@state.gov

# Index